ENCYCLOPEDIA OF STUDENT AND YOUTH MOVEMENTS

DAVID F. BURG

Facts On File, Inc.

Encyclopedia of Student and Youth Movements

Copyright © 1998 by David F. Burg

Facts On File, Inc.
11 Penn Plaza
New York NY 10001

Library of Congress Cataloging-in-Publication Data

Burg, David F.
Encyclopedia of student and youth movements / David F. Burg.
p.   cm.
Includes bibliographical references (p.   ) and index.
1. Student movements—Encyclopedias. 2 Youth movement—Encyclopedias. 3. Students—Political activity. 4. Youth—Political activity. I. Title.
LA186.B87   1998
371.8'1—dc21   97-32408

Facts On File books are available at special discounts when purchased in bulk quantities for businesses, associations, institutions or sales promotions. Please call our Special Sales Department in New York at 212/967-8800 or 800/322-8755.

You can find Facts On File on the World Wide Web at http://www.factsonfile.com

Text design by Cathy Rincon
Cover design by Nora Wertz

Printed in the United States of America

VB Hermitage 10 9 8 7 6 5 4 3 2 1

This book is printed on acid-free paper.

To my children,

Charles Gilbert Burg

and Laura Johnson Burg

───────────────

◆

Contents

Acknowledgments

t seems that I am always indebted to the staff of the University of Kentucky M. I. King Library and the research resources of that library—I am happy once more to acknowledge the debt and to express my thanks. I also wish to thank the staff of the Transylvania University J. Douglas Gay Jr. Library, especially Kathleen C. Bryson, director. Finally, as always, I thank my wife, Helen Rendlesham Burg, who is always ready to listen to dinnertime tales.

Preface

lthough the Introduction discusses such matters as defining terms and the general nature and history of student and youth movements, something must be said here about the selection of entries. There is no pretense to exhaustiveness here. It is also initially noteworthy that student and youth movements have been especially important in certain nations, such as Germany and China, and so a preponderance of the entries reflects this reality. There are more than 100 entries for Germany alone, for example, but I would not for a moment pretend that these represent more than a fraction of the student or youth movements and events that nation has witnessed—they do, however, in my judgment, represent the most significant of those movements and events, while also revealing their diversity. It is appropriate to add here that one of my major intents in preparing this book has been to reveal how enormously varied and widespread such movements have been.

Inclusiveness, however, is simply impossible. In fact, it should be stated unabashedly at the start that far more is left out of this encyclopedia than is included. Obviously, numerous organizations, movements, demonstrations, and other events involving students or youths are missing. Their absence is partly based on a single factor: there are simply too many to include. For example, in the year 1900, when there was a total of 237,000 college and university students throughout the United States, known student organizations numbered 611—and both of these totals had increased manifoldly by 1990. As another example, it is estimated that during the single academic year 1969–70, more than 9,000 student demonstrations involving nearly two-thirds of all the colleges and universities occurred in the United States alone.

To provide entries for even a small percentage of the organizations extant in the United States or of demonstrations that marked even a single exceptional year would require far more voluminous content than this book's limits allow and would also be meaningless because the great majority of the demonstrations and organizations replicated each other in purposes and programs. So what I have tried to do is to weigh the significance of a particular subject in justifying its inclusion; I have tried, that is, to choose subjects for entries based upon some definable import. Overall, I have focused on including those events, organizations, and people that had either a large impact at the time of their appearance or a large influence on subsequent events or both. Many youth movements—for example, the Young Men's Christian Association (YMCA) and the Girl Scouts—have a lengthy and continuing history that readily justifies inclusion. Others, such as the Hitler Jugend, had a relatively brief existence but a profound political or social influence of historic consequence.

Admittedly, the choice for inclusion has sometimes been arbitrary, but in each case I have tried to make clear why the event, person, movement, organization, or cause has historic merit. I have also included, again perhaps arbitrarily, some entries whose reason for being or historic context strongly argued in favor of their receiving attention. For example, although apparently neither the International Union of Students (IUS) nor the International Student Conference (ISC) had any measurable or enduring political or other influence on students, these organizations' histories clearly evidence the impact of the cold war. In these and many other cases, I would argue that any apparent arbitrariness is defensible. That said, I should also add that I may have omitted some meritorious subjects out of simple ignorance.

The fact is that student and youth movements have attracted only slight interest among historians and sociologists until the student eruptions of the 1960s garnered massive public and media attention, and with the passing of that era the interest again subsided. Consequently, writings that trace the history and significance of student and youth movements are relatively scarce. But these movements assuredly do merit study, not only by historians and sociologists, but also by educators, political scientists, psychologists, economists, and even the public as a whole. Perhaps this book may be accepted as a beginning point for a long-term or ongoing effort to provide a more comprehensive reference work in support of that meritorious study.

Introduction

Contemporary readers most likely immediately think of the 1960s when they hear the term *student movement*. It is certainly true that the period of the sixties, spilling over into the early seventies, provided a distinct apex in both the numbers and prominence of student movements. But this wealth of movements did not materialize out of thin air; its historic precedents trace back over several centuries.

Before pursuing an overview of that history, however, it is necessary to clarify the distinction suggested in this book's title. The designation *student and youth* is most purposeful and important. Whereas it is fair to say that virtually all student movements are youth movements, not all youth movements are student movements. Both types of movements involve the young, develop from similar historic origins, frequently share similar ideals or purposes, and sometimes have significant social or political impact, although usually of short duration.

Student movements as such have been mostly instigated by university students as acts of rebellion against perceived forms of oppression—curricular, societal, political, or economic. Regardless of their historic roots, they have largely been both spontaneous and ephemeral. They have most often erupted in response to an immediate circumstance (conscription, the 1848 Revolution, the Vietnam War, as specific examples) and have focused on whatever controversies surrounded that circumstance. They have also usually been short-lived because of their leaders' aging and passing from the scene, their goals being addressed or diverted, or their activism and organizations being effectively suppressed or dispelled by the established order.

Other forms of youth movements frequently share with student movements the characteristic of presenting a counterforce to systematic oppression, but sometimes their purpose actually is to serve as a transmitter of authoritarian values. Some have been generated and led by youths; others have been created by adults *for* youths. The aims of these broader-based youth movements have been as diverse as their manifold numbers throughout history: political rebellion, religious proselytizing or reform, militarism, pacifism, civil rights, communism, entrepreneurship, and a host of other causes. Because of their more durable aims, such youth movements have often had longer-term influence than more narrowly focused student movements. But it is important to note again that both types of movements share major similarities—most notably, of course, the involvement of youths—and that both are interactive.

No doubt, some definition of *youths* is desirable as a means of orientation. As a designation of an age group, *youths* has varied enormously in different centuries and in different societies. Those who are perceived as youths in the West of the late 20th century would have been considered adults in the 13th century. In the Middle Ages, for example, children were clothed and treated as adults well before puberty; they worked alongside adults, and it was common for them to be married by age 13. English law defined an adult as a male age 14; a female, age 12. As a matter of fact, this early acceptance of children into the status of adulthood remained widespread in Western society until fairly recent times: it wasn't until this century that childhood came to be seen as extending to the age of 18 or even beyond, with modern Americans experiencing a protracted adolescence as the social norm. After all, at the turn of this century the average expected life span was only about 40 years. The major reason for protracting the period of youth was the new paramountcy of industrialization and its related commercial developments, which required increasingly sophisticated levels of training and education that mandated lengthier periods of schooling, so that middle-class and upper-class youths, at least, continued their education several years longer than before instead of joining the workforce at an early age. This trend has not only continued but intensified in recent decades. It can readily be argued that as a society increases its economy's technological base, so also does the society extend its concept of the length of youth's duration. Regardless of such historic considerations, however, for purposes of inclusion in this encyclopedia, *youth* is arbitrarily considered to fall between the ages of 12 and 24; some entries mark exceptions, with youths either younger or older than these limits, but for the most part the limits stand. They serve equally well for the designation *student*, though the great majority of those involved in student movements have been older than 16.

Although a few youth groups that might be considered movements existed even in ancient Greece and Rome—for example, the young men who surrounded Socrates—student and youth movements distinctly recognizable as such to modern observers essentially originated in the Middle Ages. Dating the origin of student movements to about A.D. 1200 is appropriate because this date approximates the founding of major universities in the West—such as, Bologna, Padua, Paris, Oxford (German universities began to emerge in the 14th century)—and consequently marks the beginnings of "town-versus-gown" and students-versus-masters conflicts. These conflicts birthed the student movements that continue into the present time. The early Middle Ages also evidenced the beginnings of nonstudent youth movements. These sometimes were economic or political in nature—for example, peasant rebellions against feudal masters that involved youths or were at times even led by youths. Others were of a religious nature—for example, the Children's Crusade of A.D. 1212. Such youth movements, in short, from their very beginnings were more diverse than their student-led counterparts. That diversity continues to the present. The widespread student movements of this century focus primarily on politics, advocating reforms or even revolution to transform political and social systems, whereas other youth movements continue to exist in such variety as to involve religion, politics, sports, performing arts, and numerous other activities.

Several characteristics distinguish the student movements of the modern era. They often espouse such goals as liberal political reforms, total freedom of speech and assembly, full legal and civil rights for minorities, and other ends conceived as ethical imperatives. In so doing they sharply contrast their own presumed moral superiority with the supposed conformity or acquiescence or cynicism of their elders. (The same actually might be said, however, of the youths who led the Children's Crusade or of the Maid of Orléans who rallied French troops against the British—so this characteristic will also apply to some youth movements.) Inherent in this advocacy of a higher ethical standard is a profound conflict between generations in which the young denounce their parents' generation in particular for presumably abandoning their formerly professed values and ideals, for a consequent loss of moral credibility, and therefore for a failure of authority. (For a presentation of this view, see Lewis Feuer's *Conflict of Generations*, published in 1969.) Recent sociological studies, however, discredit the significance of this so-called generation gap, noting that, among other things, youths who as rebels denounce their elders nonetheless later end up embracing their elders' normative values and behaviors over the long term.

The rhetoric of rebellion, nevertheless, frequently indicates that the rebel young perceive their elders' authoritativeness as parents, leaders, and exemplars as corrupted or compromised to the point of being unworthy of honor, and in fact contemptible. The contempt, of course, may assume extreme forms of expression: student advocates may denounce all who are older as well as all the social or political institutions they created or perpetuated. In doing so, they are likely to abridge or deny for others the democratic principles of free speech and open politics they so vocally espouse.

Their most extreme forms of rebelliousness find expression in revolution, violence, and murder. For student movements to foster and sanction such acts may seem truly sardonic, given their professions of moral superiority; but, as Joseph Stalin and other 20th-century revolutionary leaders have declared, a revolution validates itself and creates its own morality, so that any policy or behavior that furthers the purposes of the revolution, no matter how inhumane or destructive, proves acceptable. Opponents may find this point arguable, but the extreme student rebels' overriding of rational discourse renders the argument irrelevant. In such ways some student movements end up in apparent self-contradiction (at best) or self-immolation (at worst). After all, emotional commitment, rather than thoughtful analysis, propels the student movement towards its outcome, and emotionalism can shatter even the most admirable ideologies.

While they endure, however, many politically activist student movements generate their own momentum and with it an excitement that engages not only the movements' members but also nonstudent adherents—professors, workers, and others—energized by the movements' spirit of reform. That was certainly the case in the 1960s in the United States, Japan, and Korea, in some instances with desirable outcomes, as, for example, the forced resignation of autocratic President Syngman Rhee in Korea in 1960. More often than not, on the other hand, student movements lack defined goals—the momentum feeds on itself but drives towards no clear destination. In addition, those involved in student movements as leaders and participants, by the very nature of their student status, represent middle-class or even elitist elements of society. Consequently, those in authority generally treat student activists with greater tolerance than they would afford to other disruptive elements, although of course many confrontations have ended violently with police or soldiers attacking students or vice versa. Finally, it is almost always the case—19th-century Russian student movements being a prominent exception—that only a small percentage, 10 to 20 percent at most and sometimes less than 2 percent, of the student population actually supports a given movement, with the remainder either opposed or disinterested.

As noted, student movements often and youth movements sometimes profess political ideologies that provide their cohesiveness and guide their purposes and actions. In modern times probably the most frequently adopted ideology has been Marxism. But, of course, there are diverse interpretations of what constitutes "correct" Marxism. Thus, for example, member groups of the Zengakuren movement in Japan have been warring camps of ideologues; some professed one version or another of Trotskyism in hostile opposition to other student groups who were dedicated to more "traditional" Marxism—perhaps a long-term legacy of the 1920s struggle for power in the Soviet Union between Joseph Stalin and Leon Trotsky. In stunning contrast, both the National Socialist German Student Union and the Hitler Jugend of the 1920s and 1930s adopted the fascist views of their sponsoring Nazi Party. Despite this contrast, however, both the Japanese and German groups shared a sense of youthful idealism that was the source of their dedication to their disparate ideologies—probably a tragically misguided idealism in both cases. Ironic as it may seem, however, this youthful idealism has been a common motif through the centuries among both student and youth movements, and it is this idealism that has inspired many groups' political radicalization and activism. Ultimately some have demanded nothing less than the total reformation of their societies.

Some groups have been characterized by a quite different motivation—a pervasive alienation. They seem to have been trapped in this stage of Marxism, unable to move beyond it to a larger vision. A possible explanation for this phenomenon may be that as the period of youth has been extended into the twenties, so youths have remained dependent on adults for an extended time—not being self-sufficient, the youthful student is denied independence—and dependency may breed alienation. On the other hand, alienation was evident in both the German and Russian student movements before the advent of Marx, suggesting that it might be a factor not simply of adolescence but of indigenous politics. And alienation was most certainly prevalent among the U.S. student radicals of the 1960s and 1970s, many of whom considered all forms of Marxism to be reactionary. Alienation takes many forms, after all.

Such factors as these can also characterize other types of youth movements, although with some needed qualifications being added. Many youth movements attract adult adherents; indeed, most are organized and directed by adults. Many also effect desirable ends—inculcation of sound values, socialization, productive work, physical fitness, political involvement, public service—and over long time spans. Most have clearly defined goals. In some cases, however, as with the Hitler Jugend, these goals may actually be insidious or malignant; a few youth movements have been dedicated to violence and revolution. Although some youth movements are distinctly middle class or even elitist in their orientation, many include members of all social strata and all ethnic groups.

They are quite likely to be organized around and dedicated to a prescribed set of religious or social or civic values. (Consider, for example, the Boy Scout Law: to be trustworthy, loyal, helpful, friendly, courteous, kind, obedient, cheerful, thrifty, brave, clean, and reverent.) Some are dedicated simply to furthering artistic performance and creativity. In most cases long-term involvement in a youth movement will constitute a lifelong inheritance and influence.

It is largely in this context that historians and sociologists single out the Free German Youth Movement, in particular the Wandervogel, as probably the most significant of all modern youth movements. The free youth movement emerged near the turn of the century and endured in diverse but intent manifestations until 1933, when the Nazis came to power and suppressed all but their own new youth groups. Its significance inhered partly in the fact that it was truly, and apparently uniquely, a youth movement—a movement created by and for youths. But, as Walter Laqeuer has made clear in *Young Germany*, it was far more because this movement embodied romantic, nationalistic, idealistic, educational, and racial concepts and values with connotations that lay deep in the German psyche and ultimately evinced profound political and social effects. The Free German Youth Movement, wrote British parliamentarian R. H. S. Crossman, in its influence was the equivalent for the Germans of Eton and Harrow for the British. For one thing, many of the century's prominent German political leaders had belonged to the movement as youths, as many British leaders had attended Eton or Harrow. Some enduring influence may at least be inferred, though not precisely defined. Thus the Free German Youth Movement may provide a touchstone for evaluating the potential impact of other youth movements. (Does a former Boy Scout remember the Boy Scout Law for life?)

Similarly, the German student movement originating in the 19th century with the Burschenschaften was among the most significant in history—in this case not because of the movement's almost nonexistent revolutionary activism but because of its capacity to effect academic reforms while augmenting aristocratic and middle class social and political values. In Europe probably the most oustandingly activist student movement occurred in Russia, where university students, though small in total numbers, formed a major element of the 19th- and early 20th-century revolutionary drive to reform or overthrow the tsarist government. Student movements in the Balkans were similarly militant, resulting in the assassination of Archduke Franz Ferdinand that provided the catalyst for World War I.

The fact is that such unstable political environments as existed in Russia and the Balkans proved the most fertile soil for breeding activist student movements. By contrast, the stable democracies of Great Britain and the United States had no tradition of significant student activism. In the United States the most noteworthy period of student activism prior to the 1960s occurred in the Great Depression years, notably with the Student Strike Against War; but this movement was comparatively mild and limited. The radicalized student movements of the 1960s and 1970s had no broad historic precedent and came as a great surprise. A similar comment pertains to Japan. In Africa and India student movements are of recent origin, doubtless because of these areas' former colonial status. Latin America, however, witnessed a widespread and influential student movement that originated with the University Reform Movement in Argentina, but the focus of this movement was of course on educational reform.

It is highly noteworthy that the impact of students' movements on political or social developments has varied widely from nation to nation. For example, the student movement in China dating to the May Fourth Movement of 1919 and culminating in the Chinese Democracy Movement of 1989 has frequently been most effective in involving the general public, with major short-term or long-term consequences; as a result, successive governments in China since 1919 have taken very seriously the students' potential power to effect change and have responded accordingly—mostly with repression. In Korea and Burma, student movements have actually brought about the toppling of governments. In the United States, however, student movements have most often, as in the 1960s, been marginalized and tolerated as essentially a nuisance rather than a threat requiring repression or changes in government policies. In short, the existence, nature, vitality, and influence of student movements have varied enormously by geographic region and in accordance with differing political, social, and economic circumstances. Clearly, the same comment would generally obtain for youth movements as well.

No doubt this discussion could profitably pursue these and related ideas at much greater length, but the fundamental points are here. Student and youth movements are complementary, sometimes the same, including overlapping memberships, but sometimes different. Their clientele comes from the same basic age pool, although youth movements may often involve younger adherents than student movements. Some movements are nationwide; others are restricted and obscure. Some are long-lived; others are ephemeral. Some proceed steadily, with defined values and goals; others arise spasmodically, with inchoate purposes. Some promote change, including revolutionary change; others foster stability and continuity or even reaction. Some recruit the elite; others, the commonalty. Some appeal to nationalism, even xenophobia; others, to universality. But whatever their characteristics, once again and finally, all share the unique distinction of young people's involvement as their primary reason for being.

ENCYCLOPEDIA OF
STUDENT AND YOUTH
MOVEMENTS

Abbeys of Misrule (France) organized youth groups common in both peasant villages and cities from the 13th century and enduring in some form in certain areas into the 19th century. Sometimes termed "Kingdoms of Youth" or *sociétés joyeuses*, the abbeys were actually of serious intent, as their use of carnivals, riotous behavior, charivaris, masks, and other forms of misrule provided important means of enforcing community mores. For example, a husband who was beaten by his wife would be mocked by being ridden through town seated backward on an ass during an abbey carnival parade; a widower who married a younger woman would be harassed by charivaris until he paid the abbey youths a "fine"—perhaps a means of trying to preserve the pool of nubile women for the younger men. Unfaithful spouses also were subjected to the abbeys' mockery. In the cities, crowded with apprentices and more stratified by social classes, the abbeys' civic role underwent transformation as early as the 16th century, with their organization and focus on civil order confined to distinct neighborhoods or with political and religious leaders rather than aberrant individuals often becoming the subjects of their public derision. The forms of derision were most often literary, comic, and theatrical; one Paris Abbey, the *enfants sans souci*, in about 1550 even organized as a semiprofessional troupe of actors.

Comprised of unmarried males in their adolescence to midtwenties, each Abbey gave its leader a name such as *abbot, king, prince of youth, prince of fools,* or *prince of pleasure*. Some abbeys functioned like courts, even holding mock trials. As abbeys or kingdoms, the youth groups could assume authority over others while also providing camaraderie and even brotherhood among their members. Their forms of misrule, as inversions of community standards or rule, exemplified disorder meant to reinforce order. The misrule also helped to define and to reinforce what their own standards of behavior should be as adults in the future, especially in the state of marriage—thus affording a socializing process for the youths. Most prevalent in France, Abbeys of Misrule also existed in rural areas throughout numerous other European nations, including Germany, Switzerland, Italy, Romania, and Hungary.

Bibliography: Natalie Zemon Davis, "The Reasons of Misrule: Youth Groups and Charivaris in Sixteenth-Century France," *Past and Present*, 50 (1971), 41–75.

Academic Legion *See* VIENNA UPRISING OF 1848.

Action Command of Indonesian Students (KAMI) (Indonesia) an organization formed on October 25, 1965 by leaders of various student associations meeting at the home of Major General Sjarif Thajeb, minister of higher education and science. The leaders were acting on the minister's suggestion that an entirely new student organization be created. A "national union of students," KAMI thus emerged in the aftermath of the October 1 coup d'état; it soon became the most politically powerful student organization in Indonesia, even though some groups chose not to join. On January 10, 1966, during a student rally supported by the military at the Faculty of Medicine of the University of Indonesia in Djakarta, KAMI issued "Three Demands of the Indonesian People," dissolving the INDONESIAN COMMUNIST PARTY (PKI), replacing the cabinet of President Sukarno's government, and lowering the prices of goods. Students were especially displeased with the price of gasoline, which made bus fares and thus the cost of getting to lectures very expensive, so they began a boycott of classes and street demonstrations to protest bus fares. They won public support by publicizing their demands through graffiti and posters that chastised the government for the cost of living. On January 12 they made a "long march" to Senajan, where members of Parliament were convened, to push their demands. The next day the Djarkata city government lowered bus fares to their earlier level. On January 14 KAMI members forced their way into the offices of the state-owned oil company, Pertamin, and compelled the company director to sign a decree lowering the price of gasoline. These victories gave KAMI political stature, and on January 15 Sukarno invited KAMI representatives to attend a meeting of the cabinet at Bogor; he also met personally with a student delegation.

Sukarno lowered some prices, but on January 20 he publicly criticized KAMI at a rally that then erupted into a riot. The students called a moratorium on demonstrations during the religious holidays but returned to the streets on February 2. After Sukarno dismissed a cabinet minister who sympathized with their three demands, KAMI staged a mass rally on February 23; on February 24, joined by high school students belonging to the Action Command of Indonesian High School Youth (KAPPI), KAMI tried to prevent the arrival at the presidential palace of new ministers who were to be installed that day; the confrontation with the palace guards resulted in the deaths of two students. The next day, tens of thousands of people, including military personnel, turned out in support of KAMI, while Sukarno banned student demonstrations and ordered that KAMI be dissolved. Following a February 28 rally addressed by Sukarno, nationalistic students from the Indonesian National Student Movement (GMNI), augmented by youth- and labor-group members organized by the Indonesian National Party (PNI), marched on the University of Indonesia—on the way they were joined by armed supporters—intent on wreaking destruction. But troops from the Jakarta garrison, acting on a request by KAMI, intervened to protect the university and KAMI members.

On March 3 the government ordered the university closed, and it was thereafter occupied by troops who allowed the students to continue their protests. On March 4 about 3,000 KAMI members convened at the university to create a military-style defense group; KAMI also broadcast protest messages over its clandestine Radio Ampera. On March 5 the students demonstrated in the streets of Djakarta. Newspaper and public support for KAMI grew, and students at Bandung Institute of Technology organized additional support. Three thousand members of KAPPI joined KAMI's struggle on March 7 and occupied the Ministry of Basic Education. On March 10 KAMI members forced their way into the Consulate General of the Chinese People's Republic and vandalized the rooms. On March 11 KAMI members again blocked access to the presidential palace, forcing cabinet members to arrive by helicopter. As some cabinet members voiced dissent over Sukarno's response to the student protests, word arrived that troops were deploying on the outskirts of the city; Sukarno left by helicopter for his palace in Bogor. General Suharto visited Sukarno there and persuaded him to issue a public decree conferring extensive

powers on Suharto to restore order and stability—the 11 March Order. With this new authority, Suharto on March 12 banned the PKI. Pursuing their second demand for changes in the cabinet, KAMI students captured several of Sukarno's ministers, held them at the university for interrogation, and then turned them over to the military. Suharto had 16 ministers taken into custody, ostensibly for their own protection, and then replaced them. The students' actions also helped uncover information that compromised Sukarno, leading to demands that the Provisional People's Consultative Assembly (MPRS) be convened in special session. After deliberations, the MPRS stripped Sukarno of his positions and titles and, on March 12, 1967, named Suharto acting president. Thus KAMI, with the support of KAPPI, was instrumental in achieving both the dissolution of the PKI and the end of the Sukarno government, ushering in the "New Order" in Indonesia. As a result KAMI gained special recognition, its publications were widely read, and its radio broadcasts were widely disseminated; 13 KAMI representatives were awarded positions in Parliament. It must be noted, however, that throughout the months of protest, KAMI had tacit and even open military support because the military believed KAMI's activities provided a valuable means of rallying public sentiment against the government. By 1970 KAMI had become sidetracked through disunity and lack of leadership.

Action Français (France) a political organization associated with Roman Catholicism that has a student affiliate, the Étudiants de la Restauration Nationale. Action Française was founded on June 20, 1899, its major tenets being nationalism, monarchism, and anti-Semitism. The Vatican declared it heretical after World War I, and it was banned after World War II but continued in operation. The student affiliate publishes a newspaper entitled *Amitiés Françaises Universitaires*.

African Resistance Movement (ARM) (South Africa) a militant movement formed in 1960–61 consisting largely of white former leaders of the NATIONAL UNION OF SOUTH AFRICAN STUDENTS (NUSAS) and other students opposed to apartheid. The group sabotaged rail lines and blew up electric power transmitters in the Cape and Witwatersrand areas. Many of the members were arrested and others fled the country during the "July raids" of 1964, which brought the movement to an end. Although their sabotage activities had targeted property only, one ARM member did set off a bomb in the Johannesburg railway station and was executed for murder. The government used the ARM connection with the NUSAS as an excuse to harass the NUSAS.

African Students' Association (ASA) (South Africa) an organization of African students formed in 1961 following a student strike that protested South Africa's being declared a republic. The ASA was affiliated with the banned African National Congress (ANC). It predominated at the nonwhite Fort Hare University College and University of the Natal, but there were so few African students in South Africa that the ASA's membership and funding both remained limited. Harassed by the government because of its ANC ties, the ASA disappeared within South Africa and came to exist only in exile.

Afrikaner Student League (Afrikaanse Studentebond (ASB) (South Africa) an organization formed in 1948 through a merger of the Afrikaner National Student League (Afrikaanse Nationale Studentenbond, ANSB) and the Federation of White South African Students. The ANSB, formed by Afrikaner students who had withdrawn from the NATIONAL UNION OF SOUTH AFRICAN STUDENTS (NUSAS) in the mid-1930s, had evidenced strong sympathy for the Nazis and therefore fell out of favor following Germany's defeat in 1945. The ASB tried to restore the patina of respectability to Afrikaner nationalism, and from the 1950s on it was the largest student organization in South Africa, attaining a membership of 28,000 in the mid-1960s. The ASB strongly supported the National Party, which came to power in 1948, and its policy of apartheid and also advocated segregated universities. The ASB consistently opposed the NUSAS, accusing it of promoting left-wing, anti-Christian, anti-Afrikaner, and treasonable policies.

Agrupación Femenina Universitaria (Argentina) a women-students group formed at the University of La Plata in September 1945. The Women's University Group supported the restoration of constitutional and democratic operations at the university (the military government had seized control of the universities) and appealed to women nationwide to agitate for the restoration of civil liberties. The new group represented one of the first instances of women students' involvement in politics. Similar women's groups were formed at individual faculties at the University of Buenos Aires.

Air Cadets (Great Britain) officially the Air Defence Cadet Corps (ADCC), an organization for boys founded in 1938 by the Air League of the British Empire to foster members' capabilities in flying and other aspects of aviation. By the end of 1940, with Great Britain involved in fighting World War II, the corps consisted of 204 squadrons with about 20,000 members. Boys could become full members at age 15 $1/2$. In February 1941 the Air Ministry assumed control of the ADCC, transforming its role to fulfill the then important purpose of providing boys with pretraining to prepare them for later service in the Royal Air Force.

Akademische Freischar (Germany) a youth organization founded in 1907 that was devoted to a "new way of life" (that is, a reformed life); to a "free student" program of nonpartisan understanding of political, religious, and cultural viewpoints; and to promoting the spirit of the WANDERVOGEL movement. The Akademische Freischar advocated reforms in student life that included elimination of dueling and other "outmoded" behavioral customs. It was involved in the larger "free student" movement that organized the Erster Freideutscher Jugendtag held at HÖHE MEISSNER in 1913 and thus had served as a precursor of the FREIDEUTSCHE JUGEND movement.

Akademische Gilden (Germany) a youth movement of the 1920s that joined together two concepts: the fraternity and the *Männerbund* (a mystical male bond). The movement adopted roaming and fencing as training methods, observed pagan festivals, promoted the *Volk* concept, and rejected contacts with "alien races."

Akademisch-Wissenschaftliches Wehramt (AWA, Academic-Scholarly Military Office) (Germany) an agency formed in 1931 to coordinate and direct nationwide the military sport programs, such as "war sport" camps, sponsored by diverse groups for university students. AWA regional offices were set up at most universities. The *Hochschulring* placed its military training programs under AWA control. Participating students received record books in which to note their progress in completing the successive steps in the military training.

Akhil Bharatiya Vidyarthi Parishad (All-India Students' Organization, commonly known as Vidyarthi Parishad) (India) a supposedly nonpolitical organization founded in Bombay in 1955 by students and instructors previously involved with the RASHTRIYA SWAYAMSEVAK SANGH (RSS). Evidence suggests Vidyarthi Parishad represents the youth of such right-wing Hindu communalist parties as the Jan Sangh (People's Party), as many of the group's members and representatives in its National Council are former members of the RSS. Although advocating negotiations and cooperation among students, teachers, and administrators, Vidyarthi Parishad has participated in strikes and demonstrations. The organization is especially strong in the northern states, partly because it has been an advocate of Hindi as the national language. It has also emphasized providing social services, such as modest scholarships, libraries of textbooks for underprivileged students, and other programs.

Albanian Student Protests (Albania) a series of protests by Albanian university students in December 1990 that prodded the Communist government, led by Ramiz Alia, into effecting broad political reforms. The first protest occurred on December 8 and focused on poor living conditions in student dormitories; the following day the protest escalated. On December 12, a day after a meeting of the Central Committee, the government announced that an opposition party would be formed. This was a concession to political pluralism that the government hoped would placate the public while helping to alleviate Albania's isolation from other European states at a time when Communist rule was toppling throughout the former client states of the Soviet Union. But the student unrest now erupted into riots in four large cities in northern Albania. Determined to avoid bloodshed, Alia decided on further reforms. The Presidium of the People's Assembly gave formal approval to a decree accepting a multiparty political system for Albania on December 18. On December 19 the Albanian Democratic Party received official recognition. On December 28 the Council of Ministers granted legal status to the first opposition newspaper and established a commission to draft legislation relating to the press, radio, television, and publishing media. On December 31 the government published a draft of a new constitution containing 129 articles that, among other things, would end bans against foreign investments and religion and pave the way for parliamentary democracy. Thus the students' first protest set in motion a series of protests and governmental reactions that amounted to a bloodless revolution. This revolution, however, proved more chimerical than substantive. As the ensuing multiparty election unfolded, the well-funded Communists, the Albanian Party of Labor (APL), manipulated the entire process and ignored the cities where opposition was centered to concentrate on attaining broadscale victory in rural areas. Consequently, the election of March 31, 1991 confirmed the APL's ongoing control of the government, with the Democratic Party garnering only one-third of the vote. The riots that followed in some cities were violently repressed.

Aldermaston March (Great Britain) a demonstration supporting nuclear disarmament that was initially organized by the Emergency Committee for Direct Action against Nuclear War (founded in 1957 by Bertrand Russell, J. B Priestly, and other prominent Britons); the first march occurred on April 4, 1958. On that day 4,000 people began the demonstration march from Aldermaston to Trafalgar Square (85 kilometers [53 miles]). A surprisingly large percentage of the marchers were youths, and it was young people who came to comprise the great majority of the antinuclear movement adherents through the CAMPAIGN FOR NUCLEAR DISARMAMENT (CND) that succeeded the Emergency Committee in 1958. The CND organized the second Aldermaston March, held in 1959, that generated 16,000 marchers, most of them youths, and thousands more sympathizers and proved such a success that it gave a major boost to the Ban the Bomb movement and secured the march's place as an annual event of growing significance. For example, the Aldermaston March of April 1962 drew at least 40,000 marchers (perhaps even 100,000 by some estimates), again largely a demonstration of and by young people.

Alianza de la Juventud Nacionalista (Argentina) an ultranationalistic youth group of the 1940s and 1950s affiliated with the right-wing Legión Civica Argentina. Members of the Alliance of Nationalist Youth were used by the military government of the era to attack university student demonstrators and violently break up protest demonstrations and marches. The alliance also had a student branch, the Sindicato Universitario Argentino.

Alianza Popular Revolucionaria Americana (APRA) (Peru) a student movement formed in 1924 for the purpose of promoting political reform—the first such movement indigenously created in Latin America. A shift in Peruvian governance provided the catalyst for APRA's founding. Prior to World War I, governments headed by José Pardo in 1904–08 and 1915–19 and by Augusto Leguía in 1908–12 had pursued reformist policies, including improvements in working conditions and living standards. But after Leguía was reelected president in 1919, he seized dictatorial power. Although he continued reforms—expanding the school system, ending the Indians' serfdom, extending the franchise to all literate males 21 and older—he also practiced repression by censoring the press, jailing political opponents, and violating provisions of the constitution. In response, students organized an opposition headquartered at the University of San Marcos in Lima and demanded an end to the dictatorship. During a demonstration against Leguía by students and workers on May 23, 1923, government troops attacked the demonstrators, leaving a student and a worker dead. The government immediately closed the university and jailed or exiled many student leaders. Among the exiles was Victor Raúl Haya de la Torre, president of the FEDERACIÓN DE ESTUDIANTES DE PERU (FEP), who founded APRA in Mexico City. The movement's doctrine, known as *Aprismo*, combined elements of Russian Marxism, socialism, humanism, and Mexican revolutionary concepts. *Aprismo's* major tenets called for opposition to Yankee imperialism, political unity throughout Latin America, nationalization of land and industries, internationalization of the Panama Canal, and forming solidarity with oppressed classes and all peoples. Devotees of the APRA movement assumed the epithet *Apristas*. In Peru, where the Apristas attained their greatest strength and the support of the developing middle class, the movement also advocated integration of the Indians and free elections to install a government that would guarantee personal liberties. APRA also inspired the organization of similar movements in Venezuela, Cuba, Paraguay, Guatamala, and other Latin American nations.

All-Bengal Students' Association (India) a provincial student organization founded in the 1920s. The association claimed to have 20,000 members by 1929.

All-Burma Students' Union (Burma) a university students' organization that arose out of the Rangoon University Strike in 1936. A leader in its formation was AUNG SAN.

All-Burma Youth Organization (ABYO) (Burma) a successor to the EAST ASIATIC YOUTH LEAGUE (EAYL) formed in 1944. ABYO members participated in both the resistance movement against the Japanese occupation and in the Burma National Army. Following World War II the ABYO became affiliated with the Anti-Fascist People's Freedom League (AFPFL), whose principal leader was AUNG SAN.

All-China Federation of Democratic Youth (ACFDY) (China) a national umbrella organization of youth groups established in May 1949. The membership was totally disparate, ranging from the COMMUNIST YOUTH LEAGUE (CYL) to the YOUNG MEN'S CHRISTIAN ASSOCIATION (YMCA).

Allgemeine Deutsche Burschenbund (Germany) a union of reform BURSCHENSCHAFTEN formed in the latter part of the 19th century. In the 1880s the Burschenbund passed resolutions to admit all German students to membership, regardless of their religion. Subsequent pressure from Austrian fraternities advocating a virulent anti-Semitism, which exerted influence in all the German fraternities, led the Burschenbund in October 1919 to deny memberships to new Jewish applicants.

Allgemeine Deutscher Waffenring (ADW, General German Society of Dueling Fraternities) (Germany) a nationwide association of university-student dueling fraternities founded in 1920. In May 1933, following Adolf Hitler's consolidation of power, the society rewrote its constitution to require that all its member fraternities exclude Jews and Freemasons.

Alliance of Students in Shanghai from All Provinces (Ko-sheng liu Hu hsueh-sheng tsung-hui) (China) an organization formed in 1906 through the efforts of students who had returned from studying in Japan after the government there imposed restrictions on them. Although short-lived, the alliance was significant as the first attempt in modern China to form a nationwide union of students to focus on political, social, and cultural reforms. Its goals were also notably ambitious and included creating a national parliament, publishing newspapers and magazines, promoting self-government in all provinces, encouraging study abroad, teaching the national language to eliminate dialects, organizing art clubs, encouraging construction of railroads, and studying social conditions in outlying provinces. The alliance was a forerunner of the student organizations that arose out of the MAY FOURTH MOVEMENT.

All-India College Students Conference (India) a first annual meeting held in Nagpur on December 25–26, 1920 to coordinate the student political movement generated by students' involvement in the NON-COOPERATION MOVEMENT (NCO). The conference passed a resolution supporting the boycott of government-funded universities advocated by the NCO. The conference convened annually thereafter throughout the 1920s, with the active support of militant and left-wing leaders of the Indian National Congress (Congress Party), including Jawaharlal Nehru. The annual conferences each attracted some 3,000 student delegates from all of India. They were addressed by leaders of the Congress Party, whose nationalistic views they supported.

All-India Muslim Students' Federation (India) an organization for Muslim students founded in 1937 by the Muslim League. The federation had no involvement in the independence movement but focused instead on securing rights for Muslims. The student members were largely adherents of Mohammed Ali Jinnah, leader of the Muslim League, who had for decades advocated a single independent India with cooperation between Muslims and Hindus but now supported a separate Muslim state (Pakistan) because of the near total political dominance the Hindu-led Indian National Congress had attained. Following the creation of a separate and independent Pakistan in 1947, the Muslim students' federation's influence became negligible, as the majority of Indian Muslims concentrated in the new state while most of its resident Hindus fled to India.

All-India Students' Congress (AISC) (India) a nationalist-oriented organization founded in January 1945 at the eighth session of the ALL-INDIA STUDENTS' FEDERATION (AISF), partly out of opposition to communist-dominated student groups, including the AISF; its national office was in Bombay. The AISC claimed a membership of more than 100,000 (and perhaps 300,000) in early 1945. The largest and thus the most significant nationalist student movement at the time, the AISC advocated opposition to communism while supporting the effort to end British rule. At its 1946 session, held in Delhi and attended by Jawharlal Nehru and other leaders of the Indian National Congress (Congress Party), the AISC emphasized campus issues and ventured to assert some independence from the Congress Party (no party leaders attended the 1947 session). With the success of the independence movement in 1947, the Students' Congress lost its major raison d'être, and it disbanded in 1948.

All India Students' Federation (AISF)   (India) a national organization that arose out of Indian university students' involvement in Mahatma Ghandi's civil disobedience movement of the 1930s in opposition to the British colonial administration. The All India Students' Federation (AISF) was founded in 1936. Its purpose was to serve as an umbrella organization to speak for the nationwide student movement, and it set up affiliates in all the Indian provinces. The AISF advocated radical and nationalist politics and accommodated communists, socialists, and followers of Ghandi. Each year the AISF held a national conference that coincided with that of the Indian National Congress. The AISF conferences attracted about 3,000 delegates. Dissension erupted at the 1938 conference and again at the Nagpur conference in December 1940, attended by about 400 delegates representing 40,000 members. At this meeting communist members imposed their views on the AISF—support for the Soviet Union (USSR) and opposition to the Congress Socialist Party founded in the thirties. The socialists walked out, splitting the AISF into two groups. The split weakened the student movement and generated increasing factionalism, although the AISF continued to exist under communist control into contemporary times, becoming India's oldest student organization. During the cold war years, the organization received some financial support from the Soviet Union. The AISF lost some of its student support because of communists' opposition, including insurrection in some provinces, to the government of Jawharlal Nehru following independence; but after 1955 it focused mostly on university issues (such as, tuition cost, teachers' salaries, improved facilities), although retaining its communist orientation. Because of its militancy, the AISF achieved successes during the wave of student demonstrations in 1966, when nationwide there were an exceptional 2,206 demonstrations, 480 of which resulted in violence.

Bibliography: Philip G. Altbach, "The Transformation of the Indian Student Movement," *Asian Survey*, 6, no. 8 (August 1966), 448–460.

All-Russian Christian-Social Union for the Liberation of the People   (Russia) a small, secret movement of young intellectuals and professionals, ages 20 to 33, who advocated increased freedom of expression during the late 1960s. Many were tried and sentenced to prison during 1967–68. Seven members of the movement publicly protested against the Russian invasion of Czechoslovakia on August 21, 1968 by demonstrating in Red Square on August 25, 1968 and were subsequently imprisoned. Most members of the movement were living in the West by 1980.

All-Russia Student Strike of 1899   (Russia) a nationwide student strike that began at St. Petersburg University in February 1899. It was traditional for students to celebrate the university's founding on February 8 each year, but disruptions in the preceeding few years led the rector to warn that any drunken or rowdy behavior that year would be severely punished. The warning offended students, who had beforehand decided to tone down their behavior, and they interrupted the rector's speech at the anniversary ceremony with howling. When students left the auditorium, they discovered police blocking the Dvortsovyi Bridge, which they intended to cross from Vasilevskii Island into the central city, so they headed for the Nikolaevskii Bridge. At Rumiantsev Square they were accosted by mounted police. The students threw snowballs, and the police attacked them with whips. Students and public alike registered outrage—it might be acceptable to beat peasants on the street, but students were supposed to enjoy a favored status. Students called a general meeting for February 9 at which they elected an organization committee and called for a strike to close the university; their demands included an official investigation and assurances of the rights of personal inviolability and of all citizens to file complaints against the police. The issue of police brutality elicited support from students at all the other schools in the city.

In addition, the organization committee sent representatives to other towns to arouse support. In response, on February 15, students at Moscow University and Moscow Technological Institute voted to strike. Within two weeks of the Rumiantsev Square incident universities throughout the nation had joined the strike in a show of student solidarity. The provincial students added demands, including reforms in the system of awarding financial aid. Police arrested hundreds of students; 68 St. Petersburg University students were jailed. The St. Petersburg faculty council on February 16 called for release of the arrested students, withdrawal of police from the campus, and a temporary closing of the university. On February 20 Tsar Nicholas II appointed the Vannovskii Commission to investigate the protests and arrests. Because the government was not offering to release and reinstate the arrested students, the St. Petersburg Organization Committee decided to continue the strike; but some students were wavering, and a March 1 meeting was called to determine a course of action. It was decided to end the strike; students at Moscow University made the same choice on March 5.

The strike's impact was not over, however. The St. Petersburg Organization Committee released a manifesto declaring that the strike's real purpose had been a protest against the entire autocratic system and denouncing those who had not come to the strikers' support. The committee called a meeting on March 16 where about 1,000 students voted to resume the strike; on March 17 more than 1,400 students met and confirmed the vote. On March 18 the administration closed the university, suspending all the students and giving them five days in which to apply for readmission. The strike also resumed at Moscow University and other provincial universities. On March 20 and 21 the police rounded up the members of the organizing committee and expelled them from St. Petersburg. Police also invaded the campus, and on March 31 they arrested 540 student demonstrators. At Moscow 840 students were expelled from the university, and almost 200 more were expelled from the city. In April the strike began to dissipate under the effects of the hundreds of arrests and expulsions. Hoping to provide new direction for the student movement, the Executive Council of Moscow University called an all-Russia student conference for the end of April. But before the conference could begin, the police arrested all the delegates—students from Tomsk, Kazan, Warsaw, Odessa, Kharkov, Kiev, and Iur'ev as well as Moscow and St. Petersburg—bringing the 1899 strike to an end.

The All-Russia Student Strike was a harbinger. The Vannovskii Commission's final report largely favored the students' position, saying that the strike resulted from their dissatisfaction with living conditions and the university system. The report called for a number of reforms, including augmenting course assignments and professors' supervision of students and repealing the 1884 Statute's ban on ZEMLYACHESTVA and other student organizations. The Ministry of Education announced that new dormitories would be built and the professoriat would be expanded, but that students would be required to enroll at universities nearest to the districts where they had attended secondary school, thus restricting their options. The government issued the 29 July Temporary Rules, mandating specially created boards to conscript into military service students who were involved in disorders. In April 1900 the Ministry of Education sent a circular to university administrators warning that the student movement's purpose was to foment political opposition to the government. Most of the students arrested during the strike were reinstated.

Apparently little had changed, but the students had demonstrated the capability of launching a mass movement. The strike was the first nationwide and ongoing student protest that was focused mostly on one major issue—personal inviolability. Many of the students involved were inspired to become more activist, as the Vannovskii Commission's report opened up the possibility of getting the government's attention through protest. The strike also renewed a sense of solidarity among students and generated a desire to create an ideology for the student movement as a whole. In addition, the strike provided an example for the general public of the possibilities of effective collective action through a focus on goals that had wide support and thus avoided divisiveness. The students would soon be heard from again. (*See*, for example, KIEV UNIVERSITY UPRISING, KAZAN SQUARE DEMONSTRATION, REVOLUTION OF 1905.)

Bibliography: Samuel D. Kassow, *Students, Professors, and the State in Tsarist Russia* (Berkeley: University of California Press, 1989).

All-Union Leninist Communist League of Youth *See* KOMSOMOL.

Altwandervogel (Germany) one of the major groups to emerge from the split in the WANDERVOGEL that occurred in June 1904. Karl FISCHER was the first leader of the Altwandervogel as "Gross Bachant." After Fischer left for China in October 1906 the Altwandervogel itself split, with a new group called the Jungwandervogel breaking away under the influence of Wilhelm Jansen. The Altwandervogel was among those youth groups that survived World War I and the postwar economic and political crises largely intact.

Bibliography: Walter Laqueur, *Young Germany: A History of the German Youth Movement* (New York: Basic Books, 1962).

American Association of University Students for Academic Freedom (AAUSAF) (United States) an organization founded at the University of Washington in 1951 in reaction to McCarthyism and related threats to academic freedom. The AAUSAF, although never a major movement, became nationwide through cooperation with the American Association of University Professors and other student groups. It published the *Academic Freedom Newsletter* to report on perceived threats to academic freedom at universities throughout the nation.

American Boy Scouts *See* AMERICAN CADETS.

American Cadets (United States) an organization for boys based on the BOY SCOUTS and originally established as the American Boy Scouts (ABS) in May 1910 by the Hearst newspaper chain as a gimmick to increase circulation. Although denounced as a fraud by William Randolph Hearst, the ABS persisted as a competitor of the BOY SCOUTS OF AMERICA (BSA), which decried the ABS for drilling its members with real rifles, obliging them to solicit funds, and creating confusion with the BSA among the public. The BSA finally won a charter from Congress in 1916 as the official scouting organization in the United States and then brought legal action against the ABS, now renamed the United States Boy Scouts (USBS). In response the USBS became the American Cadets in 1918. The American Cadets' leadership increasingly emphasized nationalism, and the organization died out in the years following World War I.

American Legion (United States) an organization of former armed services personnel that promotes its goals for youths through a variety of programs. Among these is Boys' State, a program that provides high school juniors with training in the procedures and functions of local and state governments; the American Legion Auxiliary offers a similar program for girls through Girls' State and Girls' Nation. The legion also sponsors Boys' Clubs and Boy Scout troops. Through its youth groups, Sons of the American Legion, whose members are sons of legionnaires, the legion promotes the "Ten Ideals:" patriotism, health, knowledge, training, honor, faith, helpfulness, courtesy, reverence, and comradeship. Members of the sons may earn awards for their attainments that exemplify leadership and service.

American Red Cross Youth   (United States) a variety of volunteer and service programs conducted by the American Red Cross, involving youths from elementary through high school levels. Overall, the intent of these programs is to promote health and safety, human services, and intercultural and international relations. The youth programs originated with creation of the American Junior Red Cross in 1917 and are supported by the Red Cross Youth Service Fund. Red Cross Youth publishes and distributes two magazines. *American Junior Red Cross News* is for students in junior and senior high schools. Teachers oversee the Red Cross Youth programs in elementary schools and serve as advisers to student leaders of the programs in junior and senior high schools. Red Cross Youth programs are also provided worldwide.

American Student Union (ASU)   (United States) a significant antiwar and antifascist organization formed during a convention of colleges and universities held at the YOUNG MEN'S CHRISTIAN ASSOCIATION (YMCA) in Columbus, Ohio in late December 1935. Initially, the NATIONAL STUDENT LEAGUE (NSL) and the STUDENT LEAGUE FOR INDUSTRIAL DEMOCRACY (SLID) provided the impetus for the formation of ASU by joining together to propose a united student movement, and the ASU was their progeny. Some 427 delegates representing 76 universities and colleges, 37 high schools, and 22 student councils attended the ASU founding convention—they claimed to represent more than 150,000 students. The delegates voted to promote racial equality, to demand that Reserve Officer Training Corps (ROTC) programs be optional, to advocate legislation providing educational opportunities to low-income youths, and to support the OXFORD PLEDGE but also "collective security" measures against fascism, among other positions. Following the convention, ASU membership quickly grew to 6,000 with chapters and other affiliated groups at numerous campuses, including more than 100 high schools. Later conventions favored academic freedom, educational reforms, support of the Spanish Loyalists, and ending racial discrimination but argued rancorously over whether to support the Soviet Union. A 21-member National Executive Committee, which remained effectively under NSL control, had the power to make decisions on programs, demonstrations, and other policies during the periods between the national conventions. The national staff headquartered in New York City also had considerable power. During the years 1936 to 1938, ASU published its own journal, *Student Advocate*, with a circulation of 30,000, in editions for both universities and high schools. First appearing in February 1936, it comprised a combination of the NSL's journal *Student Review* and SLID's journal *Student Outlook*. The ASU supported several labor-union strikes, but its major activity was organizing antiwar strikes (*see* STUDENT STRIKE AGAINST WAR). By the time of its December 1937 convention, ASU was advocating embargoes against belligerent nations and a boycott of Japanese goods. ASU's convention in 1938, when the organization had a membership of 20,000, withdrew support for the Oxford Pledge in favor of advocating "collective security;" but this year marked the organization's peak. Socialist-oriented members objected to stances favoring intervention abroad and began to withdraw from the ASU. As the major force within the UNITED FRONT, the ASU, like the United Front itself, began to decline after 1938, especially following signing of the nonaggression pact between the Soviet Union and Nazi Germany in August 1939, which sundered the unity of the student movement. At its 1939 convention, under the control of communist leaders, the delegates voted 322 to 49 against a resolution opposing the Soviet Union's November–December invasion of Finland, which had outraged the American public; the move resulted in a huge erosion of student support for the ASU. In 1940, disgruntled over the communist student groups' slavish support of the Soviet Union, liberal student groups abandoned the ASU, whose membership plummeted to 2,000. Following the end of 1941, with the Japanese attack on Pearl Harbor and U.S. entry into World War II, ASU effectively dissolved.

Bibliography: Robert Cohen, *When the Old Left Was Young: Student Radicals and America's First Mass Student Movement, 1929–1941* (New York: Oxford University Press, 1993).

American Turnerbund   (United States) a federation of Turner societies for youths modeled upon the TURNVEREIN and begun in 1848 by Friedrich Hecker, who had been exiled from Prussia because of his involvement in the unsuccessful Revolution of 1848. Hecker founded a turnverein in Cincinnati on November 21, 1848 that still exists; another was founded in Philadelphia on May 15, 1849, and by 1850 six turnvereins existed and established the American Turnerbund. The Turnerbund gymnastic societies, like their German predecessors, promote physical fitness through exercise and gymnastics. They also foster intellectual growth and character-building through lectures, debates, and other programs.

American Youth Congress (AYC)   (United States) a conglomerate or umbrella organization of numerous diverse student and youth groups founded in the summer of 1934 by representatives of more than 1,000 student and youth groups meeting in New York City. Considered for a while to be the "spokesman" for American youth, the AYC's membership by 1935 included 500 clubs and 846 organizations and other affiliates, among them church and student groups, the BOY SCOUTS, and the YOUNG COMMUNIST LEAGUE; in 1939 AYC claimed to have 4.7 million affiliated members. From its start, the AYC took a liberal and activist position, advocating the creation of a national antiwar movement by youths, abolishment of the CIVILIAN CONSERVATION CORPS (CCC) because its regimen was militaristic, and support for the right of workers to join unions of their choice. At its second convention in July 1935 at Detroit, the AYC adopted a Declaration of Rights of American Youth which supported academic freedom, laws to aid minorities, unemployment insurance, abolition of child labor, and peace. Considering the NATIONAL YOUTH ADMINISTRATION (NYA) programs inadequate, the AYC at the end of 1935 proposed an American Youth Act with scholarship and employment programs more generous than the NYA's, to be paid for by a special tax on the wealthy. Although the American Youth Act was introduced as a bill in Congress annually through 1940, except in 1939, it never moved beyond committee consideration, even though the AYC sent groups of youths to Washington to lobby for its passage in 1936 and 1937. Eleanor Roosevelt was a major backer of the AYC, and she arranged an AYC meeting at the White House that President Roosevelt addressed— the only student group he ever spoke to there. The AYC was also the only youth group to have representation on the advisory committee of the NYA. By 1939 the AYC claimed nearly 5 million youths as affiliate members. Since AYC's leadership was revealed to be largely communist-oriented, however, the organization suffered decline after the 1939 nonaggression pact between the Soviet Union and Nazi Germany and subsequent events; Mrs. Roosevelt, criticized personally by AYC leaders, also fell out with the group. The AYC began to advocate isolationism, whereas its previous position had supported collective security. The Youth Congress Citizenship Institute sponsored by the AYC in February 1940 in Washington alienated liberals because of both the isolationist view and the opposition to aiding Finland that AYC leaders advocated; it also generated a confrontation with President Roosevelt. Disaffected groups began to abandon the AYC thereafter. The AYC demonstrated against passage of the Lend-Lease Act in February 1941, its last lobbying effort in the capital. The German invasion of the Soviet Union in June 1941 proved a fatal blow.

Bibliography: Robert Cohen, *When the Old Left Was Young: Student Radicals and America's First Mass Student Movement, 1929–1941* (New York: Oxford University Press, 1993).

American Youth for Democracy (AYD) (United States) a Communist-controlled youth and student orga-nization founded in October 1943 as the successor to the AMERICAN STUDENT UNION. The AYD's Intercollegiate Division then claimed to have 1,400 members. Although AYD advocated moderate positions on issues, by 1947 it was plagued with charges of being a "subversive" or "Communist front" organization. Among its foes was the House Un-American Activities Committee (HUAC). The attacks imperiled AYD's existence, and some universities banned the group. In effect it became subsumed into the YOUNG PROGRESSIVES OF AMERICA (YPA), created in 1948.

American Youth Foundation (AYF) (United States) a nondenominational Christian organization founded in 1924. The organization's focus is on training youths to become Christian leaders through developing their mental, physical, social, and religious capabilities. AYF operates a camp in Michigan and one in New Hampshire.

American Youth Hostels (AYH) (United States) a U.S. organization modeled upon a program founded in Germany and dedicated to fostering interpersonal understanding through educational and recreational travel, outdoor activities, lectures, and other activities. The organization's emphasis on travel is supported by a system of hostels, or lodges, that provide inexpensive overnight accommodations for members. The National Association of German Youth Hostels (and its offshoots in Europe), originated by Richard Schirrmann, a teacher, in 1909 in conjunction with the WANDERVOGEL, inspired establishment of the AYH by two U.S. teachers, Isabel and Monroe Smith, who experienced hosteling while on a European trip. They founded the first youth hostel, and thereby the AYH, in Northfield, Massachusetts in 1934.

Ampo Bund *See* ANTI-AMPO STRUGGLE.

Amsterdam Anti-War Congress (World Congress Against War) (Netherlands) an international peace meeting organized by communists that convened in Amsterdam in August 1932 and was important to the U.S. student movement of the 1930s in providing a major impetus for that movement's antiwar effort. Among the leaders of the Congress were U.S. author Sherwood Anderson and French novelist Henri Barbusse, who telegraphed the NATIONAL STUDENT LEAGUE (NSL) (which had sent Joseph Clark as its representative to the congress) and requested that the NSL organize a student antiwar conference in the United States. Inspired to action, the NSL organized the STUDENT CONGRESS AGAINST WAR, which met in Chicago in December 1932.

Anti-Ampo Struggle (Japan) a major movement of 1959–60 opposing revision of the Japan-U.S. Security Treaty signed in 1951 and resulting in the government's resignation. (*Ampo* is a contraction of *Nichibei Anzen*

Banners wave above a packed crowd of demonstrators parading before the Japanese Diet in Tokyo on November 27, 1959. They called for an end to the Japanese-U.S. Security Pact and the resignation of the Kishi government. In the foreground are flat-topped hats of Japanese police. (AP/WIDE WORLD PHOTOS)

Hosho Joyaku, the Japanese name for the Security Treaty.) Opposition to a renewed and revised treaty was especially strong in the Socialist and Communist Parties but became widespread when Prime Minister Nobusuke Kishi pushed hard for approval. In March 1959, 13 sponsors formed the People's Council for Preventing Revision of the Security Treaty (Ampo Jayaku Kaitei Soshi Kokumin Kaigi), which involved 134 different groups, the most important being the Japan Socialist Party, the General Council of Trade Unions (Sohyo), and ZEN-GAKUREN. To keep control over Zengakuren's militancy, the leaders put the student group in the Joint Struggle Council of Youths and Students, but the tactic failed—one reason being that the Anti-Ampo Struggle split the Japan Socialist Party, with conservative members breaking away to form the Democratic Socialist Party (DSP). Also in March 1959 a Tokyo district-court judge

declared the original Security Treaty unconstitutional, providing a morale boost for treaty opponents. The People's Council decided to stage a series of "united actions," peaceable rallies. These were ineffectual, until the Zengakuren, which fell under control of its militant Kyosanshugisha Domei (Communist League) segment in June, decided on its own course during the rallies. On November 27, as the People's Council leaders tried to present a petition at the gates of the Diet House (seat of the parliament, Diet) as part of their eighth United Action, 1,000 students rushed through the gates, storming the Diet House. Some 6,000 more students and laborers followed, occupying the grounds. Altogether 80,000 protestors, watched by 5,000 police, joined in the Tokyo rally and 500,000 marched nationwide, but it was the attack on the Diet House that got the government's attention.

The Diet responded by introducing a bill (never passed) to restrict demonstrations in the Diet House area, and police arrested two Zengakuren leaders. Kishi planned to fly to Washington on January 16 to sign the new Security Treaty, so about 700 students from the Zengakuren occupied the lobby and tried to prevent his departure; 2,000 police dispersed them and arrested 76. On April 26, as the Diet was debating the treaty, the People's Council again tried to present a petition, and again their Zengakuren contingent (3,000 students) stormed the Diet House, intent on breaking in; 17 leaders were arrested. On May 20, after the government announced that the treaty would be put to a vote, students and laborers demonstrated at the Diet, and 300 Zengakuren members invaded the gardens of the prime minister's house next to the Diet House.

On June 10, in preparation for a scheduled visit in July by President Eisenhower, the president's Press Secretary James Hagerty arrived in Tokyo; Zengakuren members mobbed, pummeled, and detained his car at the airport. A U.S. Marine helicopter finally rescued him. This disruption, known as the Hagerty Incident, received worldwide newspaper attention and nearly convinced the Japanese government to cancel Eisenhower's visit. Instead, the government decided to crack down on the students. But on June 15, in a planned master stroke, 15,000 students marched past the Diet House and staged a sit-in at the Metropolitan Police Station while another group of Zengakuren members forced their way into the Diet compound at an entrance on the opposite side of the building. They clashed with police, and during the melee a woman student was crushed to death at about 7:00 P.M.—news of her death spurred the students to greater violence. The struggle endured into the early morning of June 16, when the police were issued tear gas and managed to disperse the demonstrators; the final toll was hundreds injured and 348 arrested. On June 18 some 330,000 demonstrators wearing black armbands surrounded the Diet House. On June 22 there was a general strike, on June 24, a national funeral was observed for the dead student, and thereafter the demonstrations slowly petered out. Although the Diet ratified the treaty, the consequences of the demonstrations included both a cancellation of Eisenhower's visit and the resignation of Prime Minister Kishi.

Bibliography: Stuart J. Dowsey, ed., *Zengakuren: Japan's Revolutionary Students* (Berkeley, Calif.: Ishi Press, 1970)

Anti-Ayub Khan Protests (Pakistan) a series of protest demonstrations in 1968–69 against the government of President Mohammad Ayub Khan initiated by students that finally forced him from office. The demonstrations originated in Rawalpindi, where students marched during early November 1968 to protest against police confiscation of contraband goods they had purchased while in Landi Kotal, on the border to the north

of Peshawar, and to demand return of the goods. During a confrontation between police and the protestors, one student was killed. A student eruption followed, so violent that army units had to be called in to restore order. From these totally nonpolitical incidents emerged ongoing protests with major political repercussions. Aggrieved students raised issues relating to administration of the higher-education system and standards for passing examinations; they were especially incensed by penalties imposed by the terms of the university ordinance approved by the Ayub Khan regime, which included confiscation of their degrees if the students engaged in political activities. As their demonstrations continued on November 11, someone fired a shot at Ayub Khan while he was speaking at a meeting in Peshawar. Concerned over the political ramifications of the students' demonstrations and the shooting, and fearful that opponents would use the demonstrations to promote a campaign against the regime, the government had Zulfikar Ali Bhutto, leader of the Pakistan People's Party (PPP), and other opposition political leaders arrested under authority of the Defense of Pakistan Rules.

The arrests set off more student demonstrations, as Bhutto had supported the students' demands. Now the student protestors' focus shifted to such political issues as reconstituting the parliament, releasing Bhutto and other political prisoners, and restoring civil rights. The demonstrations became self-perpetuating, as every time a student protestor was killed by the police, an enlarged wave of protests followed. So the protests grew and continued into mid-February 1969, by which time the thousands of students who demonstrated in each of Pakistan's major cities had been joined by women and such professional groups as the bar associations and some labor unions. Since the police were unable to control the demonstrations, the Ayub Khan regime relented, freeing Bhutto and rescinding the university ordinance. But the shift in strategy came too late, as labor unions took control of and promoted the protest demonstrations, pressing demands for improved wages and work conditions along with economic and political reforms. In some areas, their strikes closed down industries and shut off inflows of capital, leading fearful industrialists to prod the government about committing troops to end the uprisings. The regime appointed new governors for East and West Pakistan but to little effect. On March 25, conceding loss of control, Ayub Khan declared martial law and publicly announced that the government would be handed over to the military. The following day Ayub Khan resigned from the presidency; General Yahya Khan, army commander-in-chief, succeeded him. Bhutto won the presidency in the elections held in 1970.

Anti-Christian Movement (China) a nationwide protest in 1924–25 to discredit and to denounce Christian missionary activities involving student and youth groups. It was preceded by a similar movement in 1922, but the 1924 movement was notable for its Marxist orientation—the COMMUNIST YOUTH LEAGUE (CYL) was prominent in the movement. Students at missionary schools went on strike in protest against mandatory Bible classes, efforts to restrict students' participation in patriotic protests, missionary domination of universities, and related concerns. Students at Shanghai University were the first to form an "anti-Christian alliance" (in February 1924) and provided the leadership generating the organization and propaganda for the Anti-Christian Movement.

Anti-Hindi Students' Action Committee   (India) an organization active in the Tamil-speaking areas of India in 1965. The students generated demonstrations and strikes in southern India in opposition to the central government's plan to adopt Hindi as the national language; they also supported retention of English as the language used in classes in the local universities. The riots that arose out of the students' agitation resulted in 50 deaths, extensive damage, and a national crisis that forced the government to postpone enacting the Hindi language plan.

Anti-Hunger, Anti–Civil War Movement   (China) a student movement of 1947 protesting against the civil war between the forces of the Kuomintang (KMT) and those of the CHINESE COMMUNIST PARTY (CCP) and the hyperinflation (and consequent high costs for food) resulting from it. Although the origins of the movement trace to 1946, its major expression began in May 1947. On May 20 thousands of students from Nanjing schools and from schools and universities in Shanghai, Hangzhou, and other cities held a protest march in Nanjing resulting in the MAY 20TH TRAGEDY which galvanized student support for the movement. The students planned mass demonstrations nationwide to be held on June 2, which they designated as Anti–Civil War Day. Largely because of widespread police arrests of dissident students and the central government's organizing of loyalist youths and demonstrations supporting the government, Anti–Civil War Day did not occur. The government's repressive tactics backfired over the longer term, however, and public support for the students' movement apparently increased.

Anti-Menderes Coup   (Turkey) a coup d'état, preceded by massive student demonstrations, that toppled the Democratic Party government headed by Prime Minister Adnan Menderes. The Democratic Party came into power in 1950, and as the decade proceeded Menderes imposed increasingly repressive measures against his political opposition, the press, and other organizations; 2,000 of his political opponents were jailed. At the end of

Students from Istanbul University march through downtown Istanbul on April 28, 1960, in demonstration against the regime of Turkish Prime Minister Adnan Menderes. The scene turned to one of bloodshed a few minutes later when the students clashed with police. At least four persons were killed and scores of others injured. (AP/WIDE WORLD PHOTOS)

April 1960, he mandated a committee to investigate the rival Republican Peasants' Nation Party (RPP) and gave the committee sufficient powers to silence public opponents of the regime. This act ignited student protests centered at the Law Faculty in Istanbul and the Political Science Faculty in Ankara. About 1,500 students gathered in protest on the campus of Istanbul University. Police invaded the campus and attempted to arrest some of the protestors; a female student knocked down one policeman with her high-heeled shoe, and the police reacted by opening fire, killing one student and wounding others. When the university president informed the police that it was illegal for them to be on the campus, they attacked him and dragged him off to a station. Outraged students swelled the number of protestors to 5,000. The students forced the police to return the president to the campus; upon his return he tried in vain to persuade the students to disperse. Mounted police attacked as others hurled tear gas into the crowd of student demonstrators. Students jabbed cigarettes against the horses' stomachs, causing them to rear up and throw their riders. Again the police opened fire, and 20 students fell wounded. The bloody clash ended with 30 students wounded and 7 dead. Police and army tanks prevented the students from marching into the city center.

The government closed the universities for a month, but the student protests continued on through May and formed the major public opposition to the Menderes government. A thousand cadets from the Military Academy in Istanbul launched a spontaneous march to the residence of President Celal Bayar but were persuaded to stop short of their goal by their commanders. On April 28 the government imposed martial law. But the military had become disaffected as a result of Menderes's policies; and on May 3 the commander of the land forces, Gen. Cemal Gursel, demanded that political reforms be instituted. When his demand was refused he resigned. On May 27 officers and cadets from the war colleges in Istanbul and Ankara staged a bloodless coup; created a governing National Unity Committee of 38 men headed by Gursel; and imprisoned Menderes, President Bayar, and other Democratic Party leaders. Although the military had organized and effected the coup, students took some justifiable credit for the role their precoup protests had played in the government's overthrow. Consequently, with an assumed sense of power and virtue, they pursued a more active and outspoken role. They staged successful walkouts in 1960 and 1961, for example, in protests over poor food, inadequate supplies of books, and unpopular instructors. In 1962 they trashed the offices of two newspapers and the Justice Party (a successor to the outlawed Democratic Party) in Istanbul. And in 1963 they held a massive street demonstration opposing the release from prison of former President Bayar, who needed medical attention.

Anti-Park Protests   (Korea) student demonstrations against President Park Chung Hee of South Korea in 1978 and 1979. When the delegates to the National Conference for Unification voted unanimously in July 1978 to reelect Park for six more years, it appeared that he was being awarded the presidency permanently, and protest followed, especially among students. As demonstrations erupted on university campuses, the government's Central Intelligence Agency stationed agents at colleges and universities. When clashes between students and the National Police continued, many students were arrested and tried. Students and other groups pushed for political reforms during 1979. As an act of conciliation, the government on August 15 released 871 political prisoners, among them about 60 students and professors, but the protests continued. On October 16 and 17, several thousand students in Pusan demonstrated, their violent confrontations with police resulting in many deaths and widespread destruction and the imposition of martial law. The student protests then spread to Masan, Ch'ang-won, Kwangju, and other cities—the most threatening student uprising since the APRIL REVOLUTION of 1960. The gov-

ernment feared that many thousands of students would take to the streets in Seoul as well, and an internal governmental crisis ensued. But on October 26 the director of the Central Intelligence Agency, Kim Jae Kyu, assassinated Park. This shock quieted the protesters, and students turned their attention to demands for reforms at the universities.

Anti-Slavery Movement   (United States) a movement initiated by adults but involving autonomous student groups at many colleges and universities beginning in 1833. The first such group, the Auxiliary Anti-Slavery Society, was formed at Amherst College; by 1834 it included one-fourth of the student body. In the fall of that year, the college's president, Herman Humphrey, suggested that the group disband; when the students refused, he enlisted the support of the faculty in dissolving the society in March 1835. Other antislavery groups, some involved in the Underground Railroad, were established at University of Michigan, Oberlin College, Williams College, University of Illinois, Bowdoin College, Dartmouth College, Miami (Ohio) University, and New York University. When trustees ordered an antislavery group at Lane Theological Seminary in Cincinnati, Ohio, to disband, the group denounced the trustees and moved to Oberlin, where it earned the epithet Rebels.

Anti-Soviet Movement   (China) a student movement of February 23–26, 1946 centered in Shanghai that protested the ongoing presence of troops from the Soviet Union in Manchuria. The protestors also considered the Soviet troops responsible for the killing of a young engineer, Zhang Xinfu, while he was traveling through an area of North China that was under Soviet control. The movement began with the February 23 demonstration that coincided with the 28th-anniversary celebration of the founding of the Russian Red Army, being held at the Soviet consulate. Its high point was a massive memorial service for Zhang on February 26 held at Aurora University; this involved 30,000 students, as well as other groups, who marched in the city streets following the service.

Anti-Yoyogi Zengakuren   (Japan) a student organization formed in 1962 at a time when the ZENGAKUREN was fractured by factionalism. Yoyogi is the district in Tokyo where the Japan Communist Party (JCP) was headquartered, so the name signified the new group's opposition to the JCP. The Anti-Yoyogi Zengakuren was formed by the conjoining of four Zengakuren factions: Marugakudo (Marxist Student League), Shagakudo (Socialist Student League), Shaseido (Socialist Youth League), and the Front (Socialist Student Front). The Anti-Yoyogi group also fractured, but during the late 1960s it was a dominant power in the Zengakuren.

Anytown, USA   (United States) a leadership program for youths of high school age founded in 1957 and sponsored by the National Conference (formerly the National Conference of Christians and Jews). Anytown is a week-long workshop conducted in a camp setting. Workshop discussions focus on religious, racial, gender, and ethical issues and are facilitated by advisors who are teachers, clergy, business persons, or professionals in other fields. Swimming, hiking, volleyball, and other recreational activities are also part of the program. Delegates are chosen by their high schools or by sponsoring agencies.

April Revolution   (Korea) a student-initiated revolt against Syngman Rhee, the dictatorial president of the Republic of Korea (South Korea) in April 1960. Rhee's government claimed that he had won 90 percent of the votes cast in the March 15 presidential election (he had received only 55 percent in the 1956 election); students concluded that the 1960 election had been rigged. (It was later revealed by the minister of the interior that he had required letters of resignation from all mayors and police chiefs in the nation and had informed them that their resignations would be final if they failed to attain Rhee's reelection; in addition, the national police director had ballot boxes stuffed with votes favoring Rhee.) University and secondary school students reacted by staging massive and ongoing street demonstrations against Rhee in Seoul and four other major cities. Protestors in Masan had already demonstrated on election day; when the body of a student was found with a tear-gas cannister lodged in his eye, rioting erupted and many were wounded in clashes with the police.

The Masan protest evoked a sympathetic student demonstration at Korea University in Seoul on April 18 that was brutally suppressed. In response, on April 19 other students joined the Korea University students and staged a strident street protest—the "Righteous Student Uprising of April 19." Since the dubious election precipitated the demonstrations, the protestors understandably chanted slogans demanding democracy and free elections, but their implicit target was Rhee's domestic policies and the government's apparent incapacity to modernize the economy. Adults, who did not participate, nevertheless stood on the sidewalks and applauded the students' actions as they invaded homes of wealthy members of Rhee's Liberal Party, burned police stations, and marched on the government buildings. Confrontations with police generated sizable casualties, and students and others demanded that Rhee and his cabinet resign, the March 15 election be nullified, corrupt officials be forced out of the government, and political reforms be instituted to enhance or improve the democratic process. The government declared martial law and mobilized troops to move against the demonstrators since the police were unable to control them. But on April 20 the army refused to take action against the student demonstrators. The rioting and demonstrating continued every day.

On April 25 occurred another huge demonstration, with more than 300 professors from Seoul National University supporting the students by demonstrating on the National Assembly building's steps; that night troops and officers manning tanks joined the students in a tribute to those students who had been killed in earlier demonstrations. On April 26 a delegation of five students accompanied by Army Chief of Staff General Song Yo Chan went to Rhee's palace and delivered an ultimatum to him. On April 27 Rhee resigned and accepted exile in Hawaii. An emergency session of the National Assembly, attended by only 105 of the 231 members, voted unanimously in favor of a resolution supporting Rhee's resignation, new elections, and a new constitution as student leaders watched and cheered from the galleries. The assembly also appointed Foreign Minister Ho Chong to lead a caretaker government. The First Republic had come to an end.

The April Revolution is a rare example of student protestors achieving the overthrow of a government. During the six months following their success, the students comprised the dominant influence in Korean politics. Through their continuing demonstrations they forced politicians to accept their demands for punishment of Liberal politicians involved in the rigged March election, programs to stimulate economic growth, and other policies. In July 1960 radical students, especially students at Seoul National University, joined together to form the Student League for National Unification. But student influence on national politics peaked with a final spontaneous demonstration on October 11, when students stormed into the National Assembly's proceedings and commandeered the rostrum to demand that penalties be imposed on those Liberal politicians who were guilty of corrupting the March election. Afterward, student influence quickly waned. Sundered by factionalism and corrupted leadership, the students were unable to create a national organization to give themselves a continuing strong voice on the national stage. In May 1961, with the support of the United States government and U.S. troops, a military junta took control of the government, ending the short-lived Second Republic that had been initiated in August 1960.

Bibliography: Andrew C. Nahm, *Korea: Tradition and Transformation* (Elizabeth, N.J.: Hollym International Corporation, 1988).

Apristas   *See* ALIANZA POPULAR REVOLUCIONARIA AMERICANA (APRA).

Arbeiter Jugend (Working Youth)   (Germany) a Socialist-oriented organization for working-class youths up to age 20 that eventuated from an amalgam of Socialist groups founded before World War I. (*See* SOCIALIST

YOUTH MOVEMENT.) The Arbeiter Jugend, which published a newspaper of the same name, claimed 65,000 members in the 1920s. Its program emphasized rationalism and Marxism rather than the romanticism or nationalism that characterized other German youth groups. Although the Arbeiter Jugend disclaimed any political-party affiliation, it did have one connection with the Social Democrat Party in that it selected certain youths to be "functionaries" whose choice for this honor was sanctioned by party officials.

Arbeitsdienst (Work Service) (Germany) a youth movement established during the Weimar Republic. The movement entailed forming work camps where youths would engage in voluntary work service with the intention of fostering cooperation, community living, physical fitness, and self-government. The first camps were set up in 1925. When the Great Depression hit after 1929, the work-service program provided jobs to relieve unemployment, and in June 1931 the Weimar government created an extensive work-service program including public works projects and vocational education. This program was supported by the DEUTSCHE STUDENTENSCHAFT, a regional unit that also formed work camps in southwestern Germany. Student councils also set up camps. The camps involved unemployed workers as well as students. The NATIONAL SOCIALIST GERMAN STUDENT UNION supported the camps, hoping to gain control of them to propagandize the students, but the Student Union also strongly advocated making student work service a compulsory program that would require one year of service by every high school graduate. In June 1933 the Deutsche Studentenschaft, now in the Student Union's control, mandated participation in work service for all students, a requirement the Interior Ministry sanctioned in February 1934. On July 1, 1935 the Reichstag approved a law requiring all youths to perform work service. Many of the youths were involved in agricultural work—a means of facilitating the dissemination of Nazi ideology across the countryside.

Arc de Triomphe Anti-Occupation Demonstration (France) a march to the Arc de Triomphe by university students on November 11, 1940 (anniversary of the World War I armistice) in protest against the German occupation of Paris. Many of the participants were killed during the protest or were deported to Germany.

Artamanen (Germany) a right-wing youth movement, an element of the Volkisch movement, begun in 1924 whose members were dedicated to an agrarian ideology that rejected the mechanized, urbanized modern world while idealizing "noble" German peasants. Young male members formed groups that volunteered their labors on agricultural estates, mostly in eastern or northern Germany; by 1929 some 2,000 were involved in such work.

Artamanen was noteworthy in that at least two young men associated with it, Heinrich Himmler and Richard Walther Darre, became important Nazi functionaries—Himmler as the powerful head of the Schutzstaffeln (SS) and Darre as minister of agriculture. It was Darre who provided the ideology that underpinned the Landdienst program of the HITLER JUGEND. The Nazis' political power and youth movement brought an end to Artamanen, many of whose members gravitated into the SS.

Article 28 Protests (Argentina) a renewed struggle over the issue of adopting Article 28 of Law 6403 allowing the creation of private universities (all extant schools were public). Following the DELL'ORO MAINI struggle, the issue had receded from consideration; but Arturo Frondizi, inaugurated in May 1958 as the first civilian president since 1938, revived consideration of Article 28 in August 1958. Although formerly a Reformista (supporter of the UNIVERSITY REFORM PROGRAM AND MOVEMENT), Frondizi hoped to broaden his support among Catholics by this move. The student federations strongly objected to Article 28 on the grounds that it would permit establishment of private Catholic universities, free of government regulation and having the mandate to award professional licenses to graduates in medicine and law. Among the students' major supporters was Risieri Frondizi, rector of the University of Buenos Aires and brother of the president, who on September 4 spoke out publicly and led a student march to the Congress to protest against passage of the article. The student federations organized strikes at all the universities, and Reformistas fought with Catholics over the occupation of university buildings. The FEDERACIÓN UNIVERSITARIA ARGENTINA organized a public rally and parades that brought more than 250,000 protestors to the Plaza Congreso in Buenos Aires on September 19. On September 26 the Chamber of Deputies defeated Article 28, but a new bill introduced in the Senate that would allow creation of private universities regulated by the government and lacking the ability to award professional licenses passed both chambers of the Congress to become law. The student federations had won a partial victory but at the cost of splitting the student movement. For example, LIGA DE ESTUDIANTES HUMANISTAS at five of the University of Buenos Aires faculties withdrew from the university federation. In addition, a variety of splinter factions representing political ideologies ranging from communism to Peronism came into being at the universities during the decade following the 1955 initiation of the Article 28 struggle.

Assassination of Alexander II *See* EXECUTIVE COMMITTEE OF THE SOCIAL-REVOLUTIONARY PARTY.

Association Catholique de la Jeunesse Française (ACJF) (France) an organization for Roman Catholic youths formed by Count Albert de Mun in 1886. The ACJF's membership was open to youths from all social strata, and Christian socialism comprised its basic ideology. In the 1920s, however, the ACJF began to divide into five subgroups based on activity—workers, farmers, fishermen and sailors, students, and "independents." The first of these subgroups, the Jeunesse Ouvrière Chrétienne (JOC), was established in 1927 following pressure by young workers in the ACJF for its creation. The subgroup for students, the JEUNESSE ÉTUDIANTE CHRÉTIENNE (JEC) was formed in 1929—its members and others who sympathized with its views referred to themselves as *jecistes*. In 1954 the JOC and the JEC began to disagree over the role of the ACJF, with the former advocating its becoming a forum for leaders of the subgroups that might take a position on an issue only by unanimous agreement of the subgroup leaders. The JEC leaders disagreed on the grounds that such a role would result in separating the JEC from the other subgroups. The Roman Catholic church hierarchy in November 1956 tried to settle the dispute by siding with the JEC's position on the ACJF's organization, while ruling that the ACJF should be devoted either to social or political activism but not both and clearly supporting the former. This view alienated the JEC, whose leaders were involved in criticizing French prosecution of the Algerian War and in promoting political reforms to make French society and universities more equalitarian. Consequently, in 1957 some 80 JEC leaders resigned en masse; subsequently, the JEC effectively disappeared from the universities.

Association des Étudiants Musulmans Nord-Africains (AEMNA)   (France) an organization for university students from Algeria, Morocco, and Tunisia founded in Paris in 1927. AEMNA's ostensible purpose was promotion of a united and independent North Africa, but it had minimal clout, especially as nationalist movements developed in each of the three North African states and demanded independence and autonomy, not unity. In 1950 AEMNA set up a permanent secretariat to plan for a unified North African student union, but within a few years separate student unions had been created in each state—UNION GÉNÉRALE DES ÉTUDIANTS MUSULMANS ALGÉRIENS (UGEMA), for example, in Algeria.

Association Générale des Étudiants (AGE)   (France) the first local organization for French university students as such without religious or political affiliations of any kind. The first association, Société des Étudiants, was founded in 1877 at the University of Nancy, and in the 1880s similar societies were formed at the universities of Bordeaux, Paris, and Lyon. During the 1880s, these societies overall changed their name to Association Générale des Étudiants. By 1900 (when there were only 29,000 university students, more than 12,000 of them in Paris) all French university towns had such AGE organizations.

They were devoted to promoting social and recreational activities. The AGE chapters formed the UNION NATIONALE DES ÉTUDIANTS DE FRANCE in 1907. Each AGE chapter may be differently organized, either as a federation of individual associated student organizations or as an overall unit whose executive committee is chosen by votes of all the individual student members.

Association Générale des Étudiants de Lovanium (AGEL)   (Congo) the student organization formed in 1960 at Lovanium University, which was established in 1954 at Kimuenza near Léopoldville (Kinshasa) by the Roman Catholic mission and named after the University of Louvain (Belgium). AGEL sponsored a noteworthy general strike that began March 8, 1964, following celebration of the university's 10th anniversary. The strike, supported by the entire student body, lasted for a week, with student barricades preventing access to the university. The students demanded creation of a joint student-staff administration, hiring of internationally respected professors, and improved living conditions. Although effective, the strike ultimately failed after the students agreed to end it in return for creation of a committee comprised of students, professors, and administrators to study their demands—the committee had only advisory power and accomplished nothing. But the strike, as the first en-masse student uprising in the Congo, set a precedent. At the same time it revealed how severely limited the students' ability to effect change was because of their failure to exploit an initial advantage and to define a long-term vision of what the university should be. In February 1967 AGEL staged another strike, this one in response to the suspension of five students; in retaliation the administration canceled all classes, expelled all 1,950 students, and brought in army troops to occupy the campus and remove barricades. AGEL grudgingly agreed to end the strike and to accept collective readmission of the students.

Association of Jewish Youth (AJY)   (Great Britain) an umbrella organization with which 60 or more clubs and groups, such as the JEWISH LADS' BRIGADE, are affiliated. The AJY's stated purpose is "to foster devotion to Judaism and to maintain the highest standards of citizenship and the spirit of loyalty to the Queen, country and religion." Thus the AJY emphasizes religion and has an advisory committee on religion, but for many of its member groups sports and social activities are primary (although synagogues are commonly their places of meeting), and many have gentile members.

Asunción Protests   (Paraguay) ongoing student protests in May and June 1959 against the government of President Alfredo Stroessner. After assuming office on August 15, 1954, Stroessner consolidated his power, imposed press censorship, and imprisoned political opponents. In 1956, at the recommendation of the International Monetary Fund (IMF), he agreed to effect an economic austerity program in an effort to revive Paraguay's economy, which had never recovered from the devastating effects of the Civil War of 1947. The austerity program, however, proved very unpopular with farmers, businesspeople, politicians, the military, and laborers—virtually everybody, that is. Under mounting pressure, Stroessner, on April 1, 1959, announced an end to press censorship, release of political prisoners, and a future election for delegates to a constitutional convention that would be open to all political parties. Street rallies supporting these policies ensued, but opponents pushed for more reforms and the dismissal of Stroessner's security chief. Then when the government announced an increase in bus fares in May, students from the National University flooded Asunción's main square in protests that evolved into rioting. The students overturned cars and buses, and smashed store windows. Police intervened, and a battle between them and the students ensued, with 80 protestors being injured and 100 arrested, including three opposition members of congress. Stroessner took the advice of his military officers and cracked down, rescinding his brief reforms, and regaining control by June 4. The government purged instructors from the National University and members from the students' Federación Universitaria Paraguaya (FUP) and decreed that no student could graduate without a good-conduct certificate from the police. Although students remained sufficiently defiant to continue some modest demonstrating, essentially they were quiet for the next 10 years. The challenge to Stroessner failed totally.

Ateneo Universitario (Argentina) a cultural organization, formed in 1914 under the leadership of José Maria Monner Sans, of students from the various faculties (disciplines or departments) of the University of Buenos Aires. The group began to publish in 1915 a magazine entitled *Ideas* that contained articles on political, social, and philosophical subjects. The Ateneo was important as an advocate of university reform, and among its members were several youths who become active participants in the UNIVERSITY REFORM PROGRAM AND MOVEMENT of 1918. The Ateneo disbanded in 1920.

Atlanta Students Sit-In (United States) a demonstration by 200 students from Atlanta University, including

prestigious Morehouse College, on March 15, 1960. Inspired by the GREENSBORO (North Carolina) SIT-IN, the students marched to 10 sites where food was served, including bus and train stations, the state capitol, and the Federal Building, to demand service in an effort to desegregate the facilities. About a dozen of the protestors led by Julian Bond entered the municipal cafeteria, where they were refused service, arrested, and sent to the jail known as Big Rock. The students were arraigned for trespassing, conspiracy in restraint of trade, and other charges and returned to jail; they were bailed out after several hours. Although the demonstration failed in its objectives, the effort and the experience of jail provided the impetus for many of the students' continuing involvement in the Civil Rights movement. Bond, as the most prominent example, would serve for four years as public relations director for the STUDENT NONVIOLENT COORDINATING COMMITTEE (SNNC).

Aung San (1914?–1947) (Burma) student leader while attending Rangoon University. He was secretary of the Rangoon University Students' Union (RASU) and, consequently, along with U Nu (*see* NU, U), a major leader of the RANGOON UNIVERSITY STUDENTS' STRIKE of 1936, for which he was temporarily suspended and jailed. Aung San was a member of the Thakin movement, a nationalist group dedicated to achieving Burmese independence. (Burma was then a part of India and thus British colony.) Aung San became secretary of the militantly nationalist Dobama Asiayone (We Burmans Association) in 1939 and was forced to flee to Japan. He returned with the Japanese military in 1941 to raise a guerrilla force to oppose the British. Becoming convinced that the Japanese would not grant Burma independence, in early 1945 he switched allegiances to the Allies. As founder in 1944 of the Anti-Fascist People's Freedom League (AFPFL) and major general of the Burmese National Army, he was the primary leader of the independence movement, earning the epithet *Bogyoke* (Great General). In early 1947, Aung San secured an agreement for Burmese independence in 1948 from British prime minister Clement Atlee. His AFPFL won a huge majority in the constitutional assembly, making him de facto prime minister. But on July 19 he and six colleagues were assassinated on order of rival U Saw.

B

Baader-Meinhof Gang (Germany) a group of young terrorists who called themselves the Red Army Faction, initiated in 1968 by Andreas Baader, then 25, and his consort Gudrun Ensslin. At its peak the gang had 21 members, 12 of whom were women; all were young except for the woman whose name formed part of the gang's, Ulrike Meinhof, born in 1934 and a divorced mother of two children. All were university students or graduates except for Baader, and several, including Meinhof, were impelled toward revolutionary action by the police killing of Benno Ohnesorg in June 1967, the catalyst for vaulting the SOZIALISTISCHER DEUTSCHER STUDENTENBUND (SDS) into prominence. The gang's original members' first terrorist act was setting fire to a Frankfurt department store on April 2, 1968. Ulrike Meinhof became involved by attending the Frankfurt trial of Baader and Ensslin. She later visited Baader in jail in Berlin (he had violated parole) and then helped him to escape in May 1970. She went underground with him and joined the Red Army Faction to become an urban guerrilla. The gang perpetrated many acts of terror, the most heinous occurring in May 1972 when they bombed a United States military facility in Heidelberg and killed four soldiers. They also tried to kill a federal judge and wounded his wife, and attacked the Springer Publishing Company in Hamburg and wounded 17 employees. The gang expected their attacks to inspire a mass uprising. Some gang members were killed in shootouts; others defected to become witnesses for the leaders' prosecutors. Baader was arrested during a shootout on June 1, 1972 in Frankfurt along with Jan-Carl Raspe, formerly a member of WEST BERLIN KOMMUNE 2, and Holger Klaus Meins, who died of a hunger strike in prison on November 7, 1974. Meinhof was arrested on June 15, 1972. (She hanged herself in her cell in May 1976.) In 1975 six remnants of the gang, now calling themselves Commando Holger Meins, occupied the German embassy in Stockholm and took hostages in an effort to force the German government to free Baader, Meinhof, Ensslin, and Raspe; but the government held firm against them. The gang killed two of their hostages; the others, including the ambassador, managed to escape, although some were wounded when one of the gang mistakenly set off a bomb. Police killed two of the gang members and arrested the others.

Bibliography: L. Becker, *Hitler's Children: The Story of the Baader-Meinhof Terrorist Gang* (Philadelphia: Lippincott, 1977).

Baden-Powell, Robert S. S. (1857–1941) (Great Britain) founder of the BOY SCOUTS. Baden-Powell was born in London, England, and educated at the Rose Hill School in Tunbridge Wells and the Charterhouse School (1870–76), where he was a member of the CADET FORCE. After graduating he served with the 13th Hussars in India until 1883, earning the rank of captain. Baden-Powell served in Basutoland (Lesotho), in the 1888 Zulu War, and after 1889 as intelligence officer for the Mediterranean region. In 1895–96 he served in West and Central Africa. Promoted to colonel in 1897, he served for two years in India as commander of a cavalry unit and then was returned to Africa in 1899 to raise two battalions of Mounted Rifles and to organize the police in the North West Frontier of Cape Colony. Here he gained fame and promotion to major-general for his successful defense of Mafeking (Mafeteng) against a siege by the Boers (October 12, 1899–May 17, 1900).

Baden-Powell returned to England in 1901 on sick leave; in 1903 he became inspector general of cavalry and established the Cavalry School in Wiltshire in 1904. Since his 1899 military textbook *Aids to Scouting for N.C.O.'s and Men* was being used as a manual to train boys in woodcraft, Baden-Powell conceived the idea of organizing boys for scouting. He held an experimental boy-scout camp on Brownsea Island off the Dorset coast,

July 29–August 9, 1907, which birthed the movement. Baden-Powell resigned from the army in 1910 to devote his full time to the Boy Scouts and in the same year, with his sister Agnes, organized the GIRL GUIDES, which his wife Lady Olave also promoted. In 1916, Baden-Powell set up the Wolf Cubs for boys under age 11. In 1920 at the first international Boy Scout Jamboree held in London, he was named Chief Scout. Baden-Powell became a baronet in 1922 and a baron in 1929. In poor health after 1934, Baden-Powell announced his retirement as head of the Boy Scouts during the Dutch World Jamboree in 1937. He spent his final years in Kenya, where he died on January 8, 1941.

Bibliography: Ernest Edwin Reynolds, *Baden-Powell*, 2nd. ed. (London: Oxford University Press, 1957).

Balmashov, Stepan (1881–1902) (Russia) student assassin. In February 1902 the government sentenced about 400 students at Moscow University to expulsion from the university and banishment to Siberia. Minister of the Interior Dmitri Sipyagin, who had been appointed to the post by Tsar Nicholas II in 1899, carried out this sentence without any trial being held. In retaliation, Balmashov assassinated Sipyagin in April. The 21-year-old Balmashov was a student and a member of the Social Revolutionary Party, or Social Revolutionaries (SR). He was executed. These events generated a new nationwide strike by university students, resulting in banishment to Siberia, again without trial, of 115 Moscow and St. Petersburg students by Sipyagin's successor, Vyacheslav Plehve. Negative reaction in Russia and abroad prodded Plehve to relent, and he sent an emissary to Siberia to negotiate with the students. When the students rejected negotiation, Plehve counseled the tsar to pardon the students, although he forbade their living in any university town. Plehve himself was assassinated on July 28, 1904 by another student SR member, Yegor Sazonov, who threw a bomb under Plehve's carriage while Plehve was en route to see the tsar in St. Petersburg.

Bands of Hope (Great Britain) temperance societies for juveniles who pledged themselves to abstain from consuming alcoholic beverages. The first Band of Hope was founded in Leeds in Yorkshire in 1847. Other Bands of Hope followed in other cities, and a Band of Hope Union was formed in 1851. The societies spread throughout the United Kingdom, and just prior to World War I their memberships totaled 15,000. This figure was, however, far below the membership in the Church of England's Temperance Society's juvenile section, which had nearly 500,000 adherents. Some Bands of Hope existed in the United States as well.

Bibliography: Lillian Shiman, "The Band of Hope Movement: Respectable Recreation for Working Class Children," *Victorian Studies* 17, No. 1 (September 1973), 49–74.

Battle of Chicago (United States) a series of demonstrations, brutally suppressed by the police, that occurred in conjunction with the Democratic National Convention held August 25–29, 1968 in Chicago. Three groups were involved in organizing the demonstrations: the Youth International Party (Yippies), the NATIONAL MOBILIZATION COMMITTEE TO END THE WAR IN VIETNAM (MOBE), and the Coalition for an Open Convention. The yippies, led by Abbie HOFFMAN, had planned a Festival of Life as a counterpart to the convention, which was expected to nominate Hubert Humphrey—the current vice president and presumed supporter of the Vietnam War—for the presidency. Mobe, led by David Dellinger, planned an antiwar protest in conjunction with the yippie's festival. The coalition was comprised of young supporters of Senator Eugene McCarthy, an antiwar candidate for the Democratic nomination. About 2,500 yippies descended on Chicago after weeks of propagandistic articles from the radical press about what they

The sharp contrast of war and peace occurred when this group of antiwar demonstrators surrounded a statue honoring John A. Logan, a Union forces general during the Civil War, in Chicago on August 28, 1968. The demonstrators were part of a march protesting actions taken by police and Mayor James Daley during the Democratic National Convention. (AP/WIDE WORLD PHOTOS)

intended to do. These articles had so unnerved Chicago Mayor James Daley that he planned to respond with repressive police intervention. He assigned 11,900 police on 12 shifts to the task, and he had the Amphitheatre, site of the convention, surrounded by a chainlink-and-barbed-wire fence. There were also more than 5,500 National Guard troops and about 7,500 soldiers on standby.

The demonstrators, joined by an array of flower children and hippies (*see* HIPPIE MOVEMENT), numbered about 10,000 altogether (the organizers had expected 100,000). They convened in Grant Park and Lincoln Park and elsewhere along Michigan Avenue and demonstrated for a week before and during the convention. Daley refused to give the protestors permits to march in the streets or to sleep in the city parks. They marched anyhow on August 28 and again on the following day—out of Grant Park toward the Loop and the Amphitheatre; the police attacked them with clubs, tear gas, and Mace. Police sergeants repeatedly lost control over their men, who, in a frenzy, indiscriminately attacked not only yippies but also reporters and bystanders. The beatings left several hundred people injured and in need of medical attention, and the police arrested 650 demonstrators. The police also raided McCarthy's campaign headquarters, accusing the occupants of hurling garbage and epithets at them. In addition, the police attacked 63 reporters and photographers among the 300 who covered the convention and the demonstrations.

Unfortunately for Mayor Daley and the conventioneers, most of the action was covered live and broadcast on television, horrifying much of the public. Although Humphrey won the nomination, the Democratic Party emerged badly divided, and the tumult within the convention and on the streets of Chicago constituted a major cause—perhaps *the* major cause—of Humphrey's defeat in the November election to Richard M. Nixon. A 233-page report issued on December 1 by the National Commission on the Causes and Prevention of Violence condemned the Chicago police for being excessively brutal and staging in effect a "police riot." Nine policemen had already been suspended and one had resigned, with four others recommended for dismissal. Finally, the Battle of Chicago eventuated in the tumultuous trial for conspiracy of eight demonstrators arrested during the protests. (*See* CHICAGO 8 TRIAL.)

Bibliography: James Miller, *"Democracy is in the Streets": From Port Huron to the Siege of Chicago* (New York: Simon and Schuster, 1987).

Battle of Morningside Heights   *See* COLUMBIA UNIVERSITY STUDENT REVOLT.

Bawdy House Riots of 1668   (Great Britain) three days of rioting in London by crowds comprised mostly of apprentices (youths age 14 to 22) who attacked and demolished brothels in various areas of the city. (As one of the leaders on all three days was Peter Messenger, the uprisings are also known as the Messenger Riots.) The riots began on March 23, Easter Monday, in Poplar; the next day, about 500 rioters destroyed establishments in the major brothel districts of Moorfields, East Smithfield, Shoreditch, and Holborn. On March 25 a final uprising occurred in Moorfields that involved a huge crowd of apprentices, supported by residents of Southwark. The rioters were reputedly armed with iron bars, pole axes, and other weapons, and they marched in regiments headed by captains and flying green banners. On March 24, the second day of the riots, Charles II called out militia, the king's lifeguards, and other forces to suppress the riots; and many rioters were arrested and jailed. Later that day other rioters attacked New Prison at Clerkwell, freed some of those who had been arrested and repeated the attack on March 25. On March 27 the lord mayor of the city and his forces dispersed the rioters. The riots were significant because their scale and duration was unprecedented and because the rioters shouted such political slogans as "Down with the redcoats" and "Reformation and reducement" while calling for the king to grant "liberty of conscience" and promising a bloody May Day if he did not. In short, the riots were ostensibly a political protest against the monarchy and religious persecution. The government, fearing that the riots represented a larger scheme including civil war, charged 15 of the ringleaders with high treason for waging war on the king.

Bibliography: T. J. G. Harris, "The Bawdy House Riots of 1668," *Historical Journal*, 29 (1986).

Beat Generation   (United States) initially a literary movement of the 1950s that defined an ideology for disaffected, rebellious youth of that decade. The incipience of the Beats occurred in New York in the 1940s among young men—notably Allen Ginsberg and Jack Kerouac—who were students of Columbia University (or had been, in Kerouac's case). They took the term *beat*, suggesting emotional or physical exhaustion, from the language of a Times Square thief and male prostitute; later, however, Kerouac equated it with *beatific*. The Beats borrowed lingo from black hipsters and black jazz musicians. As a movement, the Beat generation may be said to have begun on October 13, 1955 when several writers read from their own works at the Gallery Six in San Francisco, most notably Ginsberg, whose dramatic reading of his poem *Howl* provided the movement's voice, temper, and credo. *Howl and Other Poems* (1956) became one of the most widely read books of the decade. In December 1955 Viking agreed to publish Kerouac's novel *On the Road*, written in 1951 but not published until September 1957, which presented an alternative American lifestyle that would resonate through the 1960s. Following the *Sputnik* launch in 1957, members of the Beat generation became referred to, sometimes derisively, as *beatniks*, a term coined by Herb Caen, a columnist for the *San Francisco Chronicle*. The Beats scandalized the general public through their indulgence in blatant sex, homosexuality, drunkenness, drug use, admiration for criminals, and other attitudes and forms of behavior that violated the conventional mores. They also advocated Buddhist concepts, especially in the work of Gary Snyder. Although the Beat generation's impact was primarily social and cultural, it had longer-term political implications and provided the prototype for the counterculture of the 1960s through its social anarchism, its denunciation of U.S. materialism, and its use of marijuana and other drugs.

Beloved Community (United States) essentially a generic term derived from Christianity, used by Martin Luther King, Jr., and adopted to express the ideal of a totally integrated and accepting community among the black and white students involved in the Civil Rights movement of the early 1960s; also applied to a small group of Nashville, Tennessee students from Fisk University and the American Baptist Theological Seminary in Nashville, Tennessee who were involved in that city's civil rights movement under the leadership of James Lawson, an African American minister born in the North. The Beloved Community of Nashville originated the sit-in at city restaurants and lunch counters in 1959, a year before the famous GREENSBORO, North Carolina SIT-INS. Although their initial effort proved unsuccessful, it gained credibility following the success of the Greensboro sit-ins, with hundreds of students thereafter joining the Nashville movement to desegregate downtown stores.

Bengal Language Demonstrations (Pakistan) student protests in 1952 against the recognition of Urdu as the official state language of Pakistan. In January 1952 Prime Minister Khwaja Nazimuddin, who—although a Bengali (East Pakistan)—spoke Urdu, announced that Urdu alone would be accepted as Pakistan's state language. In February Bengali students organized demonstrations against this policy, and the police response to the demonstrations resulted in the deaths of several students. Subsequently, many Bengali students were among the most militant participants involved in the movement to gain autonomy not just from Pakistan as a nation but from East Pakistan. In December 1971, following months of civil war and intervention by the Indian army, East Pakistan separated from West Pakistan to become the independent state of Bangladesh, thus ending the union of the two areas as the nation of Pakistan that had originated in 1947.

Berkeley "People's Park" Riots (United States) a series of riots involving University of California students and faculty members during May 1969 in Berkeley, California concerning the use of a vacant field near the campus. The field, measuring 445 by 275 feet, was a site for construction of planned student housing. On April 20 about 500 university students, joined by hippies (*see* HIPPIE MOVEMENT) and faculty members, rented a bulldozer and laid sod and planted flowers in the field, preparatory to adding swings, benches, and sculpture to transform the site into a "people's park." University Chancellor Roger W. Heyns decided to reclaim university possession by surrounding the field with a fence and excluding unauthorized persons. On May 15, after police ejected people from the park so that work could begin on the fence, the president-elect of the student body rallied about 2,000 students at Sproul Hall to take over the park. They were met by sheriff's deputies, who sprayed tear gas to disperse them and, when that failed, used riot guns to shoot birdseed at the protestors. Police and the National Guard, called up by Governor Ronald Reagan, also intervened. Reagan imposed a curfew—he had already declared Berkeley in a state of extreme emergency following demonstrations in February. Protests and arrests continued for the next three days. On May 19 a nonstudent died from birdseed-shot wounds inflicted during the May 15 confrontation, and on May 20 about 2,000 students, accompanied by more than two dozen faculty, staged a silent "funeral march." They encountered police and National Guard troops hurling tear gas, intent especially on dispersing 500 demonstrators marching to Heyns's house shouting "Murderer!" A Guard helicopter dusted the protestors and the campus with a powder substance that had been used against the Vietcong in the Vietnam War. On May 22 the Academic Senate requested an investigation by the Justice Department and overwhelmingly supported continuing the people's park, as did 85 percent of nearly 20,000 students who voted on the issue. A federal judge issued a restraining order against the sheriff, and the city council voted 5 to 4 in favor of lifting the emergency and withdrawing the troops. On May 24 Reagan had 1,700 of the National Guard troops withdrawn but continued the state of emergency.

Berkeley Student Revolt (United States) a major, longlasting uprising of students at the University of California at Berkeley in 1964 that had probably the most far-reaching impact of any U.S. student movement in this century. There was no precedent in the history of U.S. universities for the Berkeley Revolt, which began in September 1964 and continued until January 1965. The immediate cause of the revolt was university officials' claim that a strip of land at the entrance to the campus, believed by students and faculty to be city property, actually belonged to the university and that, consequently, university regulations on political activities pertained to any activities on this site. The strip of land had been to this time the traditional site for students' political fund

A student speaker uses the roof of a police car to address a large group of University of California students in front of Sproul Hall in Berkeley on October 1, 1964. The demonstrations were in protest against administrative restrictions on campus political activity.   (AP/WIDE WORLD PHOTOS)

raising and for events staged by off-campus political action groups, with the assurance that there would be no interference by university authorities. Now those authorities ordered student activists to remove their tables and political literature from the strip.

In response, students rapidly mobilized to protest, setting up tables on the strip on September 29 in defiance of the ban. They also formed the FREE SPEECH MOVEMENT (FSM), which demanded major changes in university regulations concerning student political activities on the campus. On October 1 campus police arrested Jack Weinberg, a graduate student/CONGRESS OF RACIAL EQUALITY (CORE) activist, and placed him in a police car. Students surrounded the car through the night so that it could not be moved. The university administration reached an agree-

ment that freed Weinberg, and the students celebrated a victory. Then, near the end of November, university regents called in four student leaders to respond to charges that they had committed violent acts during the October standoff. One of these students, Mario SAVIO, a spokesman for the FSM, was accused of biting a policeman's thigh. On December 1 student leaders gave the regents an ultimatum: they had 24 hours to drop the charges. The regents refused, and students seized Sproul Hall, the administration building. Savio gave a rousing speech, characterizing the university as an "odious" machine that the students must stop; folksinger Joan Baez sang "We Shall Overcome," and a thousand students occupied Sproul Hall. The police arrested 814 students during a largely nonviolent confrontation—most were quickly bailed out.

On December 3 students went on strike. On December 7 the university's president, Clark Kerr spoke to a crowd of 18,000. When Savio tried to speak after Kerr, he was dragged away by police but then allowed to return; he announced a meeting to be held later. On December 8 the faculty met, debated obstreperously, and voted in favor of there being no restrictions on what could be said in public speeches. It appeared that the students had attained their ends, but the lingering effects of the revolt were many. Throughout the weeks from September to year's end the battle had been continuous, with numerous meetings and demonstrations, frequent violations of the university's regulations and local laws, police incursions onto the campus, several sit-ins, and ongoing disruption of classes—all of which took a toll. The governor and many legislators became involved in the disputes; alumni and others throughout the state chose sides and mailed letters voicing their opinions. The university seemed near collapse, prominent professors left, and the chancellor and the president were forced to resign.

For the nation as a whole the Berkeley Student Revolt proved an influential event. For one thing, it became a symbol for students everywhere. It proved the potential effectiveness of student movements—that with organization, protests, strikes, sit-ins, rallies, vigils, and seizure of buildings, they could attain their demands. The revolt focused nationwide media attention on the student movement. It also focused attention on some problems that afflicted higher education, such as the issue of academic freedom; the relevancy of curricular requirements; the cumbersome bureaucracy of university administrations; the frequent failure of communication among students, teachers, and administrators; and impersonality resulting from the huge size of some institutions ("multiversities"). In addition, the revolt made clear that university campuses, and not just government centers or public buildings, were viable sites for student political protest. The fallout from the revolt also had long-term political consequences, as it was a contributing factor in Ronald Reagan's 1966 election as governor of California.

Bibliography: Seymour Martin Lipset and Sheldon S. Wolin, eds., *The Berkeley Student Revolt* (Garden City, N.Y.: Doubleday Anchor Books, 1965).

Berlin Anti-Shah Protest (Germany) a student demonstration against Shah Reza Pahlevi of Iran on June 2, 1967, significant because it climaxed in a classic and planned police riot and in the deliberate murder of a student. Opposed to arrests and torture of political opponents in Iran, West Berlin students staged protest demonstrations against the Shah of Iran on June 2 while he was on a state visit to the city. The demonstrations culminated in the evening at the Berlin Opera House, where the shah attended a performance of *The Magic Flute*. Police had erected a barricade and stood in a phalanx before the opera house, armed with rubber truncheons, confronting the students and onlookers. Despite some beatings by the police, the student demonstrators remained nonviolent. When the shah arrived along with Iranian secret-service agents, who earlier in the day had attacked and beaten student demonstrators, some students threw smoke bombs, eggs, and tomatoes, although the great majority remained calm. As the students attempted to leave shortly after 8:00 P.M., following the shah's entry into the building, the police—their ranks swelled by new arrivals—attacked without any warning. They brutally beat students, onlookers, ambulance nurses and doctors, even elderly bystanders. The police dragged students into a nearby parking lot and there beat them senseless. A 26-year-old graduate student, Benno Ohnesorg, not a demonstrator but an onlooker and a pacifist, rushed to the lot and was beaten to the ground. When he later tried to rise and run away, police captured him and beat him into unconsciousness. As two policemen held him under the arms to carry him to a police car, a plainclothes man rushed up from behind, raised his service revolver, and shot Ohnesorg in the back of the skull. With a major hunk of his skull blown away, Ohnesorg died in the hospital. Both the mayor and the police chief, who had planned the police attack, tried to gloss over the entire event and issued false statements to the press, but there were dozens of witnesses to the riot and the execution. The police chief and others involved were forced to resign, but the policeman who committed the murder was acquitted and continued in service.

About 20,000 students from throughout West Germany attended the funeral of Ohnesorg in Hanover on June 9. While in Hanover, they held a mass meeting on the subject of "the university in democracy," which resulted in the creation of the Extraparliamentary Opposition (Äusserparlamentarische Opposition). The Hanover meeting also generated a kind of manifesto that defined the students' sense of the crisis that afflicted both the university and the larger society—a failure of industrialism and authoritarianism—and that advocated university reform and radical political changes not just in West Germany but internationally. The statement described Ohnesorg's killing as no accident but rather the outcome of a deliberate policy to eliminate any minority opposition within West German society. The meeting propelled Rudi DUTSCHKE and Bernd Rabehl of the SOZIALISTISCHER DEUTSCHER STUDENTENBUND (SDS) into the leadership of the student movement, and the Hanover statement resonated throughout France and Italy as well as West Germany as a rallying cry for student opposition.

Berlin Uprising of 1848 (Germany), a major event of the Revolution of 1848 that swept much of Europe and nearly all the German states. On March 13 a throng of workers met in the Tiergarten and drafted a petition demanding that Prussian King Friedrich Wilhelm IV ini-

Police carry away a demonstrator at the Hamburg, West Germany, city hall where about 200 people protested the state visit of Shah Mohammed Reza Pahlevi of Iran and his wife, Empress Farah. The imperial couple arrived from Berlin where bloody fighting had broken out between demonstrators and police. (AP/WIDE WORLD PHOTOS)

tiate policies to counteract high levels of unemployment resulting from the 1846–47 economic crisis, which was exacerbated by failed harvests. On March 18 a demonstration to support the creation of a Berlin militia and a Prussian parliament, along with the granting of a free press, became transformed into overt, riotous rebellion accompanied by the erection of street barricades. The king's troops killed more than 200 rioters. Although this was a popular uprising involving mostly workers, activist democratic students from the University of Berlin played a major role. At least 100 students manned the barricades erected on March 19. Students also visited the local machine shops and succeeded in persuading the workers to become involved in the uprising. Among the most radical students was Gustav Adolf Schoffel, expelled from Heidelberg University in February for distributing communist literature to the local peasantry, who came to Berlin with the hope of matriculating at the university. Schoffel published a paper for the uprising entitled *Volksfreund*, which he dated "Year One of Freedom." He also

organized a march on the palace of Friedrich Wilhelm IV, but he was grievously disaffected when only 1,500 demonstrators turned out for it. After being imprisoned for six months, he joined the revolution in Baden and was killed there in 1849.

Big Brothers of America (United States and Canada), an organization whose primary purpose is to team one man with one boy to foster a relationship of friendship and mentoring that promotes the boy's development into a mature person of solid character. A clerk of the Children's Court in New York, Ernest K. Coulter, began the Big Brothers in December 1904 by securing the commitment of 40 members of the Men's Club of the Central Presbyterian Church each to form a personal relationship with one boy in an effort to preclude the boy's becoming involved in illegal behavior. Thirteen Big Brother associations in the United States and Canada joined together in 1946 to establish Big Brothers of America, headquartered in Philadelphia. Men volunteers (big brothers) are assisted by the organization's professional staff to develop a helpful relationship with their little brothers. The little brothers, ages 8–17, are usually fatherless and frequently prone to social maladjustments, emotional disturbances, delinquency, or other personal problems—hence the need for guidance from a mature, stable, responsible big brother.

Black Band (Germany), a remnant of the Christian Boy Scouts that continued to function clandestinely after their scouting organization was absorbed by the HITLER JUGEND in 1934. The so-called Black Band was comprised of youths from working-class backgrounds and left-wing associations who opposed Fascism. They attacked members of the Hitler Jugend's police-style Streifendienst (SRD, Patrol Service) when possible; in turn they were blamed by the SRD for various disruptive acts and overt resistance to SRD attacks that led in some cases to being arrested. The Black Band represented at least a modest resistance to Nazi repression and managed to survive until 1945.

Black Hand (Bosnia-Herzogovina) known as Ujedinjenje Ili Smrt (Union or Death) in Serbo-Croatian, a clandestine Serbian revolutionary group formed in 1911 and headed by Colonel Dragutin Dimitrijević. The Black Hand was devoted to overthrowing rule by the Austro-Hungarian Empire and the Ottomans in the Balkans region through propaganda, terrorism, and other means. It organized cells of revolutionaries throughout Bosnia. Officers and even government officials comprised much of the Black Hand's membership, which also included many students and other youths, including Gavrilo PRINCIP, the assassin of Archduke Franz Ferdinand.

Black Panthers (Israel) a youth group formed in Jerusalem in 1971 whose membership consisted of juvenile, slum-dwelling Oriental Jews, mostly Moroccans, who were regarded as a lower caste by other Israelis (many of them were delinquents). Fairly representative of similar groups, the Black Panthers originated in the Musrara area of Jerusalem formerly inhabited by Arabs whom Jewish immigrants had replaced after the 1948 War of Independence. Aggrieved by the advantageous treatment afforded a huge influx of immigrants from Eastern Europe while their own community suffered neglect, the Black Panthers staged a series of 14 demonstrations during 1971 and 1972, the first a protest at the Jerusalem City Hall on March 3, 1971, that resulted in six Panthers being arrested. Many of the protests gathered as many as 5,000 demonstrators, including university students and anti-Zionists; some erupted into violent confrontations with the police.

The Black Panthers did not oppose the Israeli government but advocated several reforms, including the elimination of slums and improved housing, increased education and employment opportunities for Oriental Jews, free housing for the most needy, "equal rights for all ethnic groups," and representation of Oriental Jews in all Israeli institutions. The central government, however, then headed by Golda Meir, responded hostilely and attempted to suppress the Black Panther movement and to discredit its leaders as Marxists. The Black Panther leaders turned to Leftist politics, including ties with the Communists. They merged their movement with the Israeli Democrats but were unable to secure a seat in the Knesset; the two groups split in 1977.

Bibliography: Shlomo Hasson, *Urban Social Movements in Jerusalem: The Protest of the Second Generation* (Albany: State University of New York Press, 1993).

Black Panthers (United States) an organization of young African American males formed in Oakland, California on October 15, 1966 by Bobby SEALE and Huey P. NEWTON. The organization's full name was the Black Panther Party for Self-Defense, and its basic philosophy was spelled out in the Ten Point Program derived from the views of Algerian freedom fighter Franz Fanon. The Panthers accepted the concept that African Americans existed as an oppressed black colony within a white mother nation, so that their long-term goal was to liberate blacks from colonial status. Their party platform demanded that blacks have freedom to decide their own destinies, control over their own communities, decent housing, quality education, justice, exemption from serving in the military, and freedom from control by the white power structure. The group's immediate purpose was to combat police brutality by trailing police officers who operated in black ghetto areas to make sure they did not harass blacks. The Black Panthers received broad media attention in this effort because they openly carried automatic weapons and spoke militantly. The Panthers also provided such community-service programs as free breakfasts, medical assistance, and "liberation" schools. The organization espoused a socialist political agenda. Its major leaders were Seale, Newton, and Eldridge CLEAVER. Members wore black berets, powder-blue shirts, black leather jackets, and black trousers. The Black Panthers gained widespread public attention on February 1, 1966 when 20 Panthers armed with pistols and shotguns (legal at the time) accompanied Malcolm X's widow through the San Francisco International Airport and to the locale of her speaking engagement—the Panther leaders were admirers of Malcolm X. In May 1967, as the California legislature debated a bill banning the carrying of weapons, heavily armed Black Panther members appeared in the capital city, Sacramento, thus garnering more media attention.

Although radical and assertive, the Panthers initially were not violent revolutionaries or racist or separatist, and they actively joined with predominantly white

Black Panther national chairman Bobby Seale (left) wears a colt 45 and defense minister Huey Newton, a bandolier and shotgun. The FBI arrested Bobby Seale in Berkeley after he was charged in New Haven, Connecticut with the kidnapping and slaying of a Black Panther party member there. Huey Newton was convicted of voluntary manslaughter in the death of a police officer. (AP/WIDE WORLD PHOTOS)

groups to further their goals of ending oppression and economic exploitation. For example, the Black Panthers allied themselves with the STUDENTS FOR A DEMOCRATIC SOCIETY (SDS) and actively participated in the Chicago convention of SDS that began June 18, 1969; however, the remarks a Panther made while addressing the convention offended and angered the women delegates, and the Panthers' alliance with SDS ended soon after the meeting, with Seale accusing SDS members of being "a bunch of jive bourgeois chauvinists." Thereafter, among the groups the Panthers did align themselves with was WEATHERMAN, an SDS faction whose tactics were hardly peaceable.

The Panthers were perceived by the police and by white society as menacing; this perception generated their decline through police attacks, killings, and jailings. Police arrested Newton on October 28, 1967 and charged him with kidnapping and killing a policeman; they arrested Cleaver on January 16, 1968 (he later fled the country); Seale was arrested for murder on August 19, 1969 and was sentenced to four years in jail. Twenty-

one Panthers were indicted on April 2, 1969 in New York City on charges of plotting to bomb a Bronx police station, to blow up Penn Central Railroad tracks, and to set off bombs in midtown department stores, including Macy's and Bloomingdale's; on December 6, 1969 Chicago police killed two Panther leaders and injured several others during a raid. There were other raids, killings, and arrests during 1969 in New Haven (Connecticut), Brooklyn, Sacramento, Los Angeles, and repeatedly in Chicago; during June the FBI conducted a series of raids on Panther field offices. Two Panthers were killed by members of a rival group on January 17, 1969 during a student meeting at the University of California at Los Angeles (UCLA) to discuss choosing a director for a new Afro-American Studies Center. On January 20, 1970 the Black Panther headquarters in Jersey city, New Jersey, was splattered with gasoline and set afire. A three-day series of shootouts, August 29–31, 1970 in Philadelphia, between Panthers and police resulted in the death of one police officer, the wounding of six other police officers, and the arrest of 14 persons charged with assault with intent to kill. In Detroit on October 25, 1970, 15 Panther-affiliated militants armed with high-powered rifles and ensconced in an armored carrier confronted police for nine hours before surrendering without a shot fired. In May 1973 the Panthers effected a revival when Seale, then chairman of the group, came in second in the Oakland mayoral election, but under Seale's leadership the Panthers moved increasingly toward providing services, such as lunch programs and small business enterprises, and away from the militancy that had generated such widespread violent responses.

Black Power Movement   (United States) a militant, confrontational movement of young African Americans, supported by some whites, that emerged out of the originally nonviolent march from Memphis to Jackson, Mississippi, begun by James Meredith on June 5, 1966. On June 6, although accompanied by FBI agents, police, and admirers, Meredith was shot by a white man but not seriously injured. The shooting instigated others to join him, however, including Martin Luther King, Jr., and Stokely CARMICHAEL, leader of the STUDENT NONVIOLENT COORDINATING COMMITTEE (SNCC). As the march ensued the participants disputed the appropriate direction for the Civil Rights movement to take, and Carmichael emerged triumphant with his advocacy of Black Power. Carmichael approached defining the movement in a speech given at Berkeley on November 19, 1966 as follows:

> This country knows what power is and knows it very well . . . So it knows what black power is. But the question is, why do white people in this country associate black power with violence? Because of their own inability to deal with blackness . . . We

are concerned with getting the things we want, the things that we have to have to be able to function. The question is . . . will white people overcome their racism and allow that to happen in this country? If that does not happen, brothers and sisters, we have no choice, but to say very clearly, move on over, or we're going to move on over you.

On the other hand, he also defined *Black Power* quite benignly as "a call for black people in this country to unite, to recognize their heritage, to build a sense of community"; and he advocated that blacks create their own goals and institutions, rejecting those racist organizations and values found in U.S. society. Other black leaders defined *Black Power* as a concept of racial pride and constructive empowerment; still others denounced it as black racism, a menace, and a threat to integration. But Carmichael opposed integration anyhow as an affirmation of presumed white superiority, and youthful black militants adopted his view. White resistance and scattered urban riots occurred in the aftermath of Carmichael's Black Power advocacy. Although black militancy began to wain by the end of the 1960s, the Black Power movement clearly influenced the rhetoric, goals, and tactics adopted by several organizations, such as the BLACK PANTHERS, and events, such as the Afro-American Society Uprising at Cornell University (*see* CORNELL AFRO-AMERICAN SOCIETY REVOLT).

Bibliography: Stokely Carmichael and Charles V. Hamilton, *Black Power: The Politics of Liberation in America* (New York: Vintage Books, 1967).

Blanqui, Louis-Auguste (1805–1881) (France) socialist revolutionary whose speeches, writings, and concepts formed a major influence on student movements. Blanqui studied law and medicine in Paris during the years 1818–24, and in 1827 he joined the student demonstrations against the restored monarchy. Following Louis-Philippe's assumption of power in 1830, Blanqui began to organize secret societies because he believed that well-organized conspirators would be needed to overthrow the government. The abortive May 12, 1839 insurrection by one of these conspiratorial groups resulted in Blanqui's imprisonment for life. Judged to be dying, he was released after the Revolution of 1848 but was again imprisoned. Released once more in 1859, he returned to organizing secret societies; he was imprisoned again in 1891 and then escaped to Belgium in 1865. Thereafter he made clandestine trips to Paris, where he helped organize Blanquist groups of students. He published a manual for urban guerrilla warfare in 1868. Blanqui supported the French cause during the 1870 Franco-Prussian War, but the Blanquists tried to overthrow the provisional government set up after Napoleon III was deposed on the grounds that it was failing to defend Paris against German attack. He was arrested and imprisoned in 1871 and again set free in

1879. He spent the last two years of his life as a journalist and political speaker. Blanqui advocated revolution and establishment of a temporary dictatorship to effect the transformation to a full socialist society through confiscation of wealth and nationalization of industry. He also advocated general public education and the creation of associations to oversee agricultural and industrial production.

Blanquism (France) the socialist political philosophy of Louis-Auguste BLANQUI that attracted many students and guided their involvement in revolutionary movements. Blanquists were involved in several attempts to overthrow the French government, notably on May 12, 1839, October 31, 1870, and January 22, 1871—all unsuccessful.

Bloody May Day (Japan) a violent protest demonstration on May Day 1952 that resulted in a student and a laborer being killed. The protest occurred a few days after Japan gained independence from the Allied Occupation; its target was the government's proposed Anti-Subversive Activities Law aimed against the political left. About 20,000 students and laborers attempted to storm the Imperial Palace in Tokyo, guarded by riot police armed with handguns. The rioters stoned the police, who arrested 1,213 of the demonstrators; 1,470 people, including police officers, were injured. The law was approved by the Diet on September 4, 1952. In the election that soon followed, the Japanese Communist Party (JCP) lost all 35 of its seats in the Diet.

Bloody Sunday (Russia) Sunday, January 9, 1905, when a massacre occurred outside the Winter Palace in St. Petersburg—at the time Russia was involved in the Russo-Japanese War. On this day Father Georgii Gapon led an estimated 50,000 to 100,000 peaceable, hymn-singing workers in a march to the Winter Palace, where they intended to present a petition (already made public on January 7) to Tsar Nicholas II, who actually was in Tsarkoye Selo (Pushkin) outside St. Petersburg. Addressing the tsar as a benevolent patriarch, the petition described the poverty and disenfranchisement that workers experienced and requested the tsar to institute numerous reforms, including releasing political prisoners from prisons, issuing a proclamation of "freedom and inviolability of the person," freedom of speech and press, "equality of all before the law," freedom to organize associations and unions, an eight-hour workday, "normal wage rates," and other reforms. As a large group led by Father Gapon approached the Narva Gate, a bugler signaled soldiers to open fire—about 40 people were instantly killed or wounded. Elsewhere, soldiers began to shoot indiscrimanately. Outraged demonstrators rampaged through the city streets, shouting and throwing stones; some workers attacked students, blaming them for the massacre. The final official toll of the massacre was 130 killed and 299 seriously wounded.

Although not directly involving students or youths (it occurred while students were on Christmas vacation), Bloody Sunday must be noted because it proved a catalysmic event for the student movement. Students evidenced almost uniform bitterness and rage throughout Russia. On February 8 about 3,000 students gathered at Moscow University, tore to pieces a portrait of the tsar, displayed a red flag, and voted unanimously to strike until September 1; they also demanded both political reforms and changes in university governance. Similar meetings were held at every institution of higher learning as students returned from the holiday, and all voted to strike until September 1; many also issued a call for a constituent assembly. No prior event occurring outside the universities had served to galvanize the student movement into such a uniform response. During February, virtually every institute of higher learning in the nation was closed down. Now the nation stood on the threshold of the violent REVOLUTION OF 1905, in which the students would play a critical role.

Bibliography: Abraham Ascher, *The Revolution of 1905: Russia in Disarray* (Stanford: Stanford University Press, 1988).

Blue-Coat Schools   *See* CHARITY SCHOOLS.

Blue Shirt Society (Lanyishe)

(China) a clandestine quasi-fascist organization formed in the early 1930s by Chiang Kai-shek's followers, who were rabidly anticommunist. Since its organizers headed military-training programs at the schools, they recruited many students as Blue Shirts. Student members of the Blue Shirt Society were active in trying to prevent radicalization of the DECEMBER NINTH MOVEMENT and in furthering the NEW LIFE MOVEMENT. The Blue Shirts were disbanded in 1944; the THREE PEOPLE'S PRINCIPLES YOUTH CORPS, although a public organization, served as the group's successor on university campuses.

Bibliography: Maria Hsia Chang, *The Chinese Blue Shirts: Fascism and Developmental Nationalism* (Berkeley: University of California Press, 1985).

B'nai B'rith Youth Organization (BBYO)

(United States) a Jewish youth movement founded in 1924. The B'nai B'rith itself, the largest Jewish service organization in the world, began as a fraternal organization founded by German Jews in 1843 in New York City. The BBYO formed by B'nai B'rith is the largest movement for Jewish youths in the world. It is comprised of three organizations: Aleph Zadik Aleph for teenage boys, B'nai B'rith Girls for teenage girls, and B'nai B'rith Young Adults for youths of age 18–26. BBYO programs emphasize Judaic heritage; civic responsibilities; and social, cultural, and sports activities.

Bologna, University of

(Italy) one of the two earliest still extant European universities, with its origins tracing to the early 12th century, founded by, and as an organization of, students who belonged to guilds known as *universitates*. The two most important of these expatriot-student societies that formed the basis of the university were the *citramontani* and the *ultramontani*. The University of Bologna, literally a guild or corporation (from the Latin *universitas*) of students created to provide for mutual aid and protection, similar to the economic guilds of the era, was officially recognized in A.D. 1158 by a grant of rights and privileges from Emperor Frederick Barbarossa entitled *Privilegium Scholasticum* (althouqh neither the town nor the university was specifically named in the grant), which promised imperial protection to persons traveling to or from Italy to pursue scholarly studies. The students initially organized as a university—a union, in effect—to bargain for reasonable prices for rooms and goods and thus prevent the townspeople from taking unfair advantage of their presence through profiteering. In 1217 the students organized their first protest boycott, literally leaving Bologna for three years, until both masters and townspeople gave in to their demands. The students' union exacted concessions from the masters, binding the masters to adhere to a set of regulations that guaranteed that the students would receive value for their money. The regulations, for example, prevented masters' absences and controlled the length and content of lectures. From the town, the students won concessions on taxes and food and rent costs. In Bologna there were actually several "universities" composed of "nations" of students led by rectors. Since the students themselves comprised the university—the University of Bologna had no fixed residence until 1562, when by order of Pope Pius IV, a building was constructed to house it—the students had the bargaining power conferred by mobility. That is, if their terms were not met to their satisfaction, they could move the university elsewhere. This mobility was no small weapon, as estimates indicate that during the period from the 12th to the 15th centuries the students numbered from 3,000 to 5,000. To protect themselves, the Bologna masters formed "gilds" (or *collegia*), which established qualifications for student admission that had to be attested by examination. The combined universities and gilds eventuated in the university as it exists today (and as the term is now understood). It should probably be noted, as a contrast, that the other early great European university, the University of Paris, was also a corporation—but a corporation of masters, not of students, and therefore not a *student movement* even in the broad sense of the term being applied here. It was the early university at Bologna that established historic precedents for student primacy or dominance in the transactions of universities.

Bombay Presidency Students' Federation (India) provincial student organization founded in 1936.

Bombay Students' Brotherhood (India) a group dedicated to social reforms, the Students' Brotherhood was founded at Bombay University in the 1890s and exemplified a new type of organization in contrast to the traditional university literary and cultural societies that provided forums for discussing Western culture and thought. The Brotherhood focused on Indian issues and advocated a "modernism" that included reforms of the caste system and women's status. Unlike the great majority of organizations at the time, the Brotherhood offered membership to women.

Bibliography: "The Bombay Students' Brotherhood," *Modern Review*, 14 (March 1914), 264.

Bowie State College Protest (United States) a strike by students at Bowie State College in Bowie, Maryland in March 1968. Bowie State was a predominantly black college with 500 students. About 300 of the students staged a boycott of classes March 27–29 and demanded creation of black history courses and improvements in housing, facilities, and teaching. They occupied the administration building on March 29, sealed off the campus, and demanded a meeting with Governor Spiro Agnew. On March 30 Agnew rejected the demand, and the students ended their protest. On April 4, however, 225 of the Bowie students staged a sit-in at the State House in Annapolis to demand a meeting with Agnew. When they refused to leave the building, all were arrested. In August at the Republican National Convention held in Miami, Florida, which was marked by violent protests in the black section of the city, Agnew became the party's nominee for the vice presidency—to be Richard Nixon's running mate in his successful bid for the presidency. Among the new vice-president's early assignments from President Nixon was discussions with the state governors on ways to control violence on college and university campuses.

Boxers (China) essentially a youth movement that emerged in 1899 and ostensibly derived from one or more of the many secret societies. It was possibly (but probably not) an outgrowth of the White Lotus Sect that traced its origins to about 1674 and the first reign of the Qing dynasty; however, the Boxer movement itself lacked the organization of such earlier societies and was short-lived. The name *Boxers* does not refer to pugilism, although some predecessor groups of this name learned martial arts; the Boxers practiced rituals leading to a trance state that effected possession by gods, meant to make them invulnerable to the weapons brought in from the West; the Boxers were the first among similar groups to practice this ritual. The Boxers, or "Spirit Boxers," as they called themselves (later equated with the Boxers

United in Righteousness), originated in 1896 in northwest Shandong in poor villages above the Yellow River as peaceful groups that fostered protection of their homes, but they soon (in 1898) became an anti-Christian and antiforeigner movement. Their discipline included these tenets: "Do not covet wealth. Do not lust after women. Do not disobey your parents. Do not violate Imperial laws. Eradicate the foreigners. Kill corrupt officials." Like other secret societies, the Spirit Boxers welcomed and recruited boys age 12 and older and even some younger than 10; all the members were male and nearly all were under age 20, mostly in their late teens; most were peasants or agricultural workers. Boxer discipline forbade sexual contact with women. The youths referred to each other as "Brother-Disciple," and the leader of each group was the "Senior Brother-Disciple."

The Boxers gained especial attention in the West through the Boxer Uprising (commonly but misleadingly known as the Boxer Rebellion) of 1900. The uprising in the spring and summer of 1899 in Pingyuan county originated in anti-Christian attacks by Boxers that resulted in the arrest and execution of some of their leaders—this in turn spurred the Boxers' rapid spread. On October 18, 1899 a group of more than 1,000 Boxers assembled at the Senluo Temple and attacked an infantry troop of more than 400 that was sent to disperse them; the Boxers killed 3, wounded 10, and drove off the rest. The troops regrouped, brought up reinforcements, and attacked the Boxers, killing at least 27 and driving the others into flight. The battle of Senluo Temple enhanced the Boxers' stature among the populace and brought more recruits to their campaign to "Support the Qing, destroy the foreign." As government authorities attempted to suppress the Boxers in one area they gained new leaders and groups in other areas. Attacks on Christians, including raids on fortified Christian missions, increased, and the Boxers' opposition to foreigners had widespread public support. By May 1900 the Boxers were nearing the outskirts of Beijing, and battles between Qing dynasty troops and Boxers occurred at various sites in Zhili province. On May 16 troops led by Colonel Yang Futong killed 60 Boxers at Laishui, but on May 22 the Boxers ambushed and killed Yang and some of his men.

Emissaries of the Great Powers complained to the Quing government and threatened intervention; in April the governments of Great Britain, France, and the United States had dispatched gunboats. Following their success at Laishui, the Boxers occupied Zhuzhou and destroyed the railway lines to Beijing. An international force of 2,000 troops set out from Tianjin, repairing railway tracks as they slowly advanced; but Boxer attacks, resulting in the deaths of 62 and the wounding of 212, forced them back to Tianjin. By June thousands of Boxers were flowing into both Beijing and Tianjin. By this time many were wearing uniforms that included either a red or a yellow turban bearing charms or a red robe and a black bandanna. In addition, Boxer units comprised entirely of girls and young women had been formed—the Red Lanterns Shining. The various groups communicated with each other through wall posters.

The Boxers were thought capable of certain types of magic, including restricting fires so that they burned only Christian houses and churches; on June 16, however, a fire they set in southern Beijing defied the magic and destroyed thousands of residences and 1,800 shops. Weakened by numerous debacles following the Sino-Japanese War, the imperial Qing government evidenced support for (and some fear of) the Boxers, whose members cooperated with imperial troops in opposing foreigners' encroachments. The court issued a "delaration of war" on June 21 and in Beijing laid siege to the foreign legations. The Boxers were in effect turned loose to expand their attacks on foreigners, and hundreds of foreigners and thousands of Chinese Christians died as a result. Imperial troops were responsible for executing scores of foreigners. The court enlisted 30,000 Boxers as a corps to protect Beijing against attacks by foreign forces. About 10,000 Boxers unsuccessfully laid siege to the city's Roman Catholic Northern Cathedral, where 3,000 Christians and 40 French and Italian marines had taken refuge. Interestingly, the Boxers also arrested and executed 70 members of the White Lotus Sect in Beijing.

On July 13 forces of the Great Powers launched a full-scale attack on Tianjin, driving the Boxers and imperial troops from the city and inflicting perhaps 3,000 losses on the latter, including one of the army's best generals. Alarmed by the loss, the imperial court moderated its stance, ceased shelling the legation buildings in Beijing, and made efforts to negotiate a settlement while at the same time executing five ministers who advocated accommodating the Great Powers. On August 4 an expedition of 20,000 troops—half of them Japanese and many of the rest Russian and Indian soldiers under British command—set out from Tianjin to attack Beijing, torching villages as they proceeded. They easily defeated forces sent to oppose them and entered Beijing on August 14. The court fled, eventually arriving in Xi'an. The victorious foreigners pillaged Beijing and scoured the nearby countryside looking for Boxers to execute; they killed many innocents, raped, looted, and burned. The vengeful killings and the imperial court's banning of the Boxers eliminated the Boxer movement. The Great Powers imposed reparations, executions, and troop emplacements as terms of settlement. The Russians occupied Manchuria. The Qing Dynasty, further weakened by these events, would come to an end with the 1911 Revolution.

Bibliography: Joseph W. Esherick, *The Origins of the Boxer Uprising* (Berkeley: University of California Press, 1987).

Boys' Brigade (Great Britain) the first of the major British youth movements to take its inspiration from military tradition, the Boys' Brigade originated in Scotland. William Alexander SMITH founded the Brigade at the Mission Hall in West Glagow on October 4, 1883. It was designed largely as an organization for boys who were too old for the SUNDAY SCHOOL movement but too young for the YOUNG MEN'S CHRISTIAN ASSOCIATION (YMCA) (roughly ages 13–17). Members of the first Brigade (later the Glasgow Company) were recruited almost entirely from the families of skilled laborers and of such white collar groups as clerks, grocers, and salespeople. Pillbox caps, belts, and haversacks comprised their uniform, they drilled with dummy rifles, and their discipline was strict. The group's crest was an anchor; its motto, "Sure and Stedfast" (*sic*, from St. Paul's Epistle to the Hebrews); its goal, "the advancement of Christ's Kingdom among Boys, and the promotion of habits of Reverence, Discipline, Self-Respect, and all that tends towards a true Christian Manliness." In addition, it fostered another motto: "Remember now thy Creator in the days of thy youth." The primary objective of the Boys' Brigade was thus made abundantly clear from the start. (In 1893 the promotion of Obedience was added.) Captain was the group's highest rank.

Smith held a meeting on January 26, 1885 at his home in Hillhead to organize the Boys' Brigade into a national movement, and thereafter for 20 years it developed rapidly from the original company, by the end of the century attaining 812 companies with more than 35,000 members throughout the United Kingdom. The great majority of the member boys were affiliated with the Presbyterian Church, but the Anglican and Methodist churches were also well represented. The organization's journal was entitled *The Boys' Brigade Gazette*. The Boys' Brigade encountered competition for members when the BOY SCOUTS began activity in 1907–08. During World War I the War Office pressured the organization's leaders to transform the Brigade into a CADET FORCE administered by the Territorials. Smith resisted the pressure, but following his death in May 1914 individual companies were granted permission to make the choice of becoming cadet forces. Any association with the military ended in 1924. In 1926 the Boys' Brigade merged with the BOYS' LIFE BRIGADE, and the organization grew steadily through the 1930s, achieving a peak membership of nearly 97,000 in 1934 and more than 2,800 companies in 1939. Following World War II, the more popular Boy Scouts displaced the Boys' Brigade, which declined steadily in membership to only 63,000 by 1970.

The Boys' Brigade also spread to the United States, and in 1894 the United Boys' Brigades of America (UBBA) was formed in an effort to draw the independent groups together. Within two years UBBA had perhaps

15,000 members, but it shifted the emphases of the original British Boys Brigade toward nationalism and militarism, with a heavy focus on drilling, maneuvers, and occasional mock battles, and thereby caused its own eventual decline. Initially, membership was limited to boys age 12 to 18, but in 1912, after membership had already rapidly declined, the minimum age was lowered to 10 in an unsuccessful effort to increase recruits. UBBA was displaced by the BOY SCOUTS OF AMERICA (BSA) as the leading organization for boys in Great Britain.

Bibliography: John Springhall, ed., Brian Fraser, and Michael Hoare, *Sure and Stedfast: A History of the Boys' Brigade, 1883 to 1983* (London: Collins, 1983).

Boys' Clubs Movement   (Great Britain) a movement to create institutes and clubs to provide recreation, entertainment, socializing, educational opportunities, health instruction, and moral guidance for adolescent boys that apparently originated with the Dover Youths' Institute, which was founded in about 1857 by the Reverend Henry White, and a Youths' Club founded in about 1858 at Bayswater by a Charles Baker. The boys' clubs concept was publicly advocated by the Reverend Arthur Sweatman, an Anglican priest, in the early 1860s as a means of providing boys with the services and amenities offered to adult males by Men's Clubs, which did not wish to accommodate youths. Sweatman founded the Islington Youths' Institute in St. George's Hall in the London borough of Islington in October 1860 when he was 26 years old. In 1863, when 25-year-old Edward Tabrum assumed Sweatman's responsibilities at the institute, it had 160 members and a waiting list of 85. At this time several other youth institutes had been established in other areas of London, and, according to Sweatman, summer excursions had become part of their routines. (Sweatman moved to Canada in 1865 to become headmaster of a boys' college in London, Ontario; in 1879 he became bishop of Toronto and later, archbishop.) The first true boys' club was the Cyprus Boys' Clubs founded in 1872 in the Parish of St. John the Divine in Kennington to serve the needs of working class boys; it survived until World War I.

During the 1880s scores of other boys' clubs, most of them under sponsorship of the Church of England, were established in London, Manchester, Bristol, Liverpool, and cities throughout Britain. Other denominations also formed clubs. The first of the Roman Catholic Boys' Clubs was founded in 1894 in London at St. Francis Church in Notting Dale, with a membership of 136 youths ages 14 to 22. The first two Jewish Boys' Clubs, also established in London, were founded in 1896 in Whitechapel and in 1898 in Fitzroy Square. The early Jewish Boys' Clubs were noteworthy for their excellent training in chess, writing, drama, boxing, gymnastics, and physical fitness.

In most cities, federations of boys' clubs were created, and at a conference held in Toynbee Hall in October 1925, representatives from these groups formed the National Association of Boys' Clubs (NABC). The NABC admitted any local federation with officers and at least four member clubs and individual clubs in areas lacking federations; by 1930 the NABC comprised 17 federations with 837 clubs plus 107 individual clubs. The NABC adopted *The Boy*, previously produced by Cambridge University undergraduates, as its official publication. Also in 1930, at its annual conference, the NABC adopted *Principles and Aims of the Boys' Club Movement*, which, as its title indicates, defined the philosophy and purposes of the movement—essentially the promotion of fitness in mind, body, and spirit; citizenship; self-government; sportsmanship; and patriotism. The NABC grew steadily and by 1952 it boasted 2,560 clubs with 190,000 members—a total membership ranking it second only to the BOY SCOUTS among organizations for boys in Great Britain, and well ahead of the BOYS' BRIGADE, the CHURCH LADS' BRIGADE, and the CADET FORCES.

Bibliography: Waldo McG. Eagar, *Making Men: The History of Boys' Clubs and Related Movements in Great Britain* (London: University of London Press, 1953).

Boys' Clubs of America   (United States) a nationwide organization of clubs serving disadvantaged boys modeled after British examples of Protestant church efforts to address the problems of urban youth. Boys' Clubs began as local and independent programs, with the first such organization founded in Hartford, Connecticut in 1860, but the first club to use the name was the Boys' Club of the City of New York that originated at the Wilson Mission in 1876. In 1892 New York City had 31 Boys' Clubs, 27 of them sponsored by a church, a mission, or a church-associated organization; by 1914 the city had more than 500 clubs, now under the aegis of the local board of education. Autonomous clubs with a membership of at least 100 in varied cities joined together in 1905 to form the Federated Boys' Clubs (later the Boys' Clubs of America, FBC). The first president was the renowned Jacob Riis (1849–1914), photographer, social reformer, and author of *How the Other Half Lives: Studies Among the Tenements of New York* (1890). By the time of Riis's death, the FBC had 110 member clubs with a total of more than 108,000 boys. From the beginning, Boys' Clubs afforded to boys age 7–17 of all races and backgrounds "a home away from home," "a place to go and a way to grow." Consequently, a club building is crucial to the organization's mission in each locale; depending on their resources, many clubs provide swimming pools and gymnasiums, and most have shops, music rooms, libraries, and game rooms. Programs include sports, crafts, theater, fine arts, woodworking, and other activities; in the past, many clubs offered classes in carpentry, printing, and other manual skills. Other groups, such as BOY SCOUT troops, are frequently sponsored and created within individual Boys' Clubs. Each club is operated by professionally trained staff. Now the Boys and Girls Clubs of America, the organization is headquartered in Atlanta and has a total membership of 2 million.

Boy Scouts   (Great Britain) an organization dedicated to training boys age 11 through 14 in citizenship; camping, swimming, and other outdoor activities; and in responsible and humanitarian behavior. The Boy Scouts was founded in 1907 by Robert S. S. BADEN-POWELL, a British cavalry officer, with the able public relations assistance of Arthur Pearson, owner of the *Daily Express*. Both men were interested in promoting patriotism, social reforms, and amelioration of class conflicts and in providing a form of training in morality and physical activity that would build character and prevent decadence. Baden-Powell's precedents in creating the Boy Scouts were the BOYS' BRIGADE and the YOUNG MEN'S CHRISTIAN ASSOCIATION (YMCA). He organized the first camp, July 29–August 9, 1907, on Brownsea Island in Poole Harbor off Dorset; 20 boys participated. The movement quickly gained adherents as Baden-Powell's military handbook *Aids to Scouting*, which he adapted for use by boys and renamed *Scouting for Boys*, was published in six biweekly installments. Boys avidly collected these installments, formed their own troops, and asked adults to serve as scoutmasters. Very soon a boy scout headquarters with a managing secretary was established at Westminster; county scout councils and district scout councils were set up, with a governing council, an executive committee, and a chief scout (Baden-Powell) presiding at the top. The organization's journal, published by Pearson, was *The Scout*. The Boy Scouts also quickly spread to other nations, initially to Chile, Canada, Australia, New Zealand, and South Africa, and by 1910 to Sweden, France, Norway, Mexico, Argentina, and the United States. Now worldwide, Scouting is autonomous in each nation but grants recognition to an international headquarters—in London until 1958 and since then in Ottawa.

Scouts train in such activities as woodlore, swimming, camping, sailing, and hiking; as they progress they receive badges for the achievement, with the highest level of achievement designated the Queen's Scout Badge (Eagle Scout Badge in the United States). Scouting features a variety of symbols and the famous motto "Be prepared." Local troops hold regular meetings; since 1920 international conclaves, "world jamborees," have been held every four years. In 1916, Lord Baden-Powell founded an identical movement for younger boys called the Wolf Cubs (in the United States, the Cub Scouts). Groups such as the Rovers, the Sea Explorers, and the Explorers were set up for boys older than 14. (The Rovers, set up in 1918 partly to accommodate youths returning from the war, was intended for young men;

and, although the age limits were left indefinite, members were mostly between age 18 and 23 but also ranged much beyond that. The activities and purposes of the Rovers remained rather ill defined, however; its membership peaked in the 1930s at less than 40,000, and in 1966 it was abolished.)

During World War I Lord Baden-Powell formed the Scout Defence Corps to train young men in methods of defending Great Britain. Boy Scouts who passed the recruitment test for entry into the corps, which included expertise in rifle shooting and military drill, were awarded "red feathers." Rover sections for boys older than 14 were added in 1919. During the 1920s and 1930s the Boy Scouts became an increasingly socially inclusive movement, advocating internationalism and brotherhood; by 1930 membership in Great Britain had risen to 422,000 (from 232,000 in 1920). Membership suffered somewhat from the effects of the Great Depression. Baden-Powell, in ill health, announced his reignation as chief scout in 1937.

Boy Scouts celebrate Washington's Birthday at Federal Hall in New York City.   (AP/WIDE WORLD PHOTOS)

Boy Scouts of America (BSA)   (United States) the U.S. offshoot of the BOY SCOUTS founded in 1910. During a sojourn in London in 1909 U.S. publisher William D. Boyce was guided by a Boy Scout to an address he was seeking on a foggy night. When the boy refused a tip because he was doing a "good turn" as a Scout, Boyce inquired about the Boy Scouts, and the boy led him to Lord Baden-Powell's office. Impressed with what he learned about scouting, Boyce returned home and, with other interested persons, founded and incorporated the Boy Scouts of America on February 10, 1910. A secretary of the YOUNG MEN'S CHRISTIAN ASSOCIATION (YMCA), Edgar Robinson, who deemed it best that all the woodcraft-oriented groups for boys be unified in a single organization, was a major force in creating the BSA. President William Howard Taft was honorary president; Ernest Thompson Seton, founder of the WOODCRAFT RANGERS, was Chief Scout. A Washington, D. C. lawyer and active participant in the capital city's YMCA, James E. West, became the first Chief Scout Executive and served until 1943. Artist Dan Beard, founder of the SONS OF DANIEL BOONE, served on the national commission from the beginning until his death in 1941 and wrote and illustrated articles for *Boys' Life*, the official magazine of the BSA. In 1911 appeared the first *Handbook for Boys* and the Scout Oath and Scout Law (both adapted from the original British versions), uniforms, and badges. With the backing of the YMCA and its supporters, the BSA grew rapidly and in 1916 it finally won a Congressional charter as the official boys' scouting organization in the United States. By 1920 the BSA had more than 376,500 members; in that year, along with scouts from 32 other nations, 301 U.S. scouts attended the First World Jamboree in England. (Since then, World Jamborees have been held every four years.)

The BSA held its first National Jamboree in 1937 in Washington, D.C., where, at the invitation of President Franklin D. Roosevelt, more than 27,000 scouts from across the nation camped beside the Washington Monument. The BSA grew rapidly, becoming the largest organization for youths in the United States—by the end of West's tenure in 1943, membership had reached 1.5 million. In 1930 the BSA established the Cub Scouts for boys age 8–10; by 1970 there were nearly 2.5 million boys in the Cub Scouts. Boy Scouts itself is for boys between 11 and 17 years of age, divided into "troops" of 30 to 35, with an adult scoutmaster but with boys themselves in key leadership roles such as patrol leader. Scouts earn merit badges and promotions for their achievements, the beginning rank being tenderfoot and the highest ranks being star, life, and eagle. There are also auxiliary groups for older boys. These include Sea Scouts begun in 1912, Explorer Scouts begun in 1935, and Air Explorers begun in 1941. Since 1959 most of the Explorer posts have been vocationally oriented. In 1971 girls were formally admitted to membership in the Explorer Scouts. The BSA had a total membership of 3.8 million in 1996.

Boys' Life Brigade   (Great Britain) begun in the fall of 1899, the Boys' Life Brigade was intended from the start to be a nonmilitary organization because of objections that Nonconformist (non-Anglican) clergy had to the BOYS' BRIGADE's military orientation. The founder was the Reverend John Brown Paton (1830–1911) a Congregational minister who had served as principal of the Congregational Institute in Nottingham from 1863 to 1898. Paton persuaded the Nonconformist churches' National Sunday School Union to sponsor the Boys' Life Brigade, with himself as president of the new youth movement. The Paton Company, as the first unit was entitled, was set up in Nottingham; it used life-saving drills rather than military drills as its core discipline. The concept gained adherents, and by 1914 there were 400 companies (mostly associated with Nonconformist churches) and a total membership exceeding 15,000 boys. In 1901 the Girls' Life Brigade was formed as a sister movement of the boys' organization. Following lengthy negotiations, the Boys' Life Brigade merged with the Boys' Brigade in 1926, with the two groups' respective symbol, a red cross and an anchor, forming the merged movement's crest.

Bibliography: John Springhall, *Youth, Empire and Society: British Youth Movements, 1883–1940* (London: Croom Helm, 1977).

Boys of 1928   (Venezuela) students of the Central University in Caracas who, having learned of the UNIVERSITY REFORM PROGRAM AND MOVEMENT in Argentina and other revolutionary efforts in other Latin American nations, launched a political reform campaign through public speeches critical of the dictatorship of Juan Vincente Gómez, the Tyrant of the Andes, in power since 1908. Among this outspoken group of students was Rómulo Betancourt, then a 20-year-old law student and later (1945–48 and 1959–64) president of Venezuela. The students were arrested and imprisoned. Released in April, they began open demonstrations and then a revolution, seizing Gómez's Miraflores Palace and attacking the main military barracks in Caracas. But because the rebellious students were unable to garner support from the public or the military, both intimidated by the Gómez regime, their revolution failed and the leaders, including Betancourt, were exiled. Betancourt returned in 1936 but was sent into exile again in 1939 and then was permitted to return in 1941. In 1945 Betancourt and a group of military officers staged a coup that installed Betancourt as president with a promise of free elections, which occurred in 1947. But in 1948 General Pérez Jiménez seized power, and Betancourt and the other Boys of 1928 returned to exile. In 1958 Betancourt returned as president following the successful VENEZUELAN REVOLU-

TION. *See also* FEDERACIÓN DE ESTUDIANTES DE VENEZUELA (FEV) and WEEK OF THE STUDENT.

Brathay Hall (Great Britain) a character-development movement for youths founded in 1946 and endowed by Francis Scott, chairman of the Provincial Insurance Company and owner of Brathay Hall, built in 1790 in the Lake District at the north end of Windermere. Although similiar to OUTWARD BOUND in purpose and program, Brathay Hall Trust operates only this one facility and focuses its effort more precisely on general education and training, with all courses open to both male and female youths age 16 to 21. Consequently, Brathay Hall offers not only outdoor activities but also courses in drama, painting, and other art forms—the emphasis being on self-discipline and self-discovery rather than on the instructors' evaluations. As part of the center's program the Brathay Exploration Group organizes and conducts expeditions within Great Britain and abroad.

Bratnia Pomoc (Brotherly Help) (Poland) a national student organization operative during the 1920s to which more than 60 percent of university students belonged. Formed during the economic adversity following World War I, Bratnia Pomoc promoted self-help among students, with sponsorship of student-operated printing presses; soap, boot, and polish factories; a book bindery; and other facilities. It also conducted programs to provide students with housing, clothing, textbooks, scientific instruments, and medical services.

Bravo Release Strike (Argentina) a strike by students at the University of Buenos Aires (UBA) to secure Ernesto Mario Bravo's release from prison. Bravo, a chemistry student in the Faculty of Exact Sciences, was arrested in May 1951 and imprisoned by the Perónist police for his political activities. Unable to acquire information about Bravo, his fellow students at the faculty agreed on June 9 to go on strike until he was released, and students at the other UBA faculties joined the boycott in support of their effort. The strike lasted for several days and resulted in the arrest of about 50 students. The Federación Universitaria de Buenos Aires then issued demands that Bravo and all the other arrested students be released, that the police be withdrawn from the faculties, and that the striking students be allowed to return to their studies when the boycott ended. On June 21 the government acceded to these demands—a major victory for the Argentine student movement, especially in the repressive environment created by Juan Perón's government.

Brüderschaften (Germany) autonomous but church-based youth fraternities extant throughout the rural communities of Germany and parts of Switzerland during the 16th and 17th centuries. Although each group varied somewhat from the others, all had certain shared features and purposes. In Germany a boy entered the communal group usually at the time of confirmation (age 14) and remained a member until marriage, unless his bachelorhood extended to the age of 30, when he would likely be expelled from the group. The main *Brüderschaften* were comprised of young males, but frequently villages had subordinate groups of young women as well. New members underwent an initiation ritual that apparently in some cases included hazing. An age hierarchy marked the group's organization, and older members—that is, those in their twenties—were in control of the *Brüderschaft* until leaving it because of marriage. The *Brüderschaft* had no economic purpose, but it performed certain important civic and moral functions. In some communities the members filled the role of the local militia, and in many villages they were given prominent roles in such church festivals and processions as Easter and Pentecost. Probably their most important role was to regulate courtship rituals and access to nubile young women; tactics (such as, bundling, ridicule, effigies, mockery, and even violence) discouraged sexual congress before betrothal, promiscuous behavior by a woman, or encroachments by spinsters, widows, or older women and older men that were seen as threatening the social pairings of the local youths. In at least one instance—the *Bubenbrüderschaft* of Mittenwald organized in 1645—and perhaps others a *Brüderschaft* became transformed into a Christian brotherhood. Such a transformation was more common among the confréries, youth groups in France similar to the *Brüderschaften* but more closely tied to the church.

Budapest Technical University Resolution (Hungary) a statement of 16 demands adopted unanimously by about 5,000 students assembled at the Budapest Technical University on October 22, 1956—the eve of the HUNGARIAN REVOLUTION. The demands included the withdrawal of Soviet forces from Hungary; elections by secret ballot within the Hungarian Communist Party (CPH); dismissal of Stalinists from positions of authority in the CPH and the reinstatement of Imre Nagy to the CPH; public trials of Mihály Farkas and other repressive Stalinist members of Mátyás Rákosi's government; general elections open to many political parties; equality in relations between Hungary and the Soviet Union; reforms in economic, agricultural, and industrial policies; the release of political prisoners; freedom of the press; removal of Stalin's statue from Budapest; a declaration of solidarity with Poland; and the convening of a youth parliament and the placement of a wreath at the statue of General Józéf Bem, a hero of the Revolution of 1848. This final demand proved a catalyst of the revolution that followed.

Budi Utomo (Indonesia) a nationalist organization founded in 1908 by Indonesian medical students. Budi

Utomo, which means "noble endeavor," was humanist in ideology and advocated improvements in agriculture, education, and commerce. Although it failed to attract a large following and never expanded beyond Java, Budi Utomo is considered to have been the first organization dedicated to Indonesian nationalism—hence its significance, however circumscribed its influence.

Buenos Aires University Occupation   (Argentina) an uprising in October 1945 in which the students occupied the Faculty of Exact Sciences at the University of Buenos Aires. In support of the university's autonomy in a climate of repression imposed by the military government, the students seized the faculty building on October 2 and barricaded the doors and windows. Police and ultranationalists surrounded the building, fired shots and threw stones at the windows, and closed down the water and electricity services to the building. One student was killed by a random shot. The students survived by bringing water and food in via a pulley system connected to adjacent buildings. On October 6 police charged into the building and arrested all the occupants. Nearly 1,600 students, including 149 women, and six professors were arrested in the building or in connection with the occupation. All were released after 7–10 days. Student seizures of buildings also occurred at the universities of the Littoral and La Plata, with equivalent results. When the students were released from custody the government also restored administrative control of the universities to the elected rectors.

Bund   (Japan) *See* KYOSANSHUGISHA DOMEI.

Bund der Jungen   (Germany) a secret organization of radical students at 10 universities spread throughout Germany that was begun in 1821. The Bund's purpose was a revolution that would unite the German states under the authority of an elected and representative government. Karl FOLLEN provided guidance to the Bund from exile in Switzerland. Although the Bund itself was short lived, dying out in 1823, it helped inspire a liberal and even radical direction among some student groups within the BURSCHENSCHAFTEN that eventuated in creation of GERMANIA.

Bund Deutscher Mädel (BDM, Association of German Girls)   (Germany) a Nazi Party organization founded in 1922 for girls and young women age 14 to 21 (following membership in the HITLER JUGEND from age 10 to 14). Membership in the BDM remained low through the 1920s and early 1930s, reaching slightly more than 19,000 in 1933 (the year Adolf Hitler became chancellor); but in 1939 total membership exceeded 1.9 million. During the war years, the BDM provided civic welfare, health care, and other forms of assistance. The BDM was widely involved in the Eastern Action, providing various support services for ethnic Germans and German settlers in occupied territories beginning in 1940. A primary goal of the BDM was to instill the idea that it was each girl's patriotic and moral duty to birth children for the Third Reich. Each BDM member spent her 18th year working on a farm—this was called the Land Jahr—as a part of the Landdienst (Land Service) program of the Reichsjugendführung (RJF, National Youth Directorate), the government agency in charge of youth organizations. The girls worked both in the fields and in the households, living either in camps or in farm homes.

Bunde   (Germany) an umbrella term for numerous groups that arose within the German youth movement during the years between the end of World War I (1918) and the Nazi accession to power (1933). However disparate in their ideologies and programs, virtually all the *Bunde* shared the overriding concept and goal of the *Bund*—a single, unified, united German youth movement. The largest and probably most important of the *Bunde* was the DEUTSCHE FREISCHAR. But the *Bunde* groups were legion and included the Adler und Falken, Freischar Schill, Geusen, and other extreme right-wing groups; the moderate Jungnationale Bund, known as Junabu; paramilitary groups such as Jungdo and Oberland; and even Catholic and Protestant groups such as QUICKBORN, Neudeutschland, Christdeutscher Bund, and Bund Deutscher Jungenvereine that found the Bund concept attractive during these years.

The Nazi regime disbanded the *Bunde* in June 1933, but their members in many cases maintained association through meetings and letters, although avoiding any public activities. They were under the watchful eye of the Gestapo and the HITLER JUGEND's private police, however, and thus destined to suppression. Most *Bunde* members accepted Nazism; others resisted, and some of them were incarcerated in prison or concentration camps or were executed; a few were executed after involvement in the failed attempt to assassinate Hitler in July 1944. The government promulgated the Hitler Jugend statute on December 1, 1936 that terminated the semilegal status of confessional Protestant and Catholic youth groups, making the Hitler Jugend the only officially recognized and acceptable youth movement. The Nazi ban on the *Bunde* was restated in February 1936 and in May 1937. In May 1935 the Gestapo was ordered to compile lists of all former *Bunde* members, and in July 1939 another ban was issued, this one listing the Deutsche Freischar, the Deutsche Jungenschaft (*see* KOBEL, Eberhard), and a dozen other *Bunde* specifically. The ensuing war sealed their fate. Following the war, many of the *Bunde* were revived and new ones were created—in both cases different in nature from their forebears.

Bibliography: Walter Laqueur, *Young Germany: A History of the German Youth Movement* (New York: Basic Books, 1962).

Bund Jüdischer Corporationen (BJC) (Germany) an umbrella organization of various Jewish student groups, such as the Verein Jüdischer Studenten an der Universität Berlin, founded in 1902. The BJC was formed largely in response to the anti-Semitism that then prevailed within many student organizations, notably the VEREIN DEUTSCHER STUDENTEN. Dedicated to both the intellectual and physical development of its members, the BJC promoted "active participation in Jewish life" and other tenets that clearly implied a program of separateness from gentile Germans.

Burlington Riot (United States) a violent youth uprising in Burlington, North Carolina in May 1969. Seventeen black youths marched on the administration building of the integrated Walter Williams High School on May 16 to protest because an African American had not been elected as a cheerleader. Police arrested them, setting off an uprising by black youths, who firebombed two stores and began to loot them. When police arrived to quell the riot, they experienced sniper fire. A 16-year-old boy died in the ensuing police crossfire; 29 were arrested. The mayor imposed a curfew the next day, and the governor sent 400 troops of the National Guard to restore order in the town.

Burschenschaften (Germany) German university student organizations (*Burschen* means "youngsters" or "lads") that originally advocated patriotism, German unification, egalitarianism, liberal causes, and Christian values. The first Burschenschaft was organized at the University of Jena in 1815 with the patronage of the grand duke of Saxe-Weimar. The movement spread rapidly among other German universities and by 1818 had established a comprehensive organization (the Allgemeine Deutsche Burschenschaft) including these individual groups. The Burschenschaft students staged joint demonstrations at the WARTBURG FESTIVAL in 1817; and in March 1819 a secret group among them known as the GIESSENER SCHWARZEN germinated Burschenschafter Karl SAND's assassination of August von Kotzebue, a German dramatist in service to Alexander I, the repressive tsar of Russia.

These and other revolutionary events alarmed German government officials, and representatives of several of the states, prodded by Prince Metternich of Austria, met together in August 1819 at Carlsbad and promulgated the CARLSBAD DECREES—a series of resolutions, many of them subsequently rendered into laws by the federal diet, intended to suppress liberal developments.

As a result, the Burschenschaften went underground. Also in 1819 the Burschenschaften excluded Jews from membership—a policy that was reversed in 1830. The Burschenschaften reemerged to take part in the 1830 revolution, were suppressed again after 1833, and emerged yet again to participate in the German Revolution of 1848, when the laws opposing them were abrogated. Following German unification in 1871, the Burschenschaften changed course to advocate militant nationalism and, especially in the century's final decade, a virulent anti-Semitism, a policy that some of the member groups did strongly oppose but with little success. In 1886–87 the *Burschenschaftliche Blatter*, a sophisticated student journal, began publication; it promoted closer association among both current and former (Alte Herren) Burschenschaften members. The journal originally remained neutral on the issue of anti-Semitism but then in 1891–92 began to allow publication of opposing views, so the controversy raged in its pages over the next five years. It also gradually turned to the advocacy of German nationalism.

After becoming chancellor in 1933, Adolf Hitler supported subsuming the Burschenschaften into the Nazi Party's NATIONAL SOCIALIST GERMAN STUDENT UNION. At that time the Burschenschaften professed to have 12,634 member groups. The Burschenschaften reappeared once again after World War II but as social clubs with no political purpose. (*See also* individual groups, such as KORPS, GERMANIA, ALLGEMEINE DEUTSCHER WAFFENRING, etc.)

Bibliography: Lewis Feuer, *Conflict of Generations: The Character and Significance of Student Movements* (New York: Basic Books, 1969)

Buske, Ernst (1894–1930) (Germany) leader of the DEUTSCHE FREISCHAR and the most significant figure in the enormously important youth movement of post-World War I Germany. Buske was born in Pomerania. A member of the ALTWANDERVOGEL, he studied law and became legal representative of a peasants' association in the northwest. Buske was excused from service in World War I because he had only one arm. At age 24 he became a leader of the youth movement, acknowledged as the premier leader by all the others in the movement (some called him "General"). In 1926 Buske helped found and became leader of the Deutsche Freischar. He was responsible for the Freischar's orientation of idealism and practicality without the nationalistic, militaristic, or romantic claptrap that characterized some youth groups. His untimely death in February 1930 was a major loss to the youth movement.

Cadet Force   (Great Britain) a voluntary youth military organization whose early membership was comprised mostly of middle-class boys. The cadets originated spontaneously at some of the major public (private) schools in 1859–60 as an adjunct of the Volunteer movement that revived at that time because of a military threat by Napoleon III. The Volunteers Act of 1863 empowered the War Office to formally authorize the formation of cadet units. Thereafter, increasing numbers of public schools set up cadet or rifle corps associated with Volunteer units, for which they served as preservice training organizations. In 1886 the government granted authority to organize cadet units independent of the Volunteers. Thus in that year the East London Cadet Corps was founded at Toynbee Hall University Settlement under the leadership of Sir Francis Fletcher Vane to organize boys from working-class families and instill in them the virtues of physical exercise, discipline, obedience, self-reliance, and patriotism. Henry Nevinson quickly succeeded Vane. His assistant, Toynbee Hall Resident William Ingham Brooke, moved to Southwark in 1887 to establish the Red Cross Boys' Club and later (May 30, 1889), with the wholehearted support of reformer Octavia Hill, the Southwark Cadet Corps. In 1891 the Southwark Cadet Corps absorbed the East London Cadet Corps and the Eton College Mission Cadet company to become the 1st London Cadet Battalion—the first English cadet battalion for working-class boys. The Army Cadet Corps overall experienced intermittent periods of strength and of weakness, depending on the health of the Volunteers and Britain's war circumstances.

The SEA CADET CORPS was formed in 1899 by the Navy League, but it traced its origins to a Naval Lads' Brigade founded by former members of the navy at Whitstable in 1856 in the aftermath of the Crimean War. The Sea Cadet Corps received official recognition from the Admiralty in 1919. The Air Training Corps, originally the Air Defence Cadet Corps, was founded in 1938 by the Air League. The Air Ministry assumed control of the corps in February 1941.

From the mid-1880s until 1910, the cadet force was mostly a nonschool, working-class movement. Thousands of cadets moved into the armed forces during World War I. But the antimilitary sentiment prevalent during the 1920s caused a 58-percent decline in the numbers of cadets during the decade—from about 119,000 in 1920 to only 49,500 in 1928. In 1930 the War Office terminated official recognition of the Cadet Force, and so Lord Allenby organized the British National Cadet Association (BNCA) in hopes of sustaining the force through private subscriptions. In 1932 the government restored official recognition and placed the BNCA in charge but did not provide financial support until 1937. When World War II began, the Cadet Force had only 20,000 members. The war stimulated recruitment, and by mid-1945 membership reached 170,000. After the war the BNCA was rechristened the Army Cadet Force Association, becoming again a preservice voluntary organization. As in the aftermath of World War I, memberships and interest declined: by the end of the 1960s there were roughly 39,000 members in the Army Cadets, 17,800 in the Sea Cadets, and 28,000 in the Air Training Corps.

Bibliography: Waldo Mc.G. Eager, *Making Men: A History of Boys' Clubs and Related Movements in Great Britain* (London: University of London Press, 1953); John Springhall, *Youth, Empire and Society: British Youth Movements, 1883–1940* (London: Croom Helm, 1977).

Cambodia Bombing Protests   (United States) nationwide student demonstrations in May 1970 against U.S. bombing of and troop deployments in Cambodia announced by President Richard Nixon on April 30, 1970. Major protests occurred at University of Maryland, Southern Illinois University, University of Wisconsin,

Ohio University, and scores of other campuses throughout the nation. Protests at Kent State University and Jackson State College were marked by tragedy. (*See* KENT STATE MASSACRE and JACKSON STATE COLLEGE RIOT.) Probably the largest of the demonstrations occurred in Washington, D.C., on May 9, when more than 60,000 protestors assembled by the New Mobilization Committee to End the War in Vietnam (New Mobe) rallied peacefully. Following the rally, however, smaller groups of student protesters staged disruptions. One group of about 700 marched to Arlington Cemetery carrying coffins covered with black cloths; another group demonstrated at the White House and tried to overturn one of the buses lined up to cordon off the area. On May 10 students from George Washington University rioted, setting cars afire, throwing stones at police and firefighters, and apparently setting off a bomb at the headquarters of the U.S. National Guard Association—police arrested about 375 of the students.

Cambridge Fifteen   (Great Britain) a group of Cambridge University students who were tried for their involvement in a 1970 demonstration. In February 1970 about 400 students staged a protest against the brutal policies of the colonels who ruled Greece at the time; they demonstrated at the Garden House Hotel, site of a Greek dinner-dance party. The demonstration was peaceful, but a group of students moved to the back of the hotel where the party room was located; they broke windows in the room, and some rushed in and fought with the police—nine were arrested. Proctors who had been with the demonstrators later provided the police with the names of 60 other protestors. Prosecutors selected 15 students to be brought to trial. The trial of the Cambridge Fifteen occurred in July 1970 and resulted in terms of 9 to 18 months for six of the defendants; seven students were acquitted. None of the defendants was charged with committing or inciting a violent crime, so the prison sentences were perceived by many as excessively harsh. Two days following the trial, about 50 students held a peaceful protest outside the Cambridge Guildhall against the severity of the sentences. Onlookers spattered them with eggs, tomatoes, rotten fruits, and flour provided by a middle-aged man and stallholders at the marketplace. Police arrived and quelled the barrage, but no one was arrested.

Cambridge Riots   (Great Britain) major town-versus-gown clashes of the 14th century that strained the joint responsibility for maintaining law and order conferred upon both the town of Cambridge and Cambridge University by the monarchy in April 1270. A dispute between students and townspeople in 1304 resulted in townspeople attacking students in their hostels. A more-serious riot occurred in 1322, when the city's mayor and bailiffs actually directed townspeople to attack the colleges and

hostels of the students, resulting in arrests and injuries to several students, the death of a priest, and destruction of books and the writs defining the university's privileges. When the university threatened to abandon Cambridge, the king ordered that the mayor, four bailiffs, and 319 other townspeople be charged and tried. Still another riot occurred in 1371, when students invaded the houses of townspeople and beat the owners and several bailiffs. These riots formed the prelude to the worst riot of all, which occurred in conjunction with the Peasants' Revolt on June 15–17, 1381. The city's mayor and burgesses joined with rebels from the countryside to attack the Barnwell Priory, Corpus Christi College, and other university property; the rioters siezed university charters and deeds and burned them. An army commanded by the Bishop of Norwich put down the rebellion. As a result of this town-gown battle, the king, by royal charter of February 17, 1382, granted Cambridge University control over regulation of market trading in the city.

Campaign for Nuclear Disarmament (CND) (Great Britain) an organization founded in January 1958 in the study of John Collins, canon of St. Paul's Cathedral. Although it was led by adults, among them the renowned mathematician Bertrand Russell, thousands of university and public school students comprised the great majority of CND's membership. The CND spearheaded the Ban the Bomb movement in Great Britain through peaceful demonstrations that sometimes resulted in arrests and jailings. The movement it began spread internationally. CND was a primary organizer of the second ALDERMASTON MARCH, and in 1963 it organized a preliminary conference for an International CND in Oxford. Since the CND's avowed major goal was to secure the Labour Party's commitment to a nonnuclear policy, failure to attain this goal led to quarrels among its leaders. Russell and others left in October 1960 to found the Committee of 100; its tactic of civil disobedience attracted many youthful adherents who decided the CND's advocacy of constitutional change was ineffectual. The Committee of 100's first mass sit-down demonstration occurred on February 18, 1961 at the building housing the Ministry of Defence. The antinuclear movement as a whole went into decline after 1962, but it had proved to be a major influence on the emergence of the NEW LEFT.

Camp Fire Girls   (United States) an organization for girls age 7–18 founded in 1910. Dr. Luther H. Gulick, an officer of the YOUNG MEN'S CHRISTIAN ASSOCIATION and founder of the BOY SCOUTS OF AMERICA, and his wife established a camp for girls called Wo-He-Lo (Work, Health, Love) at South Caseo, Maine in 1910 and also helped organize a pageant in Thedford, Vermont entitled *Camp Fire Girls*. The camp and the pageant formed the basis of Camp Fire Girls as an organization that was incorporated on May 15, 1912; its first manual also appeared that year. In 1913 the Blue Birds was formed as an auxiliary group for girls age 7–9, and in 1941 the Horizon clubs were created for girls of high school age; a Junior High Camp Fire Girls auxiliary was also created. A National Council decides on policies for the organization. From its origins, the Camp Fire Girls offered membership to any girl accepting what became the Law of the Camp Fire Girls; this includes seeking beauty, giving service, pursuing knowledge, being trustworthy, maintaining good health, glorifying work, and being happy. (Dr. Gulick believed strongly in character building and encouraging decision making for youths.) From its beginnings the organization emphasized Indian lore, with related symbolism and ceremonies. Its programs have stressed home life, creative arts, personal hobbies, outdoor crafts, sciences, business, and sports. At the Camp Fire Girls level (age 9–11) developing skills in these areas is emphasized, and girls are rewarded for their attainments with ranks of Trail-Seeker, Wood-Gatherer, and Fire-Maker. In the Junior High Camp Fire Girls (age 12–13), which stresses group activities, the ranks are Group Torch-Bearer and Individual Torch-Bearer. The Horizon clubs emphasize personal development, career pursuits, and community service, and they award Wo-He-Lo Medallions for completion of a special two-year project. In 1996 the organization, now the Camp Fire Boys and Girls, had a total membership of about 700,000.

Campus Crusade for Christ (CCC)   (United States) a nondenominational, evangelical student movement founded at the University of California at Los Angeles (UCLA) in 1951 by Bill Bright. From its beginnings, CCC has pursued a schematic approach to religious involvement, as Bright postulated "Four Spiritual Laws" that constitute the movement's ideology:

1. God *loves* you, and has a wonderful *plan* for your life.
2. Man is *sinful* and *separated* from God, thus he cannot know and experience God's love and plan for his life.
3. Jesus Christ is God's *only* provision for man's sin. Through him you can know and experience God's love and plan for your life.
4. We must individually *receive* Jesus Christ as Savior and Lord; then we can know and experience God's love and plan for our lives.

CCC has a large budget and a staff of more than 3,000 and is represented on more than 450 university and college campuses. It promotes its purposes through a variety of publications distributed at campus meetings and by individual students and through conventions. In June 1972, for example, CCC convened a week-long evangelical meeting of university and high school youths called Explo '72 at the Cotton Bowl stadium in Dallas that received impetus from the Jesus movement and attracted 75,000 participants—Honorary Chairman Billy Graham termed the meeting a "religious Woodstock." (*See* WOODSTOCK FESTIVAL.) CCC has enrolled thousands of students through conversions at such evangelical assemblages.

Candy Stripers   (United States) an organization for young women in high school who are interested in medical services. The members are hospital volunteers whose duties vary by hospital and may include reading to patients, delivering packages to rooms, working at the receiving desk, affording comfort to patients, or numerous other activities. Each hospital provides its own requirements, most likely including a minimum age for volunteering and a minimum number of hours service per year.

Carlsbad Decrees   (Germany) resolutions issued by ministers of the various German states designed, among other things, to suppress the BURSCHENSCHAFTEN. Following both the March 23, 1819 assassination of the minor playwright August von Kotzebue by the Burschenschaft student Karl SAND and a failed attempt on the life of President Ibell of Wiesbaden by another student who subsequently committed suicide in prison, powerful Austrian Foreign Minister Prince Klemens Metternich called for a conference of the German states to deal with a perceived threat of revolution. In consequence representatives from Austria, Baden, Bavaria, Hanover, Hesse, Mecklenburg, Nassau, Prussia, Saxe-Weimar-Eisenach, and Saxony met at Carlsburg in Bohemia during August 6–31, 1819. Metternich made several proposals affecting university students that the conference agreed to, including a request that the German Confederation's Diet institute a system for censoring newspapers and all other forms of periodical literature, disbanding of the Allgemeine Burschenschaft, installing agents at the schools and universities to monitor the instructors, dismissing all instructors who propounded "subversive" ideas or otherwise violated their civic responsibility, barring dismissed instructors in one state from a post in any other state, denying students expelled from one university admission to any other, barring from public office anyone who secretly remained a member of the Allgemeine Burschenschaft, and creating at Mainz a central office to investigate organizations suspected of conspiring against the government. Although the states enforced these repressive decrees with varied intensity and overall limited effect, the decrees remained officially valid until 1848, and as late as 1832 to 1836, some 1,200 students were prosecuted as members of Burschenschaften.

Carmichael, Stokely S. (June 29, 1941–)   (United States) civil rights leader and chairman of the STUDENT NONVIOLENT COORDINATING COMMITTEE (SNCC). Carmichael was born in Port-of-Spain, Trinidad and emigrated to the United States with his family in 1952. He attended the Bronx High School of Science in New

York and Howard University, earning a bachelor's degree in 1964. While at Howard he joined the CONGRESS OF RACIAL EQUALITY (CORE) in 1960 and participated in civil rights sit-ins and demonstrations in the Washington, D.C. area. In 1961 he was a FREEDOM RIDER in Mississippi and was arrested in Jackson and imprisoned for less than two months. Following his release, Carmichael joined SNCC, participating in demonstrations and voter-registration drives in the South, including the 1964 Mississippi Summer Project. Coming to disagree with other SNCC members about nonviolence, Carmichael began to advocate self-defense and banning whites from the organization. In 1965 he organized a highly successful voter-registration drive in Lowndes County, Alabama that included creating an African American political party, the Lowndes County Freedom Organization. In 1966, Carmichael was elected chairman of SNCC and transformed the organization into an advocate for "black liberation," or nationalism. Carmichael became the foremost champion and articulator of Black Power (*see* BLACK POWER MOVEMENT) following a publicized speech in Greenwood, Mississippi. He left SNCC to join the BLACK PANTHERS but later resigned over disagreement with Eldridge CLEAVER. Carmichael married South African singer Mariam Makeba in 1968, and in 1969 they moved permanently to Guinea, where he adopted the name Kwame Toure. Carmichael returned to the United States briefly in 1972, advocating Pan-Africanism and U.S. blacks' acceptance of their African cultural heritage. In more recent years he returned regularly, working as an organizer for the All-African People's Revolutionary Party.

Bibliography: Stokely S. Carmichael and Charles V. Hamilton, *Black Power: The Politics of Liberation in America* (New York: Vintage Books, 1967); Stokely Carmichael, *Stokely Speaks: Black Power Back to Pan-Africanism* (New York: Random House, 1971).

Cartell Verband (CV) (Germany) the largest Roman Catholic association of student fraternities in Germany, founded in 1867. The CV's motto was "Religion, Scholarship, Friendship," and it promoted these endeavors in trying to solidify a "Catholic consciousness" among its member chapters as a means of strengthening their resolve against Protestant hostility. It also promoted significant involvement in the Mass and other religious observances and in Catholic charitable organizations. In 1891 Pope Leo XIII forbade Catholic students' observance of the Bestimmunsmensur (ritualistic dueling) as barbaric, a move which aroused the enmity of other student organizations. During the first three decades of the 20th century and the rise of Nazism, the CV remained the largest Catholic student organization. In fact, from 1903 to 1908, the CV was the third-largest student association in Germany, and, in the spirit of the times, it committed itself to patriotism (*Vaterlandsliebe*) during a meeting at Würzburg in 1907. Although in 1930–32 the Cartell Verband had expelled students associated with the Nazi Party on the grounds that Nazism was anti-Christian, in May 1933 the organization declared its loyalty to Adolf Hitler as chancellor; at the time it claimed to have more than 10,200 members. (It should be noted that there was also a Kartell-Verband (KV) founded in 1866 as an umbrella organization of informal Catholic groups called Studentenvereine, which were originally open, nonpolitical, and flexible in their makeup but slowly evolved toward the kinds of structure, uniforms, and ritual behavior that the CV and other fraternal corporations adopted.

Catholic Boys' Brigade (Great Britain) a movement that originated in September 1896 as the South London Catholic Brigade because its founder, Father Felix Segesser (1863–1930), anticipated that the organization would not expand beyond his parish. The Catholic Boys' Brigade, like its Protestant predecesor, emphasized military training, with drills, exercise, sports, and camping. Father Sagesser, concerned to find a means of maintaining the Roman Catholic church's hold on adolescent boys, founded the group at the Dockland Students' Institute, a boys' club in Bermondsey in South East London, as a cadet-style organization to serve the sons of mostly Irish Catholic working-class families in this dock area. The boys wore caps, brown belts, and haversacks and drilled carrying sticks or broom handles (later actual rifles). The concept spread to nearby London parishes and then to other areas of Great Britain. In 1906 the Catholic Boys' Brigade's membership was estimated at 8,000, with Ireland accounting for more than half the members. The movement's journal was entitled *The Catholic Boys' Brigade Gazette*. In the years before World War I, the brigade's military nature evoked criticism, and it lapsed into obscurity, apparently becoming part of the Catholic Boy Scouts during the 1920s.

Bibliography: John Springhall, *Youth, Empire and Society: British Youth Movements, 1883–1940* (London: Croom Helm, 1977).

Catholic Boys' Brigade of the United States an organization for boys age 12 to 18 founded by the Roman Catholic church in 1915 and modeled on the BOYS' BRIGADE. In 1941, on the eve of U.S. entry into World War II, the brigade had about 40,000 members at 325 branches in 28 states, the Virgin Islands, and Canada.

Catholic Young Men's Society (Great Britain) the Roman Catholic equivalent of the YOUNG MEN'S CHRISTIAN ASSOCIATION.

Catholic Youth Organization (CYO) (United States) a nationwide youth program established by the Youth Department of the United States Catholic Conference.

As the conference lacks enforceable authority, organizations and programs of the CYO vary widely among parishes and are virtually autonomous. CYO's greatest presence has been in the largest cities. In many parishes, CYO sponsors BOY SCOUTS OF AMERICA, GIRL SCOUTS, and CAMP FIRE GIRLS groups. Many parishes sponsor the Catholic Daughters of America's Junior Program for girls age 11–18, begun in 1926, and Juniorettes for age 7–10. Columbian Squires, begun by the Knights of Columbus in 1922, involves boys age 13–18.

Centre National des Oeuvres en Faveur de la Jeunesse Scolaire et Universitaire (CNO)   (France) a government agency formed during the Great Depression for administering and coordinating all programs that provide assistance and services to students. A law approved on April 17, 1955 that granted official statutory recognition and financial support to CNO also mandated that all student organizations would share with the Ministry of Education the responsibility for making decisions affecting administration of student services—the CNO's Administrative Council would be comprised of six representatives appointed by student organizations, five representatives chosen by the Ministry of Education from 15 nominees submitted by the student organizations, and 12 representatives from the ministry or selected by the Minister of Education. In 1963 the government reduced the proportion of student representation on the Administrative Council (students would have a total of seven seats while losing the right to submit 15 nominees), but the CNO continues in its administrative duties, with authority over university housing, student restaurants, and other services.

Chaikovsky Circle   (Russia) a student group that originated as a commune in St. Petersburg in the late 1860s and was originally known as the Natanson Circle after its founder Mark Natanson, a university student. The original circle organized branches in Moscow and brought young women into its membership in the spring of 1871. The members disseminated socialist-oriented books in an effort to educate the masses in preparation for liberation, but police confiscated many of these works and arrested and deported Natanson in November 1871. Thereafter, the group was known as the Chaikovsky Circle, after a university senior who served as a business representative for the group. Although loosely organized, with no written rules and all decisions requiring unanimous consent, the circle set high standards of personal ethics. There were about 40 members in St. Petersburg and another 50 in Moscow, and the circle owned and operated a small printing press in Zurich. Among its members was Sofya Perovskaya, who later (1881) would be executed for her involvement in the assassination of Tsar Alexander II. In 1872, then age 19, Perovskaya and others in the circle began to proselytize among workers,

trying to indoctrinate them in socialism. They nearly succeeded in developing the beginnings of a labor organization but ended up in prison, along with their worker converts, in late 1873. Further arrests in early 1874 brought an end to the Chaikovsky Circle, especially as no new leadership emerged to give the group guidance. Chaikovsky himself joined a peaceable religious sect and then emigrated to the United States to join a commune in rural Kansas.

Chai Ling (1966–)   (China) a major leader of the CHINESE DEMOCRACY MOVEMENT. Chai Ling was a 23-year-old graduate student at Beijing University who was married to Feng Congde, a member of the Beijing Student Solidarity Committee, when she (Chai Ling) became general commander of the students' hunger strike in Tiananmen Square in May 1989. (*See* TIANANMEN SQUARE MASSACRE.) On May 24 she was given leadership of the Protect Tiananmen Square Headquarters that oversaw occupation of the square. Although it was announced on May 27 that students would evacuate the square on May 30, the movement renewed itself on May 30 with the appearance of the "Goddess of Democracy" created by students at the Central Academy of Fine Arts in Beijing. Chai Ling helped to set up the Democracy University in the square in early June and the sit-in at the Monument to the People's Heroes, which on June 3 was brutally suppressed by the police. (It is estimated that 20,000 to 40,000 students were arrested.) She single-handedly rallied the protesting students with an impassioned speech. Subsequently, along with WANG DAN and WUER KAIXI, Chai Ling topped the list of the 21 most wanted student protestors, issued by the government on June 9. Chai Ling went into hiding and escaped from China in 1990. Wang was released in April 1998.

Chantiers de la Jeunesse   (France) one of two major, official (sanctioned and financially supported by the government) youth organizations in Vichy France (that third of the nation purposely left unoccupied by the Germans following their conquest of France in June 1940); established on July 31, 1940. The other major youth organization was the COMPAGNONS DE FRANCE, which was voluntary. Membership in the Chantiers was compulsory for all young men of military age—the initial members were young conscripts called up just before France's surrender. Originally, their period of service in the Chantiers was five months, but it was extended to eight months in January 1941. They experienced long days of rigorous exercise and work, as well as educational and other programs intended to instill moral discipline and civic responsibility and, at least surreptitiously, to create a surrogate army. After the Germans occupied Vichy France in November 1942, the Chantiers and all other youth organizations came under their increased surveillance. On January 4, 1944 the Germans arrested the

Chantiers leader and deported him to France; on June 15, 1944 they dissolved the movement.

Bibliography: W. D. Halls, *The Youth of Vichy France* (Oxford: Clarendon Press, 1981).

Charity Schools   (Blue-Coat Schools, Great Britain) developed as a philanthropic endeavor during the reign of Queen Anne (1702–1714), when the state made no provision for educating children of the poor, Charity Schools emerged in hundreds of communities. They were founded by wealthy patrons under the auspices of the Society for Promoting Christian Knowledge, managed by local committees of governors and supported by public subscriptions exacted from shopkeepers, artisans, and others. Their purpose was to educate the children of the poor in reading, writing, moral values, and Anglicanism. The children were provided with decent clothes and placed in apprenticeship upon leaving school. By the end of Anne's reign, more than a thousand Charity Schools existed, with some 5,000 boys and girls enrolled in the London area and another 20,000 throughout England, and the concept had spread to Scotland. Inspired by concern among the upper classes over social and political unrest as well as widespread ignorance, the schools were also intended to inculcate social discipline and acceptance of the established social order; nevertheless, they constituted a major reform.

Bibliography: Mary Gwladys Jones, *The Charity School Movement: A Study of Eighteenth Century Puritanism in Action* (Hamden, Conn.: Archon Books, 1964).

Charte de Grenoble, La   (France) a charter adopted by the student congress at Grenoble on April 24, 1946 that declared the new political and social awareness of the student movement in the aftermath of World War II. The leaders of the UNION NATIONALE DES ÉTUDIANTS DE FRANCE (UNEF) and UNEF itself had been discredited by acceptance of and collaboration with the Vichy government during the war. Now student veterans of the *maquis* resistance and members of the UNION PATRIOTIQUE DES ORGANISATIONS D'ÉTUDIANTES (UPOE) assumed control of UNEF; in the Grenoble charter they declared their break with the past (students would hereafter "be in the vanguard of French youth") and outlined both their rights and duties as "intellectual workers." Their rights, the charter declared, included their right as youths "to particular consideration from society from the physical, intellectual and moral standpoints," the right "to work and live in the best possible conditions," and "to be independent, both personally and socially. . . . " Their duties included acquiring "the highest competence possible"; pursuing "truth, freedom being the first condition thereof"; defining, spreading, and defending truth; and defending "freedom against all oppression, which is the foremost consideration of an intellectual." The char-

ter thus served as an ideological guide for a UNEF resurrected as a mass democratic movement.

Chicago Democratic Convention of 1968   *See* BATTLE OF CHICAGO.

Chicago 8 Trial   (United States) the trial in September–October 1969 of the protest leaders indicted for their roles in organizing the BATTLE OF CHICAGO during the 1968 Democratic National Convention. The trial began on September 24 with eight original defendants: David Dellinger, a middle-aged pacifist; Bobby SEALE of the BLACK PANTHERS; Tom HAYDEN and Rennie Davis, founders of the STUDENTS FOR A DEMOCRATIC SOCIETY (SDS); Abbie HOFFMAN and Jerry RUBIN, organizers of the Youth International Party (Yippies); and Lee Weiner and John Froines, both teachers. Among the lawyers defending them was William Kunstler, whose role in the

Judge Julius J. Hoffman sentenced Black Panther leader Bobby Seale to four years in prison on November 7, 1969 on contempt charges. Hoffman also declared a mistrial for Seale, separating him from seven other defendants charged with conspiring to incite riot during the 1968 Democratic National Convention.   (AP/WIDE WORLD PHOTOS)

trial gained him national attention. The defendants' own tack was to heap ridicule on the charges and the court. Judge Julius J. Hoffman found Seale's behavior so disruptive that on October 29 he had Seale bound and gagged, and on November 5 he sentenced Seale to four years in prison on 16 counts of contempt of court and declared his case a mistrial to be severed from the continuing trial of the others—thereafter referred to as the Chicago 7. On October 8–11 hundreds of members of the WEATHERMAN faction of SDS had a series of demonstrations to protest the trial—their slogan was "Bring the War Home." On the first night their clash with the police resulted in 60 arrests and three protestors wounded by gunfire. Illinois Governor Richard Ogilvie ordered 2,500 troops of the National Guard to report for duty. In October the protestors attacked a police cordon in the heart of the business district; two dozen police and scores of protestors were injured, and police arrested more than 100 protestors. Altogether over the course of the three days, police arrested 290 demonstrators, including Weatherman leaders Mark Rudd and Bernardine Dohrn. The jury in the Chicago 7 trial deliberated for several days and voted to acquit all the defendants of conspiracy charges. The sentences Judge Hoffman meted out varied in severity.

Children's Aid Society (CAS) (United States) an organization for assisting orphaned, neglected, and impoverished children founded in New York City in 1853 by Protestant social reformer Charles Loring Brace (1826–90), a graduate of Union Theological Seminary and one of the motivators of the Social Gospel movement. The society provided workshops, vocational schools, and residence halls for newsboys, gang members, and other children of the streets. It also established the Kensico Farm School, as Brace believed that farm work was probably the best means of rescuing urban youths from a life of destitution. In fulfillment of this concept the CAS adopted a "placing-out program" that sent poor children from New York City to foster homes in the outlying country areas where labor was scarce; this became the society's favored program for helping city youths, and by 1860 the CAS had placed more than 5,000 children. In 1854 the CAS had expanded this concept to sending groups of children to farms in Iowa, Illinois, Michigan, and other distant states, resulting in what became known as the "Orphan's Train," which transported tens of thousands of orphans to the Midwest and West to become members of farm families—in many cases unexpectedly ending up in virtual servitude. The CAS also established (in 1853) and operated the renowned Newsboys Lodging House, a boardinghouse in New York where, for a few pennies each day, newsboys, bootblacks, and messengers could have a bed and food while also being provided physical training, a savings bank, entrepreneurial lessons, and a moral educa-

tion. (Among the men closely associated with the Newsboys Lodging House following the Civil War was Horation Alger, whose novels about "rags to riches" stories of street boys were enormously popular well into the 1920s.) The CAS was staffed by men and focused largely on boys, but women volunteers ran its programs for girls, which included a lodging house, industrial schools, and instruction in such domestic activities as cooking and sewing.

Children's Crusade (France) a spontaneous movement that arose in the summer of A.D. 1212, during a period of comparative inactivity in the Middle East but of turmoil in Languedoc and other areas of France involving the Albigensian Crusade generated by Pope Innocent III against heretics. The final goal of this children's movement was, nevertheless, to recapture the Holy Land from the Muslims, not by arms but through the force of love.

The Children's Crusade was led by two youths, a 10-year-old German boy named Nicholas from Cologne and a French shepherd boy named Stephen from a town near Vendôme. The latter professed to having experienced a vision of Christ, who appeared to him as a pilgrim and gave him a letter to deliver to the king of France. During Stephen's journey to see the king in Paris, he attracted hundreds of children and shepherds as followers. As they journeyed to Paris they chanted, "Lord God, exalt Christianity! Restore the True Cross to us!" Some of Stephen's adult followers joined the Albigensian Crusade. The majority of the followers—30,000 by some estimates—decided to travel on to the Holy Land and made their way to Marseilles, where unscrupulous merchants supposedly tricked them into boarding ships that transported them into slavery in North Africa.

The second group of crusaders led by Nicholas, whose preaching enlisted an estimated 20,000 children, traveled up the Rhine River and crossed the Alps into Lombardy, Italy, where they split up into groups. Some got as far as Genoa but could not obtain passage across the Mediterranean and so dispersed. Others reached Rome, where the pope freed them from their crusaders' vow. Although the Children's Crusade was a failure, its lingering spirit reputedly helped inspire the Fifth Crusade of 1218.

Bibliography: Jonathan Riley-Smith, *The Crusades: A Short History* (New Haven, Conn.: Yale University Press, 1989); Marcel Schwab, *The Children's Crusade* (Boston: Small, Maynard, 1898).

Children's Friend Society (Great Britain) a philanthropic organization for abandoned children founded in 1830 in West Ham by a Captain Brenton of the Royal Navy. The Children's Friend Society for the Prevention of Juvenile Vagrancy opened a house in West Ham as a refuge for waifs from workhouses, streets, and prisons; by 1837 the Brenton Asylum housed 150 boys. The Victoria Asylum for girls had meanwhile been established at

Chiswick, along with branch agencies in the British colonies. Children remained at the asylums for six months, were employed, and received occupational and general education and kind treatment. At the end of their stay the boys were sent as apprentices to the colonies. At the time, an estimated 30,000 waifs roamed the streets of London and were responsible for a large percentage of the crimes committed in the city.

Chinese Communist Party (CCP)   (China) a militant, Marxist-oriented political party founded in July 1921—one of the major outcomes of the MAY FOURTH MOVEMENT. Small local Communist Party organizations—in Shanghai and Beijing, for example—began to form in the summer and fall of 1920 as a result of the impetus of the May Fourth Movement and the encouragement of the Soviet Union, which sent delegates to China in the spring of 1920. Representatives of seven of these small groups (Mao Zedong was the delegate from Hunan) met in Shanghai to found the CCP as a revolutionary organization inspired by the October Revolution and the concepts of Marx and Lenin. In 1923 the CCP took control of publishing the monthly periodical *Xin Qingnian* (New Youth), which had achieved high repute during the May Fourth Movement. As a legatee of that movement the CCP helped to set up socialist youth groups, including in 1925 its own COMMUNIST YOUTH LEAGUE. Thousands of university students were involved in the CCP through the years. In 1948 the CCP resumed publishing the popular journal *Chinese Youth*. During the 1949 revolution and following its acquisition of power on October 1, 1949 with formation of the People's Republic of China, the CCP enrolled university students and middle school students above age 18 in political orientation and training courses and sent them as cadres throughout China to secure CCP hegemony through administrative and propagandistic programs. In 1950 in Beijing alone, an estimated 200,000 or more students completed six-month political training courses at the People's Revolutionary College and other institutions. During the early 1950s the CCP gained total control over the universities, largely with the acquiescence, and even cooperation, of the students. There were times, in fact, when the CCP itself was practically a youth movement. For example, at one time in the 1920s the average age of members of the leadership was about 26; in 1956, when membership was open to those 18 and older, about one-fourth of the party's members were 25 or younger. (It is noteworthy that in 1960 more than 40 percent of all Chinese were less than 17 years old.) *See also* GREAT PROLETARIAN CULTURAL REVOLUTION and RED GUARDS.

Chinese Democracy Movement   (China) a major student political reform movement initiated in Beijing in April 1989 that culminated in the TIANANMEN SQUARE MASSACRE. Although students' dissatisfaction had been

building for years with prodemocracy demonstrations in 1986 and 1988, the immediate catalyst for the movement's crystalization was the death on April 15, 1989 of Hu Yaobang, former head of the CHINESE COMMUNIST PARTY (CCP), whose tolerance of student demonstrations and Western political and cultural influences had earned the respect and gratitude of students but had also caused his ouster from power in January 1987 following students' prodemocracy demonstrations in late 1986. Students in Beijing held a mourning demonstration for Hu in Tiananmen Square that quickly transformed into the massive Democracy Movement.

On April 18 just after midnight, about 3,000 students began to march from the campus of Beijing University to Tiananmen Square shouting "Long live freedom! Down with bureaucracy!" At the square they were joined by several thousand students from People's University. Near dawn they tried to deliver to the Standing Committee of the National People's Congress a petition outlining seven student demands. They were outraged when no representative of the committee appeared to meet with them and they had to leave the petition with an office clerk. The petition demanded that the government (1) reappraise the career and achievements of Hu; (2) abandon the Anti-Bourgeois Liberalization campaign against Western political concepts that began in January 1987 and the Anti-Spiritual Pollution campaign against Western ideas of individualism, personal freedom, and free artistic expression that began in October 1983; (3) end press censorship and permit independent publications; (4) make public the incomes and wealth of CCP and government officials and their families; (5) rescind Beijing's Ten Provisional Articles Regulating Public Marches and Demonstrations that were drafted in 1968 to impose restrictions on demonstrating; (6) increase government expenditures for higher education; (7) present objective coverage of student demonstrations in the news media.

On April 19 and 20, the students' confrontation with authority took a different turn as they assembled and demonstrated at Xinhuamen, the entrance to Zhongnanhai—the CCP compound and living quarters of many of the nation's leaders, located about a quarter of a mile to the west of Tiananmen Square. Again they tried unsuccessfully to deliver a petition, and on the mornings of both days they clashed violently with police guards. The students claimed they were demonstrating peacefully on April 20 when the police attacked them with belts and clubs, injuring several students. In response to this "April 20 Incident" students at Beijing University began a boycott of classes. Also on April 20 they announced creation of the Beijing University Students' Solidarity Committee, independent from the CCP-backed student federation, to further the organization of the movement and to coordinate protests with other autonomous groups at other schools. In Beijing the campaign of hanging protest posters spread from the campus to walls and telephone poles throughout the city. Many of these attacked the CCP for corruption, profiteering, usurpation of power, and other evils; ironically, from beginning to end, most of the student leaders were members of the CCP.

The April 20 demonstrations in Tiananmen Square had persisted for five continuous days. Authorities announced that the square would be sealed off for the memorial service for Hu on April 22, and so tens of thousands of students poured into the square on the night of April 21. Joined by Beijing residents, the crowd reached 200,000. After the service three student representatives were permitted to approach the western entrance of the Great Hall of the People to present a petition to Premier Li Peng. They knelt there on the steps—a gesture of contrition that angered some students—but Li never appeared. By April 21 student demonstrations had erupted in other cities as well, including Shanghai, Nanjing, and Wuhan, and on April 23 representatives of 20 Beijing schools formed the Provisional Students' Federation (PSF), which declared a citywide boycott of classes. Beijing University students also began the *News Herald*, a mimeographed broadside to spread news and declarations and began liaison committees to propagandize the public.

The Politburo's Standing Committee decided to counteract student organizing by blocking the use of telephone and telegraph services. Deng Xiaoping, the supreme leader, determined to send the army against the students, although actual troop deployment was deferred by other events. The CCP paper, the *People's Daily*, transformed Deng's views into an editorial denouncing the students' demonstrations as "turmoil," the term used to define the extreme social trauma of the CULTURAL REVOLUTION and therefore a movement meriting suppression. This heavyhanded approach angered not only the students but also intellectuals, many workers, and other adult citizens. In response to the editorial, the PSF called for a massive student march on April 27. Apprised that the 38th Army had moved into positions surrounding Beijing and banned from further demonstrations by the government, students feared a violent confrontation— some wrote their wills; others decided against marching. Nevertheless, on the morning of April 27, more than 100,000 students joined the march. As the marchers approached police cordons, city residents raced forward to prevent the police from interfering. The students marched to Tiananmen Square, purposely paced through the square, and continued a circuit through the heart of Beijing cheered on by the public. There was no violence, and the march proved a great success for the student movement and a humiliation for the government.

On April 28 the PSF was reorganized as the Federation of Autonomous Student Unions of Beijing Universities and Colleges (Beijing Students' Federation), with WUER KAIXI, a 21-year-old education student at Beijing Normal University, as chairman. Most prominent among its other leaders was WANG DAN, a history student at the

university and the son of a professor. The new federation defined two primary goals: government recognition of the federation and open dialogue with the government. The government refused recognition and arranged dialogues with officially sanctioned student unions. On May 1 the Beijing Students' Federation denounced these nationally broadcast talks as charades designed to create divisions within the student movement. On May 2 federation representatives delivered a petition demanding a nationally broadcast dialogue with members of the Politburo's Standing Committee attended by Chinese and foreign journalists—the petition was rejected. The federation also pursued plans for a massive demonstration on May 4, commemorating the 70th anniversary of the MAY FOURTH MOVEMENT. About 100,000 students participated. At Tiananmen Square they listened to Wuer Kaixi read the New May Fourth Manifesto, which called on the nation to promote freedom, to accelerate political reform, to allow a free press, to eliminate corruption, to establish a democratic government, and in other ways to modernize China.

There followed several days of relative quiet. In the meantime a struggle ensued within the Politburo between the hardliners headed by Deng and a moderate faction headed by CCP chief Zhao Ziyang, with Zhao pursuing ways to enlist the support of both students and intellectuals. The struggle prevented Deng from unleashing troops to suppress the Democracy Movement, as did the May 15 arrival of Premier Mikhail Gorbachev of the Soviet Union on a state visit. But the Democracy Movement appeared to be losing momentum, until on May 13 a group of 2,000 students (mostly undergraduates from 10 Beijing schools), led by CHAI LING, a 23-year-old graduate student at Beijing Normal University who headed the Tiananmen Command Center, began a hunger strike in Tiananmen Square. The strike generated public support for the Democracy Movement and also brought university students from nearly all of China's provinces pouring into Beijing to join the cause. On May 17, as Gorbachev left for Shanghai, factory workers, high school students, clerks, businesspeople, even soldiers swelled the ranks of marchers on Changan Avenue leading to Tiananmen Square until the demonstration numbered more than 1 million participants. On May 18 the crowd was equally large, this time riding in vehicles as well as marching.

The press, encouraged by the Zhao faction, freely reported on this enormous rally and published varied appeals for governmental reforms. To strengthen Zhao's hand, his supporters tried to persuade the students to end their hunger strike in order to preclude a government crackdown, but the students remained adamant. The hardliners in the Politburo gained the upper hand, and on May 18 Premier Li Peng met with some of the student leaders prior to imposing martial law. At 9:00 A.M. on May 19, the Hunger Strikers' Group declared their

Chinese students shout with joy after breaking through a police blockade during a prodemocracy march to Tiananmen Square in central Beijing. (AP/WIDE WORLD PHOTOS)

strike at an end, transformed into a sit-in demonstration, but the Zhao faction had been defeated in the Politburo, and the government declared martial law to take effect in Beijing on May 20. During the night of May 19, as troops attempted to move into the city, huge groups of residents spontaneously massed to bar their way and protect the students. Dissension among the students on how to proceed diminished their strength, and the number encamped in Tiananmen Square, now mostly students from the provinces, declined to 40,000 or less—those determined to make a final stand. Many others advocated returning to their campuses to devise new tactics and to formulate more clearly defined theoretical positions. By May 26 all seven military commands in the nation, including that in Beijing, had fallen in line to support Li Peng and Deng. By now more than 150,000 students from the provinces had arrived in Beijing to support the movement. They rejected calls by Beijing students to

abandon Tiananmen Square and instead escalated their poster attack on Li and even on Deng. They took renewed vigor from the May 30 arrival in the square of the "Goddess of Democracy," a 33-foot-tall plaster-and-styrofoam sculpture constructed by students at the Central Academy of Fine Arts in Beijing that came to symbolize their Democracy Movement.

Students initiated plans for a Democracy University for the study of democratic theory and programs—an "open university" to be sited in the square. It was inaugurated on June 3. On June 2 a few students also began a new hunger strike, but the end of the Democracy Movement was at hand. On the afternoon and night of June 3, soldiers armed with AK-47s, truncheons, and tear gas and accompanied by tanks and armored personnel carriers assembled; at 2:00 A.M. on June 4, their onslaught on the students and residents blockading the arteries leading to Tiananmen Square began. The resisters hurled bricks and Molotov cocktails at the attackers. On Changan Avenue the army assault was especially savage. By early morning on June 4, troops encircled Tiananmen Square. Exactly what followed is not clear, but some reports indicate that after 5:00 A.M. the troops opened fire on the encamped students. Army tanks moved in to clear the square and destroy the "Goddess of Democracy." The Tiananmen Massacre—on the streets leading to the square alone—resulted in hundreds of dead, perhaps even thousands, including soldiers. Surviving students, led by Chai Ling, withdrew to the Beijing University campus. Realizing that resistance was futile, they hoped to organize a nationwide general strike, but it never occurred.

By June 6 all resistance in Beijing had ended. On June 9 television stations broadcast an address by Deng to military and political leaders in which he declared that the

The famous portrait of Chairman Mao overlooking Tiananmen Square faces off a 33-foot statue erected in the square on May 30, 1989. The statue was dubbed "The Goddess of Democracy" by students from the Central Academy of Fine Arts who modeled it after the Statue of Liberty.   (AP/WIDE WORLD PHOTOS)

government had suppressed a "counterrevolutionary rebellion," an offense punishable by death. The final toll for the June 4 massacre and its aftermath may never be known, as troops purposely cremated the bodies of the dead to hide their numbers and hospitals were forbidden to divulge information on the wounded and dead they had treated. The government issued an estimate of 300 dead, including soldiers and 36 students, and 6,000 soldiers injured along with 3,000 civilians. But doctors who had treated the victims estimated that 2,000 had died; the Chinese Red Cross estimated that 2,600 had been killed on June 4, and student groups suggested the same figure as the toll of students alone. In addition, security police arrested more than 20,000 students and intellectuals. The Democracy Movement, the most serious challenge to the government since establishment of the People's Republic of China in 1949, had been totally crushed.

Bibliography: Han Minzhu, ed., *Cries for Democracy: Writings and Speeches from the 1989 Chinese Democracy Movement* (Princeton, N.J.: Princeton University Press, 1990); Chu-yuan Cheng, *Behind the Tiananmen Massacre: Social, Political, and Economic Ferment in China* (Boulder, Colo.: Westview Press, 1990).

Chinese National Liberation Vanguard (CNLV) (China) an organization formed in Beijing on January 26, 1936 by students returned from their failed "rural crusade" to spread the DECEMBER NINTH MOVEMENT in rural areas. The CNLV came to operate as a front for the CHINESE COMMUNIST PARTY (CCP) within the student movement. By the summer of 1936, the CNLV had 1,200 active student members, who began a rural literacy program comprised largely of fostering reading of communist-oriented newspapers, tracts, and other writings, including works by Lenin. The CNLV also conducted a program to train students in guerrilla warfare. By the fall of 1936 CNLV had branches in 31 cities. The CNLV mounted a program to assist students in dealing with academic problems, managing finances, and finding employment after graduation. As war with Japan approached, the organization lost many of its adherents—a number in the wake of the SIAN INCIDENT—and was forced to scale back its activities. But its efforts had proved significant in generating support for the CCP among university students.

Chinese Students' Alliance   (United States) a nationwide organization of Chinese students studying in the United States, the first nation to which modern China sent students for education—the first students, 30 boys, arriving in 1872. The numbers of visiting students remained small until 1909 when the United States began sending Boxer Indemnity funds to China; by 1915 there were more than 1,200 Chinese students in the United States—800 of whom in colleges and universities formed the membership of the Chinese Students' Alliance. The alliance published the *Chinese Students' Monthly* in the United States and the *Chinese Students' Quarterly*, a Chinese language journal, in Shanghai. The U.S. monthly galvanized students following eruption in May 1915 of the TWENTY-ONE DEMANDS PROJECT controversy, exhorting them to return home to help save China. Many of the students did precisely that, later becoming involved with the MAY FOURTH MOVEMENT.

Chinese Youth Corps (China) one of several youth leagues formed during the Japanese occupation and the Second United Front era (1937–45) to promote loyalty to Wang Ching-wei, a rival of Chiang Kai-shek for control of the Kuomintang (KMT)—Wang formed an alliance with the Japanese. The Corps also worked to help validate the legitimacy of Wang's Puppet KMT regime in Shanghai. Another such group was the reconstituted Chinese Boy Scouts. These youth leagues were also used to support Wang's New Republic Movement, which, like Chiang's NEW LIFE MOVEMENT, promoted Sun Yat-sen's Three People's Principles and conservative social values but, unlike the New Life Movement, also advocated aiding the Japanese. It was also Wang's policy to persuade university students to join pro-Japanese youth groups that, among other things, participated in public demonstrations to further the purposes of the occupation. Naturally, following Japan's defeat in World War II, neither Wang nor his youth leagues retained any credibility.

Christian Endeavor Society *See* YOUNG PEOPLE'S SOCIETY OF CHRISTIAN ENDEAVOR.

Christian Service Brigade (CSB) (United States) an organization for boys modeled upon the BOYS' BRIGADE and the BOY SCOUTS but with an overall emphasis on religion. The CSB was founded in Glen Ellyn, Illinois in 1937 and is headquartered in Wheaton, Illinois. (There is a Canadian headquarters in Burlington, Ontario.) Groups are sited at evangelical Protestant churches and number more than 2,700 nationwide. CSB's program and uniforms resemble those of the Boy Scouts, but groups are designated *battalions* rather than *troops*. The youngest members, age 11, are known as stockades; those 12 to 18 are brigadiers; and those 19 and older are brigademen. Various levels of achievement are awarded, the highest honor being the Herald of Christ award, which is based on achievement in Bible study. CSB provides handbooks and monthly magazines for boys and leaders both—that for boys is *Venture*.

Christian Youth Council of North America a youth and student organization formed in 1934 by the leaders of 41 Protestant denominations.

Chukaku (Marxist Student League Central Core, MSL) (Japan) an important faction within the ZENGAKUREN formed in February 1963 and associated with the Japan Revolutionary Communist League National Committee. Chukaku, or MSL, was opposed to the Japan Communist Party (JCP). The faction became renowned for brutal street fighting. Chukaku was heavily involved in the HANEDA INCIDENTS and the SASEBO NAVAL BASE STRUGGLE.

Church Lads' Brigade (Great Britain) a Church of England organization inspired by the BOYS' BRIGADE. The Church Lads' Brigade (CLB) was founded by Walter Mallock Gee in 1891. Gee became secretary of the Church of England Temperance Society (CETS) Junior Division in 1889, so the CETS was instrumental in the founding, orientation, and operations of the CLB. Gee used the Boys' Brigade as his model for organizing boys who had graduated from the CETS's BANDS OF HOPE. Because William Alexander Smith had scotched the creation of an Anglican section within the Boys' Brigade, Gee decided to create the CLB, which he launched at St. Andrew's Parish Church in Fulham, London, on July 23, 1891. As a member of the Volunteers, Gee adopted a strongly militaristic organization and program for the CLB, including a full range of ranks. Initially the CLB evoked opposition and creation of rival groups by churchmen who desired an even more temperance-oriented stance than Gee took, but the CLB survived, with a Governing Brigade Council being established in 1892, the same year Gee became the CLB's secretary. Five years later, the CLB had companies in every diocese in England and Wales, but only one in Scotland. In 1908, when the BOY SCOUTS was founded, the CLB numbered 1,300 companies with 70,000 member boys. The CLB tried to counter the new competition from the Scouts by creating the Incorporated Church Scout Patrols. Recruits came largely from the families of skilled workers who attended church; yet the CLB portrayed itself as a substitute for the public (private) schools. It fostered such values as "sobriety, thrift, self-help, punctuality, obedience." The CLB's journal was entitled *The Brigade*. In 1911 the CLB aligned itself with the Territorials, applying for CADET FORCE status for its companies, thus solidifying its militarist and nationalist image. This image eventuated in declining membership for the CLB as public sentiment turned against militarism in the years between the two world wars, even though the group terminated its affiliation with the cadets in 1936. The group's membership declined significantly during the 1950s and 1960s, and by the early 1970s total members numbered about 8,000 in 320 units.

Bibliography: John Springhall, *Youth, Empire and Society: British Youth Movements, 1883–1940* (London: Croom Helm, 1977).

Church of England Young Men's Society (CEYMS) (Great Britain) an organization noteworthy for its founding in 1844 because that was the same year that the

YOUNG MEN'S CHRISTIAN ASSOCIATION (YMCA) was founded—both organizations arising from the same reform impulse. The CEYMS promoted among its young members opportunities for self-improvement that prepared them to teach in the Ragged Schools (*see* RAGGED SCHOOL UNION) and to further other social reform movements through their services.

Círculo Argentino de Estudiantes de Derecho (Argentina) an organization of law students notable for its opposition to University Reform. (*See* UNIVERSITY REFORM PROGRAM AND MOVEMENT.) The circle also supported the military dictatorship of the 1930s and sided with the ultranationalists, especially those student members of the Faculty of Law at the University of Buenos Aires.

Civilian Conservation Corps (CCC)   (United States) a program designed to provide jobs for young men ages 17 to 24 that was authorized by the Civilian Conservation Corps Reforestation Relief Act in March 1933 as part of the New Deal effort to combat unemployment during the Great Depression. The program allowed young men to volunteer for service in the CCC, which would put them to work in camps or companies of 200 devoted to such projects as planting trees, making repairs of facilities in national parks, helping to build bridges and reservoirs, controlling soil erosion, protecting wildlife, and other conservation endeavors. The youths were paid $30 per month, $25 of which was sent directly home to

The Civilian Conservation Corps's camps, which were started in 1933 to take young men off the bread lines during the Great Depression, put thousands to work. The healthy outdoor jobs they engaged in toughened many of the youth for rigors of wartime service later. The camps ceased operating in June 1942. These rugged young men were at the CCC's Camp Tomahawk in Wisconsin, where they helped fight forest fires by building fire lanes, clearing brush, and the like. (AP/WIDE WORLD PHOTOS)

their families. President Franklin D. Roosevelt appointed Robert Fechner director of the CCC.

Under Fechner's guidance, the CCC grew rapidly and captured the public's imagination and approval. The CCC attained its peak in 1935, with more than 500,000 youths in service at nearly 2,500 camps, most of which were sited west of the Mississippi River. From 1938 on, with World War II approaching, enrollment in the CCC gradually declined, and the program was ended in July 1942 against the wishes of Roosevelt, who was a dedicated conservationist. During its nine-year existence the CCC provided work for more than 3 million youths and 250,000 veterans of World War I.

Bibliography: John Salmond, *The Civilian Conservation Corps, 1933–1942: A New Deal Case Study* (Durham, N.C.: Duke University Press, 1967).

Clamshell Alliance   (United States) an organization founded in June 1976 in New Hampshire following the Public Service Corporation's announcement of plans to proceed with constructing a nuclear-power plant at Seabrook on the New Hampshire coast. Clamshell was founded by environmental activists, members of the American Friends Service Committee, and former anti-Vietnam War activists who had moved to New England in the early 1970s. COUNTERCULTURE activists and youths from Boston and other cities comprised the majority of its active supporters. Clamshell's major undertaking was a mass occupation of the power-plant site in April 1977—about 24,000 protestors participated and 1,401 were arrested. The organization also held another occupation at the site in June 1978. Although Clamshell grew rapidly, it proved unable to stop construction of the nuclear plant. The organization foundered on disagreements over tactics and leadership, and by the end of 1978 it was effectively dead. Despite its brief existence, the Clamshell Alliance was significant as the first major vehicle for countercultural, nonviolent direct action and civil disobedience; it also trained thousands of activists in nonviolent tactics and inspired the creation of numerous other alliances of environmental activists.

Cleaver, Eldridge (1935–1998)   (United States) leader of the BLACK PANTHERS and major radical activist and writer of the 1960s. Cleaver was raised in the Watts ghetto of Los Angeles. Much of his youth was spent in reformatories and prisons, where he acquired his education. Cleaver attained national renown as a writer for *Ramparts* and as minister of information for the Black Panthers formed in 1966. In a January 1968 police crackdown on the Panthers and a shoot-out in Oakland he was arrested, but while on bail he fled the country, going first to Cuba and then to Algeria. His first book, *Soul on Ice*, published in 1968, became an influential best-seller—2 million copies sold in the United States alone. Cleaver traveled in several communist nations, including the

Eldridge Cleaver, "black power" advocate and member of the Black Panther party, holds a press conference at the Algonquin Hotel in New York City to open his campaign as presidential candidate of the Peace and Freedom Party.   (AP/WIDE WORLD PHOTOS)

Soviet Union and North Korea, and he lived in Paris from 1973 to 1975. In 1975 he returned home and was again arrested; he was released on bail in August 1976. During the sixties, Cleaver gave voice to the intensity of the unrest among urban blacks and urged African Americans to pursue militant opposition to oppression by whites. In more recent years, he disavowed many of his earlier ideas, attacking communism as responsible for creating the most repressive regimes in history and advocating a militarily strong United States and destruction of the communist regime in the Soviet Union. The catalyst for his shift in ideology was President Richard Nixon's 1972 visit to the Republic of China.

Cohn-Bendit, Daniel (1945–)   (France) leader of students at the University of Paris branch at Nanterre and of the student demonstrators during the MAY REVOLT. Cohn-Bendit, a German Jew who had been born in France but returned with his family to Germany, almost accidentally became a student leader while a second-year sociology student at Nanterre. He participated in a 10-day strike in November 1967 that involved 10,000 students and the faculty and demanded university reforms. On January 8, 1968, at a time when the Nan-

terre students were reading Wilhelm Reich's books and campaigning for "sexual enlightenment," the Minister for Youth and Sports arrived to dedicate a new swimming pool. Cohn-Bendit heckled him for not mentioning sexual problems in a recent ministry white paper on student affairs. The minister responded sarcastically, and Cohn-Bendit called him a fascist. Police arrested Cohn-Bendit and planned to deport him. His student supporters fought with the police and later occupied the school's administration building. (*See* MARCH 22 MOVEMENT.) The student unrest spread to the Sorbonne, which was shut down on May 4. Cohn-Bendit became the spokesman for the Paris students during the uprising that followed. (*See* MAY REVOLT.) Many referred to him as "Dany the Red." Enemies viciously attacked Cohn-Bendit as a German Jew with such slogans as "Cohn-Bendit to Dachau!" His student defenders responded, "We are all German Jews." After the Paris May experience, Cohn-Bendit returned to Germany and tried for two years to instill revolutionary zeal in the workers at the Opel plant near Frankfurt, but with minimal success. He then turned to operating a bookshop in Frankfurt, and he published a memoir, *Der Grosse Basar*, in 1975 in both Germany and France (*Le Grand Bazar*).

Collège de France Protest   (France) demonstrations by Parisian university students in early 1848 over infringements upon academic freedom imposed by the government of King Louis Philippe. The catalyst for the demonstrations was the cancellation of a course by the popular historian Jules Michelet on January 2, 1848 at the Collège de France that was clearly politically motivated. In protest, hundreds of students demonstrated on January 6 and again on February 3—their protest was a precursor of the Revolution of 1848. A series of republican-oriented "political banquets" had been held throughout France since the summer of 1847, and now the government forbade the convening of a large banquet to be held in Paris on February 22. In response, protesting students joined with republican leaders and workers in a massive demonstration in Paris on February 22 that on the following day became a riot, with the protestors attacking the home of François Guizot, the government's chief minister. In the ensuing battle, troops killed 50 of the demonstrators. Alarmed by these events, Louis Philippe abdicated the throne on February 24, and the revolution ensued.

Collège des Commissaires   (Congo) the national governing body of the Republic of the Congo established by Colonel Joseph Mobutu in September 1960 and comprised of students and recent university graduates. The Congo had attained independence from Belgium at the end of June 1960, but it was wracked with factional conflict and a struggle for power between President Joseph Kasavubu and Prime Minister Patrice Lumumba.

Mobutu hoped to impose order and efficiency by having students trained in technical disciplines—and thus presumably proficient in applying the knowledge of these disciplines—to assume temporary control of the government. He invited them to do so, calling them home from Europe and other areas where they were studying. Each general commissioner was provided a portfolio related to his academic major—the commissioner of public health, for example, was a medical student. The College of Commissioners thus constituted a rare instance in history when control of a government was formally awarded to youths attending universities. The Collège began with good intentions and 24 members, but it soon expanded to 39 members at the behest of the student commissioners and in an effort to accommodate all regions and tribes. This ungainly size doomed the College to ineffectualness. With poorly defined roles intended to combine both executive and legislative functions, and lacking administrative and political experience, the student commissioners could not agree on policies or govern effectively. Power slowly gravitated into the control of varied factions, and the College was dissolved in February 1961—a failed experiment that discredited the mystique of the "student-technician" as a supremely capable expert.

Collegiate Anti-Militarism League

(United States) an organization founded at Columbia University in 1915 by student representatives from eastern universities. A response to the campaign for military preparedness following the 1914 outbreak of war in Europe, the league's purpose was to oppose proposals to introduce courses in military training into the curricula of the universities and also efforts to persuade students to attend military training camps. Members of the INTERCOLLEGIATE SOCIALIST SOCIETY (ISS) held two of the league's offices (secretary and treasurer), and others served as officers in subsequent years, but the ISS itself did not sponsor or support the league. During 1916 and 1917, the League produced a journal entitled *War?*

Columbia Strike

(United States) a Columbia University students' strike in April 1932—the first U.S. student strike of the Great Depression decade. The strike occurred as a response to the university administration's suspension of Reed Harris as editor of the *Columbia Spectator*, the university's newspaper for undergraduates. Harris, a journalism student, became the paper's editor in the fall of 1931. His editorials soon began to generate controversy, as he attacked the university's Reserve Officers' Training Corps (ROTC), accused the football program of being overly commercial, and pursued other problematic topics. His undoing came with an attack on the university's food service—a long-standing student complaint—but with a new twist: Harris asked for an investigation of the food service's management, which he accused of accepting rebates from food suppliers. The

administration immediately suspended Harris. In support of students' freedom of speech, the NATIONAL STUDENT LEAGUE (NSL) denounced the suspension and organized a citywide student protest and a mass demonstration. On April 4 about 2,000 incensed students gathered at the steps of Low Library and planned a campus strike, a boycott of classes, which occurred on April 6, with three-fourths of the student body joining in protest and wearing "On Strike" buttons. The students also appointed an investigative committee, which quickly defined the overriding issue involved as the right of freedom of speech and of the press. Within a week, the Columbia administration announced that there would be an investigation of the food service, and a week after that on April 20 the administration acceded to the strikers' main demand by reinstating Harris. A disgusted Harris denounced the reinstatement and "resigned." Still, the student strikers had won, and their effort is credited as constituting the beginning of the student movement of the 1930s.

Bibliography: Robert Cohen, *When the Old Left Was Young: Student Radicals and America's First Mass Student Movement, 1929–1941* (New York: Oxford University Press, 1993).

Columbia University Student Revolt

(United States) a major student uprising at Columbia University in April 1968, whose drama and impact rivaled the earlier BERKELEY STUDENT REVOLT. The ostensible catalyst for the revolt was the university's building of a gymnasium on New York City land in Morningside Park, adjacent to the Harlem ghetto that comprised the university neighborhood where Columbia was a major landlord. Although residents of the neighborhood were to be provided use of a separate facility, militant African-American leaders objected to the gymnasium as an encroachment upon the residential area. The strong Columbia chapter of STUDENTS FOR A DEMOCRATIC SOCIETY (SDS), which was campaigning against the Institute for Defense Analysis (a university consortium doing research for the Pentagon), joined this campaign with the African American opposition to the gymnasium.

On April 23 members of SDS led by Mark Rudd and of the Students' Afro-American Society joined forces and marched to the Low Library, where guards repulsed them. Shouting "Jim Crow Must Go," the students marched to the gymnasium building site, where they tore down a section of the fence. Then they occupied Hamilton Hall, the administrative building for the undergraduate college, where they held the dean prisoner for a day and closed down the classrooms. On April 24 the blacks withdrew from the mixed group but continued the occupation of Hamilton Hall. The whites moved on to occupy the Low Library, where they ransacked President Grayson Kirk's office and files, smoked Kirk's cigars, and drank his sherry. During the following days the protestors, now numbering more than 700, occupied three other buildings: the students transformed all five of the occupied buildings into "revolutionary communes." A "majority coalition" of student opponents led by athletes surrounded Low Library to prevent supplies from reaching the protestors. Classes were cancelled on April 26, and police sealed off the campus following its invasion by 250 black high school students supporting the black Columbia protestors and shouting "Black Power." On the same day H. Rap Brown and Stokely CARMICHAEL of the STUDENT NONVIOLENT COORDINATING COMMITTEE (SNCC) met with the African-American students holding Hamilton Hall to show their support in opposing the university administration's "racist policies." Kirk tried to negotiate with the protestors, but, when this effort failed, he called in the 1,000 city police early on the morning of April 30. The blacks occupying Hamilton Hall quietly surrendered, but elsewhere the police had to attack with force and remove the protestors, resulting in 132 students, 12 police officers, and four faculty members being injured and 700 persons arrested.

The "Battle of Morningside Heights," as some commentators called the event, had immediate consequences but rather indefinable long-term effects. A strike by students and some faculty resulted, with the new protest focusing on university administrative policies and the roles of students and faculty in their development. Another student-police clash occurred on May 1, police left the campus on May 2, and on May 5 the faculty voted to end classes and cancel final examinations for the term. On May 21 students again seized a building and had to be ejected by police. On June 4, a "countercommencement" was held by dissident students and faculty in protest of the traditional commencement. Construction of the gymnasium was halted, and some policies of the university were liberalized. A number of buildings had been trashed but were readily repairable. Tragically for one history professor who opposed the protest, the rebellious students had burned a 20-year accumulation of his research notes and manuscripts. Kirk, whose response to the revolt offended all sides, announced his retirement on August 23. The

Columbia students sit in at Hamilton Hall, Columbia University.   (AP/WIDE WORLD PHOTOS)

New York City police remove a demonstrator from the campus of Columbia University early in the morning of May 22, 1968. Police appeared on campus to oust a group of student demonstrators and sympathizers from Hamilton Hall, which had been seized by the demonstrators the night before. The police arrested 81 men and 50 women who had remained in the building. (AP/WIDE WORLD PHOTOS)

SDS chapter declined following the suspension of Rudd and 72 other students. The revolt initiated or at least underscored an emerging trend toward violence on university campuses instead of in off-campus confrontations and made the campus the center for launching a new U.S. revolution. (Rudd said that the controversies over the gymnasium and the Institute of Defense Analysis were both manufactured and trifling—the real cause was "to make a revolution.") The revolt also led to protests being less issues oriented and more focused on achieving a sometimes vague STUDENT POWER. Thus the Columbia student revolt was a harbinger of things to come.

Bibliography: Donald E. Phillips, *Student Protest, 1960–1970* (New York: University Press of America, 1985).

Comité d'Action Lycéens (CAL) (France) a network of lycée student groups opposed to the Vietnam War that was set up in 1967. Membership in CAL grew rapidly despite the opposition of lycée headmasters. CAL members were major participants in the MAY REVOLT of 1968.

Comité d'Action Universitaire (CAU) (Algeria) an organization formed in 1956 by right-wing French students at the University of Algiers in opposition to the independence movement headed by the FRONT DE LIBÉRATION NATIONALE (FLN). The CAU planned to create a student corps to help destroy the FLN "rebellion."

Comité de Liaison des Étudiants Révolutionnaires (CLER) (France) a student organization formed in 1961 and affiliated with the small Parti Communiste Internationaliste, a Trotskyist party. CLER had very little influence in the student movement, gaining control of only two ASSOCIATION GÉNÉRALE DES ÉTUDIANTS (AGE) chapters at provincial universities during the 1960s. In April 1968 CLER's name was changed to Fédération des Étudiants Révolutionnaires (FER). Declared illegal after the student uprisings of May and June 1968, FER changed its name to Comité pour la Défense de l'UNEF (UNION NATIONALE DES ÉTUDIANTS DE FRANCE).

Comité de Liaison et d'Information des Étudiants de France (CLIEF) (France) a student organization created on June 6, 1960 by ASSOCIATION GÉNÉRALE DES ÉTUDIANTS (AGE) members as a result of controversy within the UNION NATIONALE DES ÉTUDIANTS DE FRANCE (UNEF) concerning the Algerian War. CLIEF did not split from UNEF but propounded a progovernment view on the war.

Comité pour la Défense de l'UNEF *See* COMITÉ DE LIAISON DES ÉTUDIANTS RÉVOLUTIONNAIRES.

Commune Movement (United States) a largely rural-centered youth movement (although there were also urban communes) that burgeoned in the late 1960s, inspired by and partly a successor to the HIPPIE MOVEMENT—numerous communes, in fact, were established by hippies. A few communes were based on concepts delineated in behavioral psychologist B. F. Skinner's novel *Walden Two* (1948). Hippies abandoning Haight-Ashbury in 1968 frequently ended up at rural communes. The growth of the commune movement is suggested by the creation of the *Whole Earth Catalogue* in 1968 and its rapid expansion in sales from 1,000 in that year to 160,000 by the end of 1969; the catalogue published information on organic gardening, house building, car repairing, and similar subjects. It is estimated that by 1970 there were from 2,000 to 3,000 communes extant in the United States; there were also many communes in Great Britain and other Western nations. Many communes suffered from poor organization, some self-destructing because of anarchical operations and most plagued by transiency, promiscuity, poor finances, and lack of personal responsibility. Among the few apparently successful communes was one known as The Farm, begun in 1968 in western Tennessee. In the mid-1970s, the commune had about 600 adult residents and owed its success probably to being well ordered. The Farm supported marriage, isolated single residents by gender, frowned on premarital sex, banned extramarital sex, and promoted socialization of its children—a quite different agenda from most communes. The commune movement peaked as an attraction for youths during the early 1970s.

Communist Youth International (CYI)   an international organization founded at a meeting held in Berlin in November 1919. Representatives of leftist member groups of the International Union of Socialist Youth Organizations (IUSYO), which had been formed prior to World War I at a youth conference held in Stuttgart in 1907, comprised the delegates to the meeting; members of socialist youth organizations associated with right or centrist socialist parties were not welcome, as the allegiance of the delegates was to the Russian Bolsheviks, and they simply transformed the IUSYO into the CYI with the intent of allying it with the Communist International formed in March 1919. Consisting primarily of nonstudent working-class youths and dedicated to supporting the Bolsheviks and their new Soviet government, CYI assumed control of many groups within the international socialist youth movement. CYI's overriding purpose was to propagandize, to agitate, to demonstrate, and in any other way to foment revolution leading to development of a communist society. By 1921 the CYI was the largest politically activist youth organization in Europe. In 1923 the CYI claimed a membership of nearly 1 million with affiliated groups in 60 nations, but as the decade of the 1920s proceeded support for CYI declined precipitously, with members leaving the organization out of disillusionment over its increasing domination by the Russian KOMSOMOL and Comintern.

Communist Youth League (CYL)   (China) a youth organization created and directed by the CHINESE COMMUNIST PARTY (CCP) that originated as the SOCIALIST YOUTH LEAGUE in 1921 and was renamed in 1925. Initially having a larger membership than the CCP, the CYL claimed 2,900 members in 1925 and 35,000 in April 1927, by which time the CCP had grown to 58,000 members; both had profited from the aftereffects of the MAY 30TH MOVEMENT. Membership in CYL was open to youths ages 15 to 25. The CYL suffered decline with the CCP during the Kuomintang's suppression of the Communists beginning in 1927, and from 1928 to 1935 it did not hold a single major meeting. In November 1935 the CCP, noting that student activism was increasing, began a reorganization of the CYL, opening it to "all patriotic youth" who would resist Japanese aggrandizement, not just those with loyal ties to the CCP. As a consequence of this policy shift, the CCP announced on December 20, 1935 that the CYL's name would be changed to Resist-Japan National Salvation Youth Corps. (*See* NATIONAL SALVATION MOVEMENT.) This particular name change, however, never occurred, although several others did, including at this time a switch to the name National Salvation Youth League. About 300 delegates assembled in Yenan in April 1937 for the First Congress of Youths in

the Northwest and formed the Northwest China Association of Youths for National Salvation, comprised of young workers and peasants (many of them participants in the LONG MARCH), as an adjunct of the CYL. In 1949, as the CCP was coming to power in China, the NEW DEMOCRATIC YOUTH LEAGUE was established; beginning in 1957 it was once again known as the Communist Youth League. In 1949 the CYL had only 190,000 members, but by 1953 its membership had risen to 9 million, substantially more than the CCP's own 6.6 million membership. The membership numbers clearly reflect the CYL's mission to be a mass organization dedicated to organizing all segments of Chinese society. Most of the leadership of the CYL throughout the entire period from the 1930s to the 1950s were men who as youths had participated in the DECEMBER NINTH MOVEMENT. In the late 1960s, many of them fell victim to the excesses of the GREAT PROLETARIAN CULTURAL REVOLUTION. During the Cultural Revolution, the CYL itself was disbanded so that the RED GUARDS could benefit from undivided government attention. In the aftermath of this traumatic event, however, the CYL revived and in the early 1970s was believed to have 30 million members—about one-fifth of all the eligible youths in the nation.

Communist Youth League   (Korea) *See* KOREAN SOCIALIST WORKING YOUTH LEAGUE.

Compagnons de France   (France) one of two major, official (sanctioned and financially supported by the government) organizations for male youths (the other was the CHANTIERS DE LA JEUNESSE) in Vichy France (that third of the nation purposely left unoccupied by the Germans after their conquest of France in June 1940); the Germans banned the group from occupied France. The Compagnon, a voluntary organization for youths under 20 years of age, was established on July 24, 1940 by the Vichy government. Its principal goals were to "regenerate" youths while involving them in the "material and moral reconstruction of the nation." Its primary ideal was to instill community spirit. Forty-five members of existing youth groups initially joined in supporting the Compagnons. The organization's first camp was set up in August at Randan near Vichy. Members wore dark blue, military-style uniforms, including berets and blue shirts, and were organized in military fashion. Companies of members worked in forestry and highway services, grape harvesting, flood and land reclamation, and other endeavors for which they received daily wages. They followed a strict daily regimen that included physical-fitness training along with singing, drama, and popular arts activities. In May 1942 Jews were expelled from the movement. The number of members reached 33,000 in 1943. A similar organization for young women, Compagnes de France, was begun in 1942. The Compagnons was denounced from all sides—by Gaullists (supporters of Free France operating in exile in England), by organizations representing other collaborationists, and of course by the Resistance movement. In November 1942 the Germans occupied Vichy, and on January 21, 1944 the Compagnons was dissolved by decree, its last leader having already defected to the Maquis (Resistance).

Bibliography: W. D. Halls, *The Youth of Vichy France* (Oxford: Clarendon Press, 1981).

Confederación General Universitaria (CGU) (Argentina) a student organization formed in 1950 by the government of Juan Perón as a means of garnering support for the dictator among university students and as an alternative to the FEDERACIÓN UNIVERSITARIA ARGENTINA. The CGU had branches at all of the nation's universities but acquired relatively few members, as most students opposed Perón. Ironically, Communist students came to support the CGU because Perón, unlike his predecessors, did not suppress the Communist Party.

Confédération International des Étudiants (CIE) an international nonpolitical organization of student groups that originated as the Réunion des Étudiants Alliés when founded in Strasbourg in 1919 as a confederation of student groups existing within the Allied nations of World War I. The name was changed to CIE in 1924 in order to open the organization to students from other nations. In 1937 the League of Nations officially recognized the CIE as the representative organization of students worldwide. CIE provided a variety of service to its affiliated groups, including travel assistance, information on careers, and sponsorship of sports events such as the World University Games. The most important international student organization of its era, CIE died out after invading German troops destroyed its headquarters in Brussels in 1940. CIE did, however, serve as a prototype for the forming of subsequent organizations, in particular the INTERNATIONAL STUDENT CONFERENCE and the INTERNATIONAL UNION OF STUDENTS (IUS).

Congress of Racial Equality (CORE) (United States) a major civil rights organization of the 1950s and 1960s but originally a student organization founded in 1942 by a group of pacifist students, among them James FARMER, George Houser, and other members of the Fellowship of Reconciliation (FOR), at the Chicago Theological Seminary. CORE introduced the use of nonviolent tactics in picketing a downtown Chicago restaurant that refused service to African Americans. Its members also organized one of the first sit-ins, a 1948 protest against discrimination in the University of Kansas sports program that resulted in the CORE protestors being carried off the field of the university's football stadium. CORE used similar nonviolent tactics in protesting racial discrimination at theatres, restaurants, and other public facilities, and sponsored interracial summer institutes that attracted many students. Moving well beyond its original student base, CORE became a major national civil rights organization during the 1960s, when the organization sponsored the FREEDOM RIDERS. In 1962 CORE shifted its focus to voter registration, but it was involved in the FREEDOM SUMMER of 1964 and creation of the Mississippi Freedom Democratic Party. In the North, CORE workers organized communities to counteract the poverty and racism that afflicted urban ghetto areas. In following years, CORE became involved in the BLACK POWER MOVEMENT.

Congress Youth League (CYL) (Union of South Africa) the youth organization of the African National Congress (ANC), formally founded on Easter Sunday 1944 during an ANC meeting at the Bantu Men's Social Center in Sophiatown, a black settlement in Johannesburg. William Nkomo became the CYL's first president, but because of his leftist politics he was soon replaced by Anton Lembede. Early meetings regularly attracted about 60 members, among them Nelson Mandela and Walter Sisulu. In 1948 the CYL formally adopted a set of principles advocating African nationalism, the repeal of discriminatory laws, a provision of full citizenship to Africans, and an end to white dominance in Africa—goals to be pursued through moderation. But the National Party supported by Afrikaners gained control of the government in the May elections that year and soon instituted the repressive system of apartheid, leaving the CYL and its parent ANC little recourse but militancy.

Copenhagen University Protest (Denmark) a massive student demonstration at the University of Copenhagen in April 1968. One-fourth of the 20,000 students at the university demonstrated, demanding greater student influence in the university's operations and less dominance by professors while supporting student protestors who had occupied psychology laboratories at the school. The protest was notable as both moderate in character and a rare occurrence in Denmark.

Córdoba Manifesto (Argentina) a declaration issued by student reformers meeting in Córdoba in July 1918 that became the basis of the UNIVERSITY REFORM PROGRAM AND MOVEMENT. The manifesto indicted universities as bastions of oligarchy, nepotism, formalistic teaching, outmoded courses, and indifference to the interests of students. It declared:

> Up to now the universities have been the secular refuge of mediocrities, have provided a salary for the ignorant and a safe hospital for invalids, and what is worse, have provided a place where all forms of tyranny and insensitivity could be taught. The universities have thus come to be faithful reflections of a decadent society, offering a sad spectacle of immobile senility.

The manifesto claimed an inherent moral superiority for the young in pursuing reform:

> Youth lives in an ambience of heroism. It is disinterested and pure. It has not yet had time to become corrupt. It can never be mistaken in choosing its own teachers. . . . The acts of violence, for which we were wholly responsible, were done in behalf of pure ideas.

The manifesto called for such university reforms as open and free attendance for all those who had completed their secondary school education; institutional autonomy; student representation on all governing councils; voluntary class attendance; election of rectors by university assemblies comprised equally of student, faculty, and graduate representatives; and freedom for instructors to choose course content.

Córdoba Reform Movement *See* UNIVERSITY REFORM PROGRAM AND MOVEMENT.

Cornell Afro-American Society Revolt (United States) a demonstration by black students at Cornell University that erupted on the morning of April 19, 1969 during Parents' Weekend. African-American students at Cornell numbered 240 in a total of 13,200 during the 1968–69 academic year following a concerted recruitment effort by the university, but Cornell evidenced a racist tradition, and a series of confrontations, slights, administrative missteps, and festering issues preceded the revolt. The immediate catalyst was an incident at the black girls' cooperative: on Friday, April 18, at 3:00 A.M., someone threw a burning cross onto the porch; the campus safety patrol arrived and put out the fire but then left, leaving the girls unprotected. Members of the Afro-American Society reacted by occupying Willard Straight Hall, site of the student union, at 6:00 A.M. on April 19, expelling service personnel and parents staying in the guest rooms, and locking themselves in the building. At about 9:00 A.M. members of Delta Upsilon stormed the building; some managed entry, resulting in a fight and some injuries. Members of STUDENTS FOR A DEMOCRATIC SOCIETY (SDS) placed pickets around the building in support of the blacks. To protect themselves, the blacks brought 13 rifles and 2 shotguns into the building—apparently the first instance of students arming them-

Spokesman for the Afro-American Society at Cornell University Tom Jones (at podium) speaks to some 6,000 students during a rally on the Ithaca, New York campus in April 1969. (AP/WIDE WORLD PHOTOS)

selves during a protest in the 1960s. They demanded that reprimands that had been imposed following a December demonstration over a proposed Afro-American Studies program be lifted and that the Afro-American Society be mandated to study and report on the cross burning. An agreement was reached with the administration that provided for the blacks to leave the hall; they did so, but boldly displaying their guns—an act that increased campus tensions and incited antagonism among white students and many faculty. The antagonism took the form of rigid faculty opposition to canceling the reprimands of the December demonstrators at meetings on April 21. But sentiment began to shift to support of the black students. SDS led an occupation of Barton Hall that involved more than 8,000 students, and on April 23 the faculty voted to support canceling the reprimands and restructuring the university. The crisis was defused but with few consequential results. The Afro-American Society renamed itself the Black Liberation Front, a name that in itself perhaps suggested one of the revolt's imports: a new level of militancy in student protests that added the danger of life-threatening tactics.

Corps *See* KORPS.

Cosmopolitan Clubs (CC) (United States) a student organization initiated in 1903 with the founding of the International Club at the University of Wisconsin. The National Association of Cosmopolitan Clubs was founded in 1907, and within four years the affiliated clubs registered 2,000 members representing 60 nations. The CC advocates no political or ideological viewpoint since its purpose is to promote international understanding and good will among students. CC's journal *Cosmopolitan Student* provides information on worldwide activities. CC was among the first U.S. student organizations to become affiliated with an international organization—Fédération Internationale des Étudiants.

Counterculture (United States) a generic and plastic term that began to be in widespread use in the late 1960s to describe the overall youth movement of the period. The counterculture was essentially the creation of the hippies and the student activists of the 1964–68 period. The word *counter* expressed the youth culture's divergence from or disagreement with the prevailing adult culture. The counterculture's values found expression in folk and rock music (most especially the music of the Beatles), the use of drugs such as LSD and pot (marijuana), radically different clothing fashions, the COMMUNE MOVEMENT, and rebelliously deviant behavior. The quintessential counterculture event of the time was the WOODSTOCK FESTIVAL.

Bibliography: Theodore Roszak, *The Making of a Counter Culture* (Garden City, N.Y.: Anchor Books, 1970).

Cultural Revolution *See* GREAT PROLETARIAN CULTURAL REVOLUTION.

Dakar Student Protests (Senegal) a series of strikes and demonstrations by students of the University of Dakar during 1968–69. The protests began on May 7 and recurred on May 18, 1968, with students demonstrating and boycotting to demand that government scholarships—recently reduced to 10-month terms and allocated by examinations—be fully restored to 12-month terms. The protests were organized by the Democratic Union of Senegalese Students (UDES), which on May 25 called for a strike to begin on May 27. Disregarding government warnings of expulsion, most of the university student body participated, occupying buildings and picketing to prevent nonparticipating students from entering. On May 29 police attacked with tear gas and dispersed the strikers, leaving one student dead. Two days of street fights followed, resulting in 25 students being injured and 900 arrested. On May 30 President L. S. Senghor closed the university indefinitely. Trade-union members organized a strike in support of the students and increased wages, and the government declared a nationwide state of emergency. The strike ended on June 4. On July 20 the minister of education announced that planned reforms required closing the University of Dakar for a year, expelling all foreign students, and sending Senegalese students out of the country to study. In September government and student representatives negotiated reopening of the university and restoration of 12-month scholarships; they also agreed to involve students in devising reforms and providing safeguards to assure freedom at the university. But the truce ended on March 28, 1969 when the UDES called for a strike in protest of the expulsion of 25 students from two technical schools. Most of the university students participated, along with half of the secondary-school students. Students picketed outside university buildings in violation of the law, so on May 6 armed security forces occupied the University City (site of the student residences) and ordered students

to leave. The strike petered out. Nevertheless, on October 11 a joint French–Senegalese commission agreed on plans for reforming the university that included its "Africanization" and involving students in its governance. The university reopened on October 15 with a ruling that any student strike of more than two weeks' duration would trigger closing of the residence halls. The 1968–69 series of student protests proved an indicator of public support for a new constitution, which was endorsed by the National Assembly in February 1970.

Days of Rage (United States) four days during which the WEATHERMAN movement rampaged in Chicago, beginning October 8, 1969. Weatherman had organized what the movement called the New Red Army for the Days of Rage and hoped to generate a revolutionary movement out of the planned Chicago turmoil. Weatherman leader Mark Rudd had publicly boasted that thousands of young demonstrators would assemble for participation in the uprising, including hundreds of African Americans, but only 300 did so, including 100 Weatherwomen and few blacks. At 10:30 P.M. on October 8, they suddenly erupted from Lincoln Park armed with clubs, bottles, rocks, and bicycle chains. They stormed through the city streets, smashing parked cars, breaking windows in office buildings (including windows of the Chicago Historical Society), and shouting slogans through bullhorns. More than 2,000 police and plainclothes officers responded, and the first demonstration ended within an hour. On October 10 the Weathermen resumed the rioting, this time in the Loop business district, where police quickly suppressed them. On the two days of actual rioting, police arrested 287 Weathermen, virtually the movement's entire turnout for the riots. All of those arrested were released after $2.3 million in bail was posted, mostly by parents of the offenders. The Days of Rage, obviously not the fulfillment Weatherman

Protesters march in Chicago near the North Side during the first night of an announced four-day national action called by the Weatherman movement the New Red Army for the Days of Rage.   (AP/WIDE WORLD PHOTOS)

had hoped for, was the movement's last major public demonstration. Its fallout cost Weatherman many members, some of whom came to disagree with the concept that violence was both a means and an end in itself. One of the disenchanted remarked, "You don't need a rectal thermometer to know who the assholes are" (a play on the origin of the movement's name in the Bob Dylan song "You Don't Need a Weatherman to Know Which Way the Wind Is Blowing"). Subsequent to the Days of Rage, some Weathermen, including Rudd, held a public conference in Flint, Michigan during which they touted Ho Chi Minh, the Vietcong, and the virtues of violence, but in 1970 the movement went underground to operate in small groups to perpetrate such terroristic acts as bombings.

December Ninth Movement   (China) a massive student uprising in 1935 following Japanese military incursions into Inner Mongolia and other northern areas in an effort to create a so-called North China Autonomous Region. Protesting against Japanese aggression and also against the reluctance of Chiang Kai-shek's Kuomintang (KMT) regime in Nanjing to oppose the Japanese, students organized by the Peiping Student Union (which had been reformed on November 18) staged the largest

demonstration ever held in Beijing to that time. On December 9 students attempted to deliver a petition to the government representative in Beijing that demanded opposing creation of the "autonomous region"; conducting foreign relations openly; banning arbitrary arrests; securing the integrity of Chinese territory; terminating the civil war between armies of the KMT and of the CHINESE COMMUNIST PARTY (CCP); and assuring freedom of speech, of the press, of assembly, and of organization. Police turned the petitioners away, brutalizing some of them.

In response, the students organized a massive strike and boycotts of Japanese products and agencies. On December 16 nearly 7,800 students representing 28 institutions demonstrated in Beijing, withstanding concerted police and army efforts to disperse them. About 5,000 students, led by Tsinghua University student LU TS'UI, converged on the Shunchin Gate, where they had been promised access, only to discover the gate was locked. Lu rolled under the gate and tried to unbolt it. Seized, beaten, and held by police, Lu was finally released at 7:30 P.M. following a sit-down strike by her followers—she rolled back under the gate and led the student march back to Tsinghua University. By 8:00 P.M. the students were marching back to their dormitories and were assaulted by the police, who injured more than 380 students—85 of them severely. The demonstration strengthened the hand of the local KMT military commander in resisting Japanese pressures, which he did while denouncing the students as communist dupes.

Word of the demonstration spread nationally, generating demonstrations by youths in 16 other cities, and a total of some 65 demonstrations occurred in 32 locales by the end of December. The movement attracted public support and led to creation of the National Salvation Movement, which subsequently proved useful to the CCP's unification efforts. Enthusiasm for the December Ninth Movement tapered off fairly quickly outside Beijing, where the students had at least tacit faculty support; their attempt to disseminate the movement through a "rural crusade," however, proved ineffectual—500 students journeyed across the countryside to regale the rural masses but encountered mostly indifference. Their pilgrimage did result in student creation of the National Liberation Vanguard, which, following the students' forced return to Beijing, joined with other groups to form the CHINESE NATIONAL LIBERATION VANGUARD, a communist front within the student movement. Although the December Ninth Movement dissolved by the spring of 1936, it had proved more successful than the response to the MUKDEN INCIDENT—the Japanese did abandon their plan for an "autonomous region." The movement also served to further radicalize Chinese students—disillusioned with the KMT and its appeasement policies, they would turn increasingly to support of the CCP.

Bibliography: John Israel, *Student Nationalism in China, 1927–1937* (Stanford, Calif.: Stanford University Press, 1966); John Israel and Donald Klein, *Rebels and Bureaucrats: China's December 9ers* (Berkeley: University of California Press, 1976).

Dell'Oro Maini Protests   (Argentina) a series of student protests in the spring of 1956 intended to force the resignation of Minister of Education Atilio Dell'Oro Maini. Agitation over the minister was related to the new military government's law 6403, which rescinded the regulations of the Perón regime that governed the universities, thereby promising the restoration of their autonomy. The student federations mostly welcomed the law but objected to its Article 28, whose wording appeared to open the door to the creation of Catholic universities. (*See* ARTICLE 28 PROTEST.) The federations focused their anger on Dell'Oro Maini, who had been a member of the Liga de la Juventud Católica Argentina and was associated with Catholic and ultranationalistic organizations. Thus in April and May 1956, members of the FEDERACIÓN UNIVERSITARIA ARGENTINA began a series of protests that included occupying buildings, boycotting classes, and demonstrating outside government buildings in order to force the minister's resignation and the withdrawal of the law. Under the pressure of these

protests, Dell'Oro Maini did resign on May 16, but the law remained intact. In addition, this issue split the student movement, with Catholic organizations and the LIGA DE ESTUDIANTES HUMANITAS opposing the protests and favoring Dell'Oro Maini.

Democratic League   (China) an organization founded in 1944 to promote adoption of Western-style democracy in opposition to the Kuomintang government of Chiang Kai-shek. The league evolved from the Union of Comrades for Unity and National Reconstruction formed in 1939, which developed into the League of Democratic Groups in 1941 and then into the Democratic League. Among the member groups were student or youth organizations, such as the China Youth Party.

Demolay, Order of   (United States) a Masonic organization for boys and young men formed on March 18, 1919 in Kansas City, Missouri by Frank Land, who served as secretary-general until 1959, and a group of nine teenage boys. It is named in honor of the martyred Jacques Demolay, last grand master of the Knights Templars whom Philip IV of France had burned at the stake in 1314 in his successful effort to crush the Templars. The Order of Demolay quickly spread nationwide and to numerous foreign countries; Kansas City is the international headquarters. Membership is open to male youths age 14–21 who need not be sons or relatives of Masons to belong. The organization is distinctive for its ritual, with members being consecrated in the Initiatory Degree, committing themselves to support such virtues as courtesy, patriotism, cleanliness, and reverence; the Demolay Degree inculcates fidelity and comradeship through a ritualistic enactment of Jacques Demolay's martyrdom. Members attain honors and awards through community service, the highest honor being the Degree of Chevalier.

Deutsche Freischar   (Germany) the largest of the various BUNDE, established in 1926 through a merger of the Neupfadfinder with the Altwandervogel, one of the WANDERVOGEL groups that survived the travails of World War I and the postwar economic crises. Freischar groups, which had an average of about 16 members, existed throughout Germany but were most prevalent in the eastern states. Total membership was perhaps 12,000, mostly middle-class Protestant youths but also Catholics and a few Jews—about three-fourths being under age 18 and about 15 percent girls. Ernst BUSKE, a former member of the Altwandervogel, was the Deutsche Freischar's leader. One of the Freischar's major activities involved the concept of national labor service through the organization of numerous labor camps; here, from 60 to 100 male youths spent three weeks in communal living that included at least four hours of daily work along with an intensive educational program. The Freischar retained the idealism of earlier youth movement groups but without the extreme nationalism or fatuous romanticism that characterized so many of them. The Freischar's songbook also at least implied a healthy internationalism rather than the xenophobia preached by some other groups, as it contained the national anthems of other countries besides Germany. The Freishcar also supported political reform and was involved in an unsuccessful effort in 1930 to build a strong but moderate centrist party. Buske's untimely death in 1930 at the age of 36 deprived the Freischar of its most enlightened leader; in March 1933, two months after Hitler became chancellor, although the Freischar had opposed the mindlessness of Nazi ideology, the organization's leaders opted to join the Nazi youth movement. The eventual alternative, of course, would have been dissolution imposed by the Nazis, as occurred with all other groups the Nazis perceived as rivals.

Bibliography: Walter Laqueur, *Young Germany: A History of the German Youth Movement* (New York: Basic Books, 1962).

Deutsche Freistudentenschaft (Germany) a national umbrella organization of free-student groups formed in May 1900. The Freistudentenschaft comprised a protest movement against the exclusivity and authoritarianism of the student fraternities (corporations). It emphasized a humanistic cultivation among students, with broader knowledge as its goal; offered itself as the representative organization and spokesperson for independent students, although estimates indicated that only 15 percent or fewer of these students belonged to the organization; and to some extent promoted health, social, and civic programs for students. The Freistudentenschaft's principles and organization were democratic and parliamentarian, and, despite its sometimes indefinite voice and stature, the movement effected a significant influence among students. Because Jews and Catholics were largely excluded from the fraternities they found a haven in the Freistudentenschaft and rose to leadership positions, eliciting some anti-Semitic sentiment, and there was also some Catholic baiting, but overall the student membership sustained a liberal orientation and flatly rejected discriminatory or exclusionary policies for the organization. As World War I approached, the left wing of the movement advocated democratic and socialistic reforms.

Bibliography: Konrad H. Jarausch, *Students, Society, and Politics in Imperial Germany: The Rise of Academic Illiberalism* (Princeton, N.J.: Princeton University Press, 1982).

Deutscher Hochschulring *See* HOCHSCHULRING DEUTSCHER ART.

Deutsche Studentenschaft (Germany) a union of individual university student councils, the Deutsche Studentenschaft was formed by representatives of the councils assembled in Wurzburg during mid-July 1919. They mod-

eled the national student union's constitution upon the democratic principles of the Weimar Republic and empowered its officers to negotiate with officials of state education ministries to establish self-governing student councils that would have representation in university administrations. They also embraced the *grossdeutsch* concept (pan-Germanism) of linking the German-speaking peoples of Germany and Austria, the Sudetenland, and other areas that were formerly part of the Hapsburg Empire. Consequently, in deference to the Austrian representatives' anti-Semitic principles, they included in the constitution an ambiguous clause providing membership to all students of "German descent and mother tongue" that would allow Austrian student councils to exclude Jews while German councils dedicated to democracy included them.

This ambiguous clause immediately created tension within the Deutsche Studentenschaft and between the union and the German education ministries, which would not accept Austrian and Sudentenland councils that excluded Jews. The Deutsche Studentenschaft was organized with nine divisions called Kreise, with the Austrian universities comprising Kreis VIII and the Sudentenland and Prague universities, Kreis IX. The so-called Aryan councils of these two Kreise, which excluded "non-Aryans," represented 20 percent of the union's voting delegates and thus a menacing potential to the Republican representatives, who opposed a racially restrictive constitution. After the Republicans won control of the Deutsche Studentenschaft in 1922 the "Aryan" associations formed their own organization at a meeting in Würzburg. A conference of state education ministries meeting in Stralsund in September 1922 drafted a set of resolutions that rejected racial restrictions on membership in student associations and also in any associations with foreign student councils not recognized by the states or the university rectors after October 1, 1923. But the education ministers, not wishing to alienate the student majority that supported pan-Germanism, never enforced the resolutions, and in January 1924, beleaguered leaders of the Deutsche Studentenschaft gave in and accepted the Würzburg constitution.

Thereafter the Deutsche Studentenschaft became increasingly nationalistic and hostile toward the government of the Weimar Republic. An example of the latter stance occurred at the 1926 National Student Convention held in Bonn, where delegates endorsed student riots at the Hanover Technical Institute that forced the resignation of philosophy professor Theodor Lessing and demonstrated against the flag of the Republic—the ultimate result being loss of the union's officially recognized status in Prussia. As the NATIONAL SOCIALIST GERMAN STUDENT UNION (NAZI) gained adherents following its organization at 20 universities in the spring of 1926, the Deutsche Studentenschaft found itself in a struggle to maintain control of the student movement. In this struggle the leaders assumed rightist positions, even siding with the STAHLHELM. But at the national student convention held in Graz in 1931, Nazi delegates gained effective control of the older union. Perhaps the most egregious act of the transformed Deutsche Studentenschaft was its publication on April 12, 1933 of 12 theses "against the un-German spirit" denouncing Jewish and liberal literary works and organizing the book burnings that took place at German universities between April 26 and May 10. Any remaining semblance of independence for the union disappeared when the government appointed a Reichsstudentenführung (Reich student leadership) headed by Gustav Adolf Scheel, who coordinated control of both the Deutsche Studentenschaft and the National Socialist German Student Union.

A major program of the Deutsche Studentenschaft during its viable years in the 1920s was Studentenhilfe, a student economic assistance program headquartered in Dresden partly under the guidance of the European Student Relief Fund. Studentenhilfe arose out of the economic destitution following World War I that left many students unable to finance their educations. Studentenhilfe offices at each of the universities helped students find jobs, both while at school and while on vacation. With the payment of a fee, a student joined the Studentenhilfe corporation (similar to a cooperative), which purchased books, clothing, school supplies, and other items and sold them to the students at much-reduced prices. Besides the retail stores, Studentenhilfe provided kitchens and dining areas, laundries, and facilities for repairing clothes and shoes. Through the Studentenschaft's bank in Dresden, the Studentenhilfe program also provided loans to students who were unable to work because of disabilities or course or examination overloads.

Bibliography: Michael Stephen Steinberg, *Sabers and Brown Shirts: The German Students' Path to National Socialism, 1918–1935* (Chicago: University of Chicago Press, 1977).

Deutsch Nationalen Jugendbundes (German National Youth Union) (Germany) a nationalistic youth organization dedicated to rehabilitation of Germany during the Weimar Republic period. It quickly spread nationwide because of backing from military, academic, aristocratic, and other supporters of the former monarchy. Organized at every level down to the city, the Union had a membership of 50,000 youths.

Deutschvolkische Studentenbewegung (German Volkish Student Movement) (Germany) a schismatic movement founded in February 1924 by right-wing members of the HOCHSCHULRING DEUTSCHER ART, of which it remained a nominal part. The group's intent was militant promotion of the *Volkisch* concept (the folk community or nation). The group's honorary chairman was General Erich Ludendorff, German chief of staff in World War I. The movement attracted a purported 600 members, mostly among the free (nonfraternity) students of some of the major universities, such as Berlin, Munich, Halle, and Heidelberg. In 1925 it formed an alliance with the Austrian Volkisch-Social Student Association, whose newspaper *Der Student* spoke for both groups. The allied groups were closely tied to the Nazis and pledged loyalty to Adolf Hitler.

Deutsch-Volkische Studentenverband (DVSt) (Germany) a radically nationalistic student organization formed in 1909, whose membership was comprised of both fraternity (corporate) and independent students. Its mission was "to cultivate and propagate Germanness at the universities." Greatly influenced by Austrian rightists, the DVSt pursued a racist program of trying to expunge Jewish and foreign elements from the universities. The DVSt remained small, with only 14 chapters, but its virulent politics served as a harbinger of post-World War I political turmoil in Germany.

Directorio Revolucionario (Revolutionary Directorate) (Cuba) a clandestine student organization formed in December 1955 by members of the FEDERACIÓN ESTUDIANTIL UNIVERSITARIA (FEU) as an insurrectionary movement against the government of General Fulgencio Batista, the dictator who had seized control in a coup of March 10, 1952 that deposed the democratic government headed by President Carlos Prío. The Directorio's creation was officially announced by José Antonio Echeverría, president of FEU and head of the directorate, during a secret meeting at the University of Havana on February 24, 1956. (Echeverría had been hospitalized after being brutally beaten by police during an antigovernment protest march by University of Havana students on December 2, 1955.) The Directorio was democratic, nationalistic, and anti-Communist and advocated economic reforms, free elections, and restitution of the 1940 constitution. The Directorio supported assassinations and coordinating tactics with other anti-Batista groups as means of overthrowing the government. Echeverría and other students traveled to Mexico to meet with Fidel Castro and signed an agreement with him known as La Carta de México (The Mexican Letter, or Pact). The Directorio promised to stage riots in Havana in conjunction with Castro's planned invasion. On October 28, 1956, two Directorio members assassinated the head of Batista's Military Intelligence Service and wounded several of his friends in a planned shooting at a Havana nightclub. Castro repudiated the act. On November 30 Castro supporters staged commando raids and sabotage throughout Oriente province in anticipation of Castro's landing. The Directorio awaited word from Castro but received none until December 2, by which time Batista's forces had quelled the uprising; so the Directorio failed to riot in Havana. Castro fled into the Sierra Maestra and began a guerrilla campaign. In response to the uprising, the University of Havana closed on November 30, at first temporarily but then remaining closed until 1959, unintentionally inducing many unoccupied students to join the anti-Batista movement.

The Directorio decided that now the best means of overthrowing the government was to assassinate Batista. On March 15, 1957 armed members of the Directorio forced their way into the presidential palace and got as far as the second floor before being thwarted—15 died along with five guards. At the same time, Echeverría and other Directorio members rushed into a radio station and broadcast the announcement of Batista's presumed death and the end of his regime. Minutes afterward, police killed Echeverría and wounded several of his companions. In the following days, the regime's police hunted down and killed other members of the conspiracy as well. Then on April 20 the police killed four remaining leaders of the Directorio, including the acting president of FEU, after surrounding an apartment building in which they were hiding out on Humboldt Street in Havana; the slaughter became known as the "Humboldt event." The Directorio revived months later as the Directorio Estudiantil Revolucionaro but could not again muster its former significance, as the leaders who survived the police raids went into exile in Miami.

When they returned to Cuba in early 1958, they quarreled over tactics, one group deciding for guerrilla operations and the other returning to Havana to rebuild the underground movement there. The former group became known as the "Second Front of the Escambray," and the latter as the remnants of the Directorio led by Fauré Chomón joined Fidel Castro's JULY 26 MOVEMENT a few months before the January 1959 overthrow of Batista. At a meeting in Caracas on July 20, 1958 representatives of the Directorio had joined several other groups, including the FEU, in a pact with the July 26 Movement known as the Junta of Unity (Frente Cívico Revolucionario Democrático). When Castro arrived in Havana on January 8, 1959 the Directorio held several key sites, including police stations, radio stations, telephone exchanges, and the presidential palace. Although initially the Directorio refused to surrender their arms and appeared to offer rivalry to the July 26 Movement that threatened to erupt into fighting—Chomón objected to Castro's having said that Santiago would be the new capital when he arrived there on January 1—Castro, secure in his public backing, persuaded them to give up their weapons. He rewarded some of the student leaders with governmental posts, one being appointed minister of the interior; Chomón, who subsequently declared himself a Communist, later became ambassador to the Soviet Union and later still a cabinet minister. In July 1961, with Cuba trending rapidly toward alliance with the Soviet Union and its communist allies, the Directorio was subsumed into the Organizaciónes Revoluciónes Integradas (ORI) along with the July 26 Movement, the United Youth Movement, and the Young Pioneers.

Bibliography: Hugh Thomas, *The Cuban Revolution* (New York: Harper and Row, 1977).

Dobama Asiayone (We-Burmans Society)   (Burma) a nationalist association organized largely by university students in the early 1930s and devoted to achieving independence from Great Britain. Its ideology derived from a mixture of Marxism, the Fascist movements in Italy and Germany, and the Sinn Fein movement in Northern Ireland. Members called themselves Thakins (Masters). In 1935, when a new constitution was granted by the British, the Dobama Asiayone sponsored a parliamentary party, the Komin Kochin ("one's own king—one's own kind"). Dobama members held most of the offices in the first Burmese controlled government that was set up in August 1943. Among the organization's members were such important Burmese leaders as AUNG SAN, who joined in 1938; U NU, who joined in 1937; and Ne Win, who joined in 1936.

Dow Chemical Sit-In   (United States) a student protest sit-in against the Dow Chemical Corporation on October 18, 1967 at the University of Wisconsin. The sit-in occurred in conjunction with STOP THE DRAFT WEEK and was one of the most dramatic demonstrations of that week. It was directed against Dow because the chemical company manufactured napalm, which was used in the Vietnam War. Representatives of Dow arrived on October 17 at the Madison campus to conduct interviews of students at the Commerce Building and were picketed by about 200 protestors as they entered the building. The next morning, about 100 student protestors entered the Commerce Building and blocked the door of an office where a Dow representative was conducting interviews; others picketed outside the building. The administration agreed to call in city police. Riot police arrived. Leaders of the student protestors asked the chancellor to sign a statement requesting the Dow representatives to leave the campus and not return; he refused, and the students returned to their vigil. The police decided arrests would be necessary and the students were told they must leave the building or face arrest. But as the police tried to enter the building, the occupying students forced them out. The police battered their way in with their night sticks; they began to arrest students, hauling them outside toward their van, but they were accosted by 2,000 student protestors hurling stones, bricks, bottles, and other objects. Police responded with tear gas, but they had to call in reinforcements from the sheriff's department before the students could finally be dispersed. About 60 students received injuries during the melee; 20 police officers also were injured, a few quite seriously. On October 20 a student strike was called, and student protest leaders organized a mass rally that drew

5,000 students and 200 faculty supporters. A special faculty meeting was called, with about half of the 2,200 faculty attending. The student strike fizzled out as many of its leaders left town to participate in the MARCH ON THE PENTAGON. The faculty met again on October 23 and voted in favor of a student-faculty committee to devise policies for dealing with future obstructive demonstrations. Sixteen students involved in the protest were suspended. Protests against Dow recruiters occurred at many other campuses, but few ended so violently as at the University of Wisconsin.

Dreyfus Affair   (France) a significant political event of 1898 that involved student demonstrations. Alfred Dreyfus, a Jew and a captain in the French army serving at the War Ministry, was convicted of treason (namely, selling secrets to the Germans) in December 1894 by a court-martial whose proceedings evidenced many irregularities. He was imprisoned at Devil's Island—a scapegoat and a victim of anti-Semitism. Subsequently discovered evidence in 1896 indicated that a Major Ferdinand Esterhazy was the real culprit, but the army tried to suppress this discovery and, failing to do so, acquitted Esterhazy after a brief court-martial in January 1898. The public divided into Dreyfusards and anti-Dreyfusards, with students joining one side or the other. Protesting the Esterhazy verdict, the well-known novelist Émile Zola published a denunciation of the military leaders and a defense of Dreyfus in George Clemenceau's pro-Dreyfus newspaper *L'Aurore*. Students demonstrated in the Latin Quarter, some shouting Zola's praises, others damning him; the anti-Dreyfusards burned copies of *L'Aurore* in a bonfire near the Panthéon. In the building of the University of Paris's Faculty of Letters, students on opposing sides erupted in physical combat. Later a Major Hubert Henry admitted to forging one of the documents used to convict Dreyfus and then committed suicide. Dreyfus was retried in September 1899, found guilty, and sentenced to 10 years in prison, but the president of the Republic pardoned him.

Durango Water Rates Sit-In   (Mexico) a protest in 1972 against high water rates by about 1,500 poor residents of Durango, organized by student activists who had participated in the 1968 student movement. The students had turned their efforts to organizing urban protest movements on the issues of land and housing but discovered that the immediate concern of the urban poor in Durango was high water rates. Consequently, the students helped organize protests on that issue, including two demonstrations at the Junta Federal de Agua Potable. The 1972 sit-in at the Municipal Palace proved successful, as the government granted the reduction in the water rates that the protestors demanded. The protestors subsequently focused on land acquisition, and the

successful outcome of this effort led to their creating the Comité de Defensa Popular-Durango (CDP-Durango).

Dutschke, Rudi (1940–)   (Germany) the most prominent student leader of the 1960s and head of the SOZIALISTISCHER DEUTSCHER STUDENTENBUND (SDS). Born and raised a member of a Lutheran family in Luckenwalde, East Germany, Dutschke, in response to rumors that East Germany's borders were to be closed, moved to West Berlin, arriving shortly before the construction of the Berlin Wall in August 1961. He enrolled in the FREIE UNIVERSITÄT BERLIN (FREE UNIVERSITY OF BERLIN), where most of his friends were, like himself, escapees from East Germany (known in the slang as Abhauer). Dutschke and his friends were socialists but anti-Stalinists and antiauthoritarians, opposed to the social and political systems of the Soviet Union and Communist East Germany, and advocates of the Communist ideal that workers have control of corporations and property. They formed a group called Direct Action, which aligned with the Berlin SDS and took control of it as its leaders graduated and left. An effective speaker, Dutschke soon became the leader of SDS and its spokesman during numerous protest demonstrations in Berlin, acquiring the epithet "Red Rudi." In that role he earned the enmity of many who saw him as a menace; on April 11, 1968, during the EASTER RIOTS, a deranged opponent shot and nearly killed him. Dutschke in time recovered and, undeterred, continued to protest against oppression wherever he saw it at work—in the university, in East Germany, in the Vietnam War. In 1968 he moved to England and thereafter to Denmark. In 1974 Dutschke's doctoral dissertation was published as a book, *Attempt to Put Lenin on His Feet: Concerning the Half-Asian and the Western European Road to Socialism*. In 1975 he published an anthology entitled *The Soviet Union Solzhenitsyn, and the Western Left* for which he was coeditor and contributed one essay.

Dziady Demonstrations   (Poland) student demonstrations in January and March 1968 arising initially out of performances of Adam Mickiewicz's play *Dziady* in Warsaw. This revival production of *Dziady* emphasized passages that attacked the Russians which, when delivered on stage, elicited enthusiastic applause from audiences; consequently, the government ordered that the play be closed. Following the final performance on January 31, 1968, about 200 students marched to the Mickiewicz Monument to protest. Fifty of them were arrested, including the two leaders, who were expelled from Warsaw University. In response, students from the university and other schools protested and collected 3,000 signatures in support of the two students' readmission to the university; their effort failed. On March 8 the students began a massive demonstration that generated a three-day conflict with the police and resulted in numerous arrests. Students at the universities of Kraków, Łódź, and Poznań joined in the cause. About 8,000 students met on March 13 at Warsaw Institute of Technology and drafted a 13-point resolution. Among the resolution's demands were release of the arrested students, an end to repressive acts against students, total adherence to the civil rights guaranteed by Article 71 of the constitution, security of students on their campuses, punishment of those who had brutalized students, no more inciting of workers to attack students, and media disavowals of their broadcast or printed stories about the demonstrations. On March 21, thousands of students began a three-day sit-in to highlight these demands—the first sit-in to occur in Poland. These various efforts proved fruitless, however. Students returned to classes after schools reopened in April. In November the trials of the arrested students began, all ending with prison sentences.

East Asiatic Youth League (EAYL)　(Burma) an organization set up by the Japanese to win youth supporters for their World War II effort in East Asia. The Burmese branch was formed on June 28, 1942. The EAYL promoted physical fitness, education, public health, and other programs, including construction of public facilities. In 1945 it was succeeded by the All-Burma Youth League, an affiliate of the Anti-Fascist People's Freedom League (AFPFL), led by AUNG SAN.

Easter Riots　(Germany) a series of university student riots that erupted during the Easter holiday, April 8–14, 1968, in cities throughout West Germany. Two students were killed during a riot in Munich. Overall, in West Germany during this week, police arrested about 1,000 student demonstrators, and about 400 students received injuries. Probably of most significant consequence for the German student movement, a right-wing zealot shot its paramount leader Rudi DUTSCHKE at the Kurfürstendamm in West Berlin. Severely wounded, Dutschke was hospitalized for a long period and subsequently left West Berlin to reside in England and there pursue completion of his doctoral degree. Thus the movement lost its most prominent and most effective spokesman. Dutschke's colleagues in the SOZIALISTISCHEN DEUTSCHER STUDENTENBUND (SDS) reacted vehemently to the attempt on his life, excoriating German politicians and the public as a whole; thus they alienated any potential supporters within the "system" they hoped to radically reform while they cemented the opposition of those who were already hostile. In the aftermath of the Easter Riots, polls indicated that 65 percent of the people in the Federal Republic of Germany (West Germany) opposed student protestors, and in West Berlin the opposition reached 83 percent. Both the labor unions and the major political parties publicly dissociated themselves from any future involvement with the students. The Easter Riots therefore represented a high-water mark and turning point for the German student movement of the 1960s.

Eisenach Festival　(Germany) a large student meeting of 1848 intended to resemble the WARTBURG FESTIVAL but without the celebratory festivities. The festival followed the uprisings that erupted in most of the German states after the February Revolution in France that brought the abdication of King Louis Phillippe and the proclaiming of the Republic. The organizers—conservative BURSCHENSCHAFTEN members and more liberal Burgkeller members at the University of Jena—intended the Eisenach Festival to provide a parliamentary-style discussion of a program to free the universities from the separate states and place them under a central German authority, to achieve freedom of teaching and learning, and to repeal the legal code for students that provided for reprisal against dissidents. Some 1,200 delegates attended; they represented all but three of the German universities and the University of Vienna. The delegates voted in favor of a central authority for the universities; student freedom to move to any university of their choice; increased government funding, including paying the fees of the Privatdozenten (faculty having the lowest status); abolition of university entrance examinations for gymnasium (grammar school) graduates; abolition of semester examinations; an end to university administration of civil service examinations; permission for student representatives to serve on university governing committees and in the selection of rectors; and courses devoted to new subjects, such as political economy. They also voted in favor of abolishing the legal code for students that included the privilege, granted only to students, of the right to participate in duels; and they asked that the German National Assembly, then meeting in the Paulskirche in Frankfurt to draft a constitution for a German empire, include a clause in the constitution stripping students of special privileges.

The National Assembly included a vague clause on freedom of learning but largely ignored the Eisenach delegates' other resolutions. In any event, the National Assembly failed in its aim of nationhood and disbanded in 1849.

Enragés (France) a small and short-lived organization of student militants formed at the University of Paris campus in Nanterre in January 1968. Comprised of six hardcore radical agitators and their two dozen followers, les Enragés (the Fanatics) took their name from a group of protoanarchists of the French Revolution. Deriving their ideology from the "situationists," les Enragés staged "situations" by shouting down professors or pelting them with oranges and tomatoes and by raiding administrative offices. Among the group's spokesmen was Daniel COHN-BENDIT. Les Enragés organized a meeting on March 22, 1968 following the arrest of three students and three COMITÉS D'ACTION LYCÉENS (CAL) schoolboys for alleged involvement in explosions on March 18 and 20 at Paris offices of U.S. banks. At this meeting, students decided by a vote of 142 to 2, with 3 abstentions, to occupy the administration building—the beginning of the MARCH 22 MOVEMENT. As part of that movement les Enragés participated in the occupation of the faculty council's meeting room and subsequent events. Although they rejected the Trotskyist or Maoist leanings of other groups, they enthusiastically participated in the street riots and the occupation of the Sorbonne during the MAY REVOLT.

Epheboi (Greece) literally "those who have reached puberty," young men age 18 to 20, initially in the early fifth century B.C. from Athens but later from cities throughout Greece, who were obligated to enroll in state-controlled colleges (*ephebia*) for military training. At age 18 the Athenian youth (*ephebos*) achieved civic majority; if he was from one of the first three property classes—those who were privileged and duty-bound—and proved to be physically able, he joined the deme register, and became liable for military service, and was sent to one of the ephebia (at Munychia or Acte) for training as a member of a garrison. At the end of his first year he was reviewed; if he had performed satisfactorily, he was issued a spear and a shield to complete his equipment (he already had a broad-brimmed hat and a cloak), and he swore an oath of allegiance. For his second year he was garrisoned elsewhere in Attica or sent to participate in border patrols or even in battles. At the end of his second year, the ephebos's citizenship training was complete. Epheboi were excused from paying taxes and could not appear in court as either plaintiffs or defendants. They were also key participants in major Athenian festivals. By the end of the fourth century, the epheboi's period of military training and service was no longer obligatory and lasted only a year—in fact, at the ephebia military train-

ing was replaced with instruction in philosophy, rhetoric, art, sports, religion, and other subjects. The strict 18-to-20 age limits were dropped, and foreigners were admitted to the program, changing its character. By the end of the third century B.C. the epheboi tradition disappeared at Athens.

At Sparta the Epheboi tradition developed differently because there the state assumed charge of boys at age 7, and from age 14 to 20 they were epheboi; therefore, they entered the system at an earlier age and trained twice as long as Athenian youths (six years rather than three). At 7 the boys were organized into *agelai* ("herds") under the direction of older boys called *boagoi* ("leaders of the bull-calves"). Regarded as wild animals, the boys were meant to be tamed by training. They went naked, had neither baths nor soap, gathered reeds with their bare hands to make beds, and scavenged for food in woods or learned how to steal food. From age 10 on, they participated according to age groups in various contests, including musical and oratorical competitions, mock combat, and the notorious flogging-ordeal ceremony at the altar of Orthia that sometimes proved fatal (the boys ran a gauntlet of floggers in order to steal cheeses from the altar; the one acquiring the greatest number of cheeses won the contest). The ultimate goal of these contests was to inculcate endurance and bravery, the chief virtues of the soldier each ephebos was to become.

Epworth League (United States) an organization for youths age 9 to 25, founded in 1889 as a division of the Youth Department of the Board of Education of the Methodist Church. It provided religious, recreational, and social programs for members whose purpose was to build Christian character, further the church's development, promote friendships, and provide opportunities for self-expression and training in leadership. The organization's publication for members, *The Epworth Herald*, appeared twice a month. As an organization of the nation's second largest Protestant denomination, the Epworth League had a substantial membership, which grew rapidly to more than 1 million by 1895. Membership suffered declines in this century, however, and stood at about 550,000 before World War II.

Essex Germ Warfare Protest (Great Britain) demonstrations at the University of Essex in the summer term of 1968, when student protesters prevented a speech by a scientist from the government's biological warfare research center at Porton Down. The vice-chancellor, regarding the episode as a violation of free speech, suspended three of the students he considered to be leaders of the protest. In response, Essex students organized a sit-in that, combined with some professors' criticism of the vice-chancellor's action, effectively closed down the university and resulted in reinstatement of the suspended students and creation of committees to consider reforms at the university. The committees proposed revising the disciplinary system and other reforms, including forming committees comprised of both staff and student members. This protest constituted the first instance in Great Britain of students propounding the argument that they had the right to prevent speeches at the university by persons they perceived as proponents of ideas or institutions they considered immoral or inhumane—thus evoking the principle that freedom of speech does not extend to egregiously reprehensible acts or viewpoints. The protest's larger significance was in focusing public attention on the moral issue of conducting research to develop chemical and biological weapons. The media took up the issue and discussed operations at Porton Down. Ultimately this attention combined with other political considerations to result in the British government's proposal at the international disarmament conference in Geneva that chemical weapons be controlled.

Bibliography: Colin Crouch, *The Student Revolt* (London: Bodley Head, 1970).

ETA (Euskadi Ta Askatasuna, Basque Homeland and Liberty) (Spain) a movement formed in July 1959, comprised largely of Basque youths, in opposition to the national government of Francisco Franco. The ETA slowly evolved a structure, an ideology, and a program involving violent acts that transformed it into one of the major opponents of the Franco regime. ETA became a major force in the Basque separatist movement, using assassinations, bombings, and other terrorist acts to push its cause; it continues to pursue such activities to the present time.

Étudiants de la Restauration Nationale *See* ACTION FRANÇAIS.

Evil May Day Riots (Great Britain) an antialien uprising by apprentices (youths mostly age 14 to 22) in London on May 1, 1517, which is regarded as the archetype of the numerous London apprentices' riots that occurred during the reign of Elizabeth I and still later. Antialien sentiment had been prevalent in London for many years, fueled by the view that foreign craftsworkers residing in the city deprived natives of gainful labor. Rumors that the Crown provided special protections to foreigners that prevented Britons who brought charges against them from winning in court sparked the Evil May Day Riots. The first riot actually occurred on April 28 when youths attacked some foreigners, were arrested by the lord mayor's forces, and were imprisoned in Newgate and other prisons. Subsequently, rumors spread of a major uprising to occur on May Day, a traditional day for festivities and rioting. The lord mayor declared a curfew for that day, ordering all apprentices and servants to be confined indoors. When an alderman tried to enforce the curfew against a group of young men in Cheapside, they

resisted and roused a crowd to participate with shouts of "Prentices, prentices, clubs, clubs. Hundreds marched to Newgate and the Counter (debtors') prisons, released those jailed after the April 28 riot, and then vandalized the homes and workshops of aliens in several areas. Nobles dispersed the rioters and arrested hundreds, mostly young apprentices. The outcome was humiliating for alders of the city, as nobles and their military retinues occupied London and conducted the trials, indicating that the local officials could not preserve order on their own. The prisoners were brutally treated, and 13 were executed after the first trials on May 4. A half-dozen more were tried and executed on May 7, after which the aldermen pleaded before Henry VIII, who berated them. Then on May 22 the remaining prisoners, 400 men and boys and 11 women secured with ropes and halters, were brought before the king in Westminster Hall and there pardoned.

Executive Committee of the Social-Revolutionary Party (Russia) a terrorist cell formally organized in June 1879 within LAND AND FREEDOM. Although the executive committee's major strength existed in southern Russia rather than in Land and Freedom's St. Petersburg center, its terrorist agenda led to the parent society's demise in August 1879. Thereafter the executive committee formed the core of the People's Will, one of the two factions that reorganized as separate entities after Land and Freedom dissolved. (*See* TERRORIST SECTION OF THE PEOPLE'S WILL.) The group's seal contained an axe, a dagger, and a revolver crossed. Although never large—the total membership during its six-year life was about 50—the executive committee's terroristic actions proved most significant. On August 26, 1879, it condemned to death Tsar Alexander II. The group's first attempt on the tsar's life occurred in November 1879 when they secured dynamite under the tracks of a railroad in a plan to blow up a train carrying the tsar from Odessa, but the dynamite failed to explode. At Moscow, the end of the tsar's rail journey, the terrorists had rented a house in a suburb and excavated a tunnel running 45.7 meters (150 feet) to the railway embankment, where they planted dynamite. Here the dynamite exploded as planned, but the tsar's train had already passed the site; although the following train carrying his retinue took the blast, no one was hurt. Two other efforts by executive committee members to blow up the tsar also failed, although one at the Yellow Hall of the Winter Palace killed 11 people and wounded 56.

The next effort, however, would succeed. This time the terrorists would not only dig a tunnel and plant a mine under a roadway the tsar used frequently, but also, in case the mine failed, hurl a bomb at the tsar's carriage and thereafter, if necessary, attack with dagger and pistol. Four men in the executive committee were assigned the deed: Ignaty Grinevitsky, age 26 and a former engineering student; Timofey Mikhailov, age 21 and a boilermaker (he would back out at the last minute); Ivan Yemelyanov, age 20 and a cabinetmaker; Nikolai Rysakov, age 19 and a student. They would be assisted by two young women: Vera Figner, formerly with the MOSCOW CIRCLE, and Sofya Perovskaya, formerly with the CHAIKOVSKY CIRCLE. On March 1, 1881, while the tsar was returning from an outing at the Manege, the conspirators detonated the mine, which damaged the accompanying carriage and mortally wounded a Cossack guard and a butcher's boy. But the tsar left his carriage and lingered to commiserate with the wounded, providing Grinevitsky the chance to pitch his bomb, shattering the tsar's legs and knocking himself unconscious. Guards placed Alexander in a sleigh and hastened with him to the palace, but they neglected to treat his wounds and he bled to death. The police captured Rysakov, who, in terror, became an informer, making it possible for the police to arrest his colleagues and other members of the executive committee. Four men and two women (Perovskaya and Gesya Helfman) were tried; all were found guilty and sentenced to hang. Helfman's execution was postponed because she was pregnant. The other five were hanged on April 3, with

Rysakov being last so that he had to witness the others' deaths. No public uprising—expected by the executive committee—occurred, the many arrests rendered the executive committee ineffectual, and Alexander III abandoned his predecessor's plans for liberal measures in favor of increased autocracy.

Weakened by many arrests, the People's Will moved its headquarters to Moscow in the summer. In Moscow the executive committee revived sufficiently to pursue a new course, proclaiming its support of an anti-Semitic movement that had surfaced among workers in the Ukraine and other southern regions. The People's Will as a whole subsequently distanced itself from this tack. On March 18, 1882 an agent of the executive committee assassinated General Strelnikov, the brutal prosecutor for the military courts in the south. In May members of the committee began to make dynamite again in anticipation of revolution, but arrests quickly reduced their numbers to one—Vera Figner. Although she struggled on, trying to engender support, the executive committee never revived sufficiently to be an active force.

Bibliography: Avrahm Yarmolinsky, *Road to Revolution: A Century of Russian Radicalism* (New York: Macmillan, 1962).

Fair Bear Standards (United States) a program adopted in 1937 by the Labor Board of the Associated Students of the University of California (ASUC), the student government of the Berkeley campus, to ensure that working students received fair compensation from their employers. After an investigation in 1936 by the ASUC's Welfare Council evidenced that many Berkeley employers were underpaying student workers, the ASUC created the Labor Board to aid working students. The Fair Bear Standards adopted by the board established a minimum wage (40 cents per hour) and acceptable working conditions, and the board notified local employers of the ASUC's support for these standards. Employers who adopted the standards could display a Fair Bear sticker provided by the ASUC; those in violation would be subject to a student boycott. (*Fair Bear* referred to the university's symbol, a bruin.) Most of the employers complied with the standards, some raising wages as much as 30 percent to do so, and the boycotts proved highly effective against those who initially refused. The Fair Bear program owed its success to the support of the university administration, the student newspaper, and the undergraduate students, but this cooperation also revealed the increasing effectiveness of the student movement. The Fair Bear program attracted national attention and labor union approval, and student governments at other campuses adopted it.

Farmer, James (1920–) (United States) African-American civil rights leader and director of the CONGRESS OF RACIAL EQUALITY (CORE). Farmer was educated at Wiley College (Marshall, Texas) and Howard University. In 1942 he joined with several Christian pacifists to found CORE, dedicated to using Ghandian nonviolent methods to combat racial discrimination and segregation. Farmer participated in CORE's successful, pioneering 1947 sit-in demonstrations at two Chicago restaurants that refused service to blacks. During the 1950s, Farmer served as a field secretary for the STUDENT LEAGUE FOR INDUSTRIAL DEMOCRACY (SLID). He became national director of CORE in 1961 and in the same year organized the FREEDOM RIDERS in the South. As a Freedom Rider, he was arrested and imprisoned with others for trying to integrate a bus terminal in Jackson, Mississippi. Farmer created CORE branches nationwide, led voter-registration drives, and participated in civil rights demonstrations. In 1964 he and 300 others were arrested for demonstrating against discriminatory hiring policies at the New York World's Fair. Farmer resigned as CORE director in 1966 to become director of an adult literacy project. In 1969 he accepted a subcabinet post with the Department of Health, Education, and Welfare in the Nixon administration. He resigned in 1971, lectured widely, and served as director of the Council on Minority Planning and Strategy, headquartered in Washington. Farmer wrote *Freedom When?* (1965) and *Lay Bare the Heart: An Autobiography of the Civil Rights Movement* (1985).

Federación de Estudiantes Colombianos (FEC) (Colombia) the first nationwide student organization in Colombia, formed in 1924 as a result of national student congresses in 1922 and 1924—the first such congresses in the nation's history—convened in response to the UNIVERSITY REFORM PROGRAM AND MOVEMENT in Argentina. The FEC concentrated on attaining a unified national student movement, student representation in university governing bodies, improvements in curricula and teaching, and more qualified faculties. Unsuccessful in its reform efforts because of an unsympathetic government and a disinterested populace, the FEC assumed a more politically activist stance at the student congress held in 1928 but to little avail. A university reform law was finally passed in 1935 during the Liberal Party administration of Alfonso López Pumajero, but it granted only very limited student representation in the governance of the National University in Bogotá and limited autonomy to the university.

Federación de Estudiantes de Chile (FECH)   (Chile) a university students' organization formed in Santiago in 1906 as the result of a demonstration by students of the medical school of the University of Chile. (The university was established in 1843.) The demonstration was unusual in that the students were gathered in the Municipal Theatre to be honored for having helped to overcome a smallpox epidemic in Valparaíso; disturbed because they and their families had to sit in the galleries while the dignitaries who had come to honor them occupied all the prime seating areas, the students shouted and threw torn paper on the dignitaries. On the day following this demonstration, the president of the medical school students' organization proposed forming the federation, which since the 1930s has been known simply as FECH. In its early years, FECH was devoted mostly to providing cultural and educational programs for its members and schooling for workers. The government awarded corporate status to FECH in 1918. In 1919 FECH formed close ties with the communist-oriented Industrial Workers of the World (IWW, often referred to as the Wobblies) an affiliation that led to imprisonment for some FECH leaders.

FECH held its first national convention in June 1920, attended by 1,200 student delegates, to formalize a Declaration of Principles that emphasized a socialistic agenda, pacifism, criticism of Chilean social institutions, and achievement of justice and fraternity for everyone. To promote these principles FECH staged public demonstrations and speeches and propogandized readers through provocative articles in the student magazine *Claridad*, which became the official FECH publication in 1920. (FECH also published *Juventud*.) Reacting to FECH opposition to a popular military move against Peru, a mob of youths on July 21, 1920 invaded and trashed the FECH headquarters and removed books and magazines from the FECH library and burned them—this event continues to be memorialized by FECH. At the end of 1920, Arturo Alessandri Palma became president of Chile and freed imprisoned FECH leaders. The FECH reformists of this era became known as "the generation of 1920," and several of them later became leaders of the Socialist and Radical parties and served in the national legislature. The FECH adopted most of the reforms propounded by the important UNIVERSITY REFORM PROGRAM AND MOVEMENT begun in Argentina but made minimal effort to attain their fulfillment in Chile. In fact, in 1922 FECH began a decline that resulted in 1925 in its effective dissolution. It was reborn in 1930.

The new FECH, however, did not revive its principled and activist role of 1920. It was frequently torn by factionalism, especially conflict between socialist and communist factions, during the decade, evidencing the political conflicts in the society at large, although ameliorated by a popular front government. In 1938 the FECH sponsored the first national student convention held since 1920 and also began to publish a new official newspaper, *FECH*. The FECH returned to activism in 1956–57 with a series of demonstrations protesting price increases, especially fares on public transport, imposed by the government, with a demonstration in late March 1957 resulting in one student's death. The government declared martial law but did rescind the fare increase, although it was reinstated later without incident. By this time the FECH had become a university-centered organization, focusing primarily on achieving educational goals: this focus came to the fore in the late 1960s, when FECH spearheaded a series of demonstrations, including the occupation of administration and other buildings at the University of Chile in May–June 1968. This was a partially successful effort to effect reforms that included the granting of increased student involvement in the university's decision-making bodies.

University students comprised a major element among the supporters of Senator Salvador Allende Gossens, a founder of the Socialist Party and an avowed Marxist; on the night of his election to the presidency in October 1970, Allende addressed the public from the balcony of the FECH headquarters as thousands of youths danced in the streets. Students consequently were among the aggrieved and persecuted following Allende's death, apparently a suicide, on September 11, 1973 and the seizure of the government by a military junta led by General Augusto Pinochet Ugarte. Among the military dictatorship's first acts was the outlawing of FECH. During the remainder of the 1970s and the early 1980s, quiescence mostly prevailed on the university campuses, as military figures led the administrations at all the institutions; center-left students at the Catholic University began to regain control there in 1985, however. Campus protests erupted in May 1983 and continued into the fall in conjunction with a strike called by copper workers. In October 1984 nonpartisan students reestablished and took control of FECH through open elections. In 1985, 11 students imprisoned for advocating a strike gained national attention that forced the Pinochet government to free them, and other efforts at repression of students in 1985 backfired against the regime. But the student protestors were a distinct minority, and quiet returned to the campuses in 1986 and following years.

Bibliography: Frank Bonilla and Myron Glazer, *Student Politics in Chile* (New York: Basic Books, 1970); Pamela Constable and Arturo Valenzuela, *A Nation of Enemies: Chile Under Pinochet* (New York: W. W. Norton, 1991).

Federación de Estudiantes de Perú (FEP)   (Peru) a national federation of university students formed in

1919. The FEP spearheaded the drive for reform in Peruvian universities inspired by the UNIVERSITY REFORM PROGRAM AND MOVEMENT of Argentina, and in August 1920 its president and the president of the FEDERACIÓN UNIVERSITARIA ARGENTINA signed an agreement that allied the two groups. The university reform movement in Peru proved to be one of the most important in Latin America because it generated a political party, the Alianza Popular Revolucionara Americana (APRA or Aprista). Aprista was founded in 1924 by Victor Raúl Haya de la Torre, and many of its leaders had been active in the university reform movement during the years 1919 to 1923.

Federación de Estudiantes de Venezuela (FEV) (Venezuela) a student organization formed in 1927 as the Federación Venezolana de Estudiantes at the Central University, Venezuela's major university, in Caracas. Central University had been closed from 1912 to 1923 by Juan Vincente Gómez, the dictator who controlled Venezuela from 1908 to 1935, because of student opposition to his ruthless and brutal regime. Following the university's reopening, students had tried to organize the FEV but were thwarted by the regime's banning of the organization. Finally organized in 1927, the FEV led the opposition to Gómez, culminating in the WEEK OF THE STUDENT uprising in 1928. The FEV was again involved in demonstrations in February 1936 against General Eleázar López Contreras, who came to power following Gómez's death in January 1936. In March the FEV was reorganized as the Federación de Estudiantes de Venezuela. *See also* BOYS OF 1928.

Federación de Estudiantes Secundarios (FES) (Argentina) an organization of students in the nation's secondary schools, or *colegios*, formed in December 1952. FEDERACIÓN UNIVERSITARIA ARGENTINA (FUA) members helped to set up FES, which consequently supported FUA policies and activities in opposition to the government of Juan Perón. Prior to establishment of FES, students from the secondary schools had participated in the BRAVO RELEASE STRIKE.

Federación de Estudiantes Universitarios del Ecuador (FEUE)   (Ecuador) a national organization of university students created by statute in 1944 that has served as the spearhead of the Ecuadorian student movement. From its beginnings, the FEUE promoted the politicizing of students. A declaration by the First National Congress of FEUE held in 1944 stated that the nation's university students,

> together with the people, today more than ever should present a battle-front solidly united against imperialism, against dictatorial regimes, in favor of effective solidarity with all Latin American nations,

and supportive of the growth and strengthening of all progressive forces in the country.

During the 1950s the organization's leaders belonged to the Socialist Party, and in the 1960s the FEUE became increasingly radicalized, generating many confrontations with police and the military authorities governing the country. Many students were killed or wounded during protests in the 1960s; responding to student demonstrations in 1966 and 1970, government forces invaded and closed the Central University in Quito, and in 1968 the FEUE president was assassinated following antigovernment agitation there. Another significant incident occurred at the University of Guayaquil in 1968 after the FEUE at Central University and the University Council at Guayaquil opposed the elimination of entrance examinations—ironically, their elimination would ostensibly have made the universities more democratic. At the request of the University Council at Guayaquil, police intervened on May 29, 1968 to evict high school students who had occupied university buildings in protest of this decision and killed 15 of the protestors. Thereafter, all of the state universities voted in favor of eliminating the examinations.

Federación Estudiantil Universitaria (Federation of University Students, FEU)   (Cuba) a union of the various student groups representing each of the faculties (disciplines) at the University of Havana. FEU became an early opponent of General Fulgencio Batista, who seized power in March 1952. On April 4 about 200 students ceremonially buried a copy of the 1940 constitution as a protest, and on May 20 they staged a mass demonstration to honor the 50th anniversary of Cuba's attaining independence. Such actions by students of the FEU were perceived by Batista as threatening. During a demonstration on January 15, 1953, police killed a student (Ruben Batista), and the FEU called for a nationwide student strike in response. Student riots and demonstrations led to the closing of the University of Havana on April 14, 1953. The FEU called for another nationwide student strike after students were brutally beaten or arrested during demonstrations in Havana and Santiago on November 27, 1955. Other police attacks occurred on December 2 and 4, and the police invaded the University of Havana, wrecking the rector's office and destroying files, equipment, and furniture. As a result of these clashes, several leaders of FEU formed the DIRECTORIO REVOLUCIONARIO as an insurrectionary movement in December 1955. Later members of this movement and other students joined Fidel Castro's JULY 26 MOVEMENT, which succeeded in ousting Batista in January 1959. In October 1959 a candidate backed by the Castro government won the FEU presidency; thereafter the FEU became effectively an agency of the government, even helping to end the University of Havana's autonomy during 1960 to transform it into an institution of the state.

Federación Universitaria Argentina (FUA) (Argentina) a national federation of university students founded at the University of Buenos Aires on April 11, 1918. Members of the Federación Universitaria Buenos Aires (FUBA) supported the UNIVERSITY REFORM PROGRAM AND MOVEMENT initiated at the University of Córdoba on March 14, 1918 through encouragement of and fraternization with the Córdoba student reformists who visited the Buenos Aires campus, and they were inspired by the reform movement to create the national federation. One of the founders, Osvaldo Loudet, served as FUA's first president. The FUA was pledged to promote solidarity among all students, educational reforms, and awareness of cultural achievements and to represent Argentine students at international gatherings. On May 16 the reformists at Córdoba formed the Federación Universitaria de Córdoba (FUC), which became an affiliate of the FUA. The FUA in turn supported the University Reform Program and Movement generated at Córdoba and organized the First National Congress of University Students, which met in Córdoba July 21–29, 1918 and issued proposals for reforms at all the nation's universities. These reform proposals gave added thrust to the movement. Twelve delegates represented FUA at the Congress, and 12 delegates from each of five university federations now affiliated with FUA represented their schools. In October 1920 the FUA became the first student organization to denounce imperialism and colonialism, citing them as causes of World War I and advocating self-determination for all peoples. The FUA was an active spearhead of the Argentine student movement until 1923, when it virtually ceased to function. In addition, during the 1920s the student movement fragmented into opposed groups such as Insurrexit, a communist-oriented group formed in 1920 (it disbanded in 1935), and Grupo Concordia, an anticommunist and antianarchist group formed in 1923. FUA remained inactive through the 1920s, when largely conservative elements were in power and suppressed reform. Its revival began with a reorganization in March 1931 and with the Second National Student Congress in Buenos Aires in August 1932; the congress advocated a new national social, economic, and political system of an essentially socialistic orientation. But conservatives remained in control of the government from 1930 to 1943. Then in June 1943 a group of army officers seized control of the government, and on November 6 the Ministry of Education declared the FUA and its affiliates illegal and disbanded. Thereafter, the various federations subdivided and met secretly as smaller groups. On August 7, 1945, with the Axis fascistic powers defeated in Europe, the ban on the FUA was lifted and the FUA returned to open advocacy of a democratic government. On May 2, 1946,

President Juan Perón, now in full control of the government, assumed control of the nation's six universities; he effectively circumscribed the FUA's activities but did not dissolve the federation outright. Perón was forced from power in September 1955, and the FUA reemerged as a reform advocate. During the late 1950s and early 1960s, communist-oriented students were in control of the FUA and its affiliates; they targeted the United States for denunciation and supported the Soviet Union and Fidel Castro. The FUA is administered by a junta comprised of two representatives from each of its affiliates from whose numbers officers are selected; the junta members and the officers meet monthly and are elected annually. FUA is headquartered in Buenos Aires.

Bibliography: Richard J. Walter, *Student Politics in Argentina: The University Reform and Its Effects, 1918–1964* (New York: Basic Books, 1968).

Federación Universitaria Nacional (FUN) (Colombia) a nationwide organization recreated by communist and other leftist students in November 1963 at the beginning of a period of severe economic and political instability in Colombia. FUN organized numerous strikes during the 1960s.

Fédération des Étudiants d'Afrique Noire en France (FEANF) (France) an organization created by students from sub-Saharan Africa in Paris in 1945 that brought into federation student organizations representing the individual sub-Saharan French colonies. During its early years, FEANF was supported by the major party that advocated self-determination in the French African colonies, the Rassemblement Démocratique Africain (RDA), formed in 1946, which allied itself with the French Communist Party in the parliamentary proceedings of the Fourth Republic—an alliance FEANF strongly supported. In 1950 the RDA ended its ties with Communists, and FEANF consequently ended its ties with RDA. Following its first congress in 1951, FEANF became increasingly confrontational in protesting French colonialism and in opposing moderate African leaders, resulting sometimes in FEANF activists being expelled from France. FEANF had its own publication, *L'Étudiant de l'Afrique Noire* and was a member of the INTERNATIONAL UNION OF STUDENTS (IUS).

Fédération des Étudiants de Paris (France) a loosely organized association of the presidents of student organizations—that is, ASSOCIATION GÉNÉRALE DES ÉTUDIANTS—in Paris.

Federation for a Democratic China (FDC) (France) an organization founded in France on August 1, 1989 by WUER KAIXI, a former student leader of the CHINESE DEMOCRACY MOVEMENT; political scientist Yan Jiaqi, who had publicly supported the movement; Wan Runnan, former head of the private Stone Corporation who had supported Zhao Ziyang in his abortive power struggle with Deng Xiaoping—all of whom managed to escape to the West after the movement's suppression—and Liu Binyan, a dissident journalist who was working in the United States on a fellowship. The FDC's primary purpose was "To continue the 1989 Democracy Movement." Although the FDC did not advocate overthrow of the CHINESE COMMUNIST PARTY (CCP), it did support democratic reforms that would require a total revamping of the Chinese government and the CCP's sharing of power. The FDC had many student members but was led by liberal intellectuals and CCP reformers who had fled China. It garnered support from expatriate Chinese throughout the world and also had extensive contacts with dissident political groups in Eastern Europe.

Fédération Nationale des Associations d'Élèves en Grandes Écoles (FNAGE)   (France) an association of students in commercial and technical schools formed in June 1961 as a rival to the Union des Grandes Écoles, which was affiliated with the UNION NATIONALE DES ÉTUDIANTS DE FRANCE (UNEF) since 1958. In 1963 the FNAGE was awarded a seat on the Administrative Council of the CENTRE NATIONAL DES OEUVRES.

Fédération Nationale des Étudiants de France (FNEF)   (France) a student organization formed in June 1961 as a conservative rival to the UNION NATIONALE DES ÉTUDIANTS DE FRANCE (UNEF). Students representing various *offices* (academic disciplines), notably medicine, commerce, and law, were breaking away from UNEF in a dispute over UNEF's positions on the Algerian war and quarrels with the government. Meeting in Montpellier, students in professional *offices* founded FNEF. The government immediately recognized FNEF and provided a subsidy to the new organization (the government had ceased subsidizing UNEF). In 1963 the government awarded three seats on the Administrative Council of the CENTRE NATIONALE DES OEUVRES. FNEF opposed such UNEF proposals as government-sponsored scholarships for all students.

Federation of National University Students' Self-Governing Associations   (Japan) a nationwide organization of university student councils founded in June 1948. The federation came into being in response to the government's tripling of tuition fees (from 600 yen to 1,800 yen) because of rampant inflation. Student protests that took the form of a "nonpayment" movement had proven ineffectual in preventing the increase. But students used this failed effort as a springboard to creating a larger movement, resulting in creation of the federation, with 300 representatives from 113 state universities attending the first meeting. By the end of June some 102 universities had joined in a strike to protest the increased tuition fees, and the federation presented to the Diet (parliament) a petition signed by representatives of 82 universities. The viability the students found in unity through this federation effort provided the immediate catalyst for the formation of the ZENGAKUREN.

Bibliography: Stuart J. Dowsey, ed., *Zengakuren: Japan's Revolutionary Students* (Berkeley, Calif.: The Ishi Press, 1970).

Federation of Zionist Youth (FZY)   (Great Britain) the oldest of the English Zionist youth groups, founded in 1912. In significance it was displaced by HABONIM.

Fellowship of Youth for Peace (FYP)   (United States) a Christian-oriented (Protestant) peace advocacy organization founded in 1922 by the STUDENT VOLUNTEER MOVEMENT (SVM) and the first national student organization devoted entirely to pacifism. The FYP supported anti-ROTC efforts, sponsored educational programs, and provided speakers for campus meetings. The most active and most successful peace-advocacy organization of the 1920s, the FYP enhanced its position by merging with the Fellowship of Reconciliation, a pacifist organization for adults, in 1926.

Festival of Life   (United States) a demonstration planned by the Youth International Party (Yippies) to coincide with the 1968 Democratic National Convention in Chicago and counterbalance the convention's supposed "festival of death." In anticipation of the festival, the underground press published numerous articles that attracted the interest of potential participants and promised a gathering spiced with rock music, poetry readings, yippie political speeches, mass meditation, and other attractions. The ostensible purpose of the festival was, of course, to protest against the Vietnam War and for revolutionary political change. The leader of the yippies, Abbie HOFFMAN, declared that the yippies were "revolutionary artists. Our concept of revolution is that it's fun." But the Festival of Life turned out to be something quite different from a festival of fun as it developed in combination with other groups' demonstrations. *See* BATTLE OF CHICAGO.

Fichte Hochschulegemeinde   *See* HOCHSCHULRING DEUTSCHER ART.

Filomats   (Poland) a student secret society (*see* POLONIA) founded in 1817 at Wilno (Vilna) University. Among the Filomats' founders was the popular and accomplished Romantic poet Adam Mickiewicz (1798–1855). Initially dedicated to fostering friendships and moral growth, the society held readings and discussions of scientific and literary publications. But the Filomats slowly moved toward embracing nationalist political views, although not of a revolutionary nature. The society generated affiliates in the district's middle schools but rejected association with student secret societies in other nations or at Warsaw University, which the group considered morally suspect and reckless. The Filomats maintained their secrecy for five years, but then a spy reported on the group to Grand Duke Constantine, brother of Tsar Alexander and head of Russian governance in Poland, as being associated with other student societies, including the BURSCHENSCHAFTEN in Germany. After a student in the sixth form at the Wilno lyceum wrote on a chalkboard on May 3, 1823 "Long live the constitution of May 3," the grand duke decided to take action. (The May Third Constitution drafted in 1791 had been an unsuccessful attempt to shore up the Polish central government and to prevent foreign intervention in the nation's affairs; it was a rallying cry for Polish nationalists.) The grand duke had the chancellor of the university (director of the lyceum) arrested and ordered an intensive investigation of student secret societies by the Russian police at Wilno. As students refused to cooperate with the authorities, the investigation got nowhere until one Filomat finally confessed, resulting in the arrest of more than 100 students on the night of October 23–24, 1823—one of the largest mass arrests to that time in European history. Some 200 university students were questioned during the following months and into the summer of 1824. Twenty students received sentences, some to prison terms; most were exiled to Russia, including Mickiewicz. The affiliated groups at the middle schools were also uprooted; many of these students were sentenced to death, although the sentences were then commuted to hard labor. The Russian authorities also imposed revisions to the curriculum at Wilno University, banned certain books from the university, and increased both restrictions on and surveillance of students at the university.

Finkenschaft (Germany) an organization of unaffiliated—that is, nonfraternity, or noncorporate—students begun at the University of Leipzig in 1896. The Finken adopted a derogatory term (*der Finken* means "finches") to assert the concept of personal merit based on ability rather than memberships in a fraternity, counterpoising their independence to the exclusivity and formalism of the fraternities. The Finkenschaft concept quickly spread to Berlin, Halle, and other universities as a reform movement, the incipient free-student movement. In 1900 the free-student groups joined together in a national organization, the DEUTSCHE FREISTUDENTENSCHAFT.

First International Congress of American Students (Uruguay) a conference of students held in Montevideo, Uruguay in 1909 that was a climactic event of the decade's growing student movement in Latin America. The congress drew student representatives from Argentina, Bolivia, Brazil, Chile, Paraguay, Peru, and Uruguay. Their focus was on reform of universities throughout Latin America, so the congress served as a harbinger of

the UNIVERSITY REFORM PROGRAM AND MOVEMENT. The delegates advocated student representation in the governing bodies of the universities, revision of the examination systems, noncompulsory attendance at classes, student involvement in selecting professors, and five-year appointments for professors. Subsequent congresses at Buenos Aires in 1910 and Lima in 1912 continued the focus on such reforms.

Fischer, Karl (1881–1941) (Germany) primary founder and leader of the WANDERVOGEL movement. Fischer was born and spent most of his life in Berlin. It was there in the suburb of Steglitz that on November 4, 1901 he spearheaded the founding of the Wandervogel at a meeting of 10 people in a backroom of the Ratskeller. As the movement spread, opposition to Fischer arose, and splinter groups were formed, including the Altwandervogel headed by Fischer for a time. The initial split occurred at a meeting on June 29, 1904 at the Ratskeller that left Fischer in the minority. Weary of the conflicts, Fischer sailed for Tsingtao (Qingdao), China in October 1906 to fulfill his obligation for military service. He spent 15 years in China, returning to Berlin in 1921. Fischer became editor of a youth magazine and later served in a variety of odd jobs. After 1933 he received a monthly honorarium from the HITLER JUGEND. A lonely, melancholy, and difficult man, Fischer never married. He died in Berlin in 1941 a few weeks after the death of his mother. Following World War II, in his honor the Karl Fischer Society was created in Berlin.

Follen, Karl (1795–1840) (Germany) leader of the GIESSENER SCHWARZEN and university professor. Follen studied theology and then law at the University of Giessen, attaining his degree and becoming Privatdozent at the university in 1818. As leader of the Giessener Schwarzen Follen advocated violent overthrow of the monarchical leaders of the German states and establishment of a unified German republic. To escape suspicions about his political radicalism he moved to Jena, but following Karl SAND's assassination of August Kotzebue on March 23, 1819, Follen fled to France and then, after the assassination of the duc du Barry on January 14, 1820, to Switzerland. When Prussian authorities insisted on his return, he moved to the United States and in 1825 became professor of German at Harvard University. An abolitionist agitator, he left Harvard in 1835 and was ordained as a Unitarian minister in 1836. Follen died on January 14, 1840 aboard a steamboat that was destroyed by fire during a voyage from New York to Boston.

Forces Unies de Jeunesse Patriotique (FUJP) (France) a youth organization formed in 1943 of groups and individuals in opposition to the German occupation. Some of the members participated in the Resistance. Student members advocated liberalizing university entrance requirements, giving students a role in university governance, and other reforms to bring greater equalitarianism to higher education. After the Liberation of France by Allied forces the student members of FUJP formed the UNION PATRIOTIQUE DES ORGANISATIONS D'ÉTUDIANTS (UPOE).

Foundation for Youth and Student Affairs (FYSA) (United States) a supposedly private and independent organization established in New York City in 1952 for the purpose of supporting international student activities, including exchanges, educational programs, and other events. The FYSA's executives were mostly former officers of the NATIONAL STUDENT ASSOCIATION (NSA). The true significance of the FYSA became public knowledge in 1967 when it was revealed that the foundation was actually a primary medium for conveying Central Intelligence Agency (CIA) funds to the NSA and also to the INTERNATIONAL STUDENT CONFERENCE (ISC).

4-H Clubs (United States) an organization for youths, originally rural and small-town residents but now including city youths, which was founded as the National 4-H Club by the terms of the Smith-Lever Act of 1914. The antecedents of 4-H predate this act by many years, as rural youths in many areas were already organized into clubs based on interests in corn, poultry, canning, potatoes, cotton, or other crops and activities. By the time of the act, there were nearly 100,000 rural youths involved in such clubs. One of the two founders of 4-H was John E. Alexander, who was author of the *Boy Scout Manual* and head of the Young People's Division of International Sunday Schools.

Organized and supervised under the auspices of the Department of Agriculture Extension Service and the extension services of the state agricultural colleges, 4-H Club membership is open to all youths from 9 to 19. As originally conceived, 4-H was intended to help member youths develop into stable and productive farmers, homemakers, and citizens; in more recent years, programs involving urban-centered vocations have been added. Tens of millions of youths have been 4-H members, the great majority from farm families. Each member is required to pursue and complete a project relating to an agricultural or other vocation—for example, raising a heifer to maturity, or growing a flower or a crop to exhibit at a state fair. Each year a National 4-H Club Congress is held in Chicago and a National 4-H Conference in Washington, D.C. The concept of 4-H has spread to most of the nations in the world, and many youths involved participate in the exchange program of the International Farm Youth Exchange.

Frankfurt Putsch (Germany) an abortive attempted coup in Frankfurt am Main on April 3, 1833, when a group of radical students and young intellectuals tried to seize control of the federal treasury located in the city. Their effort had been poorly organized, and its failure led to the arrest of 1,800 suspects and the conviction of about 200 members of the local BURSCHENSCHAFTEN. The outcome sundered the student movement, as students separated into distinct Catholic and Protestant groups to pursue their opposition to secularly oriented political radicals who held anti-Christian views.

Free Church of Berkeley (United States) the exemplar and best known of the so-called Underground Churches, originally an ecumenical ministry begun in 1967 in Berkeley, California, directed by Dick York, an Episcopal minister. The Free Church's ministry was oriented to help runaways and other youths on the street who needed a "crash pad" (a place to spend the night—sometimes 90 youths per night). The ministry provided counseling on draft resistance, bad drug trips, and other problems as well as food. As the Free Church became more established, it published a monthly letter entitled *The Subversive Church*, indicative of the growing radicalization of its ministry. The Free Church was deeply involved in the BERKELEY "PEOPLE'S PARK" RIOTS.

Freedom Riders (United States) participants in a series of bus trips in the South during the summer of 1961 intended to force legal fulfillment of the Supreme Court's judgment in *Boynton v. Virginia* (1960); this decision declared segregation in railway and bus terminal accommodations illegal. The Freedom Riders strove also to invite reactions that would motivate the federal government to intervene in support of the rights of blacks in the South. The Freedom Riders were organized by James FARMER, national director of the CONGRESS OF RACIAL EQUALITY (CORE). For the first ride on May 4, 1961, Farmer and 12 others (including six young whites) boarded buses in Washington, D.C. and began a tour through Georgia, Alabama, and Mississippi en route to New Orleans. Farmer left the group before the buses entered Alabama to attend his father's funeral. The riders were attacked in Anniston, Alabama, where one of their buses was set on fire and destroyed. The second bus made it to Birmingham, where a gang of young white men beat the riders with baseball bats, lead pipes, and bicycle chains. In the wake of this violence, CORE ceased providing riders for the project, although Farmer continued his involvement and student volunteers stepped in to serve as riders on the subsequent bus trips. Throughout the summer, more than a thousand Freedom Riders traversed the South, many of them students from the STUDENT NONVIOLENT COORDINATING COMMITTEE (SNCC), and many ended up being ill-treated in prisons or jails. In September the Interstate Commerce Commission strengthened its regulations against segregated terminals; now facing the likelihood of lawsuits, communities began to drop their resistance to integrated terminals. By October three railroad companies operating in the South had desegregated their facilities, and in November the Interstate Commerce Commission banned segregated accommodations. Late in 1962 CORE announced that segregation in interstate travel had effectively ceased.

Bibliography: Robert Weisbrot, *Freedom Bound: A History of America's Civil Rights Movement* (New York: Plume (Penguin), 1991).

Freedom Summer   (United States) a civil-rights project initiated by the STUDENT NONVIOLENT COORDINATING COMMITTEE (SNCC), directed by Robert Moses, and conducted in Mississippi during the summer of 1964. About a thousand students, mostly whites, joined forces with African-American civil-rights workers to register black voters and to provide educational and health services at community centers and Freedom Schools. Altogether more than 1,000 young people participated. Before traveling to Mississippi, the students were trained in nonviolent tactics, including proper behavior when arrested, self-defense, and the way of life in the state. Three of the volunteers (James Earl Chaney, age 19; Michael Schwerner, age 24; and Andrew Goodman, age 20) who drove to Philadelphia, Mississippi to investigate a church bombing were murdered there on June 21— Goodman's first day in Mississippi. (Seven Ku Klux Klan members were convicted of the murders in 1967 but were later paroled.) Scores of other volunteers suffered beatings and arrest; facilities were bombed or set afire. One of the project's achievements was creation of the Freedom Democratic Party, which challenged the all-white Mississippi delegation at the Democratic National Convention in August 1964. Freedom Summer is also credited for speeding up passage of the Voting Rights Act of 1965 and the creation of Head Start programs and health clinics funded by the federal government.

Bibliography: Doug McAdam, *Freedom Summer* (New York: Oxford University Press, 1988).

Free Speech Movement (FSM)   (United States) the major organizational arm of the BERKELEY STUDENT REVOLT that erupted at the University of California at Berkeley in the fall of 1964. The Free Speech Movement, a coalition of 14 student groups, was organized in October by students who had participated in the 1964 Mississippi Summer Project, most prominently Mario SAVIO, the leader of the FSM. It was Savio who defined the purpose and import of FSM as a movement not only to defend the right of free speech but also to oppose the perceived dehumanization of the university. During the sit-in at Sproul Hall, he declared,

> One conception of the university, suggested by a classical Christian formulation, is that it be in the world but not of the world. The conception of

Mario Savio, leader of the Free Speech Movement at the Berkeley campus of the University of California harangues his followers during a three-hour sit-in demonstration at Sproul Hall. (AP/WIDE WORLD PHOTOS)

> [Chancellor] Clark Kerr by contrast is that the university is part and parcel of this particular stage in the history of American society; it stands to serve the needs of American industry; it is a factory that turns out a product needed by industry and government. . . . It can permit two kinds of speech: speech which encourages continuation of the status quo, and speech which advocates changes in it so radical as to be irrelevant in the foreseeable future. . . . Speech with consequences, speech in the area of civil rights, speech which some might regard as illegal, must stop.

In a series of lectures given the previous year entitled *The Uses of the University*, Kerr had in fact said that the emergent "multiversity" must accommodate the needs of industry and government. The multiversity, conceived as a factory whose impersonal manufacturing procedures produce graduates like assembly-line, identical products, was the FSM's perceived enemy. The FSM's cause, then, resonated for students at multiversities throughout the nation. More than 5,000 students regularly turned out for the FSM's demonstrations, and more than 800 were arrested during the Berkeley protests, earning sympathy from thousands of students at other universities. Capitalizing on this sympathy, the STUDENTS FOR A DEMOCRATIC SOCIETY (SDS) organized protests at numerous other multiversities, making use of FSM publications and speakers to help local chapters stage the protests.

Free University   (United States) the term used for a radical educational experiment that involved free and informal classes, usually held on university and college campuses and often taught by sympathetic faculty mem-

Laura Foner (left), a Brandeis student, and Stan Stournas, a Harvard student, lead some 200 students from five greater Boston colleges around the Harvard campus on December 8, 1964 to express support for students in their free-speech controversy at the Berkeley campus of the University of California. (AP/WIDE WORLD PHOTOS)

bers, on such subjects as techniques of civil disobedience and literature of the NEW LEFT. The free-university movement began at the University of California at Berkeley in late 1964 during the FREE SPEECH MOVE-MENT. The Free University of California was founded at Berkeley in February 1966. STUDENTS FOR A DEMOCRA-TIC SOCIETY (SDS) became especially active in creating free universities, setting up more than 100 of them in the 1965–66 academic year.

Free University of Berlin Revolt (Germany) a series of student demonstrations, strikes, and other forms of protest in the spring of 1965 at the Free University of Berlin, which had been founded in 1949 as a counter-point to the "unfree" Humboldt University in Commu-nist East Berlin. The first event was precipitated when the professor of the Philosophy Faculty, anticipating the 20th anniversary of the fall of the Third Reich, invited Karl Jaspers to address a special convocation scheduled for May 8. Jaspers's poor health prevented his acceptance, but the left-wing *Konvent* (student government) leaders who were elected in January (ironically, with the support

of right-wing representatives) learned of the professor's effort. They countered by inviting Erich Kuby, whose insulting criticisms of the Free University (including the accusation that it was a creature of the cold war) had offended members of the faculty and administration. Both the rector and the senate refused to allow Kuby to speak, but he addressed a protest meeting at the Tech-nische Hochschule, and the student leaders denounced the rector as a reactionary authoritarian who had denied Kuby's constitutional rights. This rector-student con-frontation was further exacerbated when the rector not only denied tenure to but dismissed a political science professor, trained in the United States, who had sent an open letter to a Berlin newspaper criticizing the rector and appealing for public demonstrations as a protest. From May through late July, students protested in the *Konvent* (assembly), demonstrated in the streets (some-times protesting the Vietnam War), held strikes, and demanded both the rector's resignation and equal student representation with faculty and administrators in the uni-versity's governance. The student revolt led to election of a new, liberal rector for 1965–66, but then the senate forbade any form of political-activity use of university facilities—a ban that generated more student protests and caused the ban to be rescinded. These events raised questions about repression of dissent at the university and about the viability of the Free University "model" of autonomy—other universities were governed by the states, while the Free University was governed by the senate and the rector. But older faculty members' memories of how the Nazis had taken control of the DEUTSCHE STUDENTENSCHAFT and the universities remained fresh; in addition only about 250 students (4 percent of the student body) were actually involved in the protests. *See also* FREIE UNIVERSITÄT BERLIN.

Freideutsche Jugend (Free German Youth) (Germany) an association initially of 13 youth organizations formed in October 1913 as a result of the convocation at HÖHE MEISSNER and later joined by many of the WANDERVOGEL groups. Members of the Freideutsche Jugend were committed not to use alcohol or tobacco and to promote self-determination and social and cultural reforms—"at their own initiative, on their own responsibility, and with deep sincerity"—marking a break with the adult society. In July 1913 member groups had met in Jena to try to solidify their unity before the Höhe Meissner convocation, despite representing disparate political orientations—such as nationalism, socialism, and communism—while disassociating themselves from any political party's agenda. They managed to ameliorate the Austrian groups' insistence on racial purity that would have excluded Jews, Slavs, and others to keep the movement open to all, including girls. (Anti-Semitism would resurface as an issue later, however, notably during a 1916 Freideutsche Jugend convention.) In the last years of World War I and the postwar years, the Freideutsche Jugend movement was sundered by efforts to force its adoption of right-wing or left-wing political views—a struggle that first emerged at a convention in Solling in October 1917. In spring 1918 all the major youth groups had agreed to join the Friedeutsche Jugend, but at Jena in spring 1919, about 150 members (mostly socialist oriented) of the movement convened to try to devise a means of effecting this potential unity and failed. At the 1920 convention in Hofgeismar, the political disagreements predominated. After that the Freideutscher Jugend slowly disintegrated, and by the end of 1923 it had died. It had represented probably the last viable hope of attaining the German youth movement's ideal of a single unified organization.

Freie Deutsche Jugend (FDJ) (Germany) the official state organization for youths in the former German Democratic Republic (East Germany) established following World War II, with branches initially in West Germany. Modeled after the Komsomol of the Soviet Union, FDJ became officially an adjunct of the Communist Party in April 1957. Since it was the official youth organization and essentially a monopoly, FDJ claimed a membership of millions.

Freiensozialistischen Jugend (Free Socialist Youth) (Germany) a Marxist-oriented working-class youth movement of the 1920s dedicated to work reforms for youths. The organization advocated a six-hour work day for those under age 18, apprenticeship training in state schools, the outlawing of nighttime and Sunday work by children, four weeks of annual fully paid holiday for working youths, the outlawing of work by children under 16, sixteen years of required schooling, provision for working youths of full pay and free education during school hours, and other reforms, including the abolition of military service. A communist section of the organization published its own newspaper, *The Young Guard*, having a circulation of 15,000.

Freie Universität Berlin (Free University of Berlin) (Germany) a city university founded by students and the government of West Berlin in 1948 as both an actual and symbolic defiance of the Free City of Berlin's isolation within Communist East Germany. A catalyst for its founding was a student demonstration in West Berlin on April 23, 1947—the first post-World War II student demonstration—requesting creation of a free and democratic university; both the public and the occupying Allied forces immediately backed the request. The expulsion in April 1948 of three students from Humboldt University (East Berlin) who were editors of the short-lived *Colloquium* for expressing critical views of the university in their journal also added impetus for creation of the Free University. From its beginning, the Free University was intended as a reform institution, where the dominant role of the *ordentlichen professoren* (full professors) was greatly modified, and students and teachers existed more as a community, so that the Free University would serve as an example of a new, republican type of higher education in Germany. During the 1950s, however, the Free University's administration and functions became increasingly bureaucratized. On the other hand, the students became increasingly involved with international events—for example, supporting the independence movement in Algeria.

This political involvement began to take on demonstrative form with the December 1964 protest against the West Berlin visit of Congolese Prime Minister Moise Tshombe—a protest spearheaded by the SOZIALISTISCHER DEUTSCHER STUDENTENBUND (SDS). This protest at Tempelhof Airport resulted in student demonstrators—aroused because police secretly exited Tshombe through a secondary exit to avoid the protestors; students breached a police cordon for the first time. Following in the wake of this episode in 1965 occurred the more serious FREE UNIVERSITY OF BERLIN REVOLT. The students' growing political involvement also eventuated in the BERLIN ANTI-SHAH PROTEST of 1967 and the many student protests in Berlin and throughout Germany that occurred in 1968. *See*, for example, the EASTER RIOTS and the Munich Students' Sit-down Strike.

Freie Wissenschaftliche Vereinigung (FWV) (Germany) a liberal student organization founded at Berlin University in the summer of 1881 in opposition to the nationalistic and anti-Semitic policies of the VEREIN DEUTSCHER STUDENTEN (VDS). Terming itself a "free association" dedicated to open scholarly discussion, with membership available to students of all faiths, the FWV attracted a sizable Jewish membership and spread to the universities at Breslau, Halle, Strassburg, and Leipzig. But it attracted only about one-third of the membership of the VDSt, and its chapters soon dissolved at all but Berlin University, where it endured into the early 20th century.

Freistudentenschaft *See* DEUTSCHE FREISTUDENTENSCHAFT.

Frente Popular Tierra y Libertad (FPTyL) (Mexico) an organization formed in 1976 and led by student activists who had been involved in or inspired by the 1968–71 student movement. They had subsequently turned their attention to land invasions (squatting or appropriation) in Monterrey, where extreme housing shortages afflicted the poor. Students led many of the Monterrey land invasions after 1968 in an effort to organize the urban poor into a protest movement. Notably, student militants led the Colonia Tierra y Libertad invasion, organizing the poor as a community to provide water, housing, schools, electricity, and other needs. The *colonia* succeeded in resisting government repression of the movement, enabling it to support other movements and formation of the FPTyL, led by students who had organized the *colonia*. The FPTyL included 31 *colonias populares* (poor urban neighborhoods), plus tenant groups and other associations that involved as many as 350,000 people in its work. Militant students also organized similar groups in Durango and Juchitán, providing leadership and structure for these urban protest movements.

Front de Libération Nationale (FLN) (Algeria) the major organization that promoted Algerian independence from France, founded by the young militants of the Comité Révolutionnaire d'Unité et d'Action (CRUA), which was formed in March 1954 to acquire funds and equipment to support a war of liberation and to train what became the Armée de Libération Nationale (ALN). In October 1954 CRUA reconstituted itself as the FLN, and it launched the war on November 1 with

acts of terrorism and a demand for creation of a sovereign Algeria with citizenship open to all resident Algerians. Once the war began, hundreds of students from the University of Algiers joined the FLN and the ALN. By 1956 most of the other organizations devoted to nationalism had joined the FLN, which in August of that year reorganized as a governmental body and assumed responsibility as the sole representative of Algeria in any negotiations with France. Its executive committee (CCCE) established a provisional government in exile in Tunis in 1958. The war continued until March 18, 1962 when the French signed a cease-fire agreement. A referendum conducted on July 1 resulted in a proclamation of Algerian independence two days later. The FLN became the only legal political party in the new nation.

Future Farmers of America (FFA) (United States) a nationwide, nonprofit, educational organization for students of vocational agriculture founded in Kansas City, Missouri in November 1928. FFA was afforded incorporation by Congress in 1950; it is sponsored by the Agricultural Service of the Department of Education. Membership is open to all farm youths or other students of vocational agriculture in secondary public schools; they may retain their membership for three years following graduation from high school or until the age of 21. Four ranks are awarded to members on the basis of achievement in farming, scholarship, leadership, earnings, and investment: Green Hand and Chapter Farmer awarded by individual chapters; State Farmer, by the state association; and American Farmer, by the national organization. Members may also win medals, scholarships, and cash awards. They raise animals and crops for exhibit at state and county fairs, help farmers improve farming techniques, repair buildings and equipment, and pursue other endeavors related to farming. Among the FFA's many purposes are the development of agricultural leadership and cooperation, the encouragement of improvements in farming, the promotion of character and citizenship, the fostering of scholarship, and the provision of rural recreational activities. There are chapters in all 50 states and Puerto Rico.

Future Homemakers of America (FHA) (United States) an organization formed in 1945 for students in junior high school or high school who are enrolled in home-economics classes. Sponsors of FHA are the U.S. Office of Education and the American Home Economics Association. Among its purposes are the promotion of interest in home economics, including pursuit of careers in this and related fields. FHA members provide services in both their schools and their communities, such as assisting the Red Cross, sponsoring discussions, and helping at Parent Teachers Association functions. FHA is governed by elected student officers at local, state, and national levels and also by adult advisory boards at each level. FHA publishes *Teen Times* on a quarterly basis.

Future Scientists of America (FSA)   (United States) a nationwide organization of clubs for students in grades 5 through 12 who are interested in the sciences. The National Science Teachers Association sponsors FSA. Each school-based club is essentially autonomous and develops its own programs for fostering the scientific interests of its members and encouraging learning and careers in the sciences. The national newsletter *Centrifuge* is sent to members each month.

Gakusei Rengo-kai (Student Federation) (Japan) the first student society committed to providing a nationwide organization of individual student groups. Gakusei Rengo-kai was founded at Tokyo University in 1922, and within a year it had spread throughout Japan and included high school as well as university groups. Some 40 groups comprised its membership, including SHINJIN-KAI and GYOMINKAI. Although the government tried to suppress the federation through arrests of its leaders, it held its first national meeting in 1924, when the organization had 49 member groups totaling 1,500 students. The members were polarized over defining the federation's primary purpose, one faction advocating revolutionary activism and the other the scholarly study of social problems. They compromised by adopting the purpose of propagating Marxism and remaining simply a student movement. In 1928 the minister of education ordered the presidents of the major universities to disband the so-called social science study groups, so by 1929, following the arrests of their leaders, the Gakusei Rengo-kai and its member groups were in various states of dissolution.

Gakusei Shakai Kagaku Rengo-kai (Student Federation of Social Science) (Japan) a successor to GAKU-SEI RENGO-KAI formed from that organization in 1924. At a meeting of Gakusei Rengo-kai two years after its formation, students debated whether the organization should be devoted to political theory or activism, they chose the former, generating the name change. The government consistently suppressed the organization, but the group attracted a sizable student membership and endured until 1929, when it was reorganized as the Student Group of Communist Youth.

Gallaudet University Revolution (United States) a student protest that occurred in March 1988 over the appointment of a new university president. Gallaudet University, the only college or university in the world dedicated solely to educating the deaf, was chartered by Congress in 1864 and sited in Washington, D.C. In its entire history the university had never had a deaf president. Its fourth president, Edward Merrill, retired in 1983; and his successor was short-lived in the position because of a scandal. In May 1984 the university's board of trustees, of whose 19 members only four were deaf, named Jerry Lee, then acting president and former vice president for business affairs, as president. But Lee left the position in December 1987 to become vice president of Bassett Furniture, a firm owned by Jane Bassett Spilman, chairman of the university's board—suggesting a conflict of interest on her part. To many, the moment seemed to have arrived for appointment of a deaf president. Merrill, students, alumni, and leaders of the deaf community advocated such an appointment. Many people at the university favored awarding the post to I. King Jordan, dean of the College of Arts and Sciences and former chairman of psychology, who was a Gallaudet graduate and had lost his hearing in an accident at age 22.

Although Jordan was among the three finalists, another of whom was also deaf, Spilman apparently favored the appointment of Elisabeth Zinser, then vice-chancellor for academic affairs at the University of North Carolina–Greensboro. On March 1, 1988 students and other supporters of appointing a deaf president held a rally on the university campus. On March 5–6, however, the board of trustees met secretly at the Willard Hotel and chose Zinser ostensibly on the grounds that of the three finalists she had the best administrative background.

Most of the faculty and staff, three-fourths of whom were hearing, accepted the appointment; but on the night of March 6, hundreds of disappointed students marched to the Mayflower Hotel to hear Spilman defend the choice. The following morning the students used cars to blockade the entrance gates to the university, and classes were suspended. The student protestors carried signs bearing such slogans as "Deaf President Now!" and "Deaf Power, Fight for Deaf President." That afternoon Spilman tried to address a thousand of the student protestors assembled in the university's field house. She defended Zinser's appointment as "lawful, proper, and final." Students shouted and stamped their feet in protest and then marched to the Capitol. They were not disruptive, and no arrests occurred.

On March 7 major deaf community groups, including the National Association of the Deaf, joined by the alumni association, publicly supported the students' demands. These demands were that (1) a deaf president be appointed, (2) Spilman resign, (3) the board have a majority of deaf members, and (4) there be no reprisals against the protestors. Students at state schools for the deaf held sympathy strikes; contributions poured in for the Deaf President Now Fund—$39,000 by the end of the week. To organize national and congressional lobbying efforts, a Deaf President Now Council was set up, with students, faculty, alumni, and deaf organization members.

Zinser came to Washington, D.C. on March 9 to assume the presidency immediately, rather than waiting till the end of term as she had planned. Again students blockaded the university's gates, preventing her from entering the campus. Zinser met with the four leaders of the students—Tim Rarus, Bridgetta Bourne, Greg Hlibok, and Jerry Covell, all deaf children of deaf parents. She asked them to withdraw their demands and stated that she would appoint an advisory panel and would also study Gallaudet's culture and learn sign language. Not placated, the students rejected her effort to negotiate. Nevertheless, at noon on March 9 following the meeting, Zinser declared at the National Press Club, "I am in charge"; and she promised to take whatever steps might be necessary to restore order. In the afternoon she met with Spilman; Representative David Bonior, a Democrat from Michigan; and Representative Steve Grunderson, a Republican from Wisconsin. Both congressmen, who were also Gallaudet trustees, had met earlier with student leaders and now urged Zinser to consider resigning. At the same time the Gallaudet faculty met and, by a vote of 147 to 5, asked for Spilman's resignation; they also voted 136 to 11 in support of the students' demands. Jordan announced his support of the students on March 10, describing himself as angered by the trustees' "continuing lack of confidence . . . in deaf people . . . ." On March 11, Zinser announced her resignation. On March 13, Spilman announced hers; the same day the trustees met in an emergency session and named Jordan president of the university, with Philip Bravin, a deaf IBM executive, replacing Spilman as chairman of the board.

The students had won all of their demands, except the third; but Bravin promised that as vacancies occurred newly appointed board members would be deaf whenever possible. This singular and rapidly achieved student success was deemed attributable to their entirely peaceable and polite tactics—no violence, hostility toward police, obscenities, or expressions of hatred punctuated their protests. They had taken their cue from Mohandas Ghandi and Martin Luther King Jr.; and they had organized their efforts with extreme efficiency. Their success constituted a revolution in the history of Gallaudet University, which after 124 years finally had a deaf president.

Bibliography: Harold Orlans, "The Revolution at Gallaudet," *Change* 21, No. 1 (January–February 1989), 8–18.

Gemeinschaft Studentischer Verbande (GSstV, Community of Student Leagues) (Germany) an organization of fraternity leagues formed in January 1935 by the Nazi chairman of the fraternity leagues as a countermeasure to the formation of the VOLKISCHER WAFFENRING. Admission to membership required that a fraternity belong to the ALLGEMEINE DEUTSCHER WAFFENRING (ADW) and prove it had no Freemason or "non-Aryan" members. The GSstV received official Nazi Party sanction in March 1935, so all the leagues, including those in the breakaway Volkischer Waffenring, joined it. The internecine struggles evidenced in creation of the GStV became inconsequential on May 15, 1936 when Rudolf Hess decreed that no member of any Nazi Party organization could belong to a fraternity. Thereafter the fraternities withered.

George Junior Republic (United States) a juvenile reform movement—founded in 1895 at Freeville (near Ithaca), New York, by William R. George (1866–1936)— whose major purpose was to rehabilitate urban delinquent, poor, and immigrant youths of both sexes. Because George supported racial integration as well as integration of the sexes, African Americans were admitted on a regular basis from 1897 onward. Among the Junior Republic's major supporters were Theodore Roosevelt, Washington Gladden, Stephen S. Wise, and Jacob A. Riis. When it began, the Junior Republic had about 200 citizens living on a farm of about 250 acres. What made the Junior Republic distinctive as an experiment was that its citizens were self-governing. Young men and women age 16 to 21, they wrote their own constitution and laws, elected their own officials, chose their own judges and operated their own courts, and created and administered their own penal system. The Junior Republic's motto was "Nothing without Labor," and its citizens were employed in carpentry, farming, baking, printing, public works, hotels, and restaurants. In exchange for their work, they received republic money, which they were free to spend on food, clothing, and lodging of their choice. Consequently, the most prosperous (those who were the most thrifty and hardest working) dined at the best restaurants and had the best living accommodations in the republic; the poorest ate at the "Beanery" and slept in the "Garroot," a dormitory on the top floor of the hotel. The indigent were provided free meals and lodging at the jail for three days and thereafter were arrested as vagrants and obliged to work for free. Hence, virtually everyone preferred to be gainfully employed and supported strict enforcement of the republic's laws and protection of private-property rights. Offenders were sentenced to hard labor, assigned a number, dressed in stripes (in the republic's early years), and sent to jail. The George Junior Republic generated widespread public support from various civic groups and individuals as well as voluminous articles in newspapers and magazines. The concept and apparent success of this unique institution had such great appeal that there were soon seven Junior Republics—five of them created by women's organizations—affiliated in the National Association of Junior Republics founded in 1908. There were two in New Jersey and one each in California, Maryland, Connecticut, and Pennsylvania, in addition to the original republic. Through its principles and programs, the George Junior Republic served a significant experimental role in the reform of educational and penal systems.

Bibliography: Jack M. Holl, *Juvenile Reform in the Progressive Era: William R. George and the Junior Republic Movement* (Ithaca, N.Y.: Cornell University Press, 1971).

Germania (Germany) a liberal student movement founded at the Friedrich-Alexander University in Erlangen, Bavaria in 1827 as an offshoot of the BURSCHENSCHAFTEN. The organizers invited the participation of other universities in order to disseminate the movement, but liberalism did not attract a large following in the following decade, perhaps because of the repressive effects of the 1819 CARLSBAD DECREES. Even as late as 1832–36, some 1,200 students were prosecuted for belonging to Burschenschaften.

Gesellenverbande (Germany) brotherhoods, or fraternities, of young journeymen apprentices in trades and professions that existed in the 16th and 17th centuries. Equivalent groups existed in other countries as well, such as the *compagnonnages* in France. These youths, mostly apprenticed by age 14 or even younger, were sons who were barred from inheriting family property because of a system in which the eldest son inherited everything. A brotherhood member was initiated in a ceremony that involved giving up his family name, receiving a secret nickname, undergoing a symbolic baptism, and receiving a "godfather" within the brotherhood. The brotherhood committed the member to following a code of ethics for his trade or profession that included regarding his master as a father. Brotherhoods also encouraged celibacy. Many journeymen of the Gesellenverbande entered a tradi-

tional Wanderjahr (called "tramping" in England and *tour de France* in France) during which they migrated throughout Europe, stopping at designated houses of call to practice their trade before returning home to earn their master status. The Gesellenverbande and their counterparts in other countries lasted well into the 19th century, although in altered forms, as did the tradition of the Wanderjahr.

Ghana National Students' Organization (GNSO) (Ghana) a university students' organization created in 1964 by the Convention People's Party (CPP), headed by President Kwame Nkrumah, as a rival to the NATIONAL UNION OF GHANA STUDENTS (NUGS). The latter was at the time effectively defunct because government authorities had arrested many of its leaders following NUGS's protest against Nkrumah's dictatorial intervention in judicial proceedings and removal of the chief magistrate of a special court. GNSO lost its reason for being after the February 24, 1966 army coup that ended Nkrumah's regime.

Giessener Schwarzen (Giessen Blacks) (Germany) a radical right wing of the BURSCHENSCHAFTEN, centered at the University of Giessen. The group was dedicated to nationalism and the attainment of a "pure" German nation from which those with French, Slavic, or Jewish blood would be exiled. The black sect's leader was Karl FOLLEN, and among its members was Karl SAND, the assassin of August Kotzebue.

Girl Guides (Great Britain) the girls' counterpart to the BOY SCOUTS. In September 1909 during the Boy Scouts' first major rally, held at the Crystal Palace, a group of uninvited "Girl Scouts"—dressed in scout hats and scarves and holding staves—appeared and requested an inspection from Chief Scout Robert BADEN-POWELL. As a result Baden-Powell and his sister Agnes wrote *Girl Guides: A Suggestion for Character Training for Girls*. Agnes became head of this new organization, with an office at Boy Scout Headquarters. Registration for membership in the Girl Guides began in May 1910. (The name *Guides* was borrowed from that of an Indian regiment.) In 1912 the Baden-Powells adapted *Scouting for Boys* as a handbook for the Girl Guides and entitled it *How Girls Can Help Build Up the Empire*. Both the Promise and the Law of the Guides replicated those for the Boy Scouts. In its early years, the organization faltered because of weak leadership and a weak program, but in 1925 Lord Baden-Powell attained a charter of incorporation, became chairman, and created a committee of young women to manage the organization. Success followed. In 1917 Baden-Powell rewrote the handbook, updating its ideas; it was reissued as *Girl Guiding* in 1918, the same year in which his wife Olave became chief guide. She was named world chief guide at the organization's sixth International

Guide Conference in 1930; she held this post for more than 40 years. The Girl Guides became the largest youth movement in Great Britain. The Brownies branch, created in 1924 for girls age 7 ¹/₂ to 11, is the most popular organization for girls under age 11 in Great Britain. At age 11 girls may become members of a Guide Company; and at 15 they may move up to the Rangers (Air, Sea, or Land), a branch created in 1920 for girls between 15 and 21. The Guides movement spread worldwide, although its equivalent organization in the United States and some other nations is the GIRL SCOUTS. Most of these groups belong to the World Association of Girl Guides and Girl Scouts established in 1928.

Bibliography: Alix Liddell, *The Girl Guides, 1910–1970* (London: Muller, 1970); Olave Baden-Powell, as told to Mary Drewery, *Window on My Heart* (London: Hodder and Staughton, 1973).

Girls' Clubs Movement (Great Britain) roughly contemporaneous with the BOYS' CLUBS MOVEMENT but with different purposes, a movement that began in the 1860s to provide social opportunities for girls and to prevent their falling victim to various social vices. The movement apparently dates to 1861 when Lady Kinnaird began a club for girls in her own home and a religious guild set up a girls' club in Bristol. Unlike boys clubs, such groups and later related organizations were not geared expressly to adolescents but to both girls and young women, including working women. The most tireless advocate for establishing a girls' clubs movement was Maude Stanley, who founded the Soho Club for Girls in 1880 and the Girls' Club Union (GCU) in 1883. The GCU in 1890 had 17 London clubs and 11 provincial clubs as members. The movement dwindled thereafter but revived after 1911 when the National Council of Women and the Women's Industrial Council amalgamated to form the National Organization of Girls' Clubs; in 1926 this group reorganized as the National Association of Girls' Clubs (NAGC). Through the years, membership in the NAGC went well beyond girls' clubs as such to include such groups as the GIRLS FRIENDLY SOCIETY and the YOUNG WOMEN'S CHRISTIAN ASSOCIATION (YWCA)

Girls' Clubs of America (United States) an organization for girls similar in purpose and programs to the BOYS' CLUBS OF AMERICA. The first Girls' Club was formed in Waterbury, Connecticut in 1864, but the national organization was not established until 1945 when 19 clubs joined in its creation. Although open to all girls age 6 to 18, the Girls' Clubs' primary purpose is to serve those who are disadvantaged, with a focus on building character through educational, social, health, recreational, community-service, and vocational programs. Each club has its own building; many have libraries, kitchens, game rooms, craft rooms, swimming pools, and

other amenities. Club members of high school age may compete for the Girls' Club Citizenship Award, which includes a trip to Washington, D.C. and meetings with government officials and is based on outstanding community service.

Girl Scouts (United States) an organization for girls modeled after the GIRL GUIDES of Great Britain and founded in 1912. While on a visit to England, Juliette Gordon Low decided that the United States needed a Girl Guides program; she founded the first one in Savannah, Georgia in 1912. In 1915 the organization established a national headquarters in Washington, D.C. and changed its name to Girl Scouts. The Girl Scouts grew rapidly with the impetus of World War I when they marched in parades in their khaki uniforms and sold war bonds, so that by 1920 there were 50,000 members. In 1930 membership exceeded that of the CAMP FIRE GIRLS; by 1970 the Girl Scouts had nearly 4 million members. The Girl Scout Promise commits the members to be trustworthy, helpful, loyal, courteous, "a friend to all," friendly to animals, obedient, cheerful, thrifty, and "clean in thought, word, and deed."

A fashion parade of Girl Scout uniforms from the past to the present was a feature of the 38th National Convention of the Girl Scouts in 1969, attended by 8,000 conventioneers. Modeled from left to right are the 1912 adult uniform, the 1918 uniform, the junior uniform of 1969, and the adult uniform of 1969. (AP/WIDE WORLD PHOTOS)

Girl Scout groups are organized by age, the Brownies (age 7–8) being the youngest. Junior Girl Scouts is for age 9–11. These first two groupings comprise the majority of Girl Scout members. Cadette Girl Scouts is for age 12–14; Senior Girl Scouts, age 15–17. Campus Girl Scouts was established in 1968 to promote older girls' continuing affiliation with the organization. Girls are offered training and service opportunities in numerous activities and receive badges for achieving proficiency. To augment its camping program, the organization established in 1968 the Girl Scout National Center West on a 5,265-hectare (13,000-acre) site in Wyoming. The Girl Scouts has been strongly committed to fostering friendship and harmony among girls from disparate racial, ethnic, and socioeconomic groups. In 1996 the Girl Scouts of the U.S.A. had a total membership of 3.2 million.

Girls' Friendly Society (Great Britain) an organization founded by the Church of England in 1875 for young women who leave home to work in factories. Membership categories are Candidates, age 7–11; Members, 11–14; Senior Members, 14–21; and Townsend Members, older than 21. The society operates both residential and holiday hostels. In 1877 the first U.S. branch of the society opened in Lowell, Massachusetts under the auspices of the Episcopal Church, making it one of the first Protestant organizations for girls in the nation.

Girls' Guildry (Great Britain) the first British organization for girls that required its members to wear uniforms. Modeled upon the BOYS' BRIGADE, it was founded in Glasgow in 1900 by Dr. William Francis Somerville and the older girls from his Sunday School class meeting by his invitation at the Anderson Church Hall. Following the example of their model, the members drilled and marched. Their uniform consisted of a navy blue shirt, a boater (straw hat), a white blouse, and a red sash; their badge symbol was an Eastern lamp. The stated purpose of the Girls' Guildry was to promote "capacities of womanly helpfulness" in the members. By 1903 there were 24 companies in Scotland and seven in England. In 1939, when World War II began, the Girls' Guildry had a total membership of 24,000, with 338 companies in Scotland, 131 in England, and three each in Wales and Northern Ireland. During the mid-1960s, the Girls' Guildry joined with the GIRLS' LIFE BRIGADE and the Girls' Brigade of Ireland (with combined memberships totaling 100,000 girls younger than 21) to become the Girls' Brigade; it became the Boys' Brigade's sister organization.

Girls' Life Brigade (Great Britain) an organization founded in 1902 by the National Sunday School Union as a girls' equivalent of the Boys' Life Brigade. The Brigade's Four Square Programme emphasizes spiritual, physical, educational, and social training—the first four

letters of these spelling *SPES*, the Latin word for "hope." The brigade spread worldwide, with the first overseas company established in Cape Town, South Africa in 1925. In the mid-1960s, the organization joined with the GIRLS' GUILDRY and the Girls' Brigade of Ireland—all three being sister organizations of the BOYS' BRIGADE, which had absorbed the Boys' Life Brigade—to form a single organization, the Girls' Brigade.

Gorres Ring (Germany) a student organization founded in 1926 as a Roman Catholic alternative to the HOCHSCHULRING DEUTSCHER ART. The Gorres Ring eventuated from a controversy that followed the failed Nazi Beer Hall Putsch of November 1923 in Munich. The chairman of the Munich Hochschulring, who was also editor of the organization's national publication *Deutsche Akademische Stimmen*, wrote and published a denunciation of the Roman Catholic church's alleged involvement in precluding the putsch's success. He also published articles by Nazis and other right-wingers who supported the putsch, including articles that scurrilously attacked the church and Christianity as a whole. Although the Berlin Hochschulring publicly deplored these articles, the national organization temporized. As a result, Catholic students began to break away from the Hochschulring, at first forming their own groups associated with it and finally forming the Gorres Ring. Although it took a moderate stance, the Gorres Ring supported nationalism and the folk community (Volksgemeinschaft) concepts advocated by the Hochschulring. In the early 1930s, however, the Gorres Ring moved increasingly to the Right, viewing Benito Mussolini's Italian Fascism as exemplifying an acceptable alternative to the Weimar Republic. As with other student groups, the Gorres Ring was displaced by the ascendancy of the Nazi student movement (NATIONAL SOCIALIST GERMAN STUDENT UNION) in the thirties.

Göttingen Gemeinderat (Germany) a communal council formed at the beginning of 1831 in the city of Göttingen by university students, faculty, and some townspeople as a rebellion against the Hanoverian government headed by King Wilhelm in Münster. The Hanoverian revolt had surfaced in Brunswick (Braunschweig) and Osterode and had inspired the creation of the Göttingen Gemeinderat, which assumed virtual executive and legislative powers. For more than a week, the Gemeinderat succeeded in keeping at bay both the Hanoverian military and opposition within Göttingen by supporters of Wilhelm; it then accepted the government's ultimatum that it capitulate unconditionally and peacefully.

Göttingen Seven (Die Göttingen Sieben) (Germany) seven professors dismissed from Georg August

University of Göttingen in 1837 by the infamous Ernst Augustus, recently become king of Hanover, because they protested against his arbitrary rescinding of the state's liberal 1833 constitution. Among the Göttingen Seven were the renowned historians Friedrich Dahlmann and Georg Gervinus and the philologist–folklorist Grimm Brothers, Jacob and Wilhelm. The dismissal was significant as a catalyst for student protests. Troops were sent to Göttingen to suppress the students' demonstrations there. The Göttingen Seven became instant martyrs for political liberals, and throughout Germany so-called Göttingen Associations sprang up to raise money for the professors until they could find other employment. As Jacob Grimm was ordered to leave Hanover immediately, both he and his brother departed for Kassel, where they had previously lived.

Great Proletarian Cultural Revolution (China) essentially a power struggle over ideology and policy that lasted from 1965 to 1968 in which Mao Zedong and his faction in the government and in the CHINESE COMMUNIST PARTY (CCP) purged the CCP, the universities, and the arts of those seen as opponents. Among Mao's major purposes in the Cultural Revolution was to attract young adherents to the CCP as the party of youth, to educate them politically, and to provide them with a "vanguard" role. Since 1949 the CCP had abjured youths to denounce their fathers and their bourgeois views, among other things, as a means of discarding the old Confucian values system; that effort intensified during the Cultural Revolution. Because the educational system was a priority of the Cultural Revolution, the government tried both to accommodate and to involve university students. The accommodation came on June 13, 1966 in the elimination of admissions examinations and in a move to revamp entrance requirements. At Beijing University especially, the Maoist faction involved students as activists in the political maneuvering to remove opponents. But the students' greatest involvement nationwide occurred through their service in the RED GUARDS, which entailed their absence from the universities for an entire year.

Greens (Germany) a political party officially launched in 1980, although it fielded candidates for communal elections in Schleswig-Holstein as early as 1977. The Greens' founding congresses were held in January and March 1980 and involved many veterans of the student movement of the 1960s and 1970s who had interest in socialism and environmentalism. Notable among those involved in these congresses, for example, were former student-movement leaders Daniel COHN-BENDIT and Rudi DUTSCHKE. In regional elections of the early 1980s, the Greens derived two-thirds of their support from young voters under 25. From the party's beginnings, the Greens have had sizable support among university students.

Greensboro Riot (United States) a violent student protest in Greensboro, North Carolina in May 1969 punctuated by sniper fire. The protest originated at the all-black Dudley High School on May 21, when students erupted into anger and rock throwing after a militant student was barred as a candidate in a school election. Police dispersed the high schoolers with tear gas, but students at the North Carolina Agricultural and Technical University rose to their support. Sniper fire and rock throwing at whites in cars passing the campus reportedly ensued. On May 22 a student was found dead of a sniper wound; students blamed the police, although the shot may have been fired by a student or by armed white youths in the area. The president closed the university, and the mayor imposed a curfew. On May 23 sniper fire from a dormitory impeded police movements, and troops of the National Guard entered the scene to clear the campus, using tear gas and rifle fire. Police and Guard members sprayed tear gas and smoke over the dormitory from a plane and a helicopter. They arrested 200 students and confiscated eight guns.

Greensboro Sit-In (United States) an event of the U.S. Civil Rights movement that began on February 1, 1960 in Greensboro, North Carolina. On that day four African-American students from North Carolina Agricultural and Technical College sat down at a lunch counter in a Woolworth store reserved "for whites only" and requested service. Although refused service, they stayed seated. The next day, 30 students participated in the quiet demonstration. There had been earlier, ineffectual sit-ins, but this event captured public interest. Thus was born the sit-in protest movement, making use of a nonviolent tactic for spotlighting the injustices of racial discrimination and segregation. Within only two weeks, sit-ins occurred in 15 other towns. The tactic was widely adopted and spread rapidly throughout the South, involving tens of thousands of students, both blacks and whites. The sit-ins effected an advance in the Civil Rights movement, comprised the catalyst for the subsequent student movement as a whole, inspired the nonviolence of the SAN FRANCISCO CITY HALL DEMONSTRATION and other protests through the early 1960s, and generated the creation of the STUDENT NONVIOLENT COORDINATING COMMITTEE (SNCC). The original Greensboro sit-in also eventuated in the 1963 effort by 1,000 black students from the Agricultural and Technical College to integrate two cinemas and a downtown cafeteria in Greensboro; one of their demonstrations resulted in the jailing of 241 students and another in the jailing of 600.

Gremialistas (Chile) a grouping of politically, economically, and religiously conservative middle-class and upper-middle-class students of the 1950s and 1960s,

Three Woman's College students aided African-American students here protesting refusal of five-and-dime stores to serve them at lunch counters.   (AP/WIDE WORLD PHOTOS)

mostly centered at the Catholic University. Its name derived from their advocacy of student issues only—that is, a *gremial* (guild) focus. The Gremialistas won control of the FEDERACIÓN DE ESTUDIANTES DE CHILE (FECH) in 1969. Many of the most involved Gremialistas were products of the University of Chicago's monetarist economics school, as the United States government awarded fellowships to 150 Chilean students to study at Chicago during the years 1956–61; in Chile they were referred to as the Chicago Boys, and after graduating from Chicago many of them returned to teach at the Catholic University. Many were recruited to serve in the government that succeeded Salvador Allende's in 1973. The Chicago Boys populated the Office of National Planning (ODEPLAN). During the 1970s, the Gremialista movement spread to many other university campuses besides Catholic University, and members assumed leadership roles in student governments at these campuses. From 1985 on, however, center-left students began to displace them.

Grossdeutsche Jugend (Greater German Youth Movement)   (Germany) a Nazi Party youth organization whose creation was announced in Saxony in early 1924. As other youth organizations joined it, the move-

ment formed the basis for the creation in 1926 of the HITLER JUGEND.

Grossdeutsche Jungenbund   (Germany) an umbrella organization of all the BUNDE created on March 30, 1933, in an effort to salvage the existence of the Bunde in the face of the threatened hegemony of the HITLER JUGEND. The titular leader of the Jungenbund was Admiral Adolf von Trotha (1868–1940). By April 15, however, von Trotha and other leaders had already decided to integrate the Jungenbund with the Nazi movement, although disagreements with the Hitler Jugend persisted. Then on June 17, 1933, the day Baldur von SCHIRACH became supreme Nazi youth leader, the Jungenbund was dissolved—its brief existence suggesting only futility.

Gruppi Universitaria Fascisti (GUF)   (Italy) a revolutionary Fascist student group founded in 1920 that later became a nationwide student organization, devoted to indoctrinating youths in the tenets of Italian Fascism. The GUF also provided its members a means of rising within the Fascist Party. Ironically, the party tolerated nonconformist views among GUF members, resulting later in a clandestine GUF movement that opposed the regime.

Guatemala Revolution (Guatemala) a nonviolent revolution in 1944 initiated by students at the University of San Carlos against the dictatorial government of General Jorge Ubico Castañeda. In early 1944 the students had organized the University Students Association, which petitioned the government to replace the university's dean. Surprisingly, Ubico willingly negotiated with the students. Encouraged, the students on June 22 demanded other changes, including the government's granting of autonomy to the university. Considering the new and broadened demands a challenge to his authority, Ubico immediately assembled his cabinet (he had done so only once before during his 13-year rule). The government then not only rejected the students' demands but also suspended all constitutional rights on the grounds of maintaining order. In response on June 23, the students called for a general strike, and teachers immediately came to their support. On June 24 the students initiated the strike with a demonstration in San Carlos—they marched through the city's streets to a mass assembly at the National Palace Plaza, where the Atlantic Charter was read publicly. (Drafted by President Franklin D. Roosevelt and Prime Minister Winston Churchill during their August 1941 meeting at Argentia, Newfoundland, the charter defined war aims against the Fascist powers as well as postwar goals.) They were joined by 311 prominent professionals who on the same day petitioned Ubico to resign.

Ubico's response was brutal police attacks that evening against any groups that violated the capital's curfew, and on June 25 troops occupied the city. On that day, a Sunday, a patrol of cavalry attacked a group of women dressed in mourning clothes, wounding several and killing one, a teacher. On June 26, a general protest strike closed banks, stores, schools, and offices. Students distributed leaflets urging strikers to resist peacefully and to avoid any hostile acts. The strike spread to other towns. Ubico tried to salvage the situation by firing the head of the secret police, but the strike continued. On July 1, conceding failure to end the nonviolent protest, Ubico resigned; a junta of three generals assumed control of the government and promised elections. But the junta, controlled by General Federico Ponce Vaides rigged the October 13 elections in its favor. On October 20 disaffected junior officers took control of the honor guard at the Presidential Palace, killing one loyalist in the process. General Ponce ordered loyal troops to attack the rebel officers, but assembling crowds came to their support. Students armed themselves with rifles and stones to help defend the rebels, and many troops defected to the rebel side. The junta generals took refuge in foreign embassies and were replaced by another three-man junta that promised and carried out free elections and the drafting of a new constitution. This ushered in nearly 10 years of democratic government. Thus, Guatemalan university students had instigated a peaceful revolution, but it eventuated in the need for a military coup to effect its fruition.

Bibliography: Jim Handy, *Gift of the Devil: A History of Guatemala* (Boston: South End Press, 1984).

Guy Fawkes Night Riots (Great Britain) a series of protests and riots that occurred in Oxford in 1867 in a classic town-versus-gown conflict. Guy Fawkes Night (November 5), a festival that celebrates the failure of the 1605 Gunpowder Plot to blow up the House of Lords (in which Hawkes was a co-conspirator), was in Oxford traditionally followed by a violent riot involving university and town youths; the riot was tolerated by local authorities because it allowed the youths to expend their aggressive energies. But in 1867 the town youths were joined by townspeople in a protest over the price of bread. The protestors finally gathered at Balliol College in support of a strike by stonemasons at the college. They demonstrated for two nights, causing both town and university authorities to order up troops; then instead the authorities unleashed the university student cadet corps, armed with clubs, against the protestors on the third night. A bloody riot and battle of unprecedented violence ensued that virtually constituted class warfare.

Gyominkai (Men of Dawn Society) (Japan) a student organization founded at Waseda University in 1921. Its Gyomin Kyosanto (Men of Dawn Communist Party) was the ostensible front for the underground Communist Party founded in 1921; both were suppressed by the government, and their leaders were arrested. (The Japan Communist Party was founded in Moscow on July 15, 1922 by Japanese delegates and members of the Comintern; it was suppressed into nonexistence within a year.)

Habonim   (Great Britain) probably the most important of the Zionist youth movements in Great Britain. Habonim originated in 1929 as a scouting group, but by 1934 it was formally affilliated with the Zionist movement. Its significance lay in the fact that it was the first to be involved in the British Chalutz movement—that is, Habonim encouraged its members not only to settle in Palestine but also to join a kibbutz there. By 1970 some 3,000 members had settled in Israel, some founding their own kibbutzim.

Haile Selassie I University Riots   (Ethiopia) a series of student uprisings in Addis Ababa during 1968–69 that resulted in government closings of Haile Selassie I University. An uprising erupted on March 30, 1968 in response to a fashion show that featured models in miniskirts. Students pulled models and dignitaries from their cars, threw eggs at them, and punched them. In response, the government closed the university. The student riots, joined by high-school and primary-school students, continued throughout the week, with bloody student-police clashes and 37 students arrested. Emperor Haile Selassie ordered students back to school on April 8 but to no avail, so the Ministry of Education closed all schools in Addis Ababa. Weeks passed before the students returned to classes. On March 3, 1969 students began a strike that resulted in closing the university and all the secondary schools in Addis Ababa. The students presented demands to the government that included dismissing the minister of education, increasing the education budget, ending examination fees, and revising the system for allocating scholarships. On March 7 the emperor had schools reopened and ordered students to return to classes. The students balked, and many were arrested, suspended, or expelled. On March 29 a delegation of students met with the emperor and unsuccessfully pleaded for the release of the arrested students. On April

3 university students staged a sit-in; many students were arrested and one was killed. On April 4 the students held a mock funeral and demonstration; more than 1,000 students were arrested during the two days, and four students and one teacher received five-year prison terms. The confrontations continued through the year, and during an uprising in December, government security forces shot 20 students.

Halcones (Hawks)   (Mexico) a group of right-wing, paramilitary youths affiliated with the Mexico City police, who trained them in karate and using firearms and sometimes employed them to thwart student demonstrations. For example, when a leftist-organized student street demonstration occurred in the city on June 10, 1971, trucks and buses carrying hundreds of Halcones were allowed through police barricades; as police remained aloof, the Halcones attacked the student demonstrators for almost five hours, shooting and beating them. The Halcones pursued their student victims into stores, cinemas, and a Catholic hospital. The attack left 200 students injured and 11 dead. Public protest led to the resignations of the mayor and the chief of police. A government inquiry implicated a right-wing conspiracy within the Institutional Revolutionary Party (PRI), the party in power, to discredit President Luis Echeverría, whose policies had accommodated university students' demands and promoted freedom of the press and economic reforms.

Hambach Festival   (Germany) a massive 1832 gathering of students, peasants, tradesmen, and others devoted to the cause of nationhood—the largest and most significant demonstration for German unity to that time. Nearly 30,000 participants from throughout the German states convened in 1832 at the village of Hambach near Neustadt an der Haardt, ostenibly in celebration of the anniversary of the 1818 Bavarian Constitution. The festival began with a procession to the ruins of Hambach Castle that included flags of red, black, and gold—the colors of the BURSCHENSCHAFTEN and thus of the liberation movement. The flags bore the inscription "Germany's Rebirth." Among the organizers of the Hambach Festival was a journalist named Siebenpfeiffer who presented a speech entitled "The German May" in which he extolled the crowd not to celebrate the past but to fight for "freedom and German national honor" and for reestablishing "a fatherland and a free homeland." More than 20 speakers addressed the festival participants—all denouncing German disunity and advocating freedom and nationhood. They also voiced an "eternal curse" upon the kings of the states as "traitors of the people and the whole human race." But the participants could not agree on a plan of action for creating a viable organization and a program for attaining German sovereignty. The German Confederation responded to the Hambach Festival by arresting many of the participants; increasing surveillance of students and dissidents; forbidding the public display of the red, black, and gold colors; and outlawing public statements of opposition to the Confederation.

Haneda Incidents   (Japan) a series of student protests in October–November 1967 intended to prevent Prime Minister Sato Eisaku's departure from Tokyo's Haneda Airport for visits to Southeast Asia (beginning in South Vietnam) and the United States. Viewing these trips as support for U.S. imperialism, several factions of ZEN-GAKUREN (especially the ANTI-YOYOGI ZENGAKUREN and the HANSEN SEINEN IINKAI) gathered members in Tokyo on October 7 to stop Sato from leaving for Southeast Asia the following day. On the morning of October 8, about 3,000 students with clubs and helmets traveled by public commuter trains to Haneda Airport. About 1,500 occupied a platform at Oomori Station to prevent Sato's train from reaching the airport, but they were driven off by hundreds of riot police and thereafter made their way to the airport. When the students arrived at the three bridges entering the airport, they were blocked by police armored vehicles and were forced back with water cannons when they attacked. After the students tried to set fire to the vehicles, police circled around behind their positions and attacked them on the bridges. Some students jumped into the water; one student was killed. News of the death brought more students, reinforced by workers, to join the melee, but this time they were dispersed with tear gas. Some 600 protestors and perhaps 1,000 police were injured in the struggles; 58 protestors were arrested. Meanwhile, at 10:35 A.M. Sato's plane left the airport for South Vietnam. Then on November 12 thousands of students, mostly members of the SAMPA RENGO ZENGAKUREN (with helmets, towels over their faces, wooden poles, and stones), descended on train stations to travel to Haneda and prevent Sato's departure for

the United States. This time the police—7,000 strong—were better prepared, with large shields and tear gas; they clashed with the students at the train stations and stood firm. The skirmishes ended with 564 people injured and 335 arrested. Again Sato safely flew off. The Haneda Incidents evidenced a significant increase in the use of weapons and violent tactics in Japanese student demonstrations and were largely condemned by the nation's news media.

In fall 1969 another incident occurred at Haneda, again an effort to prevent Sato from leaving for the United States. Sato was scheduled to depart on November 17, and several demonstrations took place during the preceding four days. Militant students of the Anti-Yoyogi Zengakuren and workers of the Hansen Seinen Iinkai, deterred from attacking the airport itself because 3,000 police supported by vigilantes guarded it, attempted on the afternoon of November 16 to gain control of Kamata and block the approach to the airport, while other students attacked the Tokyo Station. Using Molotov cocktails, they closed Kamata Station and fought with police through the night. Smaller demonstrations on November 17 failed to prevent Sato's arrival at and departure from Haneda Airport, although 60 international flights were canceled. Nationally about 75,000 riot police had been mobilized for the two days; more than 2,000 protestors were arrested, and 82 were injured. In Washington, D.C., on November 21 Sato and President Richard Nixon released a joint statement announcing that Okinawa would be returned to Japanese control in 1972.

Bibliography: Stuart J. Dowsey, ed., *Zengakuren: Japan's Revolutionary Students* (Berkeley, Calif.: The Ishi Press, 1970).

Hansen Gakudo (Anti-War Student League)   (Japan) an organization formed in 1952 by students disaffected by the shift of the ZENGAKUREN leadership to support of Japan Communist Party (JCP) militancy. In particular, the Hansen Gakudo objected to the JCP's policy of sending squads of students into the countryside to try to proselytize farmers and incite them to rise up against the landowners—a policy adopted from the Chinese Communists, which they considered absurd and futile.

Hansen Seinen Iinkai (Anti-War Youth Committees)   (Japan) youth organization founded on August 30, 1965 by the Socialist Party and the General Council of Trade Unions (Sohyo). Their creation was generated in reaction to U.S. bombing raids against North Vietnam and the signing of the Japan-Korea Security Treaty in June 1965. The Vietnam War and the Japan-Korea treaty were seen by left-wing political groups in Japan as imperialistic and a threat to Japanese democracy.

Hare Krishna   *See* INTERNATIONAL SOCIETY FOR KRISHNA CONSCIOUSNESS.

Harlan Miners' Strike   (United States) a strike begun in February 1931 by coalminers in Harlan County, Kentucky. This action instigated a visit by a student delegation sponsored by the recently founded NATIONAL STUDENT LEAGUE (NSL), which comprised the first political undertaking by students during the Great Depression to garner national attention. The strike had been marked by violence, with coal operators using armed thugs to attack the miners; in May 1931, for example, the thugs opened fire with machine guns, killing four people. This violence had already aroused the attention of well-known writers, including Theodore Dreiser, Lincoln Steffens, Sherwood Anderson, and John Dos Passos, who at Dreiser's instigation visited Harlan in November 1931 and again in February 1932 to investigate. It was these writers' reports on the latter visit that inspired the NSL expedition. NSL leaders in New York announced and organized the expedition, depicting it as an effort to bring humanitarian assistance to starving and beleagured miners and not as a political endeavor. They wished to avoid antagonizing Kentucky and Harlan County police and other opponents of the expedition.

Eighty students—the men dressed in coats and ties—set out from New York for Harlan County, the first group leaving by bus on March 23, 1932 with two miners as guides. Most of the students were from Columbia University, City College, Hunter College, and other New York schools, but there were also students from University of Wisconsin, University of Tennessee, University of Cincinnati, Harvard University, and Smith College. Most of the students were not NSL members. The first busload of students encountered hostility even before reaching Kentucky, where they were threatened by angry crowds and gun-wielding deputies. County prosecutor Walter B. Smith denounced them as "Yankees, aliens, and agitators" and demanded that they leave the state. Deputies escorted them to the courthouse in Middlesboro for questioning by Smith, who heaped verbal abuse on them, until the students' leader, native Mississippian and Columbia student Robert Hall, objected that their rights were being violated and they would answer no more questions. So deputies loaded them back on the bus and escorted them to the border. The second busload of students was boarded by deputies and Smith, who informed their protesting leader, "I am the law," and forced the bus to leave the state. In both encounters, deputies assaulted students; in the second bus after they were already returned to Tennessee, deputies beat the leader viciously, injuring a woman and beating another man over the head with a revolver.

Thus the expedition failed in its stated objective, but it evoked widespread media attention. The leaders made every effort to arouse sympathy for the miners by sending representatives to the governors of Kentucky and Tennessee to demand an investigation of police brutality and the denial of constitutional rights to both the miners and the students. They also sent representatives to Washington, D.C. to deliver their demands to the Justice Department and the White House. Although spurned by the governors and federal officials, including President Herbert Hoover, the students did muster some support in the Congress, where they testified before the Senate Committee on Manufactures. Their story also aroused newspaper criticism of Kentucky coal operators and officials, garnered protests from hundreds of university professors, and gained national recognition for the previously unknown NSL and consequently recruits to its membership. In addition, the expedition inspired a similar endeavor by 150 students and teachers from midwestern schools who gathered at University of Chicago and unsuccessfully attempted to travel by bus into the troubled Illinois coalfields.

Harvard Exam Week Riot   (United States) the largest student riot in the United States during 1930, notable for its violent but totally nonpolitical nature. At 11:45 P.M. on May 7, a student played taps on a bugle outside one of the school dormitories to signal that, as the exam week was ended, it was time for revelry. Students pitched lightbulbs from their dormitory windows, and about 1,500 students gathered outdoors to indulge in tumult. Police officers were unable to quell the disturbance and called out the riot squad; firefighters also arrived after students set off an alarm. Students pelted them with bottles, fruits, and other objects. The riot lasted more than an hour, resulting in the arrest of one student and the hospitalization of two others. This thoughtless indulgence occurred during the first year of the Great Depression, when millions of the unemployed were staging hunger marches in major cities.

Hayden, Tom (1940–)   prominent U.S. leader of the NEW LEFT, student protest, and antiwar movements of the 1960s. Hayden was born in Royal Oaks, Michigan in 1940 and graduated from the University of Michigan in 1961. Following graduation he worked in the Civil Rights movement and with the STUDENT NONVIOLENT COORDINATING COMMITTEE (SNCC). His civil rights work resulted in his being beaten in McComb, Mississippi in October 1961 and his later arrest with 10 other SNCC activists in Albany, Georgia. Hayden was primarily responsible for drafting the PORT HURON STATEMENT, and he served as president of the STUDENTS FOR A DEMOCRATIC SOCIETY (SDS) in 1962–63. He joined other antiwar activists in traveling to North Vietnam in 1965 and 1967 in an effort to end the Vietnam War. He participated in the COLUMBIA UNIVERSITY STUDENT REVOLT, helping to occupy one of the university buildings. Hayden and another SDS leader, Ronnie Davis, were organizers of the famous protests at the August 1968 Democratic National Convention in Chicago (see BATTLE OF CHICAGO). Subsequently he and Davis and five others were brought to trial as the Chicago Seven (*see* CHICAGO 8 TRIAL). Hayden was again arrested in May 1971 as a participant in the People's Park demonstration in Berkeley. In 1973 he married actress Jane Fonda. In the late seventies and early eighties, he was elected to and served in the California General Assembly. Hayden authored numerous books and articles.

Heimdal (Sweden) an organization formed in 1891 by conservative students at the University of Uppsala. Heimdal's overall purpose has been the defense and promotion of traditional values, including support for the state church's role. Consequently, the group has served as something of a counterforce to the VERDANDI STUDENT SOCIETY.

Hell *See* ORGANIZATION.

Hell's Angels (United States) the most widely known of the youthful West Coast motorcycle gangs that originated in the early 1950s as groups protesting against middle-class American life by pursuing an alienated, outcast, provocative, even antisocial lifestyle. These gangs had numerous names, such as Iron Horsemen, Road Rats, and Satan's Slaves, but the Hell's Angels were most prominent nationally. Hard drinking and hostile, some wore German military helmets and decorations, had

Hell's Angels from across the country parked their motorcycles outside New York City's Limelight disco, a converted church (background), to attend a benefit to raise funds for the Hell's Angels' legal defense fund. (AP/WIDE WORLD PHOTOS)

swastika tattoos, and shouted "*Sieg Heil!*" They regarded student antiwar demonstrators as traitors, however, and viciously attacked a group of University of California students who marched from Berkeley to Oakland in a protest against the Vietnam War on October 16, 1965. The Hell's Angel's "Maximum Leader" sent a telegram to President Lyndon Johnson offering the gang's services as a military force to fight the Vietcong behind the lines but were turned down. The Hell's Angels attend weekend rallies, and they have periodically staged bloody melees, such as at Altamont in 1969 and Bridgeport, Connecticut in 1975. They also established branches in England in 1969. The Hell's Angels inspired at least two movies, most notably *The Wild One* (1954) starring Marlon Brando, and Hunter Thompson's book *Hell's Angels: A Strange and Terrible Saga* (1966).

Himpunan Mahasiswa Islam (Islamic Student Association, HMI) (Indonesia) an organization founded by university students of the Islamic faith in February 1947. HMI was affiliated with the political party Masjumi, which was banned by the government in 1960 after Masjumi supported a revolution. By 1967 HMI had an estimated membership of 100,000. As an opponent of the INDONESIAN COMMUNIST PARTY (PKI) and its student affiliate, HMI gained stature after the failed coup d'état of October 1, 1965 that some elements of PKI had supported. About 5,000 students from HMI and other Islamic groups rallied on October 5 to demand that the PKI be dissolved. On October 8 members of HMI, augmented by representatives of other anticommunist groups, burned down PKI's headquarters and also pillaged and burned the home of D. N. Aidit, chairman of PKI's Central Committee: on September 29 Aidit had called for the elimination of HMI in a public address. Subsequently, HMI also attacked and burned the headquarters of the Communist Movement of Indonesian Women, the People's Youth, and the All-Indonesian Central Organization of Trade Unions. Over the following weeks, PKI was effectively destroyed and tens of thousands of its members were killed.

Hindu Student Federation (India) an organization founded in the 1930s devoted to Hindu nationalism. It advocated an ideology similar to that of the RASHTRIYA SWAYAMSEVAK SANGH, which had been founded in the preceding decade. The student federation's membership was concentrated in northern India.

Hippie Movement (United States) a youth movement also known as "the flower children" that arose in the Haight-Ashbury (Hashbury) district of San Fransisco in 1965 and that attracted adherents from throughout the country—the East Village in New York City also became an area of hippie concentration. The hippies propounded a vaguely defined philosophy and a way of life that pre-

The hippie population of San Francisco turned out on a warm spring day to parade around the Haight-Ashbury district on April 2, 1967. Young and old gathered in the streets until police called a halt and began arresting many of them for unlawful assembly.   (AP/WIDE WORLD PHOTOS)

sented an alternative to conventional society. They denounced materialism and extolled "doing your own thing," peaceful social interaction, free love, "dropping out," and drug use (primarily pot and LSD). Their publication *Kerista Speeler* advocated a religion (Kerista) of supernaturalism, fellowship, peace, and love. The hippies lived in communes ("tribes" or "families") in relative poverty. But a hippie communal group called the Diggers, who begged the food they used, fed people free in San Francisco's Golden Gate Park and Berkeley's Constitution Park; others opened "free stores" in both cities where people could take whatever they needed. Hippie rock groups such as Country Joe and the Fish, Jefferson Airplane, and the Grateful Dead flourished giving free concerts. Frequently overly passive because of drug use, hippies became the prey of victimizers—during "the summer of love" in 1967, many were killed or brutalized. It is estimated that in 1967 there were 250,000 full-time hippies in the United States. During the following year, plagued by police harassment and internal weaknesses (such as increasing use of dangerous drugs) and overwhelmed by media popularization, the hippies died out as a movement in Haight-Ashbury and elsewhere, except in

isolated communal pockets mostly in rural areas, but they had provided some enduring legacies: for example, the Jefferson Airplane and the Grateful Dead became popular commercial rock groups. The hippies also brought a renewed popularity to mystical religion and influenced the founding of encounter groups and similiar awareness-training endeavors. In addition, hippie fashion (leather shirts, beads, and long hair) influenced changes in clothing and hair styles among the general public.

Hitler Jugend (HJ, Hitler Youth)   (Germany) the Nazi Party's organization for youths of both sexes age 10 to 18 (although many older youths belonged), whose creation was announced by Adolf Hitler at the party's 1926 convention in Weimar; its origin, however, traced to a letter Hitler wrote in February 1922 demanding creation of a youth group. Hitler, who regarded the existing youth movement with contempt, appointed Kurt Gruber as head of the new Nazi youth movement. Although banned in some states, the Hitler Jugend grew, especially in Austria and northern Germany, and by 1929 claimed to have 200,000 members—a significant exaggeration, as actual membership was closer to 20,000. Their uniform included the Nazis' brown shirt and swastika armband. By 1929 Gruber was losing influence to Baldur von SCHIRACH, and in 1931 he resigned. Schirach was appointed national leader of the Hitler Jugend in June 1932, and during that year membership exploded: the organization's fall convention in Potsdam attracted about 100,000 members and supporters. In 1933, the year Adolf Hitler became chancellor, membership in all branches totaled nearly 2.3 million, and by 1939 the total exceeded 7.2 million—82 percent of the nation's existing age group. (Membership in the HJ was made compulsory in 1936 by law.)

As the youth program was organized, on March 15 in the year in which a youngster became 10, he or she registered at the local youth headquarters; after proof of "race purity" was secured, boys were inducted into the Jungvolk (JV, Young Folk) and girls into the Jungmädelgruppen (JM, Young Girls Groups) in an elaborate ceremony on April 20 (Hitler's birthday). At age 14 the boys graduated into the Hitler Jugend proper; girls, into the BUND DEUTSCHER MÄDEL. At 18 the boys entered the STURMABTEILUNG or some other military unit; after 1939 girls remained in the Bund until age 21 because they were not required to serve in the military. All members, however, could participate in massive marches as participants in the Nazis ritualistic public demonstrations.

During their years in the Hitler Jugend members were, of course, indoctrinated in Nazi beliefs, and many were processed through the organization's leadership programs to prepare them for posts in an elaborate leadership hierarchy designed to perpetuate the Hitler Jugend indefinitely. Those who did well in the regional programs were advanced to a year's training at National Leadership Schools, where they underwent rigorous physical training and absorbed a fanatical faith in Hitler.

Boys of the Hitler Youth receive instructions on how to use a rifle. (AP/WIDE WORLD PHOTOS)

Young men could then enter the Academy for Youth Leaders established at Braunschweig in 1939 and there train for leadership in the Hitler Jugend as a profession.

By the mid-1930s, leaders of the Hitler Jugend attained major influence in university student politics, with many of them holding leadership positions in the DEUTSCHE STUDENTENSCHAFT or the NATIONAL SOCIALIST GERMAN STUDENT UNION. The Hitler Jugend mounted strong opposition to the university fraternities, especially in *Wille und Macht*, the organization's major journal. Schirach spoke publicly against the fraternities and forbade Hitler Jugend members from belonging to them. He also opposed the BUNDE and all youth groups that rivaled the Hitler Jugend; on April 5, 1933 Hitler Jugend commandos took control of the offices of the Reichsausschuss (the Executive of German Youth Movements) in Berlin, and expelled Jewish and Socialist groups from membership. In the following months, all the Bunde and other groups were dissolved or subsumed into the Hitler Jugend, which became the only German youth movement. In 1933 HJ leaders created the Streifendienst (SRD, Patrol Service), a unit of members who monitored the behavior of others members and reported to authorities any deviation from prescribed conduct—an echo of the Gestapo meant to ensure uniformity and compliance.

A significant program called Landdienst (LD, Land Service), begun in 1934, involved both HJ and BDM members (more than 215,000 during the program's 10-year lifetime). LD participants spent a year (Land Jahr) encamped in a farming region occupied with farm labor. The program grew out of an idealization of agriculture, an ideology of "blood and soil" as part of the Volksgemeinschaft, and was intended to draw youths back to the soil—in effect, to transform them into peasants. In its most successful year, 1938–39, the LD program resulted in only 30 percent of the youths choosing to pursue the peasant life.

Most importantly, in 1938 and following years, through the efforts of Heinrich Himmler, head of the Schutzstaffeln (SS, Elite Echelon), and especially his influence over Artur Axmann, who succeeded Shirach in the summer of 1940, the Hitler Jugend became the major source of recruitment for new SS members. In fact, a strong mutual support system grew up between the two organizations, with thousands of HJ members moving into the Waffen–SS (Combat SS) in their late teens years; many others entered the SS-Totenkopfverbande (SS Death's Head Units), which were in charge of the concentration camps. To abet this tie, HJ youths were provided premilitary training at about 200 Wehrertüchtigungslager (WEL, Premilitary Training Camps), some 40 of which served as feeders for the SS and the remainder for the regular army; this training included instruction in firearms use and in maneuvering in varied terrains.

So conditioned were HJ youths by indoctrination, surveillance, training, and patriotic fervor that they gladly joined in Germany's sacrificial final defense as the war in Europe neared its end. They were organized as the Hitler Youth Division within the Waffen-SS or as units within the Volkssturm (People's Militia). Some 5,000 Hitler Jugend, many of them only 12 to 15 years old, participated in the Battle of Berlin (April–May 1945), joining diehard SS units in a futile effort to defend the city against invading Russian troops; only 500 of the Hitler Jugend participants survived the battle. Following Germany's surrender, some HJ members joined isolated Werewolf units to carry out guerrilla attacks against the Allies.

Bibliography: Gerhard Rempel, *Hitler's Children: The Hitler Youth and the SS* (Chapel Hill: University of North Carolina Press, 1989).

Hochschulring Deutscher Art   (Germany) a nationalist political movement within the universities begun in 1919 that promoted the concept of the folk community (Volksgemeinschaft). The Hochschulring's incipience occurred early in the year when some Berlin students involved with *Jungdeutsche Stimmen*, a right-wing youth-movement publication, formed the Fichte Hochschulgemeinde (named for philosopher Johann Fichte). In June this group, the Berlin KYFFHAUSER VERBAND, and members of the Berlin BURSCHENSCHAFTEN joined in forming the Hochschulring Deutscher Art. The Hochschulring spread quickly throughout Germany and became active both at the schools and in the larger community by means of cooperative efforts with similar groups and participation in social and political endeavors. In July 1920 representatives of 20 Hochschulringen and other groups met in Göttingen to establish the movement as a national organization. Supported by funding from the Burschenschaften, the Hochschulring became the leading movement in student politics during the 1920s as a catalyst for student disillusionment with the Weimar Republic, opposition to parliamentary democracy, anti-Marxism, and desire for a monarchical or otherwise authoritarian government and the establishment of state capitalism; it gained control of student councils at many of the universities. Although the Hochschulring did not support virulent anti-Semitism, it excluded Jews from membership on the grounds that they constituted a separate nation. The Hochschulring's official newspaper, *Deutsche Akademische Stimmen*, was published by a nationalist group in Munich. The Nazi's abortive Beer Hall Putsch on November 8, 1923 in Munich involved some members of the local Hochschulring and thus threw the movement into some disarray, as many of its members were traditional conservatives and old-style liberals who were opposed to such radical tactics. This event and an attack on the Roman Catholic church published in the *Deutsche Akademische Stimmen* revealed a basic disunity in the organization. In October 1928 the Hochschulring began a program of military training; in 1929 it joined with the STAHLHELM in conducting "war sport" camps, with the latter providing the instructors. By 1930 the Hochschulring was fading, to be displaced by other groups such as the NATIONAL SOCIALIST GERMAN STUDENT UNION, for whose fascist program the Hochschulring's views had actually helped prepare the way to acceptance among students.

Bibliography: Michael S. Steinberg, *Sabers and Brownshirts: The German Students' Path to National Socialism, 1918–1935* (Chicago: University of Chicago Press, 1977).

Hoffman, Abbie (1936–1989)   (United States) leader of the Youth International Party (Yippies) and longstanding political activist. Hoffman was born in Worcester, Massachusetts, graduated from Brandeis University (1959), and earned a master's degree (1960) in psychology from the University of California at Berkeley. He then served briefly as a civil rights worker in the South and returned to Worcester, where he was a salesman for a pharmaceutical firm and did volunteer work with minority youths. In 1966 he moved to New York City, where he managed a theater and helped organize the hippies in the East Village. (*See* HIPPIE MOVEMENT.) He attained renown as the leader of the Yippies during the 1968 antiwar demonstrations at the CHICAGO DEMOCRATIC CONVENTION and as one of the defendants in the Chicago Seven Trial. (*See* CHICAGO 8 TRIAL.) Arrested for possession of cocaine in 1973, he went underground and worked on environmental issues in Fineview, New York under the name Barry Freed. He reemerged in 1980, appearing on the television show *20/20*, and surrendered to the authorities. He served less than a year in prison. He participated in one more demonstration—a protest against the Central Intelligence Agency (CIA) at the University of Massachusetts in Amherst that also involved Amy Carter. Hoffman wrote several books, perhaps the best known being *Steal this Book* and *Revolution for the Hell of It*. He committed suicide in 1989.

Höhe Meissner   (Germany) a convocation of about 3,000 youth-movement leaders and members representing more than a dozen organizations held in October 1913 on a hill (Höhe Meissner) near Kassel as a counterdemonstration to other celebrations held throughout the centenary year of the Battle of Leipzig, considered symbolic of the Wars of Liberation. The youth groups were dismayed by the sometimes riotous behavior that characterized these other celebrations, including the official celebration at the battle site, and many came to Höhe Meissner advocating a stance against the use of tobacco and alcohol that they believed marred the celebrations—they wanted social reforms based on asceticism. Others wanted a broader reform program. The result of their discussions was the creation, effected by their leaders, of the FREIDEUTSCHE JUGEND, an association of most of the assembled groups, which still retained their own individual identities as well. They also adopted the so-called Meissner Formula:

> Free German Youth, on their own initiative, under their own responsibility, and with deep sincerity, are determined independently to shape their own lives. For the sake of this inner freedom, they will under any and all circumstances take united action. To form mutual understandings, they will have Free German Youth Days. All of these gatherings of the Free German Youth are to be free from the use of alcohol and tobacco.

A second Höhe Meissner convocation was held in August 1923 in hopes of reinvigorating the unity that was the intended goal of the Freideutsche Jugend, but the effort failed totally, although many of the disparate and disagreeing groups that now comprised the youth movement sent representatives, and by the end of the year the Freideutsche Jugend was dead.

Hornsey Affair (Great Britain) a student sit-in begun in May 1968 at the Hornsey College of Art in north London. The sit-in originated as a demand that the college grant autonomy to the student union and a sabbatical year to the union's president, but it became transformed into a revolutionary revisioning by the students of the college's entire mode of art education—a free university, in effect, designated Crouch End Commune, as the students called the occupied college. An outside committee of inquiry was appointed, and in its report the committee criticized the college's administration and proposed student representation on an advisory committee for the college. The local council of Haringey, however, had final control of the college, and when the college reopened in November, the council effected the dismissal of many students and part-time teachers implicated in the sit-in. Although ultimately failing in its objectives, the sit-in inspired similar movements at other art colleges, most notably at Guildford.

Bibliography: Students and Staff of Hornsey College of Art, *The Hornsey Affair* (Hammondsworth, England: Penguin Books, 1969).

"Hot Week" (Yugoslavia) the week of June 3–10, 1968, during which students in Belgrade and Zagreb staged protests demanding political liberalization. Students at Belgrade University pushed their cause through a sit-in. Demonstrating students voiced their support for the protesting students in France (*see* MAY REVOLT) and for the "international student revolt." The students' protest, however, never approached the level of militance then being experienced in France and Germany; it quickly dissipated after the government promised reforms and pled for peace and order in the face of the Soviet Union's threat to Yugoslovia's independence.

Howard University Sit-In (United States) students' occupation of the administration building at Howard University in March 1968 in a protest demanding institutional reforms. The sit-in culminated a four-year agitation for reforms in admissions standards, financial policies, the curriculum, and disciplinary procedures at the university. The catalyst for the sit-in was provided by "the Orangeburg Massacre" (*see* ORANGEBURG PROTEST), which inspired a sympathy demonstration for the Orangeburg protestors by 500 Howard students and a demand by the militant student group Ujamma (formed in fall 1967) that Howard be transformed into a "black university." This demand, known as the Orangeburg Ultimatum, included the resignation of President James M. Nabrit, Jr., within three weeks, the resignations of the vice-president and the dean, more courses in African-American history, reinstatement of faculty members dismissed for political activism, creation of a student judiciary committee, and other changes. The adminstration denounced the ultimatum. On March 1 at Charter Day ceremonies, students seized the stage and read a revised version of the ultimatum entitled "Definition of a Black University." When 39 of the students involved in this disruption were ordered to appear before a judiciary board on March 19, student leaders rallied 1,000 students in protest; following the rally several hundred of the students occupied the administration building. On March 20 the administration suspended classes, but more than 2,500 students remained on the campus, many of them joining the demonstrators inside or outside the administration building. On March 22 leaders of the sit-in issued 16 demands, including immediate dismissal of Nabrit, a new judiciary system, amnesty for the sit-in demonstrators, student control of disciplinary policies, and a "black-oriented curriculum." A group of trustees negotiated a settlement with the students that provided four concessions: amnesty for the sit-in demonstrators, student control of the judiciary board that would discipline the Charter Day demonstrators, a student-faculty board to review student complaints, and a vaguely worded promise to bring Howard into attunement with the times. If acceptance of students' demands was the gauge of the five-day sit-in demonstration's success, then it had to be judged a failure. It did, however, result in creation of a faculty-student committee to recommend curricular changes, creation of a student-controlled judiciary board, and other reforms. The Howard University Sit-In also inspired sit-ins at numerous other black colleges, including Fisk University, Bowie State College, and Cheyney State College.

Hsi-nan University (China) a school established in Chengdu in spring 1930 by faculty and students from the Hsi-nan Public School, a hotbed of communist agitation in Chongqing in Sichuan. After Kuomintang (KMT) authorities imprisoned or killed agitators at the Chongqing school during their drive to suppress the CHINESE COMMUNIST PARTY (CCP), the remaining faculty and about 100 students fled to Chengdu, where they recreated the school as Hsi-nan University. The new university was significant as a center for fomenting mass student movements, so the authorities ordered it closed. About 200 students opposed the order and were imprisoned; 80 of them were later tried as Communist leaders. Eventually, authorities forbade non-Sichuan students from leaving the province and imposed other restrictions that generated a terroristic repression—police and soldiers murdered students on the streets of Chengdu and other cities in the province.

Hunan Students' Association (China) a radical organization of Hunan-province students to which Mao Zedong belonged. Mao and other members of the association founded the influential periodical *Xiangjiang pinglun* (Xiang River Review) in Changsha in July 1919. During 1920–22, the association supported the movement to attain independence for Hunan province and devised the slogan "A Monroe Doctrine for Hunan" to promote the view that Hunan should stay out of the political power struggle between North China and South China. A warlord who seized power in Hunan province near the end of 1920 suppressed the student movement in 1922.

Hundred Flowers (China) a student movement of 1957 originally proposed by the CHINESE COMMUNIST PARTY (CCP) but then quickly suppressed. Conceding that students had staged some small-scale strikes in 1956, the CCP wanted to find a means of ensuring student support of government policies, especially economic construction. To this end Mao Zedong declared in a speech given in February 1957 that he would welcome the "blooming of a hundred flowers" and the "contending of a hundred schools of thought." Mao blamed "bureaucratism, subjectivism, and sectarianism" and inadequate efforts to inculcate ideology among the students as the causes of any disaffection, and he avowed that limited free expression would generate achievements in the arts and sciences and earn greater support for government policies among students. The students took the invitation to pursue free expression at face value. On May 19, 1957 they displayed the first "big character posters" containing criticisms on the so-called democratic wall at Beijing University, some of the criticisms accusing the CCP of having too much power or the government of being undemocratic; others advocating private ownership of property, university autonomy, the study of modern

Westen literature and art, and other changes. The Beijing students also formed a Hundred Flowers Society, which issued a few publications. Similar events occurred at a few other schools. The government reacted with an "antirightist" campaign to suppress the commentary, identifying 800 "rightists" at Beijing University who were put under supervision or sent off to labor camps to be "reformed"—the "antirightist" campaign at Beijing lasted until January 1958. CCP officials were sent into the universities and middle schools, imposing a new eight-hour weekly course on political orientation. Three middle-school students accused of leading a riot in Hanyang were executed. The Hundred Flowers movement came to an abrupt end, more significant by far for its suppression than for its initiation.

Hungarian Revolution (Hungary) the October 1956 national rebellion against the repressive communist regime of Mátyás Rákosi and his successor Ernö Gero initiated by university student demonstrations. Rákosi was a hated tyrant who was responsible for the murders of tens of thousands of alleged political opponents and conspirators, including László Rajk, popular hero of the Spanish Civil War, falsely charged with being the leader of antigovernment conspirators. Fearing an uprising similar to those in East Germany and Czechoslovakia (*see* WORKERS' RISING IN EAST BERLIN), the Russians had deposed Rákosi in April 1953 and replaced him with Imre Nagy, a reformist promising a "new course." Nagy freed 80,000 political prisoners and introduced policies of toleration that again alarmed the Russians, who restored Rákosi to power in April 1955. The brief taste of moderation and the revelations of torture and terror that had been inflicted on former political prisoners had a lasting effect, however.

Opposition to Rákosi grew, even within the Hungarian Communist Party (CPH). The initial spearhead of the movement to depose Rákosi was the PETÖFI CLUB created in 1956—following the launching of de-Stalinization in the USSR—by the university affiliate of the COMMUNIST YOUTH LEAGUE (KISZ). Through teaching and demonstrations, the club pressed the issue. A June 27, 1956 meeting of the Petöfi Club that lasted 12 hours became the largest demonstration against Rákosi to that time. Three days later, the premier denounced the club as "antiparty." At the end of July, the Russians removed Rákosi but put in his place the despised Ernö Gero. To placate the opposition Gero permitted a ceremonial reburial of the murdered Rajk on October 6, the day in 1849 when leaders of the War of Liberty had been hanged; more than 300,000 people attended the ceremony. The bloodless Polish Revolution in October fueled hopes of some similar development in Hungary. Now the university students, many of them members of the KISZ, began in earnest to organize a movement for achieving an independent, democratic, and socialist Hungary. They set

A truck with Hungarian youths, holding a white flag with a red cross marked in by blood, speeds through revolution-torn Budapest.
(AP/WIDE WORLD PHOTOS)

up teams who were responsible for separate activities—actual fighting; printing and disseminating leaflets; establishing communications with workers, soldiers, and government officials. At a meeting on October 22, about 5,000 students unanimously adopted the BUDAPEST TECHNICAL UNIVERSITY RESOLUTION, which spelled out their demands for change, and the students planned a major peaceful march and demonstration in Budapest for October 23 and invited workers and others to join them. Their purpose was to show support for the "POLISH OCTOBER" revolution and to present to the government the list of demands contained in the Budapest Technical University Resolution, including reinstatement of Nagy in the CPH and as premier, the removal of Soviet troops from Hungary, and ending Soviet domination of Hungary's politics and economics.

The students' march was to proceed from the statue of Sándor Petőfi on the left bank of the Danube to that of József Bem on the right bank—both men had been heroes of the 1848–49 revolution. The entirely peaceable march, which lasted for hours, garnered 300,000

demonstrators calling for independence and the installation of Nagy as premier. The demonstrators listened to speeches at Bem's statue. Then most of the crowd moved on to Parliament Square, while a group of students went to the building housing Budapest Radio to pressure the station to broadcast the students' 16 demands—these included Hungarian independence, withdrawal of Soviet troops, free elections, and freedom of speech and religion. Gero broadcast a speech denouncing the demonstrators, and his security police opened fire on the unarmed students who gathered outside the radio building—an act that, instead of intimidating the demonstrators, incited their anger and resistance. Hungarian soldiers arriving on the scene gave their weapons to the students or began to fire on the security police. Workers in suburban factories snatched arms from caches and raced to join the fight. Soldiers, who were prevented from leaving their barracks, threw their guns out to the demonstrators. News of the battle at the radio building spread to the provinces, and a full-scale nationwide rebellion ensued.

The fighting in Budapest raged into the morning of October 24, with tanks of the Soviet MVD (security police) and Soviet troops who had been stationed in the city joining in firing on the rebels. Young students, apprentices, and schoolchildren desperately battled the Soviet forces in the streets. The government broadcast an appeal for increased help from Soviet forces while announcing its recommendation that Nagy, then effectively a prisoner at the Communist Party headquarters, be appointed premier. By now most of the Hungarian troops stationed in and near Budapest had joined the rebels, bringing arms and ammunition with them. At noon on October 24, Russian deputy premier Anastas Mikoyan and Presidium member Mikhail Suslov arrived in Budapest; they placed János Kadar in the premiership and returned to Moscow with Gero. To counter the rebels, the minister of defense ordered Colonel Paul Maleter to take a tank battalion and capture Killian Barracks, sited at a controlling junction of Budapest's major east-west boulevard; Maleter did so—for the rebels.

Now the rebels had a sizable military presence and a capable military commander, but the major force driving the revolution remained the hundreds of individual fighting groups. These were comprised mostly of children and teenagers of both sexes who were adept at making and using Molotov cocktails, which proved a menace to Soviet tanks. Lionized as "freedom fighters" in the Western press, the youths and their fellow rebels successfully combated the Soviet forces through October 28, when the government offered concessions that included withdrawal of the Soviet forces from Budapest. The rebels had also gained support from industrial workers, who began to set up workers' councils in Budapest on October 24 that within three days had extended nationwide and pressured the government for reforms through petitions and a general strike. On October 25 Nagy had been freed and had begun to set up a cabinet, which took control on October 30. On November 1 Premier Nagy declared Hungary's neutrality and withdrawal from the Warsaw Pact. It seemed the rebels had triumphed. Nagy formed a coalition government on November 3. On that day also, a delegation of military officers, including Maleter, went at the invitation of the Russians to the Soviet headquarters outside Budapest to negotiate further Soviet troop withdrawals; all were arrested. On November 4 Soviet forces launched a full-scale attack on Budapest. Nagy and his colleagues found asylum in the Yugoslav Embassy—they would be duped into leaving on November 23 and arrested. From November 5 to November 22, a nationwide general strike occurred in protest of the Soviet occupation.

After occupying Budapest and the provinces, the Russians began the deportation of Hungarian youths to the USSR and informed the United Nations on November 19 that 16,000 had been deported. Many other youths were kept in prison until their 16th birthday, when they could be and were legally executed for political crimes. It is estimated that about 20,000 rebels were arrested. More than 50,000 revolutionaries had been killed during the Russian offensives, the great majority of them young men and women between 15 and 28—as was also the case with the more than 80,000 wounded. In Budapest alone, more than 10,000 youths age 15 to 23 had been killed. Nearly 230,000 Hungarians, including 7,500 university students, escaped to the West. Nagy, Maleter, and an estimated 2,000 others were executed. The Hungarian Revolution—a revolution initiated by students and other youths who comprised the largest single group among the revolutionaries, led temporarily by youths, and sustained by them to the end—had been totally crushed. It had, however, generated the most serious crisis in Eastern Europe since the then Soviet Union had imposed a communist hegemony on the region following World War II—as both the Soviet Union and the Western powers clearly recognized. Thus, commentary within the Warsaw Pact nations referred to the Hungarian insurrectionists as "counterrevolutionaries," while in the West they were called "freedom fighters."

Bibliography: Ferenc Vali, *Rift and Revolt in Hungary* (Cambridge: Harvard University Press, 1961); Hans-Georg Heinrich, *Hungary: Politics, Economics, and Society* (Boulder, Colo.: Lynne Rienner Publishers, 1986).

Imperial College Protests   (China) a series of student protests at the Imperial College during an extended period of years that comprised important precedents for the 20th-century student movement, to a large extent legitimizing the idea of students as the voice of public opinion. The first, a protest by 30,000 students led by a student named Wang Han objecting to the punishment of an honest censor, occurred in the first century B.C. during the Han dynasty and was the first instance in Chinese history of students overtly interfering in domestic politics. Another protest, an early factional dispute, occurred in the second century A.D. during the latter years of the Han dynasty; it involved students joining with intellectuals and officials to criticize the government and the role of eunuchs. Several hundred of the students and officials were subsequently imprisoned and executed. Then in 1125 during the Song dynasty, students led by Ch'en Tung (Chen Dong) unsuccessfully requested the emperor Qin Zong to have the premier and the nation's military leaders executed for malfeasance. On May 2, 1126 began the most famous of all these early student protests: Chen led a group of hundreds of students in protesting against the dismissal of Li Gang, who advocated war against the Juchen, and in petitioning the emperor to punish the premier and to formulate policies opposing aggression by invaders from the north. In less than a day, 100,000 citizens gathered to support the students. The subsequent riotous confrontation resulted in the death of 20 of the emperor's attendants and the executions of several citizen protestors held responsible, but also in revised government policies—the first time in Chinese history that students had led protests by citizens against official foreign policy. The emperor also reinstated Li Gang, and the government tried unsuccesfully to bring the protests to an end by offering students official positions and bribes. Although in 1127 Emperor Gao Zong (son of and successor to Qin Zong) had Chen Dong and numerous other students executed, further student protests marked the Sung dynasty years. In 1129 the emperor, expressing remorse for Chen's execution, awarded the student leader a posthumous official rank.

Indian National Theatre (INT)   (India) a theater company begun in 1942 by student leaders of the nationalist movement. Students comprised most of the actors involved in the INT's dramatic productions during the group's early years. The company and its affiliated student groups toured towns and villages presenting nationalist-oriented productions. INT began to attract the interest of professionals, and in 1949 it became a professional theater company.

Indonesian Communist Party (PKI)   (Indonesia) a political party formed in 1920 out of the Indies Social Democratic Association as part of the nationalist (independence) movement; later significant for its involvement in the Indonesian student movement. (Indonesia became a sovereign state in December 1949.) PKI functioned powerfully within the student movement, spreading communist precepts through its student affiliate organization, the Communist Concentration of Indonesian Student Movements (CGMI), formed in 1956 through the merger of local student groups. CGMI also supported those who had studied in the Soviet Union, Eastern Europe, or China in obtaining instructor positions in the state universities. By 1964 CGMI claimed a membership of 32,000. Among the CGMI's major adversaries was the Islamic Student Association (HIMPUNAN MAHASISWA ISLAM, HMI), an organization claiming 100,000 members in 1967. CGMI agitated to have HMI representation banned at various schools and, in September 1965, called for HMI's elimination and effected its rejection from the Presidium of the Federation of Indonesian Student Associations (PPMI). But following an abortive coup attempt in September 1965 supported by some elements of PKI, the Communists fell into disfavor. In October the HMI and other Islamic student groups demanded the banning of PKI and, joined by other anticommunist student groups, burned down PKI's headquarters and also torched the house of D. N. Aidit, the chairman of PKI's Central Committee. The new ACTION COMMAND OF INDONESIAN STUDENTS (KAMI), created on October 25, demanded the dissolution of the Communist Party and movement. In the months that followed, especially under the government of General Suharto, the PKI was effectively destroyed, with tens of thousands of communists being killed.

Intercollegiate Civic League (ICL)   (United States) a moderate student organization founded in 1905 for the purpose of generating student knowledge of and participation in political activities. The ICL did not advocate any specific political philosophy but simply fostered awareness through discussions of such issues as child labor, student voting rights, and means of becoming involved in politics locally and nationally. Within five years of its founding, ICL had 32 affiliated clubs nationwide, each club having between 30 and 100 members. It apparently dissolved in 1917.

Intercollegiate Liberal League (ILL) (United States) a moderate student organization, founded in 1919, that was devoted to fostering open minds and "development of an informed student opinion on social, industrial, political, and international questions." To serve these ends ILL's major effort was a bureau of students and other speakers who toured university campuses. ILL generated opposition from both right-wing and left-wing students, and in 1921 it merged with the National Student Conference for the Limitation of Armaments, an antiwar group, to form the NATIONAL STUDENT FORUM (NSF).

Intercollegiate Socialist Society (ISS) (United States) an organization for students founded in New York City on September 12, 1905 at the behest of socialist author Upton Sinclair. The ISS's purpose was to promote "an intelligent interest in socialism" among college and university men and women through the creation of "study clubs" and other legitimate means. (Socialist study clubs already existed at the universities of California and Wisconsin.) Jack London was chosen president; Sinclair, first vice president. London launched the ISS with a series of three lectures—at Harvard University, Grand Central Palace in New York, and Yale University. The first ISS-affiliated chapters were established at Columbia and Wesleyan universities. London resigned in May 1907 and was replaced by Graham Stokes; with Harry Laidler as organizer, the ISS began to add chapters at eastern universities, including Harvard, Princeton, Pennsylvania,

and New York. In 1910 the ISS held its first convention, with 35 delegates from seven schools attending; representatives from 12 other schools could not make it. The ISS's journal was first issued in 1913: the *Intercollegiate Socialist* (later, 1919–21, the *Socialist Review*) was the only student-oriented journal of the period devoted to politics. ISS membership probably peaked in 1915 at 2,200 dues-paying members; there were then 70 university and college chapters and 12 alumni chapters, mostly in the East and the Middle West. In 1916 there were 71 university and college chapters and 15 alumni chapters, but by 1918, following U.S. involvement in World War I, these numbers dropped to 39 and 12. Although the ISS never had any connection with the Socialist Party and consistently defined itself as an educational organization only, it was frequently confused as a party affiliate and fell victim to the public debate over war preparedness, which the party opposed. When the United States entered the war in 1917 the ISS announced itself neutral; thus the ISS appeared unpatriotic. By December 1919 only 17 college chapters remained, and the organization was under public attack. In spring 1921 the ISS ceased publishing its journal, and that summer Vice President Calvin Coolidge joined the organization's attackers. The executive committee decided to disband the ISS, and in the fall of 1921 it was reorganized as the LEAGUE FOR INDUSTRIAL DEMOCRACY (LID). During its existence, many prominent U.S. citizens were student members or were in some way associated with the ISS, including Eugene V. Debs, Norman Thomas, Walter Lippmann, Vida Scudder, Charles Beard, W.E.B. Du Bois, Heywood Broun, and Paul Douglas. However limited in its membership totals, the ISS was the most important student organization of its time, and its publications were widely read by students.

Bibliography: Max Horn, *The Intercollegiate Socialist Society, 1905–1921: Origins of the Modern American Student Movement* (Boulder, Colo.: Westview Press, 1979).

Intercollegiate Society of Individualists (ISI) (United States) an organization for university and college students founded in 1953 by the political libertarian Frank Chodorov, the editor of *analysis.* Chodorov found disturbing what he and other conservatives saw as "collectivism on the campus," so he founded ISI as a countermovement, his specific target being socialist-oriented student organizations, such as the LEAGUE FOR INDUSTRIAL DEMOCRACY. William F. Buckley, Jr. (1925–), a graduate of Yale University and author of the controversial *God and Man at Yale: The Superstitions of "Academic Freedom"* (1951), served as president. ISI was perhaps unique in that members were self-selected and that there were no meetings or proselytings. Considered by Chodorov simply "an organization of ideas," ISI distributed free literature (including its publication *The Individualist*) to both members and nonmembers. ISI began with

600 members. By 1961 membership had risen to 13,000 nationwide, and ISI's mailings of conservative publications had reached an audience of 40,000 students—a "loose confederation" of conservative youths. Thus ISI provided conservative youths with an intellectual "home"—a focus, a literature, and a realization of shared ideas and support. ISI sponsored and coordinated campus lectures by conservative intellectuals and, in 1965, founded the conservative journal *Intercollegiate Review*, which soon attained a circulation of 45,000—this during the revolutionary student movement of the 1960s. In 1966, the year of Chodorov's death, ISI changed its name, becoming the Intercollegiate Studies Institute. Buckley considered the ISI a major force in creating a large and emergent group of political conservatives.

International Antiwar Day Riot of 1968   (Japan) a major riot that occurred on October 21, designated as International Antiwar Day by Japanese left-wing political groups. The 1968 antiwar rally at the Tokyo suburb of Shinjuku held this day by members of the HANSEN SEINEN IINKAI became tumultuous when a crowd of students, workers, and others trashed the train station and threw Molotov cocktails into a police box. The riot resulted in the police invoking the Antiriot Law, reinstating the crime of "riotous assembly" not applied for the previous 16 years. On International Antiwar Day in 1969, student demonstrations and riots again occurred at Shinjuku Station but also at other stations and at Waseda University and elsewhere in the nation, closing down several railways and leading to the arrest of more than 1,500 protestors nationwide (more than 1,200 in Tokyo), the largest number of arrests ever made in a single day to that time.

International Society for Krishna Consciousness (ISKCON)   (United States and Canada) a religious youth movement, popularly known as Hare Krishna, founded in New York City in 1965 by A. C. Bhaktivedanta Swami (1896–1977), who some believed to be directly linked with the Hindu god Krishna. Bhaktivedanta arrived in New York in September 1965, lived with supporters, and began lectures and services intended to convert followers to "God-consciousness"; mostly he attracted youths who were involved in the COUNTER-CULTURE movement. The ISKCON movement's young adherents began to appear in many U.S. cities in 1966. Since then, the movement has spread virtually worldwide, including a large temple near Bombay with more than 6,000 adherents and major centers in North America sited in New York, Boston, Berkeley, Montreal, and Los Angeles; by the 1980s it had 45 centers in Europe, 35 in Asia, 40 in Latin America, and 10 in Africa. Los Angeles is headquarters for the organization and its publishing facility, which has published more than 50 volumes of Bhaktivedanta's original works and translations. Bhak-

tivedanta translated the Hindu scripture *Bhagavad-Gita*, with added statements of appreciation for his work by Allen Ginsberg, Denise Levertov, and Thomas Merton.

The ISKCON movement teaches adherents, now numbering in the tens of thousands, to seek spiritual enlightenment through devotion to Krishna—hence their chanting of the mantra that begins with the words "Hare Krishna" (O Lord Krishna) and derives from the Kalisantara Upanishad. This "Great Mantra" awakens God-consciousness, leading to the experience of Samadhi. Student, or brahmacarin, adherents follow an ascetic regimen that includes early morning devotional services; they abstain from eating meat, fish, and eggs or drinking intoxicants, tea, and coffee, and they avoid any form of sexual activity. Copulation is discouraged as an impediment to spiritual growth; it is acceptable essentially only for married couples who live outside the temple and by them only once monthly. Many adherents live in the group's temples; others seek converts among youths on city streets, where their shaved heads and diaphonous robes make them readily recognizable; they frequently sell copies of the movement's journal *Back to Godhead*. Krishna Consciousness, hierarchical and authoritarian in its organizational structure, accepts the Hindu system of castes. In 1970 Bhaktivedanta founded a Governing Body Commission comprised of 12 advanced devotees to administer the movement as an ongoing entity.

International Student Conference (ISC)   an organization of national student unions initiated at a December 1950 meeting in Stockholm of representatives from 22 unions of Western nations as a rival organization to the INTERNATIONAL UNION OF STUDENTS (IUS). Delegates met again in January 1952 in Edinburgh to establish an organizational structure, including a secretariat with limited powers—the Co-ordinating Secretariat of National Unions of Students (COSEC). The ISC was sometimes better known as COSEC, which was headquartered at Leiden in the Netherlands. The ISC's policies on economic, social, and political issues reflected those of the Western nations, but, though clearly a counterbalance to the IUS, the organization had been intended from its origins to be nonpolitical. It published a monthly journal, *The Student*, in four languages, from 1956 to 1968, and also an *Information Bulletin*, pamphlets, and diverse other pieces; sponsored special projects and conferences, notably a series of International Student Press Seminars, and both the Asian Student Press Bureau and the European Student Press Bureau; and provided student travel services. In 1962 27 delegations, including those of France and Yugoslavia, walked out of the ISC's meetings because of its refusal to seat a delegation from Puerto Rico; some delegations were also disgruntled by the ISC's refusing to condemn U.S. policies in Vietnam. Nevertheless, 1962 was probably the peak year for the ISC, as students representing unions in 80 nations, mostly non-Western, attended the Quebec conference. The ISC was covertly funded by the United States's Central Intelligence Agency (CIA), as was revealed publicly in 1967; the damaging revelation and resultant loss of funding caused the ISC's demise in February 1969.

Bibliography: Philip G. Altbach and Norman T. Uphoff, *International Student Politics* (Metuchen, N.J.: Scarecrow Press, 1973).

International Student Congress   a conference held in Mexico in 1921 that was inspired by the influence spreading throughout Latin America of the UNIVERSITY REFORM PROGRAM AND MOVEMENT, initiated three years earlier at the University of Córdoba in Argentina. University students from 23 nations, including the United States and Asian and European nations, attended the congress. The delegates issued declarations that advocated adoption of the University Reform Program by universities throughout Latin America, extension courses to serve the working classes, and opposition to militaristic and dictatorial governments in Latin America.

International Student Theater Union (ISTU)   an organization founded in 1962 to foster amateur theater groups, with membership open to all such university-associated groups. Its affiliates are based in Europe, where ISTU has sponsored four summer theater festivals in Germany, Italy, Turkey, and Yugoslavia.

International Union of Socialist Youth (IUSY)   an organization headquartered in Vienna and prominent during the 1960s that represented youths affiliated with the Social Democratic parties of various European nations. The revelation in 1968 that IUSY received funding from the American Central Intelligence Agency (CIA) plummeted the IUSY into inactivity.

International Union of Students (IUS)   a worldwide organization of university students founded in Prague, Czechoslovakia in August 1946. A committee of students representing Australia, Belgium, China, Czechoslovakia, Denmark, France, Great Britain, India, the Soviet Union, the United States, and Yugoslavia worked for a year to prepare for the organization's founding. Cold war politics, however, quickly took their toll since the group's 17-member (representing 17 nations) executive committee was dominated by communists. After a conference in Prague in 1948, the United States and Canada terminated their membership, as did other Western nations subsequently. One Western group that retained its membership was the UNION NATIONALE DES ÉTUDIANTS DE FRANCE (UNEF), which did not divorce itself from the IUS until November 1950 following the mounting unpopularity of the French Communist Party. Headquartered in Prague, the IUS was largely funded by the governments of the Soviet Union and Czechoslovakia. In 1947 the IUS began to publish a journal, *World Student News*, which has appeared in six languages. In later years, the IUS was wracked by internal conflicts that erupted especially at its periodic congresses; most notable was the political confrontation between the Soviet Union and the Republic of China, which to some extent menaced Soviet control over the IUS, and the political fallout from the Soviet Union's intervention in Czechoslovakia. Nevertheless, in 1964 students representing organizations in 87 nations attended the IUS congress, suggesting a continuing strength. Following the death of the INTERNATIONAL STUDENT CONFERENCE (ISC) in 1969, the IUS remained as the sole international student organization.

Bibliography: Philip G. Altbach and Norman T. Uphoff, *International Student Politics* (Metuchen, N.J.: Scarecrow Press, 1973).

International University Sports Federation (FISU)   an organization established in 1959, independent from both the INTERNATIONAL UNION OF STUDENTS (IUS) and the INTERNATIONAL STUDENT CONFERENCE (ISC), by student unions in Western European nations. As a sponsor of international sports events FISU has organized student olympics, Universiades, that occur every two years in diverse locales and have attracted thousands of participants from dozens of nations. FISU, headquartered in Louvain, Belgium, has consistently tried to avoid involvement in political antagonisms or issues.

International Youth Hostel Federation   a worldwide organization of youth hostel associations founded in 1932. The federation's purpose is to serve as coordinator and facilitator for the travel programs that hostel associations afford to their members. By 1970 nearly 50 national associations with 20 million individual members belonged to the federation, which sponsored more than 4,200 hostels worldwide.

Inter-Varsity Christian Fellowship (IVCF)   (United States) a nondenominational, evangelical movement actually begun in the early 1920s at Oxford and Cambridge universities in England as an intercollegiate union; it attained its greatest prominence in the United States, where it was first established in 1940. IVCF flourished in the religious revival that followed World War II and in time developed chapters at more than 400 university, college, nursing school, and other campuses. Its membership was enhanced by the rise of the JESUS MOVEMENT in the late 1960s and early 1970s. IVCF holds a national convention every third year; its 1970 convention, held at the University of Illinois, attracted 12,000 participants—apparently the largest student religious meeting ever held to that time in this nation. With a central administration and a field staff that serve as advisers, or "coaches," for campus groups, IVCF stresses individual spiritual and intellectual growth and functioning as a Christian within a student's own environment. IVCF does not conduct religious services as such but instead fosters Christianity through small action groups characterized by Bible study, prayer, discussion, and fellowship.

Intifada   (Palestine) a Palestinian uprising that began in December 1987 in the Israeli-occupied West Bank and Gaza. The catalyst for the Intifada occurred when an Israeli army tank-transport crashed into a truck carrying Palestinian workers returning to Gaza from their jobs in Israel—four of the workers were killed. The funerals of three of them at the Jabalya refugee camp on December 8 and 9 sparked the uprising. Crowds comprised mostly of teenagers demonstrated, and when Israeli soldiers arrived to disperse them, the youths hurled rocks and iron bars. The soldiers lobbed tear gas and opened fire on the demonstrators, killing a 20-year-old and injuring many others. The young protestor's death incited anger, and the uprising spread throughout Gaza and the West Bank during the next few days, launching the Intifada.

By the end of 1987, more than a dozen Palestinians had been killed and dozens more wounded, and the protests continued unabated into 1988. The Israeli military arrested hundreds of students and closed schools and universities; many of those arrested were kept in admininstrative detention or even deported. The universities remained closed for most of 1988; ironically, the closings freed students to participate more fully in the Intifada. In March 1988 the military outlawed the *shabiba*, an informal youth movement in the West Bank and Gaza whose members participated in the Intifada. In fact, children, many only seven to ten years old, formed much of the backbone of the Intifada—they were the stone throwers. They also did the work of rolling the tires they set afire and other obstructions onto roads. The ablest stonethrowers were those age 15 to 19 who were adept at using slingshots—and they were the most hunted down by Israeli troops. Youths older than 19 provided leadership in directing attacks on the troops. Among the many communal groups that emerged by early 1988 to organize and lead the Intifada was the Social Youth Movement (Shebab), formed in 1982 and affiliated with the Palestine Liberation Organization (PLO). From such communal groups arose the Unified National Leadership of the Uprising (UNLU), which provided the Intifada's organization and leadership.

Israel poured troops into Gaza and the West Bank to suppress the Intifada. In this effort, they used ruthless tactics—indiscriminate beatings, arbitrary arrests and detention, and torture; they entered homes during the night and arrested all the teenage youths they found. These tactics not only demoralized many Israeli soldiers but also incited protests by many groups within Israel that opposed their government's policies in the occupied territories. Daily confrontations occurred in the West Bank and Gaza between Israeli troops and rock-throwing Palestinian youths. To some extent the Intifada also began to employ boycotts of Israeli goods, strikes, mass violations of curfews, refusing to work in Israel, and other tactics to enhance the opposition to the Israeli occupation. As the Intifada continued, the PLO provided some leadership and direction from its headquarters in Tunis. To strike a blow against this leadership, the Israeli government authorized agents to assassinate Abu Jihad, PLO Chairman Yasir Arafat's closest aide, in April 1988. The assassination only intensified the Intifada uprising, with more violent attacks on Israeli soldiers. By the end of the first full year of the Intifada, Israeli forces had imprisoned 20,000 Palestinians, many of them teenagers and many arbitrarily imprisoned and interrogated for long periods; they had also wounded more than 20,000 and killed more than 360—all to no avail. As the Intifada continued into the 1990s, a new Israeli government headed by former Defense Minister Yitzhak Rabin, who perhaps ironically had directed the failed effort to suppress the Intifada, would seek a political solution in secret negotiations with the PLO.

Bibliography: Don Peretz, *Intifada: The Palestinian Uprising* (Boulder, Colo.: Westview Press, 1990).

Jackson State College Riot (United States) a student-police confrontation on May 17, 1970 at Jackson State College, a black school in Jackson, Mississippi. The riot resulted in the killing of two male students, one a junior at the college and the other a high school senior. The confrontation resulted after rioters—reportedly not students at the college—threw stones and bottles at white motorists passing by the campus. Police arrived, someone set fire to a car, and students congregated before a women's residence hall shouting at the police. The police, who afterwards contended they had been fired on by a sniper in the residence hall, opened fire, killing the two students and wounding nine others—all blacks. Attorney General John Mitchell visited the campus and initiated an investigation by his department. A second confrontation was avoided on May 21 when an assistant attorney general in charge of the Civil Rights Division, Jerris Leonard, intervened as students, believing bullet-riddled panels at the residence hall would be destroyed as evidence by Mississippi police, held a vigil to keep the police from confiscating them, and the FBI took control of the panels. The President's Commission on Campus Unrest held three days of public hearings in Jackson in August; in its report issued in October, the commission condemned the police for the shootings. A federal grand jury convened in Jackson was discharged in December after failing to return any indictments.

Jahn, Friedrich Ludwig (1778–1852) (Germany) founder of the TURNVEREIN and hence known as Turnvater (father of gymnastics). Jahn studied theology and languages at the universities of Halle, Göttingen, and Greifswald. He joined the Prussian army following its humiliating defeat by Napoleon's forces at the Battle of Jena (October 1806). In 1809 he went to Berlin, where he taught school. In 1810 he published *Das Deutsches Volksthum*, a treatise on German cultural nationalism that touted the Volksgemeinschaft (folk community) ideal and resurrection of the Teutonic civilization. Jahn became concerned over the demoralizing effects of the defeats Napoleon had inflicted on the Prussians, and he determined to restore morale by promoting physical fitness and moral uplift through gymnastics. In 1811 in Berlin he opened the first *Turnplatz*, an open-air gymnasium, and there taught gymnastics to youths. In 1813 Jahn helped create the Lutzow Freikorps and commanded one of its battalions in the war against Napoleon. After Napoleon's defeat in 1815, Jahn returned to Berlin as state teacher of gymnastics. In this post he helped found the first BURSCHENSCHAFTEN at Jena. In 1819, because of his advocacy of democratic views, the authorities closed his *Turnplatz* and arrested and imprisoned Jahn. He was released in 1825 but forbidden to return to Berlin. He spent the rest of his life in Freiburg. In 1840 the Prussian government awarded Jahn the Iron Cross for his service in the Napoleonic Wars. He was elected to the German National Parliament in 1848.

Jakarta Riots (Indonesia) three days of turbulence in the Indonesian capital city in January 1974 that coincided with a state visit by Japanese Prime Minister Kakuei Tanaka. The uprising was supposedly a protest against growing Japanese commercial interests in Indonesia, but in reality it amounted to an attack on the regime of General Suharto. The protests began with student demonstrations on January 14, the day of Tanaka's arrival; the students demonstrated outside the office of Suharto's ally, Lieutenant-General Ali Murtopo, and burned effigies of Tanaka and General Sudjomo Humardani, Suharto's personal assistant for economic affairs. Similar student demonstrations occurred in Bandung. On the morning of January 15, student demonstrators marched through Jakarta, demanding that Suharto dismiss Humardani, Murtopo, and Major General Soerjo and that political

The view from the bullet-riddled girls dormitory at Jackson State College where two students were killed and nine injured. Police opened fire on the building after they claimed they were fired on by snipers.   (AP/WIDE WORLD PHOTOS)

corruption be brought to an end and prices of goods be reduced. On this day, mobs of children and youths from poorer sections of the city, along with *becak* drivers, joined the students in the streets, and violent rioting ensued. The rioters attacked Japanese enterprises, such as the showrooms of the Astra Motor Company. They burned and pillaged more than 100 stores and set fire to about 650 cars, mostly Japanese. Security forces fired on the rioters in some areas of the city. After two days of riots, 11 people were dead and 130 were wounded. Although the student demonstrations may possibly have been supported by Suharto's political rivals, including General Sumitro, the rioting had been spontaneous. Suharto took advantage of the outbreak to reassert his authority, removing Sumitro from control of both the armed forces and security forces and reassigning other opponents to ambassadorships that would take them out of the country. Thus as an expression of opposition to Suharto, the student demonstrations and the riots backfired.

Japan Young Communist Alliance   (Japan) an organization for students and other youths founded in February 1946. It was an offshoot of the Japan Communist Party (JCP).

Jesus Movement   (United States) a religious movement among youths, mostly of age 14 to 24, that originated in the late 1960s; to a large extent, it grew out of the evangelical and pentecostal traditions. Most of the Jesus people of the movement's early years had some involvement with the youth culture of the time, including drug use; the majority also were of middle-class or upper-middle-class backgrounds, and it is estimated that about 30 percent were Jewish (Jews for Jesus in fact is associated with the movement). The Jesus Movement's exact origins are obscure but trace to California and such sources as the Salt Company Coffee House (opened in Hollywood in 1967 by the Hollywood Presbyterian Church) and The Living Room (opened in San Francisco's Haight-Ashbury district in 1968)—both coffeehouse establishments serving as centers for evangelical ministries. Its origins also trace to such street-corner evangelists of the same years as Sue and Tony Alamo (a converted Jew), who subsequently sited their ministry, the Christian

Indonesian students burn effigies of "economic imperialism" and "dogs of Japan" at a rally in Jakarta. The protest came as Indonesia prepared to host Prime Minister Kakuei Tanaka of Japan who was making his last stop on a five-country visit through Southeast Asia. (AP/WIDE WORLD PHOTOS)

Foundation, at a ranch near Saugus, California while maintaining their street evangelism in Los Angeles.

Whether associated with churches or having their own meeting places ("Jesus houses" or "Jesus centers"), Jesus people share in common certain beliefs and modes of expression. Their beliefs are summarized in their "One Way" maxim—that Jesus Christ represents the only means of salvation and that the Second Coming is near. They emphasize judgment and repentance, Bible study and classes, gospel and rock music, testimony, and even some speaking in tongues. In many cases, followers of the movement live in communes. Several communes exist under the direction of the Christian Foundation, for example, and several others are affiliated with the Calvary Chapel in Santa Ana; the most famous communal group is the Children of God, an offshoot of the Jesus Movement that is strongly apocalyptic and has colonies throughout North America and Europe. Jesus people have held parades and demonstrations and have disrupted rock concerts "to witness" and to promote their beliefs. The movement has fostered numerous publications, among them the Berkeley-centered World Christian Liberation Front's *Right On!* and the *Hollywood Free Paper*, both begun in 1969; *Truth* published in Spokane; and the New York Bible Society's *Great News*. The Jesus Movement has promoted its views on university campuses through the Campus Crusade for Christ and the INTER-VARSITY CHRISTIAN FELLOWSHIP. A number of celebrated entertainers have been associated with the Jesus Movement, including Johnny Cash, Arlo Guthrie, Tiny Tim, and Pat Boone.

Bibliography: Ronald M. Enroth and Edward E. Ericson, Jr., *The Jesus People: Old-Time Religion in the Age of Aquarius* (Grand Rapids, Mich.: W. B. Erdmans Publishing Company, 1972).

Jeune République, La (The Young Republic) (France) a youth movement, although not restricted to youths, begun in the early 1920s by Marc Sangnier, a Christian Democrat member of the Chamber of Deputies, and some Roman Catholic friends. It was a democratic movement whose purpose was to establish Christian principles as the norm for all areas and forms of behavior, from private to political, not only nationally but internationally. The movement was open to everyone regardless of class, religion, or occupation in an effort to promote understanding and fellowship. Members of the movement published a weekly newspaper, *La Jeune République*, and a bimonthly review, *La Démocrate*. La Jeune République also participated in international congresses and formed alliances with groups in other nations.

Jeunes Gens de Paris, Les (France) "the youth of Paris" of the late 1820s and the 1830s who were viewed by others as a definable group that became referred to as the Bohemians. The Bohemians lived in the Latin Quarter, making it a tourist mecca. They effected a contempt for work and responsibility, touted living only in the present, and wore outlandish clothes accented with long hair and beards. The Bohemians avowed an interest in Eastern religions, mysticism, alchemy, satanism, and occult subjects. Many saw Lord Byron and other Romantic poets as their heroes. There was no quite comparable group in any other major European city of the era.

Jeunesse Communiste Révolutionnaire (JCR) (France) an organization formed in March 1967 and centered at the Sorbonne in Paris by students having a nondoctrinaire Trotskyist orientation. The JCR had no affiliation with a political party. It was declared illegal after the May–June 1968 student uprising but continued under its original name.

Jeunesse du Rassemblement Démocratique Africain de Côte d'Ivoire (JRDACI) (Ivory Coast) the youth branch of the Parti Démocratique de la Côte d'Ivoire (PDCI), which was created on September 12, 1958. Provisional leaders of the JRDACI helped to set up 70 branches throughout the nation by February 1959, and the new organization's first congress occurred March 14–16, 1959. Youth delegates at the congress insisted on an autonomous constitution for the JRDACI so that it could comprise an opposition within the PDCI, the dominant political party as the Ivory Coast approached independence (achieved in August 1960). The JRDACI promoted democratic reorganization of the PDCI and free discussions of party policies. As the party saw it, the JRDACI's importance was as a training ground for future leaders of the PDCI and thus of the nation. The JRDACI foundered, however, upon a purported leftist plot to overthrow the PDCI-led government in 1962–63 that resulted in nearly two-thirds of its leaders being sentenced to prison; in 1965 the JRDACI was dissolved.

Jeunesse Étudiante Chrétienne (JEC) *See* ASSOCIATION CATHOLIQUE DE LA JEUNESSE FRANÇAISE.

Jeunesse Françiste (France) the youth movement of the Parti Françiste (Blue Shirts), a political party modeled after the Italian and Spanish Fascist movements, founded in 1933, and headquartered in Aix-en-Provence. Although the party was banned during Léon Blum's coalition administration (1936–37), it reappeared in 1941 after the German conquest of France as a collaborationist group. The Jeunesse Françiste comprised three groupings: cadets, avant-gardes (older boys), and guides (girls). Ostensibly, the Jeunesse Françiste members pursued programs fostering civic awareness and the study of Marxism, capitalism, Judaism, and other subjects, but at times they armed themselves and rallied to intimidate local officials.

Jeunesse Ouvrière Chrétienne *See* ASSOCIATION CATHOLIQUE DE LA JEUNESSE FRANÇAISE.

Jewish Lads' Brigade (Great Britain) an organization for Jewish boys inspired by and modeled on the military-style CHURCH LADS' BRIGADE. The Jewish Lads' Brigade (JLB) was essentially the creation of Colonel Albert Edward Goldsmid (1846–1904), a Zionist who envisioned the JLB as serving the sons of poor East European Jewish immigrants who were living in East London and were too young to be in the Jewish Boys' Club. In 1894 he presented his proposal for creation of the JLB to a society of Jewish intellectuals known as the Maccabeans, who ended up providing most of the funding for the youth movement in its early years. The JLB's first meeting convened in the hall of the Jews' Free School in Spitalfields in February 1895 and was attended by about 120 boys. Most of the early members came from the Jewish Board Schools in or near the Aldgate East area. After 1900 the JLB spread into other London areas, attaining an estimated membership of 1,000 in the city, with another 4,000 members throughout England. Goldsmid served as the JLB's commandant until his death in 1904. In 1913 and the years thereafter, the JLB's London social center was Camperdown House in Whitechapel. An enduring goal of the JLB was to foster the Anglicization of its boys in order to promote their assimilation into English society. In 1963 was founded a Jewish Girls' Brigade, which added such activities as first aid, cooking, and crafts to the JLB's standard military-drill routine.

Bibliography: Sidney Bunt, *Jewish Youth Work in Britain: Past, Present, and Future* (London: Bedford Square Press, 1975).

Jichikai *See* STUDENT SELF-GOVERNING ASSOCIATIONS.

"Jingo Day" Demonstration (United States) a student protest against the Reserve Officer Training Corps (ROTC) program at City College of New York (CCNY) in May 1933 renowned for the "umbrella attack." CCNY President Frederick B. Robinson, known for his efforts to suppress student protests, canceled afternoon classes for May 29, 1933 so that students could attend an annual ceremony of military exercises prior to Memorial Day. Antiwar students labeled the event "Jingo Day" and organized an antiwar rally to coincide with the military exercises. About 700 students gathered for the rally, but they were so close to assembling ROTC cadets that police ordered them to disperse. They rallied about a half-block away and began to picket the stadium where the military exercises were sited. Many tried to enter the stadium but were ejected; they gathered elsewhere and renewed the attempt. About 100 gained admittance but encountered closed doors and cadets and police who forced them back. Robinson arrived on this scene with the ROTC commander and some guests. Suddenly, he hoisted his umbrella and clobbered about a dozen students with it, supposedly in an effort to clear a path to the stadium. Some students tried to disarm him. Police intervened and escorted Robinson into the stadium. The CCNY Student Forum put out an issue of its newsletter with the headline "Robinson Runs Amok on Campus: Maddened President Attacks Students." Administration officials confiscated copies of the newsletter and suspended 29 students, three student organizations, and the student newspaper. Undaunted, students led by the NATIONAL STUDENT LEAGUE (NSL) and the STUDENT LEAGUE FOR INDUSTRIAL DEMOCRACY (SLID) held large off-campus protest rallies through the following week, ending with an "umbrella parade" that included an enlarged replica of Robinson's weapon. An American Civil Liberties Union investigation indicated that, enraged by the protestors outside the stadium, Robinson had launched the umbrella attack without provocation and therefore was responsible for the consequences. Those consequences included widespread media attention for the student antiwar movement. In fact, the movement benefited greatly from publicity and with new adherents following each of Robinson's efforts to suppress CCNY student protestors, but his jingo-day attack drew exceptional attention.

Joan of Arc (c.1412–1431) (France) a pious peasant girl who in 1429, at the age of 17, led French troops to victory over the English at Orléans during the Hundred Years' War and made possible the crowning of Charles VII as king of France. Joan began to hear "voices" when she was 13, and at 16 these voices prompted her to travel to Vaucouleurs in May 1428 in hopes of joining the dauphin's forces. Not taken seriously, she returned home but was back in Vaucouleurs the following January. This time she succeeded, and, dressed as a man and accompanied by troops, she was sent to the dauphin in Chinon. After weeks of questioning by ecclesiastics, Joan was dispatched to Orléans and there on May 6 and 7 led the French troops in successful offensives against the English and the Burgundians, causing their retreat and lifting the siege from the city. She then helped defeat the English at various sites along the Loire and achieved a major victory at Patay on June 18. She persuaded the dauphin to travel to Reims, traditional coronation site of the French kings, where he was consecrated as Charles VII on July 17 with Joan in attendance. After several other battles, including a failed attempt to take Paris, Joan was unhorsed during battle at Compiègne in May 1430 and captured by the Burgundians, who turned her over to the English. After months of interrogation by ecclesiastical authorities, she abjured her earlier testimony, in effect admitting heresy, and was sentenced to life imprisonment. Later recanting this abjuration, Joan was submitted to English secular authorities, who had her burned at the stake on May 30, 1431. Investigations 20 years later led to the annulment of her sentence, and on May 16, 1920 Joan was canonized by Pope Benedict XV. She is France's greatest heroine, and a national festival is held in her honor each year on the second Sunday in May.

Job's Daughters (United States) a Masonic organization for girls and young women founded by Ethel Mick in Omaha, Nebraska in 1921. Membership is open to youths age 12 to 20, but they must be related to a Master Mason. The organization's ritual derives from the Book of Job, and its motto is "Virtue is a quality which adorns women." Local groups are known as bethels; each must hold two fund-raising projects per year. The organization is established nationwide and in numerous foreign countries.

Johnson Affair (United States) a student protest in the fall of 1932 at City College of New York (CCNY) over the firing of Oakley Johnson, a left-wing English instructor. Johnson had been a member of the LEAGUE FOR INDUSTRIAL DEMOCRACY and the NATIONAL STUDENT LEAGUE (NSL), he publicly supported the Communist Party, and he had accompanied students on the HARLAN MINERS' STRIKE expedition. Although CCNY's President Frederick B. Robinson had been conducting an antiradical campaign at the college for over a year, the administration gave the excuse of falling enrollments in dismissing Johnson. Student newspapers called for Johnson's reinstatement, and on October 26, 1932 several hundred students staged a protest rally and marched into the administration building. Robinson called out the police, who clubbed and dispersed the demonstrators, arresting 20—the first instance of a university president requesting police action against student protestors during the Great Depression decade. In response, about 1,000 students demonstrated at the courthouse. They also held a mock trial of Robinson and Paul Linehan, director of the night school. NSL members assumed the roles of prosecutor, defense attorney, and judges with 28 witnesses testifying. The audience found both Robinson and Linehan guilty of political censorship and suppression and sentenced them to abdicating their posts. Robinson saw no humor in the trial and suspended 19 students who had organized it.

Jugendbewegung   (Germany) during the first three decades of the 20th century, the German youth movement overall, including both organized groups and inchoate, spontaneous, or localized groups as well as the spirit of the youth movement as a whole. Certain tenets or views permeated the movement: a spirit of revolt; opposition to the conventional authority of the church, the school, and the home; an emphasis on experiencing nature (a form of pantheism); a striving for self-determination; a dedication to vague religious or spiritual ideals; patriotism and a desire for German renewal. Such views were regarded as exemplifying the universal and unchanging character of youth. In 1927, the apex of the youth movement in Germany, 56 percent of the young males and 26 percent of the young females in the nation belonged to a youth organization. *See also* FREI-DEUTSCHE JUGEND.

July 26 Movement   (Cuba) a revolutionary movement led by Fidel Castro, whose purpose was to overthrow the dictatorship of Fulgencio Batista and whose name derived from an abortive effort to initiate an uprising against Batista that occurred on July 26, 1953. At dawn on that day Castro, then 26 years old, led 134 of his supporters (*fidelistas*) in a surprise attack on the Moncada military barracks at Santiago, where a thousand troops were stationed. A group led by Castro's younger brother Raúl actually captured the Palace of Justice in Santiago, but the others, poorly armed and severely outnumbered, were quickly routed, as were another band of 28 who simultaneously attacked the Bayamo barracks. The rebels killed 16 soldiers and three officers. Castro lost eight men, and on May 26 and following days about 80 more were apprehended. Most of them were summarily shot, and others tortured and brought to trial. Castro himself was captured, tried, and sentenced to 15 years in prison. The brutality of the repression and the trials ironically won Castro stature among the public. Now his movement, previously known sometimes as the Youth of the Centenary or just the Movement, would have a distinct name. Castro, Raúl, and 18 of their comrades left prison in May 1955 under an amnesty. In July, Castro left for Mexico to rebuild his guerilla force.

On November 25, 1956, sailing aboard the yacht *Granma*, Castro and 81 rebels planned to attack in Ori-

ente Province on November 30, coincidental with an uprising in Santiago led by Frank Pais. A 23-year-old student at the University of Santiago, Pais was the most effective organizer among the July 26 Movement's groups remaining in Cuba and had brought many young men and women to his cause. At dawn, Pais coordinated about 300 youths who wore red-and-black armbands representing the movement; they attacked the police headquarters, the harbor headquarters, and the Customs House, captured the first two, and set fire to the latter. Another group entered the Boniato prison and freed some political prisoners. Pais and his followers then left the city but returned on December 1 to torch the harbor headquarters and capture several public buildings—they were in effective control of Santiago. Pais's forces had killed several police officers and suffered three dead. Batista sent reinforcements to put down the uprising. The *Granma* missed the action, having foundered in rough seas, only belatedly on December 2 bringing the rebels to the west coast of Oriente, where they were quickly attacked by waiting troops. Castro, Raúl, Ernesto "Che" Guevara, and nine others managed to escape to the Sierra Maestra, where the movement began to rebuild. Students and other youths joined Castro in the mountains. Pais, who consulted with Castro in the mountains, was shot and killed by the police in Santiago on July 30, 1957.

As the July 26 Movement's strength and support slowly grew, civil war followed. Batista made one large-scale offensive against Castro in the Sierra Maestra in May 1958 that ended in both disaster and the forced withdrawal of the invading forces. In August 1958 the July 26 Movement, with the support of student groups in Santiago and Havana, began a final drive to oust Batista, who fled to the Dominican Republic on January 1, 1959, leaving Castro in control of Cuba. *See also* DIRECTORIO REVOLUCIONARIO.

Bibliography: Hugh Thomas, *The Cuban Revolution* (New York: Harper and Row, 1977).

June Tenth Incident   (Korea) a demonstration in Seoul on June 10, 1926, the funeral day of Sunjong, the last Korean emperor, who had died on April 25, 1926. A protest against Japanese rule, the demonstration involved tens of thousands of Koreans, including thousands of students, many flying the banned Korean national flag or the Red flag. At the time, there were 44 youth associations and 300 religious youth societies involved in advocacy of political, social, and economic reforms. The incident also came to be known as the Second March First Movement, referring to the MARCH FIRST MOVEMENT of 1919, although the arrest of scores of socialists and communists by the Japanese precluded any ongoing movement.

June Third Movement   (China) a term that CHINESE COMMUNIST PARTY leader Mao Zedong applied to the

MAY FOURTH MOVEMENT in order to obfuscate the primacy of the role that students and intellectuals played in that movement. June Third Movement actually refers to the time when the workers' began to provide massive support to the students' May Fourth Movement through nationwide strikes.

Jungdeutschlandbund (Germany) an organization for youths founded in 1911 and led by adults. Its primary program was military training, which initially discouraged the participation of WANDERVOGEL groups that the bund tried to involve. Many Wandervogel groups did in time join the bund to enjoy its benefits, which included savings on railroad fares. Among the bund's goals was to instill patriotism and to prepare youths for citizenship; it was also strongly antisocialistic in orientation. The bund had 750,000 members by 1914, making it the most popular youth group in the nation, but it died during World War I, which began in August of that year.

Junge Nationaldemokraten (JN) (Germany) the radical youth wing of the rightist National Democratic Party (NPD) founded in 1970 with a membership of 1,000. The JN is notable for organizing campaigns to intimidate Jews and foreign laborers, bombing a hostel for refugees in Hamburg, and merging with Neonazi groups in Berlin and northern Germany.

Junge Union (JU) (Germany) the youth affiliate of the Christian Democratic Union (CDU) that was formed during the years 1947–50 and came to power in 1949 with the election of Konrad Adenauer as chancellor of the Federal Republic. The JU, among other things, serves as a means of generating members for the CDU party.

Junior Achievement (JA) (United States) a nationwide, nonprofit organization devoted to the involvement of youths in the free enterprise system. Inspired by the success of 4-H CLUBS, Horace Moses, a paper company executive in Springfield, Massachusetts, decided to create a similar organization in urban areas to train youths for business careers. With Theodore N. Vail, former AT&T president, and Senator Murray Crane, he formed the first Junior Achievement in Springfield in 1926, open to youths age 8–12. In 1929 the organization was extended to New York and the age limits were changed to 6–21. Charles Hook, president of Armco Steel, spearheaded the effort to expand JA into a national organization, beginning with a meeting of 750 business leaders in New York on December 5, 1941. JA grew rapidly and by the 1960s had programs in 250 cities. Each JA group is a company of about 15 youths formed at the beginning of the school year; each company elects an executive committee, chooses a product to make, raises capital by selling stock (each member must own at least one share), opens a bank account, buys raw materials and tools, obtains a JA charter and pays rent, and begins production and marketing. Members earn wages and commissions established by vote and maintain budgets, accounts, and records; they apply a bookkeeping system developed by the American Institute of Certified Public Accountants. When the school year ends, the company is terminated, and any profits are distributed to the stockholders. Through this program, directed by advisers from the business community, youths learn about the processes, risks, and opportunities of business enterprise. Junior Achievement, headquartered in New York, receives financial support from corporations and other businesses.

Junior Missionary Volunteers Pathfinder Club (United States) an organization for boys and girls formed by the Seventh-Day Adventist Church in 1950. Its primary goals are to promote Christian ideals and entrance into missionary service. All youths who are at least 10 years old may join, although the Pathfinders is primarily for members of the church. Members may become club leaders with the rank of master guide through achievement of honors in numerous nature and crafts activities. Programs include hobbies, camping, art, hiking, nature lore, field trips, drills, and much more. Achievements and awards resemble those in the BOY SCOUTS OF AMERICA, but Pathfinders differ in emphasizing religion in all activities and involving both boys and girls together in the clubs. Pathfinders is now a worldwide organization.

Junior Optimist Club (United States) an organization for teenage boys founded in 1924 by the Optimist Club. Mostly centered at junior high schools, the Junior Optimist Clubs focus on recognizing and encouraging youths who are responsible and creditable. Optimists present awards to Junior Optimists for scholarship, citizenship, sportsmanship, leadership, and community service. Major programs of the Junior Optimists in support of these purposes include sponsorship of sports events and community-service activities and projects. In addition, the Optimist Club sponsors a variety of youth programs such as JUNIOR ACHIEVEMENT, BOY SCOUTS OF AMERICA, and BOYS' CLUBS OF AMERICA.

Kakukyodo *See* NIHON KAKUMEITEKI KYOSAN-SHUGISHA DOMEI.

Kakumaru (Revolutionary Marxists) (Japan) a student organization formed on July 8, 1963 by the Revolutionary Communist League (Kakukyodo, short for *Kakumeiteki Kyosanshigisha Domei*), itself founded in June 1958 in opposition to the Japan Communist Party (JCP). (*Kakumaru* is a contraction.) Kakumaru is a faction within the ZENGAKUREN; its greatest stronghold is at Waseda University and other Tokyo schools. Kakumaru controlled numerous STUDENT SELF-GOVERNING ASSOCIATIONS and also had high-school-level organizations, such as the Marxist High School Students' League in Tokyo.

KAMI *See* ACTION COMMAND OF INDONESIAN STUDENTS.

Kapp Putsch (Germany) an abortive uprising by a Freikorps in Berlin on March 13, 1920 that attempted to topple the Weimar Republic government and restore the monarchy. Its name derived from the involvement of Dr. Wolfgang Kapp, a U.S.-born, right-wing member of the Reichstag (Parliament); Kapp declared himself chancellor with the support of General Erich Ludendorff, who had been chief of staff during World War I. A sympathetic Reichswehr (army) corps failed in its duty to suppress the putsch, and the government fled to south Germany. But a general strike called by the unions secured restoration of the legal government four days later. Students were involved through their participation in the Technische Nothilfe (Technical Emergency Aid), which provided utilities and other services during the strike—at least implicit support for the putsch. In addition, students helped the army to quash uprisings in the Rhineland and Saxony-Thüringen by left-wing revolu-

tionaries opposing the Kapp Putsch. In Thüringen a student contingent, involved in the suppression of the counterinsurgency, shot 15 prisoners who were alleged to be "red guards." Despite the evidence of their culpability, a military tribunal exonerated the students, eliciting denunciations in the press and from some politicians.

Kartell-Convent (KC) (Germany) an organization of Jewish student associations (corporations) founded in 1896. The KC's purpose was to combat anti-Semitism while fostering "the education of their members as self-conscious Jews." It rejected religious and political separatism for Jews, insisting on their unity "through history, culture, and legal community with the German fatherland." The KC had its own journal, the *Kartell-Convent Blatter*.

Kartell-Verband (KV) (Germany) an organization of Roman Catholic student associations (*Studentenvereine*) founded in 1866. The KV's motto was "Religion, Scholarship, and Sociability," and its intent was to represent "the cause of Catholicism among German students." In the early years of its existence, the KV was open to members of other groups and was simple in structure, but by the end of the century it had taken on the formalism of the student fraternities, with flags, colors, and other ritualistic features.

Katholische Jugend Deutschlandes (Catholic Youth of Germany) (Germany) a youth movement of the Roman Catholic church that was headquartered in Düsseldorf and had a president, a staff, and individual chapters led mostly by priests. The Katholische Jugend was dedicated to educating youths in the tenets and worldview of the Roman Catholic church. In the 1920s, the organization published seven periodicals that had a total circulation of 200,000.

Kazan Square Demonstration (Russia) a peaceful demonstration on Sunday, March 4, 1901, in Kazan Square in St. Petersburg involving students and other protestors. The event was preceded by a planned student demonstration on February 19 at the square that authorities thought had been precluded by mass arrests of students who had met to plan the protest. But about 400 students assembled at the square for the February 19 demonstration; police arrested 244, including 128 female and 71 male students—the other 45 were nonstudent onlookers. In response, the St. Petersburg University Organization Committee (*see* ALL-RUSSIA STUDENT STRIKE OF 1899) organized the March 4 demonstration and purposely invited public participation, as the February 19 event had evoked public sympathy for the students.

A massive crowd, mostly students, gathered at Kazan Square before Kazan Cathedral on March 4. Mounted Cossacks forced the demonstrators against the cathedral's steps and blocked streets leading to the square to prevent the demonstrators from escaping. Both Cossacks and police armed with sabres and whips brutally attacked and dispersed the demonstrators, injuring about 60 and arresting 775. Many of those arrested were students, who were held for three weeks, then expelled from St. Petersburg University or other schools they attended, and finally banned from the city. But the government had not made use of the 29 July Temporary Rules, which mandated military conscription for offending students, thus suggesting a willingness to compromise. (The expulsion and banning were rescinded later in the summer in time for students to be readmitted for the fall term.)

Reports of police brutality evoked public outrage and support for the students in St. Petersburg, and the event received widespread attention as the basis of Maxim Gorky's revolutionary poem "Song of the Stormy Petrel." In a conciliatory gesture, Tsar Nicholas II announced the appointment of a commission headed by General P. S. Vannovskii to investigate the possibility of revoking the Temporary Rules and to propose reforms in the higher education system. Students felt they had cause to believe the student movement had proven an effectual means of prodding the government toward making reforms—that is, they felt they had won. They would, however, be proven wrong: the March 4 demonstration and its suppression, as it turned out, constituted one of the preludes to "BLOODY SUNDAY" and the REVOLUTION OF 1905.

Bibliography: Samuel D. Kassow, *Students, Professors, and the State in Tsarist Russia* (Berkeley: University of California Press, 1989).

Kent State Massacre (United States) a deadly confrontation between students and troops of the National Guard that resulted from riots and antiwar protests. The protests occurred on May 4, 1970 at Kent State University in Kent, Ohio, primarily in response to the sending of U.S. troops into Cambodia. Tensions had been building in Kent and at the university campus for three days preceeding the tragedy. On the night of May 1, scores of students flooded out of downtown bars and onto North Water Street, dancing and blocking traffic. When an irate motorist made threatening gestures, students climbed atop his car and shouted antiwar slogans. After someone hurled a bottle into the street, the students smashed the car's windows and windows in stores and set fires in trash cans. The mayor called out police to quell the disturbance and to enforce a curfew that the students had not known existed. The police emptied the bars and, with tear gas, forced the students back to the campus. On the night of May 2, black students who demanded increased enrollment of African Americans at Kent State joined forces with antiwar protestors in a rally at the Commons on the campus—about 800 students gathered. They attacked the Reserve Officer Training Corps (ROTC) building, breaking windows and throwing flares inside that set the building ablaze. When firefighters arrived, the protestors threw rocks at them and cut fire hoses with machetes. Police, again using tear gas, entered the fray. The mayor now requested aid from the National Guard, and Governor James Rhodes ordered about 500 troops of the guard to the campus; they had been working for three days at teamsters' strike sites. Armed with tear gas and loaded M-1 rifles and pistols, the guards helped police restore order.

Governor Rhodes arrived in Kent the next day, May 3, and condemned the protestors but refused to close the

A group of youths cluster around a wounded person as National Guards hold their weapons on Kent State University campus in Ohio. Four Kent State students were killed and nine wounded in a confrontation between students and guards. (AP/WIDE WORLD PHOTOS)

campus; he did however declare a state of emergency and forbade further demonstrations. That night, about 500 defiant students held a sit-in at a busy intersection in Kent and threw rocks at troops of the guard (now swelled in strength to about 900), who arrived to disperse them and arrested 150 in the process. Classes convened as usual on the morning of May 4, but at noon some students rang the Victory Bell and about 1,000 assembled at the Commons to test the ban on demonstrations. Another 2,000 gathered to watch. Officers in two jeeps approached from the National Guard's staging area at the ROTC building and ordered the protestors to disperse. The students responded with "Pigs off campus! We don't want your war." The jeeps withdrew, and guards, wearing helmets and gas masks, approached and began to fire tear-gas cannisters at the protestors. Students flung back some of the cannisters but also fled, with about 100 guards in pursuit. But the guards ran out of tear gas and nervously began to retreat back up the hill of the Commons. At the crest of the hill, some of them kneeled and aimed their rifles at rock-throwing students below; others stood behind them, guns raised. Suddenly they began to fire. Screaming students ran for safety; others stood in stunned silence. Four students—two women and two men, including an outstanding ROTC student, and none of them a protestor—lay dead, and nine were wounded. The shock of the massacre reverberated throughout the nation. Responding to the public's concern, President Richard Nixon on June 13 appointed the President's Commission on Campus Unrest, which investigated both the Kent State and the Jackson State tragedies. (*See* JACKSON STATE COLLEGE RIOT.) The commission, which held three days of public hearings in Kent in August, concluded that only the National Guard, no students or police, had fired shots; there were at least 54 shots fired by 29 guards. No order to fire had been given, and the only provocation had been rocks thrown by student protestors; reports of snipers were entirely false. Subsequent trials involving eight guards were held (in 1974, 1975, and 1978–79), but all were acquitted, and Ohio awarded $675,000 to parents of the dead students.

Bibliography: Peter Davies, et al., *The Truth About Kent State: A Challenge to the American Conscience* (New York: Farrar Straus, Giroux, 1973); Ottavio M. Casale, ed., *The Kent State Affair: Documents and Interpretations* (New York: Houghton Mifflin, 1971).

Key Club (United States) an organization sponsored by the Kiwanis Club for young men in high school as a service program for both their schools and their communities. The Kiwanis Club of Sacramento, California sponsored the first Key Club at a high school there in May 1925. The concept slowly spread nationwide, and in 1943 it evolved into the International Key Club and adopted a constitution and by-laws in 1946. The general office is in Chicago, where the official publication *The Keynoter* is produced. Although each Key Club is financially self-sustaining, two Kiwanis Club members are supposed to attend every meeting of the club. Key Club's overarching purpose is to provide community services that are meant to develop members' initiative, leadership, cooperation, and citizenship. Each club draws up a list of its service achievements for the year, and annual awards are presented to those clubs with the most impressive reports of achievements.

Khartoum Students' Strike (The Sudan) a protest in 1964 against General Ibrahim Abboud and his governing Military Council of The Sudan by members of the Students' Union of the University of Khartoum. The students initiated the strike in October 1964 primarily in opposition to the government's decision to place administration of the university, which was established in 1956 and had been autonomous since the founding of its first constituent college in 1903, under the authority of the Ministry of Education. The students were also protesting against government actions in the Southern Sudan, and their meetings occurred in defiance of a government ban. The student strike led to a nationwide general strike, riots, and demonstrations that eventuated in the temporary closing of the university but also in the collapse of the government. Unwilling to suppress the spreading protest, Abboud resigned as head of state and was replaced by a transitional government appointed under provisions of the constitution of 1956 that established The Sudan as a republic.

Kibbo Kift, the Woodcraft Kindred (Great Britain) a youth movement begun in August 1920 by John Hargrave, commissioner for camping and woodcraft at the BOY SCOUT Headquarters in London, and other London scoutmasters who were displeased with the nature of the scouts' involvement in World War I. *Kibbo Kift* means "proof of great strength" in an archaic version of English. Hargrave was influenced by the writings and theories of Ernest Thompson Seton and Stanley Hall (see ORDER OF WOODCRAFT CHIVALRY) and of H. G. Wells. From the latter, he derived the Kibbo Kift's emphasis on internationalism and pacifism that was written into the organization's Covenant. Although the Kibbo Kift was ostensibly socialist in its philosophy, Hargrave was autocratic and secretive, even devising a symbolic language for the group. The members' green or brown uniform included a Saxon-style cowl or jerkin, an army cloak, shorts, and sandals. Membership was always small and exclusive, peaking at 236 in 1924, when at the annual council, known as an Althing, a group representing South London cooperatives challenged Hargrave's dictatorial leadership and subsequently left the organization. By the early 1930s, Kibbo Kift had been absorbed by the Greenshirts wing of the League of the Unemployed. In 1935 the Greenshirt

Movement for Social Credit became the Social Credit Party; thus Kibbo Kift disappeared, subsumed into a political party.

Bibliography: John Hargrave, *The Confession of the Kibbo Kift* (London: Duckworth, 1927).

Kiev University Uprising (Russia) a major student demonstration at Kiev University in December 1900 that elicited an exceptionally repressive government response with assassination as a result. Students held meetings on November 13 and 15; the uprising's catalyst was the arrest of four students who had been leaders of these meetings and their sentence—internment in the university jail (kartser). Two of the students refused to enter the jail and were expelled. Responding to the expulsion, on December 7, 1900 about 700 students held a meeting at Kiev University's main auditorium and demanded reinstatement of the expelled students and elimination of the jail. Ordered to disperse, the students refused. The rector conceded his inability to control the situation, and so the governor-general of Kiev sent a detachment of mounted Cossacks and an army battalion to take control. The students presented their demands to the rector and began to leave the auditorium. The troops sent by the governor-general surrounded the building and arrested all 406 students who were present.

The government appointed a commission to try the students. Under the terms of the 29 July Temporary Rules (the government's response to the ALL-RUSSIA STUDENT STRIKE OF 1899 that mandated military conscription for student offenders), on December 31 the commission sentenced the two leaders of the original meeting to three years of military service, five other students to two years of service, and about 175 to one year of service; others received less-severe punishments. Student groups at the universities in Odessa, Moscow, and St. Petersburg reacted with calls for protest that were dampened by fear of similar reprisals under the Temporary Rules. At St. Petersburg University, the students' Organization Committee did stage a protest on January 25, 1901, but most students, fearing punishment, avoided involvement—28 of the ringleaders were sentenced to serve in the army, resulting in one's suicide.

Minister of Public Instruction Nicholas Bogolepov upheld the sentences imposed on 183 of the students and reprimanded the others, warning that if they committed another offense, their sentences would be carried out. In retaliation for the extreme severity of this punishment, students committed disruptive acts. On February 14, 1901, a disaffected former student named Peter Karpovich arrived at Bogolepov's office for an appointment and assassinated the minister, shooting him point blank with a revolver. The ensuing tensions and continuing student concerns over harsh penalties generated the KAZAN SQUARE DEMONSTRATION.

KISZ (Hungarian Communist Youth League) (Hungary) the youth wing of the Communist Party of Hungary (CPH) founded in November 1918 and therefore among the most important social organizations in Hungary. Youths age 14 to 28 comprise its membership, but KISZ has been more selective in admitting members than the similar KOMSOMOL in Russia; in 1985 about 38 percent (913,000) of those in the eligible age group belonged. But, as with Komsomol, membership provides access to higher education, careers, and CPH political involvement.

Knights of King Arthur (KOKA) (United States) an orqanization for boys founded in 1893 by Congregational clergyman William Byron Forbush. The KOKA was the most famous among a number of orders for boys based on chivalric codes of conduct; others included the Knights of the Holy Grail, the Knights Crusaders, the Knights of Methodism, the Epworth Court of Arthur, and the Knights of Valor. Each KOKA castle (the equivalent of a Boy Scout troop) was supervised and guided by a clergyman in the role of Merlin. Boys experienced three stages of membership: pages committed to obedience, service, and watchfulness; esquires committed to purity, reverence, and temperance; and knights as members of the church. They were initiated into these stages by means of pageants based on Alfred, Lord Tennyson's *Idylls of the King*, and they pledged themselves to be pure in body and heart. A forerunner of the BOY SCOUTS OF AMERICA, the KOKA had enrolled a total of 125,000 members by 1923, but it was displaced by scouting because of lack of national field workers to organize castles and round up recruits.

Kobel, Eberhard (1907–1955) (Germany) known as Tusk, the most influential youth leader of the early 1930s and founder of the distinctive Deutsche Jungenschaft. Born in Stuttgart, Kobel belonged to a WANDERVOGEL group and later to the DEUTSCHE FREISCHAR, in 1928 becoming the Freischar leader in Württemberg. He brought revolutionary changes to the Freischar publications that greatly enhanced their appeal. On November 1, 1929 he founded, with a small group, the Deutsche Jungenschaft of November 1st ("D.J.1.11"), with which he hoped to conspire to take control of the youth movement. The Junngenschaft under his charismatic leadership propounded some extraordinary concepts, including militarism based on mythical interpretations of the Samurai. Kobel joined the German Communist Party briefly in 1932. In that year, his Jungenschaft energized the youth movement, but too late. Opposed to Nazism, Kobel was arrested by the Gestapo in January 1934 but later released; in June 1934 he left for Sweden and exile in London, England. After World War II, he returned to Germany (East Berlin), where his youth movement concepts garnered revived interest and formed the basis for the creation of new BUNDE.

Kommune 1 (Germany) a communal group in Berlin during the 1960s representing the hippie wing of the local SOZIALISTISCHER DEUTSCHER STUDENTENBUND (SDS). The group attained notoriety for its mock "riot" against the 1967 visit to Berlin of Hubert Humphrey, then vice president of the United States. The "riot" proved so provocative that SDS dissociated itself from Kommune 1, but both groups nevertheless reaped the verbal wrath of the Berlin press and public. Kommune 1 incurred further wrath with the group's subsequent declaration that effectively called for the public to set fire to Berlin stores as symbols of excessive consumption. There was also a WEST BERLIN KOMMUNE 2.

Komsomol (Communist Youth League) (Russia) a Soviet organization for young people age 14 to 26 (raised to 28 in 1956) established by the Congress of Youth Associations (194 delegates representing some 120 different youth groups). The congress convened in Moscow from October 28 to November 4, 1918 and at subsequent congresses held in 1919 and 1920 to join together youth groups that had been involved in the October 1917 Revolution. The name *Komsomol* is a contraction of *Kommunistitchesky soyuz molodyozhi.* Originally Komsomol was autonomous, but the organization became an affiliate of the Communist Party at the Second Congress of Youth Associations held in 1919; at the Third Congress held in 1920, it became an adjunct of the Communist Party, its independence proving short-lived. Until the Third Congress, members of Komsomol elected their own officers; thereafter the officers were Communist Party choices.

Komsomol began with a membership of about 22,000; about 10,000 members fought at the front during the Civil War. (Only about 4 percent of the early membership was older than 23 years and through the years about 70 percent of the members have been under 23.) In 1922, with the Civil War well past, Komsomol assumed a program of health, sports, education, publication, and industrial activities for its members. Komsomol was especially involved in establishing factory schools (Fabsavutchi, or FSU) so that young workers could receive instruction while in their workplaces; the first of these had opened in February 1921. Komsomol added Lenin to its official name in the autumn of 1924 as a tribute (Vladimir Lenin died on January 21, 1924). After Joseph Stalin attained power, any remaining independence Komsomol retained disappeared; officers were removed, arrested, imprisoned, and even executed. In 1922, rival youth groups were proscribed, and from 1926 Komsomol was the only youth organization extant in the Soviet Union—at least the only officially accepted one. Its overriding purpose became the training of young people in "a communist

manner," the development of "a communist society," and the defense of the Soviet Union. Komsomol membership grew steadily, and by 1928 it reached 2 million—7 percent of all those in its targeted age group. By 1935 membership exceeded 3.5 million; in the 1950s, membership began a rapid climb, reaching nearly 42 million (65 percent of those in the eligible age group) in 1987.

Komsomol served the Communist Party's purposes through the teaching of party doctrine and the promotion of communism in schools, the army, factories, and farm communities. At both national and urban levels, the organization had numerous publications. The periodical for the Komsomol Central Committee was named *Young Guard*; that for lesser leaders and rank-and-file members was *Cell*; numerous other periodicals included *The Young Communist, The Young Proletarian,* and the Moscow journal *Young Bolshevik.* The major daily newspaper for youths is *Komsomolskaya Pravda.* Altogether Komsomol has operated three publishing houses, produced 50 million copies of books and brochures annually, and has published 230 newspapers and magazines for the young with a total run of more than 82 million copies. In 1932, during a decade of rapid urbanization and industrialization, a group of 4,000 Komsomol members founded Komsomolsk, which by 1939 grew into a city of more than 70,000 as a center of shipbuilding and machinery manufacturing.

Komsomol also set up organizations for younger youths. The first of these, the Children's Communist Organization of Young Pioneers, was formed for youths age 10 to 16 (later 10 to 14) by the Moscow Komsomol in 1922; by 1926 its membership had grown to about 2 million and by 1932, to about 5 million. The Pioneers' publication was *The Pioneer.* As an organization, the Pioneers was probably more important in serving the purpose of the Communist Party because membership (more than 20 million in the mid-1960s) was virtually universal for the age group; all were enrolled in schools, thereby enhancing the prospects for indoctrination. Each link (*zvenó*), or basic membership unit, consisted of 5 to 12 children in a classroom, who elected their own leader; links were joined together as a detachment (*otríad*) comprising all the children in a single school grade. The detachment elected a guiding council of at least three outstanding Pioneers. Both the links and the detachments functioned, of course, under adult supervision, as did the brigade (*druzhína*) consisting of the entire school. The brigade also elected a council of 3 to 15 older Pioneers, who then chose a president. The Pioneers also had nonschool facilities, including camps, directed by party and government agencies. The Pioneers and the Komsomol joined forces to form and lead an organization for youths age 8 to 11 known as Little Octobrists, whose membership approached 275,000 in 1926. The Octobrists became defunct just before World War II but was informally (not as a distinct organization) revived after 1957 as a means of preparing children for the Pioneers. All other organizations for youths besides these three were outlawed.

Membership and participation in Komsomol were a prerequisite or necessity of entry into and retention at institutes of higher learning. Participation was also considered a stepping stone to membership in the Communist Party, but following the introduction of glásnost in mid-1985, enormous disaffection with Komsomol revealed itself. Many rival youth groups began to emerge. These were accepted by the government and so today they number in the hundreds. Komsomol itself began to return to its roots, bringing back free elections of officers and pushing organizational reforms. Komsomol was enormously important in serving as a force of socialization for a society that underwent revolutionary changes, including industrial and other forms of modernization, and also for promoting advances in education and for involving youths in the political system. Through the era of perestroika, membership in komsomol remained essentially compulsory; otherwise, by one estimate of 1989, only about one-fifth of its members would have stayed in the organization. In 1987, during the perestroika period, Premier Mikhail Gorbachev criticized the organization's leadership for being old-fashioned and privileged, but Komsomol's influence over career positions and college admissions persisted. Komsomol also continued to operate three publishing houses that produced more than 230 newspapers and magazines.

Bibliography: Jim Riordan, ed., *Soviet Youth Culture* (Bloomington: Indiana University Press, 1989).

Korean Communist Youth Association (Korea) a communist organization for youths formed in 1925 by Cho Pong-am, Pak Hon-yong, and others who founded the Korean Communist Party in Seoul in April 1925. It claimed to have 32,000 members in 224 branches but was short-lived: the party itself ceased to exist by the end of the year as a result of government suppression.

Korean Socialist Working Youth League (North Korea) an organization for all youths age 15 to 30, founded in January 1946 as the Communist Youth League and renamed in May 1964. In 1980, the league had a membership of 2.7 million. The equivalent organization for all youths between age 8 and 14 is the Korean Young Pioneers, also founded in 1946.

Korps (Corps) (Germany) the most exclusive and elite student fraternities, some tracing their beginnings to the early years of the LANDSMANNSCHAFTEN. The Korps were dueling fraternities, with each member being required to participate in at least one Mensur to test his worth (the imperial government outlawed dueling in 1883, but it continued in ritualized form). The Korps were devoted to the promotion of lifelong friendships, "exemplary education as honorable students," and "character training as active and dutiful men" for their members. They had defended traditional views during the Vormarz and the Revolution of 1848. Members practiced compulsive drinking bouts (Kneipzwangen) and wore drinking caps and identifying colors. They were the first student corporations to create a national organization, the KOSENER VERBAND, established in 1855; in 1887 the Korps graduates (Alte Herren) formed their own national association, the Alte Herren Verband. As an elite the Korps served as the model for all other student corporations, especially dueling fraternities, to emulate. It is noteworthy that during the 1850s, the Korps fraternities accepted Jewish members, but as student anti-Semitism grew in virulence, largely through the efforts of the VEREIN DEUTSCHER STUDENTEN, the Korps gave in and, in 1880, adopted a policy of excluding Jews.

By the mid-1880s, however, the proportion of Korps members in university student bodies was declining, partly as a result of opposition to dueling, and reforms of the dueling system were instituted. During the late 19th and early 20th centuries, the Korps derived their values—such as obedience, courage, honor, patriotism—from the army officer corps. Former Korps members attained widespread and significant professional and political stature during the era of the German Empire, 1871 through 1918. In fact, during the decade leading up to World War I, members of the Korps' Alte Herren held far more seats in the Reichstag than any other former members of student corporations—two to three times as many seats as those held by BURSCHENSCHAFTEN graduates, for example—and their political orientation was monarchical and conservative.

Kosener Verband (Germany) probably the most elite of the KORPS fraternities, the Kosener Verband, or Kosener Senioren Convents Verband (KSC), was formed in 1855 and gradually subsumed all the local Korps chapters. It accepted as members those Korps chapters that adhered to the existing Komment (ritual customs) and the Senioren Convent (S.C.); these prohibited political stands although they promoted dueling and fulfillment of the S.C. The S.C. prescribed a hierarchy of officers (Chargierte), actives (Corpsburschen), pledges (Fuchse), and guests (Konkneipanten) which reinforced the concept of authority. In 1884 the KSC began to publish a student journal, *Akademische Monatshefte*. Its leadership dissolved the organization in September 1935 following Nazi officials' displeasure over its refusal to comply (reversed when the dissolution occurred) with a Nazi directive to expel "non-Aryan" members that would have constituted an affront, especially to the Korps' Jewish alumni who were World War I veterans. In 1933 the Kosener Verband reported having 5,544 members.

Kosovo Disturbances   (Yugoslavia-Serbia) an uprising among Albanians in the Republic of Serbia's autonomous province of Kosovo in March 1981 instigated by young teachers. The young nationalistic rebels advocated the province's eventual unification with Albania—Albanians then constituted nearly 80 percent of Kosovo's residents, the remainder being Serbs and Montenegrans.

Koto-gakko-Remmei (High School League)   (Japan) an organization for high school students formed in 1923. The league was formed by representatives from several high schools for the purpose of propagating communism among students.

Kritische Universität   (Germany) "critical university," also known as "negative university," a concept of the university transformed and radicalized—the alternative university—first fostered by West Berlin students in 1967. As the students defined it, the Kritische Universität would promote "critical theoretical reflection" and analysis to devise tools for the practical use of radical groups wanting to achieve "enlightened democratization of our society" and "liberation from the oppression of inhumanity. . . ." Thus the Kritische Universität was not a physical site with buildings but a counterforce to the existing university that would "publicly and demonstratively attack its present structures and its irrational and repressive objectives. . . ." To effect this end the students set up freewheeling "alternative courses" and disrupted existing courses, ostenibly in the service of "liberating" their fellow students and molding all students into a community. In some form, the movement spread to other university centers such as Munich, Münster, and Tübingen and also influenced the TRENT MOVEMENT, but it was not notably successful.

Bibliography: Gianni Stratera, *Death of a Utopia: The Development and Decline of Student Movements in Europe* (New York: Oxford University Press, 1975).

"Kuby Affair"   (Germany) an incident in May 1965 at the Freie Univeristät in West Berlin so named because it involved the university authorities' refusing to let the writer Erich Kuby speak at a ceremony marking the defeat of the Nazis. The authorities opposed Kuby because of remarks he had made at the university in 1958 that seemed to give philosophic support to Humboldt University in East Berlin and thereby violated the prevailing anticommunism in the West at the time. Student groups such as the SOZIALISTISCHER DEUTSCHER STU-DENTENBUND (SDS) interpreted the rejection of Kuby as proof of the university's authoritarianism, and in response they supported a large demonstration against the rector of the university. The "Kuby Affair" thus provided SDS especially with an opportunity to radicalize students that would play out in the massive and ongoing student demonstrations of 1967–68.

Kurfürstendamm Demonstration   (Germany) a student demonstration in December 1967 on the Kürfurstendamm, the great shopping center in downtown West Berlin, to protest against materialistic consumerism at Christmas time while people were dying in Vietnam. The demonstrators tried to break through police cordons set up to prevent their access to the Kurfürstendamm, resulting in the first large-scale police suppression of student demonstrators that came to characterize the confrontational protests of the following year.

Kwangju Incident   (Korea) a student uprising in October–November 1929 that generated a widespread student anti-Japanese movement (Japan then ruled Korea). The incident followed student strikes in 1927 and 1928 that included demands for "decent treatment" of Korean students by Japanese instructors at the three Korean public schools in the city—Kwangju High Common School, Kwangju Agricultural School, and Kwangju Normal School. Korean student resentment of Japanese students who called them barbarians and who mistreated Korean female students erupted into the incident— ongoing bloody fights between Korean and Japanese students that spread beyond the city. News of Korean students' arrests instigated anti-Japanese student riots throughout Korea. The riots continued for five months and involved more than 54,000 Korean students, including thousands of women, at nearly 200 schools (mostly colleges and high schools but also some primary schools). Student demonstrators demanded release of the students arrested in Kwangju and elsewhere, the end of police interference at schools, and the termination of the Japanese colonial educational policies. Authorities imprisoned or expelled hundreds of students in response, but the student anti-Japanese movement continued clandestinely.

Kyffhauser Verband der Vereine Deutscher Studenten   (Germany) a student movement founded at a convention organized by the VEREIN DEUTSCHER STU-DENTEN (VDS) at the Harz Mountains in August 1881 and named for the Kyffhauser Range in the mountains that is identified with the Hohenstaufen emperors. (A popular legend states that Friedrick Barbarossa sleeps within the range with his knights and will awaken to lead a united Germany to victory.) Champions of the monarchy, the members of the Kyffhauser Verband pledged to defend Christianity, the emperor, and German traditions: their motto was "With God for Kaiser and Reich." The movement's political program attracted members from the various fraternities despite their social or parochial differences, and the movement soon adopted the organizational form of a fraternity. The movement used demonstrations, newspaper reports, and other tactics in promoting its political agenda. It also adopted blatant anti-Semitism, which influenced the policies of other fraternities, and resurrected the Grossdeutsch concept (uniting all those of German ancestry and language). The movement's organ was the *Kyffhauser Zeitung*. The Kyffhauser Verband movement spread quickly throughout the northern universities; it was at first banned in Bavaria, however. The program of the Kyffhauser Verband in effect helped foster Nazism, and in 1933 after Adolf Hitler's seizure of power it changed its long-standing motto to "With God for Hitler and National Socialism." At that time, the organization claimed to have more than 2,300 members.

Kyosanshugisha Domei (Communist League) (Japan) a student organization formed in December 1958. About 2,000 students who had quit or been expelled from the Japan Communist Party (JCP) because of their opposition to the JCP leaders' Stalinist leanings established this rival group, also known by the abbreviation *Kyosando* or the German term *Bund*. They subsequently assumed control of the Central Committee of the ZENGAKUREN, in which they and other JCP opponents were referred to as the Mainstream.

Labor Youth League (LYL) (United States) a communist-controlled university-student organization formed in 1948 which in effect replaced the YOUNG PROGRESSIVES OF AMERICA (YPA). Its statement of principles touted the working class as "the source of progress in the modern world," denounced "big business tycoons," and advocated friendship between the United States and the Soviet Union. The new organization, born into the cold war and the onslaught of the Korean War and McCarthyism, would have little hope of success. LYL claimed to have 6,000 members, but it was never influential, probably because it was openly communist in a period of intense anticommunism. Its two publications, *Challenge* and *New Foundations*, reached a limited audience—5,000 in the case of the latter. At the LYL's 1957 convention, the delegates—of whom there were only 27—voted overwhelmingly to dissolve the organization; this occurred in the aftermath of the Soviet Union's suppression of the Hungarian Revolution and Nikita Khrushchev's denunciation of Joseph Stalin's policies.

Land and Freedom (Russia) a secret revolutionary society backed by university students that was formed in St. Petersburg in 1876 through the efforts of Mark Natanson, the founder of the CHAIKOVSKY CIRCLE. (There had been an earlier society of this name supported by Mikhail Bakunin that tried to foster an uprising in Poland in 1863 involving Russian army officers; its complete failure killed the society.) Although Natanson was arrested again in June 1877, others took his place in fulfilling the organization and activities of the society, which initially devoted itself primarily to the advocacy of equal distribution of lands among the peasants. The society raised funds through contributions and through sales of its publication *Land and Freedom*. It gained public awareness by a demonstration by more than 300 protestors, mostly students, at the Kazan Cathedral on December 6,

1876—the first public demonstration supporting revolution to be held in Russia. A 20-year-old student, Georgy PLEKHANOV, gave an impromptu speech castigating the government that led to the protestors marching down the Nevsky and shouting such slogans as "Death to the tsars!" They were attacked and beaten by police, who arrested more than 30 people, including innocent bystanders.

Land and Freedom fostered unsuccessful protests at the universities in 1878 demanding the student right to form organizations. On January 24 of that year, Vera Zasulich, then 26 and for more than a year a worker at the society's press, fired a point-blank shot into General F. Trepov, chief of police in St. Petersburg, in an attempted assassination—Trepov survived. At her trial in March, to everyone's surprise, Zasulich was found not guilty. She became an immediate heroine in Europe and was hailed as a Russian Charlotte Corday, but police tried to arrest her again as she left the prison. She was secreted away during the melee that ensued between police and her supporters, and she later fled to Geneva. Zasulich's attack on Trepov began a long period of assassinations or attempted assassinations of public officials by revolutionaries, with Land and Freedom adopting a program of disruptive tactics that included planned assassinations. This program, however, generated serious disagreement within Land and Freedom, as a major faction of the group opposed terrorism. In an attempt to bridge this disagreement, the society granted one-third of its budget to a terrorist cell within the society that called itself the EXECUTIVE COMMITTEE OF THE SOCIAL-REVOLUTIONARY PARTY, which would pursue the program of disruption. But this effort at reconciliation failed, and on August 15, 1879 Land and Freedom dissolved.

Landsmannschaften (Germany) student organizations founded in the first half of the 19th century whose membership was based primarily on students' regional origin—that is, a given university might have separate Landsmannschaften for students from Prussia, Silesia, Saxe-Coburg, and so on. Many of these groups became dueling fraternities in the late 19th century. An Allgemeine Landsmannschaftsverband, a national umbrella organization for the groups, was founded in 1868 by five chapters; it dissolved in 1877 but revived in 1882, then dissolved again briefly in 1897 and revived again in 1898. Like most of the BURSCHENSCHAFTEN, the Landsmannschaften embraced the anti-Semitism that peaked among students in the 1890s, and in 1894 many formally excluded Jews from membership.

Law for the Maintenance of the Public Peace
(Japan) a law enacted by the Diet in March 1925 at the government's request to provide for eliminating any movement the government considered menacing. The law prohibited movements or organizations dedicated to effecting or even discussing political or social reformation. Violaters of the law were subject to imprisonment for up to 10 years (the maximum penalty became execution in 1928). The first application of the law was against members of the student federation GAKUSEI RENGO-KAI at Kyoto University: 30 students were sentenced to prison. The law effectively prohibited free speech. It remained in effect until 1945, when U.S. occupation forces repealed it and freed 500 political prisoners incarcerated under its terms.

League for Industrial Democracy (LID)
(United States) successor organization to the INTERCOLLEGIATE SOCIALIST SOCIETY, founded in New York City on October 24, 1921. The re-formation was publicly announced on November 17 when LID's mission was defined as "education for a new social order based on production for public use and not for private profit." Socialist leaders Norman Thomas and Harry Laidler were appointed LID's joint executive directors. In the climate of intolerance toward left-wing politics that prevailed in the 1920s, LID made minimal efforts to organize student groups and even had its student affiliates, formerly called socialist clubs, innocuously renamed social problems clubs or liberal clubs. Some clubs did, however, participate in protests to prevent the executions of the anarchists Nicola Sacco and Bartolomeo Vanzetti. LID published a weekly newspaper entitled the *New Leader* to present democratic socialist views. LID organized national and regional conferences that addressed such issues as educational reform, U.S. foreign policy, and labor unionization; it also tried to create links between students and laborers. LID's scholastic approach and study groups had minimal appeal to students, however, and by 1929 LID had only a little more than 1,000 student members among a population of 1 million undergraduates nationwide. But in the subsequent Great Depression era of the 1930s, LID's student organization set up in 1932—the

STUDENT LEAGUE FOR INDUSTRIAL DEMOCRACY (SLID)—gained impressive strength on university campuses. LID advocated views that were opposed to communism and critical of the Soviet Union during the 1930s. When SLID became STUDENTS FOR A DEMOCRATIC SOCIETY (SDS) in 1960, LID retained its ties with the student group, but they parted ways in January 1966 because of SDS's increasing radicalism.

Let Us Vote (LUV)
(United States) a youth movement founded in late 1969 at the University of the Pacific in Stockton, California by Dennis Warren, a 21-year-old prelaw student at the university. Senator Birch Bayh of Indiana, while visiting the campus, had challenged students to launch a campaign for voting rights that inspired Warren and other students to action that resulted in creation of the movement. LUV's sole purpose was advocacy of enfranchisement for youths age 18 and older. This advocacy was pursued through dissemination of information that argued for enfranchisement on the grounds that young adults accepted civic responsibilities, desired political participation, believed in constructive dissent, and therefore deserved to be awarded the right to vote by either individual states or the federal government. While maintaining a national headquarters in Stockton, LUV grew within six weeks of its founding to include chapters at 3,000 high schools and 400 colleges and universities throughout the 50 states. LUV marketed its advocacy through Warren's guest appearances on television talk shows and through sales of sweatshirts, bumper stickers, buttons, and records.

Life Saving Scouts and Guides
(Great Britain) a Salvation Army youth organization modeled after the BOY SCOUTS. The organization was founded by the Salvation Army's Colonel Sladen in 1914. Its primary emphasis was on first aid, but by 1930 it was the second largest (after the Boy Scouts) woodcraft group in Great Britain. In 1948 the group abandoned its separate status and became a part of the Boy Scouts as the Salvation Army Scouts.

Liga de Estudiantes Humanistas
(Argentina) a student organization founded in 1950 with a largely liberal Catholic membership. The League of Humanist Students differed to some extent with the FEDERACIÓN UNIVERSITARIA ARGENTINA (FUA) philosophically but supported the FUA's efforts against Juan Perón, including the BRAVO RELEASE STRIKE. But in the years following the ouster of Perón in September 1955, the Humanistas fell out with the FUA over tactics—they opposed involvement in national politics and argued for focusing entirely on the university setting and achievement of the long-standing goals of the UNIVERSITY REFORM PROGRAM AND MOVEMENT. For example, the Humanistas refused to support the FUA over the DELL'ORO MAINI PROTESTS issue. They also opposed the

growing domination of Communists in the FUA and the individual university federations that occurred in the 1960s.

Little Commonwealth (Great Britain) a juvenile reform community modeled after the GEORGE JUNIOR REPUBLIC and established in Dorsetshire in 1913. The Little Commonwealth had the backing of an illustrious group of people, including Lord James Bryce, the Duchess of Marlborough, Earl Grey, Lady Somerset, George Montagu, and Arthur Balfour. Homer Lane, an American who had headed the Ford Junior Republic near Detroit, was the superintendent. Although the Little Commonwealth essentially adopted the economic and governmental concepts of the Junior Republic, it differed in fundamental ways from its precursor. Adult leaders were directly involved in its functions, it used the family rather than the community as its model, and it emphasized corrections over education, which was provided by a Montessori school. World War I effectively derailed the Little Commonwealth so that by 1917 there were only two families in residence, each comprised of 18 children—most of them girls. Some unscrupulous girls accused Lane of misconduct, and, although the charges were never proven, the directors decided to close the Little Commonwealth. The failed experiment did, however, leave a legacy of progressive influence on educational and penal reform in Great Britain.

Little Germany (Great Britain) an early l6th-century informal organization of young Cambridge University students and dons who met regularly at the White Horse Inn for discussions on church reform. The group became known as Little Germany because they were primarily interested in Lutheran concepts that emanated from Germany. Although not a movement as such, the radical members of Little Germany would have a significant impact on the Protestant Reformation in England. Among them were Robert Barnes, Thomas Bilney, Miles Coverdale, Thomas Cranmer, Hugh Latimer, and William Tyndale. Cardinal Wolsey ironically helped to spread the group's reformation ideas to Oxford, where he had built Cardinal College (now Christ Church) in 1526, because the Cambridge students whose transfer to the new Oxford college he sponsored were members of Little Germany.

Livelihood Associations (Japan) student organizations formed in the period of hardship following Japan's surrender (August 15, 1945) ending World War II. The associations provided cheap meals, clothes, and books for students. They constituted one of the origins of the student councils that eventuated in creation of the ZENGAKUREN.

London School of Economics Student Revolts (Great Britain) a series of protests, when the Labour Party held control of the government during the 1960s, by students of the London School of Economics and Political Science (LSE). The first concerned the issue of Rhodesian independence, raised by Rhodesia's unilateral declaration of independence in November 1965. Students marched to Rhodesia House, the embassy, and protested, with many of the left-wing groups advocating that British army troops intervene; several students were arrested. In 1966 a controversy arose concerning the appointment of the former principal of University College, Rhodesia as director of LSE, leading to a disciplinary hearing against the president of the student union for a letter he wrote to *The Times*; students held a sit-in during the hearings, and the president was not punished. On January 31, 1967 a controversy erupted over a student meeting (convened under the leadership of Marshall Bloom, a U.S. graduate student at LSE) concerning the new director; banned from the Old Theatre, a lecture hall where the union normally met, angry students among a crowd of about 600 stormed into the hall. One of the porters who tried to block their entry died of heart failure. The school was closed for a day, student leaders were accused in anonymous pamphlets of being responsible for the porter's death, and the findings of a committee of inquiry formed the basis for a disciplinary trial. Although found not guilty, two student leaders were suspended; as a result hundreds of students barricaded the Old Theatre building and staged a sit-in. After a week, when the authorities granted concessions to the suspended students, the sit-in ended. These protests in 1965–67 constituted the first outbreak of student activism in Great Britain in modern times. In the l967–68 school year the new director of LSE assumed his post without incident; the issue that had been in the background from the beginning—student participation in the LSE's governance—came to the fore. Student protestors rejected an offer by LSE governing authorities to increase student representation as insufficient. But this issue became sidetracked by demonstrations over the Vietnam War and investments in South Africa, and finally, in 1969, by a movement to destroy the iron gates at the school, causing the LSE to be closed down for three weeks and criminal charges to be brought against eight students and two lecturers. Acts of vandalism by militant students and disagreement among the students about tactics pushed the student revolts into a chaotic state, and they sputtered out. They had, however, apparently inspired protests at other schools, primarily over the issue of student participation in institutional governance.

Bibliography: Colin Crouch, *The Student Revolt* (London: Bodley Head, 1970).

Long March (China) a prolonged retreat begun in the summer of 1934 by army units (the Red Army first formed in 1927) of the CHINESE COMMUNIST PARTY (CCP) that had been effectively encircled in South China by Chiang Kai-shek's Kuomintang military forces. Faced with annihilation, the young men comprising the Red Army units retreated to the west and the north, sometimes through Japanese outposts, waging skirmishes and battles as they went, traversing mountains and swamps, to struggle their way over 6,600 miles into the northwest (northern Shaanxi) and there to retrench. During their withdrawal, the Red Army units were joined by such student or youth groups as the Taiyuan Students for National Salvation. The Long March lasted into 1937, with about 22,000 men reunited in Shaanxi and Gansu at its end. Only about one-tenth of those who undertook the march completed it—some died of exposure, some were casualties of battle, and others were deserters. Probably the most important outcome of the Long March, besides saving the remnants of the Red Army, was that Mao Zedong acquired control of the Party Military Affairs Committee and thus effectively of the army, placing him in a position to attain leadership of the CCP in the early 1940s.

Lovanium University Students' Protest   (Congo) a demonstration in June 1969 that resulted in a bloody confrontation between students and army troops. This protest followed two earlier demonstrations, the first on October 29, 1968 when students protested against economic policy statements and a reference to the Popular Movement of the Revolution (MPR) during an address by the minister of education at the university. In response, the government canceled scholarships for 1968–69 for all students who were not members of the MPR. On February 3, 1969 students at Lovanium University (later a unit of the Université Nationale de Zaire) and also at the University of the Congo at Lubumbashi had demonstrated peacefully for greater involvement in the governance of their universities. On June 4, 1969 the Lovanium University student protest, which was unauthorized, demanded larger government grants for students. The demonstrators began to march toward the center of Kinshasa, intent on presenting a list of grievances to President Joseph Mobutu. When civil authorities told them to turn back, the students ignored the warning and continued their march. Army troops opened fire on them, killing six students (a French reporter's account said 12) and wounding 12. Mobutu closed the university, had 400 students arrested for questioning, and directed armed troops to patrol the streets of the capital. On June 12 the MPR dissolved all student organizations except for its own Youth Section. On June 16 the government ordered students to return to their colleges, but the students refused. Of the students arrested for questioning, 34 were tried for rebellion, with 5 sentenced to 20 years in prison and 15 sentenced to serve 4 to 10 years. On August 8 Mobutu declared the university reopened

under increased government control; in October he declared an amnesty for all those students who had been sentenced to prison.

Lu Ts'ui (1914–   )   (China) one of the principal leaders of the DECEMBER NINTH MOVEMENT. Born in Huchou, now Wuxing, Lu became a student at Soochow University in Shanghai, but she was expelled because of her political activities, and she transferred to Tsinghua University in Beijing. She was involved early on in the December Ninth Movement, serving as Tsinghua University's representative on the steering committee that planned the December 9 demonstration. Her most famous exploit occurred during the December 16 demonstration when she led about 5,000 students to the Sunchih Gate, where they had been promised access by the police but instead found the gate locked, with a cordon of police behind it. Lu rolled under the gate and tried to unbolt it, as the startled police accosted her. While the police were beating on her, she actually spoke with foreign correspondents. Lu was held by the police, but a sit-down strike by her student followers succeeded in obtaining her release. At about 7:30 P.M., she rolled back under the gate and led the student protestors back to Tsinghua University. This exploit made her the heroine of the December Ninth Movement—she was known as the local Joan of Arc. Soldiers raided the university on February 29, 1936 to arrest her and others, but Lu fled and hid out. She traveled to Europe to represent China at the World Youth Congress held in Geneva, Switzerland, August 31–September 6, 1936. Living in Paris, she joined the CHINESE COMMUNIST PARTY (CCP). She and her husband, Jao Shu-shih, lived in the United States from 1938 to 1940. They moved to Yan-an in February 1947 and gained prominence in the CCP until Jao was accused in 1954 of plotting against the CCP. Thereafter, Lu fell into obscurity.

Lyubery   (Russia) a teenage youth cult group that emerged in the late-1970s whose members are devoted to violent opposition to Westernization. The name *Lyubery* derives from Lyubertsy, an industrial suburb of Moscow. Male members of the group train in martial arts and body building, and they supposedly eschew smoking, drinking, and drug use. Their usual uniform is a white shirt, a narrow black tie, an outdated coat, and wide, checked trousers. They profess to be upholders of traditional Russian values, and they attack aliens and devotees of Western youth culture, fashions, music, and dances. Their violence has generated protest marches in Moscow by hundreds of their teenage opponents. Lyubery is unique in Russian history, although anti-Western sentiment is a long-standing tradition among many Russians.

Manchurian Invasion Protests (China) a series of student demonstrations protesting the government's response to the Japanese invasion of Manchuria in September 1931. The Japanese launched their invasion on September 18 and quickly overran Manchuria, which they declared the independent state of Manchukuo in February 1932. Since the Japanese had exercised enormous influence in Manchuria for years and since his policy was to destroy the Chinese Communists before tackling foreign invaders, Chiang Kai-shek, head of the Kuomintang, acquiesced in the Japanese conquest. In response to the Japanese invasion, thousands of zealous students traveled to Nanjing, site of the Kuomintang government, to protest against the government's acquiescence and to advocate war with Japan. In some areas they lay across railroad tracks until they were provided with free transport to the capital. During a September 28 demonstration in Nanjing, a student mob attacked the foreign minister and nearly beat him to death. In December radical students from Beijing gained control over the demonstrations—more than 16,000 demonstrators were involved—and pushed them into a surge of violence. During this action the students roughed up Kuomintang officials and pillaged the offices of the Kuomintang party newspaper. The government retaliated by arresting and imprisoning the radical students and driving others underground; the protest movement dissipated.

Mandalay Student Protest (Burma) a demonstration in Mandalay against British rule by students at the Intermediate College and the National High School, supported by a sizable number of monks, on February 10, 1939. A bloody conflict with police occurred; 17 students and monks were killed. The bloodshed fomented public support for the students and generated other demonstrations in Mandalay and Rangoon. These and other protests drew students firmly into the Burmese nationalist movement.

Mansarover Incident (India) a demonstration in 1959 by students from Allahabad University to protest the beating of a student by the manager of a cinema named Mansarover. The resulting riot led to four people being killed, many injured, and many more arrested. A male student participant who was expelled from the university staged a hunger strike, and after a few days, press reports indicated that he was dying. The university's vice chancellor called a secret meeting of the Executive Council to try to resolve the resulting crisis, but students discovered the house where the meeting was taking place and attacked it, destroying furniture and vegetation. The intimidated Executive Council acceded to all the students' demands and subsequently all resigned.

Manson Family (United States) a group of nine girls and five boys who were, in effect, cult followers of Charles Manson, ex-convict and former resident of Haight-Ashbury (Hashbury), the hippie district of San Francisco. The "Manson family" constituted an extreme and aberrational example of the lifestyle advocated by the hippies (*see* HIPPIE MOVEMENT) and the COUNTERCULTURE. They left Hashbury with Manson in early 1968 and took up residence on the Spahn Ranch north of the San Fernando Valley. Rightly suspected by the police of stealing cars, they left the ranch after a year and encamped in the desert near Death Valley. The Manson family would come to national attention for a single heinous act. On August 9, 1969, acting on Manson's orders, four members of the family entered the Benedict Canyon home of film director Roman Polanski, who was then in London, England, and viciously murdered his pregnant wife, actress Sharon Tate, and three of her visiting friends; they also killed Polanski's caretaker, age 19, and a friend of his, age 18. Manson and four female family members were indicted for murder by a Los Angeles County grand jury on December 1; these five and a sixth family member, Charles Watson, were also indicted for the murders of Leno and Rosemary LoBianco, killed in their Beverly Hills home on August 10, 1969. Manson and two other defendants, both young women, were found guilty of seven counts of first-degree murder on January 26, 1971, and a third defendant, also a young woman, on two counts of first-degree murder. All four were convicted of conspiracy to commit murder. Watson, a 25-year-old, was convicted for both the Tate slayings, to which he confessed, and the LoBianco murders on October 12, 1971.

March Against Death   (United States) the largest antiwar demonstration in U.S. history, organized by the NEW MOBILIZATION COMMITTEE TO END THE WAR IN VIETNAM (NEW MOBE) and held in Washington, D.C. on November 15, 1969 (also the largest demonstration ever held in the capital to that time). The march drew more than 250,000 demonstrators, the great majority of them students and other youths; a parallel march in San Francisco drew at least 60,000 demonstrators (one estimate set the number at 175,000). In anticipation of trouble, the Defense Department announced on November 12 that 9,000 troops were being deployed to the Washington area. The March Against Death, however, proved entirely peaceable; the New Mobe provided thousands of parade marshalls to help the marchers and to assist the 3,000 D.C. police to maintain the peace. The demonstrations actually began on November 13 and lasted 40 hours, culminating on November 15. On November 14 more than 1,000 militants—among them members of STUDENTS FOR A DEMOCRATIC SOCIETY (SDS) and the Youth International Party (Yippies)—rallied at DuPont Circle to march to the South Vietnamese embassy. Police intercepted them with tear gas; the protestors responded violently, hurling rocks, breaking about 50 store windows, and damaging 40 police cruisers. Another splinter group of several thousand led by yippies marched on the Justice Department building to protest the Chicago 7 trial (see CHICAGO 8 TRIAL); marshalls from the March Against Death tried to maintain peace and order as police hurled tear gas into the crowd. During the melee, protestors broke windows in 50 buildings. Police arrested 135 protestors during that day. Whether peaceful or violent, the November 13–15 demonstrations had no effect: President Richard Nixon reportedly was watching a football game on television as the March Against Death paraded past the White House.

March 18th Tragedy   (China) a massacre of student and other demonstrators in Beijing that occurred on March 18, 1926. The demonstrators were led by Li Dazhao, a teacher at Beijing University who was among the prominent intellectuals involved with NEW YOUTH and also a leader of the North China branch of the CHINESE COMMUNIST PARTY (CCP). The mass demonstration was a protest against the government's surrender to demands by imperialist nations. Soldiers employed by Beijing warlord Duan Qirui opened fire on the demonstrators, killing 47, mostly students. This and other bloody events of the mid-1920s pushed radical youths increasingly toward adoption of violent tactics in place of propaganda. (Li Dazhao, viewed as culpable for his role in the massacre, was killed by warlords a year later.)

March First Movement   (Korea) movement for independence from Japan that was inspired by the ideal of self-determination expressed in Woodrow Wilson's Fourteen Points at the end of World War I and that emerged in nationwide demonstrations on March 1, 1919. Although not a student or youth movement as such, the March 1 demonstrations involved thousands of youths, and one of the groups involved early on in advocating independence was centered at the Chung-an High School. On February 28, a group of leaders involved in the independence movement issued a "declaration of independence," which they printed and distributed. Then on March 1, a separate radical group aroused residents of Seoul by proclaiming that Kojong, the former emperor who had died on February 22, had actually been assassinated and by urging Koreans to take vengeance on the Japanese. A crowd gathered at Pagoda Park and began to march through the city's streets; as they marched, shouting for independence and waving the banned Korean flag, tens of thousands joined them. Other demonstrations erupted in other cities—one estimate says a total of 2 million demonstrated nationwide. Korean students studying in Japan also demonstrated for independence on March 1 in Tokyo, Osaka, Kyoto, and other cities. The Japanese reacted with repressive measures—banning assemblies and demonstrations, searching schools and homes; their tactics resulted in the deaths of 1,600 Koreans and the injuring of another 16,000, along with the destruction of hundreds of schools, churches, and houses. Nearly 20,000 Koreans were arrested. Among them was Yu Kwan-sun, a 16-year-old girl who was tortured and died in prison. The arrests of hundreds of girls and women led to creation of the Devoted Women's Society and other women's organizations. The failed March First Movement also eventuated in formation in the 1920s of numerous socialist organizations, including youth groups, and of the short-lived Korean Communist Party (1925) and its affiliated Korean Communist Youth Association, which claimed to have 32,000 members. In addition, in May 1919 high school and university students in Seoul began a new movement with the formation of the Conference of Korean Students, although the Japanese restricted both its membership and its activities.

March on the Pentagon   (United States) a demonstration against the Vietnam War touted as a "Confrontation with the Warmakers" that occurred on October 21 and 22, 1967 as a climax to STOP THE DRAFT WEEK. Among the march's organizers were David Dellinger, chairman of the NATIONAL MOBILIZATION COMMITTEE TO END THE WAR IN VIETNAM, and Jerry RUBIN, organizer of the Vietnam Day at Berkeley. The march was preceded by a gathering of demonstrators at the Church of the Redeemer on the afternoon of October 20; they marched to the Department of Justice building, where they listened to speakers, including William Sloane Coffin, Jr., chaplain of Yale University, Dr. Benjamin Spock, and poet Robert Lowell. On October 21 about 50,000 marchers, including thousands of students, convened at the Lincoln Memorial, where they listened to more speeches. Following this rally the protestors marched arm-in-arm across the Arlington Memorial Bridge and on to the Pentagon, where the Department of Defense had assembled 1,500 police, 2,500 troops of the National Guard, 200 U. S. marshals, and 6,000 troops to defend the complex against their onslaught; in addition 20,000 troops were stationed nearby.

At the Pentagon the demonstrators gathered peaceably at the north parking lot. Then a wedge of protestors emerged from the crowd and, brandishing a North Vietnamese flag, ax handles, and clubs, launched an attack at the Pentagon's front entrance, which was protected by MPs and U.S. marshals who forced the invaders back. Another attack followed, with the protestors hurling tomatoes and bottles. During these and following skirmishes that lasted into the night, some marchers actually entered the Pentagon, but scores were brutally clubbed and bloodied by the police and troops who arrested hundreds, including novelist Norman Mailer. In the aftermath, the press generally took a dim view of the marchers. And the march itself had minimal, if any, effect on U.S. prosecution of the war or on the presidency of Lyndon Johnson, but it did signal a coming shift toward violent confrontation as the tactic antiwar protesters would adopt with increasing frequency, rather than peaceful rallies. Perhaps the most significant result of the March on the Pentagon was one of the outstanding literary works of the 1960s, Mailer's *The Armies of the Night* (1968).

Bibliography: James Miller, *"Democracy Is in the Streets:" From Port Huron to the Siege of Chicago* (New York: Simon and Schuster, 1987).

March on Washington   (United States) a demonstration to promote ending the Vietnam War, held in Washington, D.C., on April 17, 1965. The march was originally proposed by the Peace Research and Education Project of the STUDENTS FOR A DEMOCRATIC SOCIETY (SDS) in December 1964 and approved by the SDS's National Council. In organizing the march, SDS

Demonstrators against U.S. policy in Vietnam hold a sit-in in front of the East Executive Avenue gate to the White House grounds on April 20, 1965. When they refused to leave, police carried them to patrol wagons.   (AP/WIDE WORLD PHOTOS)

mailed materials requesting student support and arguing that the war was a civil war, was a lost cause because the National Liberation Front had popular support, would increase instability in Southeast Asia and thus work against U.S. interests, created the risk that both China and the Soviet Union would intervene, was not an officially declared war, wasted U.S. resources that could be used to combat poverty in the United States, and was immoral since it involved American troops in murder—persuasive analysis, as the number of march participants would indicate. SDS also argued that the march would succeed because of its goals: to break the "manipulated consensus" supporting U.S. involvement, to promote debate on the issues the war entailed, and to bring together various groups who were somehow being victimized by the war. The march was also unique in inviting participation by all political groups, including communists. Because of the communist participation, SDS's parent organization the LEAGUE FOR INDUSTRIAL DEMOCRACY (LID) and the NATIONAL COMMITTEE FOR A SANE NUCLEAR POLICY (SANE) rejected involvement. Nevertheless, the March on Washington to End the War in Vietnam was a great success, attracting 25,000 participants. The march also propelled SDS to the forefront of the antiwar movement.

March 22nd Movement   (France) a militant student movement begun at the University of Paris branch campus at Nanterre on March 22, 1968. On this day a group of students called together by LES ENRAGÉS initially gathered to protest against oppression by the police, who had arrested three university students and three COMITÉS D'ACTION LYCÉENS (CAL) schoolboys for alleged involvement in setting off bombs at American

Express offices in Paris as a protest against the Vietnam War—they supposedly were acting on the initiative of the Comité Vietnam National. The assembled students voted 142 to 2, with 3 abstentions, to occupy the administration building. The 142 supporting students, led by Daniel COHN-BENDIT, broke into the administration building and occupied the faculty council's meeting room. Emulating Fidel Castro (they called themselves *fidelistes d'Europe*), they set up the March 22nd Movement (after Castro's JULY 26 MOVEMENT) and scheduled a teach-in to protest imperialism on March 28; about 400 students took part. They also scheduled a meeting for March 29 to discuss establishing a "critical university," based upon the KRITISCHE UNIVERSITÄT concept promoted by students in West Berlin. Tension between the Cohn-Bendit faction and communist-oriented students within the movement appeared so threatening that the dean closed the Nanterre campus until April 2 in hopes of ameliorating tensions. A mass student meeting followed in which the communist groups were defeated. One of the March 22nd Movement's primary avowed purposes was to create "another Vietnam" within France. The movement's militance inspired student demonstrations during April in Paris and in other cities. As the movement spread, its avowed goals widened; Cohn-Bendit defined them as collectivization of property, abolition of inherited property, suppression of marriage, elimination of nationalism and the military, and promotion of worker solidarity. The French Communist Party denounced the movement as bourgeois. Teach-ins at Nanterre led to the further suspension of classes there, and on May 3 the movement's members gathered at the Sorbonne to become a spearhead of the student uprising that became known as the MAY REVOLT. The leader of the March 22nd Movement, Daniel Cohn-Bendit, became the primary leader of the May Revolt.

Marukusushugi Gakusei Domei (Marxist Student League)

(Japan) a student group created in 1960 by the Kakukyodo to further its activities in separation from the ZENGAKUREN.

Mass Education Speech Corps

(China) an organization created on March 23, 1919 by students at Beijing University as part of the emerging "new culture movement" to bring learning to the illiterate masses. As a part of the emerging "new cultural movement," the speech corps, typical of numerous other such organizations, provided popular lectures in both urban and rural settings on sciences, new ethics, recent social and political thinking, and other subjects. In a related endeavor, the university's student union also created a night school (January 18, 1920) to provide free classes for workers and poor children, who normally were denied access to education. These student educational programs gained momentum and expansion in the context of the MAY FOURTH MOVEMENT. The speech corps continued its work into 1923.

May Fourth Movement

(China) a revolutionary movement initiated by student demonstrations at Beijing University on May 4, 1919—the May Fourth Incident—although its immediate antecedents began in 1917 and took inspiration from the TWENTY-ONE DEMANDS PROJECT. Youthful Chinese rebels had felt hopeful that the Paris Peace Conference following World War I would restore Chinese sovereignty in Shandong Province, since China had provided the victorious Allies with 200,000 coolies to assist their effort on the Western front. In late January 1919, reports arrived in Beijing that the Allies had signed secret treaties supporting Japan's claim to Shandong Province and that the Treaty of Versailles awarded to Japan the former rights and privileges Germany had held in the province. There followed news that the Japanese had bribed Chinese warlords to accept Japanese sovereignty in Shandong. In reaction, about 100 representatives of student groups, mostly from Beijing University, met on the night of May 3 and planned a peaceful demonstration to be held the following day (Sunday) as a protest against Japan and especially its supporters within the Chinese government. On the morning of May 4 representatives from 13 Beijing colleges and universities involved in the planning met and drafted five resolutions that called for sending telegrams to organizations in China and abroad asking them to protest the Paris Peace Conference provision, for efforts to arouse public opposition, for a mass public meeting in Beijing, for creation of a permanent union of all Beijing students, and for the establishment of the route for the afternoon demonstration (to begin at the Tien-an Gate and end in the Hatamen Boulevard business district).

More than 3,000 students representing 13 colleges and universities in Beijing participated in the afternoon demonstration, gathering in the Square of Heavenly Peace at the Tien-an Gate; there government officials had failed in trying to convince them to disperse. The students walked peaceably through the city streets, gaining the admiration of both spectators and police, but their demonstration culminated in violence. Prevented from passing through the foreign legation area of Beijing, the students marched to and attacked the house of a pro-Japanese official, who managed to escape. But the students beat another official who was there and pillaged and torched the house. As night approached the police intervened against the demonstrators, arresting and imprisoning 32 students. The government declared martial law in effect in the legation area. The incident might have ended at this point, but the students met immediately to organize themselves for an ongoing protest. On May 5 student representatives convened and officially founded the STUDENT UNION OF PEKING (in full, Student Union of the Middle Schools and Institutions of

Higher Learning in Peking), the first organization of its kind in China.

As news of the Beijing demonstration spread students in Nanjing, Tianjin, Wuhan, Shanghai, and other cities staged demonstrations, while those in Beijing continued. In Shanghai, for example, students received news of the Beijing events on May 6 and began to organize a response; representing 33 schools in the city, they sent a protest telegram to the government in Beijing, and 3,000 students (the majority of the participants) joined in the Citizens' Assembly held on May 7 and the march that followed. The students received support from professors, workers, and merchants, who began to participate in the student boycott of Japanese goods. Government authorities forced the chancellor of Beijing University, who had supported the students, to resign, and police severely suppressed the student demonstrators. In response the Beijing students went on strike on May 19, and students in all the large cities throughout China followed their lead. The authorities declared martial law in Beijing at the beginning of June. The Japanese government protested the student demonstrations and boycott to the Chinese government, and they landed marines at major Chinese ports. Between June 3 and 6, police arrested 1,150 students and intellectuals in Beijing. Shanghai merchants, encouraged by the students, reacted by forming a trade strike against Japan; more than 60,000 workers joined them. The Chinese government gave in, freed those arrested in Beijing, dismissed three ministers attacked by the students on May 4, and on June 28 rejected signing the Treaty of Versailles. The Japanese did not occupy Shantung. As a result, the demonstrations and strikes ceased, but the boycott continued through the summer.

The May Fourth Movement inspired the organization of student groups nationwide, and the students sent delegates to a June 16 meeting in Shanghai that founded the NATIONAL STUDENT ASSOCIATION—a means of coordinating student activities nationwide. Other student groups in Beijing alone that emerged out of the movement included the Renaissance Society, the New People's Society, the Marxist Club, the Young Socialist Group, the Social Welfare Society, the Women's Rights Movement Alliance, and others that fostered many future members of the communist movement. In July 1919 leaders of the May Fourth Movement founded the periodical *Young China*. The ongoing force of the May Fourth Movement instigated by youths in a generational conflict with the old order created a pivotal shift in Chinese social and political values, with academics now espousing total Westernization, formation of the CHINESE COMMUNIST PARTY (CCP) by students and intellectuals involved in the movement, Sun Yat-sen's acceptance of aid from the Soviet Union and cooperation with the Chinese Communists, and other momentous developments with long-term ramifications for

China's future. One writer observed that for Chinese intellectuals May 4 was "the day Confucius died," signifying the severance with the past in favor of Marxism or other Western ideologies.

Not only did the May Fourth Movement mark the beginning of the modern student movement in China, but it also for the first time joined together two causes: the struggle for Chinese sovereignty and opposition to the traditional political and social order. It had brought together in coalition students, intellectuals, urban workers, merchants, and industrialists to effect change. In addition, the movement provided a new thrust in the effort to renew Chinese culture (the "new culture movement"), especially through creation of vernacular language and literature; it advocated the rights of women and attacked the patriarchal orientation of the family unit. Idealistic students formed associations for communal living and programs to bring education into the villages and rural areas, but the peasantry was never directly involved in the May Fourth Movement. Nonetheless, Chinese society as a whole was changed forever through the movement's long-term effects. The May Fourth Movement comprised a watershed in Chinese history, a demarcation between past and future, and, as such, one of the most significant youth movements of all time. By mutual agreement of the CCP and the Kuomintang, the 1919 watershed was for some years nationally commemorated as Youth Day, but this appellation was later changed to Literature Day and then to Culture Day. The "May Fourth Tradition," the ongoing legacy of the movement and its ideals, endured until the founding of the Communist state of the People's Republic of China in 1949.

Bibliography: Chow Tse-tsung, *The May Fourth Movement* (Cambridge: Harvard University Press, 1960).

May Revolt (France) a major student uprising in Paris during May 1968 that critically destabilized the government of the Fifth Republic headed by Charles de Gaulle. Several years of intermittent protests at universities preceded the May Revolt. These focused primarily on dormitory privileges. But at Nanterre, a suburb to the west of Paris where a branch of the University of Paris had been founded, students in November 1967 staged a strike over examination standards, class sizes, and representation on governing bodies that succeeded in achieving their demands, although the faculty resisted implementing changes. The Nanterre strike generated radicalized student agitation by groups like LES ENRAGÉS and the MARCH 22 MOVEMENT and in particular the leader Daniel COHN-BENDIT, who would become the spearhead of the May Revolt. In January 1986 there were widespread protests at many schools concerning dormitory regulations. In February the issue became the Vietnam War. At Nanterre in March and April, protests, sit-ins, and public debates led to the suspension of classes on May 2, the same day Premier Georges Pompidou left on a trip to Iran and Afghanistan.

On May 3 the Nanterre students assembled in the courtyard at the Sorbonne, along with militants from the University of Paris, to hear speeches. When right-wing students threatened to attack the crowd, the university rector asked police to clear the courtyard. The police loaded about 500 students into vans to transport them to stations where their papers could be checked. The other students, believing their compeers were being arrested, attacked the vans, hurling rocks. The police retaliated. For more than five hours the battle raged, resulting in hundreds being injured, including 80 police, and 600 students arrested. Public opinion sided with the students, and in the following days major student organizations, including the UNION NATIONAL DES ÉTUDIANTS DE FRANCE (UNEF), called for a general strike. On May 4 and 5 the student revolt, joined by CAL members, spread nationwide. Street fights marked the Latin Quarter for two weeks. Students occupied university buildings and pressed three demands: the dropping of charges against the protestors and the release of those who had been arrested, the withdrawal of the police from the university area, and reopening of the university's facilities.

On May 6 thousands of university students, lycéens, and university faculty marched past Nôtre Dame chanting "We are a tiny group" and heading for the Sorbonne, when at about 3:00 P.M., without warning, they were attacked by the police. Initially stunned, the marchers began to fight back, hurling paving stones; the police responded with tear gas and brutal beatings, not just of students but of Red Cross workers and elderly bystanders. The battle raged for 12 hours, and more than 400 people were arrested. The next day, 50,000 university students and lycéens in Paris protested for five hours at a demonstration called by UNEF at the Champs Élysées; student demonstrations also occurred in Nantes, Toulouse, Bordeaux, Lyons, Marseille, and other provincial cities. On May 10, about 20,000 students marched through Paris; police forced them back to the Latin Quarter, where the students erected nearly 30 barricades—the first time since the Paris Commune of 1871 that barricades had appeared in the city. During the afternoon and evening, the protest swelled, and that night about 30,000 protestors found themselves virtually surrounded in the Latin Quarter by cordons of police. The students overturned cars, tore up paving stones, hauled tables, chairs, and billboards—whatever they could find—to build barricades. At about 2:15 A.M. on May 11, the police attacked with tear gas; although the protestors fought back, the police broached the barricades, chased down students, and brutally beat them— and anybody else they encountered. The "Night of the Barricades" left hundreds injured and more than 80 cars destroyed. On May 11 Pompidou returned and, after consulting with De Gaulle, announced concessions to the students and the reopening of the Sorbonne. The gesture proved too late. Trade and teachers unions, sympathetic with the students, called for a one-day general strike with massive demonstrations for May 13. The students, now unopposed by the police, occupied the reopened Sorbonne. Later they also occupied the national theater, the Odéon.

The May 13 strike and demonstrations led to wildcat strikes at Renault plants, Sud-Aviation, and other manufactories throughout France. A general strike followed that involved 6 million workers, with strikers occupying factories. The so-called contagion spread to doctors, lawyers, engineers, and other professionals, a national revolt demanding reforms in the medical system, broadcasting, and other enterprises. On May 22 the government banned Cohn-Bendit, then on a mission in Germany and Holland, from returning to France. In response students rioted in the streets on May 23 and called for a massive protest march on May 24. An agreement reached by government, union, and business negotiators was rejected by union strikers. Opposition political parties on the Left publicly espoused replacing the Gaullist government, whose eroding authority seemed destined for total collapse. At this critical juncture, on May 29, De Gaulle disappeared. He was in Baden-Baden conferring with General Jacques Massu. On May 30, with a massive public rally organized in his support and with the apparent backing of the army, De Gaulle returned, made a masterful radio address announcing immediate elections, and the corner was turned. The government regained control during the next month, with the police recapturing the Odéon from students on June 14 and the Sorbonne on June 16. Then the government handily won the June 23 election despite continuing disruptive student protests, including a destructive riot on June 11, as public opinion turned against the students. The renewed government instituted university reforms and other policies, and the perceived peril receded in memory. Nevertheless, the May Revolt had generated circumstances that nearly brought down the government, raised the specter of either a communist or fascist takeover, and constituted a political and social watershed. The French were left to analyze for years what had caused the May Revolt and what it said about modern civilization.

Bibliography: Bernard E. Brown, *Protest in Paris: Anatomy of a Revolt* (Morristown, N.J.: General Learning Press, 1974).

May 30th Movement (China) a movement initiated by a student demonstration held on May 30, 1925 in the city of Shanghai. The circumstance that generated the movement was a strike by workers at a cotton mill owned and operated by the Nagai Wata Company, a Japanese-owned firm. At the beginning of February 1925, some 40 adult Chinese workers at the mill had been fired and replaced by youths who were paid less; after six of the fired workers were arrested on February 4, other workers at the mill walked off their jobs—to be joined later by the workers at 10 other factories operated by the company. Lasting nearly a month, the strike involved more than 17,000 workers, and it was supported by Shanghai University students, especially those who had been involved in educational programs to bring increased literacy to the workers. One student in fact served as the primary spokesperson for the strikers. This strike dissipated by the end of February because of compromise agreements. But then in May, another strike ensued, beginning at the same cotton mill.

The May 30th demonstration evolved from a fight on May 15 between the strikers and Japanese pistol-toting foremen—one shot a worker who died of the wounds two days later. In protest students distributed handbills, gave speeches, and demonstrated in the Shanghai International Settlement, which was controlled by foreigners, and some were arrested and jailed. They also organized a memorial gathering attended by perhaps 10,000 people on May 24, after which six students were arrested. Those arrested were scheduled for trial on May 30 despite pleas by professors and other students for their release. On May 30, in anticipation of a planned demonstration, police began to arrest student lecturers. A group of several hundred students and supporters marched down Nanjing Road and assembled at about 3:30 in front of the Laozha police station to demand release of the arrested students. A British officer ordered his anxious troops to fire on the student demonstrators, resulting in the killing of 11 unarmed demonstrators and the wounding of at least 30.

The massacre inspired the May 30th Movement, which joined together students, merchants, and workers—the SHANGHAI STUDENT UNION (SSU), the Shanghai Chamber of Commerce, and the General Union of Shanghai (formed on May 31 at the behest of the communists). The general public was incensed and aroused by the martyrdom of the murdered students, compelling proof of the victimization inflicted on the Chinese by foreign imperialists; their outrage would be perpetuated by propaganda and street theater performances produced by students and other supporters of the movement. Other martyrs were added on May 31 when students and supporters retraced the May 30th demonstrators' course along Nanjing Road, joined by shouting workers and spectators—all confronted by the police in a struggle that left more wounded and dead demonstrators.

The Federation of Workers, Merchants, and Students, created on June 2 with several students among its leaders, spearheaded the movement, demanding indemnities for the massacre victims, improved wages and working conditions for the workers, and the granting of legal rights and privileges (such as the right to vote) to the Chinese. The students, workers, and merchants went on strike, closing down foreign-owned factories; 160,000 people were on strike in June, and the strike lasted through September. On June 30 the Federation of Workers, Merchants, and Students staged a huge memorial service for the martyrs that was attended by thousands, including representatives from 150 Shanghai organizations. In August and September, the General Union of Shanghai reached agreements with the Japanese and the English, and the strikes ended; the foreign presence and influence in Shanghai remained essentially intact, however. The movement had incited a nationwide wave of supportive protests, strikes, and boycotts of foreign goods.

The May 30th Movement's longest-lasting effects were the strengthening of the drive to organize workers and create unions and the reinvigoration of the political militancy generated by the MAY FOURTH MOVEMENT. It also induced increasing numbers of students to adopt a radical antiimperialist and nationalist stance, which led many to support the Kuomintang (KMT) led by Chiang Kai-shek and many more to join the KMT's then ally, the CHINESE COMMUNIST PARTY (CCP), which had been represented in the leadership of the movement. But Chiang's brutal purge of the CCP in April 1927 caused many of these student adherents to be disaffected.

Bibliography: Richard Rigby, *The May 30th Movement* (Canberra, Australia: Griffin, 1980).

May 20th Tragedy   (China) an incident that occurred in Nanjing on May 20, 1947: students from universities in the city as well as students from Shanghai and other cities staged a march protesting the Civil War and hunger and were brutally attacked by hundreds of police, who arrested 50 of the marchers. As news of this event spread, it generated support for students' ANTI-HUNGER, ANTI-CIVIL WAR MOVEMENT, with the new nationwide rallying cry of "Fight hunger; fight civil war; fight oppression."

Memorial of the Examination Candidates   (China) a petition presented by students at the end of the first Sino-Japanese War (1894–95). The Chinese lost the war and were obliged to cede control of Formosa and Korea to the Japanese. More than 1,200 students who had gathered in Beijing for the triennial examinations sent this memorial to the emperor demanding continuation of the war.

Milice   (France) a militia force comprised mostly of youths age 18–25 established by Pierre Laval, the dictatorial leader of Vichy, France, in January 1943 at the behest of Adolf Hitler. By autumn 1943, the Milice claimed to have 29,000 members of both sexes, of whom about 10,000 participated in military and police activities, joining German forces in vicious "anti-terrorist" attacks. In February 1945 the Milice became incorporated, along with other French collaborationist military groups committed to opposing Bolshevism, into the Division

Charlemagne for the final defense of Germany. The division had a "youth section" comprised of boys age 16 to 18, many of whom participated with the fanatical Waffen-SS in the catastrophic, futile effort to defend Berlin against invading Russian troops in April–May 1945.

Minsei (Minseido, Democratic Youth League) (Japan) a faction within the ZENGAKUREN founded December 7, 1964. Its parent body was the Japan Communist Party (JCP), and so the Minsei took a pro-JCP line within the Zengakuren. In the late 1960s, the Minsei was one of the two largest and most important factions in the Zengakuren. The Minsei support parliamentary democracy, peaceful demonstrations, discussion, seminars, and other democratic programs. Their high school organization is the Minsei Koko Han (Youth League High School Group).

Mito High School Campus Liberation Struggle (Japan) a 1945 student movement dedicated to democratizing the school (now Ibaragi University). The Ministry of Education had imposed a conservative administration and faculty on this traditionally liberal school, so the students went on strike, locking themselves in a dormitory, and demanded the dismissal of the school president, the rehiring of liberal teachers, and the restoration of student management of the dormitories. Their strike succeeded after only three days, generating the movement's spread to most of the other campuses in Japan, including private universities and missionary schools. Thus the Mito struggle was a forerunner of the ZENGAKUREN.

Mods (Great Britain) a teenage grouping that emerged in London in 1960 and subsequently spread throughout Great Britain. Initially the Mods' virtual raison d'etre was clothing, and they were the major influence in the creation of the Carnaby Street fashion industry and new styles in men's fashions. Mods adopted traditionally feminine stylistic attributes: long hair, makeup, high heels, bright colors. But unlike their predecesors, the TEDDY BOYS, the Mods scorned women—the movement was at least implicitly homosexual or bisexual, and Mods were accused of effeminacy. The Mod milieu became commercialized by 1961 through Carnaby Street, the Rolling Stones, and the record industry. Mods also became identified with Soho discotheques and the drug scene (amphetamines). Mods embraced essentially conventional values while seeing themselves as individualistic. They were interested in literature, providing a market for several Mod-oriented magazines, the best known entitled *Ready Steady Go* after a television program. Mods gained notoriety for violence after groups of Mods and ROCKERS clashed during the WHITSUN DISTURBANCES of 1964.

Moscow Circle (Russia) a loosely organized group formed in early 1875 whose nucleus consisted of a band of young women in their early twenties known as "the Frietsch girls" because they had lived at a boardinghouse operated by a Frau Frietsch in Zurich, where several of them had been medical students at the university. Some of these girls, along with young Caucasian men who were separatists and whom they had met in Geneva, returned to Moscow and formed the circle. In February 1875 they adopted a constitution for the All-Russian Social-Revolutionary Organization that required members to divest themselves of all possessions and to live and work among peasants and factory workers in order to organize them into revolutionary cells, including groups devoted to terrorism. Their proselyting in the factories led to their being arrested, so that by August of 1875 the organization ceased to exist. As defendants, they were not brought to trial until March 1877 in what was known as the Trial of the Fifty. On the stand, the defendants boldly affirmed their revolutionary convictions and received harsh sentences, including exile to Siberia and hard labor—all of which garnered public sympathy for the young women.

Motherfuckers *See* UP AGAINST THE WALL: MOTHERFUCKERS.

Movimiento Nacional Socialista (Chile) the National Socialist, or Nazi, movement formally established in April 1932. Although not a political party, the Nazis had a political agenda that involved attacks on the coalition government of the Liberal and Conservative parties, including acts of violence. Much of the violence was perpetrated by the Tropas de Asalto, a group of youthful storm troopers within the Nazi movement that included university students. They tried to stage a coup prior to the 1938 presidential election, seizing a building at the university and a government building near the presidential palace, but the coup failed when no military backing resulted. The police rounded up the young Nazis–numbering 58, including 14 students—and massacred them in the government building they had seized. The Nazis subsequently dissolved but reemerged almost immediately as the Vanguardia Popular Socialista (Popular Socialist Vanguard).

Movimiento Universitario de Renovadora Orientación (MURO) (Mexico) a semisecret fascist organization at the National Autonomous University of Mexico (UNAM). MURO has advocated removing politics from the university in order to concentrate on academic pursuits, but it also opposes leftists and Jews.

Mukden Incident (China) an act of Japanese aggression in September 1931 in Manchuria—known to Western historians as the Mukden Incident—that aroused massive student protests. On September 18, 1931 near the center for the Japanese-owned South Manchurian Railway in Shenyang (Mukden), Chinese troops clashed with the railway's Japanese guards. Alleging that the Chinese had sabotaged the railway, Japan sent troops within eight hours following the incident to capture the city of Shenyang and to forcefully occupy large areas of South Manchuria—a violation of several international treaties to which Japan was a signatory. In reaction to this blatant aggression, university students in Shanghai, Nanjing, and Beijing organized Resist Japan National Salvation Associations and prepared to stage protests in an upsurge of nationalism; they called for national unity in opposing the Japanese. Students issued a call to arms; in Shanghai, for example, they demanded authorization to form "student armies" to come to the nation's defense.

Eager to push for confrontation, students in the northern and central provinces organized volunteer armies to resist the Japanese. The KMT approved creation of a Volunteers Corps as one means of controlling the student movement while appearing to take a stand that favored a military response to the Japanese, and provided military trainers for the volunteer groups. The KMT also welcomed scores of student delegations to Nanjing to petition for government intervention against the Japanese, with Chiang himself usually addressing the students, as another means of maintaining control. In Nanjing, capital of the Kuomintang (KMT) government, on September 28 more than 4,000 students marched on the Foreign Ministry to accost Foreign Minister Wang Cheng-t'ing, who was reputed to have ignored warnings of the Japanese attack. They entered the ministry, found Wang, and beat him bloody. KMT leader Chiang Kai-shek publicly chastised the students' behavior while pledging resistance to the Japanese. But after ostensibly supporting the student movement early on, the KMT reversed itself and chose a course of appeasement—that is, accommodating the Japanese and refusing to take action—which generated student disaffection with the KMT. The Shanghai Resist Japan National Association defied the government and called a week-long strike in the hope of forcing Chiang to react against the Japanese; the students held a Popular Tribunal on December 10 that intimidated local officials supposedly involved in derailing a student protest on the previous day. Demonstrations occurred at other universities, and huge delegations of students brought petitions to KMT headquarters demanding action.

Thousands of students had been involved in the protests held primarily in Nanjing and Shanghai, but to little avail—since the demonstrations did not spread nationwide, the Nanjing government could largely ignore them. In addition, the student movement began to fracture into quarelling groups, partisans of opposed radical and conservative viewpoints. Although Chiang did

announce his resignation from the government on December 15, purportedly in response to the student protests, the effect of his announcement was to dissipate the movement. On December 17 in Nanjing, police attacked, beat, and arrested student demonstrators. Students ended their strikes and returned to classes. Although their movement petered out, the students had been successful in staging mass demonstrations and in organizing a nationwide boycott of Japanese goods, with public support. Japanese forces, however, continued to advance in Manchuria.

Munich Protest of 1848 (Germany) a public outcry, prominently supported by students and generated by outrage over King Ludwig I of Bavaria's infatuation for the dancer Lola Montez, that peaked in March 1848—at the height of the Revolution of 1848. Despite his early liberalism Ludwig had pursued increasingly reactionary policies as monarch, and the Montez affair provided the final catalyst for public opposition to his reign. In March, this opposition reached such intensity that he decided to abdicate in favor of his son and heir, Maximilian II. A liberal student group, the Burschenschaft Rhenania, served as spokesman for the public protest and helped to bring about Ludwig's abdication and the forming of a more liberal government. Before vacating the throne, Ludwig granted the students' demands to convene an assembly of the Estates and to create a student militia. Subsequently, students formed a Volunteer Student Corps and a variety of representative assemblies.

Muslim Students' Union (MSU) (India) the longest-lived Muslim student organization in India, founded in 1890. Among the MSU's purposes stated in its 1920 Annual Report was providing for "the mental, moral, and material welfare of Muslim students in general." Prior to 1930, the MSU provided educational, cultural, and social programs and avoided any involvement in politics; it did, however, champion women's rights and the abolition of purdah. In the 1940s the MSU was torn by the struggle between nationalist and communalist Muslims; and after independence and the partition that created Pakistan in 1947, it survived but only in a very reduced form and with few public activities. The MSU's center in Bombay, where the MSU was headquartered, had been an important generator of future Pakistani leaders, however, including Muhammad Ali Jinnah.

Mutual Improvement Association (MIA) (United States) a youth organization sponsored by the Church of Jesus Christ of Latter-day Saints (Mormons). Origins of the MIA, or Mutual, trace to Mormon President Brigham Young's creation of a church association for young women on November 28, 1869 and another for young men on June 10, 1875. MIA is open to any interested youths, including non-Mormons, age 12 and older and is divided into an organization for young men (YMMIA) and one for young women (YWMIA), which function cooperatively. MIA programs feature weekly meetings; religious instruction; art, social, recreational, and sports activities. MIA adopted the BOY SCOUTS OF AMERICA as its program for boys age 12 and 13; and the Boy Scouts' Explorers for age 14–17. The MIA girls' program for age 12 and 13 is the Beehive, begun in 1914; MIA Maid is for age 14 and 15; and Laurel is for age 16 and 17. MIA also provides social and cultural programs for young men and women above high school age, including young married couples.

Nanterre Student Protests   *See* MARCH 22ND MOVE-MENT and MAY REVOLT.

Narita New Airport Struggle   (Japan) demonstrations by students, workers, and Narita residents in 1967–68 against construction of a new airport at Narita to serve Tokyo. The new airport (to replace Haneda) was deemed necessary to accommodate supersonic airplanes. Narita residents began to demonstrate against it in the fall of 1967; they were joined by workers and members of ZEN-GAKUREN, who believed the airport would be used to support the U.S. war effort in Vietnam, in February and March 1968. The student demonstrators clashed with police on February 26 and March 10, with many being arrested. The struggle peaked in a March 31 demonstration by about 2,400 protestors (including about 800 students) who marched to the Narita City Hall and there battled the police. The demonstrations succeeded only in delaying construction of the airport.

Narodniki (Populists)   (Russia) a movement of the mid-1870s promoted by university students and intellectuals to bring agrarian socialism to the Russian countryside. The concepts fostered by the Narodniki derived largely from essays by Peter Lavrov published under a pseudonym in 1868–69 as *Historical Letters*. The basic concept was to "go to the people" and educate them in socialistic reform. Consequently, beginning in 1872, hundreds of students donned peasant dress and went into rural areas to work on farms or as teachers in order to educate the peasants. In 1873–74, the numbers of these young zealots swelled to nearly 2,000 as Russian students ordered home from Switzerland by the government joined their crusade. Although the peasants reacted to the students with hostility or indifference, the authorities saw them as a genuine threat. Between 1873 and 1877, police interrogated 1,600 Narodniki, and 525 were held for

trial; of these 79 were sent into exile. This government repression effectively killed the Narodniki movement.

National Autonomous University Strike   (Mexico) a strike by students of the National Autonomous University of Mexico (UNAM) in Mexico City during early 1987 in protest against sweeping university reforms mandated by the federal government. The reforms had been decreed while students were on vacation during 1986 and generated protest because of their major repercussions, which included making it nearly impossible for lower-income students to attend the university. The student strike of 1987 eventuated in victory, as the government rescinded most of the reforms.

National Committee for a Sane Nuclear Policy (SANE)   (United States) a nationwide organization formed in New York in 1957; a student affiliate group was founded in the following year that had chapters at most major universities in the country. SANE advocated international nuclear disarmament and supported the Nuclear Test Ban Treaty of 1962 and subsequent weapons-control agreements. More left-wing than its parent organization, the Student SANE attracted communist and pro-Soviet members, leading to attacks by senators and members of Congress. These included the threat of public hearings on communist infiltration into the parent organization, which in consequence insisted that these elements be ejected from the Student SANE in favor of a pro-West stance. The Student SANE rejected this policy, causing SANE to suspend the student organization in 1962; its decline followed quickly thereafter.

National Conference on Students and Politics (United States) a conference held in Washington, D.C., in December 1933 that comprised a predecessor for the UNITED FRONT. The conference was significant for the wide range of student groups that sponsored and organized it: NATIONAL STUDENT FEDERATION (NSF), STUDENT LEAGUE FOR INDUSTRIAL DEMOCRACY (SLID), NATIONAL STUDENT LEAGUE (NSL), International Student Service, League of Nations Association, YOUNG MEN'S CHRISTIAN ASSOCIATION (YMCA), and YOUNG WOMEN'S CHRISTIAN ASSOCIATION (YWCA). Eleanor Roosevelt presented the keynote address, and representatives of the Roosevelt administration participated. Students from throughout the nation attended and wrangled over such issues as pacifism, fascism, armaments, racism, and tariffs. The conference received major coverage by the newspaper press. It also established an organization of the same name as a means of involving students in ongoing concern with major foreign and domestic issues. The conference's board of advisors included Charles Beard, Norman Thomas, Reinhold Niebuhr, John Dewey, and Senator Robert Wagner.

National Council of Methodist Youth (NCMY) (United States) the umbrella youth services organization of the Methodist Church—one of the nation's largest denominations—founded in 1941 with a membership of more than 1 million youths. NCMY programs have included work camps, regional meetings, and social services; it has mostly advocated liberal positions on national issues—such as opposition to ROTC and universal military training in the mid-1950s. A later significant offshoot of NCMY is the Methodist Student Movement.

National Council of University Students of India (NCUSI) (India) an organization founded in 1960 to replace the failed NATIONAL UNION OF STUDENTS. The NCUSI also suffered from political manipulation during the cold-war years, receiving financial support from Western nations. It has pursued moderate tactics, advocating students' cooperation with university administrators. The NCUSI, unlike other Indian student organizations, has not been a mass movement but an organization of student leaders. By the late 1960s the NCUSI had representation at fewer than half of India's 66 universities and a smaller membership than its rival ALL-INDIA STUDENTS' FEDERATION. Neither the NCUSI nor the AISF, however, could justifiably claim to be representative of India's students, as both did during international meetings.

National Federation of Catholic College Students (NFCCS) (United States) the most activist Roman Catholic organization that attempted to unify Catholic university students. Founded in 1937, the NFCCS sponsored such events as Interracial Justice Week, supported civil rights, and opposed universal military training during the 1950s.

National Grange (United States) a nationwide organization of farm families that, at its local organizational level known as a Subordinate Grange, sponsors Juvenile Granges for youths age 5 to 14. Programs of the Juvenile Grange include educational and social activities and community projects. Subordinate Granges also sponsor BOY SCOUTS OF AMERICA troops and 4-H CLUBS and participate in the Grange Interstate Youth Exchange and International Hospitality Plan.

National Liberation Front *See* FRONT DE LIBÉRATION NATIONALE (FLN).

National Liberation Vanguards of China (NLVC) (China) a pro-communist student organization formed in Beijing on February 1, 1936 that was committed to the liberation of China and was initially comprised largely of leftist students of the DECEMBER NINTH MOVEMENT. Organized according to Leninist tenets, with secret cells of three to five members, the NLVC was from its beginning communist oriented, and it soon became an adjunct of the COMMUNIST YOUTH LEAGUE (CYL). It was through their involvement in the NLVC that many of the December 9ers eventually found their way into membership in the CHINESE COMMUNIST PARTY (CCP). In spring and summer 1936, the NLVC trained students in guerrilla war tactics and held maneuvers to prepare them for fighting the Japanese, who had already occupied large areas of China. By June, membership had grown from the original 300 to more than 1,300, and by the end of the year there were more than 2,000 members. But the SIAN INCIDENT made the NLVC's continuation precarious, as did the advancing Japanese. So NLVC members left Beijing, and many relocated in south-central China, as did thousands of other students and faculty from other university cities. Thereafter, the NLVC members served as guerrillas in the war against Japan. The number involved peaked in late 1938 to an estimated 20,000; as a result of internecine rivalries with the CYL and other groups, the NLVC apparently withered away into effective nonexistence shortly thereafter, although it was not officially dissolved until 1949 and the creation of the NEW DEMOCRATIC YOUTH LEAGUE.

Bibliography: John Israel and Donald W. Klein, *Rebels and Bureaucrats: China's December 9ers* (Berkeley: University of California Press, 1976).

National Mobilization Committee to End the War in Vietnam (Mobe) (United States) a coalition of about 100 antiwar organizations (a large percentage of them student groups) representing the political spectrum from Left to Right, formed in 1968. Among the Mobe's significant undertakings was its major role in organizing the demonstrations in Chicago during the 1968 Democratic National Convention. (*See* BATTLE OF CHICAGO.) The

Mobe also organized the "counterinaugural" of January 19–20 in Washington, D.C. as a peaceful antiwar demonstration to coincide with Richard M. Nixon's inauguration as president. The demonstrators numbered about 6,000, and on January 19 they held a counterinaugural parade, marching in the opposite direction from that the official parade route would take. Twenty-two were arrested when scuffles occurred at the end of the parade. Among the demonstrators on January 20 were elements representing STUDENTS FOR A DEMOCRATIC SOCIETY (SDS) and Co-Aim (the Committee for an Anti-Imperialist Movement), who decided to ignore Mobe's call for peaceful protest and adopted violent tactics. A group of about 300 of them hurled rocks and bottles at Nixon's limousine while shouting obscenities as the president-elect was transported to the inaugural site. Mobe's successor, the "New Mobe," also organized two other significant events: the VIETNAM MORATORIUM DAY and the MARCH AGAINST DEATH.

National Newman Club Federation　(United States) the largest national Roman Catholic organization for university and college students, founded in 1915. It was named for British cleric John Henry Cardinal Newman.

National Reconstruction Movement　(Korea) a movement created in fall 1961 by the military junta government of South Korea (Republic of Korea). The government ordered university student-government associations to participate; most did so at least tacitly by adding the term *reconstruction* to their names, but the Seoul National University student government refused to comply and suffered no retaliation.

National Salvation Corps of Chinese Students Studying in Japan (Jiuguotuan)　(Japan) as its name suggests, an association of Chinese students in Japan founded in 1918 to provide organization for the students in carrying out rallies and demonstrations in Tokyo protesting perceived Japanese imperialism. Later they protested, in particular, the terms of the Treaty of Paris following World War I that, among other objectionable terms, awarded Japan jurisdiction over Shantung (Shandong) Province. In May 1919 members of the Jiuguotuan returned en masse to China, making their headquarters in Shanghai and agitating for mass demonstrations against the Japanese. Thus they became deeply involved in the important MAY FOURTH MOVEMENT. The Jiuguotuan students were also invited to join the SHANGHAI STUDENT UNION (SSU).

National Salvation Movement　(China) a movement generated by reaction to Japanese aggrandizement in late 1935. Japan demanded that the government of China grant creation of an "autonomous region" in North China, and the Kuomintang government of Chiang Kai-shek made an ambiguous response. Fearful that North China might suffer the fate of Manchuria, students at Yenching University and Tsinghua University staged massive demonstrations on December 9 and December 16, 1935—known as the DECEMBER NINTH MOVEMENT—that eventuated in creation of the National Salvation Movement in early 1936. The movement's primary purpose was to advocate a national united front, joining the Kuomintang (Nationalist Party) and the CHINESE COMMUNIST PARTY (CCP, led by Mao Zedong) in opposition to Japan. Although supported by students of the December Ninth Movement, the National Salvation Movement as an organization comprised a loose coalition of businesspeople, bankers, professors, journalists, lawyers, and military leaders; it was centered in Shanghai, where the International Settlement and the French Concession provided some protection against political reprisals (the Japanese, however, occupied the city from 1937 to 1945). To show their support of the movement, many student groups adopted the words *National Salvation* as part of their names; for example, on April 25, 1936, the Peiping (Beijing) Student Union changed its name to the Peiping Student National Salvation Union (PSNSU), thus emphasizing its support of the boycott against Japanese goods and other forms of opposition to Japan. The Japanese occupation suppressed the National Salvation Movement, arresting many of its members; remnants of the movement took refuge in the Northwest.

National Salvation Youth Corps　(China) a Leftist organization formed in November 1937 in Wuhan with leadership provided by members of the NATIONAL LIBERATION VANGUARDS OF CHINA (NLVC). The youth corps quickly spread into Hubei, Henan, Anhui, Hunan, Sichuan, and other areas, garnering tens of thousands of members—in Wuhan alone there were 5,000 members. In its drive against the Communists, however, the Kuomintang effectively brought an end to the corps in 1938.

National Socialist German Student Union (Nationalsozialistischer Deutscher Studentbund)　(Germany) the university student organization of the Nazi Party (National Socialist German Workers' Party), officially launched in 1925. Although a Nazi student group had existed in Munich in 1922, the first official Nazi student organization was formed at the University of Leipzig in November 1925, and the Student Union itself was founded on February 20, 1926 at the University of Munich. The Student Union appealed primarily to free (nonfraternity) students and made a major effort to enroll youths from the working class. It toned down Nazi concepts, especially racist and antiintellectual ones, to adapt the movement to the academic community, affording lip service to university ideals of free speech and autonomy. Its newspaper, *Nationalsozialistische Hochschulbriefe*, solicited the involvement of poorer students in the movement and touted student links with the workers in a populist program. In the year of its founding, the Student Union claimed to have units at 20 schools and began to hold annual national conventions. In September, the organization came under the guidance of Nazi Party leaders, and the party also provided some funding. As with party members, Student Union members wore uniforms comprised of brown shirts, Swastika armbands, and jackboots.

In the summer of 1928 the party leaders chose Baldur von SCHIRACH, closely allied with Adolf Hitler, as leader of the National Socialist German Student Union. Under Schirach the organization abandoned the student-worker emphasis and sought to recruit students from all walks, including fraternity members; it sponsored lectures and other educational programs, held discussions on Nazi concepts, and presented Nazi leaders as campus speakers for purposes of proselytizing. Discussions ranged about many subjects, such as foreign policy, capitalism, economics, race, and anthropology, all providing Nazi interpretations with a veneer of scholarship that made them palatable in the university context. In 1929 the organization founded a Nazi student journal, the *Akademischer Beobachter*, with Schirach as editor, as another means of propagandizing, including portraying the Student Union as the champion of academic freedom and university autonomy. Through these varied efforts, Nazism came to seem compatible with the thinking of an array of fraternity and other groups who had for years espoused right-wing, nationalistic, or folk-community views. Student Union activists also won elections to student councils (at some schools winning majority representation) and became members of the BURSCHENSHAFTEN and other student organizations to promote Nazi views from within these groups. They also secured the key leadership positions in the DEUTSCHE STUDENTENSCHAFT. At the beginning of the thirties, Student Union members began increasingly to organize violent demonstrations against Leftist political rallies and professors whom they opposed—a tactic that both civil and university authorities failed to counteract. Thus, although by 1932 a sizable countermovement had developed within the Deutsche Studentenschaft and the academic establishment, the Student Union was poised to subvert the older student organizations and take total control of the overall student movement following Hitler's appointment as chancellor in January 1933. By summer 1935, that control was secured, and by summer 1936, the National Socialist German Student Union was in effect the only extant student organization in Germany.

Bibliography: Michael S. Steinberg, *Sabers and Brown Shirts: The German Students' Path to National Socialism, 1918–1935* (Chicago: University of Chicago Press, 1977).

National Student Association (China) a student organization aligned with the Communist Party. Founded in May 1936, the association to some extent was meant to replace its predecessor of the same name (see below).

National Student Association (NSA) (China) an organization of students intended to support the national government, founded on June 16, 1919 and headquartered in Shanghai. In April 1927, when the Kuomintang (KMT) led by Chiang Kai-shek purged communists in the Party Purification Movement (including the killing of the NSA's 22-year-old communist chairman), the headquarters was moved to Wuhan. Subsequently, communist influence in NSA was eliminated. NSA was actively involved in the protest that followed the TSINAN INCIDENT. The NSA advocated a strong youth movement not dominated by the KMT, a position that led to friction with KMT leaders. In 1929 the Ministry of Training banned the organization.

National Student Association (NSA) (United States) a nationwide organization of university student-government councils founded in September 1947 at a convention assembled for this purpose at the University of Wisconsin. The convention attracted 800 delegates representing 351 universities and colleges and 20 national organizations. They drafted a constitution that rested decisions about policy in an annual congress, which would elect officers and a National Supervisory Board with broad powers to interpret NSA policies. They also drafted a Student Bill of Rights, whose tenets included support for academic freedom, the right to an education, and rejection of racial, religious, or political forms of discrimination. Since NSA was a federation, members of all affiliated organizations automatically became NSA members; consequently, it claimed more than 1 million members, and, even though this membership was largely inactive and involuntary, the claim was enough to make NSA the presumed speaker for U.S. students. The organization's publication was entitled *Student Government Bulletin*.

The NSA became actively involved in international student activities, helping to organize the INTERNATIONAL STUDENT CONFERENCE (ISC) following NSA's withdrawal from the INTERNATIONAL UNION OF STUDENTS (IUS) in 1948. The NSA was especially involved internationally after 1953, when the FOUNDATION FOR YOUTH AND STUDENT AFFAIRS (FYSA) began to fund its international activities. NSA in fact provided more than half of the ISC's annual budget while also sponsoring and funding numerous of its own programs, including the Foreign Student Leadership Project (begun in 1956); annually, this project brought 15 foreign students to this country for a year of study and travel.

NSA devoted its energies to student issues and concerns (although members became active in the Civil

Rights movement) until its 1960 Congress; here, a majority of the delegates voted in favor of formulating and advocating positions on national social and political issues. As the positions to be taken were liberal, conservative dissidents broke away to form the Association of Student Governments. The NSA's liberal image, including its opposition to the Vietnam War, was badly corroded by public revelation in 1967 that for 15 years the Central Intelligence Agency (CIA) had been covertly providing about 80 percent of the NSA's annual budget and that NSA officers had provided intelligence reports to the CIA. The secrecy of this covert relationship had been maintained by the CIA's recruitment of NSA officers as intelligence liaisons and the CIA's threats of prosecution under terms of the National Security Act if the students revealed the relationship. The NSA broke its tie with the CIA and thereafter became increasingly militant in its opposition to the Vietnam War. It also discontinued its annual International Student Relations Seminars (ISRS), begun in 1952, which informed attendees about developments in the international student movement.

National Student Christian Federation (NSCF) (United States) a federation of Protestant university student groups, including the YOUNG MEN'S CHRISTIAN ASSOCIATION (YMCA), the YOUNG WOMEN'S CHRISTIAN ASSOCIATION (YWCA), the United Student Christian Council (USCC), the Student Volunteer Movement, and the Inter-Seminary Movement, founded in 1944 and originally titled the United Student Christian Council—the name change occurred in 1951. The organization's name was changed once again in 1966, through merger, into the United Christian Movement (UCM), which disbanded in 1969. Its major publication was *Motive*. NSCF participated in international movements, prominently the World Student Christian Federation. The NSCF from its origins until its demise was significant as a force for Protestant student ecumenism.

National Student Federation (NSF) (United States) a liberal, nationwide student organization founded in December 1926 at a meeting in Ann Arbor, Michigan. Two groups were responsible for the organization of NSF: a National Student Federation of America, modeled after European student unions and formed by representatives of seven Western universities in January 1925, and the Intercollegiate World Court Conference held at Princeton University in December 1925 that attracted representatives from 245 colleges and universities, mostly in the East. This conference promoted support for U.S. membership in the World Court, but the delegates also expressed the desire to form a permanent student organization similar to those national groups extant in Europe. Delegates representing these two groups (and the student governments of 200 schools) met at Ann Arbor and formed the NSF in 1926 as a federation of student governments—the nation's first such federation. The NSF, claiming 400,000 members in 1928, emerged as the nation's most important student organization and was viewed as the speaker for U.S. students. It operated a headquarters in New York City, held annual conventions, provided a travel program that took many students to Europe, and served as an information clearinghouse for student governments.

During the early years of the Great Depression (1930–32), Edward R. Murrow—then recently graduated from Washington State College and later renowned as a war correspondent and head of CBS News—served as president of the NSF. Murrow castigated university students for their apathy regarding national and international economic and political problems; he originated a radio news show, *University on the Air*, broadcast by CBS as part of the effort to arouse student involvement in important issues. NSF also began to publish *National Student Mirror* in 1933 as an organ of communication that endured for three years; later, NSF published a weekly entitled *NSFA Reporter*. The NSF's political disinterestedness was suggested by its annual convention held in December 1933 where delegates rejected one proposal to boycott the 1936 Olympics in Germany and another to condemn university censorship of student publications while managing to avoid any discussion of war. But in 1934 NSF established a National Institute for Public Affairs to foster discussions and conferences on national issues, and in 1935 it produced a series of issues-centered radio programs broadcast by CBS. Since NSF did not take stands on anything more controversial than such campus-centered issues as freedom of the student press, it began to lose out to more radical groups. NSF disbanded in 1946, but it served as the prototype for the NATIONAL STUDENT ASSOCIATION (NSA) founded the next year.

National Student Forum (NSF) (United States) the first significant national student organization, formed in 1921 through the merger of the INTERCOLLEGIATE LIBERAL LEAGUE (ILL) and the National Student Conference for the Limitation of Armaments. NSF grew rapidly and by the end of 1923 had branches at 25 colleges and universities and individual members at 300. In addition, through its journal *New Student*, the organization reached a national audience of politically active students until May 1929, when it ceased publication. In 1928, many members of the journal's staff had left to join the LEAGUE FOR INDUSTRIAL DEMOCRACY (LID), and in 1929 NSF itself disbanded to become part of LID. An executive committee of 30 persons (20 students, 5 alumni, and 5 faculty) governed NSF. Although liberal in orientation, NSF did not espouse a defined political ideology. Its major activities included a national conference and sponsorship of regional and local meetings devoted to key contemporary issues. Its most important activity, however, was the seven-year publication of *New Student*, which carried articles on international affairs, academic concerns, sex, national politics, educational reform, and a host of other subjects covering nearly the entire gamut of U.S. life.

National Student League (NSL) (United States) a communist-oriented university-students' organization founded in December 1931 in New York City under the name New York Student League and rechristened as the National Student League in February 1932. Founding of the NSL evolved from an effort by Frederick B. Robinson, the virulently antiradical president of City College of New York (CCNY), to suppress *Frontiers*, a magazine founded by Harry Magdoff in February 1931 and modeled after the Marxist *New Masses*, because its first issue advocated the abolition of the Reserve Officer Training Corps (ROTC) program at CCNY. Robinson had copies of *Frontiers* confiscated and suspended 11 involved students; in response CCNY activists organized a citywide student campaign against censorship and a strike threat that convinced the CCNY trustees to authorize publication of the magazine and to reinstate the suspended students. This successful student campaign, which created contacts among students in schools throughout New York City, eventuated in creation of the NSL, with Magdoff as one of the founders. The NSL and the STUDENT LEAGUE FOR INDUSTRIAL DEMOCRACY (SLID) comprised the Left's effort to organize university students, but NSL was distinctive in having communists among its leadership, in advocating a genuine national student movement, and in promoting an activist and even militant response to social and political problems.

Dedicated to nationwide organizing for the purpose of addressing campus problems and effecting student protests, NSL grew quickly. It gained national publicity when a busload of NSL members traveled to Harlan County, Kentucky to assist coalminers involved in a bitter strike: the local police authorities drove them from the county, but the episode gave NSL an organizational boost. (*See* HARLAN MINERS' STRIKE.) NSL also grew by participating in local campus controversies, such as organizing a protest against tuition increases at the New York City colleges in 1932 and organizing a strike at Columbia University concerning dismissal of the student newspaper's editor for criticizing the administration. (*See* COLUMBIA STRIKE.) In 1932 it organized a high school unit, working especially on organizing in the New York City schools. From its origin in 1931, the NSL published a journal entitled *Student Review* that spread its advocacy until the journal's failure in December 1933 for lack of funding. By 1933, NSL had organized 129 local chapters. NSL advocated worker-student cooperation; opposition to ROTC, racism, and imperialist wars (antiimperialist wars were acceptable). NSL cosponsored an antiwar conference held in Chicago in December 1933 that advocated

the termination of ROTC and the Morrill Act's provisions. Perhaps NSL's most renowned activity was the instigation of a nationwide student strike, cosponsored by SLID, protesting war preparations. The strike originated on April 13, 1934 when 25,000 students demonstrated—an unprecedented event in U.S. history. (*See* STUDENT STRIKE AGAINST WAR.) For a second strike in 1935, youths representing such groups as the NATIONAL COUNCIL OF METHODIST YOUTH and the AMERICAN YOUTH CONGRESS joined in. At the end of 1935 NSL joined with SLID in forming the AMERICAN STUDENT UNION (ASU) and effectively lost its individual identity, but during its short existence it had been a major force in organizing student activism and attracting students to communism.

Bibliography: James Wechsler, *Revolt on the Campus* (New York: Colvici, Friede, 1935); Robert Cohen, *When the Old Left Was Young: Student Radicals and America's First Mass Student Movement, 1929–1941* (New York: Oxford University Press, 1993).

National Turkish Students' Federation (TMTF) (Turkey) a government supported student organization formed in 1960. The TMTF receives funding from the government and is obligated to maintain political neutrality. Its leaders and members, however, have been sympathetic to Leftist party policies.

National Turkish Students' Union (MTTB) (Turkey) a government supported student organization formed in 1960. The MTTB, like its counterpart NATIONAL TURKISH STUDENTS' FEDERATION, receives funding from the government and is obligated to maintain political neutrality. The group's sympathies, however, have been generally progovernment.

National Unification League (Korea) a South Korean (Republic of Korea) student organization formed in November 1960 whose primary purpose was promotion of unification between North Korea and South Korea. The political ideology of the members was socialist, nationalist, and both anti-American and anticommunist. The league disseminated its own publications and sponsored discussions and demonstrations, but its leftist orientation limited its memberships, even though most Korean students supported a nationalistic ideology. The military junta that seized power in a May 1961 coup banned student organizations, except for student governments, and as a means of enforcement of the ban, the junta arrested the leaders of student organizations. Officers of the league, because of their socialist leanings, were tried and given lengthy prison sentences. The ban lasted until 1963, although the junta did allow participation in international student meetings supporting the United Nations.

National Union of Ghana Students (NUGS) (Ghana) an organization formed in 1958 as a successor to the National Union of Gold Coast Students. NUGS was bold enough to voice opposition to policies imposed by the government of Kwame NKRUMAH and his Convention People's Party (CPP). For example, in January 1964 NUGS protested against deportation orders served on six faculty members of the University of Ghana at Legon, but police dispersed their demonstration, and the government closed all three national universities for over two weeks in retaliation. The CCP-controlled press joined in condemning the students, and the CCP established student publications and required students to take "orientation" courses. The party and the government pursued these and a variety of other means to suppress NUGS, including creation of a rival organization (THE GHANA NATIONAL STUDENTS' ORGANIZATION), and by 1965 NUGS had effectively ceased to exist. Following the February 24, 1966 army coup that seized control of the government while Nkrumah was in China, NUGS revived and began to focus on issues related to students' rights.

National Union of Nigerian Students (NUNS) (Nigeria) a nationwide university student organization initiated by the Students' Union of the University College of Ibadan in 1956. It includes student councils of the colleges at Ife, Zaria, and Nsukka. NUNS has protested against corruption in the Nigerian government, apartheid in South Africa, and French nuclear-weapons tests in the Sahara Desert.

National Union of Northern Rhodesia Students (NUNRS) (Zambia, former Northern Rhodesia) an organization formed in 1963 at a time when no university existed in Northern Rhodesia. Students from Europe, the University College in Salibury (Southern Rhodesia), and Northern Rhodesia technical and postsecondary schools convened in Lusaka and created NUNRS.

National Union of Rhodesian Students (NURS) (Rhodesia) an organization formed in 1963 by African students at the University of Rhodesia. Members of NURS supported the political cause of the Zimbabwe nationalist movement. In 1980 Rhodesia became the Republic of Zimbabwe, with African majority rule.

National Union of School Students (NUSS) (Great Britain) an organization founded in 1968 following the MAY REVOLT in France. In 1973 it was estimated to have 10,000 members. The NUSS gained public attention during demonstrations in London in 1972, when the organization's reform policies had the support of perhaps 60 percent of the school pupils in the nation.

National Union of South African Students (NUSAS) (South Africa) the oldest student organization in South Africa, formed in 1924. Its original primary purpose was to promote cooperation and integration among Afrikaner and English students (the political unification of South Africa occurred in 1910), but it had little success in this endeavor because of the Afrikaners' opposition to the NUSAS's liberalism and internationalism. NUSAS also discouraged membership by nonwhites. Thus ethnic fragmenting seemed inevitable, and in the 1930s students at the universities where Afrikaans was the language of instruction (Stellenbosch, Potchefstroom, and Pretoria) broke away over the issue of extending membership to Fort Hare University College (nonwhite) and formed their own organization, the Afrikaner National Student League (Afrikaanse Nasionale Studentebond, or ANSB), which later merged with another group to become the AFRIKANER STUDENT LEAGUE. Thereafter NUSAS represented mostly the English language universities (Cape Town, Witwatersrand, Natal, and Rhodes) and a liberal view but remained relatively small and inconsequential. In 1945, however, NUSAS broadened its base by extending membership to Fort Hare and other nonwhite schools. With the victory of the Nationalist Party in the 1948 national election and the coming of apartheid, the nonwhite and left-wing white elements united in pressing the NUSA to take a stand for political and social equality, but by 1955 they had lost out to more conservative elements that were intent on focusing strictly on issues affecting student welfare. Government efforts to impose racially discriminatory policies at the universities, however, alarmed many students, and in 1957 the NUSAS adopted the Universal Declaration of Human Rights as its basic policy, thus denouncing apartheid. From 1957 to 1959, the NUSAS conducted a program of marches and other events opposing the imposition of apartheid at the universities but without success. Accusing the organization of being a revolutionary movement, the government harassed and condemned the NUSAS during the 1960s, arresting or banning some of its leaders and raiding its headquarters in Cape Town, but it did not outlaw the organization.

National Union of Students (NUS) (Great Britain) an organization formed in 1922 with the intention of including all the student unions of all the universities and university colleges in the nation for the first time in British history. It derived from the Inter-University Association, begun after World War I, which included only the so-called redbrick universities (not Cambridge, London, or Oxford). Its formation was spurred by students who had been delegates to the CONFÉDÉRATION INTERNATIONAL DES ÉTUDIANTS, who desired to create a British union that would serve as a counterweight to the anti-German positions taken by the UNION NATIONALE DES ÉTUDIANTS DE FRANCE (UNEF). The NUS, however, largely devoted its efforts to obtaining reduced foreign travel fares and other benefits for students rather than pushing any political or academic agenda. By the 1960s, the NUS had adopted activist policies, demanding student representation in university governing bodies, an end to the means test for student grants, improved student accommodations, increased health services, and other benefits.

National Union of Students (NUS)   (India) a nonpolitical student organization established in 1950 by the Indian National Congress in a joint venture with the socialists. At Jawaharlal Nehru's request, the Socialists agreed to join in sponsoring formation of the NUS, which was initiated at a large conference in Bombay that both Nehru and the Socialist leader Jayaprakash Narayan addressed. Ironically, outside political influences and the student leaders' own identification with political parties aborted the NUS's proposed noninvolvement in politics. Many university administrations rejected having NUS groups at their schools because of its being manipulated by outside political groups. The NUS also suffered from lack of funds, student indifference, and factionalism; by 1958 it was moribund.

National Youth Administration   (United States) an agency within the Works Progress Administration (WPA) created by executive order of President Franklin D. Roosevelt on June 26, 1935. The National Youth Administration (NYA), headed by Aubrey Williams, was a government program directed specifically at organizing and serving U.S. youths, mostly between 16 and 24. It coordinated government efforts to support needy college students, promote vocational education and training, reduce transiency among youths, and provide relief and jobs to youths—all intended to prevent the U.S.'s young people from becoming lifelong victims of the Great Depression's economic devastation. Through a system of grants to high school and college students, the NYA tried to enhance their skills development while keeping them out of the job market; through its jobs program for nonstudents, the NYA provided assistance to 300,000 youths per year by 1937. Many of the involved nonstudents initially worked in developing parks and recreational facilities, cleaning public buildings, and similar tasks; in 1937, however, the NYA changed its approach to emphasize work that provided training and then, in 1939, to employing youths in the defense industries. The NYA also created job placement services, community residences for youths from rural areas, and special programs for African Americans. By 1940 the NYA had provided part-time work for more than 2 million students—representing 12 percent of all college and university students. The agency also provided jobs for an additional 2.6 million other youths. As World War II proceeded, the NYA's working youths became totally involved in the defense industries, and the agency devoted a major effort to obtaining jobs for young women and African Americans in these industries. Wartime budget restrictions caused the NYA's death in 1943. Throughout its existence, the NYA was headed by Aubrey Williams.

Bibliography: Ernest K. Lindley and Betty Lindley, *A New Deal for Youth: The Story of the National Youth Administration* (New York: Viking, 1938); John A. Salmond, *A Southern Rebel, the Life and Times of Aubrey Willis Williams, 1890–1965* (Chapel Hill: University of North Carolina Press, 1983).

National Youth Alliance (NYA)   (United States) an extremist, antiestablishment organization formed after the 1968 presidential election by youths, mostly in the 18-to-21 age group, who had supported George Wallace and his American Independent Party during the election as members of Youth for Wallace. In the spring of 1969, NYA claimed to have 3,000 dues-paying members. The NYA proposed to form an alliance of students and young workers—a Right Front—allied against the Left, which ironically also supported a student-worker alliance; like the NEW LEFT, the NYA opposed conservative economics and "bourgeois values." NYA members overtly professed belief in white supremacy and advocated "white studies" courses in colleges and universities to teach the superiority of the white race—a far more openly racist stand than that taken by Wallace's adult backers—and many of its leaders were publicly professed anti-Semites. The NYA was also more militant than the majority of Wallace backers, calling for a "Right Front terror" to eliminate the Left. Again like the New Left, however, the NYA opposed the Vietnam War and wars in general as a means for a rapacious economic system to maintain employment levels and for ambitious politicians to garner votes while "America's finest young men have been murdered." Such views were advocated in the NYA's publication *Statecraft.*

Natural Science for Youth Foundation   (United States) an organization founded in 1961 to promote creation of natural science centers, school nature centers, and children's museums to promote education in nature and conservation for youths. The foundation provides a variety of services—planning, programming, financing, staffing—for the establishment of such centers and has helped to create more than 100 nature centers for youths throughout the nation.

Neformalnye   (Russia) "informal groups" of youths that began to emerge largely in the post-Stalinist era rather than organized associations or movements; consequently, they were of enormous significance as counterpoints to the officially sanctioned KOMSOMOL. In 1988 during the Perestroika period, for example, the newspaper *Pravda* estimated that 50 percent of the Soviet Union's young people belonged to some 30,000 *neformalnye* (also referred to as *samodeyatel'nye initsiativy*, "independent initiatives"); surveys conducted among high-school-age youths in Moscow in 1987 indicated that more than 70 percent belonged to "informal groups." In the late-1950s, such groups centered mostly on music, but in the 1960s they included hippies and rock-music followers. (*See* HIPPIE MOVEMENT.) In subsequent years, *neformalnye* have been formed through affiliation with such widely varied phenomena as HARE KRISHNA, Islam, Christianity, drug use, soccer teams, and neofascism. Among recent groups are the LYUBERY, devoted to anti-Western views, martial arts, and violent opposition to hippies; and the *fashisty*, in some cases genuine ideological fascists and in others anti-Semites who adapt as their symbols the swastika and other trappings of Nazism. Some more-or-less organized "informal groups" of youths have focused on politics—for example, the Federation of Socialist Clubs formed in the late 1980s to promote support for perestroika. But the majority of the *neformalnye* have been assumed to be those—in 1985 estimated at 100,000—who could be called "groupies," followers of pop- and rock-music bands, or just devotees of these forms of music. All *neformalnye*, however, are seen as a whole to constitute a counterculture within Russian society.

Bibliography: Jim Riordan, ed., *Soviet Youth Culture* (Bloomington: Indiana University Press, 1989).

New Democratic Youth League (NDYL) (China) a nationwide youth organization created in 1949 by the CHINESE COMMUNIST PARTY (CCP) to rejuvenate the COMMUNIST YOUTH LEAGUE. The NDYL held its first congress in April 1949. From 1957, the NYDL was known once again simply as the Communist Youth League.

New Left (United States) a youth movement involving a variety of groups and organizations that began to emerge in the early 1960s. The STUDENTS FOR A DEMOCRATIC SOCIETY (SDS) meeting at Port Huron, Michigan in 1962 called for the formation of a "New Left" whose defining of public issues would help people "see the political, social and economic sources of their private troubles and organize to change society." The ideology of the New Left was spelled out in the PORT HURON STATEMENT, which made clear that the SDS at least believed that university students would generate this movement because the universities accommodated political life, existed nationwide, condoned controversy, were populated by youths who matured after World War II, and comprised a good meeting ground for liberal and socialist elements that could effect a political synthesis. The statement declared,

> A new left must transform modern complexity into issues that can be understood and felt close up by every human being. It must give form to the feelings of helplessness and indifference, so that people may see the political, social and economic sources of their private troubles and organize to change society.

The New Left's origins lay in the 1950s. Its name derived from a publication, *The New Left Review*, begun by Leftists in Great Britain in the late 1950s who were disaffected by the Hungarian Revolution and Nikita Khrushchev's revelations about Joseph Stalin. The Civil Rights movement, especially the STUDENT NONVIOLENT COORDINATING COMMITTEE (SNCC), was also a major influence. The articulation of the New Left ideology in the Port Huron Statement, however, created immediate friction with the "old Left" sponsor of SDS, the LEAGUE FOR INDUSTRIAL DEMOCRACY. Central to the New Left program would be rejection of the Marxist view of social and economic divisions resulting from capitalist exploitation and disillusionment with New Deal and other liberal efforts to reform the social system. The New Left saw the basic problems afflicting society as militarism, racism, and poverty, and its leaders set out to devise projects and tactics to reorient the political system to address these problems while generating a class-free society marked by unity through individual political action. They promoted creation of an alliance among various powerless groups, not dominated by a strong central leadership, but this effort resulted by 1967 in the increasing fragmentation of the movement into separate groups—students, blacks, poor whites, and antiwar activists. This fragmentation became painfully evident at the SDS annual meeting held in June 1969, which signaled the coming death of the New Left as a movement, as SDS itself divided into warring factions. Among the groups involved to some extent in the New Left movement, besides SDS, were the Student Nonviolent Coordinating Committee (SNCC), WEATHERMAN, the YOUNG SOCIALIST ALLIANCE (YSA), the Progressive Labor (PL) movement, and various peace groups. By 1972 the New Left had effectively dissolved, even as an underground movement.

Bibliography: George R. Vickers, *The Formation of the New Left* (Lexington, Mass.: Lexington Books, 1975).

New Life Movement (China) a movement begun in 1934 by Chiang Kai-shek, leader of the Kuomintang (KMT), to reorient the Chinese people toward conservative social and political views; among the movement's primary promoters were members of such youth groups as the BLUE SHIRT SOCIETY and the THREE PEOPLE'S PRINCIPLES YOUTH CORPS. The movement expropriated the organizational and propagandistic tactics of the MAY FOURTH MOVEMENT to further such goals as convincing the public to embrace traditional Confucian moral values while also supporting Chiang. Despite the students' proselyting efforts, however, the New Life Movement never gained widespread support among the general public.

Newman Clubs *See* NATIONAL NEWMAN CLUB FEDERATION.

New May Fourth Movement (China) student demonstrations that began in Shanghai in May 1947. The demonstrators protested against the civil war being waged between the communist and Kuomintang forces and also against inflation and financial speculation. The student movement spread to Beijing, Nanjing, Shenyang, and other cities. During demonstrations in Tianjin and Nanjing on May 20, the police attacked the protesting students, injuring and arresting sizable numbers. This suppression inspired more student demonstrations, resulting in more suppression and arrests— 13,000 were arrested during May and June. The killing of a student in Hangzhou by a secret service agent in the autumn generated an eruption of student strikes that transformed the movement into "the movement for the protection of civil rights."

New Mobilization Committee to End the War in Vietnam (New Mobe)   See NATIONAL MOBILIZATION COMMITTEE TO END THE WAR IN VIETNAM.

New People's Study Society (Hsin-min hsueh hui) (China) a student organization formed in Changsha on April 18, 1918, one of many such student and youth organizations inspired by *New Youth*. The society is noteworthy simply because it was founded by Mao Zedong, then a student at Hunan Province First Normal School, and his friends. Although the society attained no particular significance within the "new thought" movement, it was responsible for recruiting and organizing students in Hunan Province to participate in the work-study program by pursuing their studies in France.

New Tide Society (China) a small but influential reform organization formed on November 18, 1918 by 21 Beijing University student members, many of whom later participated in the MAY FOURTH MOVEMENT initiated in 1919. The society published the monthly journal *Hsin ch'ao* ("New Tide"), bearing the English subtitle *Renaissance*. Members of the society formed the vanguard of the so-called new thought movement, whose advocates supported modernization, democracy, liberalism, individualism, women's independence, and other concepts imported from the West while opposing traditional values associated with Confucianism and questioning prevalent religious and superstitious values. The movement also championed intellectual and cultural reforms, including use of the vernacular language and a literary revolution. The "new thought" movement's basic principles were summarized in its use of two nicknames: "Mr. Democracy" and "Mr. Science." The New Tide Society increased its membership and reorganized on August 15, 1920, but by the end of the year, the *New Tide* journal had ceased publication because most of the society's leaders had gone to study in Great Britain or the United States, and in 1921 the society atrophied into nonexistence.

Newton, Huey P. (1942–1989) (United States) a founder and leader of the BLACK PANTHERS. Newton was born in Monroe, Louisiana. In October 1966 he joined Bobby SEALE as cofounder of the Black Panthers, and a year later Newton became the movement's foremost celebrity when he was indicted for the alleged murder of an Oakland, California police officer. The case and the trial became a celebrated cause, with a nationwide "Free Huey" campaign that attracted hundreds of new members to the Panthers and the creation of new chapters. Newton was convicted of voluntary manslaughter in July 1968, but the state supreme court overturned the verdict in 1970 and Newton was released from prison. While he was imprisoned, however, the Panthers dwindled, wracked by factionalism and a national campaign against them by the Federal Bureau of Investigation (FBI). Newton was arrested and jailed repeatedly on varied criminal charges. In August 1989 he was murdered outside an Oakland "crack" house.

New Utrecht High School Protest (United States) an organized protest by Leftist students at New Utrecht High School in Brooklyn in 1930. The primary leader of the protest was Joseph Clark, a member of the YOUNG COMMUNIST LEAGUE (YCL) and later a founder of the NATIONAL STUDENT LEAGUE (NSL); in 1930 he helped establish the History Club at the school to provide a forum for student discussion of radical issues. When school authorities tried to close down the club, Clark and his fellow YCL activists responded with militant protests. They also organized a boycott against milk because the price was raised. Other students enthusiastically joined the boycott, successfully pressuring the school administration to roll back the price increase. These protests comprised a rare instance of high-school-student militancy in the early years of the Great Depression and presaged things to come in the university student movement of the 1930s (see STUDENT STRIKE AGAINST WAR, for example).

New York Draft Riots (United States) three days of rioting in New York City, July 13–15, 1863, ostensibly in protest of a conscription law approved on March 3 that defined all able-bodied males age 20 to 45 eligible for military service; selections would be made by drawings but with a provision that a draftee could either provide a substitute or buy exemption for $300 (perceived by many as a benefit for the rich). Violent antidraft riots erupted in many areas—Ohio, Kentucky, Pennsylvania, Indiana, New Jersey, Illinois, and especially in areas of pro-Southern sentiment—but the worst riots occurred in New York City, where there was sizable pro-Southern and antiblack sentiment. Drawings in the city began on July 11, and the riots that followed constituted "New York's bloodiest week"—the worst urban riots in U.S. history prior to the 1960s. Although the ringleaders of the rioting were not identified, teenaged and younger children comprised a major portion of the thousands of rioters involved, many of whom belonged to the organized street gangs of the impoverished Five Points area in south Manhattan. For example, it was a crowd comprised mostly of teenage boys that unsuccessfully tried to attack the mayor's home on Fifth Avenue and, after being repelled, moved on to pillage and burn the Colored Orphan Asylum, home to 200 African-American children. The full extent of the carnage during the three days of rioting is not known, but estimates place the death toll in the hundreds, among them miraculously only three police officers. (It should be noted, however, that for political motives, contemporary newspaper accounts greatly exaggerated the rioting's extent, destruction, mayhem, and killing.) Ten regiments of Union Army troops sent by Secretary of War Edwin Stanton arrived by July 18 to ensure the restoration of order, and the draft drawings resumed.

Bibliography: James McCague, *The Second Rebellion: The Story of the New York City Draft Riots of 1863* (New York: Dial, 1968).

New Youth (China) a leftist monthly journal (Chinese title *Hsin ch'ing-nien*) founded in Shanghai in September 1915 by the intellectual and revolutionary Chen Duxiu (Ch'en Tu-hsiu, 1879–1942), a participant in both the 1911 and 1913 revolutions. As editor of *New Youth*, which was subtitled *La Jeunesse*, Chen advocated a cultural break with the past and creation of new literary, social, and educational movements through adoption of Western concepts and techniques. Thus *New Youth* became probably the major speaker for the so-called new thought movement among university students and intellectuals and inspired the formation of numerous student organizations to promote "new thought." Editorially the journal opposed monarchy and the Confucian social system, promoting democracy, liberalism, equality of the sexes, science and technology, literary and language reforms. Chen appealed directly to students to spearhead the cultural revolution. In this effort, he published in *New Youth*, his widely known "Call to Youth," which entailed the six principles he elaborated: "Be independent, not servile; be progressive, not conservative; be aggressive, not retiring; be cosmopolitan, not isolationist; be utilitarian, not formalistic; be scientific, not imaginative." In this call, Chen asserted, "All our traditional ethics, law, scholarship, rites, and customs are survivals of feudalism. When compared with the achievement of the white race, there is a difference of a thousand years in thought, although we live in the same period." He ended with the battle cry for reform, "Youth, take up the task!" His appeal increased after he was appointed dean of the arts faculty at Beijing University in 1917; students used articles in *New Youth* as the stimulant and basis for discussions helping to formulate the concepts that infused the MAY FOURTH MOVEMENT. Chen was involved in the May Fourth Movement both through

his ideas and his presence, for which he lost his university post and was imprisoned for three months. Chen was the primary founder of the CHINESE COMMUNIST PARTY (CCP) (officially dated July 1921) and served as its first secretary general; *New Youth* then became the CCP's official publication. The journal had been managed and published by the New Youth Society, founded in September 1919, but the liberal members of the society abandoned it when the journal became an organ of the CCP, and the society was dissolved in October 1921. The secret police suppressed the journal in Shanghai, and publishing operations were moved to Canton (Guangzhou). The final edition of *New Youth* was dated July 1, 1922, but the magazine reemerged briefly in 1923–24.

Nihilism (Russia) a movement of the 1860s and 1870s among university and technical-school students that began as a repudiation of prevailing social and artistic values and eventuated in political terrorism. The term *nihilism* derived from Ivan Turgenev's novel *Fathers and Sons* published in 1862. Though misapplied and rejected by the students as inappropriate, the term was used to encompass the students' values that were evidenced in their behavior, manners, appearance, and ideals—long hair for men, short hair for women, speech intended to shock, slovenly dress, blue spectacles, contempt for the arts, admiration for artisans, defiance of respectability, self-contained egoism, implied atheism, and sexual freedom. The spokesman for the Nihilists during the years 1861–66 was Dmitri Pisarev (1840–68), who became a student at St. Petersburg University in 1856. Pisarev propagated the idea that no certain truths or criteria for behavior existed and that there should be no restrictions on how a person might develop. In the 1870s, despite government efforts to repress the young rebels, the Nihilists numbered several thousand. Nihilism was an extreme manifestation of a growing intellectual and moral reformation that had a significant impact on politics as the Nihilists came to embrace socialism and terrorism. One of Nihilism's final political expressions may be seen in the work of the Executive Committee of the Social Revolutionary Party.

Bibliography: Daniel R. Brower, *Training the Nihilists: Education and Radicalism in Tsarist Russia* (Ithaca, N.Y.: Cornell University Press, 1975).

Nihon Kakumeiteki Kyosanshugisha Domei (Japan Revolutionary Communist League) (Japan) an organization known as Kakukyodo that was formed in December 1957 and attracted a large number of student adherents who constituted a faction within the ZENGAKUREN. Founded in the aftermath of de-Stalinization in the Soviet Union, the Kakukyodo followed the writings of Trotsky.

Nihon University Struggle (Japan) next to the TOKYO UNIVERSITY STRUGGLE the most important demonstrations by students at a Japanese university, in 1968. The Tokyo Tax Office's disclosure in February 1968 that the sum of 2 billion yen ($5.5 million) was missing from the university's accounts provided the spark for the struggle. On May 22 the Economics Department joined with the Junior College Students Associations to protest the shoddy accounting practices of the Student Section in the administration. The following day when members of the students associations met, the administration had them closed up in the building where they convened, angering the students and inspiring a protest march by 2,000. On May 27 the students formed the Nihon University All-Campus Joint Struggle Council, known as Nichidai Zenkyoto. The Zenkyoto demanded that the administration hold bargaining sessions to discuss student complaints—a demand the administration refused. Reputedly encouraged by the administration, right-wing students began to harass the Zenkyoto. In response 10,000 students on June 4 held a sit-down strike, surrounding the university's main building and demanding a bargaining session. The session was held on June 11 and attended by 10,000 students who were attacked by right-wing students; the administration called in the police to disperse the Zenkyoto students. Consequently, students in several of the university's departments barricaded their buildings and called strikes. On July 20 the president and trustees began to negotiate with the students and promised a bargaining session on August 4. The students demonstrated again; the police were again called in, arresting 68 students; and the administration reneged on its promise and requested a court injunction, which was granted, against the students' barricading of the law and economics departments' buildings. On September 4 the police removed these barricades, and their intervention galvanized general student unity that resulted in strikes and barricades at all the departments. On September 30, at a mass meeting with 15,000 students, the president promised to meet students' demands, including formation of a student self-governing association, resolving the issue of false salary payments, resignation of the trustees, and a bargaining session to be held October 3. But he reneged on the meeting and instead had Zenkyoto leaders arrested. On October 31 he annulled his promise of September 30th.

The struggle continued. On November 11, right-wing elements attacked students who barricaded the Art Department but failed to dislodge them; police accomplished the task on November 12. On November 22, about 2,000 members of the Nichidai Zenkyoto rallied with students at Tokyo University's Yasuda Hall in support of the "Nihon and Tokyo University Struggles' Victory." In the early months of 1969, however, with many of their leaders arrested, the student barricades collapsed under police attack, the last falling on February 18, and the struggle came to an end or moved underground.

Although ending in failure, the struggle was significant in that Nihon University (a private school) was Japan's largest, with a student body of 90,000, and, unlike the conflicts at Tokyo University and other campuses, this struggle was not marred by warring radicalized factions.

Bibliography: Stuart J. Dowsey, ed., *Zengakuren: Japan's Revolutionary Students* (Berkeley, Calif.: The Ishi Press, 1970).

Nishihara Loans Protests   (China) student protests in 1918 provoked by a loan agreement with Japan and one of the precursors of the MAY FOURTH MOVEMENT. Japan had extended numerous loans to China during the decade; the largest for China's participation in World War I provided for equipping troops, and other loans provided for arms and ammunition. To guarantee these loans, China granted a Japanese bank consortium control of mines, forests, and railways in the Northeast as well as certain revenues, such as those generated by the stamp duty. By the terms of the Nishihara loans of early 1918, Japan was granted authority to "cooperate" in controlling the Chinese army and navy. In reaction, some 2,000 students at Beijing University staged a demonstration outside the residence of the president of the Republic. Chinese students studying in Japan left there in protest and formed the Students' Assembly for the National Welfare. Students in Shanghai, Tianjin, and Fuzhou also demonstrated. The protests were supported by the Beijing newspapers and by the National Federation of Chinese Chambers of Commerce.

Nkrumah, Kwame (1909–1972)   (Ghana) African political leader who masterminded the nonviolent movement that achieved independence for Ghana (the former Gold Coast, where he was born) in 1957 and became its first premier and president. While a student in the United States—he earned degrees from Lincoln University and the University of Pennsylvania—Nkrumah reorganized and became president of the AFRICAN STUDENTS' ASSOCIATION. In 1945 he went to Great Britain and pursued his studies at the London School of Economics and Political Science. While there he became vice president of the WEST AFRICAN STUDENTS UNION and a leader of "The Circle." He returned to the Gold Coast in 1947 to begin the independence movement. Nkrumah formed the Convention People's Party (CCP) in 1950. He was elected prime minister in 1952 and continued to head the government following independence in 1957. Nkrumah became president when Ghana became a republic in 1960. While visiting China he was toppled by an army coup d'état on February 24, 1966 and received sanctuary in Guinea. Nkrumah died in Bucharest, Romania.

Noches Tristes (Sad Nights)   (Mexico) weeks of almost nightly student confrontations with riot police (*granaderos*) in Mexico City from the end of July until early October 1968. The primary catalyst for the confrontations was a July 23 brawl between students from the National Autonomous University of Mexico (UNAM) and the National Polytechnic Institute (IPN) in which the *granaderos*, rather than the Mexico City police, intervened. They chased students into a vocational school affiliated with IPN and there brutally beat not only the students but also professors and janitors. The Noches Tristes confrontations began on July 26, when students representing the IPN's Federación Nacional de Estudiantes Técnicos (FNET) and the UNAM's Communist Youth Organization staged separate demonstrations—the former to protest *granaderos* brutality during the July 23 brawl and to demand disbanding of the *granaderos*, and the latter to commemorate Fidel Castro's JULY 26 MOVEMENT, a demonstration that had been planned in advance. These demonstrations, which inadvertently mingled, were peaceful, and the students dispersed with some from both groups assembling at the Zocalo, site of the presidential palace, where the *granaderos* brutally attacked them. That evening at two high schools, hundreds of youths, some having participated in the earlier demonstrations, barricaded themselves in the school buildings in protest, using captured buses as barricades. They remained for three days as police and army troops occupied other buildings to prevent students from occupying them. Then on July 29, police and troops besieged the barricaded students; the battle lasted until July 31, with 30 of those involved being injured, several students killed, and many arrested. As a result of these incidents, huge ongoing demonstrations in support of the students occurred at other high schools and at the universities in the city, leading to a momentous outcome.

Since the Olympic Games were to begin in Mexico City on October 12, as the weeks passed, official concern over the continuing disturbances grew. Schools were closed and classes suspended at the National University (UNAM). At this time, there were 80,000 students enrolled at UNAM and another 50,000 at the Polytechnic Institute in the city. For nearly two weeks, police occupied numerous schools and UNAM, the site for some of the Olympic events, and army units joined the police in opposing the demonstrators. On August 8 the students' National Strike Council (CNH), with representatives from about 150 different schools, announced six demands for ending the strike, including the freeing of all political prisoners, repealing the "Law of Social Dissolution" which provided for imprisoning political dissidents, removal of three police officers and abolishing the *granaderos*, and indemnification for the families of those who had been killed or wounded in the demonstrations. Although President Gustavo Díaz Ordaz publicly professed a desire for conciliation, government policies and responses belied his statements. In the meantime, the news media portrayed the students as dangerous revolutionaries. The largest single demonstration during the weeks of protest occurred on August 27 when 300,000 students and their supporters marched in the streets. In his state-of-the-nation speech on September 1, President Díaz Ordaz denounced the protests as subversive and conspiratorial and promised their repression while offering to negotiate—but he made no effort to begin talks.

On October 2, in an unauthorized but peaceful demonstration, about 10,000 students gathered in Tlateloco, the Plaza of the Three Cultures, to listen to speeches; spectators gathered. Soldiers and army vehicles assembled at the plaza. Someone fired shots, and panicky students and spectators tried unsuccessfully to flee the plaza. During the hour-long melee that followed, the police kept firing, killing an estimated 200 students and women and children (the official death toll was 49), arresting about 2,000 (including foreign journalists), and wounding scores of others. Horror over this tragedy led on the following day to acceptance of an unofficial armistice between the students and the police until the Olympic games had concluded. Within two days, both the Senate and the Chamber of Deputies had condemned the students and praised the police. One of the student leaders, the police announced, had confessed to involvement in a conspiracy and named those politicians and intellectuals who had funded it; all denied the charge. An outraged Octavio Paz, then ambassador to India, resigned in protest of the government's actions. The Olympic games proved a great success. Military forces were withdrawn from the IPN campus on October 29, and classes at all schools were to resume on November 4. The students' six demands were never addressed. In 1970 a judge sentenced 68 of the involved students to prison on diverse charges for terms varying from 3 to 17 years; all but 19 were released by the summer of 1971. October 2 itself came to be known as *la nueve noche triste* or Noches Tristes (the original sad night occurred in 1520 with the Aztec massacre of Cortés's troops).

The "events of '68" gained international attention and formed a watershed in Mexican history. In July 1970, the Congress repealed the Law of Social Dissolution restricting political speech, thus fulfilling one of the students' six demands; at the same time, however, the legislators revised the penal code in such ways as effectively to transfer the repealed restrictions and penalties to it, even providing for longer prison sentences than the repealed law had authorized. As a gesture, the Congress also approved a constitutional amendment that lowered the voting age for unmarried persons to 18. Despite its apparent failure, student resistance continued, leading to more-violent repression.

Bibliography: Arturo Escobar and Sonia E. Alvarez, eds., *The Making of Social Movements in Latin America* (Boulder, Colo.: Westview Press, 1992).

Non-Cooperation Movement (NCO) (India) the first major Indian nationalist agitation movement, initiated by Mahatma Gandhi through a manifesto he issued on March 10, 1920 and subsequently through the Indian National Congress (Congress Party) beginning in the fall of 1920, with the purpose of undermining the authority of the British Raj as a means of attaining independence. Based on nonviolent civil disobedience, the movement promoted boycotting British institutions, including schools, courts, and other official bodies, as well as British-made goods. The Non-Cooperation Movement attracted massive student support, the first Indian political movement to do so. In conjunction with the movement, Youth Leagues were organized to coordinate the student involvement. The students participated in Congress Party campaigns and meetings and in street demonstrations.

Students also went on strike to shut down universities after the Congress called for creation of National Institutions—the National College Movement. The strike, or boycott of classes, tactic was especially noteworthy in Calcutta, where on January 21, 1921 a large group of students marched in the streets, garnered increased student support in subsequent marches, and pursued a widely adopted tactic—lying side by side en masse so that other students either joined their boycott or had to walk on them to get to classes. The strike movement spread to other cities on January 27, but by the end of February, it was already declining in Calcutta and Lahore and had gained little steam elsewhere. Therefore, the strikes had no lasting effect, although those students who heeded Ghandi's call to abandon their studies altogether and devote themselves to the independence movement became full-time supporters of that movement, with long-term consequences.

The Non-Cooperation Movement itself declined following an outbreak of violence in an eastern village and Gandhi's arrest on March 10, 1922 and subsequent trial for sedition, followed by his imprisonment. Most of the National Institutions failed, and students returned to the universities and to classes, but they continued the local student organizations that the movement had generated. Gandhi was released from prison in February 1924 but did not return to active involvement in the independence movement until 1927.

Bibliography: R. C. Majumdar, *History of the Freedom Movement in India*, Vol. III (Calcutta: Firma K. L. Mukhopahyay, 1962–63).

Nu, U (1907–) (Burma) student leader while at Rangoon University. Nu received his bachelor's degree from the university in 1929, and he returned in 1934 to study law. As a law student in 1936 and known as Thakin Nu, he was president of the Rangoon University Students' Union (RUSU) and leader of the RANGOON UNIVERSITY STUDENTS' STRIKE of 1936, which resulted in his temporary suspension and jailing. Nu was a member of the Thakin movement, a nationalist group dedicated to achieving independence for Burma, which was then a British colony. (*Thakin* means "master," the required address for Burmese talking with a Briton at the time; it was adopted to mock the British while evoking the movement's goal of the Burmese becoming their own "masters.") The British jailed Nu in 1940 on a sedition charge, but he was released following the Japanese invasion of Burma in World War II. Nu became prime minister in 1948 after Burma received its independence and served in that capacity until 1958, except for a brief period in 1956–57.

Nunan Bill Protest (United States) a 1935 student lobbying effort to prevent approval of a bill introduced in the New York Legislature that would require college and university students to take a loyalty oath. At the time, New York-centered groups formed the spearhead of the 1930s student movement; concerned that if the Nunan Bill were enacted it would discourage or even prevent student protests, the STUDENT LEAGUE FOR INDUSTRIAL DEMOCRACY (SLID) and the NATIONAL STUDENT LEAGUE (NSL) cosponsored a vigorous movement opposing its passage. They supported a delegation of 500 students, under the leadership of women from Vassar College, that lobbied legislators in Albany. Student newspapers statewide supported the lobbying effort through their editorials. This intensive student pressure succeeded in securing the bill's defeat in March 1935—a clear-cut victory for the student movement.

Octobrists   *See* KOMSOMOL.

Odessa Student Congress   (Russia) a secret meeting of student delegates held at Odessa in June 1900. The meeting occurred in response to the oppressive measures taken by the government following the nationwide student strike of March 1899, which was instigated by the coalition committees of the ZEMLYACHESTVA. The Odessa congress decided to continue the student struggle with the government, which had all the delegates arrested.

Ohio State University Riot   (United States) demonstrations in April and May 1970 at the Columbus, Ohio campus. Students pressed four demands: ending the Reserve Officer Training Corps (ROTC) program at the university (a common student issue of the time), admission of 2,500 more African-American students by the fall of 1970, creating university branches in black communities to be administered by blacks, and ending all research at the university related in any way to war. When the university president refused to negotiate, students called a strike for April 29–30. Governor James A. Rhodes sent 1,200 troops of the National Guard to the campus on April 29. Guard troops and the police used tear gas and pepper gas in trying to disperse the demonstrators; 600 were arrested, 50 were suspended with denial of amnesty, and 20 were reportedly wounded by shotgun fire. On May 5 students demonstrated again, this time protesting the April 30 announcement that U.S. troops had been sent into Cambodia. They tried to close off the entrances to the campus, and two Guard members, trying to disperse them, were injured when struck by hurled bricks; the president closed the campus on May 6. On May 21, student protestors led by black militants broke windows and looted stores near the campus; the governor ordered 5,000 additional Guard troops to the campus.

Ohnesorg, Benno   *See* BERLIN ANTI-SHAH PROTEST.

Oji Camp Hospital Struggle   (Japan) a series of demonstrations against the U.S. Army hospital at Oji (in Tokyo) in February-April 1968 after the army began to bring patients directly to the hospital from Vietnam. Residents of the area began the protests in 1967; students of the ZENGAKUREN joined them for demonstrations on February 20 and March 20, 1968, ending in clashes with the police. During a demonstration on April 1, a bystander was killed when hit by a stone, and the students torched a police car. The demonstration concluded on March 8 after the Tokyo Magistrates Court issued an order outlawing further protests.

Okinawa Day Demonstrations   (Japan) student protests in Tokyo on April 28, 1969, known as Okinawa Day because on that day in 1952 the terms of the San Francisco Peace Treaty took effect, severing Okinawa from Japan. Left-wing groups agitating for the return of Okinawa to Japanese control were granted permits to demonstrate on April 28, 1969, but the government denied permission to an Anti-Yoyogi student group known as the Five Faction Alliance. (*See* ANTI-YOGOGI ZENGAKUREN.) The students decided to demonstrate anyhow, threatening to occupy the prime minister's residence and take control of the city. Police mobilized to prevent the students from succeeding by confining them to the university campuses, which the police managed to achieve during the morning of April 28, but in the afternoon, the students ceased their skirmishes with the police and rushed to the Ginza district. Here the Five Faction Alliance was joined by other students and by workers from the HANSEN SEINEN IINKAI. At first they occupied commuter railroad tracks, stopping the trains, but when the police dispersed them, the protestors raced into the back streets of the Ginza, where still other students

Leftist students (foreground), some wearing helmets, fire stones at riot police, many wearing full-length shields, near Shinbashi national railway station in the heart of Tokyo. Students demanded the return of Okinawa from U.S. rule.   (AP/WIDE WORLD PHOTOS)

Leftist students hurl stones and spray water in the direction of riot police during a demonstration in the Kanda area in Tokyo. Demonstrators demanded the return of Okinawa from U.S. rule. Police reported 30 or more officers injured, two critically. Some 300 students were arrested.   (AP/WIDE WORLD PHOTOS)

joined them. Together, they erected barricades on a street stretched from the Ginza shopping area to the Tokyo terminal station; they christened this the Ginza Liberated Area. The students held their ground until 9:00 P.M., when half withdrew from Ginza peacefully through the police lines; from the opposite end of the area, the others withdrew after setting fire to several cars.

Orangeburg Protest   (United States) demonstrations in Orangeburg, South Carolina by African-American students in February 1968. Students from predominantly black South Carolina State College and Claflin College began to demonstrate on February 5 against a segregated local bowling alley and other public facilities; they continued the protest the following day, when one police officer and seven students received injuries and police arrested 15 students. In response, the governor mobilized National Guard units. On February 7, students at the state college began to throw rocks and bottles at passing cars, until 100 state police arrived to seal off the campus;

classes were suspended, and National Guard troops arrived. On February 8, as the protest continued, a student hurled a piece of lumber that felled a state trooper; other troopers, thinking he had been shot, opened fire on the students without warning, killing three black students and wounding 34 others, including Cleveland Sellers of the STUDENT NONVIOLENT COORDINATING COMMITTEE (SNCC), who was also arrested. No guns were reported seen or found among the protestors. In response, black residents of Orangeburg announced a boycott of white-owned businesses and demanded removal of the National Guard, suspension of the troopers responsible for the shootings, elimination of segregated schools, and other measures. On February 10, the mayor appointed a biracial commission to investigate the killings. Students returned to the campus on February 28, and on March 5 the governor withdrew the National Guard and ended the state of emergency. On November 8 a federal grand jury meeting in Columbia, South Carolina rejected the indictment of nine state troopers involved in the shootings; on May 27, 1969 a federal jury in Florence, South Carolina that included two African Americans acquitted the troopers. The shooting of the three students became known as "the Orangeburg Massacre"; it provided the catalyst for the HOWARD UNIVERSITY SIT-IN.

Order of Woodcraft Chivalry (Great Britain) an organization founded by Quaker geologist and anthropologist Ernest Westlake (1856–1922) as a pacifistic alternative to the BOY SCOUTS, which he and others involved considered basically militaristic. Modeling the Order of Woodcraft Chivalry after the WOODCRAFT INDIANS of America which had been established by Ernest Thompson Seton, Westlake began the order in summer 1916 at the Quaker Secondary School, Sidcot Lodge, in Somerset. His purpose was to train youths by means of an educational method based on a Darwinian concept, generated by G. Stanley Hall, that theorized that adolescents "recapitulated" all of human cultural history as they themselves developed mentally and physically. The training included woodcrafts, rituals, and ceremonies of a pantheistic bent that were intended to help adolescents "recapitulate" the stages of human evolution. Local units of the order were called lodges. The individual lodges were members of guilds, and overseeing the entire organization was a National Council of Guidance. Westlake served as chieftain until his death in a car accident in 1922, when his son Aubrey succeeded him with the title of marshall. In 1923 the order named Seton as honorary grand chieftain. The order has remained small, never exceeding a few hundred members, mostly middle class and Quaker.

Organization (Russia) a group devoted to economic revolution that originated in 1865 within the Moscow "circle"; the circle was established in 1863 by students and a few teachers and government clerks to create and operate both producers' cooperatives and a school for boys in the city's slums. Among the leaders of the Organization was Nikolai Ishutin, a youth nicknamed "the General" by his comrades and who was an advocate of terrorism. He and a handful of others, including his cousin Dmitri Karakozov, formed a secretive and extremist band of youthful terrorists called Hell as a cell within the Organization. The members of Hell dedicated themselves to total secrecy, abandoning family and friends, assassinating political officials, killing traitors within their group, and committing suicide if necessary. Karakosov himself was determined to assassinate Tsar Alexander II. In the early spring of 1866, Karakosov traveled to St. Petersburg and disseminated a leaflet announcing his intentions to kill Alexander that was, surprisingly, ignored by the authorities. Other members of the Organization went to St. Petersburg to try to dissuade Karakosov from making an attempt on the tsar's life, but on April 4, while the tsar was approaching his carriage after visiting the Summer Garden, Karakosov shot at him but missed. Papers found on the arrested assailant incriminated the Organization, and authorities arrested all of its members and several nonmembers as well. Thirty-five youths, some only boys, were tried; Karakosov and Ishutin were sentenced to death. Karakosov, age 24, was hanged on September 3, but at the last moment Ishutin's sentence was commuted to a lifetime of hard labor. In reprisal for the attempt on the tsar's life, the government launched a wave of arrests and repression in 1866–68 known as the "white terror," which resulted in the arrests of hundreds of suspected radicals. The arrests and sentences of Karakosov and his associates brought an end to the Organization, but its influence continued through the efforts of LAND AND FREEDOM and other groups. In addition, following their release from prison, some members of the defunct Organization formed a commune called the Smorgon Academy (after a forest where gypsies trained their bears for carnival performing), which broke new ground by being the first radical political group to involve young women. The Smorgon Academy, in its turn, was eliminated through arrests of its membership made in early 1869.

Orissa Demonstrations (India) a series of student demonstrations in the state of Orissa in 1964. The demonstrations were carried out by a committee of representatives from many of the schools in the state whose leaders contended that the state's chief minister was corrupt; they demanded that he resign. The well-organized demonstrations forced the resignation of the entire state government. As the government's chief minister was a National Congress Party representative, the success of the student's effort, which was supported by some of the opposition political parties, created something of a crisis for the central government in control of the Congress.

Osmania University Strike   (India) a successful 1966 student uprising against the Andhra Pradesh government ostensibly to protect the university's autonomy. The president of the Osmania University Teachers' Association announced on October 27 that teachers would not conduct classes as a protest against the government's alleged ignoring of teachers' interests in making the appointment of a new vice chancellor, claiming that the manner in which the appointment was made violated university autonomy. On October 28 students joined in, blockading the building that housed the university administrators' offices to prevent the new vice chancellor from entering. They stoned passing vehicles, shattered streetlights, and severed telephone wires to prevent the registrar from communicating with the vice chancellor. Thereafter, they abducted the registrar to prevent his meeting with the university chancellor in Hyderabad. Violence that resulted from the continuing demonstrations forced the closing of all the businesses in Hyderabad and Secunderabad, where on October 31 police attacked a mob of 5,000 students at the railway station with lathis and tear gas. Buses and trains ceased operating for three days. On October 30, a meeting of the Osmania University Student Association drew up a list of 11 demands by the striking students. These included the maintenance of university autonomy and the insistence that the government call a meeting of government officials, teachers, and students to review legislation relating to the university's autonomy. But the demands also concerned such unrelated issues as the provision of food ration cards to city students and bus concessions to evening students. The students met with the chief minister of Andhra Pradesh, who had removed the previous vice chancellor for personal and political reasons, on November 3; they met again on November 6 when their strike ended. The chief minister had agreed to convene a meeting of students, teachers, education ministry officials, and education specialists to review the University Act and to draw up recommendations on how it could be amended to preserve university autonomy. The student strike was unusual in that it was directed against the state government and was encouraged by the faculty.

"Oust Robinson Week"   (United States) a student effort in October 1934 to force the dismissal of City College of New York (CCNY) President Frederick B. Robinson that arose out of a controversy surrounding the campus visit of a delegation of Italian Fascist students. Adamantly antiradical, Robinson banned demonstrations against the visiting Italians and on October 9, 1934 hosted a special assembly in their honor in CCNY's Great Hall that was attended by 2,000 students. After the audience jeered Robinson, he denounced them as "gutter-

snipes." When Edwin Alexander, an activist member of the NATIONAL STUDENT LEAGUE (NSL) and a representative of the Student Council who was supposed to welcome the Italians on behalf of the student body, expressed anti-Fascist views, he was forced away from the microphone and assaulted by members of the Italian Club. Students in the audience leaped onto the stage to defend Alexander, and a riot ensued. Subsequently, the administration suspended 26 demonstrators and the entire Student Council. The NSL and the STUDENT LEAGUE FOR INDUSTRIAL DEMOCRACY (SLID) organized protests against the suspensions, including a mock trial of Robinson that indicted him for violating academic freedoms and for supporting Fascism; 1,500 students attended. The groups also organized "Oust Robinson Week" to build support for Robinson's dismissal. Students demonstrated at City Hall and at the president's home, resulting in 18 being arrested. In retaliation, the administration expelled 21 of the suspended students. More than 2,000 students staged a two-hour strike and burned Robinson and Benito Mussolini in effigy. The "Oust Robinson Week" demonstrations gained public, media, and alumni support for Robinson's being fired: in December, a faculty committee reinstated the suspended and expelled students, and CCNY alumni organized a movement to secure Robinson's dismissal which, along with pressure from continuing student protests, proved ultimately successful. The movement to secure Robinson's firing comprised both a victory for student Leftists and a means of instruction in effective organization of future demonstrations. (*See also* "JINGO DAY" DEMONSTRATION.)

Outward Bound   (Great Britain) a character-training movement for youths begun in 1941 with establishment of the first Outward Bound school at Aberdovey, Wales, largely at the instigation of Kurt Hahn, a well-known educator at Gordonstoun. The success of the program led to creation of the Outward Bound Trust in 1946. Subsequently, schools were established at Eskdale, Devon, Moray, Ullswater, Rhowniar, and at numerous locales elsewhere in Europe and North America and throughout the Commonwealth. Five of the British schools serve young men only; the school at Rhowniar serves young women but also offers some courses for both sexes. Each school or association is independent (a private company with representation on the board of the Outward Bound Trust), but all share similar programs and purposes, although with some unique course offerings at different schools. The courses are residential, last about four weeks, and are attended by youths 16 to 21 years old whose fees are usually paid by their employers. Courses include not only lectures and discussions but also outdoor activities, such as sailing, swimming, canoeing, and rock climbing, that involve vigorous physical effort. Trainees are supposed to abstain from using alcohol or tobacco. The overriding purpose is to change behavior by increasing self-awareness and self-confidence. Emphasis is placed on communal living and community service. By the mid-1970s, Outward Bound was serving 6,000 youths annually, with nearly 2,000 business firms as sponsors. The staff at each school is in the charge of a warden, who has control of hiring, firing, and programming. A report on each trainee's progress and achievement is sent to the trainee's sponsoring employer. In later years, Outward Bound instituted "City Challenge," which consists of courses offered in urban locales for training in how to cope with city life. Outward Bound was the first—and remains the largest, best-known, and best-organized—undertaking of its kind for youths in Great Britain.

Oxford-Cap War   (United States) an episode of May 1842 illustrative of 19th-century town-versus-gown and class controversies. The Oxford-Cap War resulted from Harvard students' adoption of an imitation Oxford cap for their headgear. On May 14, a law student encountered an African-American townsman wearing a "black-pasteboard square cap" that burlesqued the student attire. The law student knocked the hat from the black man's head and, as the black walked away, offered to fight any white males who came to his support; none did. On May 18, a bus passed the school; atop the bus rode another townsman wearing a burlesque cap. Students attacked the bus, beat the man, and drove him and the bus driver into flight. Another confrontation occurred on May 21 in front of the Tremont House between a group of students and some town "rowdies" who ridiculed their caps, but no serious injuries resulted. Then a group of perhaps 300 Boston "rowdies," wearing disguises and burlesque pasteboard caps, staged a nighttime invasion of the Cambridge campus, where they confronted some 50 students who were reportedly armed with pistols, knives, and clubs. Faculty members milled about, trying to prevent a fracas, although President Josiah Quincy told the students to defend themselves "in *any* way" if attacked. The rowdies hurled stones at Harvard buildings, breaking several windows in the law school, and beat a student who happened by on the way to his residence; then they returned to Boston. A few other scuffles marked the conflict, but by May 24 the "war" had essentially ended. The students also soon gave up wearing Oxford caps.

Bibliography: Kenneth Wiggins Porter, "The Oxford-Cap War at Harvard," *New England Quarterly*, 14 (March 1941), 77–83.

Oxford Pledge   (Great Britain), a pacifist pledge formulated by students at Oxford University on February 9, 1933, less than 10 days following Adolf Hitler's accession to power (he became chancellor of Germany on January 30). In a totally unprecedented occurrence, the Oxford Union voted 275 to 173 in favor of this pledge to oppose participation in war. The wording of the pledge committed union members not to fight, under any circumstances, for their king or country in a future war. Adoption of the pledge startled Great Britain because the Oxford Union represented conservatism and aristocracy and in effect provided training for future British leaders. Newspapers and alumni responded with a barrage of criticisms, with alumni organizing to have both the pledge and the vote expunged from the union's minutes. In response, the union met; about one-fourth of the student body attended and voted 750 to 138 to retain the pledge. Subsequently, the Oxford Pledge won a majority at University of Glasgow, Cambridge, University College in Wales, and other universities. The Oxford Pledge, translated into an Americanized version, garnered widespread appeal in the United States, where a poll of more than 22,600 students at 65 colleges and universities in 27 states conducted by Brown University's student newspaper indicated that 39 percent of those polled supported a pacifist position; another 33 percent asserted that they would not serve in the military unless the nation itself was invaded; 72 percent said they would refuse to fight in an overseas war. Student councils at numerous universities adopted the U.S. version of the Oxford Pledge. The STUDENT LEAGUE FOR INDUSTRIAL DEMOCRACY (SLID) organized a nationwide "peace strike" in April 1934 using the pledge as the strike's focus. The NATIONAL STUDENT LEAGUE (NSL) also became a sponsor of the strike, which, although poorly publicized, generated demonstrations by 25,000 students (15,000 of them in New York City). The participants and those who took part in another 1935 antiwar strike organized by the NSL adopted their own version of the Oxford Pledge: "We pledge not to support the government of the United States in any war it may conduct." So the Oxford Pledge added impetus to the significant student antiwar movement of the 1930s. (*See* STUDENT STRIKE AGAINST WAR.)

Palestinian Resistance Movement (Palestine) a Palestinian nationalist movement, ongoing since Israel was founded in 1948, whose major purpose since the Six-Day War of June 1967 (and Israel's subsequent unification of Jerusalem) has been the end of Israeli control of the West Bank and Gaza. Although not a student or youth movement as such, the Palestinian Resistance Movement has depended heavily on the participation of students and even young children. High school and university students frequently formed the vanguard of the demonstration marches that were a standard form of Palestinian protest for more than two decades. The Israeli military responded by closing Palestinian schools and universities for long periods. Among the most significant protests was an uprising that began in November 1981, as Israel tried to effect Military Order 947, which would establish a Palestinian civil administration in the West Bank and Gaza as a means of undercutting the Palestine Liberation Organization (PLO). The PLO, founded in 1964, was credited as the speaker for the Palestinians. Students at the West Bank universities of Bethlehem, Hebron, an-Najah, and Bir Zeit initiated the 1981 protest; in response, the Israeli military closed the universities, in some cases for months. But the unrest spread and continued into the spring of 1982, with strikes and riots. (*See also* INTIFADA.)

Pan-African Student Conference (PASC) a conference of student groups from throughout Africa held at irregular intervals. The first PAC was held in Kampala in July 1958.

Paris, University of (France) one of the earliest universities, although founded by the masters rather than the students (as at BOLOGNA [UNIVERSITY]), but the scene of an early town-versus-gown riot that won special status for students. In the year 1200, after a wealthy German student's servant was ejected from a tavern for disparaging the wine, a group of German students invaded the tavern and beat the innkeeper. In response, Paris townspeople led by the city provost attacked the students and killed several of them. The Paris university masters, threatening to withdraw the university from the city, appealed to King Philip Augustus for restitution. Seeing a chance to diminish the papacy's influence over the university and to prevent economic losses for the city if the university left, the king granted the masters' appeal. The provost was not only removed from office but sentenced to life in prison, and the king issued a charter that granted special privileges to the students as *clerici* (having the rights and benefits of clergy) and to the masters. Both were made exempt from taxes and from arrest except for capital crimes. Another student riot in 1229 resulted in the university's being granted a charter. Bibulous students disputed their tavern bill, were thrown out, and returned with reinforcements to trash the tavern and harass the local townspeople. When in reaction Queen Blanche ordered the provost and police to punish the students, these officials' fulfillment of the order resulted in several dead and numerous wounded students. The arts faculty masters protested to the king but got no response, so they withdrew their part of the university from Paris and stayed away for three years; the theology faculty, however, remained in the city. To effect the reunification of the university in Paris, Pope Gregory IX in 1231 issued a bull that in effect granted to the university the masters' long-desired official charter of incorporation—and under papal protection.

Participatory Democracy (United States) a central concept of the NEW LEFT defined, although quite ambiguously, in the PORT HURON STATEMENT, as follows:

That decision making of basic social consequence be carried on by public groupings;

—that politics be seen positively as the art of collectively creating an acceptable pattern of social relations;

—that politics has the function of bringing people out of isolation and into community, thus being a necessary, though not sufficient, means of finding meaning in personal life;

—that the political order should serve to clarify problems in a way instrumental to their solution; it should provide outlets for the expression of personal grievance and aspiration; opposing views should be organized so as to illuminate choices and facilitate attainment of goals; channels should be commonly available to relate men to knowledge and power so that private problems . . . are formulated as general issues.

Given this definition, different groups and individuals within the New Left movement envisioned "participatory democracy" differently. The thrust of the concept, however, promoted personal political empowerment, and it was seen as a call for students in particular to seize the initiative in demanding that empowerment.

Bibliography: James Miller, *"Democracy is in the Streets": From Port Huron to the Siege of Chicago* (New York: Simon and Schuster, 1987).

Peace Strikes of the 1930s   (United States) a series of national student antiwar demonstrations during 1934–38 that constituted probably the major effort of the national student movement of the 1930s. *See* STUDENT STRIKE AGAINST WAR.

People's Movement of 1989   *See* CHINESE DEMOCRACY MOVEMENT.

People's Will   *See* TERRORIST SECTION OF THE PEOPLE'S WILL.

Perhimpoenan Indonesia (Indonesian Association) (Netherlands) an organization of Indonesian students studying in the Netherlands, formed in the early 1920s. Perhimpoenan revamped its predecessor organization to become a militant movement—one of the first Indonesian groups to advocate independence and national unity for Indonesia. It published a journal entitled *Indonesia Merdeka* (*Free Indonesia*). Five members of Perhimpoenan, led by University of Rotterdam student Mohammad Hatta, attended a congress of the League Against Colonial Suppression and Imperialism held in Brussels in 1927 and secured a resolution from the congress endorsing Indonesian independence. Perhimpoenan was put on trial at The Hague in March 1928. Many members of Perhimpoenan became leaders in various fields after returning to Indonesia, including Hatta, who, upon the declaration of Indonesia's independence on August 17, 1945, became the new nation's first vice president.

Petöfi Club   (Hungary) an organization founded in 1956 by the university affiliate of the Communist Youth League (DISZ). (The club was named for Sándor Petöfi, a poet and national hero who had died fighting against the Russian troops sent into Hungary by Tsar Nicholas I in 1849 to crush the War of Liberty (1848–49). The troops had been requested by Habsburg Emperor Francis Joseph, whose Austrian troops had been unable to quell the rebellious Hungarians.) In the immediate aftermath of the de-Stalinization policy begun in February 1956, students were able to obtain government permission to form the Petöfi Club (or Petöfi Circle), whose primary purpose was to hold free discussions. The club conducted teach-ins that frequently concluded with demands for the resignation of the repressive Premier Mátyás Rikósi, known as "the Stalin of Hungary." They also pressed for his replacement by the reformist Imre Nagy, who had served as premier from June 1953 until April 1955, when the Russians, alarmed by Nagy's freeing of 80,000 political prisoners and toleration of free speech, had Rikósi returned to power. Forums and discussions conducted by the club attracted thousands of people, including Nagy himself and such other prominent dissidents as György Lukács and Géza Losonczy. The Petöfi Club's demonstrations—most notably a mass demonstration that the group organized on October 23, 1956—provided a major impetus for the student uprisings that eventuated in the HUNGARIAN REVOLUTION.

Petrashevski Circle   (Russia) the best known of the "circles" (as they were called) of young radicals in St. Petersburg during the 1840s, the Petrashevski Circle was formed in 1846. The circle devoted itself mostly to discussions of Fourier's theories and other utopian concepts and to denunciations of prevalent social evils rather than to an advocacy of revolt. It was short-lived, nevertheless, destroyed in 1849 by a series of arrests and trials of its members. The Petrashevski Circle is perhaps especially noteworthy in that among its enthusiastic members was the novelist Fyodor Dostoyevsky, who joined the circle in 1847. On April 23, 1849 Dostoevsky and 30 other members of the circle were arrested and imprisoned in the fortress of St. Peter and St. Paul. All were condemned to death on December 23, but as they were being prepared for execution, they were informed that the sentence had been commuted to exile in Siberia. Dostoevsky left on December 24 for Siberia, where he spent four years.

Pioneer Girls   (United States) an evangelical Christian organization for girls founded in October 1939 as a subsidiary of the CHRISTIAN SERVICE BRIGADE. Originally named the *Girls' Guild*, the organization assumed the name *Pioneer Girls* in September 1941 and became autonomous. Like the CSB, it has headquarters in Wheaton, Illinois and Burlington, Ontario. Groups are sited at churches, and members are trained to attain "personal knowledge of Christ as Savior" and "effective Christian leadership and service." Member groups are organized according to school age. Girls in grades 3 to 6 are Pilgrims; in grades 7 to 9, Colonists; in high school, Explorers. Groups meet weekly to pursue Bible study, service projects, and other activities. Pioneer Girls operates nearly two dozen camps in the United States and Canada, all entitled *Camp Cherith*, and a leadership training center in Michigan. In 1970 there were more than 100,000 members at more than 2,500 churches.

Pioneers   *See* KOMSOMOL.

Plekhanov, Georgy (1856–1918)   (Russia) revolutionary and theoretical proponent of Marxism born in Gudalovka, Russia. In 1873 he became a student at the Konstantinovskoe Military School in St. Petersburg. Interested in organizing factory workers, he joined LAND AND FREEDOM and was a leader of the society's 1876 demonstration at Kazan Cathedral. As a political agitator he contributed articles to *Land and Freedom*, the society's publication, but he opposed the society's move toward terrorism and formed a short-lived splinter group promoting mass protests instead. To avoid being arrested, Plekhanov went abroad, settling in Geneva. There Plekhanov helped form Liberation of Labor, a Marxist revolutionary organization, and wrote several books, including his major works *Socialism and Political Struggle* (1883) and *Our Differences* (1885), that established the theoretical basis for Russian Marxism. In the 1890s, Vladimir Lenin became an adherent of Liberation of Labor. Plekhanov returned to Russia in 1917. He died in Terioki, Finland.

Police Athletic League (PAL)   (United States) an organization that provides recreational activities for youths living in areas with high rates of juvenile crime or delinquency. PAL originated in the 1930s as a program fostered by police juvenile aid bureaus, but it became a private, nonprofit organization supported by donations, off-duty police officers, and professional staff. Its strongest presence has been in major cities in the East, where the program is operated mostly by professionals from recreation departments, with police involvement declining.

Polonia   (Poland) secret societies of Polish university students that began in 1816 in Breslau and Berlin and spread to Warsaw University and other Polish universities. The Polonia were inspired by the BURSCHEN-SCHAFTEN; and their rituals derived largely from those of the Freemasonry movement, to which many Polish students also belonged. Initially devoted to such purposes

as comradeship, learning, and humanitarianism, the secret societies soon embraced Romantic literature and the ideals of Rousseau and evolved into nationalistic, patriotic groups opposed to political oppression. Minority activists within the secret societies plotted against Russian dominance and were subjects of surveillance by government spies. At Warsaw University, the largest of the student societies was Gospoda Akademicka (The Students' Inn), which police raided in 1820. Another major student society at Warsaw University was Panta Koina (All United), which was founded by Ludwik Mauersberger in December 1817 and disbanded in 1821. Perceiving the student societies as a threat, the government banned all secret societies through a proclamation issued on November 6, 1821, forcing students to organize underground groups if they wished to continue their activities. Police harassed and arrested members of several societies; for example, they arrested and imprisoned Panta Koina's former members in 1822 but later released them following an investigation. Mauersberger, however, died in January 1823 of tuberculosis that he had contracted while in prison. Although remnants of the secret societies persisted clandestinely and a few new societies were created, the banning and police repression effectively destroyed the role that some of the societies had played in advocating nationalism and liberalization. Consequently, neither members of the societies nor other students had any significant involvement in the Polish insurrection that began on November 30, 1830. (*See also* FILOMATS and UNION OF FREE POLES.)

Bibliography: Frank W. Thackeray, *Antecedents of Revolution; Alexander I and the Polish Kingdom, 1815–1825* (New York: Columbia University Press, 1980).

Port Huron Statement   (United States) the founding document of STUDENTS FOR A DEMOCRATIC SOCIETY (SDS), issued in June 1962 during SDS's organizational meeting at Port Huron, Michigan. Composed by the SDS's first president, Tom HAYDEN, with revisions by other delegates, the statement defined broad goals that became widely adopted by the U.S. student movement as a whole and therefore comprised one of the movement's seminal documents. The Port Huron Statement declares in part:

> We seek the establishment of a democracy of individual participation with two central aims: that the individual share in those social decisions determining the quality and direction of his life, and that society be organized to encourage independence in men and to provide the media for their common participation. . . .
> Every effort to end the Cold War and expand the process of world industrialization is an effort hostile to people and institutions whose interests lie in perpetuation of the East-West military threat and the postponement of change in the "have not"

nations of the world. Every such effort, too, is bound to establish greater democracy in America. The major goals of a domestic effort would be:

1. America must abolish its political stalemate.
2. Mechanisms of voluntary association must be created through which political information can be imparted and political participation encouraged.
3. Institutions and practices which stifle dissent should be abolished, and the promotion of peaceful dissent should be actively promoted.
4. Corporations must be made publicly responsible.
5. The allocation of resources must be based on social needs. A truly "public sector" must be established, and its nature debated and planned.
6. America should concentrate on its genuine social priorities: abolish squalor, terminate neglect, and establish an environment for people to live in with dignity and creativeness.

The statement outlined the concept of PARTICIPATORY DEMOCRACY and also the nature of the NEW LEFT movement. From its composition and the 1962 convention emerged the leadership of SDS as the spearhead of the New Left. The Port Huron Statement defined those values that were apparently most widely shared by U.S. students—or at least students with an activist bent. Between the time of its composition and its first actual publication in 1964, some 20,000 mimeographed copies were disseminated.

Bibliography: James Miller, *"Democracy is in the Streets": From Port Huron to the Siege of Chicago* (New York: Simon and Schuster, 1987). (*See* Miller's Appendix for complete Port Huron Statement.)

Prague Spring (Czechoslovakia) a reformation and liberalization of the Czechoslovakian government and society that eventuated from activities begun in the fall of 1967, the initial and catalytic event being a student demonstration on October 31. On that night, there was a power failure in the Strahov district of Prague—a common occurrence actually—but about 1,000 students living in the district left their rooms carrying candles and assembled in the streets. They processed through the streets shouting "We want light! We want to study! We want light!" Police appeared to bar the march and amassed enough strength to attempt dispersing the students. Those students at the front of the march could not retreat before the police cars because of the massed crowd to their rear. The police attacked with clubs and tear gas as television cameras recorded the scene. The following day, newspaper reports falsified the event, castigating the students as hooligans and capitalist stooges who had attacked innocent police officers. Angered by these news reports, students prepared and disseminated their own version of what had happened, revealing the brutality of the police attack; they began a public cam-

paign against the "lack of freedom and humanism" in Czechoslovakia that gained the support of young workers and intellectuals.

Their campaign gave impetus to a movement among the majority of the Central Committee of the Communist Party that resulted in Antonín Novotný's loss of the positions of president and first secretary of the Czechoslovak Communist Party. Alexander Dubček became first secretary of the party on January 5, 1968 and began to institute political, social, and cultural reforms referred to as the Prague Spring—an effort to transform communism and to create "Czechoslovakia's Road to Socialism." The period of liberalization ended on August 21, 1968 when military units from the Soviet Union and its Warsaw Pact allies invaded Czechoslovakia to suppress Dubček's reform movement. The invaders dissolved the Czech Student Union as part of the suppression. Students and members of youth organizations held discussions in the street with troops of the occupying forces, questioning them on how the intervention could be justified. In November, university students staged a general strike and joined with workers in a futile effort to defend the liberalization that Dubček had brought. To protest the Soviet suppression and support freedom of speech, a student named Jan Palach immolated himself by fire at the statue of St. Wenceslas in the heart of Prague on January 16, 1969. Hundreds of thousands of marchers paraded by the site to commemorate Palach's act, but the Prague Spring had died.

Presentation Day Protest   (Rhodesia) a demonstration by African students at the July 16, 1966 graduation ceremonies at the University of Rhodesia. The students were promoting the nationalist movement while also protesting against the commencement speaker, the South African principal of the University of Capetown, and ministers of Prime Minister Ian Smith's government who were attending as guests. The student protestors waved placards denouncing Smith's recent Unilateral Declaration of Independence that illegally established Rhodesian independence from Great Britain; they also disrupted the ceremony with singing, shouting, and waving placards that denounced the ministers. Jostling and fistfights occurred. In response, university authorities expelled 31 students; civil authorities later placed nine students, including three Europeans and an Asian, in restriction in their homes and arrested nine faculty members. The principal closed the university for nearly a month. Later the student leaders and their faculty advisors were expelled from Rhodesia, and police raided the homes of students who had been leaders in the NATIONAL UNION OF RHODESIAN STUDENTS (NURS).

Primer Congreso Iberoamericana de Estudiantes   a 1931 congress of Latin American students that convened in Mexico—the first of its kind. It was noteworthy for the period, when many nations in the area had totalitarian governments, because the students issued declarations opposing dictatorship while supporting democratic government, separation of church and state, laws to protect minorities, redistribution of wealth, and other social programs. The students also advocated boycotts and other methods of combating imperialism.

Princeton IDA Protest   (United States) a sit-in by Princeton University students in October 1968 at the building housing the Communications Research Division (CRD) of the Institute for Defense Analysis (IDA). The IDA was a research institute affiliated with 12 sponsoring universities, including Princeton; it conducted scientific research for the Department of Defense that included chemical and biological warfare. The Princeton University chapter of STUDENTS FOR A DEMOCRATIC SOCIETY (SDS) targeted the IDA for protest on the grounds that its activities violated the ideal of free and open scholarly research that the university was committed to. On October 23, 1968, the Monday following the MARCH ON THE PENTAGON, about 70 SDS members began a sit-in at the entrance to the CRD building, which was adjacent to the university campus, preventing CRD personnel from entering. In the afternoon, police arrested 31 of the demonstrators (the others had left to attend classes or to have lunch). Faculty pressures following the arrests resulted in an open meeting attended by 500, at which President Robert F. Goheen announced that he would appoint a faculty committee to review the relationship between the university and IDA. The Kelly Report, later issued by the committee, called for IDA to end the sponsorship affiliations of the 12 universities and stated that, if IDA refused to do so, then Princeton should unilaterally end its association with IDA; the full faculty endorsed the report. As a result, Princeton moved to end its association with IDA, and protests against affiliation with IDA emerged at Columbia University, the University of Chicago, and other schools. The successful student protest strengthened the SDS's role at traditionally conservative Princeton, as indicated in the election of an SDS activist as student body president in April and in the chapter's ability to assemble 1,000 students for a demonstration on May 2.

Princip, Gavrilo (1894–1918)   (Bosnia-Herzegovina) born in Oblaj, Bosnia, a South Slav nationalist who on June 28, 1914 assassinated Archduke Franz Ferdinand, heir to the Austro-Hungarian throne of the Habsburgs, and his wife Sophia while they were on an official visit in Sarajevo—an act that became the catalyst for launching World War I. Princip was a member of the clandestine BLACK HAND, which trained him in terrorism as a part of the group's effort to overthrow the Austro-Hungarian Empire's rule in the Balkans. He and four other Black Hand youths waited for the archduke's procession through the streets of Sarajevo; one threw a bomb that bounced off the archduke's car and exploded under the following car. A short while later, while en route to the hospital to visit an officer who had been wounded during the blast, the archduke's driver made a wrong turn; during the confusion that followed, Princip stepped forward and shot the archduke and duchess, killing them on the spot. Austro-Hungary held Serbia responsible for the deaths and declared war on July 28, triggering the terms of treaties that obliged Russia to intervene in Serbia's support and drew Germany, Great Britain, Italy, and other nations as well into the ensuing war. Princip was tried in October 1914 and sentenced to 20 years in prison, the maximum possible penalty for an offender under the age of 20, as Princip was at the time of the killings. He died of tuberculosis in a hospital near the prison.

Pro-Campos Demonstration   (Puerto Rico) a pro-independence student demonstration at the University of Puerto Rico on December 17, 1947 to celebrate the return home of Nationalist revolutionary Pedro Albizu Campos; he had been released from prison after serving a six-year sentence for conspiring to end the United States' governance of Puerto Rico violently. During the demonstration, students lowered the U.S. flag that flew over the university tower and replaced it with the Puerto Rican Nationalists' flag. The university suspended three student leaders of the demonstration. The legacy of this demonstration eventuated in a student strike and riots a few months later in 1948 after the chancellor refused to allow Campos to speak on the campus. Students occupied classrooms and fought with police, resulting in the official closing of the university and the expulsion or suspension of many students. The chancellor also disbanded the student government organization (General Council of Students) and the student newspaper, barred any form of partisan political activity from the campus, and made class attendance mandatory.

Progressive Youth Organizing Committee (PYOC) (United States) a communist controlled university-student organization formed in 1960 by students previously associated with the LABOR YOUTH LEAGUE (LYL). Although PYOC and its magazine *New Horizons for Youth* focused largely on issues of interest to students, including the growing concern with civil rights, it proved to have limited appeal. Consequently, it was short-lived, being replaced by the W. E. B. DuBois Clubs founded in 1963.

Provos   (Netherlands) a small movement, comprised mostly of young people but joined by older adults, that was centered in Amsterdam during the 1960s and proved significant because of the enormous public attention it garnered. The term *Provo*, an abbreviation of *provocateur*, rather ironically derived from a doctoral dissertation entitled "Background to the Behavior of Young Trouble-

Makers" submitted at Utrecht University in January 1965 in which the doctoral candidate referred to one element of the troublemakers (street groups who indulged in provocative behavior for diversion) as "Provos." Some graduate students, writers, and other intellectuals who learned of the dissertation adopted the term for themselves. In May 1965 one group of Provos began to participate in "happenings" that were staged by a jester-magician at the Het Lieverdje (Little Rascal) statue; these happenings protested cigarette smoking, consumerism, overseriousness, and other perceived failings. The Provos adopted bizarre mottoes and buffoonery as forms of protest. Copies of a magazine entitled *Provo* that first appeared in Amsterdam in July 1965 were immediately confiscated because the contents were viewed as offensive—the confiscation, of course, assured the magazine's success. The Provos were not an organized movement but simply individuals who shared a disdain for conformity, bureaucracy, and other aspects of modern life. Provos wore white clothing, adopting the color white as symbolic of cleaning up air pollution and other urban ills; they had "White Campaigns" to address such problems. Although nonviolent, protests by Provos evoked violent police reactions, severe jail sentences, and widespread media attention. Media coverage generated Provo groups or imitators in other cities, but the Provo phenomenon had effectively died out by the middle of 1967.

Quickborn (Germany) a Roman Catholic youth movement devoted to hiking (or rambling) begun in 1909. Quickborn attempted to bridge the gaps between French and German youths in the years before World War I. Quickborn opposed the use of alcohol and tobacco. From 1924 to 1933 a priest, Romano Guardini, co-publisher of *Schildgenossen*, headed the movement; he was also head of the youth center Rothenfels between 1926 and 1939. In 1921 Father Guardini described the movement's roving pursuits as intended to create mutual dependency; it was antisocialist as well.

Quit India Movement (India) a nonviolent independence movement launched against British rule when the Congress Party (or Indian National Congress), led by Mahatma Ghandi and Jawaharlal Nehru, approved the Quit India resolution on August 8, 1942 during an All-India Congress Committee meeting in Bombay; the resolution called for a "do or die" nationwide effort to resist the British in every possible way, except violence, and demanded that Great Britain "Quit India" before the Indians would agree to fight on the side of the Allies in World War II. On August 9 the government had Ghandi, Nehru, and numerous other Congress leaders arrested and imprisoned, depriving the movement of its leadership and of leaders who had espoused nonviolence. Ironically, news of the arrests generated nonviolent demonstrations (*hartals*) throughout India, to which the government responded with repressive measures, including some instances of firing on demonstrators. This repression evoked violent revolt in response, with massive groups of protestors sabotaging, destroying, or torching railways, telegraph offices, police stations, government buildings, and homes of government officials. The violent protests continued for weeks. By the end of 1942 official countermeasures resulted in more than 1,000 deaths (and perhaps ten times that figure), more than 3,000 wounded, and more than 60,000 arrested, with about 26,000 brought to trial; military losses were eleven killed and seven wounded.

University students played a critical role in the Quit India Movement, except for communist groups, such as the ALL-INDIA STUDENTS' FEDERATION, which supported Great Britain's war aims as a means of aiding the Soviet Union against Germany. Massive nationalist student protests closed most of the country's universities at varied times and for long periods; for example, a student strike closed most of the colleges in Bombay for three months, until November 3. Nationwide, students staged daily demonstrations, committed acts of sabotage, and tried to disrupt British administrative efforts in their support of the Congress Party's independence drive. Students were less committed to nonviolent tactics than were Ghandi's main followers, and violent episodes did mark the protest as nationwide protesters destroyed 318 police stations and police and soldiers killed 940 people. After Congress leaders, including Ghandi and Nehru, were arrested, students assumed some of the movement's leadership positions, served as liaisons between the movement and leaders of the underground, published outlawed newspapers, and operated a secret radio station. Thousands of students were expelled from their schools, and thousands went to jail. Student militancy, now aroused, continued until the independence movement succeeded in 1947, but 1942 was the highwater mark for massive student participation in the independence struggle. The students increasingly joined in the Ghandi nonviolent civil disobedience movement or focused their attention on campus issues following some disillusionment with the compromises that congressional leaders made in an effort to avoid bloodshed.

Bibliography: R. C. Majumdar, *History of the Freedom Movement in India*, Vol. III (Calcutta: Firma K. L. Mukhopadhyay, 1962–63).

Quito Protest (Ecuador) a street demonstration by students of the Central University of Quito that occurred on April 25, 1907. The students were protesting against President Eloy Alfaro's awarding a contract to a foreign firm to build a railroad into the Oriente jungles in exchange for receiving large tracts of land; they were also protesting violations of the right to vote. The authorities brutally put down the protest, killing three students and wounding many. This incident comprised Ecuadorian students' first real involvement in the nation's politics.

Radicals (Switzerland) a movement of nationalistic students and middle-class citizens centered in largely Protestant and urban cantons that emerged in 1839 in response to the "regeneration" of the Swiss cantons. The Radicals constituted an opposition to the interests of those cantons that were largely Catholic and rural. They promoted ending the near-autonomy of the cantons, creating a centralized authority, and instituting such reforms as universal suffrage and broader civil liberties. They held the Catholic church responsible for retarding Swiss cultural and educational development. The Radicals' conflict with their political opponents in at least 10 of the cantons became so severe between 1839 and 1845 that it threatened at times to erupt into civil war.

Ragged School Union (RSU) (Great Britain) the umbrella organization, formed in 1844, of the Ragged School movement in London. Ragged Schools, which became established in cities throughout Great Britain, were so called because they served the poorest children—dirty and unkempt, shoddily dressed and often shoeless—of the nation's city slums. Although there were precedents, including several schools founded for poor children in London slums from 1798 to 1838 by a tailor named Thomas Cranfield, the first so-named Ragged School was established in 1841 in Field Lane, Smithfield by Andrew Walker of the London City Mission. Lord Shaftesbury became interested in 1843, volunteered as a teacher, and was elected president of the RSU upon its formation as the overall organization for the Ragged Schools of London in 1844. His involvement gave the movement both prominence and respectability, attracting donations, so that the movement quickly expanded. In 1867 the RSU had 226 Sunday Ragged Schools, 204 Day Schools, and 207 Evening Schools serving 26,000 children, taught mostly by volunteer teachers of evangelical religious orientation, as Shaftes-

bury was. The well-known reformer Octavia Hill served as a Ragged School teacher for many years, and General Charles George Gordon, who had attained English-hero status from his military exploits in China, was a volunteer teacher at a Ragged School in Gravesend. In the 1870s, after the government assumed responsibility for general education, the numbers of Ragged Schools began a swift decline. Determined to continue its work with poor adolescents, the RSU shifted to founding and operating YOUTHS' INSTITUTES. Some volunteers involved in the Ragged Schools movement, however, adopted a less religion-centered view and left the movement to set up BOYS' CLUBS as an alternative. The RSU and other groups also founded for indigent youths Boys' Refuges or Boys' Homes whose purposes and services differed substantially from those of the Ragged School movement. By 1887 the RSU was serving fewer than 1,700 children.

Bibliography: Waldo McG. Eagar, *Making Men: The History of the Boys' Clubs and Related Movements in Great Britain* (London: University of London Press, 1953).

Rags (Great Britain) a term coined around 1900 for undergraduate students' rowdy displays. Rags exemplify the age-old town-versus-gown confrontations, with the students regarding their rowdiness as great fun, while the townspeople see it as a nuisance at best.

Rainbow Girls (Order of the Rainbow) (United States) a Christian-oriented (Protestant) Masonic organization for girls and young women age 12 to 20, founded in 1922. Membership is open to daughters of members of the Eastern Star or the Masons or to friends of Rainbow Girls members. Overseeing the order is a Supreme Assembly headquartered in McAlester, Oklahoma; the Grand Assembly operates at the state level. Each local assembly is operated by 20 officers and an adult adviser and is self-sustaining. The assemblies sponsor fund-raising projects for their operation and also provide services to their communities. Members may earn points and medals for their services to the order or demerits for failure to fulfill obligations.

Rangoon Student Riots (Burma) a series of student rebellions in fall 1953 at the University of Rangoon, that were significant in the Burmese national context, especially as the university had opened in a state of turmoil in December 1920. In September 1953, when registrations proved larger than the number of hostel beds available, students simply preempted beds assigned to others; when university authorities requested that they give up the beds and wait for official assignments, the students ignored the plea and assumed a contemptuous view of the authorities when they made no move to enforce their request. In the wake of the authorities' waffling occurred student-union elections, with candidates of the Socialist and government-backed Democratic Student Organization pitted against the Communist-backed Progressives. When they seemed likely to lose, the Progressives, who had campaigned raucously, entered the polling place and destroyed the ballots. Again, the university authorities did nothing. Then the authorities announced their decision to shorten the customary one-month vacation to two weeks, and the entire student body rebelled. They formed a Full-Month Implementation Committee, issued an ultimatum, and called a strike for September 29. The university authorities appealed to Prime Minister U NU to resolve the issue. He accepted responsibility, made a public appeal over the radio, and condemned student behavior (including attacks on police cars), but the student strike was allowed to run its course for the entirety of September 29. On September 30 military police and fire brigades invaded the campus, arrested the strike leaders, and dispersed the other students; some shots were fired, but few people were seriously injured. Two thousand students who applied for special leave were allowed to go home; others remained to march through Rangoon and demand release of the strike leaders. Some of the leaders were expelled or lost their scholarships, but all the other students were readmitted to the university without penalty. Altogether a fairly moderate rebellion, the Rangoon riots were, unlike later student riots in other nations, entirely internal—the creatures of institutional policy.

Rangoon University Students' Strike (Burma) a strike organized by the Rangoon University Students' Union (RUSU) that began on February 25, 1936 and constituted the second student strike in Burma (the first was the UNIVERSITY ACT PROTEST of 1920). The strike was significant less for what it accomplished than for its leadership, members of the nationalist Thakin movement. (*Thakin*, the Burmese word for "master," which had to be used in addressing all Britons unless the Britons had more significant titles, was adopted by the movement to deride the British and to signify the movement's goal of Burmese becoming their own masters.) The primary leader of the students' strike was Thakin Nu, then 29 years old, president of the RUSU, and a law student; in 1948, following Burma's independence, he would become the first elected prime minister as U NU (Mr. Tender). The other leader was AUNG SAN, approximately 22 years old and secretary of the RUSU; he later became military leader of the nationalist effort and served in effect as prime minister in 1946–47, until his assassination. Both Nu and Aung San were arrested and suspended from the university but later reinstated. Although the student strike promoted democratization of the university administration and various curricular reforms, its actual underlying intent was opposition to British rule, and during a demonstration at the British Secretariat, police killed a student named Aung Gyaw, who became a martyr for the student protestors. The students garnered public support throughout Burma in pursuing a boycott, but their strike soon ended.

Rashtra Seva Dal (RSD) (India) a socialist youth organization founded in the 1940s as a counterpoint to the RASHTRIYA SWAYAMSEVAK SANGH (RSS). Unlike the RSS, the RSD pursued a secular ideology that included opposition to the caste system and support of intercaste marriages, but its program was also comprised of drilling, physical training, and social activities. The RSD's leadership was controlled by socialist students, and its greatest strength was in Maharashtra.

Rashtriya Swayamsevak Sangh (RSS) (India) a militant right-wing Hindu movement, founded in Nagpur in 1925, whose membership was comprised mostly of high-school-age youths. The RSS advocated Hindu nationalism (including Hindi as the official national language) and traditional Hindu values, including perpetuating the caste system. As a corollary to these views, the RSS also opposed westernization, while encouraging anti-Muslim and anti-Christian sentiments among Hindus. Many university students, especially in the rural schools, were attracted to the RSS and its paramilitary program. The RSS did not participate in the independence movement, publicly professing no ambitions in politics but only in furthering a Hindu cultural renaissance. The RSS was centered entirely in Maharashtra until 1937, when it began to spread nationally; by 1938 the organization had 40,000 members, and by 1950 it had a half-million members in the Bombay state alone. In the 1940s, the movement's membership numbered in the hundreds of thousands. In 1948 a member of the RSS assassinated Mahatma Gandhi.

Red Army Faction *See* BAADER-MEINHOF GANG.

Red Guards (China) cadres of university and middle school students that were organized as paramilitary units in mid-1966 to promote the purposes of the CHINESE COMMUNIST PARTY (CCP) during the GREAT PROLETARIAN CULTURAL REVOLUTION of 1966–69. Mao Zedong saw the Cultural Revolution as a means of counteracting his opponents in the CCP, neutralizing the bureaucracy, rededicating youths to the long-term success of the Chinese communist revolution, and eliminating any lingering bourgeois tendencies that students might harbor, among other things. The Eleventh Plenum accomplished these purposes, demoting such Mao opponents as Deng Xiaoping, promoting such Mao allies as Lin Biao, and unleashing the Red Guards to help purge the CCP apparatus. The Red Guards (Hung-wei Ping), comprised of 22 million young people age 15 to 21, were named after the army units that Mao had organized in 1927, and they received moral and material support from Mao and Lin Biao.

Members of the Red Guards perceived their duty to be fulfillment of the revolution through purging from society all remnants of the pre-communist culture—a duty that certainly encouraged xenophobia. In this effort, they used varied means, including publications, wall posters, reciting the contents of *Quotations from Chairman Mao* (the "little red book"), demonstrations, and in some cases intimidation or violence. They rallied to such slogans as "There can be no construction without destruction" and "To rebel is justified," and they communicated through "big character posters" plastered on walls in Beijing and other cities. The Red Guards were encouraged to attack "class enemies," officials, and professors and even to kill, pillage, and burn. During the year following August 1966, an estimated 50 million of these youths traveled across the countryside. For food and shelter they depended on the resident populace in areas they traversed, but their periodic eruptions into acts of mass hysteria and brutality earned public enmity. Each Red Guard unit was led by a young officer from the Kung An Pu (Ministry of Public Safety), who identified the Red Guards' enemies. All members were pressed into conformity—refusing to behave in uniformity with other Red Guards invited arrest or death. They could travel free on railroads and boats, but in remote areas they had to march long distances, frequently encountering hostile peasants and villagers who drove them away; consequently, tens of thousands starved or froze to death.

Red Guard units first appeared in universities and middle schools throughout the nation and pursued their purpose by condemning "bourgeois" teachers and administrators, courses deemed to be impractical in their applications, and admissions and job placement policies that favored academically qualified students over "politically qualified" students from worker, peasant, or military backgrounds. As they surged across the nation in 1966–67, the Red Guard units attacked lower-level CCP committees, most of which owed their appointments to Deng's Secretariat. Beatings and furious battles resulted. Some local committees created their own Red Guard units to protect themselves, thus compounding the confusion engendered by the Cultural Revolution.

Beginning on August 18, 1966 and for weeks thereafter through November 26, Red Guard units, comprised of an estimated 11 million members, converged on Beijing for a series of eight gigantic rallies that were reviewed by Mao and Lin Biao and for meetings with Mao. The government assigned 100,000 troops from the People's Liberation Army to monitor the Red Guards, live with them, advise them, and maintain order. But the presence of Red Guards in such huge numbers severely strained the city's transportation, housing, food, and other services and also the patience of some CCP officials as Red Guard groups disrupted factories, attacked foreign diplomats, and erupted in intense factional disputes that threatened to eventuate in anarchy. Consequently, on October 31, all travel by Red Guards was suspended for five days, and the army assumed control of their movements. The rally on November 25–26 was pronounced the last until spring. Early in 1967 the government encouraged the Red Guard units to disperse into

Red Guards in Beijing perform a skit, "Down with U.S. Imperialism!", during a demonstration against Burma's anti-Chinese demonstrations. (AP/WIDE WORLD PHOTOS)

the countryside and to learn the values of the peasants. In the fall of that year, the universities and middle schools that had been closed down by the Cultural Revolution were reopening, and over the coming months the Red Guard movement slowly dissolved. What it had meant remains somewhat problematic, but the Red Guards constituted a massive nationwide youth movement that brought together millions of young people in a shared experience, rededicating them to a new social order while permitting them a certain degree of spontaneity and autonomy. It also took them away from their schools for a year, with some long-term educational and economic consequences.

Bibliography: Jeffrey N. Wasserstrom and Elizabeth J. Perry, eds., *Popular Protest and Political Culture in Modern China* (Boulder, Colo.: Westview Press, 1992).

Registration of Girls and Boys Order   (Great Britain) a government decree of 1941 (the second year of World War II) that stipulated that all British youths age 16 or over must register with their local education authorities. Any youth found not to belong to a youth movement at the time of registration was required to appear before a panel of interviewers, who advised an appropriate movement for the youth to join. Although joining a youth movement was not made compulsory by the order, the effect was to swell the ranks of the CADET FORCE and other organizations.

Reichsbundes der Deutsch Demokratischen Jugendvereine (German Democratic Youth Movement) (Germany) a nationwide youth organization of the 1920s affiliated with the German Democratic Party. With a membership of about 20,000, the youth group published its own periodical, *Die Demokratischen Jugend.*

Revolution of 1905   (Russia) a period of massive strikes by workers and students that were ongoing through most of the year and peaked in October 1905. This revolutionary movement arose largely in reaction to BLOODY SUNDAY but also in response to the humiliating surrender of Port Arthur to the Japanese in January, the Russian defeat at Mukden in March, and the loss of Russia's Baltic Fleet at the Tsushima Straits in May as the Russo-Japanese War approached its end. The strikes began in January. Students at virtually all the institutes of higher learning called a strike to last until September. The protests spread to secondary schools and seminaries and included demands for reforms in the entire educational system, such as curricular changes, reduced costs, students being free to hold meetings, and parents being allowed to participate in the schools' governance. In response to this growing agitation for educational reform, the government finally issued a decree on August 27 (the 27 August Rules) that rescinded the 1884 regulation by restoring autonomy to institutes of higher learn-

ing, allowing faculties to elect deans and rectors and students to hold meetings. Perhaps most notably for ensuing events, the rules made it possible for students to hold political meetings.

As the workers' strikes spread and revolutionary groups agitated for genuine revolution, the students were obliged to define a role in the unfolding disruptions. Through the initiative of a group at Moscow University, an All-Russian Student Congress convened at Vyborg, Finland, on September 1, with representatives of 23 institutes of higher learning throughout Russia attending. At the congress occurred an unsuccessful effort to create a central agency to lead a united student movement; in addition, there was a call to end the general student strike in favor of returning to the universities and transforming them into centers of revolutionary agitation.

The St. Petersburg University Coalition Council, which had helped to organize the Vyborg congress, and other groups participated in a meeting of 2,000 students in the university's main auditorium on September 13 to consider the issue of reopening the university. Following debate, they voted 1,702 to 243 in favor of a resolution to do so. The resolution also supported revolution, an armed uprising followed by the convening of a constituent assembly. Student groups at other universities passed similar resolutions. At Moscow University, some 4,000 students met on September 7; a majority of those who stayed to the meeting's end approved what became known as the Second Moscow Resolution, which called for reopening the university as a "revolutionary base." Odessa, Kazan, and other provincial universities followed this resolution as their model. These various resolutions committed the student movement to radical politics—at least in word, though not fully in deed, as the majority of students remained moderate, not committed to activism.

What followed were meetings that involved students with workers and the increasing radicalization of both groups. Since the government's 27 August Rules had granted autonomy to the universities, police did not try to stop radical political meetings held on the campuses, especially at Moscow University; these were attended also by railway workers, women, soldiers, civil servants, teachers, and high school students. These meetings proved both very popular and very successful and were attended by thousands—for example, 4,000 at a meeting on September 20 at the University of Kazan and 13,000 on October 15 at St. Petersburg University. Student organizers also used the meetings to solicit money from the attendees to buy weapons or to support strike funds.

In late September, a strike movement began in Moscow; in October it spread to St. Petersburg and other cities. On October 8, the Moscow railroad workers went on strike; the strike spread, so that by October 13 the nation's transport system had come to a dead halt. A general strike followed, supported by government employees, professionals, even some businesspeople. The strikes brought still more workers to the universities for political and organizational meetings. Inspired by this general ferment, students went on strike at 48 of the nation's 58 seminaries to demand better living conditions and other reforms; in October students created such serious disorders at the theological academies in St. Petersburg, Moscow, Kazan, and Kiev that the administrations suspended classes. Rightists blamed students for the general strike. In Odessa, Kazan, Kiev, and Kharkov, mobs attacked the universities; students and workers erected barricades on the campuses to keep them out. In Moscow, butchers and milkmen who were put out of work by the strikes attacked and beat students and invaded the university on October 15; the next day, a military guard called in by the rector to protect the students from the mob escorted them off the campus. At the same time, the governor general of St. Petersburg, backed by troops who surrounded the campus, closed St. Petersburg University to any future political meetings. Fearing the worst, the government decided to close all the universities.

On October 17, a beleaguered Tsar Nicholas II issued an imperial manifesto (later known as the October Manifesto) that promised to grant "freedom of conscience, speech, assembly, and association," to give representation in the Duma to "those classes of the population that are now completely deprived of electoral rights," and to increase the powers of the Duma, which would now have to approve all laws. The manifesto also provided a vague offer of universal suffrage in the future. In short, the October Manifesto seemed to promise a constitutional monarchy, although a constitution was not specifically mentioned. Leftists claimed victory. Triumphant demonstrators, including high school and university students, celebrated with street marches, but the nobility, the church hierarchy, and those who had lost jobs because of the general strike were not happy. A rumor spread that students and Jews had forced the tsar to sign the manifesto by holding him hostage. Counterrevolutionary mobs erupted in riots and pogroms against Jews, students, professionals, with beatings and killings.

Administrators and faculty councils were faced with deciding whether to reopen the universities. At Moscow University, fearful that revolutionaries would seize control of the university if it reopened, the faculty council, at the urging of the rector, voted 61 to 5 on November 7 to keep the institution closed. Other universities followed this lead; with only a few exceptions, the Russian higher education institutions remained closed until September 1906. When the schools did reopen, the barriers to women and Jews had fallen, enrollments nearly doubled, and the student movement's ideology changed. Since the preeminence of workers in the Revolution of 1905 had apparently obviated students' political importance, the movement adopted "student professionalism"—a focus on economic needs, such as mutual aid and other forms of financial assistance, rather than political confronta-

tion. The government's new 11 June 1907 Rules banned institutionwide student-government organizations and any student meetings not strictly academic in nature. Students voted against responding with a national strike. But further repressive moves—renewing restrictions on admission of Jews and women, forcing student organizations to disband—instigated the student strike of September 1908; it failed, however, from a lack of public support.

Bibliography: Abraham Ascher, *The Revolution of 1905: Russia in Disarray* (Stanford, Calif.: Stanford University Press, 1988); Samuel D. Kassow, *Students, Professors, and the State in Tsarist Russia* (Berkeley: University of California Press, 1989).

Revolution of 1930   (Argentina) a coup by military leaders on September 6, 1930 that was largely motivated by antigovernment demonstrations by University of Buenos Aires students. On August 31 university students, joining a growing opposition to the Radical party government headed by Hipólito Irigoyen, released a declaration calling for policy changes to deal with corruption, inefficiency, and the depression. If their demands were not met, the students vowed to demonstrate in the streets. The catalytic event occurred on September 4 when, following a rally at the Faculty of Medicine, several thousand students marched through the streets of Buenos Aires to the Plaza de Mayo, site of the Casa Rosada (the presidential offices and seat of the government), and demanded Irigoyen's resignation. Police brandishing sabers moved in to disperse the students, and someone began to shoot, wounding several students and one police officer. The students accused the police of brutality and continued the demonstration for several hours until they finally dispersed. The shootings and the death of one of the wounded students elicited public sympathy for the students and their cause. On September 5, Irigoyen turned over control of the government to the vice president, and the cabinet declared a virtual state of emergency. On September 6, army troops headed by two generals marched to the Casa Rosada and seized control of the government, ousting the Radical ministers and installing military officers in their place. The students supported the coup—a rare instance of student demonstrators backing a government takeover by conservative forces, for which the students later received major criticism. In a declaration, the students expressed pride in their involvement in toppling the government and urged the restoration of civilian democratic government, with the military serving only as caretakers. But when the military held on to control of the government, the students joined the opposition. In subsequent years, the military government arrested proreform students and faculty.

Revolution of 1957   (Colombia) an uprising in May 1957, known as "the days of May," that was initiated by student demonstrations and led to the ouster of General Gustavo Rojas Pinilla from the presidency. Rojas had come to power through a coup d'état on June 13, 1953 that toppled the government of Laureano Gómez Castro. The public initially welcomed the coup, as Rojas promised a restoration of peace and justice. But the new regime quickly turned repressive, censoring the press and attempting to retain power through the military; it was also weakened by rising inflation, unpopular tax policies, and corruption. Students became a major source of opposition to the regime; during a student demonstration against Rojas in June 1954, police killed several of the protestors. When in May 1957 Rojas tried to have a constituent assembly that Gomez had convened award him the presidency for another four years, student protestors took to the streets. The student demonstrations inspired a nationwide strike, the so-called civic strike that students helped maintain; many businesses and both major political parties, the Conservatives and the Liberals, joined the strike. The army on May 10 forced Rojas into exile in the United States. He returned in October 1958 and was impeached, but in 1962 he reappeared on the political scene. Except for the Revolution of 1957, students' efforts to influence Colombian political events have been largely intermittent and ephemeral, despite an ongoing militancy among a minority of students in opposition to successive governments well into the 1980s.

Bibliography: Robert H. Dix, *The Politics of Colombia* (New York: Praeger, 1987).

Rico Assassination (Cuba) an incident of October 28, 1956 when several students associated with the DIRECTORIO REVOLUCIONARIO and its leader José Antonio Echevarría attacked some police and army officers as they were leaving the Montmartre night club in the Vedado area of Havana. The students, led by Juan Pedro Carbo Servia, a medical student, fired on the officers, who were accompanied by women, killing Colonel Blanco Rico, chief of military intelligence, and wounding Colonel Marcelo Tarbenilla, son of the chief of staff, and his wife. In their search for the assassins, the police entered the Haitian Embassy, where several Cubans had sought sanctuary; they shot and killed some of the Cuban refugees and seized the others, whom they later executed—a death toll of 10. The Rico assassination also worked against student interests, as Rico was among the few officers who opposed torturing persons detained for interrogation. At the time, many students were involved in acts of sabotage and terror as part of the resistance to the dictatorial government of General Fulgencio Batista.

Río Piedras Language Demonstration (Puerto Rico) a one-day strike in November 1946 by students at the main campus (Río Piedras) of the University of Puerto Rico to protest President Harry Truman's veto of a bill passed by the Puerto Rican legislature that mandated Spanish be used as the official language of instruction in all Puerto Rican schools. About 6,000 students (approximately two-thirds of the campus student body) participated in the demonstration. This was apparently the first student-protest demonstration held at the campus since the university's founding in 1902. Spanish subsequently became the official language of the Puerto Rican public schools in 1948, with English receiving emphasis as a preferred subject.

Rockers (Great Britain) a teenage grouping of the early 1960s whose adherents were mostly working class. Rockers expressed largely conventional or even reactionary social and political values, with a touch of xenophobia. Rockers, devoted to their motorbikes, wore motorcycle-style jackets and cycle gear and emphasized masculinity—even the women, dominated by male Rockers, dressed masculinely. They garnered a reputation for violence, especially following the clashes between groups of MODS and Rockers during the WHITSUN DISTURBANCES.

Rodriguistas (Manuel Rodríguez Patriotic Front) (Chile) an urban guerrilla youth movement formed by the Communist Party in 1980. Many of the Rodriguistas came from the impoverished areas of cities where unemployment rates were extreme. They joined with other youth groups in carrying on a form of urban warfare against the regime of General Augusto Pinochet Ugarte during the years 1983–86, committing thousands of dynamitings and acts of sabotage and hundreds of kidnappings and attempted assassinations. The Rodriguistas planned a major terrorist attack and stored weapons in the village of Vallenar in anticipation, but security forces thwarted their plot, confiscating the weapons cache, which included a huge quantity of explosives, 3,000 automatic rifles, 2 million rounds of ammunition, and 275 rocket launchers. Frustrated by the loss, the Rodriguistas decided to fulfill Operation Twentieth Century, probably their most daring exploit: the assassination of Pinochet. Two dozen of the front's guerrillas made the attempt on Pinochet's life on the evening of September 7, 1986 as the president's motorcade left his mansion in suburban Melocoton to drive into Santiago. The Rodriguistas attacked with rocket and machine-gun fire, damaging several cars and killing five bodyguards. They launched a rocket that hit the president's Mercedes but failed to explode; Pinochet escaped, his driver speedily turning about and racing back to the mansion. Pinochet's attackers also escaped, disappearing into the city. The president took vengeance with repression of the Left, torture, and armed attacks, one of which in 1987 left 12 Rodriguistas dead. Nine of the Rodriguistas involved in the assassination attempt were hunted down and sentenced to death. Although the Communist Party decided to abandon terrorist tactics following this repression, the

Rodriguistas rejected this policy change and continued acts of sabotage and attempted assassinations until Pinochet's regime came to an end in 1989.

Rogaku-kai (Association of Laborers and Students) (Japan) an organization formed in 1918 comprising a federation of the Yuai-kai, the first national workers organization, and students of the universities in Tokyo and Kyoto. Rogaku-kai gave birth to SHINJIN-KAI.

Rubin, Jerry (1938–1994) (United States) antiwar activist, organizer of the Youth International Party (Yippies) and defendant in the Chicago Seven trial (*see* CHICAGO 8 TRIAL). Rubin was born in Cincinnati, where his father was a union organizer, and became a graduate student at the University of California at Berkeley during the BERKELEY STUDENT REVOLT and the later protests against the Vietnam War. In late 1967 he joined with Abbie HOFFMAN and others to form the yippies and to plan the "Festival of Life" to coincide with the Democratic National Convention in 1968. The antiwar protests during the convention resulted in the Chicago Seven trial, where Rubin was found guilty of intent to riot; the verdict was overturned on appeal. Rubin later became involved in various self-awareness programs such as EST and in Wall Street investment banking, which made him wealthy. He died in the hospital of heart failure two weeks after being injured when hit by a car while jaywalking in Los Angeles.

St. Daniel's Night (Spain) a university student demonstration in Madrid on April 10, 1865 (St. Daniel's Night). The students assembled in central Madrid to protest the firing of Emilio Castelar, a professor at the University of Madrid who was dismissed because he had criticized Queen Isabella II. Troops sent to disperse the protestors wounded 100 students and killed 9. The massacre elicited widespread public comment and constituted a major prelude to the Spanish Revolution of 1868. The revolution resulted in the overthrow of Isabella II, who left Spain to reside in Paris.

Saint-Just, Louis de (1767–1794) (France) youngest and perhaps most zealous leader of the Reign of Terror. After a brief sojourn in Paris at the age of 19 ended in his mother's having him incarcerated in a reformatory for several months, Saint-Just settled in Soissons, near his hometown, in 1787. He served as clerk to the public prosecutor, studied at Reims, and received his law degree in 1788. In 1789, he anonymously published an erotic epic poem that was confiscated by authorities, and for safety he hid in the home of a friend in Paris, then mired in the frenzy of the French Revolution. Saint-Just became a supporter of the ruthless Robespierre, sought a seat in the General Assembly, and, in 1791, published *Esprit de la Révolution et de la Constitution de France*, which advocated sovereignty for the people. Barred from the General Assembly because he was too young, Saint-Just complained, "I am a slave of my adolescence!" He won election to the National Convention in September 1792, about a month after his 25th birthday. An uncomprising champion of the extreme Left, he became a member of the Committee of Public Safety, the small governing group of the Reign of Terror, in May 1793. He succeeded Robespierre, was elected president of the convention, and successfully led French troops against the Austrians at Fleurus. He secured passage of the Ventôse Decrees, which provided for expropriating property of the wealthy for distribution to the poor and advocated radical changes envisioning a communal society. But his tyrannical behavior and advocacy of mass executions aroused dread and loathing among his opponents. Arrested on July 27, 1794, he was sent to the guillotine the next day—dead at the age of 26.

St. Petersburg Anti-Statute Protest (Russia) a protest in the autumn of 1861 by students of the University of St. Petersburg against a university statute approved by Tsar Nicholas I the preceding May that would severely reduce the number of government scholarships and would abolish the students' right to hold meetings. (At St. Petersburg, nearly two-thirds of the students needed financial aid, and, ironically, the nation's universities had only recently been opened to expanded enrollment, with the number of students at St. Petersburg quadrupling. But authorities wished to prevent any possibility of revolutionary activity among the students.) In July, the minister of education—a conservative who had replaced a more liberal minister who was dismissed following student agitation in the spring—added to the statute's retrictions still more stringent regulations of his own. Tuition was increased 50 rubles, sufficient to weed out some poor students and to create financial hardship for others. And a new handbook delineating the new regulations was issued, with the requirement that every student must sign it. These measures united students in opposition; as a result, when the students returned from the vacation period, they began to organize in collective protest.

Students held numerous meetings, notably on September 23, when the university's buildings were still locked because registration would not begin until the following week. The students broke into a locked auditorium to hold their protest meeting, where they decided that all who accepted the new regulations would be ostracized and that the handbooks would be signed but disobeyed and also burned. In response, authorities kept the university buildings locked on September 25 when registration was to begin, so the students marched through the city streets to the home of the rector—the first such demonstration march in Russian history. When the authorities refused to compromise, the students met on October 10 and decided to stage a boycott of classes, scheduled to begin the following day. On October 11, only 70 students out of an estimated 1,400 who planned to attend classes actually did so, while other students demonstrated outside the buildings but were dispersed by police. On October 12, a much larger crowd of demonstrators assembled. Police and soldiers arrested and imprisoned several hundred of the protesting students, but the protests continued. So many were arrested that the city's jails overflowed and many had to be sent to the naval fortress at Kronstadt for imprisonment.

But the strike succeeded: by the end of October, only 20 percent of the students who had enrolled were actually attending classes. After two months, the jailed students were released, although scores of them were deported to distant provinces. Conceding that the university could not return to normal operations, authorities closed it in December indefinitely; it would not reopen until autumn 1863. Significantly, however, the St. Petersburg student protest had spread to other cities, including Moscow, where students who demonstrated at the governor's mansion were attacked, injured, and arrested. The protests ultimately failed, and in 1863 new university statutes granted increased autonomy to faculties while prohibiting the formation of any corporate student organizations or assemblies. The students held assemblies despite their illegality and thus kept alive the spirit of unity. Their meetings also nurtured political dissent, and many veterans of the 1861 strike became members of opposition groups such as LAND AND FREEDOM.

St. Petersburg Student Strike of 1899   *See* ZEMLYACHESTVA.

St. Scholastica's Day Riot   (Great Britain) probably the most famous town-versus-gown riot that occurred in medieval England—on February 10, 1355 in Oxford. The disturbance began in a tavern near Carfax when a group of clerks (or clerics, as all university students were involved in ecclesiastical study) complained about the wine. The wine merchant replied caustically, and they threw the wine goblet at his head. The innkeeper's friends rang the bell of St. Martin's Church, assembling a mob of men armed with bows and arrows and other weapons. They attacked the students as they passed by, and, when the university chancellor appeared to try to quell the disturbance, they attacked him. The outraged chancellor then rang the St. Martin's Church bell to assemble a mob of armed students. The ensuing battle lasted until nightfall. Miraculously, no one was killed or mortally wounded, but the battle had only begun. On the following day, about 80 armed townspeople who had been stationed at St. Giles's Church attacked students in Beaumont who were walking after having dined. One student was killed and others were wounded. Another general battle followed this assault; the townspeople, supported by others from the countryside, overwhelmed the students, killing and maiming and also pillaging the students' halls. This battle also ended after nightfall. But the next day, the townspeople returned for more mayhem, invading the students' houses and killing or wounding any who resisted and, reputedly, scalping some of the clerics. This carnage was apparently too much. In retaliation, King Edward III established an inquiry that resulted in the king's abrogation of both the university's and the town's privileges and in the imprisonment of several of the townspeople in the tower of London. The king then later returned the privileges, with those of the town reduced and those of the university increased, granting Oxford University jurisdiction over the city. In addition, the Bishop of Lincoln put the townspeople under a year-long interdiction and required that the mayor, bailiffs, and 60 leading burghers attend St. Mary's Church on every St. Scholastica's Day to pray for the souls of the murdered students—a ceremony that continued until 1825. Each was also required to donate a penny, 40 of which would go to support 40 penurious students. The St. Scholastica's Day riot was significant in its results—namely, establishing the paramountcy of the university in Oxford civic affairs, with the chancellor acquiring increased powers, including control over market trading.

Bibliography: W. A. Pantin, *Oxford Life in Oxford Archives* (Oxford: Clarendon Press, 1972).

Salvation Army Youth Programs   (United States) a diversity of services for youths, including Red Shield Youth Centers, offered by the Salvation Army, a Christian-oriented (Protestant) international organization that originated in England in 1865. The Salvation Army provides boys' clubs and camps for girls and boys. Among its groups serving girls are the Sunbeams for age 10–13 and the Girl Guards for age 14–18. Their programs resemble those of the GIRL SCOUTS but with an emphasis on religious instruction and Sunday School attendance.

Samajwadi Yuvak Sabha (Socialist Student Organization)   (India) an organization founded in 1953 by the Indian Socialist Party. The SYS, which suffered from conflicts among the Indian socialists, probably attained no more than 5,000 student members nationwide, with its strength localized in northern provinces. In some locales, SYS activist gained leadership roles during the widespread student demonstrations of 1966.

Sampa Rengo (Three Faction Alliance)   (Japan) an alliance formed in 1962 among three factions of the ZEN-GAKUREN. At the time, the Zengakuren was wracked with factionalism and power struggles, and the alliance hoped to achieve control of the STUDENT SELF-GOVERNING ASSOCIATIONS. The three factions creating the alliance were SHASEIDO, SHAGAKUDO, and Kozo Kaikaku-ha, or Kokaiha (Structural Reform Faction of the Front); the first two were major forces in the Zengakuren. The alliance also wished to organize the opposition to a University Control Bill proposed by the government of Prime Minister Hayato Ikeda. Disputes within the member factions and expulsion of the Front group led to the alliance's being reformed in September 1963. So the original group's life was brief, but Sampa Rengo continued in its new guise. In December 1966 the group reconstituted itself as the Sampa Zengakuren.

Samurai Skyjack   (Japan) a famous incident in which nine members of the SEKIGUN hijacked a Japanese Airlines (JAL) jetliner on March 31, 1970. The JAL flight was from Tokyo to Fukuoka, and as soon as it was airborne, the Sekigun members pulled out short swords and pipe bombs, entered the cockpit, and demanded that the pilot fly the plane to Pyongyang, North Korea. When the pilot asserted they must first land at Fukuoka Airport to refuel, the skyjackers agreed and proceeded to tie up the 122 passengers, using rope and vinyl cords they had brought on board. At Fukuoka Airport, authorities agreed to allow the plane to proceed to North Korea, and the skyjackers released 23 of the passengers. They disembarked past a Sekigun brandishing his sword—his image was broadcast worldwide over television, inspiring the news media to refer to the exploit as the "Samurai skyjack." The plane took off and, escorted by fighter planes, reached the eastern coast of South Korea, where South Korean fighter planes assumed the escort duty. At the 38th parallel, the plane flew along the border, turned north into North Korean air space, and then suddenly turned west. Signaled that it was approaching Pyongyang Airport, the plane subsequently landed at what was actually Kimpo Airport at Seoul, South Korea. Angered by the ruse, the Sekigun students threatened to blow up the plane and settled in for a siege. The plane sat on the tarmac through April 1 and 2. On April 3, the Japanese parliamentary vice minister of transport offered to replace the passengers as a hostage. After a delay while a Socialist Party member of the Diet was flown in to satisfy the Sekigun skyjackers of the vice minister's identity, the exchange was effected; in the afternoon the plane left at about 6:00 P.M. for Pyongyang, arriving there at about 7:20 P.M. The plane, its crew, and the vice minister returned to Japan on April 5. The skyjacking had lasted 84 hours.

Sand, Karl (1795–1820)   (Germany) the assassin of August Kotzebue (1761–1819). Sand was a theology student at the University of Jena, where he belonged to the GIESSENER SCHWARZEN wing of the BURSCHEN-SCHAFTEN. Born in Weimar, Kotzebue was well known for his novels and plays, including some highly satiric works. He had served as a Russian official in St. Petersburg and in Estonia, had married a Russian, and was suspected of being a Russian agent at the time of his death. He also published magazine articles that scoffed at German pretensions to liberty and nationhood, while attacking the student movement—hence earning the hatred of the young German revolutionaries. Kotzebue resided in Mannheim, where Sand stabbed him in the throat on March 23, 1819. Sand then turned his dagger on himself but survived. He was tried for murder, sentenced to death, and beheaded on May 20, 1820. Sand was a follower of Karl FOLLEN, who tried unsuccessfully to rally other students to march on Mannheim and liberate Sand. With his death, Sand became a hero for the activist students, but his assassination of Kotzebue served as the prime impetus for the conference that adopted the CARLSBAD DECREES for the suppression of the Burschenschaften.

SANE   *See* NATIONAL COMMITTEE FOR A SANE NUCLEAR POLICY.

San Francisco City Hall Demonstration   (United States) a protest in May 1960 against hearings by the House Un-American Activities Committee (HUAC). A subcommittee of HUAC was in the city to investigate communism in northern California, having subpoenaed numerous individuals to testify. Two weeks beforehand, a student organization at the University of California at Berkeley called SLATE began to organize a demonstration to protest against HUAC's perceived violation of the civil liberties of those people who had previously testified at its hearings. On the second day of the hearings (May 9), some 400 protestors, mostly students, disrupted the HUAC hearings on the second floor of the city hall; the police sprayed them with fire hoses, clubbed many, and forcibly dragged them out to the street. The confrontation resulted in 12 persons injured (including 8 police) and 64 arrests. Sixty-three of those arrested were released; the remaining protestor, a student at the university, was later tried and acquitted. On May 10, the number of protestors swelled to 5,000 in response to the previous day's confrontation.

In organizing the demonstration, the students had garnered 2,000 signatures on a petition requesting cancellation of the HUAC subcommittee hearings and the disbandment of HUAC. The SLATE organizers called for a nonviolent protest at the hearings. Altogether, about 1,000 students attended the hearings on May 8 and 9, many of them professing neutral views of the proceedings, but on the day of the police confrontation, all were attacked, generating increased sympathy among still other students. The demonstration was significant for adoption of the nonviolent tactics of the Civil Rights movement. In addition, it resulted in a marked shift in many students' views from neutrality and noncommitment to political involvement and activism. In short, the demonstration inspired the political radicalization of many University of California students.

San Francisco State College Uprising (United States) a series of student demonstrations on the campus of San Francisco State College culminating in confrontations with the city police during December 1968. The uprising began with a violent protest on December 6, 1967 involving racial issues. The protest generated opposition to the college president, John Summerskill, by members of the state-college system board of trustees, who condemned him for not calling in the police to restore order. In February 1968, Summerskill announced his resignation, to take effect in September, and denounced the administration of Governor Ronald Reagan for not providing constructive leadership for higher education. In May, the chancellor of the state-college system announced that Summerskill's resignation would become effective immediately; he was replaced on May 30 by Robert Smith. Smith thereafter earned the wrath of the state trustees by refusing to appoint to a nonteaching position George Mason Murray, a member of the BLACK PANTHERS and the college's Black Student Union who had publicly advocated violence—he had made an at least implicit call to kill the president, the governor, members of the Supreme Court, and others. On October 31, the chancellor ordered Murray's suspension; Smith complied but suspended Murray with pay. In response, students called a strike to begin November 6.

Smith closed the college on November 13 because of ongoing disturbances and violence; on November 18 the board of trustees, headed by Reagan as an ex officio member, ordered it reopened. Acknowledging his inability to resolve the varied conflicts, Smith resigned on November 26; S. I. Hayakawa, a well-known semanticist, was named acting president. Classes resumed on December 2 with police keeping order. But on December 5 and the days following, repeated clashes occurred between police and students resulting in 85 arrests. On December 6, Hayakawa granted some of the student demands, including creation of a black studies program and appointment of a nonwhite director of student financial aid, but he refused to grant amnesty to suspended students and insisted that police remain on campus. After two weeks of violent police-student confrontations, Hayakawa closed the college on December 13 for an early Christmas holiday. Student protests, supported by teachers, resumed in January 1969; a large rally on January 23 resulted in 483 arrests. Reagan publicly praised Hayakawa for his strong response to the ongoing protests. Hayakawa served as president of the college through 1972; on the basis of the reputation he had

gained, he was elected to the United States Senate in 1976. On January 7, 1969 in his state-of-the-state message, Reagan asked the legislature to pass a law, to be submitted later, that would forcefully remove "criminal anarchists and latter-day Fascists" from California college and university campuses by expelling troublemaking students and instructors. Reagan, who in January 1969 also sent state police to quell an uprising at the University of California at Berkeley, was elected president of the United States in 1980.

San Marcos Student Strike (Peru) a long-lasting strike initiated in early 1919 by the students of the University of San Marcos in Lima; the oldest university on the continent (founded in 1551), it was perceived by the students to be trappped in the past, so they pressured the Peruvian government into granting reforms. Inspired by the UNIVERSITY REFORM PROGRAM AND MOVEMENT in Argentina, the San Marcos students agitated for revisions in university regulations to bring them up to date, for student participation in the university's governing councils, for open competition in the selection of professors, for academic freedom, and for prohibition of the church from influencing university operations. The student strike lasted for four months, earned the support of workers, and finally attained success. The national legislature passed legislation that included most of the student demands.

Sanqintuan *See* THREE PEOPLE'S PRINCIPLES YOUTH CORPS.

Santa Barbara Riots (United States) a series of uprisings by students at the University of California at Santa Barbara during the winter and spring months of 1970. An initial protest over a faculty firing in spring 1969 had left the Santa Barbara campus in continuing tension. On February 24, 1970 students rioted, hurling rocks and bottles at police, in Isla Vista, the town adjoining the campus where about 9,000 students resided. The riot erupted after police arrested two students who were accused of arson and resisting arrest. Demonstrations continued on February 25, after William Kunstler, defense lawyer in the CHICAGO 8 trial, addressed the students. During the night rioting broke out again, and students firebombed the Bank of America branch in Isla Vista. Twenty-five sheriff's deputies received injuries, and 36 students were arrested. Governor Ronald Reagan visited Santa Barbara on February 26 and laid part of the blame on Kunstler for the riots of the previous night; rioting resumed on February 26, and the National Guard was called up the next day. On April 16, violent rioting recurred in Isla Vista following several hours of speeches, including one by Nancy Rubin, wife of Jerry RUBIN, leader of the Youth International Party (Yippies). Rubin himself had been barred from speaking in Isla Vista by both university and county officials. A police attack set off the riot; four students were wounded by birdshot fired by the police. On April 17, students threw rocks and set fires. The next day, during the ongoing rioting a student was killed, apparently by a ricocheting bullet from a police officer's rifle, as he walked out of the Bank of America branch that had been destroyed by fire in February (it had reopened in March).

Santiago Uprising   *See* JULY 26 MOVEMENT.

Sasebo Naval Base Struggle   (Japan) demonstrations against the arrival of a United States nuclear aircraft carrier in January 1968. The USS *Enterprise* and its escort vessels, with the permission of the Japanese government, were scheduled to arrive at the Sasebo Naval Base on January 19 while en route to South Vietnam. Arguing that the nuclear aircraft-carrier's visit might initiate the creation of nuclear bases in Japan, the ZENGAKUREN planned demonstrations to try to prevent the visit. Somewhat fewer than 1,000 students traveled to Fukuoka, where they made their base at Kyushu University. On January 17, they approached the base via its entry bridge, which was guarded by barbed wire, armored vehicles, and Japanese riot police armed with water cannons and tear gas. The police handily repulsed the students, chasing some of them into a nearby hospital and firing tear gas into the building—this generated a public outcry. On January 18, students had another ineffectual clash with the police. The *Enterprise* entered the harbor as scheduled the next day; the students demonstrated again and fought with the police. On January 20, the students collected money on the street corners of Fukuoka. The next day there was a final effort: four students waded across the Sasebo River, climbed over a wire fence, and entered the base; they were immediately arrested. The *Enterprise* sailed out on January 23, and the students left for Tokyo.

Savio, Mario (1942–1996)   (United States) leader of the FREE SPEECH MOVEMENT (FSM) at the University of California at Berkeley during the BERKELEY STUDENT REVOLT of 1964–65. Born and raised in New York, the son of Italian immigrants, Savio graduated at the top of his high school class of 1,200. He attended Manhattan College and Queens College (where he majored in philosophy) before beginning graduate studies at Berkeley after his family moved to California. Savio spent the summer of 1963 in Taxco, Mexico, helping to construct a laundry to protect the residents against cholera. During summer 1964 as a member of the STUDENT NONVIOLENT COORDINATING COMMITTEE (SNNC), he participated as a teacher in the FREEDOM SUMMER in Mississippi. An effective orator, he was very persuasive in addressing the demonstrators during the 1964–65 student protests at Berkeley. Savio was arrested during one of the demonstrations for biting a police officer on the

thigh; he was also involved in the second student strike in December 1966. Savio continued to be politically active through the years and was involved with the opposition to Proposition 209 (intended to end affirmative action in California) when he died of a massive heart attack in November 1996.

Schirach, Baldur von (1907–1974)   (Germany) Nazi youth leader and governor of Vienna. Born in Berlin to an aristocratic German father and an American mother, two of whose ancestors had signed the Declaration of Independence, von Schirach joined the Nazi Party in 1924 while a student at the University of Munich. Reading Henry Ford's *The International Jew* and other works had converted him to anti-Semitism; he also strongly opposed Christianity and the aristocracy. He devoted himself to organizing high school and university students for the Nazis and proved outstanding at the task. Well regarded by Adolf Hitler, to whom he was blindly committed, von Schirach was put in charge of the NATIONAL SOCIALIST GERMAN STUDENT UNION in 1929 and became Reich Youth Leader of the party in 1931. In 1933, having enrolled hundreds of thousands of young people in the Nazi youth movement, he organized a huge youth march for Hitler in Potsdam. In May of that year, at age 26, he was appointed Leader of the Youth of the German Reich. At this time his cult following rivaled that of Hitler, and by 1936 the HITLER JUGEND he headed numbered 6 million members. In his propagandizing to recruit youths, von Schirach appealed to pagan romanticism, militarism, and patriotism; members of the Hitler Jugend were drilled in the Nazi concepts of discipline and leadership that were spelled out in his book *Die Hitler-Jugend* (1934), which was designed to transform them into "master race" examplars.

In 1932, von Schirach published two best-sellers, *Hitler, wie ihn Keiner Kennt*, illustrated with photos by his father-in-law Heinrich Hoffmann (Hitler's official photographer), and *Triumph des Willens* (the same title as Leni Riefenstahl's famous film about the 1934 Nazi Party rally at Nürnberg). In 1934, von Schirach published a book of poems and a collection of short biographies of Nazi leaders. He enlisted in the army in 1940 and served in France, earning an Iron Cross. But palace intriguers had undermined his influence with Hitler as the war ensued, and in 1940 he was removed as youth leader and named Gauleiter and governor of Vienna.

At the Nürnberg trials following the war, von Schirach denied knowledge of the genocide of the Jews and denounced Hitler; he was sentenced to 20 years, serving his imprisonment with Rudolf Hess and Albert Speer at Spandau Prison in Berlin. After his release in 1966, he published a memoir, *Ich Glaubte an Hitler* (1967), in which he tried to explain the deadly fascination Hitler effected in himself and other German youths, accepted guilt for not being involved in preventing the death camps, and voiced his concern that a revival of Nazism be thwarted. Von Schirach lived out his life in relative seclusion and died at Kroev.

Sea Cadet Corps   (Great Britain) an organization for boys formed in 1899 by the Navy League and granted official recognition by the Admiralty in 1919. Its predecessor was the Naval Lads' Brigade, founded at Whitstable by a group of former navy men in 1856 following the Crimean War, and other brigades formed subsequently elsewhere. The organization's primary purpose was to train boys in seamanship and to nurture their admiration for the Royal Navy. In 1940, as World War II commenced, the Sea Cadet Corps had 100 units with a total membership of 7,500 boys age 14 to 18.

Seale, Bobby (1936–)   (United States) civil rights leader and cofounder (with Huey P. NEWTON) and chairman of the BLACK PANTHER party. Seale and Newton composed the Ten Point Program that comprised the constitution of the Black Panthers. He was also a writer and editor for the party newspaper, *Black Panther*. A political militant and powerful speaker, Seale was among the leaders arrested during the riots at the CHICAGO DEMOCRATIC CONVENTION of 1968. He gained special notoriety during the resulting CHICAGO 8 TRIAL when Judge Julius Hoffman ordered that he be bound and gagged. Seale was charged with murder in New Haven, Connecticut but was acquitted—the trial resulted in a hung jury. He had become a cause célèbre, however, even in Europe. In 1970 in Frankfurt, Germany, his proponents (including Daniel COHN-BENDIT) organized a Black Panther Solidarity Committee, which demanded his release from prison. In several countries, March 6, 1971 was declared International Solidarity Day for Bobby Seale. His release soon followed. In spring 1973, Seale ran in the Oakland, California mayoral election against the incumbent and came in second with 20 percent of the vote. Seale wrote a history of the Black Panthers entitled *Seize the Time: The Story of the Black Panther Party and Huey P. Newton* (1968) and *A Lonely Rage* (1978).

Sea Training Association (STA)   (Great Britain) a character-development program for youths founded in 1966 and based at Bosham in Sussex. Although similar in conception to OUTWARD BOUND, STA is distinctive in that its program is sea-based—the first such in Great Britain. Trainees take a two-week, 800-mile cruise aboard a schooner, doing all the crew work involved in the ship's sailing operations from climbing the rigging to cleaning decks. Each crew has three watches, a cycle of four hours on duty and eight hours off. This strenuous routine constitutes the entire physical- and character-development scheme. STA originated in 1955 to race the last of the square-rigged sailing ships in England and

ended up in 1966 building and outfitting two schooners for this youth training program, which provides cruises for both male and female youths.

Second Great Awakening   (United States) a Protestant revivalist movement that swept across the nation section by section during the years 1790 to 1840. The Second Great Awakening, unlike its predecessor (the Great Awakening of the 1740s and 1750s), was notable for its massive involvement of adolescents and other youths; according to contemporary accounts, they comprised the great majority of those who experienced conversions during the revivals—in fact, in many areas youths actually initiated the majority of the revivals. Conversion occurred with adolescents as young as 7 to 13, although most of the converts were older than 13 and the majority were girls. In addition, the awakening inspired a zeal for missionary work among young students. This zeal first emerged among the Society of Brethren formed in 1808 at Williams College. Several members of the society moved on to Andover Theology Seminary, recently established to counter the burgeoning of Unitarianism at Harvard Divinity School; in 1810 they asked the Congregational General Association of Massachusetts to provide them guidance on becoming missionaries. The young petitioners were mostly intent on becoming missionaries to "the heathen in Asia." In response to their request, the association appointed the American Board of Commissioners for Foreign Missions to provide support. Extensive U.S. missionary work abroad, however, did not occur until nearer the end of the century, but the awakening also inspired many youths to become involved in home missionary work that took them into every state in the Union.

Segni Affair   (France) a student demonstration that occurred in February 1964 concurrent with a state visit to Paris by Italian President Segni. Although Segni was to be escorted at the Sorbonne by Minister of Education Christian Fouchet, the demonstration had nothing to do with his visit and had been scheduled beforehand as a protest against Fouchet's refusal to discuss some educational reforms with student leaders of the various ASSOCI-ATIONS GÉNÉRALE DES ÉTUDIANTS (AGE) of the University of Paris's five faculties (academic disciplines). These reforms included student representation in decision making at the faculties. Concerned that the demonstration, scheduled for February 21, might erupt into violence (thus alienating the public) but lacking the power to stop it, leaders of the National Bureau of the UNION NATIONALE DES ÉTUDIANTS DE FRANCE (UNEF) decided to make the demonstration nationwide in hopes of keeping it peaceable and under UNEF discipline. Confusion over the demonstration was compounded by disagreement among member groups of UNEF, a UNEF letter to President Segni expressing respect and seeking his tolerance, a letter containing an ultimatum sent to Premier Georges Pompidou by members of the Paris-Letters Faculty AGE, and a ban imposed on the demonstration by the prefect of police. The government demanded that UNEF cancel the demonstration, warning of varied consequences, including the termination of subsidies to UNEF and the prosecution of UNEF leaders. The government also closed the Sorbonne and the Faculty of Science and posted guards, and 5,000 police and security officers swarmed through the Latin Quarter. UNEF cancelled the original demonstration but assembled some 3,000 students on the Right Bank to demonstrate at the railroad stations. The protest generated clashes with police, injury to several police officers and students, and the arrest of 163 people. Four students were arraigned, including one (Christian Desobry) who was accused of hitting a police officer and was sentenced to eight days in jail—the first time a UNEF member had ever been sentenced for any act that had occurred during a demonstration. The sentencing hardened UNEF's resolve and elicited the sympathy of other student groups. On February 26, more than 5,000 students assembled for a peaceful demonstration in the Sorbonne's courtyard and demanded that Desobry be released immediately. And throughout France, AGE members held demonstrations to demand Desobry's release; some of these resulted in violence, injuries, and arrests. The Ministry of Education terminated subsidies to UNEF and contacts with UNEF, effectively rendering UNEF moneyless and powerless in subsequent years. Thus the Segni Affair marked a significant turning point for the French student movement.

Sekigun (Red Army Faction)   (Japan) a militant faction of the Socialist Student League (SHAGAKUDO) that was formed in September 1969. As a faction within the ZENGAKUREN, the Sekigun added a new dimension to student protests by making pipe bombs for the November 1969 effort to prevent Prime Minister Sato from flying to the United States. (*See* HANEDA INCIDENTS.) The group advocated worldwide revolution, including the overthrow of the Communist governments in the Soviet Union and China. It was heavily suppressed by the police, who imprisoned 200 of its members. The still at-large leaders decided to flee the country, leading to the Sekigun's most famous exploit—the hijack of a Japan Airlines jetliner on March 31, 1970. (*See* SAMURAI SKYJACK.)

September 18th Incident   *See* MUKDEN INCIDENT.

Shagakudo   *See* SHAKAISHUGI GAKUSEI DOMEI.

Shakaishugi Gakusei Domei (Socialist Student League)   (Japan) an organization formed in May 1958 and known as Shagakudo. It developed out of the Hansen Gakusei Domei. Not associated in any way with the Japan Socialist Party, the Shagakudo's orientation was neverthe-

less Marxist Socialism. The Shagakudo advocated the "Massen Strike" to generate civil war. This tactic involved using university campuses as bases and involving workers, farmers, and others in mass strikes that would instigate the civil war.

Shakaishugi Seinen Domei (Socialist Youth League)   (Japan) a mostly student organization known as Shaseido and formed in 1960 under the auspices of the Japan Socialist Party. In orientation, the students were more radical than the party.

Shanghai Student Union (SSU)   (China) an association of citywide students, founded in 1919 through the impetus of the MAY FOURTH MOVEMENT and as a means of better-organizing student participation in that movement. The SSU was initiated through preliminary meetings held on May 8 and 9 and officially founded during a meeting held on May 11, 1919; the meeting, held at the headquarters of the Chinese World Students Association, was attended by delegates from 61 schools in the city. The SSU was organized as separate and specialized departments, each having a director and assistant director, with distinct branch unions—an unusually bureaucratic structure for a student association. The SSU organized the student strike that was begun on May 26 as part of the ongoing May Fourth Movement and in support of the students in Beijing, who were already on strike. At least 12,000 students participated in the Shanghai strike. SSU branches also sent groups of student lecturers into the nearby villages to apprise the residents of unfolding events in the movement, and SSU students assumed the roles of surrogate police and other officials to ensure city merchants' compliance with the boycott of Japanese goods supported by the movement. The SSU was also involved in the MAY 30TH MOVEMENT of 1925–26.

Bibliography: Jeffrey N. Wasserstrom, *Student Protests in Twentieth-Century China: The View from Shanghai* (Stanford: Stanford University Press, 1991).

Shaseido   *See* SHAKAISHUGI SEINEN DOMEI.

Shingakudo (New Student League)   (Japan) a student organization formed on October 19, 1969 by the Komeito, a political party representing the reformed Buddhist sect, Soka Gakkai. The organization was also called Shingakusei Domei. Its stance was politically moderate and antiwar. In 1970, the Shingakudo claimed a membership of 270,000 at 315 universities, making it one of the largest student organizations in Japan.

Shin Gakusei Domei   *See* SHINGAKUDO.

Shinjin-kai (Society of New Men, or Enlightened Man Society)   (Japan) a well-known and influential student organization that was formed in 1918—the first national association of students. At the end of World War I democratic and socialistic political philosophies swept over Japan, creating a context for the creation of numerous organizations that espoused progressive ideologies. The Shinjin-kai was among the most influential of these. It was founded by a group of students at Tokyo University who were followers of Professor Sakuzo Yoshino, the leader of Taisho. Shinjin-kai adopted the Russian expression *V Narod!* (To the Masses!) as its maxim. The society published the journal *Democracy*, sponsored lectures, studied social theory, interpreted books by foreign authors, and enlisted the membership of workers as well as students through the organization of a labor movement. It was the leading student organization until 1921(?), when the GYOMINKAI (MEN OF DAWN SOCIETY) was founded. In 1928, the minister of education ordered the presidents of the major universities to disband all the so-called social-science study groups, so that by 1929, following the arrests of its leaders, Shinjin-kai was in decline.

Shoeblack Society   (Great Britain) an organization for indigent, neglected, unemployed, and homeless boys founded in London in 1851 by J. McGregor. The society is of some historic note because it was an offshoot of the RAGGED SCHOOL UNION and because McGregor's intent was to provide the boys with work, cleaning the shoes of foreign visitors come to London to see the Great Exhibition. As it turned out, the British liked the boys' shoecleaning service, and the idea spread to other cities—for example, the Liverpool Shoeblack Society was established in that city in 1862. The London Shoeblack Society and others provided dormitories as quarters for the homeless boys.

Shrove Tuesday Riots   (Great Britain) an ongoing series of uprisings by apprentices (mostly youths of age 14 to 22) in London, especially during the early 17th century. The apprentices rioted each Shrove Tuesday, the day before Ash Wednesday, 24 times during the period 1605–1641, often attacking and demolishing brothels as an act of justice (brothels were illegal) on this confessional day before the beginning of Lent. Occasionally, these ritualistic riots became excessively violent, as in 1671 when they erupted in three different areas of the city and involved extensive destruction.

Sian Incident   (China) in effect an army mutiny, with student participation, in Xi'an (Sian), capital of Shaanxi Province, in December 1936 that resulted in the kidnapping of Chiang Kai-shek. The Sian Incident was an outgrowth of the Japanese invasion of Manchuria and agitation for a united front, bringing together Kuomintang (KMT) forces headed by Chiang and the Red Army of the CHINESE COMMUNIST PARTY (CCP) in opposition to the Japanese. This agitation was largely spearheaded by the residual DECEMBER NINTH MOVEMENT. Chang Hsueh-liang (known as the Young Marshall), commander of the Northeast Army headquartered at Xi'an, favored the united front; he had the support of students who had come to Xi'an from Beijing following the December Ninth Movement to work with the troops and also with the civilian residents in fostering nationalist sentiment, at Chang's invitation. Two hundred of these students comprised a special regiment within the Northeast Army and were being trained to become officers. The presence of the students led Chiang Kai-shek, who planned to use the Northeast Army against the Red Army, to accuse Chang Hsueh-liang of harboring communists. On December 9, 1936, thousands of students commemorated the anniversary of the December Ninth Movement by marching from Xi'an to Chiang's suburban headquarters at Lin-tong to petition for ending the civil war and fighting the Japanese. After police shot and wounded two of the students, Chang intervened, halted the march, and personally delivered the students' petition. Enraged that Chang Hsueh-liang supported the students, Chiang Kai-shek severely reprimanded Chang, who thereafter decided on rebellion. Students from Beijing formed part of the hand-picked regiment that staged the December 12 rebellion and captured Generalissimo Chiang. While left-wing students nationwide applauded the kidnapping, which the CCP also praised, the Sian Incident ironically culminated in evisceration of the Leftist student movement. Students supporting the KMT mobilized massive student support for Chiang and pressed for his release. After promising to back formation of a new United Front, Chiang was released on December 25 and, voluntarily accompanied by Chang, returned to the capital, Nanjing. There Chang was imprisoned. (He remained in prison through World War II and after 1949 existed under house arrest on Taiwan.) Reversing the CCP's stand, Mao Zedong supported and welcomed Chiang's release, generating great confusion among left-wing students. Chiang fulfilled the promise to form a United Front and became the nation's undisputed leader. Right-wingers within the KMT created the militaristic Sanmin chu-i Youth Corps, which was dedicated to Chiang as supreme leader, after the example of the HITLER JUGEND. The Northeast Army left Sian to be occupied by troops from Nanjing, and many of the former Beijing students in Xi'an, not knowing where else to turn, trekked northward to join the Red Army. The Sian Incident thus marked the ultimate end of the December Ninth Movement.

Siege of Chicago   *See* BATTLE OF CHICAGO.

Simon Commission Protests   (India) a series of student demonstrations against a British committee of inquiry (the Simon Commission) that visited India in 1928 to review problems related to Indian independence and self-rule and to draft proposals concerning Indian self-government. The Indian National Congress (Congress Party) opposed the commission because there were no Indian nationalists in its membership and called for a show of mass public disapproval of the commission. Students received this call with enthusiasm and embraced the job of organizing demonstrations. In Bombay, where the members of the Simon Commission disembarked, students held a one-day strike, approved a resolution opposing the commission, and staged a demonstration that resulted in some student protestors being injured by police. This demonstration inspired others by students in most of the country's larger cities. These were the first demonstrations in India to be organized on a nationwide scale entirely by students.

Situationists (Great Britain) an individualistic, left-wing student protest group formed during the demonstrations of the 1960s. The group's philosophy was to reject all constraints, existing systems, and accepted forms of protest in order to be totally spontaneous. During such protests as the LONDON SCHOOL OF ECONOMICS REVOLT, they sprayed painted walls and released balloons, but they also revealed courage and commitment in many acts. The Situationists espoused their own brand of socialism—distinct from traditional Marxist views.

Skinheads a youth grouping that apparently originated in Great Britain in the late 1960s but since has appeared throughout the Western nations. The term *Skinheads* derives from their shaved heads. They are conservative, working-class, even reactionary in political and social values and are also xenophobic. The Skinheads' first significant appearance in England occurred at a sit-in in Piccadilly in summer 1969; they were also involved that year in attacks on Pakistanis in Leeds and East London. Xenophobia seems to characterize Skinheads everywhere; for example, in Germany, where Skinheads are identified with neo-Nazism, they have been involved in violent attacks on Turkish resident workers and other foreigners during the 1980s and 1990s.

SLATE (Slate of Candidates) (United States) a student political organization that was formed at the University of California at Berkeley in early 1958 by a coalition of students representing Leftist, cooperative, independent, and religious groups. Originally entitled Toward an Active Student Community (TASC), the organization assumed the name SLATE because it presented for offices in the Berkeley student government a "slate" of candidates who represented opposition to the fraternity members who usually controlled the offices. SLATE's platform included the end of discrimination in

fraternities and sororities, the assurance of fair prices for student housing, the securing of academic freedom, and the provision of equitable wages to student employees. The SLATE candidates lost the election but succeeded in publicizing their platform; in the following academic year, the regents, and the faculty senate approved regulations that prohibited discriminatory restrictions in fraternity and sorority charters. They also obligated faculty members to safeguard students' civil liberties through such means as maintaining the confidentiality of their political views. SLATE also sponsored the convening of similar student political groups, such as POLIT at the University of Chicago and VOICE at the University of Michigan, in an annual conference, the first one held in summer 1959.

SLATE organized petition drives, picketing, and protests against the execution of Caryl Chessman, who was sentenced to die at San Quentin for forcing two women to perform fellatio. (The Chessman case inspired probably the most significant opposition to capital punishment in U.S. history to that time; Chessman was nevertheless executed in 1960.) In addition, SLATE organized the picketing of local stores as a show of support for the Civil Rights movement. SLATE was also responsible for organizing the SAN FRANCISCO CITY HALL DEMONSTRATION against the House Un-American Activities Committee in May 1960. Although SLATE had no more than 200 active members as the latter demonstration unfolded, the group managed to mobilize some 5,000 protestors.

Smith, Sir William Alexander (1854–1914) (Great Britain) founder of the BOYS' BRIGADE. Smith was born on Oct. 27, 1854 near Thurso, Scotland, the eldest of three sons. He attended the Miller Institution but left the school following his father's death in 1868. His mother sold the family's home and sent him to live with and work for her brother, owner of a wholesale soft-goods business in Glasgow. In 1872 he joined the YMCA. Influenced by attending the British crusade of U.S. evangelists Dwight Moody and Ira Sankey, Smith joined the College Free Church in 1874. That same year, he also became a member of the 1st Lanarkshire Rifles, a Glasgow volunteer regiment. In 1879, Smith went into business for himself as a wholesale soft-goods dealer. He was secretary of the Sunday School Teachers' Society and member of a Young Men's Club that formed the core of the Boys' Brigade he founded in 1883. In 1888, Smith left his business to serve as the first full-time secretary of the brigade. His two sons by his first marriage (his first wife died in 1898) also became involved with the brigade. His second wife died following a trip to the United States. Smith died on May 8, 1914 while attending a meeting of Boys' Brigade executives in London.

Bibliography: Roger S. Peacock, *Pioneer of Boyhood: The Story of Sir William A. Smith* (Glasgow: Boys Brigade, 1954).

Socialist Association of Young Workers (SAYW) (Russia) a "class-organization of proletarian youth" formed in the Narva district of St. Petersburg in spring 1917. Its organizers were members of the WORK AND LIGHT league who opposed that league's nonpolitical program in favor of political involvement. The SAYW embraced the ideology of the proletarian class struggle, and 3 of its 11-man executive committee members were young Bolsheviks; the eldest of them, V. Alexeiev, age 21, became the league's principle leader. The SAYW advocated enfranchisement of 18-year-olds, a six-hour workday, and the outlawing of nighttime work for juveniles, and it adopted the Bolshevik Party's program of struggle to overthrow capitalism. At Work and Light's August 1917 conference, the SAYW won the ideological struggle, as the delegates voted to join with SAYW. The SAYW was among the more important of the many precursors of KOMSOMOL.

Socialist Youth Corps (China), a youth organization formed by the CHINESE COMMUNIST PARTY (CCP).

Socialist Youth International (SYI) the first politically oriented international student organization, founded in 1907.

Socialist Youth League (SYL) (China) a youth organization formed through the leadership of Chang T'ai-lei and Ch'en Tu-hsiu (founder of NEW YOUTH) in August 1920 that was the forerunner of the COMMUNIST YOUTH LEAGUE. Its membership was open to youths of age 15 to 28 (later 25). Sundered by conflicting views of socialism, anarchism, and communism, the SYL disbanded in May 1921 but was reconstituted in November 1921 in Shanghai with a Leninist orientation. The SYL held its First National Congress in Canton in May 1922, attended by 25 delegates who represented 2,000 members of 15 branches; it elected a governing executive committee. Although more influential than its parent, the CHINESE COMMUNIST PARTY (CCP) which was officially established on July 1, 1921, the SYL, because of its work with students, peasants, and laborers, was meant to serve as a means of recruiting new members for the fledgling CCP. During 1922 and most of 1923, the SYL published *Pioneer*; in October 1923 it began to publish *Chinese Youth*. At its second congress, held in Canton in August 1923, there were 30 delegates representing an estimated 6,000 members; this indicated rapid, although misleading, growth—the numbers subsequently declined precipitately to 2,500, probably as a result of controversy over the CCP's formation of a United Front with the Kuomintang. At the beginning of 1925, with its membership revived, the SYL held its Third Congress, at which it was decided to change the organization's name to Communist Youth League.

Socialist Youth League (SYL) (United States) a small national student and youth organization founded in 1946 as an affiliate of the Independent Socialist League. Within five years of its founding, SYL had established chapters at 25 colleges and universities. Marxist but anti-Stalinist in orientation, SYL belonged to the so-called THIRD CAMP. Among its publications was the periodical *Anvil and Student Partisan*. Although SYL sponsored a few demonstrations, its major effort was educational—meetings, lectures, conferences—including participation in the programs of other student organizations. In 1954 SYL merged with the YOUNG PEOPLES' SOCIALIST LEAGUE (YPSL) to form the Young Socialist League (YSL), except for a conservative faction which continued as the YPSL. Then in 1957 the YSL became subsumed into this ongoing YPSL, except for some YSL dissidents who broke away to form the American Youth for Socialism; which in 1959 became the YOUNG SOCIALIST ALLIANCE (YSA).

Socialist Youth Movement (Germany) an umbrella term (also called the Socialist Workers Youth Movement) for a movement that originated in different cities as distinct groups that were founded and led by adult socialist workers. The first of these groups was formed in Berlin in June 1904 following the suicide of a young apprentice who had suffered abuse by his master. Another and totally separate group was formed in Mannheim in September 1904. From Berlin, the movement spread through the northern cities; from Mannheim, through southern Germany. The government, regarding it as subversive, tried to suppress the movement with passage in 1908 of the Law of Association, which outlawed political work involving youths. The two groups survived the suppression and merged, founding a periodical entitled *Arbeiter Jugend* that attained a circulation of 100,000 by 1913. Among other causes, the Socialist Youth Movement opposed the military and military training—one reason for their near dissolution during World War I. They also suffered from the disunity that afflicted the Social Democratic Party after 1916, even though the youth movement tried to maintain a certain independence from the party. The movement revived following the war, but after 1933 it went the way of all things opposed by the Nazis. *See also* ARBEITER JUGEND.

Social Science Study Groups (Japan) student organizations that originated in the 1920s for the study of social science, not then part of the Japanese university curriculum. Their orientation was generally Marxist, or socialistic. Probably the inspiration for these groups was SHINJIN-KAI. The groups went into eclipse in the World War II period but were revived after the war, again with a largely Marxist orientation. The groups advocated joint control of universities by students and faculty, democratization of campuses, student self-government, and formation of a student front in opposition to the government, among other goals.

Société des Étudiants   *See* ASSOCIATION GÉNÉRALE DES ÉTUDIANTS.

Society for the Study of Marxism   (China) an organization established by students at the Beijing University near the end of 1918. The students were supported by Li Dazhao, head librarian of the university and later a leader in the CHINESE COMMUNIST PARTY (CCP).

Society of Union and Progress   (Turkey) a revolutionary political movement formed by students in the secular universities. Supposedly, the society originated in 1889 when four students in the medical school of the Turkish military organized themselves as opponents of the government. They quickly won support among students at other institutes of higher education in Istanbul, and in time their organization assumed the name Society of Union and Progress. The society in 1896 staged a coup that failed, but it nevertheless continued to attract new supporters, especially among cadets at the military academy whose Westernized secular education generated impatience with the government. When these cadets graduated, they went on to form revolutionary cells wherever they were stationed in the Ottoman military.

Sokols   (Czechoslovakia) gymnastic societies for the young that were similar in program and purposes to the German TURNVEREIN. The first Sokol (the Bohemian word for "hawk" or "falcon") was established in Prague in 1862. The Sokols emphasize physical fitness and a communal spirit that is attained through a program of mass calisthenics and gymnastics. They sponsor gymnastic festivals that involve thousands of youths. The Sokol movement came to the United States in 1867 when the first Sokol opened in New York City. The American Sokol Union represents scores of Sokols throughout the United States, which were created to serve youths of Czech descent.

Sons of Daniel Boone   (United States) an organization for boys that was begun by Daniel Carter Beard (1850–1941) in 1905. Beard, referred to as Uncle Dan, was an outdoorsman and a writer for *Recreation* magazine and of guidebooks for boys, such as *American Boys' Handy Book* (1882), that sold well and widely. The Sons of Daniel Boone emphasized the outdoors as a means of developing manliness and toughness, but it never flourished through lack of organization. Renamed as the Boy Pioneers, it survived only into the 1920s. Beard, however, was also involved, at least in a titular fashion, in the organization of the BOY SCOUTS OF AMERICA.

Sorbonne Explosion   (France) a massive student demonstration in 1963 at the University of Paris, the first of several protests to demand improved classroom, library, and living conditions. As a result of a baby boom after World War II and of government lack of foresight and planning to accommodate the resultant large numbers of students, university classrooms were exceedingly overcrowded, with no room for half of the students to get in to hear lectures; textbooks and copies of lectures were very expensive; living quarters were inadequate and expensive. Thus, students began to protest. In 1962, government authorities banned public protests by university students but made no effort to rectify the physical conditions that caused the protests. Finally in November 1963, about 10,000 students at the Sorbonne defied the ban and protested against the poor conditions. Some 4,500 police were sent against them throughout the Latin Quarter, attacking students with clubs and fists, spraying them with fire hoses, and arresting scores of them. On the following day, 300,000 students at the nation's 23 universities went on general strike, joined by half of the professors. In February 1964, the UNION NATIONALE DES ÉTUDIANTS DE FRANCE (UNEF) called for new demonstrations; they were again put down by the police.

Southern Negro Youth Congress (SNYC)   (United States) an organization founded in 1937, led by blacks, headquartered in Richmond, Virginia, and devoted to promoting racial equality. The three student founders of SNYC, Louis Burnham, James Jackson, and Edward Strong, had served as leaders in the AMERICAN STUDENT UNION (ASU) and the AMERICAN YOUTH CONGRESS (AYC); all three were communists (SNYC was the youth affiliate of the communist-controlled National Negro Congress). From its beginnings, SNYC was involved in civil rights and labor issues in the larger society, not just with campus concerns. For example, SNYC organized strikes in support of improved wages and working conditions for black workers in Richmond tobacco-processing plants, and they advocated an antilynching law that was being considered by Congress. SNYC's first convention, the All Southern Negro Youth Conference, occurred in Richmond in February 1937; it focused on achieving improved economic and political opportunities for African Americans. SNYC also promoted cultural programs; it set up the Negro Community Theater in Richmond and the People's Community Theater in New Orleans as a means of fostering black pride. In its first year, SNYC established youth councils in communities throughout Virginia, North Carolina, Alabama, and Tennessee.

Sozialistischer Deutscher Studentenbund (German Socialist Student Union, SDS)   (Germany) an organization for university students formed by the Social

Gendarmes with clubs in hand charge some of the 1,500 students who massed near the Sorbonne in Paris's Latin Quarter on November 7, 1963, protesting the government's education policies. Students demanded the resignation of Education Minister Christian Fouchet and threw mud at the police. (AP/WIDE WORLD PHOTOS)

Democratic Party (SDP) in Hamburg in 1946. Although the SDP's intent was to affiliate students more closely with the party, conflicts arose between the SDP and the SDS, especially after the SDP repudiated orthodox Marxism at its 1959 congress in favor of a policy of, in effect, reforming capitalism—a repudiation the SDS refused to embrace. The party terminated funding for SDS in July 1960 and, in 1961, banned simultaneous membership in the SDS and the SDP. The SDS members then moved increasingly leftward politically and participated in protests against the Vietnam War and other political causes. The expanded horizon resulted from a spontaneous student demonstration against Moise Tshombe, prime minister of the Democratic Republic of the Congo, during his visit to Berlin on December 18, 1964—they threw tomatoes at his car and denounced him as the "murderer of [Patrice] Lumumba." This event awakened SDS to Third World issues and struggles, and

the Vietnam War became a central focus for the group. On February 4, 1966 its members demonstrated against the war, demanding U.S. withdrawal, throwing eggs at America House, and lowering the U.S. flag to half staff. When the president of the Free University apologized for this attack, SDS expressed outrage. The West Berlin SDS came into increasing national prominence after the group's involvement in a protest against Vice President Hubert Humphrey on April 6, 1967 and another against a state visit by the Shah of Iran on June 2, 1967 that culminated in a police officer's killing of a student, Benno Ohnesorg. (*See* BERLIN ANTI-SHAH PROTEST.) Some 20,000 students marched in the procession that accompanied Ohnesorg's coffin to the Berlin border, and his funeral in Hanover on June 9 resulted in a manifesto for radical political change and in the formation of the Extraparliamentary Opposition (Ausserparlamentarische Opposition), led by SDS, which itself was soon led by

Rudi DUTSCHKE. On February 18, 1968, SDS conducted a protest march in West Berlin against the Vietnam War which generated a counterprotest three days later by 100,000 Berliners who condemned Dutschke. On April 11, 1968 just before Easter, a lone gunman tried to shoot Dutschke; in response, student riots erupted throughout Germany, resulting in two deaths in Munich. SDS's leadership role began to decline as many new radical groups emerged during the 1968–69 winter, and in March 1970 SDS dissolved itself.

Spartakus (Germany) officially the Marxistischer Studentenbund Spartakus, an extreme left-wing student group that originated as part of the SOZIALISTISCHER DEUTSCHER STUDENTENBUND (SDS) and the German Communist Party (DKP) but then declared independence from its parent. By the mid-1970s, Spartakus claimed 4,500 members (6,100 by 1980) on 110 university campuses, making it the largest left-wing student group in West Germany. Spartakus published the *Röte Blatter*, which had a circulation of 30,000 in 1981 when it held effective control of many of the university student parliaments and constituted a strong influence in university politics. Spartakus adhered to the party line of, and received some funding from, the Soviet Union. (It should be noted that the DKP also had two other youth organizations: the Sozialistische Deutsche Arbeitsjugend for young apprentices, students, and workers; and the Junge Pioniere for children. In 1981, the former had about 35,000 members; the latter, about 3,000.)

Stahlhelm, Bund der Frontsoldaten (Steel Helmet, Union of Frontsoldiers) (Germany) an organization of World War I veterans that recruited university students and provided such programs for them as paramilitary training and "war sport" camps. The Stahlhelm set up its first student auxiliaries in 1923. In October 1929, it formed the Stahlhelm-Studentenring Langemark as a separate student organization. Even after Adolf Hitler became chancellor in January 1933, the Stalhelm groups remained independent; fraternity students joined them as a preferred alternative to belonging to the NATIONAL SOCIALIST GERMAN STUDENT UNION or the STURMABTEILUNG (SA). In July 1933, however, the Stahlhelm Studentenring Langemark placed itself under the authority of the Student Union; in April 1934 it ceased to exist, subsumed completely into the Student Union.

Stilyagi (Russia) youths of the 1950s and 1960s, similar to the TEDDY BOYS of Great Britain, who pursued a rather Bohemian, self-indulgent lifestyle that was devoted to leisure pursuits and minimal work that outraged political officials. Like the Teddy Boys, the *stilyagi* had their own bizarre forms of clothing. They wore oversize shoes, loud neckties and socks, and padded jackets with loud check designs, and they sported elaborately styled hair. They cultivated Western leisure pursuits, including jazz music and dance fads, and adopted U.S. slang terms and English nicknames. The government at national and local levels waged campaigns against the *stilyagi* as idle violaters of social mores.

Stockholm Riot (Sweden) a spontaneous mass hysteria involving about 3,000 youths (more than two-thirds of them under 21 years old) that erupted on New Years Eve 1957 in Stockholm. The marauding youths hurled cans and other missiles at police and tried to frighten the police horses with fire crackers. They forced motorists to stop and tore off their cars' doors. The riot comprised the most violent youth-gang uprising of the decade in Sweden.

Stockholm University Protest (Sweden) a student demonstration in May 1968 at the University of Stockholm to protest against a proposed curricular change. When authorities suggested the creation of 35 distinct fields of study in the liberal arts (or philosophy) faculties, students protested that the change would diminish their traditional freedom to choose courses of study. Several hundred students occupied the union building during the protest, which was noteworthy not only for its moderation but also for its rarity—very few student demonstrations occurred in Sweden, even during this year of massive and violent student uprisings worldwide.

Stop the Draft Week (United States) the week of October 16–21, 1967, marked by mostly student-organized demonstrations and protests against the Selective Service System and the Vietnam War. During the week demonstrations occurred throughout the nation at which university students and other young men handed in their draft cards to be collected and sent to the Justice Department. Among the most significant demonstrations was the siege of the Oakland Induction Center, which involved perhaps 20,000 protestors, a large percentage of them students from Berkeley. The siege lasted for days and involved clashes between police and protestors over control of a 20-block area of Oakland that left a police officer and 24 protestors hospitalized. The Oakland conflict was one of the week's events that indicated a shift in protest tactics "from dissent to resistance"—the adoption of political disruption and violent confrontation as protest techniques. Another significant event of the week was the DOW CHEMICAL SIT-IN. Stop the Draft Week culminated in the famous MARCH ON THE PENTAGON.

Street Gangs not a definable movement but a nearly universal urban youth phenomenon—extant in at least every major city of Asia, Europe, Latin America, and North America. These youth groups have traditionally identified themselves with their city neighborhoods, joining together as a means of demonstrating solidarity and to do battle with groups from other neighborhoods and, in more recent eras, with immigrants from other nations. The gangs' origins in Europe trace to the Middle Ages. In Florence during the decade 1380–1390, for example, two groups known as Berta and Magroni reportedly battled each other for 50 consecutive nights. It was especially common for such groups to fight each other during carnival periods. This gang warfare sometimes resulted in deaths, as, for example, in Douai in the 16th century. Every nation has its own terms for street gangs, usually pejorative in connotation—in Germany, for example, they have been referred to as *Meuten* (packs of hounds) and *Rudel* (herds or wolfpacks). Although they have undergone varied changes through the years—in particular following the industrialization of the 19th century—street gangs continue to the present time and have proliferated. A few gangs are accorded individual entries in this encyclopedia.

Probably the most notorious contemporary gang in the United States is the Crips—along with their rivals the Bloods. The Crips, or Eight-Tray Gangster Crips, originated in south-central Los Angeles in the 1960s and came into national notoriety in the 1980s because of increasing gang killings in the city. In fact, in 1984, there were 212 gang killings in Los Angeles county; by 1991, the number had surged to 721. In 1992, the Los Angeles district attorney's office estimated that there were 125,000 to 130,000 gang members in the county, but this figure included even innocuous informal groups. A White House conference of May 1996 announced a total of more than 16,000 gangs with more than 500,000 members nationwide; the conference declared that gangs could now be found in 800 cities and towns—up from

Former Five Duce Crips members Charles Rache (center) and Michael Baker (left) with fellow gang members in South Central Los Angeles. The two along with about 25 other gang members showed up at the African-American Unity Center to support Brotherhood Crusade leader Danny Bakewell and former pro football player Jim Brown in an anticipatory call for peace following the verdict pending in the Rodney King civil rights trial. (AP/WIDE WORLD PHOTOS)

only 100 in 1970—including 80 percent of all cities with populations exceeding 100,000. Some gangs, now highly organized with hierarchies, turf maps, and systems for collecting "internal taxes," had "franchised" themselves, opening branches in smaller towns. The Crips themselves are now represented by branches in most major U.S. cities.

Student (Russia) an activist student journal begun in 1903 by Grigory Nestroyev, a former student at Kharkov University whose involvement in the student movement there had resulted in his arrest in 1902. Essentially socialistic in his politics, Nestroyev used *Student* to advocate national unity in the student movement. To this end, *Student* organized a three-day national student conference in Odessa in November 1903. Delegates attended from the universities in St. Petersburg, Moscow, Kharkov, Odessa, Kiev, and Riga. They drafted a statement that defined the principles of the future student movement and called for creation of coalition councils with student representatives of the Social Democrats, Social Revolutionaries, and other political groups. The statement also urged the banning of ZEMLYACHESTVA (student societies) that were not politically oriented, so that in the future the student movement would be devoted to revolutionary politics. The great majority of students at the universities rejected implementing these principles in favor of continuing to pursue students' own nonpolitical corporate and academic issues.

Student Christian Movement (United States) an inclusive term for what historically has been primarily the university campus affiliates of the YOUNG MEN'S CHRISTIAN ASSOCIATION and the YOUNG WOMEN'S CHRISTIAN ASSOCIATION but also including a myriad of groups representing the Roman Catholic and Protestant denominations. This movement has been at times, such as during the 1920s when it included an estimated 5 percent of the undergraduate population, the most important of all student movements with respect to numbers of students who were actively involved.

Student Congress Against War (United States) a conference held in Chicago in December 1932—among the first such conferences convened as part of the important student antiwar movement of the 1930s. The conference was organized by the NATIONAL STUDENT LEAGUE (NSL) and supported by other student groups, including the student wing of the LEAGUE FOR INDUSTRIAL DEMOCRACY (LID). The Chicago congress was inspired by the AMSTERDAM ANTIWAR CONGRESS (or World Congress Against War) held in Amsterdam the previous August. The Chicago congress drew 680 student delegates from 89 colleges and universities in 30 states. They represented a broad array of groups, including Christian fundamentalists and labor delegates, but the majority were Leftists. Among those attending was the famous Chicago settlement-house leader Jane Addams, who had received the Nobel Peace Prize in 1931; she presented an address to the congress condemning all wars of any kind—a bone of contention for many Leftists who opposed only imperialistic wars. Given the disparateness of the groups represented, the congress was marked, not surprisingly, by raging disputes among Communist, pacifist, and socialist delegates. The congress nevertheless adopted resolutions that supported official U.S. recognition of the Soviet Union, opposed wars of imperialism, advocated a nationwide student antiwar campaign, and called for organization of a movement to abolish Reserve Officer Training Corps (ROTC) programs. Delegates also denounced the World Court and the League of Nations as irrelevant. The congress helped set the stage for the broader peace movement to come and also brought together students of disparate political views under the single banner of peace at a critical juncture— Adolf Hitler would become chancellor of Germany about a month later, on January 30, 1933. On January 22, 1933, a southern California Student Conference Against War convened at University of California at Los Angeles, with 300 students representing 29 California schools attending; Upton Sinclair presented the keynote address. Similar conferences were held at Columbia University and New York University in fall 1933. The student antiwar movement was definitely launched.

Bibliography: Ralph S. Brax, *The First Student Movement: Student Activism in the United States During the 1930s* (Port Washington, N.Y.: Kennikat Press, 1981).

Student Cooperatives (United States) associations of students formed during the Great Depression to save expenses through communal room and board provided in student-owned and/or student-operated dormitories. Cooperatives were formed at Texas A&M University, University of Idaho, University of Michigan, and a few other schools in 1932. At Michigan, for example, the Socialist Club set up a boardinghouse for 30 students who were charged $2.00 per day for room and board and in exchange had to work at the house for a designated number of hours each week. Cooperatives quickly became popular, and by 1938 more than 100 campuses had cooperative boardinghouses that provided housing and meals for more than 70,000 students. Some cooperatives branched into other endeavors also, such as operating book and supply stores, laundries, cafeterias, and restaurants.

Student Defenders of Democracy (SDD) (United States) a prowar student organization, apparently the largest of several, founded in January 1941. Gaining a membership of 5,000 during its first year, SDD supported the Lend-Lease program and increased aid to the Allies, while also promoting civil rights and labor union-

ization. SDD published a journal entitled *SOS* (for *Sweethearts of Servicemen*). In October 1941, the organization joined with the Student League for Progressive Action and other prowar groups to establish a Student Merger Committee; in December 1941 these groups all merged to form the STUDENT LEAGUE OF AMERICA (SLA).

Student Defense Corps (Korea) an organization established by the Liberal Party of Syngman Rhee, first president (1948–60) of the Republic of Korea (South Korea). The corps' purpose was to regiment students to support Rhee's government, including the staging of demonstrations.

Studentenbund (Germany) a paramilitary organization for university students that was formed by the Nazi Party in 1932. All members of the NATIONAL SOCIALIST GERMAN STUDENT UNION were required to train for six months with the STURMABTEILUNG (SA), followed by two years with the Studentenbund, and then return to the SA or to join the Schutzstaffel (SS). The Studentenbund aroused opposition from both the SA and the SS, and it disappeared after the Nazis came to power in 1933.

Studententag (Germany) an annual university-students convention that was held during the years of the Weimar Republic (1919–33).

Studentischer Verbandedienst (Student Fraternity League Service) (Germany) an organization of student fraternities formed in spring 1932 in opposition to the NATIONAL SOCIALIST GERMAN STUDENT UNION. The league tried to persuade student councils throughout Germany and Austria to vote Student Union members out of office in a belated but promising effort to prevent them from taking total control of the DEUTSCHE STUDENTENSCHAFT. The league later changed its name to Hochschulpolitische Arbeitsgemeinschaft (University-Political Study Group). Their opposition, along with that of other groups, to the Student Union appeared on the verge of success by the end of 1932, but Adolf Hitler's becoming chancellor in January 1933 derailed its momentum.

Student League for Industrial Democracy (SLID) (United States) the youth wing of the LEAGUE FOR INDUSTRIAL DEMOCRACY (LID) that was formed in 1932. LID's student section had succeeded well and numbered 3,000 members in 1930 so that at its 1931 conference held at Union Theological Seminary, LID prepared the preliminary organizational work to create SLID as a separate student branch. In December 1932 LID officially created SLID to organize students, promote LID's original educational goals, support labor-union strikes, stage protests over academic issues, and otherwise pursue a more activist role on university campuses. SLID received financial and administrative support from LID. Within a year of its founding, SLID had chapters at more than 50 colleges and universities. SLID, whose leaders were socialist oriented, opposed communists and was critical of the Soviet Union, but it attracted liberal students of varied political views and formed links with other student groups. In 1933, SLID became the first U.S. affiliate of the International Socialist Students' Federation (ISSF). The year 1934 was a peak moment for SLID: the organization helped to mobilize the first nationwide STUDENT STRIKE AGAINST WAR, which involved 150,000 students. In 1935 Joseph P. Lash, perhaps the most important student leader of the decade, became SLID's executive secretary. (Lash also became a personal friend of Eleanor Roosevelt; in 1964 he published a memoir of her and, in 1971, the well-known *Eleanor and Franklin*.) Despite SLID's anticommunist stance, in 1935 it merged with the NATIONAL STUDENT LEAGUE (NSL) to form the AMERICAN STUDENT UNION (ASU), which thereafter overshadowed SLID. When the ASU effectively disbanded after 1941, SLID resumed its original identity but never regained its earlier stature; from 1936 to 1945, it had hardly any separate representation at colleges and universities. After World War II, LID returned to funding SLID, but the student group remained small, with 400 members in 15 chapters in 1947 and a peak memberships of 500 and 25 chapters in the 1950s. During the 1950s, SLID maintained its anticommunist stance and its opposition to the Soviet Union, while supporting the Marshall Plan, academic freedom, civil liberties, and racial tolerance. But its membership and budget both remained small during the decade, and its 1958 convention drew only 13 delegates. In 1960, SLID changed its name to STUDENTS FOR A DEMOCRATIC SOCIETY (SDS) and adopted the Civil Rights movement as a major cause. In the 1930s, SLID had sponsored a journal originally entitled *Revolt* and later, *Student Outlook*; in the 1950s it had a journal entitled *SLID Voice* and other publications; in 1959 it began to publish a new magazine entitled *Venture*. One of the most important student organizations of the 1930s, SLID counted among its members numerous persons who attained renown in subsequent years, including Daniel Bell, James FARMER, Sidney Hook, Max Lerner, Talcott Parsons, Walter Reuther, Will Rogers, and William Shirer.

Bibliography: Ralph S. Brax, *The First Student Movement: Student Activism in the United States During the 1930s* (Port Washington, N.Y.: Kennikat Press, 1981).

Student League of America (SLA) (United States) a prowar student organization that was formed in December 1941 through the merger of the STUDENT DEFENDERS OF DEMOCRACY (SDD) and other prowar groups. SLA promoted programs by which students could support the U.S. war effort. It was also supported by the NATIONAL STUDENT FEDERATION of America.

Student Nonviolent Coordinating Committee (SNCC) (United States) a student organization that was dedicated to achieving desegregation through nonviolent means; it was an outgrowth of the GREENSBORO SIT-INS in 1960. The initial inspiration for creating SNCC occurred at a conference at Shaw University in April 1960, where Martin Luther King, Jr., and other civil rights leaders urged the 200 attending delegates to become affiliated with the Southern Christian Leadership Conference (SCLC) or some other major civil rights group. In response, they formed a temporary coordinating committee to maintain communication among student groups at various campuses. Subsequently, they met as the Temporary Student Nonviolent Coordinating Committee, which elected Marion Barry (thereafter first chairman of SNNC and later mayor of Washington, D.C.) as chairman; they were presented with a statement of purpose, drafted by Rev. James Lawson on May 14, 1960, that was formally adopted by SNNC at a meeting in October 1960 when the word *Temporary* was dropped from the organization's name. The statement reads in part:

> We affirm the philosophical or religious ideal of nonviolence as the foundation of our purpose, the pre-supposition of our faith, and the manner of our action. Nonviolence as it grows from Judaic-Christian traditions seeks a social order of justice permeated by love. Integration of human endeavor represent the crucial first step towards such a society. . . . By appealing to conscience and standing on the moral nature of human existence, nonviolence nurtures the atmosphere in which reconciliation and justice become actual possibilities.

SNNC adhered to these ideals during its early years, especially under the guidance of James Forman, who became executive secretary in 1961. SNNC pursued both direct action and voter registration activities, participating as FREEDOM RIDERS and in FREEDOM SUMMER and registering voters in Mississippi and other Southern states. SNNC participated in demonstrations that involved more than 70,000 white and black students in about 50 towns and cities in the South in 1961 alone and resulted in the desegregation of restaurants and other establishments. In 1966, Stokely CARMICHAEL became SNNC's leader, and the organization shifted to a militant and confrontational approach, including intimidation and violence; under his leadership and that of H. Rap Brown, it adopted the BLACK POWER program and excluded whites from membership. SNNC declined rapidly during the late 1960s. In July 1969, the organization dropped *Nonviolent* from its name, replacing it with *National*; Brown, who had stepped down in 1968, also resumed the chairmanship.

Bibliography: Clayborne Carson, *In Struggle: SNCC and the Black Awakening of the 1960s* (Cambridge: Harvard University Press, 1981).

Student Peace Union (SPU)   (United States) the largest and most significant U.S. student organization of its time; devoted to pacifism, it was founded in April 1959 as a Midwestern "regional student peace organization." Chicago-area pacifist students, who were affiliated with the American Friends Service Committee (AFSC), convened a conference in Chicago that officially established SPU. Assisted by members of the AFSC, the SPU spread nationwide; by 1963 it had 60 chapters and claimed 4,000 student members, and its monthly *Bulletin* had a national circulation exceeding 8,000. The SPU reflected the THIRD CAMP position in charging both the Soviet Union and the United States with responsibility for the nuclear arms race and the cold war. The SPU sponsored lectures, debates, and discussions; organized anti-ROTC protests and regional peace demonstrations; and supported the Civil Rights movement. Perhaps SPU's most noted event was the WASHINGTON ACTION PROJECT of February 1962 that brought to Washington 8,000 to 10,000 protestors for the largest pacifist demonstration in the capital since the 1930s. Leadership of the SPU by 1962 was largely in the control of members of the YOUNG PEOPLE'S SOCIALIST LEAGUE (YPSL). By summer 1964 SPU was declining rapidly, and so the delegates to the annual convention voted to disband the organization. Its decline resulted from the signing of the partial nuclear-test-ban treaty between the United States and the Soviet Union in November 1963 and from the shift of national attention to the Civil Rights movement. In 1966 it dissolved.

Student Power   (United States) a major ideological principle and shibboleth of the student movement of the second half of the 1960s and into the 1970s. Definitions of the concepts underlying "student power" varied from group to group, but essentially it entailed achieving and asserting the ability both to influence and to make decisions concerning university policies and also, to some extent, to effect reforms of the U.S. social, economic, and political systems. Implicit in the term were student determination to play a larger role in making decisions on curricula, admissions policies, and investment of endowment funds; the achievement of a "reconstructuring" of the university that shifted power from administrators and boards to students and faculty; the attainment of "freedom" for students; and, for some student movement groups, the effecting of revolutionary changes in U.S. politics and society. Implicit in the term also was the use of force, if necessary, to achieve these ends.

Students' Brotherhood   (India) probably the most significant student organization of its era in Bombay, where it was founded in 1889. The brotherhood was devoted mostly to intellectual, cultural, and social interests; from 1907 to 1914 it published the *Students' Brotherhood Quarterly* containing articles on literary and cultural subjects. Its members were also active in Hindu, Muslim, and Parsi student organizations. The brotherhood showed a rare activism during the 1927–28 academic year when the percentage of students who passed the matriculation examination declined sharply; in response, the brotherhood protested and called for a student street demonstration. About 150 students began a march to the convocation hall where the senate of the University of Bombay was meeting; as the demonstrators proceeded, their numbers swelled to include 10,000 protestors. They forced the senate to review the examination results. The brotherhood reprised this effort in 1936 in response to the so-called Matriculation Massacre, when the university authorities' decision to require increased competence in English resulted in a jump in failures. Joining with the Bombay Students' Union, the brotherhood organized a student protest that attracted 20,000 demonstrators. The students continued to press the issue, again storming into a meeting of the university senate and demanding that passing marks for the exam be raised from 20 percent to 44 percent. The students won the administration's offer to those who had failed the opportunity to take a second exam, but after only 21 percent passed this exam, the protest slowly died out. During June of the same year, inspired by the Matriculation Massacre effort, the brotherhood and the union convened an all-city students' conference that drew 1,000 students and drafted a Students' Charter—a precedent-setting document that influenced student groups throughout the nation. The charter reaffirmed the right to freedom of "thought, speech, and association" and demanded that the government recognize student organizations as equivalent to organizations of merchants or workers and act through them to promote the well-being of students and to encourage "self-government, discipline, and teamwork" among students. In subsequent years, as students became increasingly politicized in response to the nationalist movement, the Students' Brotherhood's influence waned, and the organization died out after 1940.

Bibliography: Philip G. Altbach, *Student Politics in Bombay* (Bombay and New York: Asia Publishing House, 1965).

Students' Congress   (India) a political organization for university students formed and sponsored by the Indian National Congress (founded 1885). The Students' Congress supported Indian National Congress Party candidates in elections, and whenever Congress leaders were arrested for their activities opposing the British Raj, Students' Congress members assumed the leadership of the Congress. Following the achievement of Independence in 1947 and the Congress Party's control of the new government, the Congress disbanded the Students' Congress in 1948 and tried to establish nonpolitical student organizations, such as the NATIONAL UNION OF STUDENTS (NUS), in it place.

Student Self-Governing Associations   (Japan) essentially student councils founded at the universities during the late 1940s. Students meeting at Waseda University in May 1946 adopted the idea of student self-government and called a meeting of nationwide student representatives on the issue in June that resulted in November in creation of the National Student Self-Governing Union. The union is dedicated to the establishment of student councils, the polling of students, and the effecting of campus democratization. In January 1947, Tokyo University became the first to form a student self-governing association (*jichikai*) that was acceded to by the administration; other universities quickly followed. The nature of the associations varies somewhat among campuses, with the larger universities having a separate association for each department or faculty. The associations coordinate student activities and administer student facilities (dormitories, canteens, etc.). All students are automatically enrolled. Each association is headed by a committee that is supported by student fees and elected by the student members (all automatically enrolled at the time of registration) which elects a standing committee with a chairman.

Students for a Democratic Society (SDS) (United States) an organization founded (assuming its name) in 1960 (*see* STUDENT LEAGUE FOR INDUSTRIAL DEMOCRACY) but formally established at Port Huron, Michigan in June 1962 that is generally considered to have constituted the vanguard of the U.S. student movement of the 1960s and also probably the major element within the NEW LEFT movement. In its original manifestation as the Student League for Industrial Democracy (SLID), the organization was a student offshoot of the LEAGUE FOR INDUSTRIAL DEMOCRACY (LID) of which University of Michigan students had gained control; now as SDS, it became an independent organization inspired by the STUDENT NONVIOLENT COORDINATING COMMITTEE (SNCC) but with broader and more distinctly political goals than those of the civil rights organization. About 60 university students (mostly undergraduates) representing 11 institutions attended the Port Huron meeting that founded the new, independent SDS; they chose Tom HAYDEN to be SDS's first president. Hayden, a graduate of the University of Michigan, drafted the PORT HURON STATEMENT that defined the new group's broad goals.

SDS grew rapidly in numbers of both chapters and individual members because of its emphasis on varied issues rather than a single issue, the intellectual capabilities of its leaders, its accommodation of varied political views, and other strengths. By 1964, there were 27 chapters with 1,200 members, and the following year membership jumped to more than 4,000 in 125 chapters. This large one-year growth resulted from interest generated by the FREE SPEECH MOVEMENT (FSM) at the University of California at Berkeley in fall 1964 and increasing antiwar sentiment as the Vietnam War escalated. By 1968, there were chapters at nearly 300 colleges and universities with a total of about 30,000 individual members. But the group's effectiveness in attracting nonmember supporters for its rallies and demonstrations far exceeded the strength suggested by these numbers. During its first four years, SDS focused on achieving political and social reforms through peaceful and organizational activities such as TEACH-INS that opposed the Vietnam War. One of its major undertakings was the Economic Research and Action Project (ERAP), begun in August 1963 and designed primarily to educate university students about the realities of working class life as a prelude to organizing community groups—an indication of SDS's original interest in diverse issues. The Political Education Project (PEP) of 1964 promoted SDS involvement in the presidential and congressional election of that year, and the Peace Research and Education Project (PREP) was designed to educate students about foreign policy issues. Perhaps SDS's most noteworthy project was organization of the MARCH ON WASHINGTON to end the war in Vietnam of April 1965, which earned SDS major stature as a leader of the antiwar movement.

Following a meeting in June 1966, the focus of SDS shifted to the achievement of university reforms that would improve the quality of students' lives. From 1968 on, however, SDS's goal was STUDENT POWER—in SDS's case a confrontational effort to change not just the university system but to unite with workers, Mexican Americans, or other groups to achieve power within the political system to force reforms. At a December 1968 convention, an extreme leftist faction maneuvered the founding of a new youth organization named the Revolutionary Youth Movement (RYM), but the RYM in turn would fracture into WEATHERMAN and a less-militant left-wing group called RYM-II. Each of these groups claimed to be the real SDS, and the factionalism clearly foreshadowed the decline of the SDS as a viable organization. Its members did participate in the "counterinaugural" in January 1969 (*see* NATIONAL MOBILIZATION COMMITTEE TO END THE WAR IN VIETNAM), in the MARCH AGAINST DEATH in November 1969, and in other antiwar demonstrations. In October 1969, the Weatherman SDS staged a violent demonstration in Chicago as a protest of the CHICAGO 8 TRIAL. SDS held its final annual convention in the Chicago Coliseum in June 1969, with some 1,500 delegates attending. It was here that the Weatherman group emerged as a separatist group and irreparable fragmentation occurred. SDS's demise appeared well in process when 13 of its leaders were indicted by a grand jury in Detroit, Michigan, on July 23, 1970 for "conspiring to bomb and kill." Within a year, the SDS had ceased to exist, and the indicted leaders had gone underground.

Bibliography: Kirkpatrick Sale, *SDS* (New York: Random House, 1973).

Students for America (SFA) (United States) a conservative, nationalistic organization that originated in

Los Angeles in 1951 as the National Collegiate Mac-Arthur Clubs, its initial purpose being to promote General Douglas MacArthur as the Republican Party's presidential nominee for 1952. Failing in that effort, it became the SFA in 1952. The group published a monthly newspaper entitled *American Student*. Although SFA emphasized educational issues, it was dedicated to opposing left-wing politics at universities and colleges and hired a national security director to monitor radical views espoused by students and faculty members. SFA claimed to have 2,500 members at 120 schools in 1954. The SFA attacked the NATIONAL STUDENT ASSOCIATION (NSA) as a communist front organization and encouraged its members to infiltrate left-wing groups and report their activities to government authorities. Although SFA never achieved major impact and effectively died out after 1955, it did evidence the influence of McCarthyism on university campuses.

Students for Democratic Action (SDA) (United States) a politically liberal student organization that was founded in 1948 with the sponsorship and financial support of Americans for Democratic Action (ADA). Following its 1948 organizational drive, the SDA had chapters on 148 university and college campuses and a total membership of 5,000 students, but its membership fell off after 1950, partly reflecting an overall decline in the student movement during this period. By 1955 there were only 65 chapters with a total of 2,000 members. SDA joined with other groups, including the NATIONAL STUDENT ASSOCIATION (NSA) and the CONGRESS OF RACIAL EQUALITY (CORE), to foster its own advocacy of civil rights and other causes, but it consistently remained virulently anticommunist, although socialist groups were active within its membership. SDA actively participated in political campaigns, supported the United Nations and economic recovery aid to Europe, opposed universal military training, and promoted civil rights, civil liberties, and academic freedom. Although a relatively small organization, SDA was probably the most important student political organization of the 1950s—certainly the most important liberal organization. But it suffered from radical students' attacks on its anticommunist stance, from internal dissension, and from burdensome interference by its ADA mentors. In 1959, SDA disbanded by merging with ADA.

Students for McCarthy (United States) an organization of thousands of university and college students who supported the candidacy of Senator Eugene McCarthy of Minnesota in the 1968 presidential election. Many of these students worked in McCarthy's primary campaigns. The male students shaved their beards, got short haircuts, and donned mainstream clothing in order not to offend conservative voters. Attracted to McCarthy because of his longstanding opposition to the Vietnam War,

students joined in his grass-roots campaign, helping with fund raising, organization, and canvassing. So many young people were involved in the McCarthy campaign that it garnered the epithet "children's crusade" in the news media.

Students' Representative Council (Great Britain) the first British students' union, the Students' Representative Council (SRC) was founded at the University of Edinburgh in 1884. Inspired by visiting the University of Strasburg during the previous year, Fitzroy Bell created the plan for the council. By one account, the SRC was actualized following an election for university rector won by the candidate of the University Conservative Association, which thereafter invited the members of the opposition group, the University Liberal Association, to dinner. At the dinner, it was proposed that this initial union be made permanent, resulting in the first SRC. Within a few years, SRCs were established at all the other Scottish universities. Fitzroy Bell, one of the first presidents of the Edinburgh SRC, later served as secretary of the Scottish Universities Commission.

Bibliography: Michael Sanderson, ed., *The Universities in the Nineteenth Century* (London: Routledge and Kegan Paul, 1975).

Students' Society for National Salvation (China) an organization, originally named the Patriotic Society of Students, that was formed in summer 1918 by student representatives meeting in Shanghai. This effort to unify the student movement was part of the save-the-nation movement; it resulted from adverse reaction to the secretly negotiated Sino-Japanese Military Mutual Assistance Conventions by which the Chinese government awarded Japan the right to station troops in Manchuria and Outer Mongolia, to assign Japanese officers for training Chinese army and navy personnel, and other concessions. Although kept secret by the two governments, news of the negotiations and partial contents of the conventions were revealed in newspaper accounts, resulting in public outrage over the Chinese government's pro-Japanese stance and the burgeoning of the save-the-nation movement. On May 21, 1918, about 2,000 students from colleges and schools in Beijing demonstrated against the conventions, visiting the office of the president to demand annulment of the agreements; the president placated them with promises. Similar demonstrations occurred in Shanghai, Tianjin, and other cities, requesting local governments to pressure the central government in Beijing. Although the student demonstrations died down, merchants joined the protests by meeting and petitioning the government. Out of these demonstrations, a precursor of the MAY FOURTH MOVEMENT, came the impetus to form the Students' Society for National Salvation, itself a forerunner of the STUDENT UNION OF PEKING. The society, with the particular support of students at the National University of Beijing, began to publish *The Citizen Magazine* on January 1, 1919. The journal advocated a patriotic uprising and thus went beyond the literary and intellectual revolution spearheaded by the NEW TIDE SOCIETY's *Renaissance*.

Student Strike Against War (United States) a major event that was initiated in April 1934 to foster the student antiwar movement of the 1930s. Organized by the STUDENT LEAGUE FOR INDUSTRIAL DEMOCRACY (SLID) and the NATIONAL STUDENT LEAGUE (NSL) and arising out of those two groups' experience with the COLUMBIA STRIKE, the antiwar strike occurred on April 13 beginning at 11:00 A.M. and lasting only one hour, with students otherwise attending classes regularly throughout the day. (The strike was purposely set for the day and time in 1917 when Congress had declared war on Germany in order to capitalize on U.S. disillusionment with World War I and "the Great Betrayal of 1917.") About 25,000 students participated, mostly at East Coast schools, with the largest percentage of them in New York City. Participants took the OXFORD PLEDGE. There were counterdemonstrations at some schools, including Harvard and Johns Hopkins, and administrative opposition at others, including Oklahoma and Syracuse. Nevertheless, although it had not been very well planned and organized, the strike was a great success and garnered wide media attention. As the first antiwar strike of the decade and the largest student political demonstration in U.S. history to that time, the event bolstered the peace movement significantly and marked an end to prevalent apathy among U.S. students.

That truth is evidenced in the second Student Strike Against War, which occurred on April 12, 1935, was better organized than the first strike, and involved the efforts of numerous groups besides SLID and NSL, including the YOUNG MEN'S CHRISTIAN ASSOCIATION (YMCA), the YOUNG WOMEN'S CHRISTIAN ASSOCIATION (YWCA), the National Council of Methodist Youth, and numerous student government bodies. The strike attracted the participation of 175,000 students at more than 130 campuses nationwide. In New York City 10,000 strikers demonstrated. At University of California at Berkeley, 4,000 demonstrated—the university's first antiwar strike; at University of Chicago, 3,500; at University of Minnesota, 3,000; at University of Pennylvania, 2,500; at many smaller schools like Oberlin and DePauw, more than 1,000. Again, there was opposition at some schools from some student groups and administrators, including President Nicholas Murray Butler of Columbia University. But, again, the third Student Strike Against War, held April 22, 1936, proved the increasingly widespread appeal of the student antiwar movement. This time, a record number of students participated—more than 350,000 nationwide out of a total student population of 1 million. No U.S. student movement before or since has involved such a large percentage of the national student body. Unfortunately for the student antiwar movement, however, eruption of the Spanish Civil War in July 1936 and formation of the Rome-Berlin Axis in October 1936, which linked the Fascist powers Italy and Germany, presaged events that would derail any hopes of avoiding involvement in a future world war.

Bibliography: Robert Cohen, *When the Old Left Was Young: Student Radicals and America's First Mass Student Movement, 1929–1941* (New York: Oxford University Press, 1993).

Student Strike of 1911 (Russia) a nationwide strike by students that began in January 1911 following issuance of a government circular on January 11 that banned student meetings on the premises of institutions of higher learning and that obligated faculty councils to call in police to arrest students who participated in any such meetings—a clear attack on the institutions' autonomy. The strike originated in a January 23 meeting of the St. Petersburg City Coalition Council, which included students and a representative from Moscow. The strike, which involved both universities and technical institutes, became nationwide by the first week of February. Massive arrests of students resulted, with police invading campuses uninvited. As a sidelight of the strike, more than a third of the faculty at Moscow University resigned in protest over the firing of three of their colleagues who had objected to police incursions; most never returned—a severe blow to the university's academic viability. This elicited a statement of protest from 66 industrialists, challenging the government's policies. The student strike and the Moscow professors' resignations called into question presumed progressive development at the universities and reflected the extent of discontent among the middle class. As the strike persisted, the government's response was simple repression. Besides mass arrests, 1,871 students were expelled and another 4,406 were suspended (at the time, nationwide, there were about 100,000 students). Thus the strike ended unsuccessfully, but the repression increased public disaffection with the government.

Bibliography: Samuel D. Kassow, *Students, Professors, and the State in Tsarist Russia.* (Berkeley: University of California Press, 1989).

Students' Union for the Salvation of the Country (China) an organization that was formed in 1918 by students at Canton University.

Student Union of Peking (China) (full name—the Student Union of the Middle Schools and Institutions of Higher Learning in Peking [Beijing]) an organization of students founded on May 6, 1919, two days following the initial protest event of the MAY FOURTH MOVEMENT. The union's defined purpose was "to facilitate the performance of students' duties and to promote the welfare of the nation." Given the prominent cause of the moment—

opposition to Japanese aggrandizement of Chinese territory—the union's primary goals entailed restoration of Shandong, a boycott of Japanese goods, punishment of pro-Japanese ministers in the government (regarded as traitors), and an end to government by warlords. The union was comprised of two councils: the legislative council, formed of two representatives from each school involved, met weekly to define policies and draft resolutions, and the executive council, elected by the student bodies of the involved schools, was charged with carrying out the policies. Finances were to be provided by the students. The union was significant for several reasons: it was the first united student organization formed on a citywide basis in Chinese history—and the first successful effort to unify Beijing students; the first student organization with active, joint participation of both male and female students; the model for similar organizations established by students in major cities across China in the following weeks and years; and the impetus for founding of the Student Union of the Republic of China in June 1919. The union was, of course, also a major force in the ongoing May Fourth Movement.

Student Union of Tientsin   (China) (full name the Student Union of the Middle Schools and Institutes of Higher Learning in Tientsin [Tianjin]) an organization that was founded on May 14, 1919 as a result of spreading support for the MAY FOURTH MOVEMENT and modeled upon the STUDENT UNION OF PEKING (Beijing). The Tianjin union was noteworthy in that Chou En-lai, who had been a student in Japan and returned home after the May Fourth Incident, became editor of the union's daily newspaper, *Journal of the Student Union*, which had a circulation exceeding 20,000. His future wife, Teng Yingch'ao, then a student at the First Girls' Normal School and a leader in the Tientsin Association of Women Patriotic Comrades (founded on May 25, 1919), was also a member of the union, heading its speech department. Both, of course, later became leaders of the CHINESE COMMUNIST PARTY (CCP). The Tianjin union became a major supporter of the May Fourth Movement, joining in the national student strike on May 23 with the participation of 10,000 students in the city.

Student Volunteer Movement)   (United States) a nondenominational Protestant organization founded by Christian evangelist Dwight L. Moody (1837–1899) in 1886 and formally organized in 1888 at his Northfield, Massachusetts base of operations. The movement's purpose was to enlist university and college students as volunteers for foreign missionary service. Its motto was "The evangelization of the world in this generation." By 1898, a year before Moody's death, more than a thousand students (men and women) had enlisted in the movement and been sent overseas as missionaries. During the next 20 years thousands more followed them.

Study Group on Military Matters   (Japan) a proposed promilitary student organization at Waseda University. Following World War I, the Japanese military advocated military training of youths, and the government supported the employment of surplus officers in the universities. In this context, in 1923 officials planned to found the Study Group on Military Matters at Waseda University as a promilitary organization for students. The first meeting was to be attended by generals, the university president, and professors. But an assemblage of 5,000 students, half of the university's student population, met in opposition and aborted the Study Group's founding.

Sturmabteilung (SA)   (Germany) storm troopers, also known as the Brownshirts, the SA was a paramilitary organization of the Nazi Party formed in 1921 and reorganized in 1930. SA members were known for their brutality in street fighting used as a means of intimidating political opponents of the Nazi Party, many of whom they murdered. The SA vigorously recruited university-student members for paramilitary training; in July 1933 it gained control over the program of war sports, or military sports, for students. In September of that year, Adolf Hitler, who had become chancellor in January, ordered that an SA office be established at every university in Germany. Thereafter, separate SA units were formed at each university, and fraternities were required to have their members belong to the SA or to the Schutzstaffel (SS) or the STAHLHELM. Many students found ways of avoiding service in the SA, however. By 1933 the SA, under the command of Ernst Rohm since its reorganization, numbered 2 million members and was twice the size of the regular army—a cause of concern to the Officer Corps. Fearing that he might lose the army's support because of the SA's prominence and Rohm's ambitions to control the army, Hitler ordered the SS to murder Rohm and hundreds of his henchmen on June 30, 1934—known as "the night of the long knives." Afterwards, the SA offices at the universities became defunct, and universal conscription that was begun in March 1935 obviated the need for paramilitary training. The SA quickly dissolved.

Sukarno (1901–1970)   (Indonesia) dominant political figure in Indonesia for 40 years and leader of the nation's independence movement. Born in Surabaya, East Java, Sukarno graduated from the Bandung Technical Institute in 1926 with a degree in engineering (architecture). In that year he helped to found the General Study Club for which he served as secretary and through which he launched his political career. He also published *Nationalism, Islam, and Marxism*, in which he promoted unity of the nation's diverse political groups to oppose Dutch control of Indonesia. On July 4, 1927, he formed the Indonesian National Association, renamed Indonesian National Party (Partai Nasional Indonesia, PNI) in 1928; in December 1927 he brought the existing seven Indonesian parties into a confederation and became the spearhead of the independence movement. On December 29, 1929, Dutch authorities arrrested Sukarno; he was sentenced to four years in prison. His sentence was commuted, and on December 31, 1931, he was freed and returned to lead the independence movement. He was arrested again in 1933 and exiled to Flores; he remained in exile until 1942, following Japanese occupation of Indonesia. In 1945, he became president of an independent Indonesia, which formally received sovereignty from the Dutch in December 1949. Sukarno remained president until September 30, 1965, when he was ousted in a coup led by General Suharto.

Sunday School (Great Britain) a program for the religious instruction of children, the Sunday school was purportedly conceived by Robert Raikes (1736–1811), although precedents existed decades before Raikes began his work and the great majority of Sunday schools were locally created. Since many children worked six days per week in factories, which provided no time for their education, Raikes, who published a newspaper in Gloucester and advocated prison reforms, deemed the Sunday school as the means of preventing children from joining the ranks of criminals. Supported by his Anglican priest, Raikes established the reputedly first Sunday school in Gloucester in 1780, with lay people serving as teachers in their own homes. Through articles Raikes wrote for his newspaper, interest in the idea grew, and Sunday schools sprang up throughout Great Britain. By the time of Raikes's death, the movement, now fully associated with the churches, reportedly involved 500,000 British children. By 1850 more than 2 million children age 5 to 15 were enrolled in Sunday schools in England. The Sunday school movement also spread to the Continent and to North America, where it attained especially wide acceptance among the Protestant churches. In 1830, there were reportedly 570,000 youths enrolled in Sunday schools in Canada and the United States. Although enrollments declined as a result of the severe disruptions caused by the Panic of 1837 and the U.S. Civil War, they climbed again abruptly during the 1870s and thereafter throughout the remainder of the 19th century to nearly 7 million in 1880 and close to 12 million by 1893.

Bibliography: Thomas Walter Laqueur, *Religion and Respectability: Sunday Schools and Working Class Culture, 1780–1850* (New Haven, Conn.: Yale University Press, 1976).

Sunday School Union (Great Britain) probably the most significant of the interdenominational organizations involved in promotion of Sunday schools, founded in London in 1803 by a group of activists, ranging in age from 18 to 25, who were already involved in the SUNDAY SCHOOL movement. They produced a pamphlet on how to organize a Sunday school and in 1805 began to publish the long-lived *Youth's Magazine*. In 1812 the union became

a public organization, holding its first open meeting in May. Essentially an organization of teachers and also a publishing house, the union by 1833 could claim the membership of more than 40 percent of the schools and nearly 60 percent of the students in England. In 1835, more than 7,800 schools, nearly 111,000 teachers, and almost 910,000 students were affiliated with the Union.

Sveriges forenade studentkarer (National Union of Students, SFS) (Sweden) the first national organization of Swedish students, formed in 1921 in response to appeals by organizations in other nations for cooperative efforts among European students. SFS constitutes a confederation of the student unions of 35 Swedish institutes of higher learning, with a membership of virtually all the students in the nation. The chairman of SFS is a full-time employee, making this position a stepping stone to political power—for example, former Prime Minister Olof Palme had served as SFS chairman. In keeping with its origins, SFS concentrated on international issues until the late 1940s, when it became involved in the student trade-union movement. It has also been active in recent years in gaining benefits for students, such as improved housing accommodations and reduced railway fares.

Swingjungen (Swing Youth or Swingers) (Germany) a youth gang of several hundred that formed in Hamburg in 1939–40. The gang was labeled *Swingers* because of their taste for U.S. music and English clothes. Although not politically motivated, Swingers attacked members of the HITLER JUGEND (HJ), in particular the HJ's police-style Streifendienst (SRD, Patrol Service) and otherwise aggravated Nazi authorities. Heinrich Himmler, head of the Schutzstaffeln (SS), in 1942 had some of the ringleaders incarcerated in concentration camps and brutalized, but the Swingers survived and spread to Berlin, Saarbrücken, Dresden, Vienna, and other cities. The Swingers typified a form of youthful defiance of the Nazi regime but a defiance that did not become genuine revolt. Still, such gangs openly opposed the compliant homogeneity that was represented by the HJ and thereby incited oppression. The Mutineers in Leipzig, for example, suffered hundreds of arrests between November 1942 and January 1943—157 were imprisoned outright. Similar gangs existed in cities throughout Germany in these years.

Symbionese Liberation Army (SLA) (United States) a small group of militant young revolutionaries formed in Oakland, California in spring 1973. Several of them were former university students who had been visiting prisoners at Vacaville and secretly teaching them Maoist revolutionary concepts. When one of the prisoners, a black named Donald DeFreeze who called himself Cinque Mtume, escaped in March 1973 and was hidden by a student member of the group, he became their leader in forming the SLA and called himself their field marshall. On November 6, 1973, some members of the SLA assassinated the Oakland school superintendent, an African American named Marcus Foster, because he had allowed police surveillance. But the SLA's most notorious act was kidnapping Patty Hearst, daughter of newspaper publisher Randolph Hearst, from her Berkeley apartment on February 5, 1974. The ensuing story of the Hearst family's offer of $2 million for food donations to the needy as a ransom and Hearst's April 4 announcement that she was voluntarily joining the SLA, followed by her being videotaped while participating in an armed robbery of a San Francisco bank, was ongoing front-page news. Most of the SLA members were killed during a shootout with the police on May 17, 1974 in Los Angeles while Hearst remained underground. She was caught by the FBI on September 18, 1975 and found guilty of bank robbery on March 20, 1976. The story became the subject of several books, television documentaries, movies, and even plays.

Teach-ins (United States) a peaceful tactic involving speeches, songs, and marches that inaugurated the peace movement in protest against the Vietnam War during the 1960s. The first teach-in occurred on March 24, 1965 at the University of Michigan, where a group of faculty had planned a moratorium on classes to present a day of lectures and seminars on the war. When the moratorium aroused opposition, they decided on an all-night convocation of the same nature instead; 3,000 students and professors gathered for it—only 500 had been expected. Both students and professors spoke. The participants sang songs, imbibed cookies and coffee, and held a torchlight walk; the teach-in lasted through the night and into the next morning. This first teach-in inspired others at more than 100 campuses. One held at the University of California at Berkeley proved the largest: it attracted 12,000 students, who listened to antiwar speeches by Benjamin Spock, Norman Thomas, Senator Ernest Gruening, Norman Mailer, and many others and were entertained by Dick Gregory, satirists known as The Committee, folk singers, and other performers. In response to the teach-ins, the Johnson administration sent a three-man "truth team" to several Midwest campuses to speak to students and support the war. A National Teach-in was held on May 15 at the Sheraton Park Hotel in Washington, where academic experts debated the war.

Teddy Boys (Great Britain) not an organized youth movement but an urban-centered phenomenon of the 1950s that involved mostly working-class adolescents (including girls); they defined themselves as a distinct youth subculture through a "uniform" and certain patterns of behavior—all of which witnessed a significant break with pre-World War II generations of British youth. The uniform was a modified and flamboyant Edwardian style (hence the name *Teddy boys*) first popularized by youths from the Elephant and Castle area of London, who presumably were adapting a revival of the style by the gentlemen's fashion arbiters of Saville Row in 1948–50. It included a draped jacket with a velvet collar and padded shoulders, a slim-jim tie, a flowery waistcoat, tapered drainpipe trousers, and shoes with thick crepe soles—the clothing accented by a "D.A."—a bushy, or wavy hairstyle including large sideburns. The name *Teddy boy* was coined by the press in the spring of 1954. Teddy boys and their girlfriends frequented cinemas and dance halls and were early fans of rock 'n' roll. The Teddy boy movement peaked in 1956 when Greater London alone had about 30,000 Teddy boys and thousands more were found in the provincial cities.

Two members of the Edwardians, a group of youngsters of the 1950s who adopted the styles of a half-century before. Staid old Londoners called the Edwardians "Teddy Boys" and regarded their velvet-collared jackets and calf-clinging drainpipe pants as the uniform of juvenile delinquency. Some of them were involved in gang fights. (AP/WIDE WORLD PHOTOS)

Although not organized as gangs, the Teddies came to prominence during a period when Britain was experiencing a precipitous rise in adolescent criminality that the press identified with them, branding the Teddy boys as a menace. The primary catalyst for the press's view was an altercation (termed a "battle" by the press) between two groups, totaling about 50 Teddy boys, that occurred on the station platforms at St. Mary Cray in Kent on April 24, 1954. They fought with fence staves and fire buckets until police arrived and shut them up in the ticket hall. This and other incidents caused the Teddy boys to be identified as "gangs," "hooligans," and "thugs" and thus made them targets of press, police, and public antagonism. The Teddy boys were perpetrators of the rock 'n' roll riots of 1955–56 inspired by the film *Rock Around the Clock* starring Bill Haley and the Comets. These riots gained so much attention that they probably inspired similar rock 'n' roll riots in cities throughout Europe (such riots were reported in more than 500 cities on three continents, however). There were counterparts to the Teddies in attitude and deportment in other nations, such as the *blousons noirs* in France and the *halbstarken* in Germany. Teddy boys also became deeply involved in the North Kensington race riots of 1958 in Nottingham and Notting Hill, which they started. By 1960 the Teddy boy phenomenon had effectively disappeared, but it left a legacy of adult suspicion and hostility towards youths.

Temporary Rules Strike   (Russia) student demonstrations against the Temporary Rules on Student Organizations announced by the government in November 1901. The new rules revised the 1884 Statute that had outlawed all student organizations and meetings; yet they were so restrictive as to leave things effectively unchanged. The Temporary Rules allowed students to set up such organizations as discussion groups, libraries, music clubs, and drama clubs but provided that these organizations could meet only under the supervision of a professor appointed by the rector; general meetings were still forbidden. In protest, the students' Executive Committee at Moscow University met on January 29, 1902 and called for a general meeting of students on February 9 to determine a response. Although the Executive Committee members were arrested on January 31, hundreds of students, aware that a student meeting at St. Petersburg University on February 5 had voted to strike in protest, assembled in the university auditorium on February 9. They passed a resolution supporting freedom of speech, the right to strike, an eight-hour workday, removal of all restrictions on aliens, and a constituent assembly and the promise to back their demands with force. The resolution appeared to be a radical departure. The police arrived at the campus and arrested 509 of the assembled students. On February 20, the government sentenced 95 of the students to exile in Siberia for from two to four years; another 567 students, some jailed since February 9, received jail sen-

tences. Similar strikes, mass arrests, and punishments also occurred at St. Petersburg and other universities. In August 1902, a government minister visited the students who had been sent to Siberia to offer amnesty, and subsequently all were released but continued under police supervision.

Bibliography: Samuel D. Kassow, *Students, Professors, and the State in Tsarist Russia* (Berkeley: University of California Press, 1989).

Terrorist Section of the People's Will   (Russia) a group of students representing 12 fraternities at the University of St. Petersburg who organized themselves as a terrorist movement in 1886. They used the name *People's Will* even though that society was dead and none of the Terrorist Section's members had any connection to it. They determined to assassinate Tsar Alexander III. Three members of the Terrorist Section, armed with bombs, loitered on the Nevsky Prospekt on March 1, 1887 (anniversary of the assassination of Alexander II), awaiting the appearance of the tsar's carriage, but they had aroused suspicion and were taken into custody, thus ending the threat of "the second March the first." Two of the would-be assassins pleaded guilty and talked, leading to the arrest of the other members of the Terrorist Section and their organization's demise. The twelve men and three women arrested were sentenced to death, but the sentences of all but five of the men were commuted to imprisonment or hard labor. The five condemned men were executed on May 8. One of them was Alexander Ulyanov, a leader of the Terrorist Section whose 17-year-old younger brother reputedly swore revenge for his death. The brother would later take the name Vladimir Lenin.

Third Camp   (United States) an umbrella term for a group of socialist-oriented student groups of the 1950s that maintained an independent political posture by rejecting the policies of both the Socialist and Communist parties, while at the same time rejecting the policies of the governments of the United States and the Soviet Union. Prominent among them were the YOUNG PEOPLES' SOCIALIST LEAGUE (YPSL) and the SOCIALIST YOUTH LEAGUE (SYL).

Three People's Principles Youth Corps (Sanqintuan) (China) a youth organization that was formed in 1939 and controlled by leaders of the Kuomintang Party (KMT) of Chiang Kai-shek. One of its purposes was to be a counterforce to the CHINESE COMMUNIST PARTY (CCP) and its COMMUNIST YOUTH LEAGUE on university campuses. The Three People's Principles themselves, inherited from Sun Yat-sen but modified by Chiang, were Science, Democracy, and Patriotism. Members of the Sanqintuan served not only as opponents of the Communists and supporters of Chiang, but also as advocates of the NEW LIFE MOVEMENT. The Sanqintuan also functioned as a parent group for the Boy Scouts and the Girl Scouts. After 1945, during the years of the Civil War, members of the Sanqintuan supported the KMT by attacking communist demonstrators.

Tiananmen Incident   (China) a student demonstration in Tiananmen Square in Beijing on April 5, 1976. Long since disillusioned with revolutionary zealotry following the excesses of the GREAT PROLETARIAN CULTURAL REVOLUTION and the near destruction of the universities (they had only reopened in 1971), Chinese university students used the occasion of a public mourning ceremony for the late Premier Chou En-lai to demonstrate political dissidence. Thousands of students joined thousands of other citizens in a mass demonstration in the square that actually served as a forum for veiled criticism of the Maoist extremists. Police attacked, beat, and jailed demonstrators, quickly bringing the incident to an end. The Maoists heaped blame for the demonstration on Chou's protege Deng Xiaoping, who fled to safety in South China. Following the death of Mao Zedong and the arrest of the Gang of Four, however, Deng became leader of a new coalition government in December 1978.

Tiananmen Square Massacre   *See* CHINESE DEMOCRACY MOVEMENT.

Timişoara Revolution   (Romania) a revolt that began in Timişoara on December 16, 1989, initiating the Romanian revolution that overthrew the brutal Communist dictator Nicolae Ceauşescu. Youths comprised the majority of the Timişoara revolutionaries—university students, children, and secondary school pupils—although all segments of the populace participated in the uprising. Among the groups involved were the Europe Society, Timişoara journalism students; the December 16 Confederation, an organization of young people in Timis County; Timşez, an organization of young Hungarians in Timişoara; and the Society of Young Journalists. The unarmed rebels fought against the army, the militia, and the Securitate (secret police), enduring mass arrests and murders along with violent confrontation. But on December 21, they had secured Timişoara as a free city governed by the Romanian Democratic Front. More than 100,000 residents gathered in the city's Opera Square, fraternizing with soldiers who had joined their cause and chanting "We are ready to die!" and "Down with communism!" Spreading from Timişoara, the revolution swept the nation. On December 22, Ceauşescu and his hated wife fled from the rooftop of the Central Committee building located in the Palace Square of the capital, Bucharest, leaving both the government they had controlled and the Romanian Communist Party (RCP) in swift and total collapse. The Ceauşescus were captured,

tried, and executed by firing squad on December 26. Dissident members of the RCP, however, gained control of the government in the aftermath of the revolution—to the distress of the Timişoara rebels, whose demands had included free elections. On November 17, 1990, the RCP announced its official reorganization as the Socialist Labor Party, a change in name only.

Tiranë Demonstration   (Albania) a demonstration by youths on July 2, 1990 in Tiranë, the capital city, intended to prod the Communist government of Ramiz Alia into making broader reforms than the few changes already announced in foreign policy (reestablishing diplomatic relations with the United States and the Soviet Union) and the legal system (making it possible to obtain passports for travel outside Albania, lowering penalties for defection—previously considered treason). In the aftermath of the demonstration, thousands of people sought refuge in foreign embassies in Tiranë, and nearly 5,000, mostly young people, were allowed to leave the country, taking advantage of the reform in granting passports. The mass exodus shocked the government, which introduced ameliorative new economic and political measures at the Communist Party's plenum on July 6 and 7 and replaced hardliners in the Politburo.

Tojiren (Tokyo Liaison Council of Student Self-governing Associations)   (Japan) a student organization formed on April 20, 1961 by Japan Communist Party members of ZENGAKUREN who opposed the policies of the Mainstream that controlled Zengakuren. The name is an abbreviation for *Tokyo-to Gakusei Jichikai Renraku Kaigi*. Tojiren served as a rival group to the Mainstream and evolved out of conflicts over policies for the ANTI-AMPO STRUGGLE. During a meeting that rivaled the Zengakuren's 16th National Congress Tajiren was transformed into Zenjiren (Zenkoku Gakusei Jichikai Renraku Kaigai)—a change in name only. The Zenjiren itself collapsed in 1963.

Tokyo University Struggle   (Japan) a major series of ongoing student demonstrations and strikes—the longest and most important of the time—running throughout 1968 and into 1969. The catalyst for the struggle was changes in the system of Medical Department internships that were proposed in December 1967 as a Doctors' Registration Bill in the Diet that students opposed. After the administration repeatedly refused to discuss the changes with them, the students formed the Medical Department Struggle Council on January 27, 1968 and initiated a strike and a boycott of graduation examinations on January 29. Representatives of the council tried to meet with the hospital director on February 19 but instead were met by the senior assistant of the medical staff; an ensuing scuffle led to rumors and misunderstandings that resulted in 17 students being penalized, 4 with expulsion, by the Medical Department faculty. In reaction, students in other departments began to support the medical students' struggle. The students prevented graduation ceremonies on March 28. About 6,000 students gathered on June 20 and decided to stage a universitywide strike of indefinite duration. When the Diet approved the Doctors' Registration Bill, in reaction the struggle council decided to occupy Yasuda Hall, an auditorium with a tall clock tower that symbolized Tokyo University. On July 5 at a general meeting in the occupied building, the students formed the Tokyo University All-Campus Joint Struggle Council, comprised of graduate students and known as Todai Zenkyoto. On July 16, the Zenkyoto presented seven demands; in response on August 10, the university offered a peace plan, and the director of the hospital and the dean of the medical department announced that they would resign.

On August 22, medical students declared the strike over, but when the new dean refused to meet with them, the struggle resumed and escalated, and during September and October, students in all the university's departments went on strike and barricaded buildings. On November 1, conceding failure, the president of the university resigned. Then the students fractured into factions, with some ZENGAKUREN factions refusing to negotiate with the acting president; internecine warfare ensued. For example, 2,000 students fought to gain control of the library, occupied by the Zenkyoto, and a Kakumaru faction in the literature department forcefully held nine professors, locking the dean in his office for nine days. On November 16, the acting president agreed to negotiate with the Zenkyoto in Yasuda Hall, and they reissued their seven demands, which included voiding the punishment of the medical students, forbidding police from ever again entering the campus, and instituting some system of self-criticism of university policies. While the acting president pursued the negotiations, the minister of education favored a punitive approach. A massive demonstration at the Hongo campus on November 22 pitted 6,000 supporters of the Zenkyoto faction against 6,000 supporters of the Minsei faction, but it was kept peaceable through the intervention of 2,000 nonaligned students and professors. The factional conflict shifted to the Komaba campus, where for three weeks in December two opposed student factions occupied buildings and fought each other. The Zenkyoto and Minsei factions clashed on January 9, and police were called in for the first time since June to quell the riot that left 118 people injured and 52 students arrested. Finally on January 18, after continuing conflicts, 8,500 police equipped with tear gas, shields, and armored vehicles, entered the Hongo campus to rout the Zenkyoto from Yasuda Hall and other barricaded buildings. The siege of Yasuda Hall lasted two days and received live television coverage and worldwide news-media attention. Altogether more than 1,200 students were arrested, 375 during the siege of Yasuda Hall, which now was a total ruin. The spring entrance examinations were canceled, but peace slowly returned. The significance of this long struggle lay in the fact that Tokyo University had been regarded as the most prestigious and important national university in Japan; its prestige suffered a terrible blow. In addition, the struggle attracted support from hundreds of students throughout Japan who traveled to the campus to join the demonstrations. It was something of a prototype for similar confrontations elsewhere in 1968: out of 377 universities in Japan, 107 suffered conflicts during the year. This struggle, together with the 1968 NIHON UNIVERSITY STRUGGLE, encouraged the creation of Zenkyoto groups at all the universities and widespread adoption of such tactics as strikes and barricaded buildings for student protests.

Bibliography: Stuart J. Dowsey, ed., *Zengakuren: Japan's Revolutionary Students* (Berkeley, Calif.: The Ishi Press, 1970).

Toller, Ernst (1893–1939) (Germany) revolutionary leader, playwright, and poet. Toller, who believed he represented "the youth of a whole generation," served in World War I and then returned to being a student at the University of Munich, where as a leader he showed an unusual ability to identify with workers and their cause. In 1918 he became deputy president of the Central Committee of the Workmen's, Peasants', and Soldiers' Soviets of Bavaria. With massive student support, Toller and his committee successfully staged a revolution, seizing control of the local government and setting up the Bavarian Soviet Republic, with Toller as president, in Munich in April 1919. The Soviet appointed a commission of six students to devise plans for reform of the university. The revolution was suppressed and Toller was imprisoned for five years (1919–24). While in prison he wrote several expressionistic plays, including *Transfiguration* (1919), *Masses and Man* (1922), and *Brokenbow* (1924). A Jew, Toller fled Germany in 1932 and presented lectures elsewhere in Europe opposing the Nazis. Toller emigrated to the United States in 1933 and published an autobiography, *I Was a German*, in the same year. He worked briefly and unsuccessfully as a script writer in Hollywood. Impoverished and depressed, Toller committed suicide in New York City.

Tolstoi Demonstrations (Russia) student demonstrations following the death of the renowned author Leo Tolstoi on November 7, 1910. On November 8 students at institutions of higher learning nationwide spontaneously conducted memorial services and issued resolutions that called upon students to memorialize Tolstoi by assuming leadership of a movement against capital punishment. Demonstrations continued through the week until November 15 and were especially spirited in St. Petersburg, where thousands of students repeatedly tried to demonstrate at the Nevski Prospekt and were dispersed by police. Although the demonstrations had no overt political intent, government authorities perceived them to be menacing as a potential catalyst for reviving the worker-student coalition of the REVOLUTION OF 1905. The arrest of student demonstrators instigated an unsuccessful effort to mount a student strike as a protest in support of the arrested students—an issue that festered into 1911. The Tolstoi Demonstrations thus served as a harbinger of the STUDENT STRIKE OF 1911.

"To the People" Movement   *See* NARODNIKI.

Transcendental Meditation (TM)   (United States) a movement begun in the late 1960s, not a youth movement as such but with a majority of its adherents under age 25. TM became virtually a worldwide movement, but its major impact occurred in the United States among college and university students; it gained many adherents in Germany, Great Britain, and other European nations as well. The leader of the movement, Maharishi Mahesh Yogi, first gained widespread attention in 1967, probably because the Beatles were then prominent among his devotees. Interest in TM burgeoned among U.S. students, and in 1969 Stanford University became the first school to offer a course in the Science of Creative Intelligence, the method and content of the Maharishi's teachings. By 1972, at least 10 universities had courses in TM—there were an estimated 250,000 U.S. devotees by then and more than 400 student groups practicing TM. The primary discipline for TM devotees is to meditate twice daily for 15 or 20 minutes as a means of attaining awareness and self-realization, a higher consciousness.

Trent Movement   (Italy) a student movement centered at the Institute of Social Sciences in Trent that began in 1965. The institute was founded as a private institution in 1962 by Roman Catholic groups associated with the Christian Democratic Party and became the first school in Italy allowed to offer a degree in sociology. Although sited in a highly conservative Catholic region, the institute attracted students from thoroughout Italy who embraced activism. They organized demonstrations and sit-ins and occupied the school in the successful cause of getting Parliament to grant the institute legal authority to award a degree in sociology, rather than a proposed degree in "political science with a sociological orientation." Winning this battle amounted to a radical change in Italian higher education, especially as the prevailing view was hostile to sociology and denied its status as a distinct social science. Virtually the entire student body at the institute was involved in the movement, participating in occupation of the school, conducting seminars, and preparing documents to support the movement's purposes. As the Trent Movement burgeoned in 1967–68, the involved students broadened their goals to include increased student participation in the institute's governance (student power), curricular changes, and a revolutionary view of the university's role in society. They modeled this revolutionary view of the university on the KRITISCHE UNIVERSITÄT concept and conceived of the university as the generator of political total confrontation (*contestazione globale*). The Trent Movement was the first student movement in Italy to use such protest tactics as occupying buildings and disrupting classes, but its professed ideals were distinctly derivative of Marxism.

Trinchera   (Cuba) a student organization formed at the University of Havana in 1959 in opposition to the increasing power of Communists within the government of Fidel Castro. The leaders of Trinchera (the Trench) had previously belonged to the Catholic University Association (Agrupación Católica). Their purpose was to arouse the Cuban people against the communist threat through articles in their newspaper (*Trinchera*), demonstrations, and other means. Trinchera members demonstrated against Anastas Mikoyan, vice premier of the Soviet Union, when he visited Cuba in February 1960, and 20 were arrested. In March they demonstrated in support of a television and radio commentator who opposed the communists; they were brutally beaten by members of the FEDERACIÓN ESTUDIANTIL UNIVERSITARIA (FEU) and the FEU's student militias. DRE leaders then helped form the Directorio Revolucionario Estudiantil (Revolutionary Student Directorate, DRE) at the University of Havana as a part of the Revolutionary Recovery Movement (MRR) in an effort to develop a student underground. The DRE advocated nationalism, social justice, democracy, and property rights in articles in *Trinchera*. In late 1960, DRE began a campaign of bombings, in January 1961 its members sabotaged the Havana electric power plant, and in February they helped to set up a nationwide student strike. Some DRE members began guerrilla action in Oriente province in April 1961. In the repression that followed the Bay of Pigs invasion, DRE members were imprisoned or executed or escaped into exile.

Tsinan Incident   (China) a military clash that occurred on May 3, 1928 between units of the Northern Expedition dispatched to Shandong Province by the Kuomintang (KMT), with enthusiastic student support, to subdue the warlords there and the Japanese troops supposedly sent to protect Japanese citizens in Jinan (Tsinan), capital of the province. KMT leaders voiced outrage over the incident as another example of humiliating foreign interference in China, and student associations rose to the occasion by organizing a nationwide protest against the Japanese. On May 24, the NATIONAL STUDENT ASSOCIATION (NSA) consummated the protest's national scope by proclaiming a boycott of Japanese goods. The protest movement created a dilemma for the KMT, which feared that it might fall to communist control, but the KMT also profited from its nationalistic fervor and therefore rejected Japanese demands that the movement be banned by responding that it broke no laws and so could not legally be suppressed. The Shanghai Student Union (SSU) had exacerbated the KMT's problem by organizing a three-day strike and a rally but complied with KMT desires by adhering to restrictions against inflammatory speeches and parades; on May 17 the SSU announced its rally had raised $24,000 to support the Northern Expedition. On May 9, the 13th anniversary of the TWENTY-ONE DEMANDS PROTEST, students at the private schools in Beijing observed National Humiliation Day. The following week, Beijing students staged a one-day protest walkout that closed the city's schools. By the end of May, the foreign relations crisis resulting from the Tsinan Incident was in process of diplomatic resolution, but the students continued their boycott of Japanese goods. The incident had longer-term repercussions also, as it led the KMT to create a 17-year program of anti-Japanese educational indoctrination that involved classes in history, geography, and other subjects. In addition, for students, Japan became the new target for antiimperialist denunciations, replacing Great Britain in the role of foreign devil.

Tsinghua University Protest   (China) a student uprising on February 18, 1936 in resistance to government efforts to suppress agitation at universities in Beijing arising out of the DECEMBER NINTH MOVEMENT. Several hundred police officers attacked the campus at dawn; students, aroused by the alarms of student sentries, rushed to the defense. They drove off the invaders, pelting them with steamed bread provided for the police officers' breakfast and trashing their vehicles. Responding to student protests, the chancellor visited the mayor's office to request an explanation of the police attack, while the students assembled to plan further resistance. The chancellor returned with eight police officers intent on arresting 47 students wanted by authorities. Students seized the police officers as prisoners. In response that evening, more than 500 police and a regiment from the 29th Army invaded the campus. Forewarned of their coming, left-wing student leaders had already fled, but the police interrogated 600 students and arrested 21. Police also raided Beijing University the same day. These and other raids quieted student demonstrations for a few weeks.

Tupumaros   (Uruguay) an urban guerrilla ring comprised mostly of students, both men and women, that was initiated by the militant faction of the Uruguayan Socialist Party in 1962–63. The group took its name from Tupac Amaru, an ancient Inca king. Raul Sendic, a law student at the University of the Republic, was the leader of the Socialist militant faction and the major organizer of the Tupumaros. This faction had worked nonviolently to organize the sugarcane workers and to promote improvements in their working conditions, but failure of this effort pushed them into organizing the Tupumaros and adopting terrorism and armed conflict. The Tupumaros challenged the government's legitimacy during the 1960s through bank robberies, staged kidnappings of foreign diplomats and prominent Uruguayans, and the uncovering of government corruption, while successfully combating police suppression over the years. Among the Tupumaros's most famous escapades was holding British ambassador Geoffrey Jackson hostage for eight months during 1971. Thereafter, the Uruguayan army crushed Tupumaros and then launched a successful coup d'état in June 1973. Before its demise, Tupumaros had been the best organized and most successful group of its kind in Latin America; many of the group's members were students in the architecture, arts, and medicine programs at the University of the Republic, where the Tupumaros held secret meetings.

Turin University Occupation   (Italy) a student movement that began in November 1967 at Turin University, with students occupying the university's faculty (department) sites and other buildings. The occupation lasted for nearly seven months. Initially, the students were protesting the university administration's decision to move the university's headquarters without having consulted with the students to determine their views on the move; their protest also included advocacy of structural and other academic reforms that had been promised by successive national governments for about 10 years. As the occupation endured, the students' cause increasingly embraced the larger issues of political, economic, and social reform; but its basic thrust remained an attack on authoritarianism, which in the university was personified by the *professori ordinari* system. The Turin student movement spread throughout Italy, with occupations, sit-ins, and other forms of student protest erupting at other universities from December 1967 until June 1968.

Turkish Students' Strike   (Turkey) a widespread students' strike in 1876 demanding governmental changes at a time when Turkey was bankrupt and appeared on the verge of dissolution. The strike began in Istanbul, spreading among the religious schools (*medrese*). The students acquired arms and organized mass meetings held at mosques. They drafted a petition to demand that the grand vizier and the leaders of the religious establishment resign. The government complied by dismissing these officials. Although the religious students' movement arose in sympathy with the Young Ottomans, the students rejected the other goals of the Young Ottomans, such as the instituting of a constitution and a parliament.

Turnerschaft (VC)   (Germany) a university student fraternity formed in 1885 that evolved from the TURN-VEREIN movement. It was a full-fledged dueling fraternity (*schlagende Verbindung*) with the motto *mens sana in corpore sano* (a sound mind in a sound body). The VC published a newspaper entitled *Akademische Turnerzeitung*. In the 1890s, the VC joined the nationalistic movement, adopting an advocacy of pan-Germanism and anti-Semitism.

Turnverein   (Germany) an association that fostered gymnastics for young men, begun by Friedrich Ludwig JAHN in Berlin in 1811. The ostensible purpose of the original *Turnverein* program was to strengthen the young men's bodies so that they would be prepared when war with Napoleon came. Jahn developed much of the gymnastic equipment still in use in the *Turnverein* gymnasiums, including the horizontal bar, the side horse, the vaulting horse, and parallel bars. *Turnverein* training emphasized achieving physical fitness and good health through exercise and also encouraged patriotism. During the Revolution of 1848, many *Turnverein* members supported the revolutionaries and consequently were forced by the triumphant monarchy to leave Germany; they established *Turnvereins* in the nations where they settled. One of the movement's legatees, the Deutsche Turnerschaft (German Gymnastic Association), organized youth divisions for those between 13 and 17 years of age that by 1884 had an enrollment of 30,000, rising to 184,000 in 1912. In addition, in the latter year 62,000 schoolboys and 25,000 schoolgirls were involved.

Twenty-One Demands Protest   (China) massive student demonstrations against demands placed on China by the Japanese government in 1915. Japan presented the Twenty-One Demands in January to the government of Yüan Shih-k'ai, the first president of the Chinese Republic although a former military commander for the Manchu (Qing) dynasty (China's last dynasty, which lost power in 1911). Central to these demands was the provision that China recognize Japanese authority and dominance in Shandong, Inner Mongolia, Manchuria, the southeastern coastal provinces, and the Yangtze (Chang) River valley. One article in the demands provided for the appointment of Japanese "advisers" to key posts in the civil administration, the army, the government, and the police and assumed for Japan the right to supply most of China's armaments. Public disclosure of the Twenty-One Demands generated opposition and a movement to boycott Japanese goods. But Yüan Shi-kai, probably having no means to resist, accepted the demands on May 25. In protest, Chinese students staged demonstrations nationwide, and Chinese students studying in Japan returned home to join the protests, which constituted a precursor to the MAY FOURTH MOVEMENT.

Unbedingten, Die   (Germany) a radical student group within the BURSCHENSCHAFTEN that Karl FOLLEN helped to found at Jena in 1818–19. The term *Unbedingten* ("absolutists" or "unconditionals") defined the group's extreme sense of rightness and mission. One of the group's members was Karl SAND.

União Nacional des Etudantes (National Union of Students, UNE)   (Brazil) a national federation of state and local student groups that was formed in 1938, during the first regime (1930–45) of Getúlio Vargas. By 1947, radical nationalistic students had control of UNE, resulting in clashes with police and periodic closings of its Rio de Janeiro headquarters. But by the end of 1950, more moderate students were in control. UNE advocated university reforms, including increased funding and more scholarships, and opposed sending troops to Korea as part of the United Nations force. For 10 years, UNE had promoted creation of a national petroleum monopoly known as Petrobas, which was established in 1953; subsequently, Petrobras provided UNE with funding. A major event for UNE was participation with workers and Rio's Metropolitan Union of Students (UME) in massive demonstrations in Rio in late May 1956 to protest a 100 percent increase in trolley fares. The protesters blockaded intersections and overturned trolleys to prevent the movement of traffic. President Kubitschek ordered the militia to suppress the demonstrations, resulting in 150 arrests and several wounded protestors. Demonstrations erupted in other cities, students arrived in Rio from other universities to support the protest, and UME students called for a nationwide three-day strike. Kubitschek met with the presidents of UNE and UME, and the trolley fares were halved—a clear-cut student victory. In addition, the federal government began to subsidize UNE and the individual student unions. In the years following 1956 the leadership of UNE gravitated toward radical Leftist politics, consistently denouncing United States "imperialism," defending Cuba, and advocating revolution throughout Latin America. In 1962, UNE launched a campaign to achieve one-third representation of students on faculty councils, but despite a two-month strike the campaign fell short. On November 9, 1964 the government of Humberto Castelo Branco legally terminated UNE through the Suplicy Law, but it persisted in a much-reduced state, even holding sparsely attended congresses in 1965 and 1966.

Union Chrétienne de Jeunes Gens   (France) the first youth organization in France, formed in about 1840.

Union des Étudiants Communistes (UEC)   (France) an organization for students created in 1956 by the Parti Communiste Français (PCF, French Communist Party) following the HUNGARIAN REVOLUTION, which was disillusioning for many students. Barred from memberships in the National Bureau of the UNION NATIONAL DES ÉTUDIANTS DE FRANCE (UNEF) during the Algerian War, UEC began to capture UNEF leadership posts in the early 1960s but lost influence in UNEF later in the decade. In 1961, Trotskyist students broke away from UEC to form the Comité de Liaison des Étudiants Révolutionnaire (CLER). From 1963 to 1965, other UEC members broke with the official policies of the PCF, rejecting Stalinism while advocating a democratic openness and cooperation with other left-wing student groups in support of UNEF policies. Members were especially outraged by the PCF's backing of François Mitterand in the 1965 presidential election. In response, the party purged dissidents from the UEC during 1965–67, while at the same time other members fell away to found rival groups, effectively dissipating the UEC's viability. Some of the purged students founded the Jeunesse Communiste Révolutionaire (JCR) in 1966. By 1968, the UEC had lost so many members that only about 1,500 remained in its ranks. The UEC published its own magazine entitled *Clarté*.

Union des Jeunes Filles de France (France) a youth organization for girls that was established by the Parti Communiste Français (PCF, French Communist Party).

Union des Jeunesses Communistes (UJCML) (France) a youth organization that was established by the Parti Communiste Français (PCF, French Communist Party) and was controlled by its Central Committee.

Unione Nazionale Universitaria Rappresentativa Italiana (UNURI) (Italy) a national university-students' union that was founded in 1947. Through the 1950s UNURI focused on university and student issues; students who represented the coalition of the Socialist and Christian Democratic parties were in control. UNURI supported student occupation of the University of Rome in 1960 that was actually the work of Intesa, a Catholic organization, and an association of communist and socialist students known as UGI. The occupation was intended to demonstrate student opposition to a law to reform higher education that was proposed by the government of Amintore Fanfani, but when it was revealed how few students were actually involved, the protest failed totally, damaging UNURI's credibility. After 1963, UNURI lost support among students, and in 1968, the very "year of the student" marked by student uprisings in many other nations, the organization dissolved itself. The Italian student scene was left to relatively small and regional organizations.

Union Générale des Étudiants Congolais (UGEC) (Congo) a national student organization that was founded by a congress that met at Lovanium on May 4–7, 1961 and was attended by students from Belgium, France, and the United States as well as Lovanium University. UGEC elected as its first president Henri Takizala, who had been a commissioner in the COLLÈGE DES COMMISSAIRES and also a leader of the Union Nationale des Étudiants du Congo et du Ruanda-Urundi, formed in March 1961. The congress also passed a resolution deploring the Congo's political circumstances and advocating creation of a "Government of Public Safety" to rule for two years, as well as a resolution that advocated expanding adult education, ensuring autonomy for the universities, and adapting curricula to African conditions. These resolutions were ignored. But at its second congress held in Léopoldville (Kinshasa) in August 1963, a time of labor strikes and government repression, UGEC adopted an activist stance together with a new slogan, "All for the People and their Revolution!" The delegates declared the assassinated Patrice Lumumba a national hero, denounced the actions of the failed Collège des Commis-

saires, and advocated such causes as nationalization of private property, improved working conditions for laborers, and antiimperialism. UGEC's new student leaders voiced a militant view that aroused opposition from some students. And the factionalism that erupted following Moise Tshombe's return to power in July 1964 tore UGEC apart, dispelling its political viability. But UGEC began to revive after a third congress in October 1966, which approved radical resolutions, such as one calling for a single-party socialist state with a "people's army" to hunt down reactionaries. UGEC's recovery stemmed partly from the role of Joseph Mobutu, who had seized the presidency in November 1965, showed a willingness to work with the student organization, and tried to bring university-trained individuals into the administration.

Bibliography: Donald K. Emmerson, ed., *Students and Politics in Developing Nations* (New York: Praeger, 1968).

Union Générale des Étudiants de Côte d'Ivoire (UGECI) (Ivory Coast) a student association that was formed in 1956 by the Association des Étudiants de Côte d'Ivoire en France (AECIF) and the Association Générale des Étudiants et des Élève de Côte d'Ivoire (AGEECI). The AECIF, founded in 1948, was affiliated with the Parti Démocratique de Côte d'Ivoire (PDCI) with ties to the French Communist Party and later with the FÉDÉRATION DES ÉTUDIANTS D'AFRIQUE NOIRE EN FRANCE (FEANF) and through it with the INTERNATIONAL UNION OF STUDENTS (IUS). The AGEECI was formed in 1952 by Ivory Coast students in French West Africa—most of them centered in Dakar, Sénégal. All of these student groups were significant in that the majority of Ivory Coast leaders following the achievement of independence from France in 1960 had been officers of one of them, and these groups had thus served as political training grounds. The PDCI controlled the government after independence.

l'Union Générale des Étudiants du Québec (UGEQ) (Canada) a syndicalist political organization of student groups that was formed in 1963 and 1964 in Quebec. The catalyst for its founding was the provincial assembly's granting of suffrage to persons age 18 and older in February 1963. In March the Association Générale des Étudiants de l'Université de Montréal (AGEUM) convened a conference that was attended by students from universities in the Montreal area who formed a provisional UGEQ committee. Other student organizations throughout Québec became involved, and on April 1, 1964 they staged a march on the city of Québec that solidified the movement and led to formal creation of UGEQ in November 1964. Implicit in UGEQ's founding were English-French antagonisms and the issue of French separatism that plague Québec in particular and Canada as a whole, because to become UGEQ members, student organizations were required to withdraw from the national federation of all Canadian students, the Canadian Union of Students (CUS)—a requirement justified on the grounds of differences in language, culture, and aspirations. As a consequence student organizations at many schools, notably McGill University in Montreal, rejected membership in UGEQ.

Union Générale des Étudiants Musulmans Algériens (UGEMA)

(France) an organization of Muslim Algerian university students that was founded in Paris in July 1955, when Algeria was a French colony involved in a war for liberation and independence—the war began November 1, 1954. The sons of French *colons* controlled the Association Générale des Étudiants (AGE) at the University of Algiers, where Muslim students were barred from forming a union of their own. UGEMA was therefore founded in France with the ostensible purpose of promoting the Algerian national culture (namely, the Arabic language and the Islamic faith) as a way of sidestepping French law, while also, because it was Muslim by name, preventing membership by French Algerians. UGEMA had sections in 25 nations where Algerian students were studying.

UGEMA of course supported the war for Algerian independence and the FRONT DE LIBÉRATION NATIONALE (FLN) which directed the independence movement. At its second congress, held in Paris in March 1956, UGEMA approved a resolution that advocated Algerian independence, which resulted in the arrest of many Muslim students in France and Algeria. The brutal torture and murder of a young Muslim student at a *lycée* in Algiers goaded the UGEMA Algiers section to action, with its leaders on May 16, 1956 calling for a boycott of classes and for all Muslim students to join the FLN's Army of National Liberation (ALN). Supported by UGEMA's leadership in Paris, the boycott proved a great success; nearly all of the 520 Algerian students at the Univerity of Algiers went on strike, and they were joined by more than 5,000 high school students throughout Algeria. UGEMA also was most effective in disseminating information and propaganda that won support for the independence movement among student groups worldwide, including both the INTERNATIONAL STUDENT CONFERENCE (ISC) and the INTERNATIONAL UNION OF STUDENTS (IUS). Consequently, French authorities tried to suppress UGEMA through arrests, torture, and executions—UGEMA's president, for example was arrested in February 1957 and held without a proper trial for four years. On January 22, 1958, the French government declared UGEMA banned and subsequently arrested the members of its executive committee along with 50 other student leaders who were rounded up throughout France. When released the UGEMA leaders fled to Switzerland and established the organization's headquarters in Lausanne; later they moved the headquarters to Tunis.

In December 1961 the provisional government of the FLN in Tunis disbanded the UGEMA executive committee and placed its own nine-man University Section in control of the student group—an act that seriously threatened UGEMA's survival. Following Algerian independence in July 1962, rival factions threw the nation into civil war, which further threatened UGEMA's viability as the factionalism sundered its unity. The fragmentation evidenced itself at the fifth congress held in Algiers in September, which ended in chaos. The August 1963 congress voted to rename UGEMA; it became the UNION NATIONALE DES ÉTUDIANTS ALGÉRIENS (UNEA)

Bibliography: Donald K. Emmerson, ed., *Students and Politics in Developing Nations* (New York: Praeger, 1968).

Union Générale des Étudiants Tunisiens (UGET)

(France) an organization of Tunisian students that was founded at a secret meeting in Paris in July 1952. UGET supported the Neo-Destours Party's opposition to French control of Tunisia and became so closely linked to the party in the years following the achievement of independence in 1956 that it lacked credibility among students and was at times even the object of student protests.

Unión Latinoamericana

a continentwide organization that was formed in March 1925 by intellectuals who had been involved with the UNIVERSITY REFORM PROGRAM AND MOVEMENT. Antiimperialist and antimilitarist, the union advocated free education and university reform throughout Latin America and also democratic government and nationalization of natural resources. Its causes were supported by the ALIANZA POPULAR REVOLUCIONARIA AMERICANA and by student federations throughout Latin America.

Union Nationale des Étudiants Algériens (UNEA)

(Algeria) the successor organization to the UNION GENERALE DES ÉTUDIANTS MUSULMANS ALGÉRIENS (UGEMA), with the new name being adopted in August 1963, a year following Algerian independence. The early leaders of UNEA were supporters of the Algerian Communist Party's policies. UNEA expressed its major national goals as opposition to "colonialism, neocolonialism, and imperialism" and support for creating a "socialist economy." It also called, unsuccessfully, for university reforms that would have awarded students increased power. UNEA also supported membership in the communist-oriented INTERNATIONAL UNION OF STUDENTS (IUS). In early 1965, however, with the support of President Ahmed Ben Bella, student members of the FRONT DE LIBÉRATION NATIONALE (FLN) finally gained control of UNEA with the intent of ending its communist leanings. Then on June 19, 1965, Colonel Houari Boumedienne seized control of the government in a coup d'état; when about a thousand pro-Ben Bella students marched in Algiers in protest, Boumedienne sent troops against them. At the end of January 1966, members of the Algiers section of UNEA staged a demonstration that involved 1,500 students and resulted in the arrest of more than 30 students. The demonstration inspired a strike by most of the 8,000 students at the University of Algiers. But neither the demonstrations nor the strike gained anything, and leaders who supported Boumedienne and his policies assumed control of UNEA.

Union Nationale des Étudiants de France (UNEF) (France) a national federation of the Associations d'Étudiants at each of the universities. UNEF was founded on May 4, 1907 at a meeting of delegates from ASSOCIATION GÉNÉRALE DES ÉTUDIANTS chapters that represented various universities assembled at Lille. Like the individual chapters that formed its membership, UNEF played a minor role before World War I, effecting no real unity or national purpose. After the war, as middle-class youths swelled the numbers of students (58,000 in 1926, double the 1900 figure), UNEF's role changed. Especially following the advent of the Great Depression of the 1930s, its purpose focused on achieving subsidized housing, grants, and health and other benefits from the government. But a lack of national unity or involvement in politics left UNEF with weak leadership, preventing it from becoming a strong umbrella organization and advocate.

During World War II, the organization cooperated with the Vichy government and thus lost credibility as a representative organization of students (many of whom participated in the Resistance). Consequently, after the war, at the 1946 Grenoble Convention, students sympathetic to the Resistance were able to win control of UNEF's leadership positions on its National Bureau (executive committee). They transformed UNEF into a democratic advocacy organization, fostering demonstrations and strikes to promote students' causes. A UNEF-sponsored strike in 1947 won reduced university fees and government grants for students. A 1948 strike won a students' health service, administered by students and funded by the National Health Service, that included free medical care, clinics, and mental hospitals. In 1950 UNEF began to advocate that the government award students a salary, but liberal or left-wing students lost control of the leadership in the same year, regaining it in 1956. For the next five years, UNEF was preoccupied with the issue of independence for Algeria, which its membership came to support.

General Charles DeGaulle, who came to power in 1958, disliked UNEF's opposition to his policies and curtailed its influence. Probably the major issue then confronting the French government was the Algerian independence movement; in June 1960, after four years of bickering over the issue and of refusal to recognize the UNION GÉNÉRALE DES ÉTUDIANTS MUSULMANS ALGÉRIENS (UGEMA), UNEF publicly supported independence for Algeria and joined with UGEMA in requesting that the French government negotiate with the FRONT DE LIBÉRATION NATIONALE (FLN) to bring the war of liberation in Algeria to a close. UNEF organized mass demonstrations against the war in Algeria; assisted students to avoid being drafted into the military; and supported the Front Universitaire Antifasciste (FUA), another student organization whose sole purpose was to fight against the regime and the Organization de l'Armée Secrète (OAS), the right-wing group that promoted repression in Algeria and waged war against the Arabs. In the 1960s and 1970s, UNEF adopted an ideology termed "revolutionary syndicalism," which advocated PARTICIPATORY DEMOCRACY within both the universities and the society at large.

Bibliography: A. Belden Fields, *Student Politics in France: A Study of the Union Nationale des Étudiants de France* (New York: Basic Books, 1970).

Union Nationale des Étudiants en Médecine (France) an organization that was created in March 1961 by students representing several schools of medicine, which divorced themselves from association with the UNION NATIONALE DES ÉTUDIANTS DE FRANCE (UNEF) because of its political positions. The new association announced its intent to be apolitical.

Union Nationale des Étudiants Marocains (UNEM) (Morocco) an organization of Morrocan students that was formed in summer 1956, following the attainment of Morrocan independence. UNEM was effectively controlled by the radical faction of the Istiqlal Party led by Mehdi Ben Barka and later (1959) became aligned with the radical Union National des Forces Populaires (UNFP)—thus incurring the monarchy's opposition. During the 1960s, UNEM staged strikes and demonstrations in Casablanca, Fez, and Rabat against the government.

Union of Free Poles (Poland) a student secret society (*see* POLONIA) that was founded at Warsaw University in late 1819 by L. Piatkiewicz and W. Heltman. The Union of Free Poles differed from most other student secret societies in that its members were dedicated to political activism and conspiratorial dealings with secret societies in other nations, their intent being to liberate Poland from Russian rule and to reunite the nation under a liberal government. Like other student secret societies, however, the union modeled its organization upon that of the Masons and consisted of lodges, the highest one with only five members and led by a grand master in charge of the union's overall organization and activities. To spread the union's views, the leadership in early 1821 established a periodical entitled *Dekada Polska* (*The Polish Decade*), edited by Piatkiewicz and Heltman. Through this periodical, they disseminated numerous liberal articles that had appeared in French and German publications and provided accounts of revolutionary activities in other nations. But when they published the May Third Constitution on its 30th anniversary, the government cracked down. (The May Third Constitution, approved on May 3, 1791, had proven an unsuccessful effort to strengthen the Polish central government and prevent foreign interventions in Poland but nevertheless provided a rallying cry for Polish nationalists.) Grand Duke Constantine, Tsar Alexander's brother and the governmental head in Warsaw, arrested Piatkiewicz and Heltman, deporting the former to Austrian Poland and sentencing the latter to serve as a private in the Russian army. The harsh life of the army broke Heltman's will, and in the summer of 1823 he confessed, providing authorities with information about the union's purposes and membership. Although numerous arrests followed, other members had been prepared, had destroyed documents, and refused to confess during a six-month investigation; consequently, no punishments were inflicted—except an added sentence imposed on Heltman. But the union ceased to exist.

Union Patriotique des Organisations d'Étudiants (UPOE) (France) a union of student organizations that was founded at the end of World War II as an affiliate of the Union Patriotique des Organisations de Jeunesse, the youth organization that succeeded the FORCES UNIÉS DE JEUNESSE PATRIOTIQUE (FUJP). The UPOE was largely dominated by liberal Roman Catholic students who were affiliated with the JEUNESSE ÉTUDIANTE CHRÉTIENNE and by communist-oriented students.

Unitas Verband (Germany) a small Roman Catholic fraternity association that was founded in 1853 for theological students. Its purpose was the promotion of "morality, scholarship, and friendship." In 1887 Unitas opened its membership to nontheological students. Unitas had only 700 members in 1913, rising to only 2,438 in 1933. Unitas was unique among the Catholic fraternities in protesting against acceptance of the NATIONAL SOCIALIST GERMAN STUDENT UNION's order of January 1934 that they must accept Protestant members; it gave in, but with the insistence that Protestant members would have to hold separate religious services. Unitas was also the last Catholic fraternity to survive under Nazism, finally disbanding in July 1938 after the police ordered all Catholic fraternities dissolved.

United Boys' Brigades of America (United States) the U.S. offshoot of the BOYS' BRIGADE, a semimilitary organization for boys dedicated to instilling "true Christian manliness." The organization's programs include drill, Bible study, religious instruction, sports, camping, physical training, hiking, and other activities. Groups are open to boys age 12 and older. Each group is commanded

by a captain who must be at least 21 and lieutenants who are at least 18 years old. Membership has always been small and declined during the 1960s. The Boys' Brigades' headquarters is in Baltimore.

United Front (United States) a unity movement among disparate student organizations during the years 1934–39. The United Front was possible during these years because of basic agreement on policies advocated: opposition to war and promotion of peace, "collective security" in opposing fascism, and at least moral support of the Loyalists in the Spanish Civil War. These causes or goals brought together socialist, communist, isolationist, and liberal groups, most prominently in the AMERICAN STUDENT UNION (ASU), as the United Front, even though the groups maintained differing ideologies. The United Front collapsed soon after the Soviet Union concluded a nonaggression pact with Nazi Germany on August 24, 1939 that set the stage for the September 1 invasion of Poland and the beginning of World War II. The break resulted from the communist-oriented student groups' shift to advocating U.S. aid for the Allies and the Soviet Union, while other groups continued to support U.S. neutrality.

United States Student Assembly (USSA) (United States) a confederation of anticommunist, liberal student groups that was formed in 1943. During the World War II years, the USSA supported the U.S. military effort. When it peaked after the war in 1946, with representation at more than 70 colleges and universities and a membership of 3,000, the USSA devoted its energies to relief aid for war-ravaged nations. In April 1947 the USSA became an affiliate of Americans for Democratic Action as the STUDENTS FOR DEMOCRATIC ACTION (SDA).

United Student Peace Committee (USPC) (United States) a broadly based organization of Leftist, liberal, and pacifist antiwar groups that was formed in 1937 and that coordinated the student peace strike of that year (see STUDENT STRIKE AGAINST WAR). The USPC became the 1937 strike coordinator at the behest of the AMERICAN STUDENT UNION (ASU). The USPC's involvement brought into the antiwar demonstration the support of its constituent members, including the NATIONAL COUNCIL OF METHODIST YOUTH, the national councils of the student affiliates of the YOUNG MEN'S CHRISTIAN ASSOCIATION (YMCA) and the YOUNG WOMEN'S CHRISTIAN ASSOCIATION (YWCA), various other student religious groups, the NATIONAL STUDENT FEDERATION (NSF), the AMERICAN YOUTH CONGRESS (AYC), and the ASU—thus greatly broadening the base of the antiwar strike and the potential pool of demonstrators. The USPC, was predominantly pacifist, though also essentially isolationist or at least noninterventionist, in orientation. It participated in the 1938 antiwar strike but less overtly because of controversy over supporting collective security or interventionist measures.

United World Federalists (UWF)   (United States) a movement that advocated world government, begun by university students in 1942. By 1945, UWF had chapters at colleges and universities in 25 states, and in 1946 they held a national conference that established UWF as a national organization with 2,500 student members. The new organization published a newspaper entitled *The Student Federalist* and promoted creation in 1947 of a UWF for nonstudent adults that attained a membership of 40,000. The student UWF peaked in 1949 with a membership of 5,800. The federalists focused on the United Nations as the potential progenitor of a world government, but dissensions within that organization and the conflicts of the burgeoning cold war doomed their hopes. By 1950 the UWF was in decline, never to effect a significant impact.

Universidad Central de Venezuela Protests (Venezuela) a series of violent student demonstrations and strikes at the Universidad Central de Venezuela (UCV), following an order issued on December 14, 1966 by the government of President Raúl Leoni that directed armed police to occupy the university. The order constituted a reinterpretation of university autonomy, allowing government authorities to invade the campus and take control of access to it through occupation of nearby streets. Students reacted with violent protests, and the government responded by closing down the UCV in early 1967. The conflict generated a fierce rivalry between the Partido Comunista de Venezuela (PCV) and the Movimiento de Izquierda Revolucionaria (MIR) political forces at the UCV, with the PCV advocating resolving the conflict through negotiations and the MIR promoting ongoing student strikes. The Leoni government, however, refused to compromise, and the student protests petered out, with student elections in 1968 indicating that a majority favored accommodation and negotiations.

University Act Protest   (Burma) the first student political movement in Burma (then a province of British-ruled India) that was formed as a protest against the stipulations of the University Act of 1920. At the time, Burma had two institutions of higher learning, Rangoon College (founded in 1884 as an affiliate of the University of Calcutta), and a Baptist school, Judson College, established in 1894—neither of which awarded degrees. The University Act of 1920 proposed creation of an independent residential university but set very high standards of qualification for entrance; those who failed to qualify could be admitted on a probationary status. Burmese students opposed these entrance qualifications and organized a protest strike for December 4, 1920. The strike quickly gained the support of secondary school students,

Burmese politicians, and the general public. The student protestors demanded creation of a system of schools devoted to instruction in Burmese language, literature, and history and in technology. Toward this end, they set up such schools at Buddhist monasteries and other sites, with both students and monks serving as teachers. The system spread throughout Burma, but, plagued by lack of funding and never recognized by the Department of Education, the system collapsed in 1922. The student strike itself failed within a year, never attaining the students' major goals. It was important, however, for the nationwide support and coalition of political groups it generated and for the stature it gained for students as a future political force.

University Christian Movement (UCM)   (United States) a Protestant ecumenical student movement founded in 1966. The UCM subsumed the NATIONAL STUDENT CHRISTIAN FEDERATION (NSCF). The UCM in turn fell victim to the turmoil generated by the NEW LEFT student movement and disbanded in 1969.

University Federation for Independence (FUPI) (Puerto Rico) a militant student organization that was begun in 1956 at the main campus (Río Piedras) of the University of Puerto Rico. It has been the largest politically oriented student organization, with a membership of a few hundred, and the most left-wing in Puerto Rico; although small, its influence is extensive. FUPI claimed to be the successor to the General Council of Students (the student government organization dissolved by the chancellor in 1948 following the PRO-CAMPOS DEMONSTRATIONS) and thus the representative organization for the entire student body. FUPI is dedicated to achieving Puerto Rican independence and upholding the interests of students. It has advocated autonomy for and democratic processes within the university and, within the larger society, the end of militarism, racism, political repression, and other injustices. Events related to the 1964 gubernatorial election led to FUPI's attainment of some major goals. FUPI organized an electoral boycott as a means of highlighting Puerto Rico's "colonial" status, while at the same time the group advocated university co-government involving students, professors, and administrators. FUPI hecklers were injured at a rally by the small University Federation of Anti-Communists (FAU) and in response staged a protest march through the campus on October 28—a violation of university regulations. Student sympathizers joined them. The police were called in and dispersed the demonstrators, leading to a riot supported by still other students that involved stone throwing, tear gas, burning police cars, and the arrest of 11 students. The chancellor closed the campus until November 5, but these events had galvanized student and faculty support for reforms. On October 29, an assemblage of 5,000 protestors marched to the Capital Building in San Juan.

These protests and continuing pressure resulted in legislation granting a campus student government and other reforms at the University of Puerto Rico. FUPI was a major organizer of a March 11, 1971 demonstration for Puerto Rican independence at Río Piedras; the demonstration spawned a battle with Reserve Officer Training Corps (ROTC) students and rioting, with shooting and rock throwing, that resulted in the death of one ROTC student and two police officers and the wounding of 50 students, police officers, and professors. Students then raged through Río Piedras, attacking shops with U.S. affiliations, breaking windows, and setting fires. Police arrested 64 students on March 12 for involvement in the riots; on March 17 a 20-year-old student was arraigned for killing one of the police officers during the riots.

Bibliography: Arthur Liebman, *The Politics of Puerto Rican University Students* (Austin: University Press of Texas, 1970).

University Reform Program and Movement (Argentina) a movement of enormous and long-lasting significance for all of Latin America that was begun by students at the University of Córdoba in 1918. On March 14, 1918, the students' Comité pro-Reforma at Córdoba announced a general strike, including boycotting classes, to start on April 1 when the school year began and to last until their reform demands were accepted. The students' initial manifesto criticized the university for intellectual dishonesty, a failure to adhere to scientific objectivity, religious influence on the curriculum, and dictatorial administration. University officials rejected their demands, and so on March 31 the Comité pro-Reforma staged a rally in the city to generate public support. Faced with empty classrooms on April 1, officials closed the university until the student strike ended. The students sent a delegation and the administration sent two professors to Buenos Aires who met with university officials and the minister of education. The professors argued that reforms were neeeded but that the students' demands were excessive. In response, the minister of education sent his attorney general, José Matienzo, to Córdoba to investigate and to propose remedial measures. Arriving on April 16, Matienzo proposed the resumption of normal operations while he conducted his investigation, and the students acceded by ending their strike. Matienzo's report blamed stagnant membership in the academic councils for the problems at Córdoba and proposed periodic council elections with full faculty participation—a proposal President Hipólito Irigoyen instituted by decree on May 7. The decree meant that all administrative posts at the University of Córdoba were vacant and were to be filled by elections at the end of May.

Encouraged by this result, the students formed the Federación Universitaria de Córdoba (FUC) to replace the Comité pro-Reforma and to pursue attainment of their remaining reform demands. The FUC aligned itself with the recently formed FEDERACIÓN UNIVERSITARIA ARGENTINA (FUA) and began to publish a periodical to advocate reform. But when the students' candidate for rector lost to a conservative candidate in the June 15 election, the students rioted, took control of the university's buildings, and then marched through the streets of Córdoba. Although a group of conservative students and professors formed the Comité por Defensa de la Universidad to oppose the reformists, the Córdoba reform movement now gained nationwide support from students at other schools and from a variety of newspapers, liberal organizations, and political parties. Thus university reform became a national issue. The reformists increased the pressure, a highlight of their campaign being the First National Congress of University Students convened in Córdoba on July 21 and attended by 12 delegates from each of the five university federations who met for eight days. The congress issued a statement of proposals known as the CÓRDOBA MANIFESTO that included university autonomy, competitive selection and periodic review of professors, free university education open to all qualified applicants, optional class attendance, extension classes for members of the working class, and other reforms.

Soon after the congress, Irigoyen appointed a liberal intellectual as a new intervenor to visit Córdoba, and on August 7 the conservative rector announced his resignation. Because of opposition from conservatives, however, Irigoyen replaced his original intervenor appointee with his Minister of Education José Salinas. As Salinas's arrival was deferred and the university's shutdown extended to nearly three months, the reformists' impatience grew; on September 9, a group of 83 FUC members occupied and barricaded the university's buildings and declared themselves in control. They sent a message to Salinas advising him of their action and urging him to come to Córdoba soon. Troops invaded the university and arrested the students, but they had won their goal: Salinas arrived on September 12. Greeted by enthusiastic students, Salinas assumed direction of the university, interviewed administrators and students, and returned to Buenos Aires to report to the president. On October 7, 1918, Irigoyen issued a decree that instituted nearly all the reforms demanded by the University of Córdoba student reformists, including student representation on the university governing councils, periodic council elections, more flexible examination procedures, optional class attendance, and greater freedom to professors in choosing lecture materials. In addition, Salinas appointed some new administrators and professors who were approved by the students.

Considered the most influential movement in the history of Latin American education, the university reform movement generated a significant legacy. That legacy included founding the Federación Universitaria Argentina (FUA); establishing the precedent of using rallies, demonstrations, manifestoes, and congresses to garner public and media attention and support; arranging meetings and interviews with government officials; staging riots, occupation of buildings, or other actions leading to confrontations with police and other authorities; and involving university student organizations in national affairs. The university reform movement promoted greater student involvement in university administrations, with student representation on governing boards; competitive selection of instructors rather than appointment by aristocrats; fixed terms of appointment for instructors (about seven years), after which they could be reappointed following academic review; student involvement in the academic-review process; liberalization of university entrance requirements; financial aid programs for students; abolishing tuition fees; grading based entirely on examinations; students' right to repeat courses as often as desired and to attend only those lectures of their choice; and adherence to the principle that students should be civic-minded and devoted to improving their communities. This program revealed a major shift in opening the universities, until now the sinecures of the aristocracy, to the middle and lower socioeconomic classes. It spurred the modernization of Argentina's universities as agents of progress and change rather than conservatism. The university reform program spread quickly, being adopted in 1919 at universities in Chile, Cuba, Mexico, Ecuador, and subsequently throughout Latin America, with 18 nations enacting into law some or all of the reform proposals. The movement generally succeeded in institutionalizing the principle of university autonomy—although at times universities have been closed by dictatorial governments—and participation of students in governing boards (*Co-Gobierno*), with a representation usually comprising from one-fourth to one-third of each board's membership. Students are also strongly represented in most faculty councils.

Unfortunately and rather ironically, the first governmental effort to undo university reform occurred in its birthplace, Argentina, where Máximo Marcelo T. de Alvear succeeded Irigoyen in 1922. Alvear threw his support to reactionaries in the universities who did their best to overturn or gut reforms during his presidency, which lasted until 1928. The Argentine universities thereafter continued to suffer from suppression of reforms and violations of their autonomy through the reign of Juan Perón, who was overthrown in 1955.

Bibliography: Richard J. Walter, *Student Politics in Argentina: The University Reform and Its Effects, 1918–1964* (New York: Basic Books, 1968).

Up Against the Wall: Motherfuckers   (United States) an offbeat and anarchistic youth group within the NEW LEFT of the late 1960s, notable for its members' uninhibited, pseudo-proletarian lifestyle, including an argot replete with profuse obscenities. Typical of their antics was a New York Motherfuckers' march up Sixth Avenue, carrying garbage gathered from the streets in the Lower East Side and dumping it before the Lincoln Center as a protest against materialism and high culture's indifference toward street people. Motherfuckers also disrupted meetings of the STUDENTS FOR A DEMOCRATIC SOCIETY (SDS) to protest what they regarded as the New Left's vapid political rhetoric and wrangling.

Up With People   (United States), a unique program for youths of all nations that began in 1965 to promote international understanding and cooperation, along with personal development through involvement in international travel, community service, educational programs, and performing arts. Each year, Up With People involves more than 700 college-age (17 to 25) students representing 20 to 30 different nations in a program of travel, service, and education that lasts for 11 months. The participants are divided into five casts that travel together worldwide; they live with more than 80 host families in the communities that they visit in different nations. Participants experience training in business management through daily involvement in the program's operations, including public relations, sales, finances, advance promotion of performances, planning events, public speaking, and internships. In each community that they visit, they participate in some community service, such as programs for school children, conservation projects, and building houses for the homeless with Habitat for Humanity. In each community they also provide a staged performance that involves them in singing, dancing, stagecraft, and instrumental music. During the year, the students travel about 30,000 miles and enjoy participating in local festivals, visiting historic sites, and learning about different national cultures, languages, art, folklore, politics, and religions. More than 17,000 youths from 79 different nations have participated in this program. Up With People is headquartered in Broomfield, Colorado.

Valle Giulia Protest   (Italy) a student demonstration at the Valle Giulia in Rome on March 1, 1968 that erupted into a vicious riot and a furious battle with the police. While suppressing the protestors, the police arrested more than 250 students. The brutal violence of the police response aroused large-scale newspaper and public sympathy for the students and opposition to the police. This outcome constituted a victory for the protestors, a turning point for the Italian student movement, and a crisis for the Christian Democratic-Socialist coalition national government, as the Socialists threatened to abandon the coalition if the repression of student demonstrators—the policy of the interior ministry—continued.

Velvet Revolution   (Czechoslovakia) the peaceful transfer of government control after the mass resignations of the neo-Stalinist leaders of the governing Central Committee, the Presidium, and the Secretariat in November 1989, following massive nationwide demonstrations to protest brutal police suppression of a student demonstration on November 17. The student demonstration had been totally nonviolent: young women placed flowers on the shields of riot police officers; in Wenceslas Square the students lit candles in memory of those who had died during the suppression of the PRAGUE SPRING of 1968. But police attacked the students with fury. The subsequent protests and resulting nonviolent revolution were spearheaded by university students and artists. Among the groups involved was the Union of Socialist Youth, which demanded the government's resignation. The widespread protests involved numerous recently formed dissident groups (including the Civic Forum), led to a general strike on November 27, and culminated in selection of a new government—a government in which, for the first time in 40 years, Communists did not comprise the majority. Alexander Dubcek, leader of the Prague Spring, became chairman of the Federal

Assembly on December 28, and on December 29 Václav Havel was elected president. The momentous end of Communist domination in Czechoslovakia had eventuated from an initial student protest.

Venezuelan Revolution   (Venezuela) a popular uprising of 1958 that was initiated by students of the Central University in Caracas against the dictatorship of Pérez Jiménez; he had come to power through a military coup in November 1948 that overthrew a democratically elected government. The Jiménez regime had banned political activity, temporarily closed universities, censured the press, and suppressed labor unions, terrorizing the public while enriching officials through corrupt business dealings. Jiménez's security police repeatedly assassinated secretaries of the Acción Democrática Party (ADP), which had formerly held the presidency and whose leadership was in exile. Students at Central University continued to protest against the regime, which closed the university temporarily in 1952 to discourage their protests. At the end of 1955, students secretly organized a National University Front to oppose the regime, and during the next two years they made preparations for its overthrow. A sham plebiscite held in December 1957 to validate Jiménez's "re-election" to another five-year term generated creation of an underground conspiracy (the Patriotic Junta) by suppressed political parties that formed an alliance with the National University Front. On January 1, 1958, air force jets dive-bombed the palace as a sign to military conspirators to attack the regime, but this revolt emerged too slowly and was quickly put down by military units loyal to Jiménez. Jiménez made a few concessions, however, including dismissal of the minister of the interior and the head of the security police, in an effort to preclude further opposition.

But students at the Central University plotted a revolution, which they began on January 14 with a massive demonstration and pursued with ongoing street riots. They were soon joined by thousands of workers and unemployed slum dwellers. The protestors erected barricades in the streets of Caracas and torched buses and trucks. Efforts by the military and the secret police to suppress the riots proved unsuccessful. Many intellectuals and businesspeople joined in denouncing the Jiménez regime; and members of the BOYS OF 1928, including former president Rómulo Betancourt, threw their support to the students, the "boys of 1958." Clergy and others joined the demonstrations, and navy destroyers moved into position to shell the city if Jiménez did not abdicate. During the night of January 22, Jiménez fled to safety in the Dominican Republic as students, now joined by rebellious troops, attacked and occupied the headquarters of the security police. A civilian-military junta governed Venezuela for the next year, and then Betancourt was elected president. When the Betancourt government was threatened by a coup in July 1958 after only six months in office, the Central University students, joined by the faculty, again took to the streets, armed themselves with Molotov cocktails, and occupied defensive positions throughout Caracas to uphold the democratic government. Workers and slum dwellers again came to their support, and the coup was thwarted. Betancourt visited the university to thank the students for their support; in March 1964 he completed his term of office—the first democratically elected president to do so in 134 years.

Bibliography: Judith Ewell, *Venezuela: A Century of Change.* (Stanford, Calif.: Stanford University Press, 1984).

Venezuelan University Reform Protests   (Venezuela) an ongoing series of student protests in 1969–71 against reforms in higher education proposed by the government of President Rafael Caldera. The proposed reforms would impose restrictions on university autonomy and on student voting rights and also limitations on the terms of service for university officials—an effort to get rid of incompetent administrators and instructors. Violent protests had occurred at the Universidad de los Andes in 1969 and 1970, with students at the Universidad Central de Venezuela (UCV) joining the fray. In March 1971, high school students in Caracas joined the protests, which subsequently spread nationwide. At the time, students were also protesting against United States involvement in Vietnam. Nevertheless, the government finally succeeded in instituting the reforms.

Verbindungen   (Germany) university student fraternities, mostly formed following the Revolution of 1848. These were local but later joined in associations. The fraternities took many forms, such as the KORPS and the BURSCHENSCHAFTEN; some were dueling societies while others were little more than drinking clubs. The government of Prussia in 1878 banned schoolboys from

visiting taverns, the Verbindungen hangouts, and the interior minister argued that the Verbindungen constituted a danger both to students and to family life. Creation of the fraternity associations induced former fraternity members known as *alte Herren* (old fellows) to become supportive, donating funds for houses and activities, providing an employment network, serving as public spokesmen for the interests of the fraternities and their student members.

Verdandi Student Society   (Sweden) an organization that formed in 1882 at the University of Uppsala and was largely concerned with "cultural radicalism." Through the years Verdandi held discussions and symposia and published writings on controversial issues, including equality of the sexes, the failings of Christianity, abortion, atheism, class stratifications, and the role of the military. During the 1960s, when Verdandi comprised one of the largest student organizations in Sweden, the group's focus shifted to include issues relating to dictatorial regimes, the Vietnam War, the developing nations, and other subjects of international political concern. Verdandi's avowed philosophic orientation in considering all issues is "radical humanism."

Verein Deutscher Studenten (VDSt, Association of German Students)   (Germany) a student association that was founded in December 1880 at Berlin University for both fraternity (corporation) and nonfraternity members. During 1881, the VDSt quickly spread to Leipzig, Halle, Breslau, and other universities. Its initial purpose was "to affirm and cultivate German national consciousness," and it was open to all matriculated students "of German descent." But the VDSt soon restricted membership to Christians only. It became the student torchbearer not only of monarchical nationalism but also of virulent anti-Semitism. The VDSt organized the nationalistic Hartz Mountain meeting—an apparent imitation of the WARTBURG FESTIVAL—held on August 6, 1881 that was attended by 600 students and 200 nonstudent supporters. Although opposed by other more liberal student groups that objected to its program of perceived "religious persecution, class, or race hatred" and the advocacy of anti-Semitism, the VDSt gained enormous influence and was able to take effective control of and to politicize the student movement, forcing it rightward in the decades leading up to World War I. *See also* KYFFHAUSER VERBAND DER VEREINE DEUTSCHER.

Bibliography: Konrad H. Jarausch, *Students, Society, and Politics in Imperial Germany: The Rise of Academic Illiberalism* (Princeton, N.J.: Princeton University Press, 1982).

Versailles Treaty Protest   (Germany) a student demonstration held in Berlin on June 28, 1929, the anniversary of the signing of the Treaty of Versailles. Students from the University of Berlin and the Berlin Technical Institute had planned a peaceful demonstration to protest the treaty, but the Prussian government forbade faculty participation, an act the students considered a blow against academic freedom, and they reacted violently. About 1,500 students gathered at the Hegelplatz on the morning of June 28 for the protest. When the speeches were finished, they shouted for the protestors to march to the Ministry of Culture and confront Carl Heinrich Becker, the minister of culture responsible for educational policy. At the ministry, police reported, the students tried to storm the building; the police fired shots into the air and then attacked the students with billy clubs. The students dispersed but then gathered at the presidential palace and sang "Deutschland über Alles." Again the police dispersed them, and they assembled at the university, only to be driven off once more.

Veterans of Future Wars (VFW)　(United States) in effect an antiwar protest organization that was formed by Princeton University students early in the spring semester of 1936. The founders of the VFW were conservative Democrats whose purpose was to deride paying a bonus to World War I veterans as an example of "extravagant" government spending. The group's primary tenet was to demand the payment of veterans' bonuses in advance. Their position parodied the bonuses promised to veterans through legislation passed by Congress in 1925 and again in 1931 but not scheduled for payment until 1945—a circumstance that, combined with the effects of the Great Depression, inspired the 1932 march on Washington by the Bonus Expeditionary Force (Bonus Army), composed of unemployed veterans. Within a month after its founding, VFW chapters had sprung up at 50 campuses, and these became aligned with the antiwar movement through involvement in the STUDENT STRIKE AGAINST WAR of April 1936. (The Princeton founders rejected participation in the strike.) The VFW marchers contributed a satiric touch to the strike, with about 1,200 VFW members at the University of Washington staging a funeral for the "unknown soldier of tomorrow" that featured students masquerading as Adolf Hitler, Benito Mussolini, and J. P. Morgan as pallbearers. At Columbia University, 200 members of the VFW's William Randolph Hearst Post No. 1 marched down Broadway with 20 members of the university's band, preceded by a drum major twirling a crutch in place of a baton. A VFW women's auxiliary, the Association of Gold Star Mothers of Future Veterans, began at Vassar and then spread to other schools.

Vidyarthi Parishad　*See* AKHIL BHARATIYA VIDYARTHI PARISHAD.

Vienna Uprising of 1848　(Austria) the major event of the Revolution of 1848 in Austria, the uprising was instigated and led by University of Vienna students. Following the February Revolution in France that resulted in abdication of King Louis Phillippe, a group of medical students petitioned the Habsburg Emperor Ferdinand I to grant freedom of the press and speech, academic freedom, and a constitution. The Viennese police requested the professors to exercise control over the students before the petition was offered to the entire student body for signatures, but the appeal of rebellion had spread among the students, and the effort proved futile. When their petition went unanswered, the students organized a street demonstration. Police fired on the demonstrators, killing an 18-year-old mathematics student. The rebellious students, joined by workers, erected barricades in the streets of Vienna on March 12. The uprising forced the resignation on the following day of Prince Klemens Metternich, foreign minister of Austria for 39 years, who fled to England. The students demanded to be given arms, and the government acceded, ordering the armory to provide arms to anyone who could prove he was a student by answering questions in Latin. The armed students formed the Academic Legion, whose companies elected most of the members of a Committee of Safety.

Although the government promised to institute reforms (on March 15 Emperor Ferdinand I agreed to allow a constitution and freedom of the press), demonstrations continued through the succeeding weeks, with the rebel students in effective control of managing the capital. On April 25, the government proclaimed a new constitution, which was initially well received, but opposition soon arose, and on May 5 students protested, demanding revisions. On May 7, a Political Central Committee of the National Guard comprised of representatives of the National Guard and the students was formed; on May 10, with its membership swollen to 200, the committee offered an alternative constitution. The government obliged the commander of the National Guard to order the committee to disband but was finally forced to agree to the committee's demands in response to the order—agreeing to rescind the order, to formulate a new electoral law, and to preclude military intervention except at the National Guard's request. Conservative city residents demanded that the university be closed, but some 10,000 workers from outside the city along with the National Guard joined the students in response. The emperor and his family left the city on May 17, entrusting the government to the Committee of Safety.

Responding to criticism, the Academic Legion met to decide whether to disband and on May 21 decided to continue in operation; on May 22 the students agreed to allow closing of the university until October. On May 25 the government reversed itself and tried to force disbandment of the Academic Legion by sending in the military. Students and workers erected scores of barricades, and the government was again forced to rescind the order to disband the legion. Citizen sympathizers provided funds for food and drink for the Academic Legion, whose student patrols maintained order in the city and offered its citizens numerous services, including medical care and legal counsel. By the fall, however, the Academic Legion's cohesiveness had dwindled through resignations and faltering discipline, and militant workers operated outside the legion's control. A violent confrontation between the Academic Legion and the military on October 6 left Vienna in chaos. Armies commanded by Prince Alfred Windischgrätz, Austrian commandant at Prague who had successfully suppressed the rebellion there, and Josip Jelačić, governor of Croatia, attacked Vienna; the Legion rallied to fight courageously though futilely. On October 31 the conquering army took control of the city. By November 1 the Academic Legion had been disbanded and the revolutionary leaders had either fled or were under arrest. In December, Ferdinand I abdicated in favor of Franz Joseph; a new government headed by Prince Felix Schwarzenberg declared the constitution agreed to by Ferdinand not legally binding; in February 1849 the University of Vienna reopened; by summer 1849, the empire had returned to its prerevolutionary status.

Bibliography: R. J. Rath, *The Viennese Revolution of 1848.* (Austin: University of Texas Press, 1957).

Vietnam Moratorium Day (United States) October 15, 1969, unique in U.S. history as a day of nationwide and nationally coordinated demonstrations for peace—in this instance in support of a peace agreement to end the Vietnam War. Tens of thousands of university and high school students participated, along with adults from every walk of life. As a continuation of the Vietnam Moratorium on November 15, a huge march on Washington was staged to protest against the war. More than 250,000 people participated, making it the largest antiwar demonstration ever held in Washington.

Vietnam Summer (United States) a period of demonstrations during summer 1967 supporting a peaceful end to the Vietnam War. The Vietnam Summer was modeled after the FREEDOM SUMMER of 1964, and 200 youths organized the event. About 20,000 students participated nationwide.

Hippies celebrate "the war is over." (AP/WIDE WORLD PHOTOS)

Volkischer Waffenring (Volkisch Dueling Society) (Germany) an organization that was formed on December 15, 1934 by five dueling fraternity leagues that had withdrawn from the ALLGEMEINE DEUTSCHER WAFFENRING (ADW) while accusing the other ADW leagues of failing to purge their memberships of Jews and Freemasons. The five leagues—TURNERSCHAFT, Deutsche Sangerschaft, Deutsche Wehrschaft, Deutsche Burschenschaft, and Naumburger Thing—vowed to enforce the strictures of membership in the Nazi Party for their own members, including proof of "Aryan" ancestry dating back as far as January 1, 1800. They also expanded the honor code to include not merely a personal insult but any insult to the entire Volk community—the honor to be restored by a duel resulting in bloodshed.

Wachensturm (Germany) "storming of the guard-house" in Frankfurt on April 3, 1833 by about 50 radical students and instructors; they occupied several public buildings in the city in hopes of seizing control of the city and the Diet of the German Confederation that convened in the city and thereby fomenting a general revolution. These activists represented a conspiratorial movement, formed in reaction to the political repression following the HAMBACH FESTIVAL and were mostly affiliated with BURSCHENSCHAFTEN at Heidelberg and other universities in the region. Their act of rebellion, however, was quite feeble and easily suppressed, and it generated no support from the public. In fact, its result was increased repression by government authorities punctuated by mass arrests—about 1,800 people, 1,200 of them Burschenschaften members, went to jail. Thirty-nine Burschenschaften members jailed by the Prussian authorities were sentenced to death, although their sentences were later commuted to life terms; 150 others were sentenced to long terms in prison, where they experienced brutal treatment. Of the Wachensturm conspirators themselves, 11 were sentenced to life in prison. After Friedrich Wilhelm IV became king in 1840, he granted an amnesty to the Wachensturm conspirators and many others imprisoned during the repression that followed their abortive plot.

Wall Street Demonstrations (United States) student antiwar protests staged on Wall Street in New York City in May 1970 that were distinctive for generating opposition by construction workers. On May 8, protesting students gathered on Wall Street were suddenly attacked by construction workers wearing hard hats and shouting "All the way U.S.A" and "Love it or leave it." The resulting melee left 70 persons injured, including three police officers. The workers then invaded City Hall and forced city officials to raise to full staff the U.S. flag flying at half

staff in tribute to the students killed in the KENT STATE MASSACRE on May 4. The following day during a press conference, Mayor John Lindsay condemned the violence of the construction workers and castigated the police for failing to stop the workers' rampage. On May 11, about 2,000 construction workers marched down Wall Street carrying signs demanding Lindsay's impeachment, but the police successfully controlled the demonstrators. On May 12 about 1,000 students, hailing from a dozen business graduate schools in the East and wearing short hair and coats with ties, assembled on Wall Street to protest against the Vietnam War as representatives of the "Establishment." Construction workers assembled across from the students and beyond the police barricades to shout their opposition.

Wandervogel (Birds of Passage or Ramblers) (Germany) a youth movement that was founded on November 4, 1901 by a group including five youth leaders; they were meeting in a room of the Ratskeller in Steglitz, a Berlin suburb, ostensibly acting at the behest of Karl FISCHER, then 20 years old. Its origins traced to a rambling group, formed in 1896 by Hermann Hoffmann, whom Fischer had served as an aide. In part a revolt against a rigid school curriculum and restrictions imposed at home and at church, the movement afforded liberating weekend hikes into the countryside and quickly spread throughout the cities of the northern German states. (Largely a Protestant movement, it fared less well in the predominantly Catholic southern states.) Its development was assisted by a Parents and Friends Advisory Council that Fischer set up. Disagreements between Fischer as the movement's primary leader and other leaders who objected to his authoritarianism resulted in breakaway groups—one called the Altewandervogel was temporarily headed by Fischer—but all the groups shared a common origin and similar purposes. These reflected a

A group of construction workers wearing their traditional hard hats and carrying American flags bulled their way into a group of antiwar demonstrators gathered in front of the New York Stock Exchange (in background). The workers then led an impromptu parade up lower Broadway to City Hall chanting "Impeach Lindsay."   (AP/WIDE WORLD PHOTOS)

certain rebelliousness, spontaneity, and individuality, but they were tempered by middle-class values and under the direction of young adults like Fischer. The movement's rural wanderings on hiking and camping expeditions to enjoy freedom and companionship away from schools and parents led to a revival in folk music, dances, and festivals, along with inculcating a back-to-nature spirit.

Membership in the movement was extended to girls during the years 1906–11—a revolutionary move for the era. (Although Fischer and other leaders envisioned the Wandervogel as open to everyone equally, it evolved into a middle-class movement attracting few, if any, of the urban poor.) Members were mostly between the age of 12 and 19, and group leaders were usually only a few years older than 19. Each group (*Gruppe*) was comprised of about 8 to 20 members; groups were united into branches (*Orstgruppen*) and branches, into a single provincewide organization called a *Gau*. In the privacy of their individual group "Nests," members were encouraged to express themselves freely. The movement's members adopted the casual greeting "Heil" as a break with conventional formality and as an expression of comradeship and equality. They soon had informal uniforms (lederhosen and dirndles), badges, and ranks, although overall it was highly democratic in both admission to membership and procedures and rejected the paramilitarism embraced by other groups, such as the Deutscher Pfadfinderbund founded in 1911 as the German counterpart of the English BOY SCOUTS. In addition to hiking expeditions, the groups participated in sports competitions, group singing, and amateur theatrical performances. The organization's journal was entitled *Der Wandervogel*. It was largely Wandervogel youths who gathered at HÖHE MEISSNER during the 1913 celebrations of the centennial of the Battle of Leipzig and there founded the FREIDEUTSCHE JUGEND (FREE GERMAN YOUTH). Disagreement between Fischer and others over the direction and policies of the Wandervogel led to the movement's being sundered into two groups in 1908. The movement suffered some disruption as many of its members entered military service during World War I, but it revived and thrived in the 1920s—finally to be killed off by the Nazis in 1933.

The Wandervogel movement, although given to shallow philosophizing and perhaps involving no more than 60,000 youths altogether, left some significant legacies. Prominent among these was the movement's revival of and contribution to German folk music. The group collected and published folk songs and disseminated them through a song book and choral and orchestral performances. In the process, they also revived the use of the lute and the guitar. The movement's first song book, compiled and edited by Hans Breuer and entitled *Zupfgeigenhansol*, was enormously popular. The Wandervogel's major legacy, however, was a shared experience—an intense comradeship or bonding among the members—that held lifelong weight for its devotees and profoundly influenced the German view of adolescence, with resultant long-term social effects. Many of Germany's leaders in politics, religion, and other pursuits in the post-World War I decades had been members of the Wandervogel.

Bibliography: Walter Laqueur, *Young Germany: A History of the German Youth Movement* (New York: Basic Books, 1962).

Wang Dan (1965–)   (China) the most prominent leader of the CHINESE DEMOCRACY MOVEMENT. The son of a Beijing University professor of geology and a history student at the university, Wang founded a journal devoted to political reform entitled *New May Fourth*, in honor of the MAY FOURTH MOVEMENT, and also in spring 1989 established "Democracy Salons" at the university for student discussions of democratic reforms. Wang was a major leader of the Autonomous Student Union of Beijing Universities, which organized the student hunger strike in Tiananmen Square. On April 3, 1989, 12 days prior to the death of the popular leader Hu

Student leader Wang Dan of Beijing University at a Saturday evening press conference in Tiananmen Square calls for a citywide march the following Tuesday after which the students would quit their occupation of the square.   (AP/WIDE WORLD PHOTOS)

Yaobang, his group announced a nationwide democracy movement by mounting a poster at the Beijing University "Triangle," where both official and unofficial notices were posted. Wang was a leader of the student group that met with Premier Li Peng on May 18. His name topped the list, issued on June 9, of the 21 student leaders of the Tiananmen Square democracy demonstrations who were most wanted by government authorities. Unsuccessful in attempting to escape China, Wang returned to Beijing in July and was arrested by the secret police. He served three-and-a-half years in prison, but on his release he continued to criticize the government in writings that were published abroad. In May 1995, he was again arrested, and in November 1996 he was sentenced to serve 11 years in prison. He was released in April 1998.

Warsaw Riots   (Poland) a four-day series of riots by students and other youths that occurred in October 1957. The catalyst for the riots was the government's closing of *Po Prostu*, a publication for youths and students that, since the Polish October Revolution of 1956, had become increasingly critical of the government while also advocating political liberalization. On October 3, 1957, having heard that *Po Prostu* was being closed, about 2,000 students from Warsaw Polytechnic gathered at Narutowicz Square, site of the city's largest student hostel, to protest. Police attacked them with clubs and tear gas, and a three-hour battle ensued that also involved some people who were leaving services at nearby churches. In the evening, the government asked administrators of all the higher education institutions in the city to request their students to avoid committing illegal acts. (No students from the University of Warsaw participated in the riots.) On the next evening, about 4,000 students gathered for a scheduled rally in the Central Courtyard at Warsaw Polytechnic, where an independent member of Parliament addressed them and tried to ameliorate the tensions. Afterwards, the students wrote a resolution asking

the government to reinstitute publication of *Po Prostu*. After the rally's leader was assured by police stationed outside that the students would be given safe conduct, they began to leave. The police attacked them, and another battle of several hours followed, with the police injuring 20 students and arresting 30 (they released all but 8 the next morning). On October 5 and 6, the riots burgeoned as working-class youths and others joined in, and the rioters attacked police and military patrols. Three student delegates presented the resolution about *Po Prostu* to Prime Minister Wladyslaw Gomulka on October 6 and were later arrested. As nonstudents now formed the bulk of the demonstrators and the riots continued on October 7, the Polytechnic students publicly began to disassociate themselves and call for an end to the disturbances. Students from the University of Warsaw, where the humanities were paramount, had never been involved.

Students gathered at Warsaw Polytechnic, a high technical college in the Polish capital, on October 4, 1957 to protest the banning of the student newspaper Po Prostu. *Rioting broke out after the meeting when the students marched to Communist Party headquarters.* (AP/WIDE WORLD PHOTOS)

Warsaw Student Protests (Poland) demonstrations and riots by University of Warsaw students in March 1968. The protests arose out of a ban on performing *Dziady*, a Romantic drama written in 1823 by Adam Mickiewicz and admired as a poetic evocation of Polish national freedom. The play celebrates Polish patriots' efforts to attain independence from the tsar of Russia, and the performances resonated widely in 1968, not only for students but for middle-class Poles who longed for freedom from domination by the Soviet Union. Fearful of the potential consequences, authorities closed down the production, charging that it might "stir up anti-Soviet feelings." Students collected 3,145 signatures on a petition protesting the ban to present to the *sejm* (Parliament), despite opposition from the Communist youth organization. In response, authorities expelled from the University of Warsaw two student leaders accused of responsibility for collecting the signatures; communist militants entered the university grounds and attacked students and faculty members; police harassed students, and newspapers denounced them. To protest the expulsion, students demonstrated on March 8. Police teargassed the protestors and set dogs upon them; 112 protestors had to be treated at hospitals, many of them for dog bites. Police targeted women students for brutal treatment, killing one.

This and subsequent clashes with police led to a mass student meeting on March 21 where the students decided to occupy the university and Warsaw Polytechnic. Initially, the student protestors had advocated liberalization; now they attacked the authoritarianism of the government itself and demanded a new democratic system. Their most evocative slogan declared, "There is no bread without freedom." Their opponents' propaganda struck a distinctly anti-Semitic tone, as several of the student leaders were Jews. The student protest spread to Łódź, Poznań, Wroclaw, and other cities, gaining support among the public. The students' occupation of the University of Warsaw lasted only two days—it was brutally suppressed by the police. By the end of March, hundreds of students and many professors had been expelled from the nation's universities, and many intellectuals were removed from the Communist Party. By April, the student movement was moribund. It had, however, been a harbinger of the workers' uprisings in 1971 in Gdańsk and Gdynia and the Solidarity movement that followed.

Wartburg Festival (Germany), a massive meeting of students that convened at the Wartburg Mountain (where Martin Luther had stayed in 1521–22 following the Edict of Worms) on October 17, 1817—the first such meeting in modern history. With the patronage of Grand Duke Karl Augustus of Saxe-Weimar-Eisenach, about 1,500 BURSCHENSCHAFTEN members, nearly half of them (accompanied by four professors) from the University of Jena where the Burschenschaft was founded in 1815, came together; their ostensible purpose was to commemorate the Reformation initiated by Luther and the Battle of Leipzig (where, on October 16–19, 1813, a combined force of Austrian, Prussian, Russian, and Swedish troops defeated Napoleon's army and ended the emperor's rule east of the Rhine). The students held a torchlight parade and burned items that symbolized oppression, including a copy of the *Code Napoléon*. On the following day, speakers exhorted the assemblage to pursue goals of social reform, unity, idealism, republicanism, brotherhood, and solidarity; some also proposed expelling Jews from the universities. All Europe took note of the event as a portent of a politicized and perhaps radicalized student movement. On the anniversary of the Wartburg Festival in 1819, delegates from the Burschenchaften met to organize the ALLGEMEINE DEUTSCHE BURSCHENBUND (Universal German Students' Association).

Bibliography: Heinrich von Treitschke, *History of Germany in the Nineteenth Century*, Vol. III, Translated by Eden and Cedar Paul (New York: McBride, Nast, and Company, 1915).

Warwick Student Protest (Great Britain) a demonstration during the 1969–70 Lent term at the University of Warwick, during which students occupying a university office building ransacked the vice chancellor's secret files. They discovered documents indicating that head teachers had provided the administration with information on students' political views that may have been used in reference materials submitted to prospective employers. They also found documents relating to University College, Rhodesia, and thus to the Rhodesian independence controversy, and others indicating that the Rootes Group, a U.S.-owned car manufacturer with ties to the university, had complained about a teacher who was a vocal critic of private enterprise. The students made public the contents of these documents, generating protests and sit-ins at other universities, demanding that their files be opened to public scrutiny.

Waseda All Campus Joint Struggle Committee (Waseda Zenkyoto) (Japan) a committee formed in 1962 at Waseda University that was comprised mainly of students belonging to KAKUMARU and SAMPA RENGO. Its primary reason for existence was to secure student management of a New Student Hall that was completed at the university in 1965. In November 1965, the committee demanded that the university grant management of the building to students and that each student organization (there were 600 on the campus) be given a room to use in the building. The administration refused. In December, a few hundred students demonstrated and later held a sit-down strike that ended with the invasion of an office building and the administration's calling in the Tokyo police. But on December 20, the University Council voted to increase tuition fees beginning in the next term and thereby added another issue. On January 6, 1966, the joint struggle committee reorganized itself and took the name All Campus Joint Student Hall and Tuition Fee Struggle Council. Law Department students began a strike on January 18 that spread to other departments. Negotiations between the University Council and the Joint Struggle Council collapsed on February 10, and about 500 students occupied the main office building. Three days later, right-wing students attacked them, and police intervened to quell the fight and eject the students. Students occupied the building again on February 20. The following day, about 3,000 police arrived at the university administration's request and again removed students' barricades and ejected the protestors. When the police left, the students returned. The police returned, arresting 203 students, and stayed at the campus until March 19, the day of the entrance examinations. As spring passed, the protest began to dwindle, students defected, barricades came down, and one by one the strikes came to an end. Following the university president's resignation on April 24, the protest dissolved. The administration punished 40 students, expelling 10, all of whom were involved in the protest, and the issues were left unresolved. The significance of this struggle was that it initiated the period of major disturbances at Japanese universities; typical of the nature of those disturbances were students who presented demands, negotiated with administrators, occupied buildings, staged strikes, and boycotted classes and examinations. Periodic continuing protests hit Waseda thereafter for years.

Bibliography: Stuart J. Dowsey, ed., *Zengakuren: Japan's Revolutionary Students* (Berkeley, Calif.: The Ishi Press, 1970).

Waseda Factional Battle (Japan) an armed fight between two factions within the Revolutionary Communist League (a member group of the ZENGAKUREN) that occurred at Waseda University on July 2, 1964. One of the factions was supported by members of three other Zengakuren factions—SHAGAKUDO, SHASEIDO, and the Front. The battle is important in that it marked the first time that students were armed with clubs and wore helmets. Thereafter students in the ANTI-YOYOGI ZENGAKUREN regularly wore plastic hardhats, with each faction adopting a different color of hat to expedite identification.

Washington Action Project (United States) a student peace movement that culminated in a peaceful demonstration in Washington, D.C., on February 17, 1962. More than 5,000 students from throughout the nation converged on the capital city to present to the Congress, the State Department, and the White House their request that the government create initiatives to forestall the arms race and negotiate a disarmament agreement with suitable controls. They supported a bill in Congress that would mandate United States purchase of half of a United Nations peace bond issue, asked for increased funding for the Peace Corps and the Disarmament Commission, and expressed opposition to a bill that would provide $700 million for civil defense. They also picketed at each locale. The students were generally received with politeness, but some members of Congress censured their effort.

Washington Peace March *See* MARCH ON WASHINGTON.

Washington State College Protest (United States) one of the largest campus protests of the 1930s concerning student issues and notable for its immediate success. WSC students formed the Students' Liberty Association, which was comprised of members of fraternities and sororities and the student government—not a militant group—to organize the protest, which began at exactly 11:15 A.M. on May 5, 1936. More than 3,000 students participated. The protestors desired "a voice—a representation in the administration," which for the time was a radical view, but their specific demands were fairly modest. These policy changes included an end to compulsory class attendance and the extension of closing times for dormitories both during the week and on weekends. The students announced that if a committee of faculty and administrators did not accept these demands, then students would close down the college by staging a total strike; they rejected the administration's request for time to investigate the demands by insisting on a straightforward yes or no answer to each. The committee met immediately and agreed to all the students' demands.

Weatherman (United States) the most radical, fanatic, and militant NEW LEFT group, comprising one faction of STUDENTS FOR A DEMOCRATIC SOCIETY (SDS) that emerged as a separate entity from the fragmentation of SDS during and after its June 1969 annual meeting in Chicago. Weatherman took its name from a Bob Dylan song, "You Don't Need a Weatherman to Know Which Way the Wind Is Blowing," which was also the title of a six-page article the group prepared for *New Left Notes* that was distributed among all the delegates to the convention. There were 11 drafters of this article, among them Bernardine Dohrn, Terry Robbins, and Mark Rudd. The article emphasized SDS's total support of the civil rights struggle, promoted the young as the vanguard of the fight against U.S. "imperialism," called for creation of a mass movement in the Third World, and supported the formation of a revolutionary conspiracy, directed by a single general staff in this country. Weatherman gained control of the SDS National Office and renamed it the Weather Bureau. The group advocated support of all liberation movements in this and other nations and opening a new front—a sort of Red Guard comprised of alienated youth—in the United States to pursue the liberation struggle. Militant confrontation was central to the Weatherman program, and members were trained in violence techniques. One of the group's early exploits in summer 1969 was marching with red flags at working-class beaches in Detroit, which resulted in bloody brawling. In Pittsburgh, a group of 75 Weatherwomen, some baring their breasts, occupied a high school, tied up five Quaker teachers, and ran amuck through the halls shouting "Jailbreak!" The police arrested 25 of them. They staged similar incidents at colleges in Detroit and in Cambridge, Massachusetts and also disrupted the Davis Cup championship in September 1969. Weatherman organized the New Red Army in the fall of 1969 in preparation for attacking the "pig power structure" in Chicago, but when they gathered in the city in October for the DAYS OF RAGE, only 200 Weathermen and 100 Weatherwomen out of an anticipated 5,000 showed up. They marched through the streets, breaking windows in cars and office buildings and attacking a police cordon. During the course of the rioting police arrested 287 of the New Red Army demonstrators.

Shortly after participating in the huge 1970 antiwar demonstration in Washington, which was organized by the NEW MOBILIZATION COMMITTEE TO END THE WAR IN VIETNAM (New Mobe), the Weatherman movement went underground in small groups to conduct a guerrilla war campaign of bombing, burning, and vandalizing; they now called themselves the Weather Underground. Three of them, including Terry Robbins, died when a time bomb they were preparing exploded in a Manhattan town house on March 6, 1970; two others survived the explosion. Weather Underground claimed responsibility for a June 9, 1970 time-bomb explosion at the central police headquarters in New York City that did extensive damage to the five-storey building's second storey. On July 23, 1970, a federal grand jury in Detroit brought indictments against 13 Weathermen on the charge of a conspiracy to commit bombings through a group of underground terrorists operating nationwide. On December 24 of that year, however, a statement issued by Weatherman leader Bernardine Dohrn indicated that the group was rededicating itself to a "cultural revolution" and moving away from violent tactics. Nevertheless, the Weather Underground claimed responsibility for a bomb explosion in the Capitol in the early morning of May 1, 1971, that caused no injuries but did $300,000 worth of damage and generated major concern in Congress over the building's security. The underground published a book entitled *Prairie Fire* and in late 1974 another booklet chronicling their activities, but by that time the movement was effectively dead.

Bibliography: Harold Jacobs, ed., *Weatherman* (Berkeley, Calif.: Ramparts Press, 1970).

Week of Action   (France) nationwide strikes held in November 1963 by students and teachers. The Week of Action, November 21–30, was organized by the UNION NATIONALE DES ÉTUDIANTS DE FRANCE (UNEF) joined by several teachers' unions. The teachers wanted increased funding for salaries, added faculty positions, and diminished authority over university affairs for government representatives operating at local levels. UNEF supported these demands and also called for increased funding for facilities, research, and scholarships. In addition, UNEF was protesting the reduction in student representation on the Administrative Council of the CENTRE NATIONALE DES OEUVRES (CNO) that was effected in October. Students and faculty members held six days of strikes during the Week of Action to promote their demands. The protesters planned to meet at the Paris headquarters of UNEF on November 29 and march to the Faculty of Science; but the teachers withdrew when the city prefect banned a march as an interference with public life and commerce, although he sanctioned a meeting held indoors or in an enclosed space. The teachers met in the courtyard of the Institut Poincare, but UNEF chose to fulfill the planned march. Thousands of students managed to breach police cordons and demonstrate; there was minimal confrontation, but some students were injured and about 150 were arrested. An official hearing followed, but no legal action was taken against UNEF. The Week of Action evoked media support for the teachers and students but no response to their demands from the government.

Week of Protest   (Rhodesia) a student protest during the week of May 18–23, 1969 against a proposed revision of the Rhodesian constitution that would permanently prevent majority African rule. The Week of Protest constituted the first time in Rhodesia's history that a large number of both native African and white European students joined together to oppose the government's movement to institute apartheid and to secure European political supremacy for the future in Rhodesia. A significant minority among the white students at the University of Rhodesia supported the Week of Protest, although two whites solicited signatures on a petition opposing the protest. (The government headed by Prime Minister Ian Smith had illegally declared Rhodesian independence from Great Britain in 1964 and then in 1970 declared the nation a republic with the franchise racially divided to ensure European control. In 1980 Rhodesia became the Republic of Zimbabwe, with majority African rule.)

Week of the Student   (Venezuela) a massive and spontaneous student protest against the dictatorial government of Juan Vincente Gómez (in power from 1908 through 1935) in February 1928 that marked the beginning of the student movement in Venezuela. The Week

Seated in the middle of the Boulevard Saint Germain in the Latin Quarter of Paris on November 29, 1963 are university students demonstrating for more classrooms, professors, and facilities. Police later scattered the students, broke up the demonstration, and arrested more than 150 persons. (AP/WIDE WORLD PHOTOS)

of the Student was planned by members of the recently formed Federación de Estudiantes Venezolanos (FEV) (*see* FEDERACIÓN DE ESTUDIANTES DE VENEZUELA) at the Central University (UCV) in Caracas as a series of social, cultural, and fund-raising events, but from the very first speech it became a demonstration against Gómez. Several students were arrested, and many more volunteered for arrest to show their support. As a result, other street protests ensued, with workers, women, and others joining the students. Most of the arrested students were released, and they became involved with a group of young army officers, military college students, and young professionals, in the April 7 military rebellion that attempted to overthrow Gómez in the wake of the students' protests. The coup attempt failed, largely because of poor coordination and organization. Those students involved, along with the military conspirators, including Gómez's own son López, were imprisoned or put to work on road construction projects; some escaped

into exile. (Gómez's son fell ill in prison and died soon after.) Gómez outlawed the FEV and cracked down on UCV. Participants in the student demonstrations were in later years referred to as the generation of '28 or the BOYS OF 1928.

In 1936, following Gómez's death in December 1935, national political parties were formed, and the student movement split into groups affiliated with these parties, which in some cases were led by former student leaders who had returned from exile. However, the FEV, which had been secretly reorganized in 1934–35, took initial leadership of the movement against Gómez's successor Eleázar López Contreras, who as minister of war had been responsible for suppressing the Week of the Students' uprising. The FEV served as the instigator of a huge demonstration on February 14, 1936 that turned into a riot with attacks on the homes of government ministers; police fired on the crowds, killing and wounding many. These were the largest demonstrations in 25 years, and their impact nudged López into issuing the February Program of social and economic reforms, which included revamping the educational system, providing funding for public health and assistance, reforming the tax and banking systems, and expanding transportation and communication networks, and attacking governmental corruption.

Wehrschaften　(Germany) radically right-wing dueling fraternities whose members wore swastikas. Around 1930, they became informally related to the Nazi Party. In spring 1933, they aligned themselves with the party's policies, adopted the Fuhrer principle—a single leader with unlimited dictatorial powers—and established subdivisions called *gaue* run by *gauleiters*. They also required their members to become active participants in the Nazi Party, the STURMABTEILUNG (SA), or the Schutzstaffel (SS).

Weld, Theodore Dwight (1803–1895)　(United States) student antislavery leader prominent in the 1830s. Weld was a ministerial student at the Lane Seminary in Cincinnati, Ohio when, in May 1834, he participated in debates in which he converted Southern students to support of abolition; when the administration headed by President Lyman Beecher frustrated their plans to support emancipation, Weld led 53 students who withdrew from the seminary and enrolled at newly opened Oberlin College—all became proselyters throughout the Midwest for the abolition cause. Later in 1834, Weld dropped out of school to work for the American Antislavery Society as an organizer, recruiter, and trainer. Among his converts were Henry Ward Beecher, James G. Birney, and Harriet Beecher Stowe. Following his marriage in 1838, he left the movement for private life and settled in Belleville, New Jersey. Weld published several antislavery tracts, including *The Bible Against Slavery* (1837) and *Slavery As It Is* (1839).

West African Students' Union (WASU)　(Great Britain) a politically oriented movement dedicated to achieving sovereignty for Africans through peaceful means. Founded in London, England in 1925 by Lapido Solanke, a Nigerian student, the West African Students' Union (WASU) held regular discussion meetings of West African students, many of whom later became leaders of their nations. During 1929–33, Solanke made a fundraising tour of West Africa and established WASU branches in Sierra Leone, Ghana, Nigeria, and other states. After 1930, in England, WASU advocated opposition to British colonialism and created alignments with the Labour Party and other left-wing groups. WASU remained strong through the period of World War II and included among its members in those years such future leaders as Kwame Nkrumah and Jomo Kenyatta. In 1946 WASU helped to organize the INTERNATIONAL UNION OF STUDENTS (IUS), a movement led by communists, and thereafter aligned itself increasingly with policies of the Soviet Union. After 1960 WASU slowly declined in leadership, membership, and advocacy.

Bibliography:　Donald K. Emmerson, "African Student Organizations: The Politics of Discontent," *African Report*, 10 (May 1965).

West Berlin Kommune 2 (K2)　(Germany) the better known of two youth communes (the other was KOMMUNE 1) created in West Berlin in early 1967. This urban commune experiment, whose avowed goal was the "Revolutionization of the Bourgeois Individual," proved a failure and died out in June 1968, a victim of housekeeping, sexual, psychological, and social problems that could not be resolved by its members. K2 gained renown primarily because one of its members, Jan-Carl Raspe, became a member of the BAADER-MEINHOF GANG.

Whampoa Military Academy　(China) a military school established in Whampoa (Huang pu) near Canton (Guangzhou) in May 1924 by Kuomintang (Nationalist Party) leader Sun Yat-sen. The academy was established by and under the command of Chiang Kai-shek, with the aid of the Soviet Union. Chou En-lai served as deputy head of the education department. The academy's purpose was to provide young men with military training and ideological indoctrination in the service of the Kuomintang and its program of national revolution. It opened in June with 490 cadets. On June 23, 1925, the Whampoa cadets staged a march in Canton to protest British soldiers' killing of student demonstrators in the Shanghai International Settlement in May, triggering the MAY 30TH MOVEMENT. British and French machine gunners shot them down.

White Rose　(Germany) a group of student rebels against Nazism centered at the University of Munich in 1943. The leaders were Hans Scholl, a medical student age 25, and his sister Sophie, a philosophy student age 21, who both attended the university. They maintained contact with anti-Nazi conspirators in Berlin, and through their "White Rose Letters," as their writings were referred to, they spread their anti-Nazi message to other universities. In February 1943 the *gauleiter* of Bavaria, who had been provided a file of White Rose Letters by the Gestapo, spoke to the University of Munich student body, announcing that males unfit for military duty would be given other tasks and luridly urging females to reproduce for the Fatherland—offering his adjutants to do the fathering. The offended students ejected the *gauleiter* and his Gestapo and SS guards from the hall and staged a street demonstration against the Nazis—the first public protest against the Nazis since they had come to power in January 1933. The Scholls began to distribute pamphlets agitating for a student uprising. On February 19, a building superintendent who saw them disbursing pamphlets from a balcony betrayed the Scholls to the Gestapo. They were arrested and beaten (Sophie's leg was broken). Tried in a People's Court, they were found guilty of treason and sentenced to death. Both were hanged. A few days following their execution, several other students and the rebels' mentor Kurt Huber, a philosophy professor, were executed. The White Rose group in Hamburg, which was tentatively planning to blow up bridges there, suffered a similar fate, with 30 of its members being executed.

Whitsun Disturbances   (Great Britain) an outbreak of violence by youths, mostly MODS and ROCKERS, at Brighton, Margate, and other seaside resort beaches during the May 1964 Whitsun weekend holiday. Youths plus tens of thousands of adults poured onto the beaches for the three-day weekend, and all behaved peaceably from Friday through Saturday, despite the fact that teenage Mods and Rockers were denied sleeping accommodations and food services at local inns and restaurants. The beaches were also being patroled by exceptionally large contingents of police, mounted or on foot with dogs, suggesting widespread hostility toward the teenagers. At Margate on Monday, fighting erupted between groups of Mods and Rockers, and there were disturbances at the station buffet and on the promenade—all resulting in about 30 people being injured and a few thousand pounds worth of damages. The disturbances were minor actually, but they became significant because the police arrested hundreds of youths, the popular press portrayed the youths as despicable vermin and thus incited widespread adult hostility toward youngsters, and judges sentenced the youths to extraordinarily severe jail terms or fines. Ironically, a sizable proportion of those arrested and sentenced were neither Mods nor Rockers but teenagers from quite respectable backgrounds who, for one reason or another, were swept up in the disturbances.

Wilde Cliquen   (Germany) a union that represented numerous street gangs from the North, South, East, and West Rings of Berlin formed by the gangs in 1927, a time of economic and political instability in Germany. Among the individual gangs involved were Tartarenblut, Wolfsblut, Sing Sing, Blutiger Knochen, Apachenblut, Galgenvogel, and a host of others with equally fearsome names. Many of these gangs had their own flags; members' distinctive costumes included colorful ribbons, plumes, and edelweiss as a symbol of freedom. The Wilde Cliquen's primary purpose was opposition to politically oriented youth groups, especially the HITLER JUGEND.

Wingolf   (Germany) a national organization of Protestant university students that was officially founded in 1852 but having earlier antecedents. Wingolf, or Wingolfsbund, rejected the dueling tradition prevalent among German fraternities of the time and condemned the excessive drinking and other perceived moral infractions of the fraternities. It began to publish a student journal, *Wingolfsblatter*, in 1872. Although Protestant, Wingolf accepted Catholic members but excluded Jews. About 20 percent of the Wingolf membership were theological students. Initially nonpolitical, in the 1880s and 1890s, the Wingolf accepted the nationalistic sentiments then prevalent among student organizations.

Wissenschaftlicher Vereine   (Germany) informal student societies that were devoted to scholarship, learned discussion, and conviviality and were generated by reading groups at universities during the 1850s and 1860s. Many joined together in national associations based on the primary subject matter that members were interested in—math, sciences, philosophy, theology, languages, etc. For example, the Arnstadter Verband Mathematischer und Naturwissenschaftlicher Vereine was formed in 1868; the Goslarer Verband Naturwissenschaftlicher und Medizinischer Vereine, in 1898. The Wissenschaftlicher Vereine provided opportunity to pursue scholarly discourse—the investigation of scientific and other concepts—including lectures and specialized libraries. Since they forbade politics, their membership might come from diverse other groups, such as the BURSCHENSCHAFTEN, but because many of the fraternities decried the groups' informality, some of them gravitated toward adopting colors and other customs of the fraternities. In 1910, they joined together into a national association, the Deutsche Wissenschafter Verband (DWV), comprised of 81 chapters, making it one of the four largest student associations of the time. Like most of the other student associations, the DWV adopted a strongly nationalistic position.

Woodcraft Folk   (Great Britain) also known as the Federation of Cooperative Woodcraft Fellowship, a movement for boys formed on December 19, 1925 by four woodcraft fellowships that were comprised of fewer than 70 members who met in Peckham. They chose a charter and declaration and elected 20-year-old Leslie Paul as headman. Paul had been leader of the dissidents who had challenged John Hargrave's leadership of KIBBO KIFT the year before. The Woodcraft Folk's orientation was pacifist, socialist, and internationalist. With most of its members coming from the working class, the Woodcraft Folk achieved greater success than similar groups, its membership reaching more than 4,500 in 1938, including more than 3,700 Pioneers and Elfins and more than 770 adult members. Membership fell off in the 1940s but began to recover in the 1960s; by the late 1970s it totaled 15,000.

Bibliography: Leslie Paul, *The Republic of Children* (London: Allen and Unwin, 1938).

Woodcraft Indians   (United States) an organization for boys founded in 1902 by naturalist Ernest Thompson Seton (1860–1946), author of the popular book *Wild Animals I Have Known* (1898). (Seton was also involved in founding the BOY SCOUTS OF AMERICA.) The purpose of the Woodcraft Indians was to educate boys in woodslore and nature studies, and it originated in Seton's inviting boys to camp at his Connecticut estate. Members experienced camping, Indian lore, nature studies, and related activities and could earn awards through achievement in these activities. There were no uniforms or efforts to reinforce moral strictures and build character. But the organization did not develop because it lacked effective national organization and unification.

Woodcraft Rangers   (United States) the only woodcraft organization for boys and girls to survive into modern times but confined to Los Angeles County. In the 1970s, it had a membership of about 6,000, ages even through the teens, and was divided into 300 "tribes." Its primary emphasis is on training for citizenship, with instruction in Indian lore and crafts and outdoor living. It operates four camps.

Woodstock Festival   (United States) not a movement as such but certainly a massive youth rally and an historic countercultural event that gathered as many as 400,000 youths from throughout the nation at a folk-rock music festival held August 15–18, 1969 on the 600-acre farm of Max Yasgur near Bethel, New York in the Catskill Mountains. Performing musicians and groups included Janis Joplin; Joan Baez; Crosby, Stills, Nash, and Young; Richie Havens; Sly and the Family Stone; the Creedence Clearwater Revival; The Who; Jimi Hendrix; Canned Heat; Ravi Shankar; and The Grateful Dead. The attendance was so unexpectedly huge that organization and sanitation failed; ticket sales and food services collapsed. The roads were impassable because of traffic jams and abandoned cars, so the organizers had to commandeer helicopters to bring in food, water, and medicines. Rains turned the grounds into a quagmire, inspiring many to strip naked to cope. Although drug use was abundant, the crowd remained cooperative and peaceable overall; 100 were arrested, but the police showed great restraint and avoided enforcing drug laws. One young man died of a drug overdose, and another was killed when a tractor rode over his sleeping bag. The youths who attended regarded the festival as an idyllic, perhaps even beatific, event; for many others, it was a revelation that the nation had developed a worrisome mass drug culture.

Work and Light   (Russia) the first league of young workers, formed in the Viborg district of St. Petersburg in May 1917 under the leadership of a student named P. Shevtsov. Work and Light disclaimed involvement in the revolutionary movement or with any political party in favor of the ideals of brotherhood, intellectual and moral maturity, learning, and personal and national welfare. Its goals were to found schools, youth hostels, theaters, and clubs and to sponsor excursions. This program failed to elicit wide support because of the revolutionary context of the time and other young workers' enthusiasm for political ideology and class struggle. Consequently, at the group's conference on August 18, 1917, which was attended by 179 delegates, Bolsheviks were in control, and the conference voted unanimously (there were six abstentions) to join the rival SOCIALIST ASSOCIATION OF YOUNG WORKERS. A few days after the conference, Work and Light disbanded.

Workers' Rising in East Berlin   (Germany) a protest demonstration of June 16, 1953 by workers and youths that developed into a full-scale riot. Known in the West as the Workers' Rising in East Berlin, it was nevertheless largely a youth uprising that the East German government found sufficiently threatening to call in Russian troops and tanks to suppress the rioters. Apparently, this was the first such incident of Soviet armed intervention to crush a revolt in one of Russia's satellite states. Similar rebellions by workers and youths also occurred at this time in Magdeburg, Halle, Leipzig, and other East German industrial cities and in Pilsen (Plzeň), Czechoslovakia—all smashed by Russian troops and tanks.

World Assembly of Youth (WAY)   an international organization that was founded in 1949 at a conference attended by representatives from 38 nations. Many of the groups involved in WAY's founding were noncommunist organizations that had withdrawn from the WORLD FEDERATION OF DEMOCRATIC YOUTH (WFDY). By the mid-

A crowd estimated at up to 400,000 people invaded a rural area of New York's Catskill Mountains near White Lake on the weekend of August 15–18, 1969 to attend a nearly nonstop rock music festival. (AP/WIDE WORLD PHOTO)

1960s, youth groups representing nearly 110 nations were attending WAY's annual assemblies.

World Association of Girl Guides and Girl Scouts an international organization of the affiliated GIRL GUIDES and GIRL SCOUTS groups in scores of nations. The association was formed in 1928 to promote international understanding through meetings and programs involving members of Guides and Scouts groups from diverse nations.

World Federation of Democratic Youth (WFDY) an international organization founded at a conference held in London on November 10–11, 1945 that was attended by 150 representatives from 38 nations. Communist dominated from its origin, WFDY sometimes joined with the INTERNATIONAL UNION OF STUDENTS (IUS) to sponsor conferences. From 1947 through the 1960s, the WFDY sponsored a series of World Youth Festivals (funded by the Soviet Union and the governments of Eastern European nations) that were significant for their scale—the largest ones attracting 35,000 youths from throughout the world. The festivals served both as cultural exchanges and as forums for advancing communist political views and were therefore largely boycotted by Western student groups.

World Student Christian Federation (WSCF) an international Protestant organization founded in 1896. John Mott, a U.S. philanthropist, was instrumental in its creation. Headquartered in Geneva, Switzerland, WSCF fostered missionary work and served as coordinator of programs among Protestant groups in numerous nations. During the Great Depression, the WSCF shifted to a greater focus on political and social issues and became more activist in its policy. WSCF receives major funding from the World Council of Churches. It publishes books, pamphlets, and a quarterly journal and sponsors international conferences.

World Youth Congress (WYC) an international organization founded in 1936 (its first meeting was held in Geneva) and sponsored by the League of Nations Organization to promote cooperation and peace among the world's youths. The WYC's second meeting, held in New York City and at Vassar College in Poughkeepsie in 1938, was the largest youth meeting of the 1930s decade: more than 500 delegates representing 53 nations attended. Mayor Fiorello La Guardia addressed the opening session in New York that drew a crowd of 22,000, and Eleanor Roosevelt spoke to the work session in Poughkeepsie. NBC radio also broadcast a program on the Congress. The Congress supported collective security measures opposing fascist aggression and adopted the Vassar Peace Pact, which pledged WYC members to pressure their respective governments not only to prevent or halt aggression but also to avoid supporting aggression through financial or material aid.

Wuer Kaixi (1968–   ) (China) one of the three principal student leaders of the CHINESE DEMOCRACY MOVEMENT along with WANG DAN and CHAI LING. Also known as Werkesh Daolat, Wuer was a student at Beijing University who led a student sit-in at the headquarters of the CHINESE COMMUNIST PARTY (CCP) Central Committee on April 20, 1989. He was one of the organizers, along with Wang Dan, of the Autonomous Student Union of Beijing Universities and became leader of that group. An organizer of the Tiananmen Square demonstrations, Wuer was also one of the student leaders at the May 18 meeting with Premier Li Peng at which the students' demands were presented. With Wang Dan and Chai Ling, he topped the list of the 21 most-wanted students that was issued following the bloody June 4 suppression of the Tiananmen Square demonstrations. Wuer escaped to France and subsequently to the United States, where he became a student at Harvard University and vice president of the Chinese Democratic Front.

Xin Qingnian *See* NEW YOUTH.

Yippies *See* HOFFMAN, ABBIE; RUBIN, JERRY.

Young Americans for Freedom (YAF) (United States) an organization founded in 1960 that became the most significant of several politically conservative organizations for university students and other youths. YAF began at a conference that attracted 100 delegates from 44 colleges and was held at the Connecticut estate of William F. Buckley, Jr., who spearheaded the YAF's founding. Conceived as an activist organization, YAF advocated free enterprise and anticommunism and defended the House Un-American Activities Committee (HUAC) against attack by liberal groups. It began to publish a monthly journal, *Young Guard*, in 1961. In the aftermath of Barry Goldwater's 1964 campaign for the presidency, prominently supported by members of the organization, the YAF claimed to have representation on 200 university campuses and a nationwide membership of more than 30,000 youths; by 1970 membership purportedly exceeded 50,000—about 60 percent of these being university or college students. Former members of YAF have served on senatorial staffs, in the Nixon administration, and in subsequent Republican administrations.

Young China (China) a periodical review founded in July 1919 by leaders of the MAY FOURTH MOVEMENT. *Young China* was named for and published by the YOUNG CHINA SOCIETY founded in Beijing in 1918.

Young China Communist Party (France) an organization formed in 1921 by Chinese students studying in France. The party's formation coincided with the founding of the CHINESE COMMUNIST PARTY (CCP). At the time, about 1,700 of the Chinese students in France were considered "student workers," living on relief in impoverished circumstances that made them more sympathetic with radical politics than their wealthier counterparts in the United States, for example. The Young China Communist Party spread its ideas through a weekly publication entitled *Lu Ou* (*Study in Europe*). Although relatively small, it was a significant movement in that several of its student leaders returned to China to join the CCP—and decades later to rank among its most important leaders. Among these students were Chou En-lai, Ch'en I, and Deng Xiaoping.

Young China Society (China) an influential organization of students (mostly returned from studying in Japan or France) and young intellectuals, including educators and writers, founded in Beijing in June 1918. The society was dedicated to the goals of opposing Japanese domination of China and "saving the country" through cultural renewal, educational reform, and political activism. It was formally established on July 1, 1919, following the impetus provided by initiation of the MAY FOURTH MOVEMENT, and then dedicated to the "ideal of creating a young China." The society published the monthlies *Young China* (begun in July 1919) and *Young World* (begun in January 1920) in Shanghai and a variety of small magazines and pamphlets in other locales. Probably most noteworthy of its endeavors was the society's creation of the first well-organized and potent movement against religion, begun in September 1920, which included banning persons with religious beliefs from being members of the society and sponsoring a series of antireligious lectures in Beijing and Nanjing (one given by Bertrand Russell) which were later published in *Young China*. Members of the society, never totaling much more than 100, quarreled among themselves over issues and political orientation (some had become secret members of the CHINESE COMMUNIST PARTY, CCP) at conferences held in 1921, 1922, and 1923. The quarrels resulted in the society's demise in 1923, with some members gravitating to the CCP and others forming the Chinese Youth Party.

Young Communist League (YCL) (United States) the Communist Party youth organization founded in 1922 for youths age 15 to 25. Originally entitled the Young Workers League, the YCL evolved from a split in the Socialist Party, whose extreme left-wingers joined the Communists in forming the Workers (Communist) Party in 1921. The YCL was an affiliate of the Young Communist International and the World Youth Congress. It was an inconsequential organization throughout the 1920s, when no effort was made to involve university students. The YCL formed the Young Pioneers of America in 1927 as a junior section of the YCL involving children under the age of 16, but this section was merged into other children's groups after 1930. In the 1930s, YCL pursued organizing on campuses, although its strength remained relatively small and was largely concentrated at universities in such urban centers as New York, Philadelphia, and Chicago. YCL claimed to have 11,000 members in 1936, with 600 branches including most of the states, and 22,000 members in 1939, more than twice the membership of the STUDENT LEAGUE FOR INDUSTRIAL DEMOCRACY (SLID); but the great majority of these members were nonstudents. YCL's influence in the student movement of the thirties decade exceeded its numbers, however, through the group's strong discipline—slavishly following the party line—and leadership involvement in other student organizations such as the AMERICAN STUDENT UNION and the NATIONAL STUDENT LEAGUE.

Young Conservatives (Germany) not an organized youth movement as such but a disparate and widespread group who shared an ideology during the years of the Weimar Republic (1919–33). The ideology included opposition to parliamentary democracy, antiintellectualism, advocacy of a nationalistic political and social revolution, admiration for irrationalism, and promotion of assertiveness in foreign relations. Especially strong in Berlin, the Young Conservatives comprised the major influence within the HOCHSCHULRING DEUTSCHER ART, and their ideas were disseminated widely among university student organizations.

Young Germany (Junges Deutschland) (Germany) 19th-century reform and literary movement. Active during the 20-year period from 1830 to 1850, the group never attracted many adherents. Its leaders and members were inspired by the French July Revolution of 1830 and advocated freedom of speech and press, a democratic state, and a national theater. Among the members were the major poets Heinrich Heine (1797–1856) and Georg Herwegh (1817–75). On December 10, 1835, referring to the members collectively as Young Germany, the German Confederation's Diet passed a resolution demanding severe censorship of their writings in all the states of the confederation.

Young India League (India) an organization that was formed in Bombay in 1906 under the leadership of B. G. Tilak. Its membership was comprised of nationalists and included Indian students who had been educated in England. Although its life was brief, the league was significant as the first formally established political organization of students in Bombay. It trained members for political leadership and gave them experience in parliamentary procedures. Thus the league constituted a forerunner of later student political organizations.

Young Intellectuals (YI) (United States) a radical student organization that was active in the early decades of the 20th century. YI's social and political agenda involved the denunciation of middle-class values, including marriage. The organization promoted the socialist and feminist movements and even anarchism; it also actively supported the Industrial Workers of the World (IWW). YI's membership was mostly centered in Ivy League and Middle West universities and apparently was never very large (no membership data exist); many members were active in the settlement-house movement during World War I. Although small, YI did constitute a forerunner of the radical student movements of later decades.

Young Italy (Giovine Italia) (Italy) patriotic movement for young men that was begun by revolutionary leader Guiseppe Mazzini in 1831. Young Italy was dedicated to the achievement of Italian independence, unification, and republican government and as such played a role in the *Risorgimento* (the Italian liberation and unification struggle). The secret society (*Carbonari*) to which Mazzini belonged had so far failed in its revolutionary and clandestine efforts to attain liberation, prompting Mazzini (then exiled in Marseilles, France) to create Young Italy to replace the *Carbonari* as a means of rallying the Italian people. Mazzini edited the movement's journal (published from 1832 to 1834), which was devoted to spreading the organization's ideas and entitled *Giovine Italia*. The movement quickly attracted adherents, mostly middle class, especially in northern Italy; by 1833 it reputedly had 60,000 members. In 1834, Mazzini expanded the concept to the rest of the continent with the creation of Young Europe; he also helped to found YOUNG GERMANY, Young Poland, and Young Switzerland. Young Italy's insurrections during the 1830s failed for lack of popular support; a planned uprising in Piedmont in 1833 was exposed, resulting in a dozen executions and Mazzini's being condemned to death in absentia. After 1837, he lived in London. With the help of others he reestablished Young Italy in 1840, primarily as a tool for creating a sense of national identity among Italians. In 1848 Mazzini ended its life by creating the Italian National Committee (Associazione Nazionale Italiana) in its place.

Young Life (United States) an interdenominational Christian organization for teenagers. Begun by a student assistant in a Texas church, the organization established a national headquarters in Dallas in 1941. Young Life has no actual members; its staff fosters clubs that meet weekly in private homes for the purpose of proselytizing and encouraging regular attendance at any church of a teenager's choice. The organization also sponsors recreational programs and operates several camps in the United States and Canada that attract thousands of teenage campers each summer. Now headquartered in Colorado Springs, Colorado, Young Life has a strong presence in the West but operates nationwide.

Young Lords (United States) an organization, founded by Puerto Rican university students in New York's Spanish Harlem as a political movement, that took its name from a Chicago street gang formed in 1965. The Young Lords proclaimed themselves a "Revolutionary Political Party" and advocated the overthrow of capitalism. To gain political support, they organized what was known as the "garbage offensive," during which on three successive Sundays their members swept streets in Spanish Harlem and loaded refuse into garbage cans to be picked up by sanitation crews. When the trash remained uncollected, the young Lords staged street demonstrations that resulted in conflicts with the city police and generated public attention. The Young Lords also organized a campaign to prevent children from eating lead-based paint; this campaign involved door-to-door visits by medical professionals to test children's urine for lead. Their most confrontational exploit was seizing a Methodist church in East Harlem on December 28, 1969 following services and occupying it for 11 days while demanding free space within the church for operating a free-breakfast program for youths living in the ghetto; police sealed off the church, and following negotiations, the Young Lords agreed to vacate the building on January 7, when 105 of them were arrested. Charges were dropped after the Young Lords and city and church officials made an agreement to operate a day-care center in the church. Through such efforts, the Young Lords hoped to pressure city authorities to be more responsive to the needs of the Puerto Rican community, but their efforts ultimately failed to bear fruit, and the organization withered.

Young Men's Buddhist Association (YMBA) (Burma) a youth organization founded in Rangoon in 1906. (Burma was then a British possession.) Among its founders were several youths who later served as leaders of Burma's nationalist movement. As an ostensible rival of the YOUNG MEN'S CHRISTIAN ASSOCIATION (YMCA), created and sponsored by Christian missionaries, the YMBA was devoted to restoring Buddhism as the major religion in Burma. The YMBA became distinctly nationalistic following World War I, and its educated members became involved in the movement to achieve Burmese sovereignty. The YMBA supported the students' strike that was a major part of the UNIVERSITY ACT PROTEST of 1920.

Young Men's Christian Association (YMCA) (Great Britain) a Christian-oriented but nonsectarian organization for young men originated by George Williams (1821–1905) in London. In 1840 Williams, who worked in a drapery house, formed a group of a dozen young clerks who began to meet in Williams's room for discussions, prayers, and mutual aid with the intention of improving their spiritual lives. From this beginning on June 6, 1844, the YMCA was founded. It was originally open only to members from evangelical churches, but others were invited to attend the organization's activities. The organization quickly spread to other cities. As the YMCA grew, acquiring its own buildings and hiring professional staffs, its programs expanded and its membership broadened to include men and women, and young girls of all faiths. The YMCA also soon spread overseas, to Australia in 1850 and to the United States in 1851, with the nation's first Y founded in Boston. The Y spread so rapidly that it became possible to hold a first international conference in 1855 in Paris, attended by delegates from eight nations. The conference adopted a Basis of Alliance that defined the character and purpose of the organization that still obtains. Also in 1855, the World Alliance of YMCAs was created. In subsequent decades, the Y became a truly international organization, but its greatest development was concentrated in North America. The YMCA provides programs in sports, physical fitness, public affairs, education, citizenship, camping, counseling, and other activities. The local Ys are affiliated with national councils that belong to the World Alliance of YMCAs, which is headquartered in Geneva, Switzerland.

In the United States, the nation with the largest YMCA representation (about 2,000 branches in 1970), the organization has pioneered many programs. It introduced camping and maintains the oldest camp in the nation, Camp Dudley in New York, opened in 1885. James Naismith originated the sport of basketball at the International Young Men's Christian Association Training School (now Springfield College) in Springfield, Massachusetts, where he was a physical education teacher, on or about December 1, 1891; the Y associations quickly adopted the game, spreading its popularity. The physical director of the YMCA in Holyoke, Massachusetts, William G. Morgan, invented volleyball there in 1895. Morgan also wrote the rules of the game, published in 1897 in the North American YMCA's Athletic League's *Official Handbook*, and in 1969 the Y joined the National

Collegiate Athletic Association (NCAA) in publishing the rules of the game. The Y also sponsored the first United States volleyball tournament, held in the Brooklyn Central YMCA in 1922. The YMCA began to work on university campuses in 1858. By World War I, the Y was the largest and most significant youth group in the nation—in 1915 there were 778 YMCA groups serving university students. The YMCA initiated aid to prisoners of war during the Civil War, provided most of the welfare services for U.S. soldiers during World War I, and operated nearly 650 USOs during World War II. The Y also helped to found the BOY SCOUTS OF AMERICA, and its national secretary founded the CAMP FIRE GIRLS.

The United States organization's many integral programs include YMCA World Service, which provides financial and organizational aid to overseas Ys. Its Y-Indian Guides program serves fathers and their sons age 6 to 8 with shared activities; the equivalent club for mothers and their daughters is Y-Indian Maidens. Gra-Y is for boys age about 9 to 11. Junior Hi-Y serves boys and girls of junior-high-school age, and Hi-Y is designed for high-school-age youths of both sexes, its avowed purpose being to build character and civic-mindedness. The YMCA's offshoot Student Christian Volunteer Movement sponsors and coordinates Christian missionary work. In 1996, the membership of the YMCA in the United States alone totaled 13 million—one of the largest youth organizations in the world.

Young Men's Hebrew Association (YMHA)   (United States) an organization now sponsored through individual Jewish Community Centers but originally a forerunner of the centers. The first YMHA was formed in Baltimore in 1854; this and other early YMHAs were intended as centers for social and educational programs for German Jewish youths. The two associations with the longest continuous histories are the New York City YMHA (1874) and the Philadelphia YMHA (1875). After Jewish Community Centers became established in the 1920s, they served as central agencies for YMHAs and other services. More than 200 centers with YMHAs exist across the nation, and centers and YMHAs have spread to Europe, Latin America, Canada, Australia, India, and other nations. The centers provide meeting and game rooms, gymnasiums, swimming pools, classrooms, auditoriums, exercise rooms, and other facilities.

Young Men's Mutual Improvement Association (YMMIA)   (United States) an organization of the Church of the Latter Day Saints (Mormons) that was founded in 1875.

Young Peoples' Socialist League (YPSL)   (United States) a socialist organization for youths that was founded in 1907 by groups of young socialists in New York and Chicago. In 1913, the Socialist Party granted official backing to YPSL, but there were many disputes between party leaders and the youth group, which usually espoused more radically left-wing positions on issues. YPSL opposed U.S. participation in World War I, the period of its greatest strength; by 1919 it claimed 10,000 members, very few of them university students. In that year, however, the national secretary was revealed to have secretly joined the Communist Party—a bombshell that, together with growing postwar hostility between the Socialists and the Communists, sent the YPSL into virtual oblivion for ten years. In 1929, a group of young Socialists formed a YPSL "district organization" in New York, reviving the league; in 1932 it became an official subsidiary of the Socialist Party.

YPSL had never made more than minimal efforts to organize university students, focusing instead on youths in the working class and those in high school. During the first five years of the Great Depression, the group's leaders adopted moderate views and argued against organizing "petty bourgeois students." But at the July 1935 convention, new leadership committed to left-wing militancy came to power. Also members of the STUDENT LEAGUE FOR INDUSTRIAL DEMOCRACY (SLID), these new leaders favored the creation of a united organization for students; consequently, they supported the merger of the NATIONAL STUDENT LEAGUE (NSL) and SLID as the AMERICAN STUDENT UNION (ASU) in December 1935. In 1936, YPSL set up a National Student Committee for the purpose of organizing chapters on campuses but to negligible effect; in the same year its convention approved the OXFORD PLEDGE, supported the Congress of Industrial Organizations (CIO), and opposed imperialist wars. Members of the YPSL also helped to create the YOUTH COMMITTEE AGAINST WAR (YCAW). By 1950 YPSL had only 500 dues-paying members; in 1957 the YOUNG SOCIALIST LEAGUE merged with YPSL to form a larger YPSL. During the late 1950s and the 1960s, YPSL strongly supported the Civil Rights movement. YPSL founded the journal *Free Youth* in 1924, and it also published *Young Socialist Review* for distribution to members. Although it had negligible impact among university students, YPSL constituted the major group within what was called the THIRD CAMP—that element of the socialist student movement that maintained an independent stance by refusing to support the policies of either the Soviet Union or the United States.

Young People's Society of Christian Endeavor   (United States) an organization for interdenominational church youths founded by Dr. Francis E. Clark (1851–1927). A Congregational minister and author, Clark set up the society on February 2, 1881 at the Williston Congregational Church, which he served as minister, in Portland, Maine. From this small, local beginning, the organization grew rapidly, with Clark devoting all his time to its expansion after 1887. By 1891, the society had enrolled a half-million youths as members. Clark became president of the United Societies of Christian Endeavor and of the World's Christian Endeavor Union, an international federation. By 1908 the Young People's Society had nearly 71,000 units with 3.5 million members in the United States, Canada, Great Britain, Australia, India, South Africa, China, and Japan. Its publication, edited by Clark, was the *Christian Endeavor World* (originally entitled *The Golden Rule*).

Young Progressives of America (YPA) (United States) a communist-sponsored student and youth organization that was founded at a convention held in Philadelphia in July 1948. More than 1,900 delegates from 44 states attended the conference. The YPA they created was intended to generate support for the presidential candidacy of Henry Wallace. When Wallace lost the YPA disappeared, and there would be no significant radical organization to replace it on university campuses until 1959.

Young Russia (Russia) an underground publication that was composed by a group of university students and disseminated in Moscow in May 1862. The leader of this group and primary author of *Young Russia* was Pyotr Zaichensky, age 19 and the son of a retired army colonel. *Young Russia* was noteworthy as a call to revolution by the masses through leadership provided by "our youth" and the army. The leaflet advocated a bloody revolution, followed by such reforms as establishing a federal republic, creating peasant communes from expropriated lands, emancipation of women, nationalization of factories, and abolishing the customs of marriage and inherited wealth. The students had been distributing forbidden publications and indoctrinating peasants through "Sunday schools" they had set up. Following their discovery and arrest by the authorities, the students were able to compose *Young Russia* while incarcerated—it was printed on a press they had moved to safety outside the city. After dissemination of *Young Russia*, numerous fires broke out in Moscow—their causes or perpetrators unknown—which provided authorities an excuse to crack down. Among other repressive measures, the authorities closed down all 300 of the existing Sunday schools in the nation because the student rebels had been discovered distributing literature through their Sunday schools.

Young Socialist Alliance (YSA) (United States) a Trotskyist-oriented organization formed in 1959 by diverse groups that were disaffected with leading socialist organizations such as the YOUNG PEOPLES' SOCIALIST LEAGUE (YPSL). Among these founding groups, for example, was the American Youth for Socialism, a very small organization which itself had been created by dissident former members of the YOUNG SOCIALIST LEAGUE (YSL)—suggesting how faction-ridden the socialist youth

movement was in the 1950s. Always closely associated with the Socialist Workers Party, YSA emerged in the 1960s as the most important of the "old left" groups in the student movement. During the sixties, YSA advocated moderate positions that by the end of the decade attracted new members among those who fell away from such radicalized groups as WEATHERMAN and STUDENTS FOR A DEMOCRATIC SOCIETY (SDS). The YSA also gained adherents though its participation in many of the antiwar demonstrations that were staged in Washington during the decade.

Young Socialist League (YSL) (United States) an organization formed in 1954 through a merger of the majority of members in the YOUNG PEOPLES' SOCIALIST LEAGUE (YPSL) and the SOCIALIST YOUTH LEAGUE (SYL). In 1957, YSL merged with the radical element that had continued as the YPSL, augmenting the YPSL's strength. At that time, the majority of YSL's membership broke away to form another group (American Youth for Socialism) that in 1959 merged with other groups to become the YOUNG SOCIALIST ALLIANCE (YSA).

Young Socialists (Junge Sozialdemokraten, JUSO) (Germany) the youth organization of the Social Democratic Party (SPD) open to young people age 16 to 35 but dominated by university and grammar school students. In 1977 the Young Socialists claimed 80,000 members, but only about 16,000 of these were active—disinterestedness took a toll on the organization following the resignation of Willy Brandt as chancellor of the Federal Republic.

Young Women's Christian Association (YWCA) (Great Britain) a Christian-oriented but nonsectarian organization that was dedicated to advancing the "physical, social, intellectual, moral, and spiritual interests of young women." The YWCA was initiated in 1855 in the efforts of two separate groups that began simultaneously, one called the Prayer Union and the other the North London Home, which established Christian homes for young women. They adopted the name Young Women's Christian Association in 1859, and in 1877 the two groups merged as the YWCA; in 1884 the organization adopted a constitution. In 1913, the organization began to offer residential courses and, in 1959, Blue Triangle courses to foster communications and other relationship skills, character development and self-awareness, and knowledge of politics, current events, economics, and other subjects. Like the YOUNG MEN'S CHRISTIAN ASSOCIATION, the YWCA became an international organization. Local associations belong to national affiliates with memberships in the World YWCA founded in 1894 in London and headquartered in Geneva, Switzerland.

In the United States, the YWCA was founded in Boston in 1866; it adopted its current organizational structure in 1906, when there were 608 local associations with a total membership exceeding 186,000. Girls, age 12 and older, and women are eligible for membership in the YWCA, and, although it provides programs for all ages of both sexes, its priority is young women in their teens and early twenties; the minimum membership age of 12 was officially adopted in 1934. The organization has supported women's causes and racial integration, established homes for the elderly, provided food and clothing to hospitals and prisons, and pursued other causes. The YWCA's work with youths began in Oakland in 1881 with the Little Girls' Christian Association, and in 1918 this movement became nationally united under the name Girl Reserves, which adopted uniforms, emblems, insignias, and a code. In 1946 the name was changed to Y-Teens. Its programs include housing for young women, summer camps, and education and emphasize human relations, health, recreation, spiritual growth, creative arts, community service, and citizenship. Membership of the YWCA in the United States in 1996 totaled 1.6 million.

Young Women's Hebrew Association (YWHA) (United States) an outgrowth of the YOUNG MEN'S HEBREW ASSOCIATION (YMHA), which was formed in 1888. Some YMHAs began to offer membership to young women as early as 1868, but the first actual YWHA was founded as an auxiliary of the New York YMHA in 1888. The first autonomous YWHA also originated in New York, in 1902.

Young Women's Mutual Improvement Association (YWMIA) (United States) an organization of the Church of the Latter Day Saints (Mormons) founded by the Mormon leader Brigham Young in 1869, 22 years after the Mormons first began to settle near Salt Lake in Utah. It was thus one of the earliest Protestant organizations for girls established in the United States and even antedated its counterpart for boys, the YOUNG MEN'S MUTUAL IMPROVEMENT ASSOCIATION (YMMIA). The YWMIA was originally called the Retrenchment Association, with Young defining its purpose as "to retrench in everything that is bad and worthless and improve in everything that is good and beautiful." The YWMIA's ongoing purposes are to provide religious and moral instruction, leisure and cultural activities, and training for civic responsibilities. Membership is open to all young women older than age 12. In 1915, the YWMIA formed the Bee-Hive Girls as an adjunct for younger girls.

Young Workers' League   See YOUNG COMMUNIST LEAGUE.

Youth Abbeys   See ABBEYS OF MISRULE.

Youth Committee Against War (YCAW) (United States) originally the Youth Committee for the Oxford Pledge (YCOP) formed in late 1937 and renamed in the spring of 1938, an organization formed in 1939 by an amalgam of pacifist student groups as a counter to other student antiwar groups, such as the AMERICAN STUDENT UNION (ASU), that were largely communist dominated and in favor of supporting U.S. participation in collective security measures. The groups involved in YCAW's formation included Student Peace Service (an offshoot of the American Friends Service Committee), NATIONAL COUNCIL OF METHODIST YOUTH, YOUNG PEOPLES' SOCIALIST LEAGUE, War Resisters League, and Fellowship of Reconciliation. YCAW supported the OXFORD PLEDGE and U.S. neutrality and opposed conscription and greater expenditures for armaments. Its efforts to attract students to the YCAW's views proved largely unsuccessful during the 1938 antiwar strike (see STUDENT STRIKE AGAINST WAR). The organization also sponsored a march on Washington, D.C., to protest the Lend-Lease Bill in 1941. The most radical of the student pacifist groups, YCAW held fast to its position until the December 7, 1941 Japanese attack on Pearl Harbor.

Youth Committee for the Oxford Pledge (YCOP) See YOUTH COMMITTEE AGAINST WAR (YCAW).

Youth Congress (India) a student organization founded in 1949 by the All-India Congress Committee of the Indian National Congress Party. The Youth Congress was organized at the district level rather than being based on campuses. Although claiming 50,000 student members, it never attracted widespread student support and was perceived as a vehicle to serve the ambitions of Congress Party politicians. The organization participated in Congress Party election campaigns. It attracted increased attention in 1962, when helping to generate students' support of the government after Chinese forces invaded India. Wracked with internal conflicts, the Youth Congress was disbanded in 1965.

Youth for Christ (YFC) (United States) a nondenominational Christian organization that was founded in Chicago during World War II. The founder, a pastor named Torrey Johnson, decided to hold a rally for GIs in order to dissuade them from pursuing the distractions of the city's streets. Joining with others who were conducting similar rallies in other cities, Johnson formed YFC in 1945. The later-renowned evangelist Billy Graham was YFC's first full-time staffer. YFC sometimes used bizarre tactics to attract crowds, but in the 1950s it turned to personal evangelism rather than rallies and provided young people opportunities for Bible study, overseas ministry, leadership training, and other programs. In the 1960s, the YFC's staff focused on helping teenagers to proselytize their classmates and began a program called Lifeline to aid youths who had run afoul of the law. Camping formed a major part of Lifeline's program. YFC also sponsors Campus Life clubs and *Campus Life* magazine to address issues of concern to teenagers and to provide forums for proselytizing.

Youth Franchise Coalition (United States) a coalition formed on February 5, 1969 in Washington, D.C., comprised of nearly two dozen distinct groups whose purpose was to obtain enfranchisement for young adults ages 18 to 20. Many of the groups within the coalition were student organizations, such as the NATIONAL STUDENT ASSOCIATION and LET US VOTE, but also included were the National Association for the Advancement of Colored People (NAACP), Americans for Democratic Action, Citizens for Vote 18, Young Democratic Clubs of America, and other disparate groups. Representing a constituency numbering about 2 million, the coalition advocated the granting of voting rights through state laws or an amendment to the United States Constitution. Through the work of its student groups especially, the coalition was a major lobbyist for the 1970 Voting Rights Act.

Bibliography: Wendell W. Cultice, *Youth's Battle for the Ballot: A History of Voting Age in America* (New York: Greenwood Press, 1992).

Youth International Party *See* HOFFMAN, ABBIE.

Youth Organizations United (Y.O.U.) (United States) an organization that was formed to help improve the lives of youths living in urban ghettos. Its origins lay in the efforts of a gang leader, Carlos "Chino" Garcia, in the Lower East Side of Manhattan in the 1960s. Garcia organized other gang leaders as the Real Great Society. From this beginning, gang leaders from cities throughout the nation met in New York in the fall of 1967 and formed Y.O.U. Members recruited others to help with setting up recreation centers, training programs for dropouts, and other services. Y.O.U. has been supported financially by charitable groups and by the Coalition for Youth Action of the U.S. Department of Labor.

Youth Pilgrimage for Jobs and Education (United States) a three-day demonstration in Washington in February 1937 to focus attention on the economic deprivations affecting youths during the Great Depression. The most significant feature of the pilgrimage was a February 20 march by 3,000 young protestors representing nationwide student and youth organizations who paraded down

Pennsylvania Avenue to the White House—the first mass march on Washington. The marchers carried banners and signs, chanted slogans, and sang "American youth is on the march for jobs and education." Participants in the pilgrimage also lobbied Congress to increase assistance to youths who suffer from economic hardship and to ensure that no youths would be forced to leave school because of lack of funds.

Youth Service (Great Britain) a system initiated in 1939, and officially incorporated as part of the Education Act of 1944, to provide services to youths age 14 to 20 under the auspices of the national education system. Youth Service originated as a partnership that involved the national government, the local education authorities, the various voluntary organizations (such as the YOUNG MEN'S CHRISTIAN ASSOCIATION, church groups, and the BOYS' BRIGADE), and the youths themselves (as members of advisory committees). The Education Act of 1944 obligated local authorities, in cooperation with voluntary organizations, to provide adequate facilities and programs for youths.

Youths' Institutes (Great Britain) a movement that was begun in the late 1850s to provide for the further education of boys, largely age 13 to 19, who had left elementary school and were working in such capacities as apprentices, junior clerks, and office boys. A major impetus for their founding was to provide boys with an alternative to socializing at Men's Club, where the adult members considered them unwelcome. The first institute was the Dover Youths' Institute founded in 1857 by the Rev. Henry White, who in 1860 also started an institute at Charing Cross. Among the earliest successful institutes was the Islington Youths' Institute, which opened in St. George's Hall in Islington in October 1860. It was founded by Rev. Arthur Sweatman, pastor of St. George's Church and later archbishop of Toronto. This institute, which by 1863 had 300 members, provided a reading room and library, a recreational room, and classes in a variety of subjects. By this time, several other smaller institutes had been established in other section of London and in other cities as well. In succeeding decades, the institutes were displaced by public educational efforts, the settlement-house movement, and the founding of boys' clubs, such as the BOYS' BRIGADE, that were primarily recreational; by 1900, the institutes movement had disappeared.

Z

Zemlyachestva (Russia) late-19th- and early 20th-century societies that were formed at universities by students from the same provinces or locales. Although originating in the late 1850s, they first began to be common in the 1860s because a regulation of 1861 forbade student corporate activity; the Zemlyachestva, although also illegal by the regulation, served as a substitute for the banned groups and survived by avoiding political activity. Most served to provide mutual economic support to their members, while also promoting "moral education" and the exchange of different views. The Zemlyachestva were similar to the LANDSMANNSCHAFTEN that were formed at German universities. For example, some were comprised of Ukrainians, Georgians, Armenians, or Poles only; others, of students graduated from the same gymnasium; still others, of students from particular regions, such as the Don. Although illegal, the societies thrived. For example, one account states that in the 1890s there were about 50 such societies at St. Petersburg University, some having as many as 100 or more members, with the average membership being 30; at Moscow University there were 43 such societies with a total of about 1,700 members.

During the 1880s and 1890s especially, each Zemlyachestva elected a representative to a Coalition Committee or Coordinating Council; these committees formed a network among all the universities. This network of coalitions was responsible for calling numerous student strikes from 1897 to 1904. Probably the most important was a nationwide strike that began at St. Petersburg in February 1899 (*see* ALL-RUSSIA STUDENT STRIKE OF 1899). After 43 members of three coalition committees were arrested and expelled from the university, the strike spread to the universities in Moscow, Odessa, Kiev, Kharkov, Riga, and elsewhere. In response, the government ordered all the universities closed and had more than 3,000 students permanently expelled. The government appointed a commission of inquiry that reported its findings on student living conditions in May. Another commission was appointed, but its efforts actually resulted in greater restrictions; for example, more student inspectors were appointed and students were limited to attending universities in their native regions. The government did appropriate money to build hostels for poor students but to little effect. The Zemlyachestva were now emphatically outlawed. On July 29, 1899, Nicholas II decreed that all of the expelled students be conscripted into the army.

Zengakuren (Zen Nihon Gakusei Jichi-kai Sorengo, National Federation of Student Self-governing Associations) (Japan) a dominant nationwide organization founded in September 1948, with member groups representing virtually all the universities, both public and private. With the precedent of several nationwide organizational efforts, students convened a meeting on July 3, 1948 to make preparations for creating a united student movement; on July 6, representatives of 138 universities at the meeting decided to form an All-Japan Federation of Student Self-Governing Associations. As a result 250 student representatives from 145 universities, who were attending a three-day meeting that began on September 18, founded the Zengakuren and adopted these resolutions for its guidance: opposing "fascist-colonialistic reorganization" of education, protecting the freedom of student life and studies, opposing low wages for students' part-time work (including those paid by the postwar occupation force, Supreme Commander for the Allied Force, or SCAP), opposing fascism and protecting democracy, "unity with the battle line of youth," and freedom for student political movements. Zengakuren was headquartered at Tokyo University, with Takei Akio as chairman of its executive committee; its membership comprised 300,000 students from 145 universities.

In October 1948, the Ministry of Education proposed policies that would severely limit the student self-government movement and form the basis of a university law that would restrict student political activities; a meeting of national university presidents generally supported these proposals. In response, Zengakuren made a counterproposal for university reform whose primary tenet was creation of an independent board of publicly elected members to administer the universities, and it organized a national student opposition. After the government introduced the University Bill in the Diet, the Zengakuren on May 3, 1949 held its 5th Central Committee meeting, which resolved to oppose the bill by means of a general strike—the first of many the organization would call in subsequent years. The strike that ensued over three weeks, until May 24, involved 200,000 protesting students and forced the government to back down—Zengakuren's first of many successes. Immediately following this success, Zengakuren held its 2nd General Meeting, beginning May 28 and lasting three days, attended by representatives of 349 universities, including private schools, who reelected Takei Akio as chairman.

Although the Zengakuren began to oppose the leadership of the Japan Communist Party (JCP) following the organization's 4th Congress in May 1950, when the Ministry of Education in September proposed purging the universities of communists, the Zengakuren organized strikes and a boycott of examinations in protest. The tactics precluded the purge but also led to about 100 students being arrested and hundreds more suspended. This was the year of the Korean War's beginning, and the government, with the support of the U.S. occupation (SCAP), suppressed the JCP. The war also caused SCAP to pressure the government to conclude the Japan-U.S. Security Treaty (known as Ampo), and it was signed in September 1951. In 1952, Zengakuren installed new leaders who supported the JCP's militancy; in reaction, some students formed a new organization called HANSEN GAKUDO. At Zengakuren's 5th National Congress in 1952, only 54 universities had representatives, and in 1953 the organization weakened further because of its support for the JCP.

At its 7th National Congress in 1954, the Zengakuren shifted its policy emphasis again, advocating peace; at its 9th Congress in 1956, it moved back toward its original goals for education, along with a resolution opposing nuclear testing. In 1956–57, Zengakuren's major effort involved joining with union members and residents to oppose on-site the expansion of the U.S. air base at Sunagawa near Tokyo. Thousands of students participated during the months-long protest, and hundreds

were injured. Finally, in 1959, a Tokyo District Court judge acquitted the 9 students and 14 labor leaders of the protests on the grounds that the law under which they were arrested was unconstitutional, as also, he declared, was the Japan-U.S. Security Treaty; this event set the stage for the ANTI-AMPO STRUGGLE. The 11th National Congress in May 1958 revealed the emergence of strong factions within the Zengakuren, and in the following years, first one faction and then another predominated in Zengakuren activity, including the exceptionally rebellious events of the 1960s. (Major factions are listed in this encyclopedia; but the factions were so numerous—and frequently short-lived—that the majority cannot be included.)

The factionalism reached something of an apex in December 1964, when one group of factions structured on the foundation of the STUDENT SELF-GOVERNING ASSOCIATIONS and, calling itself the Zengakuren Unity Faction, reconstituted itself as the new Zengakuren. It announced a four-point program: to work for peace, independence, democracy, and student self-government within the universities; to establish solidarity among students; to expand and augment the organization; and to develop contacts with student movements in other areas of the world. They were immediately challenged by the ANTI-YOYOGI ZENGAKUREN, which attempted to reconstitute its various factions as a united group.

Bibliography: Stuart J. Dowsey, ed., *Zengakuren: Japan's Revolutionary Students* (Berkeley, Calif.: The Ishi Press, 1970).

Zenjiren *See* TOJIREN.

Zenkoku Zenkyoto Rengo (National Federation of the All-Campus Joint Struggle Councils) (Japan) a nationwide organization of ZENKYOTO groups that was formed on September 5, 1969. It became known simply as Zenkyoto, the same term as used for a single joint struggle council. The national Zenkyoto was comprised of several factions of the ANTI-YOYOGI ZENGAKUREN and represented individual Zenkyoto at 200 universities as it members. The national Zenkyoto had a bipolar agenda: political agitation involving street riots and university campus strikes.

Zenkyoto (All-Campus Joint Struggle Councils) (Japan) campus wide student organizations that were formed at many Japanese universities in 1968 to direct the course of confrontations with administrators. *See* the TOKYO UNIVERSITY STRUGGLE for an example. The term *Zenkyoto* also refers to the ZENKOKU ZENKYOTO RENGO.

Zurich Police Riot (Switzerland) a brutal police suppression of demonstrating youths in 1968. On June 29 and 30, 1968 about 10,000 young people gathered in

Zurich to demonstrate for creation of an autonomous youth center and against police brutality. The police turned fire hoses on them and attacked them with batons. More than 200 youths had to be hospitalized for treatment of injuries. Police arrested 250 youths, many of whom they beat and tortured. Many of the victims were stripped before the beatings; girls were beaten on their genitals; boys were beaten unconscious. It was a classic example of a police riot, described by 18 leading Swiss intellectuals in their *Zurich Manifesto* as a "pogrom against youth."

Bibliography

Altbach, Philip G. *Student Politics in America: A Historical Analysis.* New York: McGraw-Hill, 1973.

———. *Student Politics in Bombay.* Bombay and New York: Asia Publishing House, 1965.

———. "The Transformation of the Indian Student Movement," *Asian Survey* 6, no. 8 (August 1966), 448–60.

Altbach, Philip G., and Uphoff, Norman T. *The Student Internationals.* Metuchen, N.J.: Scarecrow Press, 1973.

Ascher, Abraham. *The Revolution of 1905: Russia in Disarray.* Stanford, Calif.: Stanford University Press, 1988.

Baden-Powell, Olave. *Window on My Heart.* London: Hodder and Stoughton, 1973.

Barlow, William, and Shapiro, Peter. *An End to Silence: The San Francisco State Student Movement in the 60's.* New York: Pegasus, 1971.

Becker, Jillian A. *Hitler's Children: The Story of the Baader-Meinhof Terrorist Gang.* Philadelphia: Lippincott, 1977.

Blackstone, Tessa, et al. *Students in Conflict.* London: Weidenfeld and Nicolson, 1970.

Boggs, Carl. *Social Movements and Political Power: Emerging Forms of Radicalism in the West.* Philadelphia: Temple University Press, 1986.

"The Bombay Students' Brotherhood," *Modern Review* 14 (March 1914), 264.

Bonilla, Frank, and Glazer, Myron. *Student Politics in Chile.* New York: Basic Books, 1969.

Brax, Ralph S. *The First Student Movement: Student Activism in the United States During the 1930s.* Port Washington, N.Y.: Kennikat Press, 1981.

Brower, Daniel R. *Training the Nihilists: Education and Radicalism in Tsarist Russia.* Ithaca, N.Y.: Cornell University Press, 1975.

Brown, Bernard E. *Protest in Paris: Anatomy of a Revolt.* Morristown, N.J.: General Learning Press, 1974.

Bunt, Sidney. *Jewish Youth Work in Britain: Past, Present, and Future.* London: Bedford Square Press, 1975.

Cardozier, V. R. "Student Power in Medieval Universities," *Personnel and Guidance Journal* 46 (June 1968), 944–48.

Carmichael, Stokeley. *Stokeley Speaks: Black Power Back to Pan-Africanism.* New York: Random House, 1971.

Carmichael, Stokeley, and Hamilton, Charles V. *Black Power: The Politics of Liberation in America.* New York: Vintage Books, 1967.

Carson, Clayborne. *In Struggle: SNCC and the Black Awakening of the 1960s.* Cambridge: Harvard University Press, 1981.

Casale, Ottavio M., ed. *The Kent State Affair: Documents and Interpretations.* New York: Houghton Mifflin, 1971.

Chang, Maria Hsia. *The Chinese Blue Shirts: Fascism and Developmental Nationalism.* Berkeley: University of California Press, 1985.

Chatfield, Charles, ed. *Peace Movements in America.* New York: Schocken, 1973.

Cheng, Chu-Yuan. *Behind the Tiananmen Square Massacre: Social, Political, and Economic Ferment in China.* Boulder, Colo.: Westview Press, 1990.

Chesneaux, Jean, ed. *Popular Movements and Secret Societies in China, 1840–1950.* Stanford, Calif.: Stanford University Press, 1972.

Cohen, Robert. *When the Old Left Was Young: Student Radicals and America's First Mass Student Movement, 1929–1941.* New York: Oxford University Press, 1993.

Cornell, Richard. "Students and Politics in the Communist Countries of Eastern Europe," *Daedalus* 97 (Winter 1968), 166–83.

———. *Youth and Communism.* New York: Walker, 1965.

Crouch, Colin. *The Student Revolt.* London: Bodley Head, 1970.

Cultice, Wendell W. *Youth's Battle for the Ballot: A History of Voting Age in America.* New York: Greenwood Press, 1992.

Davies, Peter, et al. *The Truth About Kent State: A Challenge to the American Conscience.* New York: Farrar, Straus, Giroux, 1973.

Davis, Natalie Zimon. "The Reasons of Misrule: Youth Groups and Charivaris in Sixteenth-Century France," *Past and Present* 50 (1971), 41–75.

DeBenedetti, Charles. *The Peace Reform in American History.* Bloomington: Indiana University Press, 1980.

DeConde, Alexander, ed. *Student Activism: Town and Gown in Historical Perspective.* New York: Scribner's, 1971.

Dix, Robert H. *The Politics of Colombia.* New York: Praeger, 1987.

Dobbs, Archibald E. *Education and Social Movements, 1700–1850.* New York: Kelley, 1919.

Doolin, Dennis J. *Communist China: The Politics of Student Opposition.* Stanford, Calif.: Hoover Institution, 1964.

Dowsey, Stuart J., ed. *Zengakuren: Japan's Revolutionary Students.* Berkeley, Calif.: Ishi Press, 1970.

Draper, Hal. *Berkeley: The New Student Revolt.* New York: Grove, 1965.

Eagar, Waldo McG. *Making Men: The History of Boys' Clubs and Related Movements in Great Britain.* London: University of London Press, 1953.

Ehrenreich, Barbara, and Ehrenreich, John. *Long March, Short Spring: The Student Uprising at Home and Abroad.* New York: Monthly Review Press, 1969.

Eichel, Lawrence, et al. *The Harvard Strike.* Boston: Houghton Mifflin, 1970.

Eisenstadt, Samuel N. *From Generation to Generation.* Glencoe, Ill.: Freis Press, 1956.

Emmerson, Donald K. "African Student Organizations: The Politics of Discontent," *African Report* 10 (May 1965), 6–12.

———, ed. *Students and Politics in Developing Nations.* New York: Praeger, 1968.

Enroth, Ronald M., and Ericson, Edward E., Jr. *The Jesus People: Old-Time Religion in the Age of Aquarius.* Grand Rapids, Mich.: W. B. Erdman Publishing Company, 1972.

Epstein, Barbara. *Political Protest and Cultural Revolution: Nonviolent Direct Action in the 1970s and 1980s.* Berkeley: University of California Press, 1991.

Escobar, Arturo, and Alvarez, Sonia E., eds. *The Making of Social Movements in Latin America.* Boulder, Colo.: Westview Press, 1992.

Esherick, Joseph W. *The Origins of the Boxer Uprising.* Berkeley: University of California Press, 1987.

Ewell, Judith. *Venezuela: A Century of Change.* Stanford, Calif.: Stanford University Press, 1984.

Fass, Paula. *The Damned and the Beautiful: American Youth in the Twenties.* New York: Oxford University Press, 1977.

Feuer, Lewis. *Conflict of Generations: The Character and Significance of Student Movements.* New York: Basic Books, 1969.

Fields, A. Belden. *Student Politics in France: A Study of the Union Nationale des Etudiants de France.* New York: Basic Books, 1970.

Fisher, Ralph. *Pattern for Soviet Youth: A Study of the Congresses of the Komsomol, 1918–1954.* New York: Columbia University Press, 1959.

Flacks, Richard. *Youth and Social Change.* Chicago: Markham, 1971.

Foster, Julian, and Long, Durward, eds. *Protest: Student Activism in America.* New York: Morrow, 1970.

Fraser, Brian, and Hoare, Michael. *Sure and Stedfast: A History of the Boys' Brigade, 1883–1983.* Edited by John Springhall. London: Collins, 1983.

Gillis, John R. *Youth and History: Tradition and Change in European Age Relations, 1700 to the Present.* New York: Academic Press, 1974.

Gitlin, Todd. *The Sixties: Years of Hope, Days of Rage.* New York: Bantam, 1987.

Grant, Joanne. *Confrontation on Campus: The Columbia Pattern for the New Protest.* New York: Signet, 1969.

Hall, Stuart, and Jefferson, Tony, eds. *Resistance through Rituals: Youth Subcultures in Post-war Britain.* New York: Holmes and Meier, 1976.

Halls, W. D. *The Youth of Vichy France.* Oxford: Clarendon Press, 1981.

Handy, Jim. *Gift of the Devil: A History of Guatamala.* Boston: South End Press, 1984.

Hanna, William John. *Independent Black Africa: The Politics of Freedom.* Chicago: Rand McNally, 1964.

Hanna, William John, et al. *University Students and African Politics.* New York: Africana Publishing Company, 1975.

Hanson, Robert F., and Carlson, Reynold E. *Organizations for Children and Youth.* Englewood Cliffs, N.J.: Prentice Hall, 1972.

Hargrave, John. *The Confession of the Kibbo Kift.* London: Duckworth, 1927.

Harris, Tim. *London Crowds in the Reign of Charles II.* Cambridge: Cambridge University Press, 1987.

Harris, T. J. G. "The Bawdy House Riots of 1668," *Historical Journal* 29 (1986), 537–56.

Harrison, James P. *The Long March to Power: A History of the Chinese Communist Party, 1921–1972.* New York: Praeger, 1972.

Hasson, Shlomo. *Urban Social Movements in Jerusalem: The Protest of the Second Generation.* Albany: State University of New York Press, 1993.

Heer, Friedrich. *Challenge of Youth.* Translated by Geoffrey Skelton. Tuscaloosa: University of Alabama Press, 1974.

Heinrich, Hans-Georg. *Hungary: Politics, Economics, and Society.* Boulder, Colo.: Lynne Rienner Publishers, 1986.

Heywood, Colin. *Childhood in Nineteenth-Century France.* Cambridge: Cambridge University Press, 1988.

High, Stanley. *The Revolt of Youth.* New York: Abingdon, 1924.

Hobsbawn, E. J. *Primitive Rebels: Studies in Archaic Forms of Social Movements in the 19th and 20th Centuries.* New York: Norton, 1959.

Holl, Jack M. *Juvenile Reform in the Progressive Era: William R. George and the Junior Republic Movement.* Ithaca, N.Y.: Cornell University Press, 1971.

Horn, Max. *The Intercollegiate Socialist Society, 1905–1921.* Boulder, Colo.: Westview Press, 1979.

Howard, John R. *The Cutting Edge: Social Movements and Social Change in America.* New York: Lippincott, 1974.

Israel, John. *Student Nationalism in China, 1927–1937.* Stanford, Calif.: Stanford University Press, 1966.

Israel, John, and Klein, Donald. *Rebels and Bureaucrats: China's December 9ers.* Berkeley: University of California Press, 1976.

Jacobs, Harold, ed. *Weatherman.* Berkeley, Calif.: Ramparts Press, 1970.

Jarausch, Konrad H. *Students, Society, and Politics in Imperial Germany: The Rise of Academic Illiberalism.* Princeton, N.J.: Princeton University Press, 1982.

Jones, Mary Gwladys. *The Charity School Movement: A Study of Eighteenth Century Puritanism in Action.* Hamden, Conn.: Archon Books, 1964.

Kantor, Harry. *The Ideology and Program of the Peruvian Aprista Movement.* New York: Octagon, 1966.

Kassof, Allen. *The Soviet Youth Program.* Cambridge: Harvard University Press, 1965.

Kassow, Samuel D. *Students, Professors, and the State in Tsarist Russia.* Berkeley: University of California Press, 1989.

Kett, Joseph F. *Rites of Passage: Adolescence in America, 1790 to the Present.* New York: Basic Books, 1977.

Kiang, Wen-Lan. *The Chinese Student Movement.* New York: King's Crown Press, 1948.

Koon, Tracy H. *Believe, Obey, Fight: Political Socialization of Youth in Fascist Italy, 1922–1943.* Chapel Hill: University of North Carolina Press, 1985.

Krauss, Ellis S. *Japanese Radicals Revisited: Student Protest in Postwar Japan.* Berkeley: University of California Press, 1974.

Lane, David. *Soviet Society Under Perestroika.* Boston: Unwin Hyman, 1990.

Laqueur, Thomas Walter. *Religion and Respectability: Sunday Schools and Working Class Culture, 1780–1850.* New Haven, Conn.: Yale University Press, 1976.

Laqueur, Walter. *Young Germany: A History of the German Youth Movement.* New York: Basic Books, 1962.

Levy, Daniel, and Szekely, Gabriel. *Mexico: Paradoxes of Stability and Change.* Boulder, Colo.: Westview Press, 1987.

Lewis, Paul H. *Socialism, Liberalism, and Dictatorship in Paraguay.* New York: Praeger, 1982.

Liebman, Arthur, et al. *Latin American University Students: A Six Nation Study.* Cambridge: Harvard University Press, 1972.

———. *The Politics of Puerto Rican University Students.* Austin: University Press of Texas, 1970.

Liddell, Alix. *The Girl Guides, 1910–1970.* New ed. London: Hodder and Stoughten, 1973.

Lindley, Ernest R., and Lindley, Betty. *A New Deal for Youth: The Story of the National Youth Administration.* New York: Viking, 1938.

Lipset, Seymour Martin. *Rebellion in the University: A History of Student Activism in America.* Woodstock, N.Y.: Beekman, 1971.

Lipset, Seymour Martin, and Altbach, Philip G., eds. *Students in Revolt.* Boston: Houghton Mifflin, 1969.

Lipset, Seymour Martin, and Raab, Earl. *The Politics of Unreason: Rightwing Extremism in America, 1790–1970.* New York: Harper and Row, 1970.

Lipset, Seymour Martin, and Schaflander, Gerald M. *Passion and Politics: Student Activism in America.* Boston: Little, Brown and Company, 1971.

Lipset, Seymour Martin, and Wolin, Sheldon S., eds. *The Berkeley Student Revolt.* Garden City, N.Y.: Doubleday Anchor Books, 1965.

McAdam, Doug. *Freedom Summer.* New York: Oxford University Press, 1988.

McCague, James. *The Second Rebellion: The Story of the New York City Draft Riots of 1863.* New York: Dial, 1968.

Macleod, David I. *Building Character in the American Boy: The Boy Scouts, YMCA, and Their Forerunners, 1870–1920.* Madison: University of Wisconsin Press, 1983.

McManus, Philip, and Schlabach, Gerald, eds. *Relentless Persistence: Nonviolent Action in Latin America.* Philadelphia: New Society Publishers, 1991.

Majumdar, Ramesh C. *History of the Freedom Movement in India.* Vol. III. Calcutta: Firma K. L. Mukhopadhyay, 1962–63.

Miller, James. *"Democracy Is in the Streets": From Port Huron to the Siege of Chicago.* New York: Simon and Schuster, 1987.

Minzhu, Han, ed. *Cries for Democracy: Writings and Speeches from the 1989 Chinese Democracy Movement.* Princeton, N.J.: Princeton University Press, 1990.

Mitterauer, Michael. *A History of Youth.* Translated by Graeme Dunphy. Oxford: Blackwell, 1992.

Mommsen, Wolfgang J., and Hirschfield, Gerhard. *Social Protest, Violence and Terror in 19th and 20th Century Europe.* New York: St. Martin, 1982.

Morris, Brian. "Ernest Thompson Seton and the Origins of the Woodcraft Movement," *Journal of Contemporary History* 5 (1970), 183–94.

Nahm, Andrew C. *Korea: Tradition and Transformation.* Elizabeth, N.J.: Hollym International Corporation, 1988.

Narsimhan, Reavathi. "Student Movements in India: A Post Independence Survey," *Indian Journal of Youth Affairs* 2 (March 1980), 37–48.

Nash, George H. *The Conservative Intellectual Movement in America Since 1945.* New York: Basic Books, 1976.

Novak, Stephen J. *The Rights of Youth: American Colleges and Student Revolt, 1789–1815.* Cambridge: Harvard University Press, 1977.

Orlans, Harold. "The Revolution at Gallaudet," *Change* 21, no. 1 (January–February 1989), 8–18.

Paloczi-Horvath, George. *Youth Up in Arms: A Political and Social World Survey, 1955–1970*. London: Weidenfeld and Nicolson, 1971.

Pantin, W. A. *Oxford Life in Oxford Archives*. Oxford: Clarendon Press, 1972.

Papadakis, Elim. *The Green Movement in West Germany*. New York: St. Martin, 1984.

Paul, Leslie. *The Republic of Children*. London: Allen and Unwin, 1938.

Peacock, Roger S. *Pioneer of Boyhood: The Story of Sir William A. Smith*. Glasgow: Boys Brigade, 1954.

Peretz, Don. *Intifada: The Palestinian Uprising*. Boulder, Colo.: Westview Press, 1990.

Phillips, Donald E. *Student Protest, 1960–1970*. New York: University Press of America, 1985.

Porter, Kenneth Wiggins. "The Oxford Cap War at Harvard," *New England Quarterly* 14 (March 1941), 77–83.

Rath, R. J. *The Viennese Revolution of 1848*. Austin: University of Texas Press, 1957.

Ray, Anil B. *Students and Politics in India*. New Delhi: Manohar, 1977.

Rempel, Gerhard. *Hitler's Children: The Hitler Youth and the SS*. Chapel Hill: University of North Carolina Press, 1989.

Reynolds, Ernest Edwin. *Baden-Powell*. 2nd ed. London: Oxford University Press, 1957.

Rigby, Richard. *The May 30th Movement*. Canberra, Australia: Griffin, 1980.

Riley-Smith, Jonathan. *The Crusades: A Short History*. New Haven, Conn.: Yale University Press, 1989.

Riordan, Jim, ed. *Soviet Youth Culture*. Bloomington: Indiana University Press, 1989.

Roberts, Kenneth; White, Graham E.; and Parker, Howard J. *The Character-Training Industry*. Newton Abbott, England: David and Charles, 1974.

Roos, Leslie L., Jr., et al. "Students and Politics in Turkey," *Daedalus* 98 (Winter 1968), 184–203.

Roszak, Theodore. *The Making of the Counter Culture*. Garden City, N.Y.: Anchor Books, 1970.

Rudy, Willis. *The Universities of Europe, 1100–1914*. Rutherford, N.J.: Fairleigh Dickinson University Press, 1984.

Sale, Kilpatrick. *SDS*. New York: Random House, 1973.

Salmond, John A. *The Civilian Conservation Corps, 1933–1942: A New Deal Case Study*. Durham, North Carolina: Duke University Press, 1967.

———. *A Southern Rebel, the Life and Times of Aubrey Willis Williams, 1890–1965*. Chapel Hill: University of North Carolina Press, 1983.

Sanderson, Michael, ed. *The Universities in the Nineteenth Century*. London: Routledge and Kegan Paul, 1975.

Schirach, Baldur von. *Ich Glaubte an Hitler*. Hamburg: Mosaik Verlag, 1967.

Schwab, Marcel. *The Children's Crusade*. Boston: Small, Maynard, 1898.

Shiman, Lillian. "The Band of Hope Movement: Respectable Recreation for Working Class Children," *Victorian Studies* 17, no. 1 (September 1973), 49–74.

Smith, David Horton. *Latin American Student Activism: Participation in Formal Volunteer Organizations by University Students in Six Latin Cultures*. Lexington, Mass.: Lexington Books, 1973.

Springhall, John. *Coming of Age: Adolescence in Britain, 1860–1960*. Dublin: Gill and Macmillan, 1986.

Springhall, John. *Youth, Empire, and Society: British Youth Movements, 1883–1940*. London: Croom Helm, 1977.

Stein, Daniel Lewis. *Living the Revolution: The Yippies in Chicago*. Indianapolis, Ind.: Bobbs-Merrill, 1969.

Steinberg, Michael Stephen. *Sabers and Brown Shirts: The German Students' Path to National Socialism*. Chicago: University of Chicago Press, 1977.

Stevens, Evelyn P. *Protest and Response in Mexico*. Cambridge: MIT Press, 1974.

Stratera, Gianni. *Death of a Utopia: The Development and Decline of Student Movements in Europe*. New York: Oxford University Press, 1975.

Students and Staff of Hornsey College of Art. *The Hornsey Affair*. Hammondsworth, England: Penguin Books, 1969.

Suchlichi, Jaime. *University Students and Revolution in Cuba, 1920–1968*. Coral Gables, Fl.: University of Miami Press, 1969.

Thackeray, Frank W. *Antecedents of Revolution: Alexander I and the Polish Kingdom, 1815–1825*. New York: Columbia University Press, 1980.

Thomas, Hugh. *The Cuban Revolution*. New York: Harper and Row, 1977.

Treitschke, Heinrich von. *History of Germany in the Nineteenth Century*. Vol. III. Translated by Eden and Cedar Paul. New York: McBride, Nast and Company, 1915–19.

Tse-tsung, Chou. *The May Fourth Movement*. Cambridge: Harvard University Press, 1960.

Unger, Irwin, and Unger, Debi. *The Movement: A History of the American New Left, 1959–1972*. New York: Dodd, Mead, 1974.

Useem, Michael. *Conscription, Protest, and Social Conflict: The Life and Death of a Draft Resistance Movement*. New York: Wiley, 1973.

———. *Protest Movements in America*. Indianapolis, Ind.: Bobbs-Merrill, 1975.

Valenzuela, Arturo. *A Nation of Enemies: Chile Under Pinochet*. New York: W. W. Norton, 1991.

Vali, Ferenc. *Rift and Revolt in Hungary*. Cambridge: Harvard University Press, 1961.

Vickers, George R. *The Formation of the New Left*. Lexington, Mass.: Lexington Books, 1975.

Walter, Richard J. *Student Politics in Argentina: The University Reform and Its Effects, 1918–1964*. New York: Basic Books, 1968.

Wasserstrom, Jeffrey N. *Student Protests in Twentieth-Century China: The View from Shanghai.* Stanford, Calif.: Stanford University Press, 1991.

Wasserstrom, Jeffrey N., and Perry, Elizabeth J., eds. *Popular Protest and Political Culture in Modern China.* Boulder Colo.: Westview Press, 1992.

Wechsler, James. *Revolt on Campus.* New York: Colvici, Friede, 1935.

Weinstein, Martin. *Uruguay: Democracy at the Crossroads.* Boulder, Colo.: Westview Press, 1988.

Weisbrot, Robert. *Freedom Bound: A History of America's Civil Rights Movement.* New York: Plume (Penguin), 1991.

Whelan, James R. *Out of the Ashes: Life, Death, and Transfiguration of Democracy in Chile, 1833–1988.* Washington, D.C.: Regnery, 1989.

Wittner, Lawrence S. *Rebels Against War: The American Peace Movement, 1941–1960.* New York: Columbia University Press, 1969.

Yarmolinsky, Avrahm. *Road to Revolution: A Century of Russian Radicalism.* New York: Macmillan, 1962.

Index